The China Record

The China Record

An Assessment of the People's Republic

FEI-LING WANG

SUNY
PRESS

Cover image from Wikimedia Commons.

Published by State University of New York Press, Albany

For information, contact State University of New York Press, Albany, NY
www.sunypress.edu

Library of Congress Cataloging-in-Publication Data

Name: Wang, Fei-Ling, author.
Title: The China record : an assessment of the People's Republic / Fei-Ling Wang.
Description: Albany : State University of New York Press, [2023] | Includes
    bibliographical references and index.
Identifiers: ISBN 9781438492278 (hardcover : alk. paper) | ISBN 9781438492285
    (ebook) | ISBN 9781438492261 (pbk. : alk. paper)
Further information is available at the Library of Congress.

10 9 8 7 6 5 4 3 2 1

To my teachers and mentors,
particularly
Augustus Richard "Dick" Norton
Soldier, Scholar
1946–2019

Contents

Figures and Tables   ix

Acknowledgments   xi

Introduction   1
    Games of Numbers: A Note on Methodology and
       Epistemology   4
    Arrangement of the Book   12

Chapter 1
Political Governance: People's Dictatorship and the Party-State   15
    The Tragedy and the Grand Detour   18
    The DNA of the Party-State: Mao Zedong Thought   22
    Déjà vu in Beijing: Xi Jinping Thought   27
    CCP Optimality and China Suboptimality   34
    People's Lives and Rights in the People's Republic   37
    Extra-Legal Means for Extra Control   44
    Thought Work, Jingoism, Officials-Standard, and Power
       Fetishism   47
    The Partocracy and the Police State   55
    The Ruling Class and the Aristocracy   64
    Intrusion, Insecurity, and Intranquility   69

Chapter 2
Economic Record: Socialism with Chinese Characteristics   85
    The China Model   86
    Incompetence and Failures: Mao's Great Famine and
       Stark Stagnation   91

Three Decades of Prodigious Growth 95
Distortions and Dysfunctions 98
Extraction and Profligacy 103
Quantitative Assessments of the Record 109
What about India? A Note on Comparison 133

Chapter 3
Social Life: Bitterness, Happiness, and Resistance 135
A Bona Fide Developing Country 134
Bitterness Eaters and Luxury Indulgers 138
Inequality and Poverty 144
Disaster Relief 153
The Elusive Happiness 159
Voting with Feet 164
Watched, Worried, Wrathful 169

Chapter 4
Spirit and Ecology: Culture, Ethics, and the Environment 175
The Officials-Standard and Society 178
The CCP Pantheon of Demigods and Chiefs 184
Moral Vacuum, Amnesia, and the Mind 189
Anecdata of Corruption 194
Academia and Education 196
"We All Fake It" 207
Publication, Antiquities, and Gastronomy 210
The Environment and Ecology 213
Superpower of Imitation 219

Epilogue: From the Record 227

Notes 231

Works and Sources Cited 287

Index 397

Figures and Tables

Figure 3.1 Divorce/Marriage Rates (Percentage) 172

Table 1.1 Legal and Extralegal Punishments in the PRC 39

Table 1.2 Size of Officialdom in the PRC 61

Table 1.3 Crime rate of segments of the Chinese society 75

Table 2.1 Two Economies, Two Indices 99

Table 2.2 Incremental Capital-Output Ratios in Asia (Selected Countries) 113

Table 2.3 Foreign Exchange Reserve, Assets, and Debt (billions of USD) 117

Table 2.4 Two Economies, Two Currencies 121

Table 2.5 Purchasing Power of People's Money 122

Table 2.6 GDP per Unit of Energy Used (Selected Countries) 130

Table 3.1 Economies in Comparison (Selected Countries, 2019–21) 139

Table 3.2 Human Development Index 1980–2020 (Selected Countries) 140

Table 3.3 Horizontal Inequality and Regional Disparity Measured by HDI 151

Table 3.4 Deadliest Earthquakes in the World (1964–2016) 154

Table 3.5 Happiness Ranking in Comparison 161

Acknowledgments

As the intended sequel to my earlier book, *The China Order* of 2017, and the second volume in my planned trilogy on China, this book is the result of an immodest effort of assessing the People's Republic of China, an immense polity that governs nearly one-fifth of all humankind.

Over the decade of working on this project, I have accumulated countless debt to people too many to be listed here individually. This book was largely drafted during the global COVID-19 pandemic of 2020–2022, when I had mostly virtual but always inspiring and rewarding contact with my colleagues and students at Georgia Institute of Technology. The following institutions, listed alphabetically, kindly hosted my related research visits over the years: European University Institute, National University of Singapore, National Sun Yat-sen University, National Taiwan University, Sciences Po, Sungkyunkwan University, Tunghai University, US Air Force Academy, University of Macau, University of Tokyo, and Yonsei University. Generous grants from the Fulbright Commission, the Georgia Tech Foundation, the Hitachi Foundation, and the Minerva Initiative helped my research. A Neal Family Grant enabled editorial assistance. I received valuable comments when I presented parts of my work at (alphabetically and in addition to the host institutions above): Academia Sinica, American Political Science Association, Auburn University, Center of Strategic and International Studies, Council on Foreign Relations, International Studies Association, Joint University of US Special Forces, Korea University, Ludwig-Maximilians-Universität, National Chengchi University, National Chungcheng University, National Chungshin University, National Tsinghua University, Peking University, Princeton University, Seoul National University, Strategic Multilayer Assessment, Sun Yat-sen University, US Military Academy (West Point),

US National War College, Universiti Kebangsaan Malaysia, University of Denver, University of Indonesia, University of Malaya, University of Pennsylvania, University of Tennessee, and Victoria University. I salute you all from the bottom of my heart.

SUNY Press made this book possible, and I was encouraged and benefited greatly by the three anonymous reviewers. Katherine Thompson and Paul Goldsman copyedited the manuscript with marvelous expertise and meticulousness. Kaylin Nolan helped with the bibliography. Of course, I am alone responsible for any imperfections that may remain. Kirk Warren designed the book cover, at my suggestion, using partially Zeng Liansong's original 1949 design of the PRC national flag.

My family and friends are always the greatest source of love and support to me. My busy wife and sisters-in-law have particularly strived hard to allow me to concentrate on this book during a global pandemic. For all that I am extremely fortunate and eternally grateful.

Finally, this book is dedicated to my teachers and mentors over the decades in several countries, particularly Doctor and Colonel (USA Infantry) and Professor Augustus Richard "Dick" Norton: a soldier, scholar, leader, and mentor who was instrumental to the start of my academic career at West Point (US Military Academy) three decades ago. On October 6, 2018, after years of not seeing each other in person and only weeks before his passing, Dick wrote me from Massachusetts with these heart-warming words: "Looking back to West Point, I remain proud that we knocked down a few barriers and invited you to join the faculty. That was a good decision indeed." I cannot agree more, and I am always grateful. Cherish Hope, Rest in Peace, my friend.

Introduction

In my 2017 book *The China Order*, I attempted to reread and analyze Chinese history and worldviews to ascertain the Chinese political tradition and ideation with an examination of the Qin-Han polity and the China Order of *tianxia* (all under heaven).[1] This book, *The China Record*, the sequel to *The China Order*, focuses on contemporary China, the People's Republic of China (PRC), with an assessment of the record of the PRC state as an alternative mode of political system and a distinctive model of socioeconomic development.

As China's economy and military are both racing to become the largest in the world, the political system of the CCP (Chinese Communist Party) that governs the PRC is increasingly impacting all of humanity, beyond shaping the fortune and future of the Chinese people. In 2021 and again in 2022, the US-led West openly concluded that the rising power of the PRC had become a systemic challenge and even an existential threat to world order and world peace.[2] A solid understanding of the Chinese mode of governance and model of socioeconomic development, therefore, has become imperative for the world, including the Chinese people. In the contemporary era of globalism and multiculturalism, it is also theoretically and practically critical to ascertain both the strengths or merits and weaknesses or flaws of the PRC system. To that aim, I hope that I am presenting a concise analysis that the reader will find holistic, accurate, and useful for understanding the achievements, deficiencies, strengths, and weaknesses of the PRC under the CCP. In addressing both the issues of viability and desirability of the CCP-PRC, I wish to develop a positive, factual statement and a normative, critical analysis of the party-state. The findings of this book I hope will aid in a policy-oriented consideration about the reality of and the strategy for the world's response to the rising Chinese power.

The assessment of the PRC in this book is based on an analysis of its organizational characteristics and operational performance in four areas: political governance, socioeconomic development, people's life, and culture and the environment. The purpose of this four-part examination is to ascertain the feasibility and appeal of the rising PRC power as a contender and substitute for the current world leadership, its ability to replace the West and particularly the United States, and the viability and desirability of Beijing's pursuit of the China Order as an alternative to the West-led Westphalian world order. Over the past seven decades, the PRC has gone through many epic ups and downs of reforms, advances, successes, failures, and reversals, with countless heroes, villains, survivors, and victims. I am fully aware that all this remarkable continuity and great changes make my immodest efforts in this book truly a task with many fascinating yet humbling challenges.

I will first examine the political governance in the PRC, the "people's democratic dictatorship" under the CCP, particularly its record of protection of the lives and rights of the Chinese people, provision of social order and security, and public services and governmental efficiency. Then I will attempt to report and assess the Chinese economy, especially its achievements and problems during recent decades, before analyzing Chinese social life and the spiritual and physical ecology of the PRC. The emphasis of this book is on the operation and impact of the CCP governance in such areas as political representation, criminal justice, fiscal and monetary policies, the state-led growth model, innovation, academia and education, inequality and poverty, disaster relief and pandemic prevention, culture and ethics, social tranquility, and the preservation of antiquities and the environment. Through the combined application of normative evaluation and comparative study of both quantitative and qualitative data, this book aspires to ascertain the nature and characteristics of the PRC. It especially intends to help address questions about the efficacy, efficiency, power, sustainability, and desirability—or the lack thereof—of the CCP-PRC as an emerging superpower and a potential world leader with a set of alternative values and norms. As a small effort to advance China studies, this book has chosen to focus on the overall record, in order to offer an assessment and diagnosis rather than attempting an all-encompassing and detailed narrative of PRC history.[3]

More specifically, this book seeks to demonstrate what the CCP-PRC has really been and truly represents. It finds political suboptimality,

socioeconomic underperformance, and cultural and environmental devastation, which the PRC state has brought to China to achieve a remarkable
CCP optimality that provides longevity and power for the regime. The
first three decades of PRC history (1949–1979) constituted a bona fide
tragedy of monumental proportions. The CCP, driven by its inner logic
and compounded by the personal ambition and incompetence of its
dictatorial leader Mao Zedong, forcefully rolled back many of the gains
and changes of the pre-PRC century (1840s–1949). The PRC became
the vehicle for the CCP's power and its simultaneous attempt to recenter
and reorder the whole world for the sake of its ultimate regime security.
For that, the CCP imposed a long and disastrous detour on China, failed
the Chinese people in many ways, and faced a much-deserved demise.[4]

The post-Mao CCP responded by retreating to the pre-PRC
nationalist trajectory and policies for its own survival. Henceforth, over
the past four decades, in an instance of great historical irony, the CCP
has been both saved and enriched by the West-led Westphalian System
it always sought to displace. The Chinese people regained considerable,
albeit still limited, socioeconomic freedom and autonomy. The Chinese
economy consequently experienced prodigious, explosive growth to lift
hundreds of millions of people out of abject poverty. The PRC gained
a wide-ranging technological sophistication (mostly imported) to obtain
a fairly complete and competitive modern industrial system. Chinese
society and daily life improved and transformed significantly, largely in
the general direction of modernization and Westernization. As will be
reported in detail in this book, a large "middle class" has emerged with
significant disposable income and properties, traveling extensively at
home and abroad. The development of written laws and the proliferation
of norms of individual rights, especially in the commercial sphere, have
enhanced predictability and trust to facilitate market-oriented businesses.
Religions and socioculture in general have experienced a reinvigoration.
The PRC has also actively participated in international cooperation,
from its weighty position in the global chain of production and massive
foreign aid, to sending large troops for UN peacekeeping missions.

However, much of the Maoist governance aimed at ensuring the
security and power of the CCP autocracy has continued in China. The
DNA of the party-state has largely remained intact. The PRC became a
giant by the numbers, strengthening itself through a gargantuan extraction
of the riches of a booming Chinese economy that has been made possible by the freer and hardworking Chinese people, and critically fueled

by the massive import of capital and technology. In aggregate, the PRC record of governance and socioeconomic development is at best average, and mostly suboptimal, if qualitatively and quantitatively assessed by the criteria of life, civil and human rights, freedom and tranquility, living standards and health care, economic efficiency and innovation, ethics and cultural development, socioeconomic justice and equality, management of natural disasters and epidemics, and preservation of antiquities and the environment. Beyond the systemic deprivation of rights and freedoms, the CCP has imposed tremendous opportunity costs on the Chinese people, causing profound and multifaceted ramifications for the Chinese social fabric, moral codes, intellectual creativity, and ecology. Some of this great impact may still be mendable and reversible, but some of it appears to be incurable if not untreatable, and has already profoundly affected peoples beyond the PRC. As the CCP continues at home and attempts to reorder other nations in its image abroad, the rising Chinese power expropriated and expended by the CCP represents a suboptimal and undesirable but feasible and formidable alternative to the existing Western leadership of the international community, impacting the future of human civilization.

Games of Numbers:
A Note on Methodology and Epistemology

A distinctive feature of the PRC state and also a profound consequence of its governance has been the systematic and widespread monopoly and manipulation of information in general and statistics in particular.[5] This has been a major hurdle to assessing China, especially with quantitative data. A short discussion of epistemology is presented here to familiarize the reader with this critical issue of methodology in the study of China, which often hampers and misleads even the most diligent observers. This quick note may also serve as an appetizer for the rich, raw, taste of the record of the CCP-PRC party-state.

In the same well-documented Qin-Han imperial tradition of information censorship for political purposes, the CCP always forcefully monopolizes all information in China, with the latest declaration of the "Party's management of [all kinds of] data."[6] By means of this monopoly, the party-state constantly and sometimes farcically omits, hides, falsifies, and destroys many records, especially quantitative data. In March 2022, for instance, Beijing released its official readout on the content of a two-hour virtual meeting between Chairman Xi Jinping and US President Joe Biden "three and a half hours" before the event actually took place.[7] As omnipresent and omnipotent as it is, the PRC state does not publish many of the kinds of statistical information other states routinely do, let alone in a precise, timely or useful way, if it bothers to collect and track the data at all. As incredible as it is strange in a country of longtime central planning, the PRC State Statistical Bureau told official media that it "has stopped collecting" data on the size of the government payroll since 2008; so far, Beijing has released the grand total number of its "civil servants" only once ever in history (in 2016).[8] This is perhaps the inevitable result of the Party's long tradition of secrecy and stern discipline for keeping the countless opaquely defined, often ad hoc, secrets; it has become second nature for officials always to strive for less transparency. To be sure, political pressure often incentivizes a government to unduly hide or twist sensitive data, even in a democracy like India or the United States. But, just like the rather usual impulses and actions of government censorship of history writing, which have long been unusually comprehensive, effective, and malevolent in the Chinese World because of its "worldwide" monopoly of information and centralized, singular censorship with force, the politicized games of numbers in the PRC are both quantitatively and qualitatively unrivaled in the world.[9] In China, the systemic totality, centralized style, and deeply internalized tradition of the CCP's number games basically face no meaningful scrutiny and challenge; while in other countries, especially in open, democratic societies, with multiple and open sources of information and fact-checking, the competition from a free media nullifying the censorship efforts often tends to speedily and significantly mitigate the problem.

Given that many international organizations like the United Nations and its affiliates mostly rely on Beijing as a source for official statistical data, the international pollution of information by the CCP's number games is a chronic problem seriously hampering and even disabling China studies and international comparison. It is an elementary but critical mistake to read and accept official PRC data as the equivalent of the much more contested and verified data from other countries. Epistemological limits, propaganda, and biased punditry tend to mislead observers, especially casual data consumers like politicians and the public, to misread and caricature the Chinese "like Voltaire's mandarins or the happy peasants of Maoist propaganda." The official Gini Coefficient in the Mao era, for example, was only 0.32, which has prompted many to still misjudge the PRC of that time as poor but equal; however, a PRC study in 2013–2014 proved that the real number of Gini Coefficient in the 1960s and 1970s was more than twice as high at the world record of 0.6–0.7.[10]

Politicized creative accounting and reporting of financial data, even for publicly traded companies, sometimes by the autonomous Chinese franchises of international accounting firms, appear to be common in the PRC. The government itself seems equally inundated by bogus data.[11] One study in 2013 asserted that the PRC GDP figure itself might have been artificially inflated by $1 trillion, or 12 percent. Two studies in 2017 and 2019 suggested that the PRC GDP was probably "overstated," while in 2021 another study using satellite-based data indicated that the PRC GDP numbers could be inflated by as much as 35 percent.[12] Official PRC media concluded in 2014 that local governments have the tradition of constantly "injecting water" into statistics at all levels, chiefly the promotion-determining GDP figures. In the fourth quarter of 2019, the officially reported GDP growth rate of 6.2 percent might in fact have been only 3.2 percent. Many counties in the relatively backward Northeast added 20 to 127 percent "water," reporting a local GDP larger than that of Hong Kong.[13] A former CCP county secretary, based on the experiences of 120 peers, concluded that "statistics in China is just a myth [. . .] we commonly have to 'technically reprocess' the numbers [and] about 30% of all [economic] data contains water." The CCP leadership itself is said to have long suspected the inaccuracy of PRC economic statistics, especially the GDP numbers. Similarly, the PRC State Statistical Bureau admitted in 2021 that its numbers about fixed asset investment in China contained a large amount of "water," up to 20 percent, from 2007 to 2019.[14] The PRC trading status may be a digital "mirage," with trade figures and especially trade balance data that could be miscalculated and overestimated by as much as 36 percent.[15] Chinese real unemployment rate is routinely "at least twice as high as" the published figure.[16] The critically important numbers related to grain and food production are likely habitually inflated. The massive local government debts, highly consequential to national financial health, are often recorded and reported in two sets of books with underreporting by as much as two-thirds.[17] Partially responsible for many disasters in the past, including the great famine in 1959–1962, the CCP's structural problem of doctoring numbers clearly remains widespread today. In May 2021, the PRC State Statistical Bureau released the seventh once-a-decade census data, after many delays, reporting a total population of 1.41 billion and other demographic information.[18] Many Chinese immediately pointed out big holes and many signs of data-doctoring in the report; and officials were compelled to quickly come out to "dispel rumors and disbeliefs."[19] At the end of 2021, the former PRC Minister of Treasury openly criticized the uselessness of Chinese economic data. In 2022, the State Statistical Bureau reported national new births 16 percent (1.75 million) higher than that reported by the Ministry of Public Security.[20] In order to booster food security, the CCP decreed the country to "return [developed] land to grain farming" (fugeng) and used satellite imagery technology to verify that to promote or penalize local officials accordingly. As a result, local governments spent massive public funds in the 2010s–2020s to fool the satellites with fake rice paddies built on baren hills, yams and beans planted on cement pavement and roads, and grain farms tilled on filled fishponds and demolished fruit orchards, vegetable greenhouses and residential dwellings.[21]

As will be further discussed later, one of the CCP's number games has been about poverty and its measurement. Beijing has long maintained a poverty line much lower than the international standard and thus greatly underreports the proportion of poor people in the PRC. Prior to 2009, the PRC set its poverty line at $0.32 per day. In that year, it revised its poverty line to an annual income of ¥2,300, which equates to a daily income of $0.50, and then revised it again to $0.99 in 2015. This is far below the UN abject poverty line of $1.25 ($1.90 in 2015) and much lower than the poverty line set by China's poorer neighbors such as the Laos, Vietnam, and Cambodia. The 2009 poverty line was about ten times the ¥200 yearly poverty line of 1985 (equivalent to US $25 at the time), while the PRC GDP grew more than fifty-six times greater and the underreported official inflation increased eleven times during this period. The PRC reported only 15 to 45 million people living in poverty in 2010 by its own standard, rather than over 200 million by the UN standard.[22]

For career advancement, CCP officials appear to routinely massage their data, just as Beijing does to all information that it thinks may impact its political legitimacy or image. Other than financial data, which many observers and analysts are fully justified in treating with suspicion, even deaths by road accidents are underreported by more than three-quarters. Scholars working for the World Health Organization (WHO) concluded that traffic deaths in the PRC totaled 276,000

(20.5 per 100,000) annually in the 2010s, but Beijing reported only 65,000 (5 per 100,000). In 2021, a flood killed hundreds of people in Zhengzhou, and the government confirmed six months later that local officials "indeed" underreported the fatalities by more than one-third.[23] In 1987, the PRC central government started to report suicide rates in China to the WHO. At eighteen to twenty-three suicides per 100,000 people, that figure remained steady as among the highest in the world until around 2008. In 2009–2011, Beijing reported a "drastic decline" in that rate—a 58 percent drop—to eight to ten suicides per 100,000, and also a drop of 63 percent and 90 percent, respectively, for rural and female suicide rates. Since then, these sensitive figures have officially remained stable as among the lowest in the world (just below the world average), but always with no researchable or verifiable breakdowns and always inconsistent with fieldwork reports published in 2014 and 2018 by PRC scholars.[24] The "uniquely PRC" pattern of higher suicide rates that had persisted among rural residents (over urbanites) and women (over men) have both completely reversed since 2011 to match the world's general pattern.[25] Needless to say, the reader would easily share my sincere wish that these profound changes, however curiously dramatic, are real. I will discuss this subject further in chapter 3.

Over the decades, comprehensive games of numbers have been both a prized tradition and a standard statecraft of the CCP. The monopoly on and selective dissemination of information help to powerfully mask the suboptimal performance in the PRC and to back up the CCP's much propagated claim of the special "superiority and advantage" of socialism (or CCP leadership, Mao's line, Deng's reform, the Chinese "way of governance," Xi's reign, or whatever is unique about the CCP-PRC system).[26] PRC scholarship on the Chinese political economy, including the few serious and interesting studies such as the quasi-institutionalist explanation of the CCP's "superior ability" to grow the Chinese economy quickly, tend to uncritically base arguments on the face value of official numbers and thus unfortunately end up mostly provisional and preposterous, even propagandistic.[27] The often applauded and admired Chinese educational system and its reliance on centralized, imperial-exam-like test scores and rote memorization are, in fact, neither superior nor beneficial to knowledge creation and economic growth, when using the real numbers of a complete dataset. Many of the official PRC numbers have been repackaged and endorsed by the Chinese franchises of Western consultancies like McKinsey Greater China.[28] Misleading and delusional exuberance easily follows: in 2013, many publications, including *The Economist*, falsely forecasted that the PRC GDP (non-PPP) would surpass the US GDP by 2019.[29] As I will show in this book and its sequel, the reading by outsiders of the nature and strategy of the PRC has been even more prone to being misleading and misconstrued. Inundated by the CCP's crafty and endless games of numbers, many influential China observers seem to have malfunctioned in a way similar to that of some renowned Western scholars such as Paul Samuelson, the first American Nobel Laureate in Economics, who repeatedly made erroneous and even laughable but widely influential assertions and predictions about the Soviet Union as late as the 1980s. Indeed, uncritical use of the big numbers from the PRC easily leads to the influential conclusion that "China is Number 1," even though the wise message may still be "Never bet against America."[30]

Both the collection and dissemination of some basic information for daily life in the PRC are also tightly controlled and often purposefully hidden or distorted. For instance, the government, in the name of national security, has monopolized map-making with its own geodetic datum called GCJ-02 (topographic map non-linear confidentiality algorithm), colloquially nicknamed the "Mars Coordinate." It uses an obfuscation algorithm to add random offsets to both the latitude and longitude of positions on maps, as opposed to using the real coordinates of the common WGS-84 (World Geodetic System). As a result, "all maps in China are inaccurate" and the coordinates of a location are commonly hundreds or even thousands of meters off on digital maps guided by GPS (Global Positioning System). With the blocking of apps like Google Earth and Google Maps, satellite navigation in the PRC has long been decoupled from the rest of the world at the expense of accuracy, convenience, and efficiency.[31]

The clever and systematic games of numbers have helped the CCP to rule with indoctrination at home and propaganda abroad. But the toll on truth, action, and morality is heavy and enduring, as I will discuss later in the book. Such games often also have disastrous and literally deadly consequences on an epic scale. For proof, one need only look at the hyperinflation of agricultural production statistics known as "launching satellites" in Mao's Great Leap Forward campaign to surpass the West in power; that numbers game caused and aggravated the Great Famine, which led to the world's worst-ever loss of human lives in peacetime, 37 million or more, in less than four years (fall 1958–spring 1962). Similarly, the COVID-19 pandemic, which originated in China in December 2019 and has affected every nation, with at least 5.5 million related fatalities worldwide by early 2022, appears to once again demonstrate the potency and lethality of the CCP's second-nature games of numbers.[32]

After the outbreak of a new coronavirus (SARS-CoV-2) causing COVID-19 in central China, the PRC state failed to adhere to its international legal obligations, instead suppressing critical information for at least three weeks (December 30, 2019–January 20, 2020).[33] In 2019 and 2020, I heard from multiple independent sources (epidemiology managers, researchers, and clinicians in Beijing, Wuhan of Hubei, and Zhejiang) about an internal CCP rule of publishing no more than 10 percent of "bad" public health information, especially numbers.[34] Courageous Chinese whistleblowers, "truth tellers," like Dr. Li Wenliang, have apparently been punished and silenced by the government from the very beginning.[35] The PRC Center for Disease Control, with its post-epidemic study of antibodies found a few months later in the population of 11 million in Wuhan (the origin of the pandemic), inadvertently provided the evidence that the PRC government indeed reported only 10 percent (50,340) of the half million infected there in early 2020.[36] Studies by the RAND Corporation and the University of Hong Kong estimated that the actual number of cases of COVID-19 infection in the PRC could be thirty-two to thirty-seven times higher than Beijing's publicly announced figures.[37] Some have suggested that Beijing has "intentionally underreported" Chinese cases and deaths "by a factor of 100 or more"; the "true" number of excess deaths caused by the virus in China in 2020–2021 was "not [the officially reported] 4,636, but something like 1.7 million" or twice that in the United States; and the real "total case fatality rate in Wuhan [. . .] was 5.6%" or "4 times higher than the fatality rate of about 1.5%" in the United States, but not the PRC's scarier, officially reported rate of 7.7 percent.[38] According to the official PRC time-series data, 14.22 million Chinese died in 2020, far more than the 9 to 10 million deaths each year from 2006 to 2019.[39] The 4.22 million or more excess deaths could be the result of gross statistical errors and discordant data manipulations, a huge spike of deaths by accidents and other diseases when the health care system was impaired by the pandemic (and the draconian quarantines), or a COVID fatality about 100 times higher than reported—or a combination of the three. A team of PRC researchers reported that, in Wuhan during a nearly three-month lockdown in 2020, "excess mortality" rose 56 percent with about 68,130 "extra deaths," including 21,230 "from covid-19 related pneumonia" (or 5.5 times the official COVID mortality of 3,869 for the city) plus thousands more "from non-covid-19 related" pneumonias that shockingly jumped thirty-five times and a rise of deaths "from non-communicable disease" like cardiovascular diseases (29% increase), diabetes (83% increase), high blood pressure (100% increase), and "other diseases" (92% increase).[40] Using the American epidemiologic criteria of "death with" rather than just "death from/of" to assess the data, deaths related to the virus in Wuhan alone could be fifteen times greater than the PRC official numbers for the whole country. If proven as such, the CCP's COVID-19 related numbers game would certainly rival those "satellites" it launched during the Great Leap Forward in both absurdity and infamy.

Even the WHO, heavily criticized for being in the CCP's pocket, has complained about Beijing's delays and poor cooperation in information reporting.[41] China has nearly one-fifth of humankind and has endured the longest effects of the virus;[42] yet the PRC's official data about the pandemic has been an extreme outlier, with tight censorship and little verifiable proof or useable details, becoming sadly useless and irrelevant to the effort to fight the virus, and has likely misinformed and misled the world in profound ways. Per research led by the PRC's own star doctor-official Academician Zhong Nanshan, the impact of the COVID-19 virus decreases by one-third for every five days earlier implementation of quarantine measures.[43] Studies from the United States and the United Kingdom have also shown that quarantine measures just a week earlier could have saved thousands of lives and even halved the death toll.[44] Therefore, if the CCP had not customarily suppressed the real information about the disease for those initial weeks, the global pandemic could have been just a local epidemic or a small endemic, with hundreds of times fewer infections and fatalities. The tenacious allegations that the virus was human-altered in and leaked from a Wuhan laboratory, due partially to the distrust aroused by CCP's rather "common" coverup and numbers game that had gone haywire this time, have been threatening to fault the PRC state much more for the pandemic.[45]

While it is impossible to assess the full extent of the CCP's many games of numbers without a total opening of the party-state's secret vaults, a general pattern and some notable characteristics appear to have existed for decades. For instance, if the numbers are perceived to be positive for the regime's image and power, or just benefiting the officials in charge, lots of adding "water" or significant data inflation is fully expected, with cases of complete fabrication frequently reported. If the numbers are deemed negative or simply unpleasant, including fatalities due to natural disasters, accidents, conflicts, and epidemics, systemic omission and massive underreporting, and even total denials, are commonplace.[46] Armed with that realization and with extra and informed efforts to judiciously select, authenticate, verify, and contextualize, I hope we may still be able to utilize official PRC data meaningfully in assessing China, with some guarded and issue-specific confidence.[47]

Arrangement of the Book

Chapter 1 covers Chinese political governance through documentation of political history and reality in the PRC. The first thirty years of the PRC was a grand detour of epic proportions. The post-Mao CCP greatly retreated from both the economy and the society for its own survival. However, the Maoist governance of the "People's Democratic Dictatorship" has continued with the same ideology of Mao Zedong Thought. A defining feature of this mode of polity is the CCP's tight control of political life, the justice system, education, resource allocation, and sociopolitical mobility. Over the decades, this party-state has been resilient, extractive, powerful, and corrupt, delivering a mixed, mostly substandard, and often disastrous governance but a distinctively optimal service to the regime itself.

Chapter 2 assesses the record of the Chinese economy. It evaluates the socioeconomic development in the PRC over the past seven decades, especially the recent years. The PRC has emerged as the world's second largest economy measured by GDP and top exporter after decades of impressive economic growth, driven and fueled by foreign capital and technology. However, the basics of the Chinese political economy, and especially the state–market and state–society relationships, remain politicized and CCP dominated. Contrary to conventional knowledge, the performance of the Chinese economy has been rather average and often suboptimal. A profound case is that the PRC fiscal and monetary policies have created a sea of red ink and countless bubbles, afflicting the economy and perpetrating inefficiency and lack of innovation. By capital return, energy consumption, and other measures, China remains a typical developing economy in the world. Two shining achievements, the high GDP growth rate and the world's largest foreign currency reserve, are much less glittering under closer scrutiny.

Chapter 3 discusses the PRC's record in the areas of quality of life, political and socioeconomic equality, social tranquility, mobility, and emigration. It also examines such issues as disaster relief, pandemic prevention, public health, birth control, and the war on poverty. The chapter reports on the vastly different lives and life chances of the Chinese people and the Chinese elites in the PRC, and how they feel about and respond to the government. Measured by the living standard and overall quality of life, China under the CCP firmly remains a developing nation, despite the state and the ruling elites having obtained a world-class wealth and lifestyle.

Chapter 4 looks at China's culture and ecology. It describes and assesses the impact of the PRC state on the Chinese spiritual and physical ecologies, including cultural development, ethics, academia and education, antiquities, and the environment. The CCP has actively attempted to control and reengineer Chinese culture, Chinese demography, and the Chinese mind. Through documenting sociocultural symptoms such as the so-called moral vacuum, culture of corruption, and the devastation of the environment and antiquities, the chapter enhances the understanding of the nature and meaning of the CCP-PRC as an alternative, competing mode of governance.

The epilogue briefly summarizes the book's findings to set the stage for further studies on the rise of China and how that may be managed. The works and sources cited, together with the notes, lists the works and sources of information utilized in the book.

1

Political Governance

People's Democratic Dictatorship and the Party-State

This chapter starts my assessment of the People's Republic of China's (PRC) record of performance under the Chinese Communist Party (CCP). In examining the governance of the CCP-led PRC, I have three aims: to ascertain the nature, composition, and characteristics of the party-state of the "People's Democratic Dictatorship"; to outline the operation and impact of this polity in the areas of protection of people's lives and rights, provision of social order and security, and governmental efficiency; and to assess the overall record of the party-state as an alternative mode of governance, and particularly its key strengths and weaknesses. In the process, I will explore the CCP's ideology, way and style of governance, sources of power, methods of control, and major achievements and deficiencies. With a firm control of political life, justice system, education, resource allocation, and sociopolitical mobility in China, the CCP-PRC party-state is found to be resilient and powerful but also corrupt and extractive, delivering a mixed record of governance—expensive, mostly suboptimal, and often disastrous for the Chinese people, but distinctively effective and even optimal for the regime itself.

More specifically, based on its structural DNA and ideological orientation, the PRC state has behaved as a revived Qin-Han polity of authoritarianism and totalitarianism, a Maoist autocracy that has mightily struggled internally and externally since day one to safeguard itself. The PRC state is generally a polity of rule of man by will, force, and ruse, instead of rule of man by law, let alone rule of law.[1] After more than seven decades, the CCP has yet to honor any of the solemn pledges for democracy it made in order to win the Chinese Civil War. The People's Republic has never had much in the way of genuine and meaningful political election. Officials at all levels of power are selected, appointed, and managed top-down by the CCP leaders, who monopolize all political power. Other than the CCP, the world's largest population has neither functional political groups nor meaningful nongovernment sociopolitical organizations. Without the people's consent through participation, the source of the party-state's legitimacy has therefore been limited to force, ruse, and performance—all are increasingly expensive and fundamentally volatile. This partocracy, often just a personal dictatorship, has imposed a long and tragic detour on China and failed the Chinese people in many ways, especially during the first three decades, largely under Mao Zedong's personal dictatorship. The record of the PRC is thus a textbook case of an authoritarian party-state, a partocracy that exhibits strong traces of a totalitarian theocracy and a personal dictatorship. The party-state systematically deprives people of their political, civil, and human rights in order to obfuscate, atomize, and depower them. Fairness, tranquility, and innovation are low while inequality, injustice, and the cost of governance are high, with the vast majority of the Chinese people, including many if not most of the Chinese elites, excluded from the political process. Some of the worst peacetime losses of human lives in world history, for example, happened under the CCP. The bloated PRC state itself is easily seen as inefficient and inferior in providing social order and public safety, beyond its rather effective and even optimal accomplishment of regime protection and enrichment. The PRC has been consistently ranked by international observers as "not free," with a declining score of freedom in recent years, peering among such countries as Azerbaijan, Central Africa, Libya, and Yemen.[2] The forceful indoctrination and manipulation of people's mind with misinformation and disinformation have been matchlessly potent in guiding the rising Chinese power, portending an alarming future for the Chinese people and the rest of the world, as will be discussed further in this book and its sequel.

The post-Mao CCP retreated and hid for its own survival for about three decades (1979–2008). Much of the Maoist polity, however, has continued in China, as the same "people's dictatorship" but veiled as a "collective leadership" instead of the Maoist personal rule.[3] The post-Mao "collective leadership," or oligarchy of a group of leaders with a "core," however, started to morph into an openly personal dictatorship after 2012 when Xi Jinping ascended to become the top leader. Since its creation, the CCP itself has always held to its "core discipline," formally formulated in 1943, that mandates unconditionally that "the individual obeys the organization; the minority obeys the majority; the subordinate obeys the superior; the whole party obeys the Central." The purpose of all that, as the Party has repeated since 2019, is to ensure that the party leads and controls everything and everyone everywhere through "two maintenances": "to maintain the centralized uniform authority and leadership of the Party Central, and most critically, to maintain the core position of General Secretary Xi Jinping in the Party Central and in the whole Party."[4] Starting in 2017, after massive purges veiled as anticorruption, Xi has restored Mao's dictatorial practice of requiring all top leaders to regularly submit their personal job reports (shuzhi) with "self-criticisms" for his comment and approval.[5] Beyond these "nauseating displays of loyalty" in the constant ideological campaigns, which characterize autocratic politics in general and CCP politics in particular, a long list of 149 "negative" acts a cadre "will be punished for" has reportedly been in use to enhance political obedience.[6] These moves have buried the nominal "collective leadership." With the amendment of the PRC Constitution in spring 2018 that removed the term limit of PRC Chairman, Xi is to be, like Mao, a singular ruler for life.[7]

In the 2020s, the PRC state emerged as a giant by the numbers, enriching and strengthening itself through a gargantuan extraction of the Chinese economy. The party-state autocracy has been so resisting of internal reform that "even under its most reform-minded leader, massacred its own people" as they peacefully demanded individual rights and political reform, such as occurred in the Tiananmen Movement in 1989. As a senior China watcher concluded in 2021, "For all the incredible change in China and the quasi-institutionalization and professionalization of the governing cadre, the fundamental structures of the party are still 100 percent intact." The PRC thus became "frozen" in its political transition by the choice of the CCP.[8] In 2021, the CCP published two front-page "proclamations," declaring that the party's "internal DNA" of socialism and communism "has not let China down" in its "rejuvenation" of the Chinese nation/civilization and that the PRC does "not let socialism down [and will] do more to promote world socialism" through the realization of the China Dream of "constructing the community of common destiny for humanity."[9] It appears that the CCP's grand objective of political influence and control in the world, therefore, is to impose, on the whole of humanity and at the expense of the democratic rule of law, a suboptimal way of governance, a pre-Enlightenment Legalist-Maoist autocracy with a colorful façade of mutilated Confucianism, pseudo-socialism and communism, blatant statism, contrived Chinese nationalism and populism, and imperialist globalism.

The Tragedy and the Grand Detour

Under the leadership of Mao Zedong, the CCP relied on force, ruses, and good fortune to win the Chinese Civil War against the KMT-ROC (the Republic of China governed by the Kuomintang or Nationalist Party) in 1946–1950.[10] This landmark event convincingly demonstrates the reversibility of historical trends and the human potential for gigantic regressions and tragedies at a continental scale. Though claiming to always be "great, glorious, and correct," the CCP in fact appears to fall far short of those worthy aims.[11] Officially named a liberated "New China" with a "people's democratic dictatorship," the PRC is in fact a great leap backward institutionally and ideologically, as it is a revived Qin-Han polity of authoritarianism, and even totalitarianism.[12] Much like BC (Before Christ) and AD (Anno Domini) or BCE (Before the Common Era) and CE (Common Era), "pre-liberation" and "post-liberation" have been the official PRC chronological divisions since 1949. The name of the CCP's military, the People's Liberation Army, implies its ostensible mission of liberating the still unliberated peoples outside the PRC. The seven-plus decades of CCP rule on the Chinese Mainland has been a vivid testimony to the remarkable staying power and governing capacity of a determined and unscrupulous autocratic regime, in a post–World War II world organized under the West-led Westphalian System. For the Chinese people (including many of the PRC ruling elites), who comprise one-fifth of humankind, this modified Qin-Han polity has wrought a grand detour of history, resulting in a colossal waste of time and opportunities for many generations. The history of the PRC is replete with some of the gravest atrocities and sacrifices in human history and a record of deficient to disastrous performance in political governance, socioeconomic development, and protection of human life and rights. In hindsight and factually, the Maoist PRC appears to be an epic China Tragedy.[13]

The CCP hypocritically but rewardingly criticized the KMT-ROC for not democratizing and liberalizing China fast and thoroughly enough.

Yet the PRC replaced the ROC's inadequate political democracy and insufficient social liberty with far less of both. Liberal writer Chu Anping (purged by Mao in 1957 as a leading Rightist) famously predicted back in 1948 that "we are struggling for freedom, yet under the rule of the KMT (ROC), the issue is more or less freedom; but if the CCP rules, the issue will be having or not having freedom."[14] Leading Chinese liberal scholar Hu Shi reportedly put it humorously but succinctly in the late 1940s: Soviet Russia had bread but no freedom, the United States had bread and freedom, the ROC had no bread but a little freedom, and the CCP came with neither bread nor freedom.[15] Indeed, Chinese intellectuals and students in the ROC enjoyed the "freest and most active" publication and assembly as well as campus activities in Chinese history all the way until the CCP's takeover in 1949. Even after 1949 when the ROC lost mainland China and underwent years of panicky anti-communist "white terror," the persecuted political and cultural dissidents in Taiwan, from Yin Hai-Guang, Lei Chen, and Bo Yang to Li Ao, all fared qualitatively better than their counterparts in the PRC.[16] Under the CCP's "people's democratic dictatorship," the clock of Chinese political development was stopped and reversed, the significant gains in political democratization and social liberalization from the last decades of the Qing Dynasty obliterated. Even in the late 1940s when a Civil War was in full swing, China still had more than 150 active and competing political parties and groups.[17] Those political parties were quickly destroyed or crippled by the CCP.

The most severe manifestation of the China Tragedy was perhaps the incredibly bloody birth and maintenance of the autocratic CCP regime, particularly Mao's personal dictatorship. Tens of millions of Chinese people died for (and against) the creation of the PRC between 1927 and 1950. Even more were killed or starved to death afterward for the survival and pursuits of the CCP, almost all during peacetime. Some examples: From 1950 to 1953, one "land reform" campaign put 2 to 4.5 million people to death, and one "suppression of counterrevolutionaries" campaign mandated the execution of a "minimum" of 0.1 percent of the then 450 million population (at least 712,000 were actually shot, exceeding the quota). In 1958 to 1962, one manmade great famine starved 37 to 45 million people to death. One "cultural revolution" caused the unnatural deaths of another 7 to 20 million in 1966 to 1976. With at least 40 million to as many as 80 million deaths, Mao's CCP was responsible for killing more of its own people than Adolf Hitler and Joseph Stalin combined.[18] In comparison, PRC scientists calculated that, from 180 BCE to 1949, the combined death toll of all major climate disasters in China was 29.9 million. In absolute numbers, if not exactly proportionally, the CCP bloodbaths by guns and famine are clearly among, if not exceeding, the worst mass murders and genocides in human history, from the Mongol conquests, Nazi Germany's Holocaust, the Soviet Union's purges, to the Khmer Rouge's mass killing. And this, as one Hong Kong observer angrily alleged, was just one of Mao's "Ten Grave Crimes" against China.[19]

Unlike the mass killings in other countries, the CCP bloodbaths remain heavily shrouded in secrecy today, and they go without much truth and reconciliation, or commemoration. Officially, these unbelievable losses of human life are still mostly whitewashed and strictly off limits to even academic studies in the PRC. The perpetrators and executioners have largely evaded accountability. They are still seen as largely justified and are even enshrined in the PRC. Mao, for instance, is increasingly defended and revered in PRC classrooms and even private living spaces as the people's hero, great savior, wise leader, national patriot, and folk deity.[20] The post-Mao CCP, under Deng, Jiang, and Hu during the time of "hiding," decided to condemn some of Mao's most obvious and egregious sins. The official *Short History of the* CCP, rewritten once every decade, for example, always devoted a whole chapter to critically describe the so-called "Cultural Revolution," the final part of Mao's reign, as "ten years of chaos and disasters" in 1991, 2001, and 2011. In 2021, however, the new, extended edition deleted the chapter. All this is insult added to injury suffered by the Chinese people, who are still meant to exalt Mao as the savior with "great benevolent governance" and the CCP as *the* Party that is forever "correct"—a reality that perhaps outmatches the most nightmarish stories of fiction. To the CCP, still, its past is just the prologue for more of the same "mission," concluded a group of foreign observers in 2022.[21]

Not just horizontally compared to contemporary countries but also vertically compared to the Qin-Han rulers in the past, the PRC (especially under Mao) has been exceptionally lethal. Mao and the CCP, after winning the throne to become what was in essence the new imperial ruler of China, did not follow the tradition of founding emperors in the past, in which it was customary to relax and allow the exhausted people to rest after the brutality of civil war—the so-called "recuperating and recovery" policy.[22] The extraordinary prolonged rule of terror, however, does not necessarily prove the CCP leaders to be especially merciless, unreasonable, or bloodthirsty when compared to other past autocratic rulers of the Chinese World. Rather, it is the tragic futility and cruel fate of restoring a Qin-Han polity in the post–World War II world that proves this: unlike most of his predecessors, Mao did not rule over the real *tianxia* (all under heaven). The CCP has never yet managed to control the entire known world. A Qin-Han polity without the China Order of world empire is destined to fight ferociously and constantly against just about all other sovereign peers for its own security and survival. To fulfill its historic mandate, the economically underperforming party-state has to face the much stronger West. In doing so, it must rely on extreme extraction and the sacrifice of its own people.

In addition to massive loss of life, the China Tragedy under Mao had a record of deficient socioeconomic development and decreased living standards for the surviving Chinese who were all caged by the CCP through the tight net of urban *danwei* (work units) and rural communes. The vast predatory extraction by the state was basically all wasted during the manmade economic depressions of the Great Leap Forward and the Cultural Revolution. Some have argued that Mao's whole "revolutions" were simply unnecessary, undesirable, and disastrous. This grand China Tragedy may even surpass another grand human tragedy in the twentieth century, the "Soviet Tragedy."[23] Essentially, the PRC under Mao is understood to have caused the Chinese people to lose many tens of millions of lives, more than thirty years of time for several generations, countless antiquities and cultural treasures, and many of their civil and human rights and freedoms, in addition to enduring heavy brainwashing, widespread damages to the traditional social and ethical fabric, and serious international humiliation and mistreatment. Looking back, almost all of this death and stagnation could have been greatly reduced or even completely avoided had Mao and the CCP not adopted policies driven by the hunger for power, ultra-selfishness, and incompetence of a revived Qin-Han autocracy.[24]

Upon Mao's death, for the sake of its own regime survival, the CCP pivoted to the pre-PRC (late Qing and Republican era) Chinese route of economic development through state capitalism, limited social liberalization, and massive but selective import from and imitation of the West. The profound results have included impressive gains in economic growth and state enrichment, which are now the basis of the rise of China or, more precisely, the rise of the PRC's state power. The hardworking Chinese people took advantage of the state's retreat from their socioeconomic activities and lifted themselves materially out of abject poverty, *in spite of* rather than *because of* the CCP. Even so, the Chinese Mainland remains stagnated in many regards decades later, with poorly defined property rights, a less independent legal system, a more polluted environment, and an authoritarian government that is more corrupt and unrestricted than the KMT-ROC of seven decades ago.[25] The CCP has failed to realize nearly all of its glorious promises for China except that it has managed to accumulate wealth and stay in power. Institutionally and ideologically, the CCP-PRC party-state today has remained essentially the same Maoist governance, impressively optimal for an autocratic regime but irrepressibly suboptimal and adverse for the Chinese people.

The DNA of the Party-State:
Mao Zedong Thought

The Maoist China Tragedy has receded considerably over the past four decades, but the political system and governing norms established by Mao nonetheless still define today's CCP-PRC party-state, shaping its strength, flaws, and ambition, and perpetuating its overall suboptimal governance. The DNA of the CCP remains intact. The long shadow of Mao, officially termed "upholding the banner of Mao Zedong Thought forever and under any circumstances," fundamentally ensures that the PRC today is institutionally and operationally still the same as that which Mao founded seven decades ago: an autocratic one-party polity, a reincarnated and hardened Qin-Han polity, "a Leninist–Stalinist party-state or partocracy" inevitably centered on a so-called "core leader" who is a strongman akin to a non-hereditary emperor, "a new dynasty of son-of-heaven plus meritocratic bureaucracy,"[26] or what classic authors have termed non-hereditary autocracy or aristocratic oligarchy.[27] This Confucian (and Marxist)-coated Legalist empire still appears as hard to change as ever without a costly implosion or explosion or, ideally, some precise and transformative gene therapy. Like before, international comparison and competition with the outside world, especially from the West, still remain the leading force for sociopolitical change in China and thus the principal threat to the CCP dictatorship.[28]

As I have attempted to outline in the prequel to this book, *The China Order*, Mao was a master of wordsmithery and ruses for power and domination, a mixed product of traditional Chinese paternalistic agrarian society and imported, often half-baked ideas that included social Darwinism and the Leninist–Stalinist version of Marxism. He was a frustrated, anarchistic rebel before joined the radical agents of Moscow-financed International Communism. In practice, Mao proved to be a shrewd and effective practitioner of Qin-Han-style Realist power politics.[29] To observers in hindsight, like the authors of two international bestsellers, Mao was

> a liar, ignoramus, fool, philistine, vandal, lecher, glutton, hedonist, drug-peddler, ghoul, bully, thug, coward, posturer, manipulator, psychopath, sadist, torturer, despot, megalomaniac and the greatest mass murderer of the twentieth century-in short, a monster, equal to or worse than Hitler and Stalin. He cared nothing about the fate of the Chinese people and his fellow human beings, or even his close friends and relatives. He was driven by bloodlust and the craving for power and sex. He ruled by terror, led by native cunning.[30]

In contrast, Mao is revered by the current CCP leadership as

> a great Marxist; a great proletarian revolutionary, strategist, and theorist; the great trailblazer of the Sinicization of Marxism; and a great Chinese patriot and national hero in modern history; the core of the first-generation leadership of the Party, and the epic great man who led the Chinese people to completely change their fate and the outlook of their country [. . .] a great figure leading the tides of the Chinese nation and world progression.[31]

In reality, Mao may not have exactly fit into the villain stereotype—he "was no racist," as all were "equally" beneath him as "the people's emperor"—but he did try to start a world war, "was responsible for the death of more people than any other dictator in the twentieth century," and drove the Chinese people "into the abyss of bloody social experiments," as observed by some of his biographers. Firsthand observations seem to suggest that Mao likely suffered from serious mental illness from the early 1950s on, characterized by deep paranoia, emotive irrationality, a dysfunctional family life, sexual overindulgence, delusions, fantasies, and an eternal fear of losing power.[32] Political psychologists might simply label Mao as a typical tyrant personality:

[a] narcissist with severe superego deficiencies (who) . . . may have some advantages in rising to power, and his behavior may be an effective response to some real-life factors, but once he has consolidated his position his reality-testing capacities diminish. Fantasies held in check when his power is limited are apt to become his guides to action. As a consequence, his behavior becomes more erratic, he runs into difficulties in meeting his goals, and his paranoid defenses become more exaggerated.[33]

In many ways, Mao Zedong was mostly analogous to Chiang Kai-shek (his chief antagonist for the rule of China) and most other ROC rulers—they were essentially military strongmen, Sinocentric and autocratic with similarly incomplete and insufficient formal education, comparable middle-class family background, strong personality and remarkable tenacity, and extraordinary talent for rallying and controlling people. They were essentially all imperial son-of-heaven wannabes. Mao and Chiang both creatively tried to substitute the Mandate of Heaven with the Mandate of the People—Chiang in fact started the famous slogan of "serve the people" in 1937, five years earlier than Mao, who used it with much greater effectiveness. According to a later-purged CCP-sympathizing intellectual, both Mao and Chiang were rogues—"Chiang is an urban gangster and Mao is a rural bandit." They both had a deep-rooted inferiority complex and a common sense of insecurity, albeit for different reasons and expressed in different ways; they both also had an exaggerated sense of ego and radical ambitions of ruling and changing China and beyond. Crucially, however, they led different political organizations with divergent internal organization, ideology, and operational dynamics. They had very dissimilar associations with intellectuals, capitalists, overseas Chinese, and foreigners. Personally, Mao was much more unbounded than Chiang in pursuing life indulgence, defying ethical confines and trusts, and disrespecting rules and formality—Mao was essentially a peasant emperor with few internal and external constraints.[34] The known notes and polemics penned by Mao in his twenties show an angry, ambitious, and extremely self-centered believer of boundless Voluntarism, moral-free individual Heroism, and a burning desire to grab the Mandate of Heaven to save, lead, and reshape China and the world, including the people's minds.[35] Unlike Chiang, who became a rather devout Christian, which, along with Confucian doctrines, may have added some internal constraints,

Mao literally believed in nothing other than raw power and "history," which he struggled all his life to write and rewrite for himself. Sadly, the people on the Chinese Mainland ended up with the worse of the two autocrats as their dictator for life. As I wrote in *The China Order*:

> In an astonishing way, Mao was as dominant and powerful, tyrannical and murderous, vulgar and selfish, and cunning and unscrupulous as any Chinese emperor. He was also as incompetent and egomaniacal in managing the country, especially the economy, and as corrupt and unethical in his personal life as any of the Chinese emperors with an ultra-luxury lifestyle and endless sexual indulgences. Mao was indeed the "freest" man, the only free man in a great nation where no one else had much freedom, to experiment at all costs with his ultra-narcissistic ultimate truth of "science for the fundamental order of the universe" that was actually recycled ideas of the China Order of the imperial times.[36]

To be fair, Mao was not born a devilish person. His thirst for power and control, reliance on force and ruses, unscrupulousness and brutality developed gradually, reinforced by his cynical view of people and society and by his success in power struggles. His deep-seated inferiority complex mixed toxically with his seemingly unlikely victories and his self-aggrandizing propaganda to make him not only ever-more arrogant, cunning, manipulative, and deceptive but also totally careless about anything other than his face and his historical position. Mao was indeed a curse for China, but he was also a creation of Chinese history, institutions, and culture. He was both a perpetrator and a victim of the China Tragedy, like nearly all of his willing and unwilling executioners. His story is, thoroughly and completely, an epic and classic tragedy.[37]

Despite all the deep resentment and well-justified distaste for Mao in the present, the shadow of Mao has loomed large since his death in 1976. As a dissident PRC historian argued in 2013, "Mao's crime is that he interrupted the progress of constitutional democracy in China and led China into the dead end of class struggle and one-party dictatorship. [. . .] He did nothing good for the Chinese people, although the CCP may be indebted to him," and thus the Party has enshrined him, however nominally and cynically, for the self-serving purpose of legitimizing its one-party rule.[38]

The Party-State Mao fostered and governed was an ecosystem uniquely suitable for any similarly dispositioned ruler. Nearly all of the top leaders and senior cadres of the CCP-PRC have been either conscious Mao worshippers or unconscious Mao followers, and probably all have sampled their fair share of Mao's plots and crimes. As in ancient times under the Qin-Han autocracy, all CCP officials behave as mini-emperors, or more preciously, mini-Maos, to their subjects and subordinates. Of course, the matter of degree is significant, as quite a few CCP officials and even leaders were evidently "better" and more conscientious and respected than others. Mao has therefore become both the source of political legitimacy and also the role model for the party-state that carries his mode of organization and governance in its DNA. His much-propagated charisma, seemingly improbable and grossly exaggerated political successes, and unscrupulous but effective ideas and tools for power struggle and rule have all become sources of legitimacy and an arsenal for his followers. In particular, Mao's successful wordsmithery in using the Mandate of the People as a substitute for the traditional Mandate of Heaven has served CCP leaders enormously well.[39]

With the flattering title of Mao Zedong Thought,[40] Mao's ideological legacy consists of a mixture of Legalist statecraft of the Qin-Han polity for herding people, imported Leninist–Stalinist totalitarianism wrapped in pseudo-Marxism (and increasingly pseudo-Confucianism in the post-Mao era), and a blend of the "dark arts" of unscrupulous and unbounded pragmatism for retaining control, exemplified by his frequently quoted "three magic weapons" for power and success: "united front, armed struggle, and Party organization." To this trinity is added the "fourth magic weapon" of propaganda and "thought work"—brainwashing and mind control through the monopoly of information and the boundless use of disinformation, which has actually been "even more important than guns" to the CCP's political power.[41] Mao perhaps indeed achieved a pinnacle of articulating the cruel but effective art of Qin-Han polity in relatively plain instructions, though he did not outline the ugly details as candidly as did his real intellectual ancestors, the authors of Legalist classics like *Guan Zi, Book of Lord Shang,* and *Han Fei Zi.*[42] Mao Zedong Thought is thus treasured, and even irreplaceable, for any self-serving authoritarian or totalitarian ruler governing through force, fear, fakery, and fraud.

Compared to democratic rule of law, authoritarianism based on the rule of man by force and ruse tends to be "natural," seductive, and even addictive to political leaders; a successful, seemingly odds-defying autocratic model of governance like Maoism is logically a treasure trove for the autocratic CCP leaders. While crucially dependent on imported (Western) goods, services, and technology, the post-Mao CCP leaders took great pains to remain adamant that Beijing will never allow a dreaded "Westernization" in China. The most "reform and open" minded leadership of Deng Xiaoping and his protégés enshrined "Four Cardinal Principles" centered on the CCP's monopoly of all political power in 1979,[43] jailed and exiled democracy activists of the so-called "Spring of Beijing," crashed the 1989 Tiananmen Uprising for political change with armored divisions, and willed this "Basic Party Line" to be followed unwaveringly "for one hundred years" until the CCP succeeds in establishing an "advanced socialism in China" that will reach the level of a developed country in terms of power and wealth.[44] This party line has been reaffirmed and elaborated ever since by Deng's successors, who have routinely pledged: "We will never have a rotating-governance by multiple-parties, nor ideological pluralism, nor checks-and-balances among the three powers [executive, legislative, judicial], nor bicameralism of legislation, nor federalism, nor privatization [of property and land ownership], nor constitutionalism, nor judicial independence," and "[we will] resolutely oppose, resist and prevent the West's so-called 'constitutional governance.'"[45] The CCP is fully determined to stick to Maoism in order to stay in power, "to lead everything everywhere," above all and forever.[46]

Déjà vu in Beijing: Xi Jinping Thought

Xi Jinping became the General Secretary of the CCP in 2012, and was the first top leader of the PRC not directly handpicked by Mao or Deng. Xi, a product of the Maoist regime whose father (a senior CCP leader) was purged and jailed for many years, quickly started emulating Mao. With a PhD degree, Xi seems rather self-conscious about his education while seen by observers as repeatedly dreaming of becoming Mao the Second or Mao the Better.[47] Backed by the mighty propaganda machine, Xi has emerged as such in the party-state, however undeservingly in the eyes of many. The Party's history has been rewritten accordingly. In 2021, the Party's mouthpiece, People's Daily, promoted "100 famous quotes about the party's 100-year history," of which Mao and Xi each had thirty quotes, while Deng had only sixteen, Jiang Zemin and Hu

Jintao each had ten, with the remaining four from other celebrated CCP leaders.[48] In November 2021, the CCP Central adopted a major resolution on its history for the third time (the first two being in 1945 and 1981). This self-written centennial history honored only five of the thirteen top leaders of the CCP by name, mentioning Xi Jinping fifteen times and Xi Jinping Thought eight times, in contrast to Mao Zedong's eleven times and Mao Zedong Thought's seven times, Deng Xiaoping's and Deng Xiaoping Theory's three times each, and Jiang Zemin and Hu Jingtao once each. It also named two "failed" party leaders (Chen Duxiu and Wang Ming) once each while the remaining six disgraced party chairmen or general secretaries were simply omitted. The lengthier official companion article aptly titled "The Irreversible Course of History" went even further, naming only three of the five, mentioning Xi seventy-seven times, Mao six times, and Deng twice.[49]

By July 2021, the CCP Central had published in many languages a total of sixty-six books "authored" by Xi, surpassing the total number of books by Mao (22), Deng (10), Jiang (8), Hu (4), and three other CCP leaders (19) combined.[50] The textbook of Xi Jinping Thought required for all Chinese students from kindergarten to graduate school is now written in an almost identical prose and similar phrases as that about Mao more than four decades ago.[51] This bewildering development, akin to full and open worship and emulation of Hitler and Stalin in today's Berlin and Moscow, is in fact logical and even inevitable given the CCP's structural DNA and internal dynamics.[52] During his formative years in the 1960s and 1970s, Xi was probably awed and shaped by Mao's power. To someone in the PRC with limited education about the outside world, Mao is indeed easily *the* model dictator. In late 2021, the CCP celebrated the "two establishments" of Xi as the supreme leader and Xi Jinping Thought as "the Marxism in contemporary China," "the Marxism of the 21st century," as well as the party-state's "guiding" ideology—a triple honor once bestowed only on Mao. Like Mao, Xi is also extolled as "the Sun" in the PRC.[53] As expected, Xi managed to prevail over his opponents and critics to secure his third term as General Secretary of the CCP to continue as the more imperious supreme leader at the Party's 20th National Congress in October 2022. As such, the PRC formally moved back to pre-Deng with the coronation of a mimic of Mao, "the great leader of the people" forever.[54] The CCP's all-out effort and heavy investment to bet on a cult of personality in a strong, Mao-like dictator with the ability and "charisma" to ensure its regime, however, could end up illustrating what Karl Marx acidly wrote about Louis Bonaparte back in 1852: "All great historical facts and personages recur twice. [. . .] Once as tragedy, and again as farce."[55]

All the sins and crimes committed by Mao are to be buried and forgotten and, better yet, spun as heroic and necessary "explorations" and revolutions for the sake of a number of grand, eye-catching causes: to liberate China and the world, to end capitalism and imperialism so as to build a communist paradise, to continue the "first cultural revolution" of the 1910s New Culture Movement with his second "cultural revolution" of 1966–1976, or, lately, to rejuvenate the great Chinese nation and civilization. Perhaps because Xi feels unable to change or improve Mao's playbook but still harbors the urge to be similarly powerful and infallible, Xi Jinping Thought is now promoted in the PRC as an outgrowth of Mao Zedong Thought to continue and "strengthen" the CCP-PRC political system. Sycophants openly claim that "to eliminate the criticisms from the West and restore cultural self-confidence, we need the third cultural revolution" to follow Mao under Xi.[56]

Xi mimicked Mao's style of double-talk to declare that, after 1911, "the Chinese people tried" but "failed" at "constitutional monarchy, restoration of the imperial system, parliamentary system, multiparty system, and presidential system," before they correctly and successfully "chose socialism." In 2013, he sternly prohibited the mention and discussion of "seven issues," including "constitutional democracy," "universal values," media and judicial independence, civil rights and civic participation, "neo-liberalism," crony capitalism, and "nihilist" examination of the CCP's past. Openly, he simply "rules out Western-style political reform for China."[57] The chief mission of the CCP, asserted Xi in 2014, "is to firmly believe in the future of communism and socialism with Chinese characteristics" and the key to China's much treasured "national independence" continues to be "the independence of [our political] route, theory, and system."[58] Soon, Xi reinvented the "Party's mission and initial commitment for the happiness of the Chinese people and for the great rejuvenation of the Chinese nation."[59] However, perhaps due to the fluidity and impossibility of both the conceptualization and the practice of delivering happiness to everyone, the Party's mission statement was further substantiated with an equally otiose but somewhat less intangible aim of "common prosperity for everyone." Semantic variations aside, the elaborate and elastic but vague metamorphosing, and all-encompassing "mission" or "commitment," appears a normative justification for an eternal

CCP autocracy that appears as grand and crafty as it is empty and illusory. First-graders have now been instructed to memorize that "only with firm CCP leadership, can [we] achieve the [dual] goal of common prosperity for everyone and the great rejuvenation of the Chinese nation," so as to "listen to and follow the Party." College students in biology have been taught to visualize how "CCP's red DNA" carries on its "infinite and eternal mission," like the DNA of all cells and animals.[60]

The CCP's political banner, "socialism with Chinese characteristics," is authoritatively defined by the top PRC official in charge of social sciences as "the people's democratic dictatorship" centered on the "the communist party control of political power." Essentially, this definition is meant to safeguard the Maoist Qin-Han polity and the CCP's monopoly of political power in perpetuity, with the "red aristocracy" of the CCP as the "perennial ruling party."[61] Citing Deng Xiaoping, who decreed that "consolidating and constructing socialism will take a long time, many and even many dozens of generations," Xi Jinping concluded that the CCP's rule will last for a very long time, a notion compatible with the entire history of the Imperial China since it has been only some seventy generations since Confucius.[62] In 2015, the new PRC National Security Law made the CCP's wish China's national law: national security was defined first and foremost as the need "to protect the regime of the people's democratic dictatorship and socialism with Chinese characteristics"; "state power" was ranked ahead of China's sovereignty and territorial integrity in order of importance; and the CCP was given the leadership of all national security work. In January 2021, a senior CCP scholar announced that "China is comprehensively returning to the historic ideology and principle of Chinese civilization [. . .] to melt the old so as to forge a new Chinese civilization [. . . and] the Chinese Communist Party is the new type of civilization."[63] Two months later, twenty-two PRC departments and ministries jointly issued a decree to reaffirm the all-around effort of "eradicating the breeding ground" for civil society organizations. Then Xi declared his party-state as the so-called "whole-process people's democracy under the CCP leadership" that is "the most extensive, most useful, and most genuine democracy" in the world.[64] Intensely indignant over the US-convened Summit for Democracy (held December 9–10, 2021), which invited 111 states including Taiwan but not the PRC, the CCP simply propagated its "whole-process" democracy as the real and the best democracy while painting the United States and the West as fake, inferior, and harmful variants of democracy.[65]

Appropriating the Maoist legacy and emulating Mao extensively and even comically, a new cult of personality has been in full bloom, especially since Xi reshuffled the top echelon of the CCP in 2017. Chairman Xi got Chairman Mao's special title of "People's Leader" and is deemed to be all-wise and almighty, one who plans for and reshapes both sky and land, fights for and moves both the heavens and the earth, "assures the people's happiness," and is full of the "four core talents" needed to be the new and desperately needed "great political leader of the whole world." Having "clearly pointed out the right direction" for dozens of endeavors and ambitions in and outside of China—from winning soccer matches, developing the internet, protecting the environment, improving education and health care, "Sinicizing religions" for their "durability," and enriching every locality and gladdening everyone to guiding the "high quality development of humankind" for "a better future of the world"—Xi is to govern the party, the country, and the globe for all people worldwide. The idea of becoming a "red emperor" equal to and exceeding Mao in stature has become the dream that guides Xi and his supporters.[66] Like before, most if not all political elites in the CCP now appear morally relative and cynical but obedient, trading dignity for security and prerogatives, with the common objective of stashing family and wealth safely, preferably abroad. The autocracy itself seems stuck striving endlessly and exhaustively for security and survival through ever-more control and power at home and abroad, with the same Maoist ambition of recentering and reordering the whole world.

The CCP quickly enshrined "Xi Jinping Thought" in both the CCP Constitution and the PRC Constitution just a few years into the Chairman's reign.[67] It is perhaps a rather typical self-aggrandizing by an overconfident ruler with an inferiority complex and his calculating cronies, a despairing move to buttress Xi's otherwise thin credentials and shaky position, or it may be that the CCP is desperately gambling on a strong, Mao-like dictator to fend off the mounting pressure for political change from within and without. "All authority goes to one," as Xi's then top lieutenant Li Zhanshu proclaimed in 2018, like a court servant in imperial times; that kind of absolute personal power was written into the CCP Constitution and fully expressed in the leadership reshuffle in 2022.[68] Xi Jinping Thought, is now formally a part of the CCP's bedazzling patchwork of ideology: "Marxism-Leninism, Mao Zedong Thought, Deng Xiaoping Theory, the Theory of Three Represents, the Scientific Outlook on Development, and Xi Jinping Thought on Socialism with

Chinese Characteristics for a New Era." The long suffix of Xi Thought, though, is wordy and awkward, perhaps reflecting a lack of confidence, a bit of modesty, poor wordsmithery, or all of the above. In an effort to substantiate and visualize his thought, Xi called for the "construction of the Party's spiritual lineage," which, according to the CCP Department of Propaganda in 2021, included the "first group" of about fifty "great spirits" ranging from "Jinggangshan Spirit" and "Yan'an Spirit" in the 1920s and 1930s to "Space Travel Spirit" and "Anti-Pandemic Spirit" in the 2020s.[69]

The indoctrination and propaganda machines all predictably geared up. According to a senior CCP cadre-scholar, Xi Jinping's idea of "community of common destiny for humanity" has been "unanimously echoed, supported and accepted by the people of all countries in the world," and Xi is fully qualified and more than ready to be the desperately needed new world leader "to govern the globe" better. Within a few years, more than two-dozen colleges, institutes, and centers were set up to study Xi Thought, including a national center on "Studies of Xi Jinping economic thought" launched in 2022. On Xi's sixty-seventh birthday in 2020, a highly promoted article by a top CCP propagandist, "on behalf of the Party," certified Xi Jinping Thought as the updated and improved "Marxism of the 21st century," advancing the original "truth" discovered "in the 19th century" and updated by Lenin-Mao-Deng "in the 20th century," to provide a complete "China solution" and lead all humankind to write "the most wonderful chapter of history in 500 years."[70] The puffery to overhaul and rule the world far exceeds Mao's, who just whimsically "changed the heaven and moved the earth" in China. The true effectiveness of the second-coming of Mao, embodied in Xi Jinping Thought, however, already seems dubious, as some CCP insiders have openly blasted Xi and called him a fraud and failure.[71]

Simply stated, and without mercilessly boring the reader with the CCP's theoretical oeuvre, the essence of Mao Thought to Xi Thought is unsurprisingly all about the total and unscrupulous control of all power (and by extension wealth and stature) in China by the party, particularly its top leader.[72] With deliberate conceptual complexity and pretentious theoretical sophistication, this wordy supreme dogma hides the simple thesis of a selfish party demanding personal power for control of everything. Xi's own summary of his Thought appears dull and dreary, perhaps a sign of the degeneration of language ability at the top echelon of the CCP. The whole "eight points of clarification and fourteen points of

perseverance" of Xi Thought essentially boils down to the blatant declaration that the CCP Party Central (read the top ruler) "must lead" (and
control) absolutely everything and everyone everywhere and forever. A
somewhat new idiom reworking Mao's old mantras of "continued revolution" and "world revolution" is Xi's expression of his China Dream: "a
Chinese style of modernization under the CCP leadership to rejuvenate
the Chinese nation" and "to continuously construct the community of
common destiny for humanity" in the world so as "to create a new kind
human civilization."[73]

As under Mao, the CCP under Xi seems to remain a well-disciplined,
highly centralized, and unscrupulously autocratic machine for control,
extraction, and mobilization. Adorned with the standard Leninist–Stalinist
bells and whistles and claiming to represent and serve the people, the
CCP continuously relies on its politicized discipline, clandestine operatives,
saturating indoctrination, and countless perks to require and procure total
loyalty, obedience, and sacrifice of its members who, according to a party
insider, behave like gangsters or "ranked slaves."[74] The Party monopolizes
every form of power in the PRC; some contemporary observers compare it
to a secret society.[75] Further, as countless CCP officials and scholars have
attempted to articulate, the PRC party-state under the guidance of Mao
Thought and Xi Thought has become "the Chinese way of governance
for the whole humanity" and "the Chinese [or wiser or better] leadership
for the world [or peace or globalization or prosperity or justice]." All this
is also wrapped up as key to the "world communist movement in the
21st century." That is, the CCP has declared, with visible actions, to
aggressively repeat "Mao's global war for a new China Order," to take
over the current (Western and US) world leadership, and to influence
and govern the whole world.[76]

It is common and perhaps useful for observers to emphasize some
of the CCP's appearances and conclude that it "has always been nationalist," "remains communist," or is now "Confucian" in nature.[77] But the
party-state is more than all that with a remarkably unchanged DNA.
Relying on "ruthlessness, ideological agility, and economic growth," and
appropriating the imperial beliefs and images of the past, the CCP has
managed to survive for a century and to rule China for seven decades.[78]
Today, one feels a sense of déjà vu with Beijing: the same institutional
structure, ideological foundation, basic style of governance, and "dark
arts" of autocratic Legalism dressed with pseudo-Communism, mutilated
Confucianism, strong statism, simulated Han-Chinese nationalism, faux

populism, and imperialist globalism that made the Maoist China Tragedy and Suboptimality continue to dominate the PRC.[79]

CCP Optimality and China Suboptimality

Tragic, tenacious, and predictably persisting in its mandate or curse, and with new energy to reorganize the world, Beijing has followed its rhetoric with concrete deeds. However, proclaiming itself to be a destined and better alternative to the West and the United States to lead and guide humanity, the PRC today is in fact still institutionally and practically the same underperforming and disaster-prone political system it has always been, evolved only from the China Tragedy under Mao to the China Suboptimality after Mao. It has remained an inferior, if not always disastrous, form of political governance.

The other side of the China Tragedy and the China Suboptimality of the PRC is its peculiar CCP Optimality. As an autocratic government, Beijing is not ineffectual or weak all the time or on all issues. Authoritarian-totalitarian government certainly can be powerful, effective, and even occasionally efficient on certain issues. In fact, an autocratic regime can outdo democratic rule of law on some focused mega-projects (by disregarding the cost), in speed (by working in quick bursts toward a monodimensional objective), in orderliness (with few messy and vacillating debates), and for the benefit of a chosen few (sometimes only the ruling group or even just the ruler himself). The PRC state indeed appears to harbor "stunning illogicality" and "unmatched absurdity" inside its leadership, according to some insiders. To the CCP rulers, however, the regime has certainly been rather clever in overcoming many odds and achieving its top objective of safeguarding absolute power and the amazing prerogatives for the small group of ruling elites in the Partocracy. The CCP-PRC is thus a powerful and even optimal machine of a centralized authoritarian-totalitarian governance for the interests of the regime, allowing it to survive its many challenges and blunders. It can be considered "weakly resilient" in a sense, if the gargantuan cost to the Chinese people is discounted or dismissed.[80] CCP Optimality and China Suboptimality fits the pattern identified by political scientists studying the sustainability of bad governance by a small "winning coalition of the selectorate" despite, or even because of, the unshakable misery of the people.[81] Doubling down on its traditional arsenal of brazen propaganda and draconian and costly campaign of "people's war on the virus," and with good luck abroad, the party-state appeared to have survived the crisis of the COVID-19 pandemic and even strengthened itself politically in 2020–2021. That said, by spring 2022, the odds appeared to have changed as the CCP got stuck with its exhaustive and exorbitant lockdowns of major cities like Shanghai, amidst the impactful Western sanctions against Moscow, its "limitless partner," following the Russian invasion of Ukraine.[82]

China Suboptimality can certainly be viewed as the price paid for CCP Optimality, squarely placing the regime's best interests against the best interests of the Chinese nation and the Chinese people. In practice, the state–society relationship in the PRC has evolved with some relaxation since Mao, to allow for certain policy adaptations and government reaction addressing imminent needs.[83] Beijing is duly acknowledged and openly envied by many autocrats (even in the West) who face more struggles and fewer successes. Although CCP Optimality is real, significant, and addictively appealing to some in and out of the PRC, it is the co-occurring China Suboptimality that distresses the people (including most if not all of the elites) and defines the CCP-PRC political system. The top-down, heavy yet fastidious autocracy has aimed at and been quite successful in achieving extreme sociopolitical atomization and marginalization of the people. CCP Optimality, which is effective, regardless of cost, in creating and maintaining this suboptimal governance means it is probably almost impossible to self-reform and change without a costly rebellion, dire disaster, or violent destruction.

The opportunity cost of the futile detour during the Maoist China Tragedy and the persistent China Suboptimality is hard to quantify but certainly gargantuan. Related to the record loss of human life in peacetime due to horrendous incompetence and brutal violence, there has been a great loss of time and opportunity for many generations of one-fifth of humankind under the rule of the CCP. The CCP paused and reversed the trend of China's economic development, social liberalization, political democratization, and rise in international stature during the previous century. It launched numerous, almost nonstop political campaigns from day one to purge, control, and eliminate anyone who dared oppose it, and to extract and accumulate resources to strengthen the state in its efforts to recenter and reorder the world. About fifty "anti-party cliques" were purged by Mao to eliminate dissidents inside the CCP alone.[84] The decades-long and thoroughly politicized education and indoctrination in the PRC has twisted and wasted, often literally and physically, the abundant raw talents of the great Chinese people. The long international isolation that the PRC endured under Mao further condemned the Chinese people to long stagnation and deep misery, missing out on decades of industrial and technological revolution, especially during the first three decades of PRC history.[85] Failure after failure cruelly reduced Mao's ambition for "world revolution" to sad and desperate scrabbles to stay in power by any means. For all its suffering, one-fifth of humankind gained almost nothing; even the "revolutionary" CCP had to return to the old, pre-1949 model of economic development and foreign policy just to survive.

A unique way to see the depth and breadth of the China Tragedy and the China Suboptimality is to observe how implausibly the CCP now justifies its past and its current record. It has become ever harder to deny its failures and atrocities even with all of its monopoly on and concealing of information, prohibition of free press and free speech, and disinformation, which can be both illogical and laughable, such as the common apologist line "it's all about paying the required tuition." For decades, Beijing has had to rely on the essentialization of its dubiously persuasive narrative of patriotism: all the "mistakes, misfortune, and hardship" that the Chinese people have suffered were just the price to be paid for China to "stand up" to achieve national independence and unification. This narrative, though, is actually irrelevant if one reads the real history, since those arguably worthwhile objectives were accomplished by the ROC long ago, by 1945 at the latest (with the exception of the Taiwan issue, which was created by the CCP itself). In recent years, an even vaguer and emptier but grander and holier, and hence mesmerizing, line of the CCP has been that, from Mao to Xi, the CCP somehow always led the people to move heaven and earth to rejuvenate the great Chinese nation/civilization and to better humankind and the world. Or in the Maoist lingo of continued Chinese Revolution and World Revolution: the party-determined "pious sacrifices by us Chinese patriots," who are implied to be the world's future ruling race, is all necessary and worthwhile. Oblivious of facts and logic as it is, such a statist and imperialist party line seems to have captured many Chines elites, including even some of the renowned liberal intellectuals who are otherwise critical of autocracy and the CCP.[86]

To fully document all the details of China Suboptimality would require many more books. For our purpose, a broad-brush portrait of the PRC record should be sufficient. The reminder of this chapter will substantiate and elaborate on the inferiority and undesirability of CCP political governance, as illustrated by its substandard and mostly deficient record of protection of life and provision of public goods, including social justice and tranquility, public security and safety, human and civil rights. The CCP is found to have systematically misinformed and disinformed the Chinese people to control their minds and behavior, thus critically hampering innovation and efficiency. I will also discuss the world-class cost of the bloated CCP-PRC partocracy and police state, which necessitates and wastes the excessive and unmonitored state extraction. The next three chapters of this book will complete the examination of China Suboptimality by assessing the records of economic, social, and cultural developments and the environment of the PRC.

People's Lives and Rights in the People's Republic

As I documented in the prequel to this book, *The China Order*, and my earlier book on China's *hukou* (household registration) system,[87] the self-styled "people's democratic dictatorship" of the CCP governs with a few key pillars and ceaseless power struggles and political purges in various forms, including the recent "anticorruption" campaigns. The CCP monopolizes all political power and forces the People's Liberation Army and People's Police to pledge total allegiance to the Party alone. The mighty *hukou* system for social control has made PRC citizenship extremely incomplete, brewing systemic and deep discrimination and exclusion, socioeconomic injustice, and spatial disparities. The state monopoly of the economy, especially land, critical and lucrative industries such as energy and finance, education, and the media has enabled the CCP to extract and disinform at world-class scale. The right to life and the civil, human, and property rights of the Chinese people, including most if not all of the elites, have been constantly compromised. The people have basically no say in how the government is formed and staffed, nor can they give meaningful input on policymaking. They have no reliable recourse for the mistakes and abuses of the party-state.

The place to start is the legal system of the People's Republic, which has treated the Chinese people very harshly. Continuing the Maoist structure and ways of governance, the post-Mao PRC has a highly opaque judicial system comprised of the "people's court" and the "people's procurators" in union with the "people's police," all under the absolute control of the CCP committees at the corresponding levels, and ultimately under the top leader's dictation. Just about all police officers, prosecutors, and judges are required to be CCP members and thus must obey the party leaders absolutely. This unified system, unsurprisingly, is suboptimal in providing security and justice for PRC citizens, including the CCP elites themselves, while constantly and egregiously violating people's civil and human rights. The PRC courts, and the entire judiciary system in general, appear to first and foremost have the "instrumentalist" mission and the political and administrative "embeddedness" for maintaining sociopolitical stability for the party-state.[88]

Under the traditional presumption of guilty as charged until proven innocent (despite the latest written laws being reworded to add, to some extent, the more universally accepted presumption of innocence until proven guilty), the PRC police have countless ways to control and punish people (see table 1.1). Unlike its counterpart in many other countries, the PRC police (even plainclothes officers) are authorized to search and check anyone at any time for no reason and "can shoot without warning."[89] Other than the extra-legal penal system to be discussed in the next section, the "people's police" (and secret police) is authorized by written law and regulations and many ad-hoc, often secret, directives (the so-called "red head-letter circulars") to detain anyone for up to thirty-seven days for any reason; such imprisonment goes by the creative names of "invitation to tea," "free vacation," various forms of investigation, and "administrative" and "preventive" detentions. The detainee is treated like an inmate but avoids a public criminal record if released without further action taken. The police can also invoke "monitored residence" or "residential surveillance" (house arrest) that is mostly solitary with elastic, sometimes infinite, duration. For the punished CCP officials, this house arrest is often the dreaded, extra-legal, *shuanggui* (double designations). Parallel to the countless Gulag-style *laogai* (reform through labor) camps for convicts, the PRC created many *laojiao* (education through labor) camps to imprison people without prosecution or court trial; these unconvicted prisoners endure forced manual labor for weeks, years, or even up to two decades.[90]

After all these prelegal actions, the PRC police can then legally arrest people for between two and fifteen months, which means a criminal record. In the 2010s and 2020s, nearly 77 percent of the prelegal detainees were subsequently "arrested."[91] Virtually all legal arrests end up

Table 1.1. Legal and Extralegal Punishments in the PRC

Action	Length	Executioner under CCP
Pre-legal		
Detention	1–37 days	Police
Monitored residence (house arrest)	flexible	Police
Legal		
Arrest	2–12 months	Police
Indictment and trial	1 day–67 months	Prosecutor/court
Imprisonment	6 months to 25 years to life	Court/police
Property confiscation	Secretive	Court/police
Capital punishment	In 7–14 days or 2 years	Court/police
Extra-legal		
Party Disciplinary Actions		
Shuanggui (house arrest)	Days to infinite	CCP discipline inspectors
Reprimand, demotion, expulsion		Supervising CCP committee
Handover to indictment		Supervising CCP committee
Laojiao (now disguised)	Weeks to 3–20 years	Police
Other punishments (e.g., fines, travel restrictions)		Police

with indictments; in the mid-2010s, 98.6 percent of the arrested were indicted; a "much-reduced" such rate of 91 percent was still reported by the Supreme People's Procuratorate in 2020. The court trial (frequently secret) can last just a few hours or as long as sixty-seven months, during which time the accused are typically held without bail. Since the police, the prosecutors, and the court are three branches of the same CCP ruling entity, an overwhelming majority (a whopping 98.4 percent to 99.4 percent in the 2010s) of indictments end with a guilty conviction.[92] The total pre-sentencing jail time (from detention to arrest and trial) can be as long as 157 months (13 years) in the PRC. For non-PRC citizens, the detention, arrest, and trial can be regulated by the consular treaties between the PRC and their home countries. For instance, US citizens can only be detained without arrest for one month (upon informing the US embassy within 48 hours), and arrested and held without indictment for up to six months. However, in many cases non-PRC citizens were held much longer than the bilateral treaties allow. A recent example is the case of Swedish citizen Gui Minhai, a Hong Kong resident and book publisher. He was kidnapped by PRC secret police in Thailand in 2015, detained, placed under house arrest for about two years, and then formally arrested in 2018 and convicted in 2020 with a prison sentence of ten years. Another case involved two Canadian citizens, Michael Kovrig and Michael Spavor, who were arrested by the PRC police and held for over two years without trial. Apparently victims of Beijing's "hostage diplomacy," the two were released only when the CFO of China's Huawei Company, Meng Wanzhou, reached a deal about the US extradition case and ended her house arrest (in her Vancouver mansion) of nearly three years.[93]

If someone has the extraordinary luck to survive all that without a guilty verdict, the compensation for the lengthy and harsh pre-sentencing jail time is usually negligible. In the early 2020s, fewer than 0.01 percent of court convictions were "corrected" or overturned on appeal, according to the PRC Supreme People's Court.[94] In contrast, in the United States, there is no equivalent of *laojiao* (education through labor) and various forms of detention or monitored residence. US legal statistics show that police arrests end with indictment in only a minority of cases. Only roughly 10 percent of all indictments in the United States ever go to trial, of which only 45 to 82 percent end with a guilty conviction.[95]

The PRC court can sentence people to prison for as little as half a year or for as long as twenty-five years or life; they can also sentence the death penalty, or the death penalty with a two-year suspension. Confiscation of "all personal property" is common (almost mandatory for all death sentences), with "the figures and details of how and what to confiscate and where the impounded funds go never revealed." CCP members, especially the party-state officials, unsurprisingly, enjoy their perks even when facing the law. According to official media, after the substitute punishment of the various "party's disciplinary actions" such as reprimands, warnings, demotions, and revocation of party membership, as many as 70 percent of law-breaking cadres who are caught end up evading arrest, indictment, and jail time.[96]

Law enforcement in the PRC (and governance in general) is seriously plagued by the degradation of the legal profession. Of the thirty-one (provincial) chief justices in the PRC in 2013, only one was reported to have passed the bar exam and only seventeen had a regular college education, with half having no prior experience related to law or policing.[97] Lawyers are clearly subordinate to the CCP's law enforcement apparatus, with frequent disbarment, jailing, or worse for those legal professionals who dare to challenge (or even disagree with) the prosecutor.[98] Money and power appear to easily procure favors for the super-rich, the well connected, and ex-officials at the police station or inside the jail. A renowned journalist in Beijing has written that "a hidden network inside the judiciary system" can fix cases for a set fee with "guaranteed results."[99] Peculiar incentives—such as that the police are often mandated to fulfill arrest and conviction quotas, and that law enforcement (police, prosecutors, and courts) is allowed to retain large portions of confiscated property and fines—inevitably brew many false prosecutions, unwarranted arrests and fines, torture and fabrication, and wrongful verdicts and executions.[100] By his own admission on official media, a top police officer took hundreds of millions in bribes in just a few years, including over ¥90 million (US $13.8 million) in cash alone from one of his subordinates seeking promotion; he then used much of that to bribe others.[101]

The "real" PRC prison population is estimated by experts outside of the PRC at roughly five million, more than 2.5 times the official figures, or twice as big as that in the United States (it would be about five times as large if US inmates convicted of marijuana possession were excluded).[102] Survivors and witnesses nearly unanimously report Chinese prisons to be extremely inhumane, with forced hard labor, deliberately cruel conditions, frequent torture, and high death rates.[103] Many wrongfully convicted individuals have reportedly languished in prison for many years or died there. Abuse and mistreatment, including serious torture, is apparently extended to famous and foreign detainees and inmates.[104] According to a seasoned defense lawyer of three decades, the PRC jails have "countless problems" of unlawfulness, abuse, torture, and corruption that "are only getting worse" and "kept behind secrecy;"

he then concluded in 2019 that "we really don't want to be prisoners of [us] Chinese."[105] Even citizens of Western countries—usually treated with special care and "privilege" as part of the PRC's deferential foreign policy—have reported hellish ordeals within the PRC judicial system in 2020, whether they were criminal suspects or just diplomatic pawns.[106]

This mighty and centralized penal system carries on its Maoist tradition of focused and draconian repression of political dissidents, as authorities assert that "in political cases there are no rights" for suspects and defendants.[107] Replacing the cardinal crime of "counterrevolution" punishable by quick execution in Mao's era, "crimes of endangering state security" have been broadly and opaquely used to persecute and eliminate political dissidents, critics, and opponents.[108] Of more than 100 million mentally ill (16 million of whom are severely impaired) in China, an unknown but significant number are reported as "decreed insane" and interned indefinitely by the police for political reasons.[109]

In 1922, the CCP declared as one of its eleven political promises that it would "abolish the death penalty." But it has in fact used executions extensively and frequently to seize power and rule ever since. As mentioned earlier, use of the death penalty in the Mao era was extremely common, often with many hundreds of thousands of people executed in groups each year. The final approval authority for execution resided with provincial, county, and even township-level CCP leaders prior to 2007.[110] In the post-Mao PRC, capital punishment remains swift and extensive. In the twenty-first century, the PRC reportedly carries out "90–95 percent of the world's total executions every year," with the exact number highly guarded as "the top of the top secrets known to maybe only ten people in Beijing."[111] In 2012, the world, excluding China, executed 680 people in fifty-eight countries, with Iran (360), Iraq (129), and Saudi Arabia (79) ranked as the top three. The PRC alone executed probably five times that total that year and was the only country that refused to release official data or details about its executions. In the 2010s, the PRC was estimated to have executed 2,000 to 5,000 people each year, lower than in the peak post-Mao years of 1983 (24,000 executions) and 2002 (12,000 executions). In 2019, Iran (251), Saudi Arabia (184), and Iraq (100) remained the top three of sixteen countries that carried out the death penalty that year, with a total of 657 known executions, while the PRC alone "executed thousands."[112]

Of the sixty-eight (55 after 2011) kinds of crimes eligible for the death penalty in the PRC, forty-two (31 after 2011) are nonviolent crimes, including seven that "endanger state security," four "economic crimes," and three crimes that "disturb social order."[113] In early 2021, a top official banker received capital punishment for his well-confessed sins that all appear to be white-collar crimes.[114] After considering the gross overuse, numerous blunders, and dubious effectiveness in fighting common crime with the death penalty in the PRC, a Chinese defense lawyer concluded in 2014 that China's death penalty was highly politicized, arbitrary, opaque, and unjust: "Chinese politics needs the death penalty, just like it needs enemies; it creates enemies without opposition and executes people without death-worthy crimes." The massive number of executions appear to have other utility: before Beijing officially declared an end to the practice in 2015, more than 90 percent of transplanted human organs in the PRC were harvested from the executed (either before or after the execution)—making the PRC the only country in the world with that practice for many decades. Interviewees, however, have suggested that the end of organ harvesting was "announced to pacify foreign critics" and that this clandestine practice has not stopped. International researchers have compiled impressive evidence to allege that the PRC has long been framing and executing people for their "suitable" organs, even harvesting organs from live victims to ensure the quality of the targeted transplants for CCP leaders.[115]

As if all this is not cruel enough, since 1983 Beijing has frequently launched national or regional "harsh strike" campaigns to control society hastily and ultra-severely, often with mandated quotas of arrests, convictions, and executions, bypassing the already opaque and expedient judiciary system. An official source shows that during the first year during which a harsh strike occurred (by October 1984), the government arrested over one million people, indicted 975,000, convicted 861,000, and executed 24,000.[116] Similar year-long harsh strike campaigns have occurred at least four times nationally since then, and many more times regionally, often for special occasions (such as in preparation for major political events and celebrations like the 60th anniversary of the PRC in 2009 or the opening of the CCP's 18th National Congress in 2012). In 2021, the CCP's Central Commission of Politics and Law declared that harsh strikes had been "normalized" to regularly "sweep the dark and eliminate the bad."[117]

Human life appears to be routinely dispensable in the PRC for political needs, rulers' convenience, and the physical elimination of any real or perceived threat. In 2008, the Chief Justice of the PRC Supreme

People's Court, Wang Shengjun, openly listed three key criteria for capital punishment: requirements by the laws, "how the society and people may feel," and the perceived impact on "the current overall sociopolitical stability." His successor, Zhou Qiang, reaffirmed in 2014 that the PRC courts respond to hot button issues and serve the CCP's ad hoc policy goals such as "to promote structural reforms of the economy and industrial upgrading," thereby executing polluters of rivers, patients who attack doctors, and venders who sell recycled sewer grease as cooking oil.[118]

Extra-Legal Means for Extra Control

The CCP-PRC governance, as essentially a rule of man by will with force and ruse, is neither rule of law nor rule by law. In 2021, PRC Supreme Court guidelines stipulated that judges should "combine legal judgement with ethical evaluation" to have "rule by law with rule by morality" under the "guidance of Xi Jinping Thought."[119] The already partisan legal system is constantly and crucially supplemented by countless unwritten codes of conduct, ever-changing internal rules, and ad hoc orders that often matter more than the published laws and rules. Extensive extra-legal institutions and measures continue to safeguard the CCP autocracy "to maintain sociopolitical stability" through evolving schemes of divide-and-rule and the spreading and sustaining of fear of the unpredictable, unaccountable, and no-recourse use of force by the state.

Mao's PRC divided and organized the Chinese population after 1949 by permanently listing large numbers of individuals and their families as class foes, unredeemable sinners, and enemies of the people and state; such individuals were to be comprehensively discriminated against, humiliated, monitored, abused, and eliminated. Mao personally set the quota for listed class/state enemies at around 5 percent at each of his numerous political campaigns and purges against various segments of the society, claiming that 95 percent of cadres and masses "are good or relatively good."[120] By the 1970s, these 5 percent enemies had expanded in categories and added up to almost half of the total population, reaching hundreds of millions and literally impacting the majority of the people in China.[121] These public enemies were originally the so-called "five black kinds," consisting of landlords, rich peasants, counterrevolutionaries, "bad people," and rightists. This gigantic list later further expanded to nine categories (with the addition of traitors, spies, capitalist roaders, and bourgeois intellectuals) in the 1960s and 1970s, with at least twenty-one subcategories of state enemies and social untouchables.[122] Mao also decided in 1952 that "landlords and rich peasants" and their extended families should stay blacklisted and specially controlled "for at least 30–50 years." This list was officially discontinued in 1979 (the last group of the listed, nearly 80,000 survivors, had their "hats taken off" only in November 1984).[123]

Maoist governance thus managed to harvest the staying power of a Qin-Han polity by recreating a world of Centralia-versus-the-rest: externally, it was the Soviet Bloc (later the Maoist world revolution and now the rejuvenation of China) and the ever-changing "friends of the Chinese people" versus the West led by the United States (and also the Soviet Bloc at one time). Internally, on the basis of categorizing the Chinese people into as many as forty-five different "classes and family-backgrounds," it was those class/state enemies and "bad people" as the permanent enemy to justify the CCP's totalitarian rule and extraction through divide and conquer.[124] In the less totalitarian post-Mao PRC, the mass campaigns of class struggle have evolved into reliance on the CCP-controlled police and the partisan criminal justice system. The multicategory class/state enemies have been replaced by the constantly updated list of anti-state criminals. Political prisoners are persecuted as common criminals for acts (or even mere words) deemed to be destabilizing to the social order, threatening state security, or working as foreign agents.[125] All local police stations in the PRC continue to maintain a secretive, extra-legal blacklist of "targeted people," comprising 1 to 5 percent of the local population, to be constantly monitored and preemptively detained. Many of the targeted people appear to be the same class/state enemies as in Mao's time.[126]

In addition to the constant and systemic harassment of the targeted people, local police, secret police, media censors, and web police often use questionable criminal charges to frame, punish, silence, imprison, and banish political dissidents. Well-known examples include Liu Xiaobo, Ai Weiwei, Xu Zhiyong, Pu Zhiqiang, Gao Zhisheng, and various social organizations and spiritual groups such as the *Falun Gong*.[127] To prevent any disorderly or disobedient acts on the streets, large numbers of town-management agents routinely strong-arm street venders, protesters, and bystanders. One data collection, "only the tip of the icebag," contained over 2,000 cases of people punished in the eight years of the Xi era (2013–2021) with fines, unemployment, and imprisonment (or "hospitalization for mental illness") for their so-called "speech crimes" (*wenziyu*)—posting words online or speaking in public (such as in a classroom)—that deviate from or question the official narratives.[128]

In 1955 (formally 1957), the CCP started the notorious extra-legal practice of *laojiao* (education through labor) system, under which local police stations, directed by local CCP committees, could send any detainee to forced-labor camps for weeks and months, up to three years or even two decades, during which time these "trainees" would go largely incommunicado with no indictment, trial, or prisoner's rights. Up to two million were incarcerated in these extra-legal camps each year during the Mao era.[129] These *laojiao* camps were at least as brutal and deadly as the larger legal *laogai* (reform through labor) camps for convicts, with an unknown but likely very large number of jail deaths.[130] This system continued until December 2013, when it was officially ended; at that time a reported 100,000 staff members were "educating" nearly 200,000 detainees in about 310 *laojiao* camps.[131] Since then, anecdotal observations have suggested that many of the *laojiao* camps have been converted to a variety of police-run facilities under guises such as mental institutions, community education and drug-rehab centers, prostitution reform camps, shelters for the destitute or "assistance centers for document-less paupers" and various "trouble makers" including appeal- and recourse-seekers, all for holding people under various pretenses outside of the formal legal process.[132] In the 2020s, the PRC police still can and do "hold and educate," and effectively "disappear," people accused of a variety of "social disturbances," including prostitution and particularly political misbehavior, for six to twenty-four months (sometimes longer) without prosecution and trial. Many dissidents and protesters are reportedly put away in mental institutions, often indefinitely.[133] In Xinjiang, for years now, massive "education" camps have detained over a million Uyghurs, a Muslim minority, with little legal process.[134]

In imperial times, the Qin-Han polity of Confucianism-coated Legalism autocracy commonly allowed the people to appeal to the government, possibly bypassing the standard levels of bureaucracy but at serious cost and often risking physical tortures and jail time, to complain about anyone in the world empire, all the way to the emperor, who was of course always infallible. The real effect of such a practice for upholding justice is clearly dubious but the anecdotal, however rare, top-down interventions delivering quick and rather soothing imperial redress have been part of the powerful myth in Chinese political culture that "the officials are bad but the emperor is good once he could hear my case." The CCP restored such a petition or *xinfang* system in the PRC as an extra-legal and "innovative" way of governance and "political participation" for the ruled to seek recourse, report abuses, vent grievances, and obtain solace by appealing to the higher rulers outside of the ordinary chain of jurisdiction.[135] Outside the appeal bureaus and offices of various levels of the government throughout the PRC, it is common to find countless people at almost any time, usually cramped in long lines and spending days to many years, their efforts often ending in financial ruin and doubtful progress in their endeavors. These peculiar scenes vividly demonstrate the depth and extent of the ineffectiveness and even failure of the PRC's legal system and the injustice, inability of expression, and powerlessness many ordinary Chinese people commonly and constantly endure. However, this extra-legal channel, which serves, in practice, mostly for venting and comforting, still apparently soils the image of the party-state, which has been frequently reported to curtail, harass, and hide these often desperate and destitute petitioners. Extreme means have been employed, including kidnapping, forced interception and repatriation, and secret, somtimes indefinite, detention in so-called "black prisons" and "mental health institutions," funded by the officials of the hometown of the petitioners.[136]

Thought Work, Jingoism, Officials-Standard, and Power Fetishism

Mind and information control has been an integral element of CCP governance and a required condition for regime survival and security. As I have attempted to demonstrate in *The China Order*, the misleading and twisted official narratives of Chinese history are just the start of the suffocation of the mind of the great Chinese people. Misinforming and disinforming the people in order to alter and control their minds and behavior have been the CCP's standard practice, paired with the carrot-and-stick of monopolized resources and force. Comprehensive, intrusive, and effective media censorship—particularly, the highly sophisticated and meticulous web-policing nicknamed the Great Firewall—is the foundation for this critical aspect of CCP governance. Mao wisely warned his top cadres in 1959 that if only one newspaper were allowed to freely report the bad news in the PRC, then the CCP regime would collapse and die "in just one week."[137]

Mao and all his successors have always highly prized "thought and political work," also known as "thought reform," "mind remodeling," "brainwashing," "coercive persuasion," "thought control," and "mind control."[138] The CCP's persistent and pervasive propaganda and systemic misinformation and disinformation aimed at mind control in PRC academia, education, and entertainment are second to none in both magnitude and impact.[139] Indeed, the CCP appears to have surpassed the Ministry of Truth described in the classic and prophetic book *1984* by George Orwell in sophistication, extensiveness, thoroughness, meticulousness, and effectiveness. The party-state seems to have practiced and perfected the Orwellian methods of propaganda such as Newspeak, Doublethink, Mutability of the Past, Memory Holes, and Prolefeed—"the rubbishy entertainment and spurious news which the Party handed out to the masses."[140] The CCP has also emulated the art of so-called "Fascist aesthetics" to mesmerize people with repetitive and majestic images and sounds as a civic liturgy to arouse mass zeal and conformity for authority, uniformity, collectivism, and might. Like the European Fascists, the Soviet Union and North Korea, which relied on these extravagant ceremonies to aggrandize and captivate, the CCP has long organized, at an accelerating pace and expanding size in recent years, large parades displaying military hardware and symbolic achievements, massive numbers of marchers well-choreographed in goosestep and spectacular human formations, and colorful slogans and enchanting melodies with subliminal messages, as illustrated by the at-all-costs celebration of the CCP's centenary in 2021.[141] In addition, the methods of social and mind control depicted in the fictional World State in the dystopian classic *Brave New World* by Aldous Huxley are evidently and effectively in use in the PRC.[142] For example, the CCP hires and deploys over two million so-called "net commentators" or "web-propaganda workers," including prisoners serving sentences plus many millions more paid "volunteers," members of the so-called "fifty-cents party," who get paid ¥ 0.5 per approved posting, to pose as common netizens to misinform and disinform within the already tightly controlled PRC cyberspace.[143] One university (Fudan in Shanghai) alone appeared to have hired over 2,000 such "web commentators" in the mid-2010s.[144]

Over the last decade, the CCP has enhanced thought work all around, particularly in schools. Just one province may hire up to 200,000 full-time thought workers as "counselors and political workers" in elementary and middle schools. The CCP Central further decreed in 2021 to "comprehensively enhance" thought work on pupils, with emphasis on "heeding General Secretary Xi" and "following the party."[145] For every 170 college students, Beijing mandates the hire of one full-time thought worker (increased 30% in four years to reach 219,000 in 2022), who enjoys higher pay and securer promotions than academic faculty members. In addition, in the 2020s, 127,000 (doubled in five years) professors were teaching "academic" courses required for all colleges students on official CCP ideology from Marxism to Mao Thought and Xi Thought.[146] In 2021–2022, to further tighten its control of education, the CCP launched a swift campaign to curb and close the popular extracurricular programs of "character/caliber (liberal arts)" education for K–12, test-prep centers, and other non-state-owned schools in order to "eliminate the shadow-education" outside of government schools, in the name of "reducing student burdens and parent expenses" but actually, as asserted by the chief PRC official in charge of out-of-school education, "to defend the state's sovereignty in education," with local government-run uniform "community care centers" as the replacement.[147] In July 2021, influential public education websites of popular science like *Daxiang Gonghui*, after being squeezed with suspensions for years, were suddenly "erased" in PRC cyberspace. Social media groups for LGBTQ (lesbian, gay, bisexual, transgender and queer) were also all "expunged" overnight. Starting in fall 2021, all Chinese students from first grade to graduate school have been instructed to learn and memorize the official text of age-specific versions of the latest Xi Jinping Thought as a required course.[148] Only approved state-owned entities can report or provide any "news" for all printing and cyber publications, including social media postings.[149] Scholars or educators who dare to disobey or doubt the thought work are routinely demoted, dismissed, harassed, humiliated, and/or imprisoned.[150]

The ideological façade of the CCP-PRC party-state, however, has gone through many colorful, unscrupulous, and often drastic changes and fusions: From the imported pseudo-Soviet socialism and communism expressed in Mao's masterful oxymoron of "people's democratic dictatorship" or "new people's democracy," to radical revolutionary totalitarianism and Han-Chinese racist-nationalism wrapped up in Mao's ideas about class struggle and world revolution, to naked materialism. And then, finally—after the moral bankruptcy, "spiritual void," and confusion created by Mao and the CCP over the years—to a revival of pre-PRC values and ideas, chiefly the well-tested and trusted imperial ideology of Qin-Han polity under the China Order: Confucianism,[151] or, more accurately, Confucianism-Legalism disguised as patriotism and populism. A particular potion of jingoist thought work involves equating China with the PRC, then conflating the PRC with the CCP and ultimately the top CCP leader, shrewdly abusing the haziness of Chinese language and culture to forge together the notions of nation, country, state, government, ruling party, and ruler. In the 2010s, Mao's successors recycled his doubletalk to propose the political oxymoron of concurrently upholding three supremacies: supremacy of the (CCP) Party's interest/cause, supremacy of the people's interest, and supremacy of the Constitution and laws.[152] In 2021 and again in 2022, Xi Jinping simply declared that, among the naturally varied kinds of democracy, the people's democratic dictatorship under the CCP leadership "is the great innovation [by the CCP . . .] the brand new contribution to human political history [. . .] the most comprehensive, most genuine, and most useful democracy in the world."[153]

Brainwashing must be backed with political repression by force and enticing rewards. After the bloody crackdown on mass resistance and protests in 1989, three successive leaders, Jiang Zemin, Hu Jintao, and Xi Jinping, have kept the pressure on dissenters high.[154] The CCP reissued its guidelines for cadre training and promotion to educate the people in Marxism-Leninism, Mao Zedong Thought, and Xi Jinping Thought so as to "affirm our belief in Marxism, prevent the disorientation under Western constitutional democracy, universal values, and civil society, [. . .] and to uphold the belief in the eventual victory of communism."[155] Codenames and euphemisms aside, the CCP is determined to continue its one-party authoritarian rule in China, the Qin-Han polity, just as it has since 1949. Despite its big splash about "comprehensively advancing the governance of the country according to law" and the constitution, for example, Beijing secretly detained and then quickly jailed an independent filmmaker who dared to make a TV documentary simply tracing the history of the constitution in China.[156] As one Beijing-based constitution scholar concluded, the PRC remains a state "with a written constitution but no constitutional governance at all."[157]

The nonstop brainwashing and mind-alteration through incentives and punishment, at the expense of truth and facts, have been remarkably effective in the PRC, although many people may be just playing along in a pragmatic, performative way. Outdoing the so-called "velvet prison" found in places like Hungary during the Cold War, censorship with aesthetics and subtlety, the CCP's control of speech and mind appears to have achieved a peerless sophistication and success. The PRC seems stuck as "a society in post-traumatic distress and collective amnesia, the latter a coping mechanism for the former," commented one Chinese student in 2020.[158] One telling sign is how the objectively disastrous leader Mao continues to have such a following, genuine or fake, in the PRC. A self-proclaimed Maoist PRC professor praised Mao, as expected, although interestingly concurred that Mao's major accomplishment was in fact just the creation of the CCP-PRC regime itself, and for that, Mao has rightfully become a god to the CCP. Many still celebrate Mao on his birthday in ways that may appear simply ludicrous to observers.[159] A sizable portion of the Chinese population (even many of Mao's past victims) sincerely believe in the culture and values of the CCP's Qin-Han polity. Some have been thoroughly misinformed by the CCP's historical narratives propagating the Party's nationalist claims, developmentalist rationalization, populist mission, and socialist credentials. They still respect Mao as a people's hero who "saved" and restored China through the PRC, an imagined accomplishment that "ought to" supersede all of Mao's other negative traits.[160]

More importantly, the CCP's resistance to political reform in the general direction of democracy and liberalization seems to enjoy substantial support from the emerging middle class and wealthy urbanites. The reasons for this profound but likely artificial, masked, and transitory lack of social demand for democracy in the PRC are multifaceted. It is perhaps good testimony to the power of the Qin-Han polity, particularly the peculiar *hukou* system, in enabling the CCP's tight control of society and shaping the preferences of the privileged elites who are all urban-based.[161] The thought work is critically important to installing various types of "false consciousness" in the minds of many Chinese elites and common folks.[162] As Chinese Legalism masters argued and European Enlightenment writers decried long ago, CCP's thought work aims to create and perpetuate autocracy and tyranny through obscuration and corruption of the people, leading to a mentality of obedience based on herd governance and "voluntary servitude."[163] Some nouveau riche capitalists-turned-CCP-operatives have pompously and insolently defended and praised the one-party rule as a superior, "post-democracy" model of politics.[164] Some Western-educated PRC scholars creatively paint the PRC as having "neutral government" that is a "globally meaningful" alternative to democracy. Converted foreigners have also attempted to sell the CCP as a "political meritocracy" that outperforms democracy.[165]

The PRC state, following classic Legalism, aspires to rule by law as opposed to adhering to rule of law, though often is just simply engaged in rule of man (*renzhi*) by force and ruse. In the PRC, the distinctive concepts of rule by law or "use the law to govern" (*yifa zhiguo*), where the ruler is above the law versus rule of law (*youfa zhiguo*), where *everyone* is under the law, especially their phonetically identical abbreviation *fazhi*, are often confused, interchangeable, and deliberately misused and mistranslated.[166] This reflects the long absence of rule of law in the Chinese culture and language, the clever official opposition to rule of law, the rulers' wish to rule by law, namely by using harsh written laws to "better" command and govern, and Beijing's deflection and silencing of criticism. In the sarcastic words of Chinese critics, it is just "rule by the leader's wish" with force and ruse.[167] In June 2020, dozens of government media outlets previously named using one *fazhi* were all ordered to change to the other *fazhi*, so as "to emphasize rule by law efforts" instead of merely "to build the legal system."[168] To the "constant question about whether the party is above the law or law is above the party," the CCP's answer is the typical "dialectic" Maoist wordsmithery that puts the top ruler, codenamed the "Party Leadership" or Party Central, indisputably above the law but asks ordinary party members and organs to operate "in obedience of the law." In Xi's words, "party leadership is the soul of [our] socialist rule by law with Chinese characteristics."[169] The CCP thus obfuscates and maybe also dilutes itself with semantic twists of the two idiosyncratic concepts, using autocratic Legalist propaganda, the classic ideal of rule by law, to eclipse and replace the principle of rule of law, so as to legitimize, beautify, and "improve" the top ruler's power, in the name of the party leadership, which is always above any law and over everything and everyone, everywhere and every time.[170]

Critically, the CCP's Communist/Confucian-Legalism, with force-induced fear and shrewd manipulation of human weaknesses, has created a comprehensive officials-standard (*guan benwei*) as the monolithic socioeconomic hierarchy to centralize and control Chinese society.[171] Just like the Qin-Han rulers in the past, the CCP appoints all officials in a top-down and centralized way to monopolize all political power, social stature, and appropriation of resources, including information. The cultural notion of the officials-standard dictates that official positions come with specific prerogatives and rewards commensurate with rank, commonly including all sorts of rent-seeking and corruption opportunities. It also maintains a controlled, sole social mobility through the approved meritocracy. Wealth, success, recognition, and a simple decent social and economic life for just about everyone in the PRC are all measured, ranked, and ultimately secured or stripped according to the CCP-determined officials-standard. Being an official or cadre in the PRC, as countless cases have confirmed, is literally synonymous with possessing unrestrained power, endless perks and luxury, and opportunities for incredible personal indulgences.[172] The central and omnipresent role of political power has thus enabled and sustained a power fetishism that has become "the largest cult" and "more powerful than any other religion or faith system" in the PRC.[173] I will further discuss later in chapters 3 and 4 the impact of the pervasive officials-standard and the permeating power-fetishism in the PRC.

The extensive obfuscation and manipulation of generations of PRC citizens through potent and toxic propaganda and internalization of the party lines are akin to a massive social-engineering experiment. The distortion of reality, manipulation of the minds, and perversions of behavior for over a billion people treated like mice or guinea pigs in a giant enclosure is certainly taking a heavy toll that should petrify all Chinese people, and the world. To social scientists and historians, the CCP has been inadvertently conducting an experiment on the human mind at a massive scale for many decades, with rich, profound, educational, and even chillingly entertaining findings to be revealed about human nature, capacity, manipulability, and receptibility (that is, if the CCP does not end up turning the whole of humankind into the same kind of guinea pigs under a new China Order for the world).[174] To the observers of the PRC-West competition, it is frightening to envisage how so many misinformed and disinformed people with increasing capacity and incompatible views and values will interact with the rest of humanity. Deep incompatibility, open hatred, failure to communicate and cooperate, and fierce and full-scale clashes with the outside world may simply become the cost of the CCP governance, particularly its thought work.

The actual result and lasting effects of this expensive and exhaustive thought work are hard to ascertain quantitatively without an independent and comprehensive field study in China, which is strictly forbidden. Empirically, the CCP's crafty thought work based on information monopoly, distortion of history and facts, and logic-defying misinformation and disinformation seems most potent during people's formative years, especially when the Chinese economy coincidentally grew well and at least the urbanites experienced a significant improvement in their living standard.[175] Over the past two decades, there has indeed been an emergence of a fairly large number of Sinocentric, West-bashing, power-fetishist, and often illogical and unreasoning CCP apologists in and out of the PRC, especially among the youth. They now have a global presence, clashing with others as the so-called "wolf warriors," "little pinks," "Putin fans," and "angry youth fed with wolf-milk."[176] Recent cases of such have been widely reported in the West. I have personally observed (and indirectly heard about), for example, many PRC high school and college graduates studying in North America, Western Europe, Japan, Korea, Hong Kong, Macau, Singapore, and Taiwan carrying with them significantly staggering and often stubborn misconceptions, fallacies, and biases about China and the world. The party-state's thought work has apparently gone abroad with the intention of dividing and disintegrating the world through misinformation, disinformation, and manipulation.[177] The impact of the CCP's grand thought work on world peace, the future of human civilization, and the fortune of the Chinese people, therefore, is disturbing and worrisome.

Still, I surmise that the CCP's mind control and mind alteration of the Chinese people are cost-ineffective over time and could be made to look increasingly inept by the West, just like so many other policies of the PRC. Thought work on impressionable young minds may be fragile and impermanent when confronted with the reality or enlightenment.[178] Many PRC scholars have tenaciously persisted in the risky efforts of writing and publishing dissenting views and un-CCP ideas, often in crafty and inexplicit language, despite consequences that can often be serious.[179] Countless acidic satires, impactful revelations, and intrepid whistleblowing by "truth tellers," along with penetrating criticism and even ferocious attacks on the CCP and its leaders on social media platforms play constant cat-and-mouse games with CCP web censors, for example, suggesting immunity to and rejection of the manipulative propaganda by many Chinese inside the PRC.[180] As I will document in detail later in this book, political cynicism and outright prevarication dominate Chinese society, and Beijing seems fully aware of that. More concretely, huge numbers of Chinese have been voting with their feet, sending their assets and families out of the PRC. With sufficient effort, a good detoxification of the CCP propaganda is clearly achievable and would be a highly efficient way of managing the rise of China. In this regard, the experiences of post–World War II Germans, Italians, and Japanese and post–Cold War Eastern Europeans, Chileans, South Koreans, and Taiwanese appear inspirational, instructional, and encouraging.

The Partocracy and the Police State

As the ladder for political and also socioeconomic upward mobility, similar to imperial officialdom with its imperial exam system in the past, the CCP has been the only game in town in the PRC with the power and fortune to attract people. The CCP itself grew from 4.5 million members in 1949 to 37 million in 1978, 80 million in 2011, and almost 97 million by 2023. It now has nearly five million branches of multiple layers covering every urban district (street and residential neighborhood), rural township and village, firm and factory (including foreign-owned and private companies), cultural and educational entity including elementary schools and kindergartens, even a pauper community. The Party mandates a party cell as the political organization everywhere there are three or more members. The CCP has always declared itself to be "pioneers of the working class" (formerly "the proletarian class" until the late 1990s) or "the workers and peasants," as its Soviet Union–designed party emblem featuring the hammer and sickle indicates. Yet, by 2021, only a paltry 6.8 percent of the 95 million party members were "workers," and 27 percent were "working in agriculture," including many party officials governing the rural population.[181] In 2021, of the 2,977 People's Delegates to the National People's Congress, a rough analysis suggested that there were likely only 25 workers, 12 peasants, 15 "employees in service industries," and 167 "technical professionals," with the rest being officials and cadres of the party-state (1,591), the military (295) and "entity and enterprise managers" (819). In 2022, of the 2,296 delegates to the CCP's 20th National Congress, there were only 192 workers, 85 peasants, and 266 "technical professionals," with the rest (75.3%) being officials, cadres, and the military.[182] Although it claims social and gender equality, the party has always been male dominated. The six dozen top leaders (members of the Politburo Standing Committee or equivalent) of the CCP in more than 100 years have all been men. In the 2020s, women constituted just 28.8 percent of the party membership; there were only nine and ten women in the 204-member nineteenth CCP Central Committee and the 205-member twentieth Central Committee, respectively; as it had been for decades, there was only one female in the nineteenth Politburo (2017–2022) but none in the twentieth Politburo (2022–2027), among the 24 to 28 "Central Leaders."[183] Of the thirty-three party chiefs of provincial regions, only one was woman; of the sixty-two "deputy-province/ministry level" leaders of the thirty-one leading PRC universities, only six were women.[184]

The CCP is the world's largest "real" party, or technically the second largest party after the very loosely organized BJP (Bharatiya Janata Party) in India.[185] It is internally undemocratic and monopolizes all political power. Highly centralized and silo-like, the CCP has a very long chain of command and reporting, with a top-heavy decision-making process that structurally and operationally may allow uniformity and micromanagement but inevitably diminishes innovation and responsiveness and raise local irresponsibility and the cost of governance in general. It owns all of China's armed forces, as well as the police and secret police; directs the media, educational, cultural, financial and industrial apparatuses; and controls all the land and the vast majority of Chinese wealth. It added a corporatist dimension to its partocracy starting in the mid-1990s, blending its identity of world communism with its self-labeling of Chinese nationalism and styling itself as a "new [human] civilization rather than just a [national] political party" by the 2020s.[186] In celebrating its 100th birthday in 2021, the CCP rebranded itself once more, going from a communist insurgence group created by the Soviet Union as a branch of its *Comintern* (Communist International) in China, to now becoming a ruling party for nationalism and populism, "the pioneers of the Chinese working class and simultaneously also the pioneers of the Chinese people and the Chinese nation," "always fighting since day one of birth" in 1921 "for the happiness [or good life or common prosperity] of the Chinese people and the rejuvenation of the Chinese nation [or Chinese civilization]"; it now "cares about the future of humankind," "always unwaveringly stands on the side of historical correctness and human progress," "has obtained major global influence" and leadership, "must continuously push the construction of the community of common human destiny," and triumph in many "great struggles" to prepare for "the once-in-a-century great world transformation" so as to better the lot of humanity.[187]

All CCP members have taken and repeated essentially the same sacred vows since the 1920s: "to carry out party decisions, strictly obey party disciplines, safeguard party secrets, be loyal to the party, actively work, struggle for my whole life to realize communism, be prepared to sacrifice everything at any time for the party and the people, and never betray the party."[188] The Party constantly expands its membership. In the first half-year of 2021, it admitted 2.3 million new members, out of a pool of 20 million applicants (half of whom were "active candidates").[189] Autocratically and opaquely led by a few at the top, the CCP is organized similar to a secret-society group of ruling elites with lifetime membership. Very few in the PRC would or could ever willingly quit the party without adverse consequences.[190] The party, with about 5 or 6 percent of the Chinese population, is an omnipresent and omnipotent "red machine" that controls *everything* and rules *everyone everywhere* in China. It is a great "selectorate" that sustains an autocratic "winning coalition" to rule continuously despite its long record of disasters, tragedies, and failures.[191]

Perhaps attempting to ensure more personal control with even fewer of the organizational constraints of an oversized and overloaded bureaucracy, the CCP rulers retain the Maoist tradition of relying on numerous, often ad hoc and secretive, bureaucracies outside the existing bureaucracy. Many of them become permanent fixtures, such as the various LSGs (leading small groups) and offices. Xi Jinping himself, beyond his four top titles in the CCP-PRC partocracy, is reported also to chair at least nine of these LSGs. Top CCP leaders routinely head the LSGs on foreign affairs, national security, economic and financial policies, administrative reform, cyber security, and Taiwan affairs. In an effort, perhaps, to make those LGCs more dignified, Xi renamed many of them "commissions" in 2018–2019.[192] These less institutionalized bureaucracies are where real decisions are made with arguably more expediency and agility, outside of the functional ministries and departments in the long chain of command. As a result, the PRC Foreign Minister, unlike his US counterpart, is often several, even two dozen, people away from the top leader in the party-state hierarchy. Below the Central level, the same multiplication and redundancy of bureaucracy occurs, with countless informal bureaucracies with impressive titles and serious budgets, often just for conspicuous mandates and frivolous works.

Under the CCP's unchallenged, unrestricted, and unmonitored control, the PRC government is an undifferentiated regime that combines the legislative, executive, and judicial powers into one, despite the nominally separate organizations of the PRC National People's Congress (NPC and its predecessor, the National People's Political Consultative Conference, which has been preserved to keep the façade of a "consultative democracy" with "non-CCP" elites),[193] the State Council, the Supreme People's Court, and the Supreme People's Procuratorate. In an authoritarian-totalitarian corporatist fashion, the CCP-PRC has integrated all government functions and powers, and incorporated the leaders of professional and business associations, social and cultural groups, and religious organizations. All churches, temples, and mosques in the PRC must be registered by the state and monitored by the state's religious management authority, with senior religious clerks commonly treated and salaried as state employees with official ranks. Some of them are in fact undercover CCP members (who are supposed to be atheists). All self-organized underground religious groups are illegal and subject to prosecution. Jailing and the death penalty are used at times to eliminate uncontrolled faith organizations and groups.[194]

Vertically, the PRC is governed by this undifferentiated premodern state at five levels (central, province, prefecture, county, township/district) with the same "seven office" party-state structure: a CCP committee, a CCP discipline inspection committee, a people's congress, a people's political consultative conference, a people's government, a people's court, and a people's procurator, plus branches of government-run "mass" organizations such as the Communist Youth League, trade union, women's association, and chamber of commerce.[195] A typical county government in the 2010s was reported on PRC social media to have ninety "standard government agencies," sixteen "mass organizations," thirty-five or more county-financed units, and fifty-five or more "other agencies and offices."[196] The gargantuan, undifferentiated government of the party-state has penetrated deeper and further than any imperial rulers in the past, in an attempt to control everyone and extract resources directly, below the township level, down to every rural village and urban neighborhood. With the omnipresent officials-standard and power fetishism, the bloated bureaucracy ranks, integrates, places, and controls the elites of all walks of life to form a corporatist ruling class with varied vested interest in the regime.[197]

This autocracy is guarded by the all-service PLA, the nationally financed and conscripted but CCP-owned military, which repeatedly pledges its "total and absolute" allegiance to the CCP party and is under a very tight and highly centralized, often personal, control by the top CCP leader.[198] It is reported that to deploy a company requires direct approval from the CCP's Central Military Commission.[199] This world's largest military by size (with a reported 2 million active duty and 1.85 million in reserve) and second largest by budget has the company of a second military, the People's Armed Police Force (PAP), that is a fully equipped all-service military with 1.5 million active duty members.[200] This parallel military is also funded and staffed by the nation but pledges its loyalty exclusively to the CCP. In the 2020s, PLA and PAP officers and civilian employees are well compensated monetarily with "the best iron rice bowl" in the PRC, and "significantly better than" civil servants and employees of state monopolies like China Tobacco and mega banks.[201]

The total size of the regular police force in the PRC is a guarded state secret, but leaked information shows that it is the world's largest in absolute size and per capita size.[202] Like the two military forces, the PRC police is also controlled at every level higher than a platoon by the dual command of an officer and a political commissar, both of whom are always required to be CCP members. Local police stations are under a centralized chain of co-command by the superior police department and the CCP committee secretary at the same local level, all ultimately commanded by the CCP Central. This "people's police" covers every corner of the land with power and freedom much greater than most if not all of its peers in the world.

Inheriting from the imperial rulers of the past and learning from the Soviet Union, the CCP also relies heavily on secret police to control and govern.[203] Other than the CCP's extremely well-equipped and funded Discipline Inspection Commission and its branches all the way down to the township level, there are at least four other vertical systems of secret police in the PRC, each with its opaque and well-funded operations and extensive networks of clandestine agents and informants: the Ministry of State Security (the equivalent of the KGB of the Soviet Union), the secret bureaus and divisions of the Ministry of Public Security (the political protection units and web police), the political commissars and intelligence networks of the PLA (for military control and external intelligence),[204] and the classified investigative reporting called "internal reference" (*neican*). Most, if not all, of the PRC's state media, like Xinhua News Agency and *People's Daily*, along with government agencies, produce and circulate internal reporting, accompanying translated foreign publications and news, with varied classifications (some dailies are for the eyes of the top seven or nine leaders only) delivered by a Classified Post System.[205] In addition, there are at least two secret security forces protecting and also monitoring senior cadres and top leaders: the Central Security Bureau and the new Special Service Bureau.[206] Wiretapping, cyber snooping, and audio and video surveillance are extremely common in China. Local governments and officials have been reported to set their secretive spy networks against each other.[207]

Besides all these already bloated bureaucracies of the unprecedented and unparalleled police state, the CCP recruits and cultivates a huge army of secret informants, including scholars, artists, and college and high school students,[208] as well as a massive force of local police station–financed "police assistants" that can number two to four times as many as the regular police officers. Over 850,000 "volunteers" and informants patrol the streets of Beijing, for example, where the oversized police force is now authorized to shoot any suspected "terrorist" without issuing a warning or self-identification. Consequently, reports on police shooting and killing civilians appeared in the highly censored PRC online media.[209] The secret informants, whether paid or volunteer, exist in every community as so-called "eyes and ears," "public security team activists" or "information personnel," including secretly recruited students placed in almost every sizable college classroom.[210] As mentioned earlier, to control and manipulate the internet, the CCP hires "at least two million" full-time online censors.[211] The large web police on average censored over 30 million postings, penalized 100,000 social media groups, and closed 500 websites per day in 2020. In addition, the Communist Youth League (CYL), the youth arm of the CCP, openly recruits and deploys over 10 million imposter bloggers and posters online, including hundreds of thousands of teenagers.[212] The many millions of robo-bloggers (including forced prison labor) working for the CCP on the internet, the so-called "fifty-cents" party, alone are pricey: at the rate of 50 cents (about $0.08) and up, they post at least 488 million deceptive writings and distracting comments on websites and social media every year, as directed by CCP officials.[213] The CCP has by far the world's largest internal spying network deploying the latest, often imported, technology for internet tracking and hacking, eavesdropping, mail inspection, facial-recognition cameras, and big data-mining to extensively monitor and control the Chinese population, especially selected segments.[214]

In order to carry out all these critical but mundane and endless tasks to centrally rule everyone and everything in a nation the size of China, while rooting out any internal contention and resistance on the smallest scale and at the earliest possible moment, the party-state itself has become the world's largest bureaucracy in absolute and relative (per capita) sizes (see table 1.2). Huge numbers of cadres (*ganbu*) are appointed and managed top down to run everything in a centralized and hierarchal system. In 1997, the PRC officially "capped" the number of cadres at 40 million, already a historical peak and world-record ratio of one cadre per every thirty-three citizens.[215] This cap was soon exceeded. In 2005, the cadres "in broad definition" were estimated to number 50 to 70 million, one per every

Table 1.2. Size of Officialdom in the PRC

Era/Comparison		Citizens per every Government Official/Cadre*
The PRC		
	Estimate by PRC scholars	18–26
	"Reform" Target set for 2019	39
	2005	26
	1998	33
	1990	37
	1950s	294
Imperial China (excluding the "personal" staff and clerks of officials)		
	Qing (1644–1911)	911
	Ming (1368–1644)	2299
	Tang (618–907)	3927
	Han (25–220)	7963
Shanxi Province (PRC, 2005)		27
Liaoning Province (PRC, 2018)		20
Foping County, Shangxi (PRC, 2020)		11
Japan (1998)		150
State of Maryland (US, 2018)		180
Bangkok Metropolis (Thailand, 2018)		120

*Excluding workers and non-cadre staff in the state-owned enterprises.

Source: Chief Editor 1998; Guoji xianqu daobao 2005; Z. Cai 2018; Diyi caijing 2021; S. Cai 2022.

twenty-three to twenty-six people (or 1 of every 10 to 15 working-aged Chinese), a ratio 30 to 200 times higher than in imperial times.[216] Since 2008, Beijing has officially "stopped collecting" such data; in 2016, "for the first time ever," and still the only time thus far, it announced the number of *gongwuyuan* (civil servants) or cadres "narrowly defined" as 7.2 million, using vague criteria and tabulations without verifiable breakdowns; the actual size of the cadres "broadly defined" on the state payroll, however, grew by 16 million over seven years to surpass 80 million in 2021, as estimated by

PRC scholars.[217] Another PRC study, using a different categorization of cadres, civil servants, and government employees, found that the total size of "government employees" grew "strongly and steadily" by 170 percent over twenty-seven years (1978–2006) and then 57 percent over thirteen years (2006–2019), twice the speed of school teachers, with an "official/citizen ratio" that increased 6.8 times from 1978 to 2019, despite the almost constant decrees calling for reducing the number of cadres to save state expenditures.[218]

In 2020, one ordinary county in Hunan Province had over 12,000 local "civil servants" for its 445,000 residents, or one per every thirty-seven residents. One extreme estimate put the ratio at one cadre per every 3 to 6 working people in the PRC. In 2018–20, one smallish county, Foping of Shangxi Province with a total population of 32,600 (8,000 in the county-seat town), had 2,991 on the government payroll—or one per every 10.9 residents (one per every 2.7 urban dwellers)—with a total annual government revenue of ¥63 million ($9.4 million) but expenditure of ¥797 million ($119 million). And similar "small and uneconomical" counties are estimated to number over 200 out of the total 2,800 counties in the PRC. In 2022, in the economically more prosperous Jiangsu Province, a county of 900,000 residents had over 15,000 "government employees" (one per every six residents), with an average pay four times more than average workers, financed by taxes and sale of the user's right of "public land"—both of which appeared to be clearly "unsustainable."[219] One study found that in PRC counties, 60 to 80 percent (even up to 120%) of the government budget routinely went just to pay the "civil servants."[220] Official media reported in 2021 that local governments often resort to speed traps and other abusive fines to generate massive revenue to cover as much as one-third of their bloated budgets. Such "administrative fines" are actually a "significant source of income" for local governments in all of the provinces; per capita fines can reach 2 percent of per capita income in many places, becoming a serious extra tax.[221] Another "supplemental revenue" appears to be the widespread practice of "eating vacuous employment," a traditional practice in Imperil China, through which local officials pocket the government pay for their nonexistent subordinates that, in just one auditing in the 2010s, were discovered to be over 162,000 in thirty provinces, 56,000 in one province (Hebei), and 66 in one district (Haidian) of Beijing city. In April 2022, it was revealed that local officials in Shanghai enlisted many "phantom volunteers" to flaunt their "community work" during the pandemic-related lockdown and pocket significant sums of government pay.[222]

Unsurprisingly, this mammoth police state partocracy costs the Chinese taxpayers astronomical sums for its own upkeep alone. One political dissident estimated that the CCP would need the total party assets of the KMT plus the total campaign spending of the notably exorbitant US presidential election to barely cover the normal expenses of its Central-level bureaucracy for just one month. By the estimate of a senior CCP official, the party-state consumes an incredible 44 percent of the PRC fiscal expenditure, more than twice as high as that in Italy (19%), which was "the highest such ratio in the West."[223] The CCP's secretive Discipline Inspection committees alone reportedly employed 810,000 "inspectors" (at least 1,000 at its headquarters) in the mid-2010s, one monitoring every eight cadres, with a "limitless budget."[224] Local governments are even more bloated and expensive. One ordinary county in central China with a population of only 780,000 could have 1,013 "leading cadres" as section and division chiefs or deputy-chiefs, plus about 10,000 cadres and state employees in a total of 673 government agencies, offices, and units, costing "more than 80 percent of all government revenue."[225] In 2019, a Chinese analysis of the masked official data concluded that the cost of "feeding" civil servants in the PRC jumped 77.5 percent in five years, outpacing GDP growth by a large margin; government spending on the cadres, excluding military and diplomacy budgets and state employees in health care and education, was about 28 percent of the total national budget, by far the highest such ratio in the world, reaching 350,000 RMB ($54,000) per person in 2018, more than five times the per capita GDP or over fourteen times the median per capita income.[226]

Unsurprisingly, to work as a state cadre has become the most popular career path in the PRC toward political power, social stature, and also easy money. In the 2021 and 2022 rounds of the national Cadre Exam, 1.6 to 2.1 million vetted applicants took part, with a placement rate of only 1.4 to 1.6 percent.[227] More than half of the 3,000 Class of 2020 PhDs from the top-ranked Tsinghua university, known for its engineering programs, for example, went to work as cadres and clerks (often just entry-level staff) in the party-state agencies; in 2021, that ratio increased further to 65.4 percent.[228] In April 2022, 138 of the 208 finalists for the entry level "civil servant" jobs, like office clerks and street management (*chengguan* or quasi-police patrol) in Beijing's Chaoyang

District, were graduate degree holders, including one PhD in physics from the prestigious Peking University.[229]

The Ruling Class and the Aristocracy

Under the CCP, the supposedly classless People's Republic is among the worst countries for socioeconomic inequality in the world, which will be examined in detail in the next chapters of this book. Politically, the bloated partocracy and police state is ruled with high rigidity, central control, and strict assimilation and stratification by an upper class, an aristocracy of elites, and ultimately a tiny and exclusive ruling group. According to some insiders and political dissidents, this entrenched CCP ruling circle consists of about "500 privileged clans [of] about 5,000 people" under "a few dozen top families" that "monopolize China."[230] Countless young, idealistic, and ambitious talents join the party-state for their pursuits, which are often noble and selfless. However, the partocracy DNA and the CCP political culture appear to do an effective job in quickly frustrating, assimilating, corrupting, or eliminating most if not all of them.[231]

The 97 million (2023) CCP members plus a very few "non-CCP member" elites who are often "undercover" party members, about 6 percent of the total population (or about 18% including their immediate families), constitute the upper class of the People's Republic. They monopolize all political power and prerogatives, most opportunities and social positions, and much of the country's wealth and income. Fieldwork by PRC scholars in the twenty-first century has revealed that in the affluent Yangtze Delta, for example, CCP membership and wealth are almost synonymous: CCP members in the region are 6.2 percent of the population but make up 67.7 percent of the top 10 percent wealthiest and highest income earners. In a supposedly socialist country led by a "party of the workers/proletarian," the Deputies of the National People's Congress on average are several times richer than US Congress members, while the Chinese per capita income is less than 20 percent of that in the United States.[232]

The 50 to 80 million CCP-PRC state cadres comprise the aptly called "public servants" (*gongwuyuan*), who are estimated to be one-fourth to one-third of the total state employees and are categorized as either leading cadres (*lingdao ganbu*) or ordinary cadres (*yiban ganbu*), corresponding to the officials (*guan*) and clerks (*li*) in imperial times.[233] At about 4 to 5 percent of the Chinese population, the cadres are overwhelmingly CCP members, and are all hired and managed by the CCP Central Department of Organization and its subordinate departments of organization of the various levels of CCP committees down to townships and companies.[234] Starting in the 1950s, the cadres were for decades ranked into a total of thirty pay scales. In the 2020s, the civil servants had twenty-seven pay scales with six to fourteen steps in each scale, with a monthly "base pay" ranging from ¥3,820 ($588) for Step Six of Scale One, to ¥290 ($45) for Step One of Scale One, a "position pay" ranging from ¥4,000 (US $615) for "Full National Level" to ¥340 (US $53) for "Clerk Level," plus several other payments, subsidies, and bonuses that are less uniform, more opaque, and can be significant in practice.[235] With its officials-standard and power-fetish culture, the CCP relies on this rather imperial-style officialdom, led by the leading cadres, to govern in the name of the People (instead of Heaven, as in earlier times).

The number of active leading cadres was estimated to be around 640,000 in the 2010s. The leading cadres are the heads and deputy-heads of all the units, offices, and other entities at the five levels of the party-state: national, province-ministry, prefecture-bureau, county-division, and township-section. Out of the total of twenty-seven base-pay scales for civil servants, the ten-layered leading cadres can be ranked from Scale 1 to Scale 24.[236] They are party and government officials, company and factory directors, bank managers, hospital heads, and school/college administrators. There is a nearly equal number of retired leading cadres who commonly enjoy full benefits with varied degrees of political influence. The active and retired leading cadres number 1.3 million, or 0.1 percent (or 0.3 percent including their immediate families) of the Chinese population. They are basically all CCP members and constitute the ruling aristocracy in the People's Republic.[237] These CCP aristocrats enjoy imperial-style authority and status. They have meticulously specified and ranked perks and benefits of all kinds, including free medical care with the best doctors and medicine that money can buy from anywhere in the world; provision of housing, servants, and private plane and train travel; special supplies of goods, services, and information; frequent free vacations for the whole family and entourage anywhere in the country (sometime overseas with creative excuses); and many other allowances and privileges for them, their family members, and their cronies. Their power and prerogatives, much more important than their salaries, are basically lifelong and evidently also often creatively inheritable.

Among the leading cadres, 40,000 to 50,000 are the active "senior cadres" (*gaogan*, above the prefecture/bureau level). An estimated additional 150,000 to 200,000 "senior non-leading cadres" also enjoy the same ranked perks without actually heading an office and thus typically with less political power; this includes the retired senior cadres. Together, this group of ruling elites of the CCP aristocracy includes around a quarter-million people, or 0.02 percent (0.06 percent including immediate family) of the Chinese population. One more stratum up among the elites of the CCP aristocracy, about 3,000 to 8,000 belong to the tiny, top coterie: the active or retired cadres ranked at or above (or "treated as equivalent" of) deputy-province/ministry. The pinnacle of the senior cadres, the top of the CCP aristocracy, is sixty-three active plus 110 retired (in 2021) deputy-national and national level cadres.[238] The senior cadres, especially those above province/ministry level, dictated by the handful of national-level cadres or often just the top leader alone, rule the party-state with unquestioned and unmonitored power and enjoy world-class luxury that often even money cannot buy. Surviving the brutal competition to become a coveted state employee, the ladder for an entry-level cadre to climb to the province-ministry level is long and steep, reportedly taking thirty-one years on the fast lane with the odds of one in 50,000.[239]

The CCP ruling elites behave every bit as authoritarian, hypocritical, and self-indulgent as any aristocrats in human history. Despite all the talk of serving the people and advancing communism, the rulers of the CCP enjoy world-class luxury with world-class inequality between them and their lower-ranked comrades, not to mention the inequality between CCP officialdom and the Chinese people. Formal salary plus opaque income like bonuses and subsidies provide the cadres with upper-middle to high incomes.[240] The salary (or ration) of the top CCP leaders was already ten times that of the lowest cadres during the Chinese Civil War. This gap quickly jumped to over 28 times in 1950, 26 times in 1952, 32 times in 1955, and 36 times in 1956. By the 2010s, the real income gap between the top-paid officials and average-paid state employees had ballooned to a breathtaking 62 to 260 times, much larger than the already huge income gap between the top 5 percent and the bottom 5 percent of the general society (estimated to be about 27 times) in the PRC. In contrast, ROC government employees had a salary gap of 15 times at its highest point in 1946.[241]

More importantly, the nonsalary perks and benefits are much more meaningful to the cadres. The internal mess halls with tiered dining rooms in Zhongnanhai, the CCP-PRC Headquarters, and many other government offices, for example, often rival the best restaurants and are almost free of charge to the cadres. Since the very beginning in 1950, the PRC has modeled itself after the Soviet Union in employing a secretive system of special provision (*tegong*) to produce and provide, exclusively according to official rank, life-time supplies of countless best-quality, pollution-free, often imported, and ultra-discounted or free goods and services, even while hundreds of millions of Chinese people were starving or barely surviving on meager rations.[242] There are also free or heavily subsidized "normal" provisions of spacious housing plus villas/resorts, transportation, medical care, education, domestic service, information, entertainment, home appliances, food, alcohol, and cigarettes. The cost of those special and "normal" provisions is immeasurably large and strictly hidden. The very existence of the cadre provisions, let alone their cost, is unknown to anyone outside the autocracy, beyond some leaked anecdata.[243]

The arrogance and selfishness of the CCP aristocracy can be shockingly blatant. During the great national famine of 1959 to 1962, for example, to ensure and increase the production of *Maotai*, a "national liquor" and a standard special-provision item for the CCP ruling elites, Beijing specially collected over 10,000 tons of life-saving grains for the distiller, while tens of thousands of people literally starved to death in the very same town where the liquor was brewed under heavy security. Before the PRC, *Maotai* production was customarily prohibited when there was a shortage in the grain supply.[244] Furthermore, for over two decades now, the CCP rulers have evidently indulged themselves in a very costly program called "981 Project for Leaders' Health," which aims at prolonging the lifespan of top leaders to 150 years, with "fully functioning body parts including sex organs," all at state expense with all the latest technology procured from all over the world, even allegedly harvesting young human organs alive for transplants and "rejuvenation."[245] Even after death, the supposedly classless and atheist People's Republic literally segregates graveyards, with walls separating ordinary people from the cadres, and designating specially curated and priced (often free) cemeteries for the senior cadres and leaders.

The special-provision system and more generally the so-called "treatment" (*daiyu*) the PRC elites enjoy based on their rank can be granted, modified, or taken away by their superiors almost at will. CCP leaders hence have an easy and powerful tool to attract, bribe, indulge, corrupt, and enslave the PRC upper class, especially the ruling elites. The shielded officials become utterly remote and insensitive to the pains of socioeconomic stagnation, poor quality of food and medicine, and environmental pollution that plague the Chinese people.[246] Political opponents and dissenting officials including retired senior cadres are often effectively deterred from unapproved action or publication by the simple threat of reducing or terminating their special treatment, especially the free and vital state-of-the-art medical care.[247]

Beyond the institutionalized prerogatives and privileges, many CCP leaders and cadres have been endlessly siphoning off a staggering amount of wealth from the Chinese people. Some of the published cases of official corruption show millions or even billions in embezzled or graft money by just some lower- to middle-level officials, often with large amounts of cash stashed in their basements. At the very top, reportedly, Premier Wen Jiabao's family owned "at least $2.7 billion" in assets and Chairman Xi Jinping's sister "made" $240 million from just one deal with the real estate group Wanda.[248] There are countless reports about how the CCP senior cadres cultivate their families (including alleged mistresses and illegitimate children) to take over power or surreptitiously sending relatives to live abroad, mostly in the West, with their massive and likely ill- or opaquely obtained fortunes. The families of three top leaders, Xi Jinping, Li Zhanshu, and Wang Yang, for example, were implicated in one such report in 2020. A 10 billion-dollar embezzlement was reported in just three of the hundreds of companies under the mega state-owned HNA Group, which went bankrupt in early 2021.[249]

One PRC journalist estimated in 2015 that at least 100,000 corrupt officials had escaped abroad with over $2 trillion in assets. Perhaps reflecting just the tip of the iceberg, the CCP's "Skynet" campaign has reportedly caught and brought back thousands of such escapees since 2014 (2,041 in 2019; 1,421 in 2020), with ¥3 billion (US $448 million) in "embezzled funds recouped on average every year."[250] Leaked confidential documents such as the Panama Papers of 2016 investigated by the International Consortium of Investigative Journalists (ICIJ), have revealed that massive amount of wealth, held by the families of top leaders, has been stashed offshore incognito and tax-free through elaborate, and most likely illegal, schemes. The Panama Papers were leaked from the Panama-based law firm Mossack Fonseca, which had eight offices in China (more than in any other country) and specialized in shell companies and tax havens worldwide. Out of the 15,000 clients of the firm from 200 countries, almost 5,000 were the rich and famous from the PRC and Hong Kong, involving the families of at least eight top CCP leaders, including Xi Jinping's brother-in-law. By 2020, as a result of the ICIJ report of the Panama Papers, the decades-old law firm closed, more than 6,500 people were investigated (with arrests, indictments, and jail sentences), over $1.2 billion was recouped in unpaid taxes and fines, and politicians resigned in eighty-two countries. However, there has been zero action in the PRC, and even the mention of the Panama Papers there has been strictly forbidden.[251]

Given the colossal price-tags and the pretenses of widely used testing and evaluation of officials, one might reasonably hope that the aristocratic CCP ruling elites would work to earn their worth, somehow resembling the so-called meritocracy of governance as opposed to democracy, that has been dreamingly praised by some inside and outside of the CCP, including certain foreign Chinese scholars publishing through prestigious outlets in the West.[252] However, as a PRC scholar sharply puts it, meritocracy versus democracy is conceptually a "false dichotomy," since democracy "*is* the genuine form of meritocracy."[253] Another PRC scholar calls the cheer for the actually nonexistent "Chinese meritocracy" an outright misappropriation of Confucianism that misreads Chinese history and an idiotic "advocacy for the premodern authoritarianism and totalitarianism."[254] Human political history everywhere has more than amply informed us that monopolistic political power without sufficient restriction necessarily leads to little merit but endless incompetence, corruption, and calamities. This appears to be exactly the case in the PRC.[255] As this book has attempted to show, the CCP autocracy has meager to no special merit in comparison, especially when considering its exorbitant cost, fallacious policies, rampant corruption, and dismal record of governance. Even the official CCP media sometimes, likely with the purposeful blessings of some top leader, admit that the party-state has been plagued by a deeply trenched "reverse elimination" (*nitaotai*) in its officialdom that "promotes bad cadres and policies while eliminating the good ones."[256] Conceptually or practically, politically or administratively, historically or contemporarily, the bloated and costly CCP autocracy seems nowhere near meritocracy.

Intrusion, Insecurity, and Intranquility

The gargantuan PRC police state is expansive, expensive, and exacting for the Chinese people, with a bloated and well-equipped law enforcement thoroughly controlled by the CCP to effectively serve the regime first and foremost. It has indeed done well in keeping the CCP rulers safely in power. This matchless leviathan financially extracts and spends more for the CCP to rule its own people than to defend the country. The CCP's "maintenance of [sociopolitical] stability" (*weiwen*) or domestic security spending is growing annually by double digits in the twenty-first century. Since 2010, it has been consistently larger than the PRC's entire national defense budget, which has been growing much faster than China's economy.[257] Beijing stopped publishing the *weiwen* budget in 2013. But a European study concluded that, under Xi Jinping, domestic security spending continued to explode at an annual rate 50 to 100 percent faster than the surging external defense expenditures, becoming ¥1.24 trillion (US $197 billion) in 2017, or 19 percent larger than the PLA coffer; still, "even these numbers exclude billions of dollars spent on security-related urban management and surveillance technology initiatives." Everywhere in the PRC, the most majestic buildings in just about every city and town commonly house the party-state agencies. To CCP ruling elites, affiliates, and aficionados in and out of the PRC, the CCP Optimality of governance has restored and encouraged the seductive Chinese imperial culture and granted the ruling coterie abundant, unmonitored, and unaccountable powers, privileges, and properties. This strong authoritarian state of pseudo-Marxist and pseudo-Confucian Legalism may be rationalized by itself to offer the Chinese people (and later the whole world) a homogenized society with more prosperity and security. An expansive and expensive "security state" has indeed been the nexus of CCP-PRC governance.[258]

To the Chinese people, and even the majority of the Chinese elites, however, this quite optimal way of ensuring the autocratic power of the CCP-PRC rulers has in fact delivered a suboptimal and undesirable governance for most if not all in the People's Republic, from the ordinary Chinese people to the elites and even the rulers themselves. CCP governance appears to be an exorbitant and even tragic regression of history—a leap backward to premodernity. "The model of our society today," commented one PRC scholar, "is especially like that of the Ming Dynasty."[259] With by far the most numerous officials and police in the world, the omnipresent party-state is consistently and expectedly inferior in providing social tranquility and protecting citizens against crimes. The Chinese people pay astronomically and endure rough intrusiveness, yet still experience a chronic shortage of security and justice, in addition to the extensive deprivation of their political, civil, and human rights. As I will summarize below, people in the PRC commonly feel unsafe and insecure.

Beyond the ordinary people, who suffer under the quite optimal execution of a suboptimal governance, Chinese elites at all levels—the educated, able, ambitious, influential, and especially the rich—who refuse to be submissive and coopted or are not submissive and controlled enough, who are simply too rich or too influential, or who are connected to the wrong officials and factions, are routinely robbed, exiled, destroyed, jailed, or even executed, with various excuses and often trumped-up charges. Even the members of the ruling CCP aristocracy often become victims. As I reported in *The China Order*, the history of the CCP is a bloody history of constant internal purges that rival the worst autocracy in human history in scale and brutality. Out of the thirteen Chinese attendees of the party's first congress in 1921, seven later quit or were expelled (four others were "martyred"), with only two (Mao Zedong and Dong Biwu) dying naturally as party members. All of the six chiefs of the CCP before Mao and three of the six since Mao have been disgraced and purged.[260] Mao himself became a family member of "counterrevolutionaries" only days after his death when his wife was jailed with that label. In the 2020s, other than Mao, only three chiefs of the CCP, Jiang, Hu, and Xi, have managed to remain unblemished, plus the still revered Deng who ruled without the title of party-chief. The infamous "meat grinder" style of power struggles and purges evidently continues inside the CCP, wherein members of the top leadership are periodically toppled, disgraced, and incarcerated for life on average one every three to five years. The CCP under Mao purged five top leaders (members of the Politburo Standing Committee) out of seventeen in twenty-seven years; it has purged nine of forty-one in the forty-two years since Mao's death.[261]

Since Deng's death in 1997, CCP leaders have used even more opaque charges of corruption or just "violation of discipline and rules" to get rid of dissenters and contenders. The seemingly orderly anticorruption operations by the secret police of the Discipline Inspection Committees (DICs), which are mostly extra-legal but effective, have become the "deadliest weapon of power struggle inside the CCP." In late 2021, the CCP formally redecreed that "protecting the core position of Xi Jinping in the Party Central and the whole Party [. . .] is the supreme political principle and fundamental political duty" of all DICs.[262] Shrewdly taking advantage of popular resentment against the widespread and rampant corruption typical of any Qin-Han-style officialdom, CCP leaders have thoroughly politicized anticorruption to selectively purge opponents and challengers, redistribute positions and rent-seeking rights, and consolidate personal power.[263] It appears to also be a handy tool for enforcing obedience in the suppression of religious minorities. For example, in April 2017, dozens of local CCP cadres and clerks in Hotan Prefecture of Xinjiang were disciplined for corruption and "rule violation," with actual offenses such as "not daring to smoke in front of the [Islamic] clergy," "not keeping a good tab on the family situations of the targeted [Muslim] people," or "underreporting the number of visitors to the [local] mosque." Two senior ethnic Uyghurs officials of the CCP in Xinjiang were sentenced to death with reprieve, and another one to life in prison, all on corruption charges; but the official media itself revealed three years later in 2021 that their real offense actually involved "daring and crafty efforts" to resist and undermine Beijing's suppression orders targeted at the Uyghurs.[264] The powerful political utility of authoritarian, top-down, and selective anticorruption is evidenced by the fact that every CCP leader since Mao has been adamant about eliminating corruption, yet none has ever tried proven methods, such as an independent judicial system, free media, publicizing and monitoring officials' personal and family assets, or political empowerment of the people through elections. Further, corruption of the ruling elites and officialdom is not only inevitable but also necessary and effective in securing the loyalty and support for an autocratic ruler, something Legalists discussed as among the dark arts of politics 2,000 years ago, and scholars have identified today in other countries.[265] As expected, the CCP has a heavy "reliance upon corruption to retain the loyalty of officials to an unelected regime."[266] The CCP's anticorruption indeed shares the same politicization, cynicism, and ineffectiveness of that of other autocracies, from the Ottoman Empire to Nazi Germany and the Soviet Bloc.[267] Therefore, after years of "iron fist" anticorruption campaigns, the CCP Central and Xi Jinping officially declared and threatened that "there [still] is no clean corner in the country, no region or agency is problem-free [of corruption], just a variation of degree."[268]

The party-state officially disclosed that it had "punished" as many as 4.2 million cadres (many ended up with rapid-fire executions, long jail sentences, and "involuntary suicides") from 1982 to 2012 on corruption or misfeasance charges, on average 140,000 a year, which equates to a shockingly high "crime rate" of almost 4 percent annually, more than ten times the crime rate for the general population. Such political purges in the name of anticorruption have intensified: in barely a decade, from 2012 to 2021, the CCP "punished" a total of 3.99 million cadres, including 484 ranked at or above province/ministry, 22,000 ranked at prefecture/bureau, and 170,000 ranked at county/division; that is about 444,000 cases a year, more than doubling the party's "crime rate" of 1982–2012, and reaching about twenty times the crime rate of the general population; in a little over three years (January 2018–June 2021), over 12,000 CCP cadres were sentenced to jail for longer than five years, with thirteen senior cadres (provincial or higher) incarcerated for life, and one executed.[269]

In 2013, the number of anticorruption cases jumped 36 percent to over 180,000, with 65,000 "leading cadres" punished, followed by increases ranging from 76 to 233 percent at different levels in the following year, perfectly reflecting the fierce power struggle associated with Xi Jinping's takeover since 2012. In 2012 to 2017, all thirty-one provincial units of the PRC had their top cadres, a total of 440, "punished"; of the 376 members of the Eighteenth CCP Central Committee (2012–17), which was not entirely installed by Xi, forty-three (11%) were purged, including one current politburo member and three just-retired politburo members (one just-retired politburo standing committee member). After consolidating power with Xi's personal staffing of the Nineteenth Central Committee in 2017, however, only two central committee members and none higher were purged in 2017 to 2022; the provincial leaders "punished" during Xi's second term also dropped 86 percent to around sixty, signaling either a sudden improvement of CCP leaders in law-abiding and ethical behavior or, more likely, a much-decreased need for using anticorruption to eliminate dissenters and promote loyalists at the top level.[270]

Extensive purges of the police itself are also evident: in less than four months in 2021, for example, 72,312 CCP cadres in law enforcement (police officers, prosecutors, and judges) were "punished," 27,364 "were investigated," and 12,576 "surrendered voluntarily to confess" their wrongdoings; in the first eight months of 2022 alone, three senior police officers (above deputy minister-level) were sentenced to death with a two-year reprieve and another one to life in prison.[271] In the 2020s, a new sign of the depth and scope of the contagious corruption in the government was the so-called endemic of "baby mega-corruptors" (*wawa jutan*): the endless cases of young (born in or after the 1990s), impatient, brazen, and boundless low-ranking cadres and even just office clerks who took bribes and embezzlements of "the mammoth amount [of tens of millions] that was before seen only in the cases of old, senior cadres."[272] Corruption appears not to abate at all inside the party-state, despite the purging of millions of cadres.

Either CCP members and cadres are much more prone to crime than the general public and this unlawfulness is in direct correlation to their ranks, or their power and prerogatives come with the special job hazard of periodical purges, or both. Even climbing with so much exertion and treachery to the very top of the PRC autocracy does not really provide much security and safety, let alone due process, if one is viewed as "belonging to the wrong clique" or is associated with a fallen leader in a power struggle. Leaked reports and memoirs suggest that, once purged, the previously almighty and worshipped cadres, large or small, are also subject to the same sort of injustice, inhumanity, abuse, physical torture, and even death in the legal and extra-legal penal systems.[273]

The hierarchical prerogatives enjoyed by the "people's servants," however, do seem to remain even when they are purged or convicted. There is reportedly deferential treatment of the purged based on rank, especially for those senior cadres who are submissive and cooperative enough or still have their patrons in power: better prison meals, roomier cells, and more attentive medical staff. Convicted senior cadres and their families commonly get easy and discreet reduction of sentences, such as commutation of a death sentence to medical parole in just five years, for example, in the reported case of Zhou Beifang.[274] In the rare case of being sentenced to die, senior cadres reportedly may request the more "humane" method of lethal injection rather than facing the standard and cheaper firing squad.

Outside of the party-state officialdom, those rich and able Chinese who are not securely connected to the winning side of power struggles in the top echelons of the CCP have been specifically targeted with extortion, confiscation, exile, imprisonment, and even execution. This is likely because those with significant money and fame who are not effectively and directly controlled by the ruler could incite and finance dissents or challenges. The party thus casts particularly vigilant, envious, and suspicious attention on anyone who has "made it" in the PRC, treating them like plump livestock or dangerously wandering fat cats ready to be sheared and diminished. The mighty police state thus diligently, routinely, and deliberately undermines and destroys the wealth-creating segments of Chinese society in service to the Party's insatiable need for power and control. The suboptimality of the CCP-PRC governance thus hurts everyone underneath it, including those able and lucky elites who have become the rich and famous in the world. This is especially detrimental to China's competitiveness and creativity, as the ambitious and the excellent are systematically caged and castrated in "the CCP's culture of fear [for its] ruthless pursuit of hierarchical power and private interests."[275]

According to media reports, many of the PRC's super-rich appear to die "unnaturally." In the period between 2003 and 2011, fifteen billionaires (average age 44) were murdered, seventeen (average age 50) committed suicide, and fourteen (average age 42) were executed by the government. During the first decade of the twenty-first century, over a dozen billionaires were jailed for multiple years, their assets confiscated. Five of the super-rich were executed, and one died in prison in his forties. "The proportion of those charged, investigated or arrested after being on [China's richest] list was 17 percent, compared to 7 percent of other entrepreneurs in the same period."[276] Among the general population of those fifteen years or older in the PRC, only about 0.14 to 0.44 percent were investigated, arrested, or charged by the police annually during 2000 to 2020 (see table 1.3).[277] In 2014, at least twenty of China's richest

Table 1.3. Crime Rate of Segments of Chinese Society

Segment	Annual Crime Rate	
General public*	0.075%	(1999–2000)
General public 15 and older*	0.11–0.44%	(1999–2019)
Entrepreneurs**	0.7%	(1998–2008)
Richest PRC citizens**	1.7%	(1998–2008)
CCP cadres***	4–5%	(2013–2016)
Senior cadres***	2%	(2013–2016)

*Crime rate here refers to police processed cases (立案).

**Crime rate here refers to cases of legal investigations, arrests, and indictments.

***Crime rate here includes extra-legal party disciplinary investigations and punishments, and legal investigations, arrests, and indictments. Senior cadre here refers to the members of the CCP Central Committee.

Source: J. Liu 2008: 131–147; L. Hu 2006; J. Bai 2010: 144–159. *Beijing Times* 2012; Xinhua January 10, 2014; CDIC August 25. 2016; F. Wang 2017: 183–184. NPC December 2020; Supreme People's Procuratorate 2020.

100, a whopping 20 percent, were in various kinds of trouble with the government—one was executed, seven were jailed, eight were under investigation, three became fugitives in exile, and one went into bankruptcy.[278] This list does not include the many pre-legal and extra-legal detentions and interrogations lasting days or even weeks, as well as the travel bans and government siphoning of assets endured by some of the richest and most famous PRC businessmen, such as Guo Guangchang of Fuxing and Wang Jianlin of Wanda. The latter was once the richest Chinese and owned the US movie theater chain AMC.[279] Indeed, "China's billionaires have a high turnover—[in one year] 106 people became billionaires but 51 dropped off the list [of about 300], illustrating the risks of doing business in China."[280]

In January 2017, Chinese-Canadian businessman Xiao Jianhua, who controlled a monstrous ¥3 trillion (over US $450 billion) conglomerate, was kidnapped by PRC secret agents from his luxurious hotel suite in Hong Kong and secretly jailed for several years before he was finally sentenced to thirteen years in prison in July 2022, his assets liquidated and confiscated. In early 2018, Hong Kong–based PRC businessman Ye Jianming, who managed over ¥1 trillion (US $150 billion) in assets, was secretly arrested and jailed without a trial while his fortune was quietly taken away; he is presumably still incarcerated. In May 2018, after more than a year of secret imprisonment, Wu Xiaohui, a PRC businessman whose company owns over ¥1 trillion (US $150 billion) in assets including the fabled hotel Waldorf Astoria New York and is Deng Xiaoping's ex-grandson-in-law, was sentenced to eighteen years in prison after a secret trial, with his multibillion-dollar assets confiscated in July 2019 and fully liquidated by September 2020. The charges against Wu were "fraudulent fund raising" and "job-related embezzlement."[281] In November 2020, iconic and somewhat dissenting businessman Sun Dawu of Hebei, his family, and senior management team were suddenly arrested, and his expansive conglomerate was taken over by the state. Months later, he received a jail sentence of eighteen years, and his entire group of twenty-eight companies, worth "at least" ¥5.1 to ¥7 billion, was auctioned off to the only bidder, a company created three days earlier, for ¥686 million.[282] Many purged super-rich are widely believed to be "white glove" tycoons, running titanic businesses for some top CCP leaders who later lost out in power struggles. In September 2021, another apparent "white glove" with close association and mega dealings with some top leaders, who similarly vanished in Fall 2017 into some secret "black cell" in Beijing, suddenly reappeared by phone, seemingly attempting to stop her ex-spouse in the United States from publishing "an insider's story of wealth, power, corruption, and vengeance in today's China."[283]

Whether out of altruism, a keen sense of self-preservation, or persuasion, Ma Yun (Jack Ma, age 55) of Alibaba and Ma Huateng (age 48) of Tencent, the PRC's equivalents of Jeff Bezos (Amazon) and Mark Zuckerberg (Facebook), "willingly" gave up their companies (each with assets of nearly ¥1 trillion) in 2019, in a move Taiwanese business reporters have described as "forced [by the CCP] to retire."[284] Online PRC reporters further tallied forty-one large, publicly traded, private companies that were "nationalized" in 2019 alone.[285] In November 2020, after just "giving up" Alibaba—the massive Chinese equivalent of Amazon, eBay, and PayPal rolled into one—Jack Ma, CCP member and the richest PRC citizen, was publicly hammered with a last-minute order to suspend the long-planned Hong Kong and Shanghai IPO (initial public offering) of the Ant Group, the financial service company he founded and controlled, reported to be the world's largest ever IPO at over $34 billion. By the end of 2020, Alibaba became the target of the CCP's opaque "anti-trust" action "based on tips." In early 2021, the mega Ant Group was taken over by the PRC state.[286] Ma's impudence toward regulators was reported as a possible reason. But this action is perhaps more reflective of the general pattern of the CCP-tycoon relationship in China and the erratic factional power struggles in the top echelons in Beijing.[287] The very few secretive and exclusive, "Masonry-like," "social and friendship" clubs "for mutual assistance," which comprised super-rich businesspeople and powerful cadres plus power brokers, such as the Taishan Society (1993–2020), the Xishan Society (2007–2014), and the Lakeside University (2015–2021), were either crushed by the CCP or "voluntarily disbanded."[288]

Many rich and famous Chinese in entertainment and media businesses have skyrocketed to a world-class level of luxury and celebrity recognition. Yet, those stars apparently must show even more submission and cooperation to the party-state to be safe and secure, sometimes professing their love of the party leaders through more than just lip-service or monetary contribution. Once their patrons fall out of power or whenever they are caught doing something "improper," such as badmouthing Mao at private dinner parties, dining or sleeping with the wrong leader, or fathering children outside of the birth-planning quota, they can be trashed, mistreated, "frozen," and punished with heavy fines or even long, secret jail sentences, just like the millions of CCP cadres who are purged or the hundreds of millions of citizens who are policed. Some of the better-known cases in recent years include the very hefty fine of ¥7.48 million (US $1.24 million) levied on Zhang Yimou, the court-favored movie director who produced the opening and closing galas of the 2008 Beijing Olympic Games and the 2022 Beijing Winter Olympic Games, for having two extra children; the astronomical ¥800 million plus (US $135 million) fine without a formal trial and a mysterious, months-long "disappearance" for the arguably best-known PRC actress Fan Bingbing for an unspecified "tax evasion"; the assets confiscation and career banishment of popular comedian Zhao Benshan for allegedly being "too close" to some losers of internal CCP power struggles; the expulsion and silencing of TV personality Bi Fujian for a politically incorrect private conversation posted online by others; and the long and often secret jailing of a host of CCTV star anchors including Rui Chenggang, Ye Yingchun, Shen Bin, and Jia Xiaoye, mostly for their associations and interactions with purged CCP leaders.[289]

On the national stage, some of the richest, most powerful, and best-known Chinese routinely endure the China Suboptimality. At subnational levels, each region's mini-dictators of the CCP treat their colleagues, rich citizens, and local celebrities similarly, with the institutionally determined greed, suspicion, distain, and vengeance against uncontrolled power and wealth. The lower-ranking members of the PRC's political, business, and sociocultural elites may evade the limelight and hide away to an extent, but they are always under the watch and pressure of the myriad local cadres, to be punished for any slight offense or inconvenience, or even just out of simple jealousy and resentment. The need and reward for them forming an expensive but uncertain patronage with power-holders are just as strong and obvious as on the national stage, and nearly as unreliable and hazardous. In the less tightly controlled PRC corners of cyberspace, one sees countless stories about local and community elites enduring ghastly or even bizarre fates at the hands of the omnipresent CCP. In the 2010s and 2020s, the CCP extensively used forced confession on TV to broadcast public shaming as a new extra-legal tool for punishment and control.[290]

The mighty PRC police state watches literally everyone. Expensive surveillance cameras, with the latest facial-recognition technology from the US, have become ubiquitous in the country. In the city of Beijing alone, more than 300,000 such cameras were installed and run by the police in 2008 to monitor the public.[291] By 2018, the PRC state purchased two-thirds of the world's facial-recognition cameras to complete the world's largest network, known as Sky Net, with over 176 million surveillance cameras, one for every eight PRC citizens, including 20 million directly run by the police. They share information instantaneously and deliver police action in person, via public speaker or cell phone, within minutes, or even seconds in sensitive places like Tiananmen Square. More sophisticated surveillance cameras now identify and record people wearing facemasks by their body shape and gait.[292] In 2020, the CCP undertook the even more ambitious Brightening Project to completely integrate all national surveillance for "instant and thorough use," "completely covering every corner" of the country. This includes a total of 276 to 450 million (or even 626 million) surveillance cameras, about one for every five, three, or two PRC citizens, to be installed by 2022, in combination with AI (artificial intelligence) and big-data analysis.[293] To accompany this network, a state-controlled "social credit" system has been under development since 2014 to rate and rank every PRC resident according to government criteria.[294] People's daily chores, financial standing, private life, political "performance," and ideological inclination are all to be constantly and comprehensively monitored and analyzed to singularly determine and regulate their rights, stature, and access to schooling and jobs, travel and housing, social services and benefits, and credit and their own assets. As I will further discuss later in the book, the draconian lockdowns of many major cities and effectively the whole country, for months at a time, in the name of containing the COVID-19 virus in 2020–2022 vividly illustrated the awesome power and brutality of the police state.

With all its expensive, legal and extra-legal, expansive and intrusive, deadly and often distasteful words and acts, the CCP still only manages to create an insecure, unsafe, and intranquil society. Anyone who visits PRC cities will notice the birdcage, or even jail-like, anti-burglary metal doors and window bars everywhere. Contract enforcement such as debt repayment and civil judgments are widely ineffective. Fraud of all kinds, fakery including large financial schemes and counterfeiting, and toxic food and medicine are daily occurrences nationwide.[295] I will discuss more of these issues later in the book. My interviewees living throughout the PRC have shared endless horror stories and cautionary tales about unsafe streets, public places, and food and services; about gruesome crimes big and small; about the comprehensive lack of trust outside of immediate family and social circles; and about how the police, police assistants, town managers, and all sorts of other "security-related" characters mistreat and brutalize people.[296]

The general sense of a lack of public security and safety, together with the rich anecdata about horrendous and often senseless crimes, suggest that the real crime rate in China is likely to be among the highest in the world—with the exception of gun violence, since private firearms are strictly prohibited in the PRC. The published Chinese crime rate, always skewed and likely doctored, appears to be just around the average world crime rate. However, the available (but rare) Chinese analyses of official data show that the PRC has experienced world-class growth of crime. The crime rate, defined as the number of police-processed cases (*li an*) per population, grew annually by 16.7 percent, much faster than economic growth, from 1986 to 2019, from 0.75 to 3.6 per thousand (1.1 to 4.4 per thousand for ages 15 and up).[297] Another Chinese study reported that the police cases represent only about 20 percent of actual crimes, thus the "real crime rate is at least 130 percent more than the official data."[298] In 2020 during the COVID-19 pandemic, the PRC officially reported a 108 percent jump in criminal arrests and 130 percent increase in indictments, with robbery and burglary cases jumping by 143 percent and 158 percent; facing a surge of juvenile crime, Beijing lowered the age of criminal prosecution to twelve.[299]

One particularly striking piece of evidence illustrating the underperformance of PRC governance has been the large and common problem of human trafficking and abuse, especially involving the massive number of kidnapped women and young children stolen from their families. This "ancient" and "traditional" crime in China has seemingly continued as a vibrant, widespread, and even "wholesale-sized" enterprise in the PRC, with gruesome consequences of exploitation, brutality, injury, and death constantly reported.[300] The per capita rate of the crimes of human trafficking and slavery in China is reportedly over ten times higher than in the West and other East Asian countries.[301] One to four million people, including many children, were reported "gone missing" in the PRC every year in the 2010s to 2020s, with only a fraction of them "ever found." The rescue and recovery rate of lost and missing children in the PRC is estimated at about 5 percent, inconceivably low when contrasted with that in the United States, which is 99 percent.[302] With the world's most extensive digital surveillance network, the PRC police have demonstrated a high efficacy in identifying and locating wanted people relevant to the "maintenance of political stability"; human trafficking and many other "real" crimes, however, frequently appear to be a low priority. The mighty *hukou* system may have critically assisted the CCP governance, but its main role related to the census appears quite suboptimal: in the mid-2010s, about 13 million people were estimated to be *hukou*-less and thus "invisible."[303]

The CCP Optimality in safeguarding the autocracy, at the expense of the China Suboptimality described above, is itself also constantly and even increasingly insecure. The ever-present political instability and social tensions in PRC are accompanied by a widespread sense of insecurity and injustice on the streets, and a sinking public credibility and authority that requires yet more force and money to salvage. In early 2022, a gruesome case of a woman trafficked and used as a sex slave and baby machine for many years in Xuzhou, in northern Jiangsu Province, the so-called "chained mother of eight," was accidentally revealed and then went viral on the internet, igniting a firestorm of public resentment and trepidation.[304] PRC social media was immediately flooded with stories and reports about the seemingly chronic, omnipresent, and massive crimes of abduction, trafficking, and servitude of people, especially children and women of childbearing age, and about police inaction, incompetence, and even complicity, despite repeated but inept official cover-ups and constant online censorship. Countless sensational, frightening, and even fear-mongering "tips" about how to deal with kidnappers and human traffickers, even in the center of major cities, popped up with a very large readership, suggesting that "the feeling of insecurity, of deprivation of protection, is very strong in the society."[305] One PRC blogger put it this way: "all sorts of freedoms that we have exchanged for safety and security have basically been swindled from us: we are not safe. The state has lied to everyone; [with neither freedom nor safety] it turns out that this is a country of slavery."[306]

Increasingly, many Chinese people tend to automatically disbelieve any and all government statements and decrees, a woeful predicament of governance classically described by the Roman historian Tacitus two millennia ago, a deadly trap and a vicious cycle of faulty and undesirable governance.[307] A semi-official Chinese survey sadly concluded that a clear majority of the Chinese people are "habitual skeptics" who either "don't trust anything the government says" or simply "lack social and public trust."[308] In April 2022, a blogger in locked-down Shanghai declared, "I'll never trust even a single word of government statements [after being shanghaied so many times by blatant lies]." One month later, another "always government-trusting" professional openly declared that her family, after their atrocious but "very common" ordeal under the draconian and "absurd" quarantine policies in Shanghai—the "best city in China," became "completely disillusioned [about the government]" and decided to "seek freedom," a common epithet for emigration, above "all other pursuits." Some daring PRC scholars have long described an irreversible sociopolitical "decay" and paralysis of governance under the CCP.[309] Xi Jinping, either following the classic autocratic playbook, which requires endless enemies, or sensing some genuine danger of instability, almost constantly calls for ever-more efforts to maintain the CCP regime, codenamed "maintain stability" (*weiwen*); a single month in early 2021 saw three blunt warnings regarding some life-and-death struggle with someone attempting to "usurp the party and state power" and endanger the party-state leadership, as reported by the CCP's mouthpiece. Only months later, Xi publicly and repeatedly issued even more "tough warnings to enemies within the Party."[310]

To be sure, the CCP governance of China has always featured frequent and violent resistance—fighting suppression from day one, with mass incarceration and execution of tens of millions.[311] While independent trade unions are outlawed and strikes are prohibited, hundreds of strikes apparently still take place in China every year.[312] Civil and criminal cases related to social protests have also "skyrocketed."[313] Before it was prohibited in 2012, PRC researchers and officials periodically reported numbers of "mass incidents," riots and protests (defined as unauthorized, usually violent clashes with the authorities "involving 20 or more people") that anecdotally included attacking and even killing police and cadres, the looting and burning of shops and vehicles, sabotage of public facilities, "terrorist attacks," and blockage of public transportation.[314] That number grew rapidly from about 8,700 in 1993 (24 per day) to 87,000 in 2005, over 180,000 in 2010, and 190,000 each year during 2011–2015 (520 per day).[315] Perhaps contrary to conventional wisdom, the more prosperous and developed Southern China has the lion's share of such riots, with Guangdong, the richest province, leading the country with 31 percent of "major" riots involving 100 people or more during 2000–2013.[316] When under the same draconian lockdown during the COVID-19 pandemic in March to May 2022, people in Shanghai, China's economic center and most cosmopolitan and internationalized metropolis, exhibited decidedly much more resistance, protests, and defiance that were anecdotally violent against the "authoritarian excess" of being "Xinjianged." In late-November 2022, barely one month after Xi secured his third term as the CCP top leader at the party's 20th National Congress, the so-called "White Paper Protesters" in Shanghai openly chanted "Xi Jinping! Step down! CCP! Step down!"[317] This seems to indicate the deep and growing conflict between the party-state and the more advanced market-oriented socio-economic development. Like a huge pot boiling under the heavy lid of police and censors, and notwithstanding the likely falsification of data by the PRC police to justify ever-more funding (which is already deemed by some PRC scholars as "unlimited and uncontrolled"[318]), Chinese society appears to be far more sociopolitically intranquil than its more liberal neighbor South Korea or its chosen rival the United States.[319]

2

Economic Record

Socialism with Chinese Characteristics

This chapter continues the examination of the CCP-PRC with an assessment of its economic record. In terms of living standards, economic efficiency, innovation, and sociocultural progress, the first three decades of the PRC under Mao Zedong were a calamity, filled with misery, regression, disasters, and crises. Combined with the record losses of human lives and the extensive deprivation of people's civil and human rights discussed in the previous chapter, the Maoist economic policies created the China Tragedy and wreaked colossal havoc in the course of "a revolution derailed."[1]

The post-Mao PRC since the 1980s has fared much better, with impressive economic growth, rapid technological advancement, and significant improvement in the standard of living. The Maoist calamity subsided, and the CCP grudgingly but wisely went into "hiding" in the interest of regime survival. The PRC selectively accepted the West-led LIO (liberal international order) of the Westphalian System in exchange for critical rescue by the West, which provided it with legitimization, technology, capital, markets, resources, and food. Beijing was compelled to relax and adjust its totalitarian control of the Chinese economy and society in order to return to the pre-1949 trajectory of state-capitalistic development and state self-strengthening through importation and imitation, financed by export and foreign capital. As a result, the post-Mao PRC has experienced a booming economy with two special shining accomplishments: rapid growth of its GDP and accumulation of a world-record foreign currency reserve. Up to 430 million Chinese people, or 30 percent of the total population, are now estimated to have considerable disposable income to constitute the purchasing power for a giant domestic consumer market that rivals in size the consumer market in the United States or the European Union.[2] I have personally witnessed the phenomenal ascent of the PRC since the late 1970s and experienced the great joy and deep pride the Chinese people rightfully feel about their socioeconomic achievements. Many, including myself, have published continually to document and applaud the decades of economic growth and social progress in China, notwithstanding the self-aggrandizement by CCP propagandists and self-interested exaltation of various salespersons.

This chapter, however, intends to go beyond the glitzy façade and the conventional wisdom to provide a balanced assessment of the PRC socioeconomic record. Here we see that the Chinese economy under the CCP has made great advancements over the past three decades with the official banner of "socialism with Chinese characteristics," but has essentially expanded on the tracks of a developmental state-directed raw capitalism, or capitalism with PRC characters. The CCP maintains its autocratic domination of the state–market relationship with excessive extraction and faulty management particularly in its fiscal and monetary policies. Inefficiency, lack of innovation, dislocations and bubbles, and inequality and poverty have all continued on a massive scale and even seriously worsened. The overall socioeconomic performance of the PRC remains quite *average* and mostly suboptimal, often underachieving, with heavy costs and great uncertainties for the long run. Comprehensively assessed, the PRC economy is still firmly stuck among the ranks of developing nations. The high GDP growth rate and the world's largest foreign currency reserve, in particular, are in fact much less glittering under a closer scrutiny.

The China Model

Volumes have been published in praise of the phenomenal and even "miraculous" economic growth in the PRC since the 1980s, attributing it to a unique and superior "China Model" of development that outperforms other economic systems.[3] As I will elaborate in this chapter, however, the four-decade PRC economic record, enchanting as it is, has showcased neither a miracle, nor a new model of economics, nor the superiority of the CCP's way of governance. The rise of the Chinese economy is highly similar to and heavily influenced by the experiences of the developmental states of Japan, South Korea, Singapore, and Taiwan, with some ideological coating of the traditional rhetoric of "moral economy." The "propelling" role of non-PRC Chinese (in Hong Kong and Taiwan) and the Chinese diaspora in general, as the source of capital, technology, managerial know-how, and export facilitation has been especially critical.[4] The PRC state deserves credit for little more than relaxing its control of the economy and allowing the Chinese people some room to make their own economic decisions, while de-isolating the country to let in international capital and foreign technology. A well-observed role of "socialism with Chinese characteristics" of the party-state, perhaps a noteworthy credit, has been its focused sustentation of mega developmentalist projects such as export-led growth and the development of infrastructure and real estate, based on its central planning apparatus of authoritarian capitalism that monopolizes resources, befriends capitalists, and controls and pacifies labor. However, as I will document later in this chapter, this role seems to have been at best a mixed blessing that has indeed led to impressive outcomes but also great costs and problems, resulting in economic growth with low and declining efficiency.[5]

Pragmatic CCP leaders like Zhao Ziyang craftily cited Moscow's expedient "New Economic Policy" in the 1920s and economic reforms by "comrades" in Eastern Europe in the 1950s–1970s to ideologically cover a return to the pre-PRC state capitalism. In the penetrating words of a legendary PRC journalist, the post-Mao reform was "just trying to go back to reconnect with the 1930s."[6] The CCP's seemingly endless "reform" since the 1980s, however, "has not been an institutional innovation" despite the official rhetoric and labels.[7] As an American sinologist analyzed, the adaptive improvisations allowed and even "directed" by the developmentalist PRC state to "use what you have" to get rich, rather than the CCP's "centralized authoritarian control," were key to the growth of the Chinese economy during the 1980s–2010s. A Chinese historian of economic theory similarly concluded in 2021 that "the evolution of macroeconomic ideas and policies in contemporary China" over the past four decades featured neither theoretic innovation nor masterful vision other than trying [various ideas] "to manage the same problem" of control versus growth for the aim of "becoming rich and powerful" so as "to surpass" the West.[8]

Any centralized and active developmental state interested in economic growth (regardless of its motives for legitimacy and power or something else) in a racially homogenous country encountering a welcoming West can certainly enjoy substantial economic growth. This is especially the case in the crucial junctures of economic "takeoff" to accumulate capital and to circumvent the Lewis Transition to absorb the large "surplus" of labor. As one PRC economist summarized, Chinese economic development has been "precisely because of the [PRC] state's gradual retreat from the economy."[9] The CCP under Deng Xiaoping and the more constrained and chastened Jiang Zemin and Hu Jintao reigns indeed yielded more room for the Chinese people to pursue profit and a comfortable life in their own ways. Less bounded, though still under the continued China Suboptimality of political governance of the party-state, the industrious and entrepreneurial Chinese people quickly proved that they are fully capable of wealth-building and economic competition, with prodigious outcomes and tremendous progress, rivaling if not surpassing any peoples of the world. A "latecomer's advantage," theorized by economists over a century ago, in utilizing the ready-made technology and the richly accumulated comparative advantage predictably boosted economic growth in the PRC.[10]

The CCP-PRC is, by its DNA, a controlling and extractive state. It has been more than adequately compensated by the booming Chinese economy for its limited, tactical, and provisional retreat from people's economic and social life. In the absence of a real political transformation, the basics of the Maoist Qin-Han polity, which have traditionally been highly seductive to Chinese political elites and also structurally path-dependent, have continued. Feeling securer and more powerful, especially under Xi Jinping, the CCP predictably and emphatically resumed its pattern of rejecting sociopolitical reform, stepping up its extraction and monopoly, repressing dissention, and resisting adherence to reigning world norms and values. Penetrating and controlling the Chinese economy like a giant China Inc. (or more precisely the CCP Inc.), the party-state has leveraged its "low human rights advantage, and tolerance by other countries [. . . and acted as if] state-owned firms are business units or subsidiaries, private firms are joint ventures, and foreign firms are franchisees of the party," as one observer concluded in 2022.[11]

The post-Mao socioeconomic performance of the PRC, therefore, remains essentially, however counterintuitively to many, quite *average* and mostly suboptimal, often underachieving and forcing the Chinese people to endlessly endure hardship, or colloquially, *chi ku* (eating bitterness). The Chinese political economy and especially the state–market relationship remain politicized and CCP-dominated. A particular kind of corruption in the PRC, so-called "access money" where entrepreneurs bribe the officials for room and assistance to start and grow, now seems to be producing more harm than good to the Chinese economy as it is increasingly unable to compete with other, much less growth-friendly but more widespread, corruptions such as thuggery and fraud. PRC fiscal and monetary policies have created a sea of red ink and countless bubbles, plaguing the Chinese economy, and perpetrating deep inefficiency and lack of innovation.[12] "Since 2009 and especially over the past 8–9 years," a PRC economist argued in Fall 2021, the "Chinese economy has basically gone ever deeper into bubbling." By capital return, energy consumption, and other measures, China remains a typical developing economy in the world. With the world's second largest GDP, the PRC appears to be an economic superpower essentially by the numbers. Two shining achievements, the high GDP growth rate and the world's largest foreign currency reserves, appear quite problematic under closer scrutiny. In the cautiously vague words of Chinese economists, the PRC economic growth has benefited from a "race to the bottom" competition at home and another abroad, which is increasingly unsustainable due to the state monopoly of land, resources, and the financial system.[13]

The reasons for the stubborn suboptimality of a country's socioeconomic performance can certainly be numerous; the same is true for the overall fortune of a nation. But influential scholars from Gunnar Myrdal and Douglass North, to Amrtye Sen and others have long considered political governance and economic institutions (and their internalization or culture), and particularly a proper state and its capable policies working with a functional market system, as the most significant factors determining economic development.[14] An econometric study employing multiple methods concluded in 2019 that "democracy does cause [economic] growth [. . .] across different levels of development," especially in the long run, "and that there are many complementarities between democratic institutions and proximate causes of economic development."[15] A United States–trained Chinese scholar has argued in this vein for the central role of political institutions in economic development and the view that democracy has "a unique advantage in promoting development." An "expert in Marxism" in the PRC also agreed that "the secret determining national wealth or poverty is the state's skill in governance."[16]

The PRC, despite its prevalence of raw, nineteenth-century-style capitalism, remains a "mostly unfree economy" as its "index of economic freedom" constantly scores "below the regional and world averages." By 2021, the very high economic freedom Hong Kong and Macau both enjoyed for decades was also deemed "lost" due to Beijing's political strangulation of the two "autonomous regions."[17] Against the intense but thus far failed CCP lobbying efforts, the West, the World Trade Organization (WTO), and large economies of the world had all certified by the 2020s that the PRC was not really a market economy, let alone a market economy with reliable rule of law.[18] In recent years, the so-called "China model" of state-capitalism is understood to have degenerated into a "party-state capitalism," with the CCP's logic of political control further displacing the market mechanism in the Chinese economy.[19] With the quick spurt of its "catch-up" growth already starting to wane, and a frenzied recreation of Mao the Second in Xi Jinping, there are strong signals of more troubled times ahead for the Chinese economy and the Chinese people, if not a total return of the Maoist calamity of the China Tragedy.

A latecomer country of economic development like China may enjoy substantial "latecomer's advantage" in terms of easy and often cheap access to world-class technology, international capital, and the vast market that trailblazing countries have already developed. However, it can also suffer from a so-called "latecomer's curse" or "latecomer's disadvantage," a phenomenon in which a once-booming developing country stagnates and declines over time, or fares worse, because of the deficit of modernization in its sociopolitical institutions. This is perhaps similar to the infamous "resource curse" or "paradox of plenty," which has doomed the economic growth and political development in many countries rich in natural resources.[20] Other than importing and imitating extant technology from the developed countries in order to grow the economy, even at an impressive pace for a while, the rulers of a latecomer state tend to have little if any reason, incentive, will, or ability to also replicate the political norms and institutions of the developed countries. These institutions and norms are in fact the hard-fought and long-tested prerequisites and essential companions of sustainable technological innovation and socioeconomic development. Such a "latecomer's curse" helps to explain why many developing countries have been stuck in the so-called "middle-income trap," unable to become developed countries. In the PRC, as Chinese scholars concluded, for over a century, "[sociopolitical-economic] institutional reform in China has always been just talk and barely touched the surface."[21] The effect of the latecomer's curse of institutional-deficit, therefore, seems persistent and aggravating, with ever-higher stakes and more pronounced severity.[22]

Incompetence and Failures:
Mao's Great Famine and Stark Stagnation

Under Mao, the CCP-PRC party-state terribly overextracted and ineptly micromanaged the Chinese economy in the interests of its regime security and foreign ambitions from 1949 to the late 1970s, resulting in repeated and monumental economic failures and humanitarian disasters. These included some of the largest peacetime losses of human life in history, as reported in the previous chapter. There was also stark socioeconomic stagnation and a deep decline in the standard of living, leading to a level of carnage that was unprecedented and unparalleled in severity and scale worldwide, according to many studies.[23]

From the very beginning, the CCP has acted with ruinous impact on the Chinese economy, seemingly by design. Amidst the massive destruction and death caused by the bloody Civil War, the CCP ran a deficit of over 65 percent from 1948 to 1950 and increased the printing of currency by 220-fold, delivering on arrival a very high inflation as a very cruel form of extraction.[24] Mao created for himself a highly centralized dictatorial power to not just govern the country but also meddle in the economy, engaging in incompetent and idiotic yet radically micro and inhumanely extractive mismanagement.[25] As a result, China's GDP was 4.7 percent of the world's total in 1955, but steadily declined to 2.5 percent in 1980, while the Japanese share rose from 2.5 percent to 10 percent during the same time. China's per capita GDP was about 20 percent of that of Japan in the early 1950s, but shrank to 10 percent in 1965.[26]

At an exorbitant cost, some noticeable growth occurred in heavy industry and infrastructure projects, including irrigation reservoirs and dams, electrical grids, and road/railroad construction, under Mao's centrally planned command economy. Also, considerable improvement transpired in the control of infectious diseases, reduction of infant mortality, and expansion of basic education. The PRC managed to test nuclear weapons in 1964 and launch a satellite in 1970, thanks mostly to the Western/American-trained Chinese scientists who returned to the PRC in the early 1950s, due chiefly to the inhospitable immigration laws in the West at the time. The United States repealed its infamous *Chinese Exclusion Act of 1882* in 1943 but only started to grant permanent residency to Chinese students after graduation in 1954.[27] The CCP actively lured back about 1,200, roughly 20 percent of the total number of Chinese students in the United States, by 1955 (though scarcely any more during the quarter-century that followed), and another 500 from other Western countries. These returned talents became critically instrumental to PRC technological endeavors. Most of the returnees were eventually mistreated and jailed, with many murdered and forced to commit suicide.[28] All of these meaningful but overexalted undertakings, however, probably would have been accomplished faster and much less painfully in a non-CCP-ruled China. Mao is due no credit but more appropriately only negatives for the regressive economic development and the meager technological advancement on the Chinese Mainland during the 1950s–1970s. Any government that could have provided the most basic political order and a sheer minimum of state services would more than likely have accomplished much more than the PRC party-state under Mao.

The CCP first destroyed Chinese agriculture with its bloody Land Reform, followed by the utopian collectivization and communes, which benefited only CCP cadres and "local hooligans," as revealed early on by one of its own "people's writers."[29] Then came the elimination of private entrepreneurship in the cities. Property rights were damaged and distorted and the market mechanism smashed to give the CCP a firm monopoly over Chinese resources and wealth. Millions of good farmers, labeled "landlords and rich peasants," were killed, persecuted, and socially castrated as class or people's enemies. Production skills and incentives were suppressed and extinguished. China's already historically low per capita grain production sank to its lowest point in 1962, at 207 kilograms, insufficient for sustaining the basic daily caloric needs of the population, even under a tight and inhumane ration system that excluded the majority rural population.[30] Aside from the tens of millions who died from starvation, living standards stagnated and declined for more than two decades for the vast majority of the Chinese people. Per capita annual consumption of basic food items sank between 1957 and 1978: grain fell from 203 to 195 kg, cooking oil from 2.4 to 1.6 kg, meat from 1.1 to 0.8 kg, poultry from 0.5 to 0.4 kg, and seafood from 4.3 to 3.2 kg. Per capita housing space also declined from 4.5 square meters in 1952, to 3.6 square meters in 1978. The per capita number of shops, newspapers, and books published all declined significantly as well. For three decades, a national rationing system of nearly all daily necessities (with local twists) barely kept the urban population alive, indulging party-state officials while basically abandoning the majority (80–85%) of the Chinese people in the countryside. In 1961, in the middle of the Great Famine, in the most "protected" capital city of Beijing, residents with local *hukou* (residency) received a ration of a maximum of 126 kg of grain and 8.5 *liang* (about 11 ounces) of meat (mostly pork) per person per year, incredibly small but "still much better than all other cities in the provinces." At the same time, the small group of CCP leaders and "approved" elites had "special provisions" that were dozens to a hundred times better, including a "daily supply of fresh meat." Shanghai, the economic center of the PRC, could not feed the thousands of babies abandoned on the streets "in a sudden wave."[31]

Under Mao, especially after the mid-1950s, the Chinese economy went through a series of cycles of recession and depression and was "generally stuck and stagnated," while only the size of the population and the magnitude of state extraction showed any significant growth. According to a retrospective analysis by later PRC economists, the economy developed very "unspectacularly" and several times endured long "stagnations and even regressions"; Chinese industrialization was low, unbalanced, and costly. "The people's standard of living was not improved at all," and labor productivity, return on investment, and energy efficiency all declined. Officially, it was admitted in 1999 that the average annual wage of urban workers in the PRC declined from ¥624 in 1957 to ¥575 in 1976.[32] Furthermore, contrary to the misplaced nostalgia for the Mao era still common among many PRC citizens today, China at the time was not just extremely poor but also quite unequal, with a world-class real Gini Coefficient reaching 0.7, double the official figure.[33]

Undersupplied and undernourished, the PRC population itself was subjected to many wanton, forced, and even bloody social engineering experiments, often in the name of some revolutionary ideology or "modern science."[34] Initially, the CCP encouraged population growth in the 1950s and 1960s.[35] Then it launched a politically motivated deurbanization as an expedient way to cope with the failure of the economy and the problem of social control in the cities. The "sending down" campaigns in the 1960s and 1970s dumped tens of millions of urban residents (mostly unemployed middle school and high school graduates) into collectivized communes, creating "lost" generations of "sent-down youth," and ensuring adverse life chances for their offspring as well.[36] Finally, the CCP adopted the harsh "national policy" (*guoce*) of invasive, often violent, and even deadly forced birth control in the late 1960s, cumulating in the infamous "one child per family" policy in 1980.[37] Under the draconian policy, in the three decades from 1980 to 2009, China officially had a total of 275 million abortions by choice, and about 100 million women had surgical sterilization.[38] Even after the policy was relaxed in the late 2010s, nine million by-choice abortions occurred every year (officially; unofficially, the number was thirteen million).[39]

The malevolent Mao-era policy of birth control was disparate and regime-protecting in nature. It later intensified and was carried on by the post-Mao CCP (with a special law in 2001) until 2015, when the CCP reversed its position, calling for two children per couple in order to stimulate the sluggish economic growth. However, at that point, it was probably "already too late to avert the demographic crisis."[40] One-third of all Chinese, about 450 million people, now live in a single-child household, in a rapidly and prematurely aging society with a vast gender imbalance.[41] All of this cruel, whiplash, social engineering has given the Chinese people deep and lasting pains; it has also evidenced the nature of the PRC as a Qin-Han polity on steroids that herds and exploits people like "livestock" or "worker bees," as noted by Chinese themselves.[42] The state birth control actions, enriching certain vested interests, such as the half-million officials in charge, profoundly raised the cost of governance and damaged people's rights, privacy, and dignity. Women's rights and bodies were routinely violated by the constant monitoring, forced abortion and sterilization, and financial losses. The social and psychological impact on the single-child generations has already revealed itself in menacing and gruesome ways.[43]

In the end, according to various studies, the whole social experiment of draconian birth control, like so many other suboptimal and tragic CCP policies, turned out to be "unnecessary" in reducing population growth, after all.[44] The demographic consequences of the four-decade birth-control policy became increasingly dire as the PRC birthrate nosedived to barely ten million births (47.3 percent girls) in 2020, equal to the total number of births in 1961 during the Great Famine (the smallest in PRC history) and about half the number of births of two decades before. This was despite the self-reversed policy of two children per couple since 2015, which quickly sprang into the hasty campaign for "three children per couple" in 2021.[45] Major socioeconomic disaster is looming in China, as a rapidly aging population, far from affluent enough to provide adequate care, faces the world's fastest decline in the birthrate.[46]

Under the impact of this long, draconian birth-planning policy, compounded by the skyrocketing cost of child-rearing, which "is almost the highest in the world in relation to per capita GDP," the Chinese people "now have almost the world's lowest desire to have children," according to a major PRC study.[47] Official data shows that the PRC birth rate declined rapidly to below 1 percent in 2020 and 0.75 percent in 2021, the lowest since 1950, and much lower than the world's average (1.8%), and the birth rates in the United States and India. With over 14 percent of its 1.4 billion people aged sixty-five or older, a "deeply aging" society, the Chinese population had a net growth of 10 million in 2012, 4.6 million in 2019, barely two million in 2020, and only 480,000 in 2021, heading "irreversibly" toward negative growth in 2022–23 for the first time since the great famine years of 1960–61.[48] The *hukou* police reported an even lower number of newborns in 2021: 8.87 million, or 16 percent fewer than the figure reported by the State Statistical Bureau—"[e]ven if all of the newborns attended college in 18 years, Chinese colleges would still be unable to fill their classrooms."[49] The lasting cost and horrific suffering and death notwithstanding, the folly and failure of its coercive social-demographic engineering are but one piece of hard evidence of the inanity and malignity of the hyperactive PRC state in disrupting people's lives. As one sarcastic Chinese netizen blogged:

> How rational we are: when with 800 million people, the mandate was one child per family; with 1.3 billion, the birth of second child was allowed; now with 1.4 billion, the policy is three children per couple.
>
> People starved to death in the 1960s, the blame was on the weather; saw the advancement of the West in the 1980s, the fault was too many people; now the economy slips, the indictment is too few people.[50]

Three Decades of Prodigious Growth

Forced by an ever-sharper international comparison and competition and the sheer economic mess at home that threatened to usher in another dynastic cycle of political collapse, Mao's successors were enticed, incentivized, and coached by foreigners to reduce state control of the economy and abandon much of Mao's utterly incompetent economic policy, starting by tolerating the largely spontaneous rural de-collectivization.[51] Essentially, after the end of the 1970s, the CCP measuredly and grudgingly relaxed its tight grip on the people, *allowing* (rather than leading, as it boasts) the Chinese economy to grow. Soon enough, the PRC literally went straight back to the economic development trajectory of the late-Qing and ROC years, characterized by state-capitalist economic development powered by a large influx of foreign capital and technology, along with hard currency income from exports.

Both pre-PRC and post-Mao Chinese history have shown that this trajectory may indeed exemplify the so-called "second-best" institutions and policies for economic growth, and is effectively the "right recipe." From 1979 to 2003, the PRC received over $107 billion in official aid alone from Western governments.[52] The industrious and entrepreneurial Chinese people have created an economic boom almost naturally and spontaneously despite the still-powerful political control, excessive extraction, bureaucratic interference, and massive corruption of the party-state.[53] PRC GDP grew for nearly a quarter-century at an officially averaged annual rate of 9 percent, jumped from the world's number ten in 1990 to number two in 2012, and has been projected to soon surpass US GDP, which has been the world's largest since the 1880s. By the somewhat controversial PPP (purchasing power parity) method, PRC GDP became the world's largest in 2015.[54] Per capita income, living standards, technological level, and infrastructure have all improved significantly, and especially dramatically in state-favored urban centers. The PRC has accumulated by far the largest foreign exchange reserve in the world, has become a major producer of many manufactured goods, and is the world's largest exporter, a truly epic leap from the near-autarky of the Maoist years.

The relatively developed (but still greatly repressed and mistreated) non-state sector has been by far the most dynamic engine of the significant growth in Chinese GDP, taxation, and employment.[55] "China's economic rise in the reform era (which began in 1978) is largely the story of the expanding role of markets and private enterprise," concluded a long-time observer of the Chinese economy in 2014: "Private firms became the major source of economic growth, virtually the sole source of job creation, and the major contributor to China's still-growing role as a global trader," as well as China's increasing outbound direct foreign investment. With 70 percent of China's fixed assets and 80 percent of government and state-bank loans, the state-owned enterprises contributed only 30 percent of China's GDP, half of the private firms' return on equity by 2016, with basically no new jobs created since 1997.[56]

Opening up to international trade and investment to return to the pre-1949 track of economic and cultural connections to the world through acceptance of the reigning world order, however reluctantly and selectively, has been the key to China's economic growth over the past four decades.[57] The post-Mao PRC, rescued by the West, has been fortunate in having an international environment of peace and cooperation since the 1980s, which is far more conducive and favorable than the environment China had in the 1920s–1940s. Joining the world almost automatically led to the economic boom by easily reaping China's potential, the cost differential of factors (especially labor) that were suppressed and accumulating for more than three decades. According to a leading PRC economist in 2014, "tapping into the long-accumulated potential energy" through connecting the two sea levels of wages between the developed economies and the depressed PRC—a differential of 80 to 100 times in the 1980s and still 10 times today—is what made China's rapid economic growth possible—"there's been no miracle."[58]

The rapid growth of the PRC economy in the 1990s–2010s, therefore, is largely a delayed correction of the low, nonexistent, or even negative growth of the 1950–1970s, made possible by a lucky and successful reconnection to the world economy. The main credit ought to go to the highly productive and "bitterness-eating" Chinese people who, for the first time in the PRC, could make considerable economic decisions on their own. Even so, the rapid growth still represents a rather average, suboptimal performance of socioeconomic development overall, at a cost much higher than average, as will be detailed below. For one thing, as one PRC scholar noted, the rapid expansion of the export-driven Chinese economy has been enabled by an ever-increasing "human rights deficit and environmental deficit." The PRC's economic boom has remained basically an expansive rather than intensive growth, fueled chiefly by state investment (the monopolized savings of the Chinese people), which constituted more than half of the PRC GDP in the 2010s with an ever-decreasing marginal return.[59] By the late 2010s, the delayed release of the competitive advantage of manufacturing based on suppressed and abused labor had started to run its course and vanish.[60] Economic growth, measured by the official GDP numbers, decelerated from 2010 (10%) to 2019 (6.2%). The acceleration of the PRC-West decoupling in the aftermath of the COVID-19 Pandemic drove Chinese GDP growth into a nosedive, hitting a forty-four-year low in 2020, with –6.5 percent in the first quarter and 2.3 percent for the year.[61]

Distortions and Dysfunctions

The relaxation of state control and reduction of mismanagement of the Chinese economy, however, are only relative. Deep structural distortions of the economy and profound dysfunctions in the economic system thus inevitably persist in the PRC. An illustration of this is the bizarre financial system that exists under a tenacious and expanding state control seeking power and plunder.[62] The expression "nine dragons managing the flood" (or too many cooks in the kitchen) seems to well characterize the PRC financial system: the CCP's Central Organization Department appoints top managers of all major financial institutions; the PRC Ministry of Treasury is "the main owner" of banks and other "legal" financial firms through a complicated arrangement that only awkwardly simulates a "stock-holding" structure; the People's Bank (PRC central bank) relays the CCP's directives as "the mother" of monetary power, while the also similarly ranked bureaucracy Banking and Insurance Regulatory Commission competes relentlessly for managerial and personnel influence over money matters. The result of all this insatiable appetite for control and extraction, constant turf wars and red tape, politicized arrangements and actions, and endless incompetence and corruption of the partocrats in charge have rendered the totally state-monopolized Chinese financial system uniquely chaotic and dysfunctional.[63] The "many oddities and dysfunctions" of the PRC stock market have made it "among the world's best means of separating investors from their wealth [. . . and] consistently one of the worst performers in Asia," observed *The Economist*.[64] Indeed, the Chinese securities exchanges have largely become a giant state-run casino for wealth extraction and financial manipulation to enrich the state, state-owned businesses, and the few insiders.[65]

Though clearly an imperfect indicator, the stock market may still illuminate the stability and growth of an economy. In 2007–08, the Chinese stock market lost two-thirds of its value. In 2015–16, another drastic downturn halved the Chinese stock market despite massive and panicky state interventions directed by Xi Jinping himself, which included arresting the brokers who did not follow government orders to sell or buy.[66] The PRC equity market has been flat ever since.[67] The leading index, the Shanghai Composite Index (SEE, created in 1991), reached its historic high of around 6,000 in October 2007, and its second high around 5,100 in mid-2015, but has crashed and stuck around 3,000 for years, roughly the same level it reached twenty years ago and less than half of its historic high of fifteen years ago (all while the PRC's GDP has nearly quadrupled). In contrast, the US Dow Jones Index also fluctuates but has been growing and reaching new highs and has more than doubled over the past fifteen years (while the US GDP grew just over 48%) (see table 2.1). The smaller Shenzhen Stock Exchange has

Table 2.1. Two Economies, Two Indices

Time	Dow Jones Industrial	Shanghai Composite	US GDP ($ billion)	PRC GDP ($ billion)
Started in the year	1885	1991	—	—
Historic peak	**36,231 (2022)**	**6,030 (2007)**	**22,996 (2021)**	**17,700 (2021)**
Jan 1991	2,501	129	6,158	383
June 2001	9,243	2,221	10,582	1,339
Mar 2007	12,114	2,937	14,452	3,550
Oct. 2007	**14,066**	**6,030**	**14,452**	**3,550**
Nov 2008*	9,625	1,720	14,713	4,594
Jan 2010	10,067	3,129	14,992	6,087
June 2015	17,947	5,166	18,219	11,016
Jan 2016	15,988	2,656	18,707	11,138
Jan 2018	25,520	3,558	20,544	13,608
Jan. 2020	**29,551**	**2,880**	**20,894**	**14,723**
March 2020**	18,592	2,745	20,894	14,723
Jan 2021	30,488	3,528	22,996	17,700
Jan 2022	36,231	3,361	22,996 (2021)	17,700 (2021)
Apr 2022***	34,049	2,886	22,996 (2021)	17,700 (2021)

*The Great Recession; **COVID-19 pandemic; ***Russian invasion of Ukraine.

The points of indices are from the same (or a neighboring) day in the month listed. Considering that PRC government allows new listings constantly while rarely delisting any, the total value of the Chinese stock market has actually declined significantly over the past two decades.

Source: Google Finance, US Department of Commerce, World Bank, accessed April 2022.

performed in largely the same way since the early 1990s. In 2021, perhaps attempting to revamp the Chinese capital market for more economic growth or to reallocate the internal capital flow for better control, Xi Jinping personally ordered the opening of the third security exchange in the PRC, the Beijing Stock Exchange.[68]

The Chinese stock market appears so irrelevant to the real economy perhaps because either it is grossly underdeveloped, suggesting the absence of a functional (let alone efficient) capital market in the world's second largest economy; or it is thoroughly rigged, signaling very serious distortions in the economy by an authoritarian state that has frightened away PRC investors even with its strict state control of capital export, or both. Two more possible explanations are that China's GDP growth is a so-called wealth-neutral or even wealth-destructive economic growth, thus creating little new wealth, or the government has been forging and inflating its economic data, or both.

Nearly four decades after the start of economic reform, private property rights (especially land rights) are still poorly defined, significantly distorted, and often simply lacking, directly hindering an efficient and innovative economy.[69] According to PRC economists, only nine countries in the world still refuse to grant private land ownership rights: "Bolivia, China, Cuba, North Korea, Vietnam and the former Soviet republics in Central Asia—all backward countries."[70] Critical industries like banking are mostly monopolized by the state "on behalf of the people." Thus, in 2008, a European Commission assessment deemed China to have failed to meet four out of five criteria that the EU sets for a market economy, and in 2014 a US Congressional body concluded that "China is not currently a market economy and is not on the path to become one in the near future."[71] Many other governments in the world, as mentioned earlier, have concurred. In 2020, the PRC government furthered its monopoly of property rights by declaring that "all public digital data shall be a new type of state-owned property." In 2021, in line with its tradition of monopoly and concealment of information, the CCP started to ban the transmission of any digital data collected by connected-automated vehicles in China to their mother companies or main servers abroad.[72]

One more way to perceive the true nature of the PRC economy and the structural causes of its inefficiency and lack of innovation is to look at its politically twisted internal financial market in general, exemplified by the enigmatic interest rates for borrowing. Since the banking sector is basically owned and strictly controlled by the party-state (private bankers could face the death penalty), Chinese interest rates do not reflect the supply and demand of capital, nor do they facilitate the efficient allocation of financial resources. The Chinese people, with one of the highest savings rates in the world, end up with a very low return or even a net loss on their savings for three reasons, all caused by the party-state. First, the thoroughly dysfunctional security market (as shown above) has systematically diminished the Chinese internal capital market. Second, the draconian state monopoly of the banking sector has left very little room for Chinese financial talent to work the magic of capitalism, other than by channeling money to serve the CCP's political agenda, such as by the creation and perpetuation of colossal bubbles throughout the country, which will be further analyzed below. Third, the lack of rule of law in the PRC has made contract enforcement and social trust—both critical to a functional capitalism—exorbitant or absent, and thus turned countless investments into sheer frauds and shocking scams. One of the many creative, widespread, and massive frauds and swindles, vaporizing hundreds of billions in investments, is P2P (peer to peer) lending, which was imported from the United States but "somehow generated frauds only in China."[73] Practically, the massive volume Chinese savings can only go into state-owned or controlled banks. The interest rate for deposits was set by the state at 0.15–0.3 percent in 2020 (1.5–3.9% for long-term CDs), comparable to that in the United States. Yet the likely underreported PRC inflation rate was more than 5.4 percent (20.6% for food) in 2020, as opposed to 0.3 percent in the United States that year.[74]

The CCP has launched numerous campaigns to "reform and modernize" the PRC's financial system over the past decades, but as a pair of Dutch scholars concluded, "The fundamental objective of reform (and digital innovation) of the financial system is not 'liberalism' per se, but to reinforce [. . . and] consolidate the CCP's overall legitimacy and ruling capacity."[75] Without exhaustively listing all the distortions and wastes caused by the PRC's dysfunctional financial system, a task obviously far beyond the scope of this book, we may amply illustrate some of the flaws of the party-state leading to wealth destruction through the "CCP-directed" multi-tiered structure of interest rates in China. The lending/investing of the massive Chinese savings is mostly controlled and directed by the government. Over 70 percent of China's fixed assets and 80 percent of government and bank loans are to the ultra-inefficient state-owned enterprises (SOEs), which contribute only 30 percent of

China's GDP and basically no new jobs since 1997.[76] The SOEs not only get the lion's share of Chinese capital and at the best rates (which can be near or even below zero), but also enjoy extremely lax conditions and monitoring. Defaults and write-offs are therefore commonplace. For other "policy allowed" private borrowing like mortgage loans, the rate in 2020 was 4.4–5 percent (versus 2.5–3.5% in the United States). With a twice as high return on equity, the non-SOE business borrowers are routinely charged a much higher rate, anecdotally at double digits, after going through endless hurdles and with widespread bribery as the enabling lubricant.

In the late 2010s, SOEs were only half as profitable as non-SOEs, with the real gap likely much larger, since SOEs tend to monopolize the most lucrative businesses like banking.[77] If a new private business becomes profitable and influential, the government often simply resorts to force, including confiscation and the death penalty, to acquire it for the state, sometimes under the cover of "joint ownership." In the words of a senior CCP official (also a financial tycoon), successful, sizeable, or "important" private enterprises in the PRC are to be "private-owned, state-managed, and party-controlled."[78] Over the past two decades, countless such cases have happened in businesses, including coal, oil, chemicals, IT, and online commerce and financing. Appointing and managing the leaders of the many dozens of large SOEs simply as minister or deputy-minister level senior "leading cadres," the CCP appears set to expand the SOE monopoly of the Chinese economy in the 2020s.[79]

For consumers and small businesses, the main sources of borrowing are the very limited credit cards issued by banks and the state-approved, quasi-credit (store) cards issued by giant online merchants like Alibaba (*zhifubao* or Alipay) and Jingdong (*baitiao*).[80] The purported interest rate for credit cards is set by the government at around 0.05 percent daily (or 18.25 percent annually). The real rates are complicated and much higher, often hidden as various incomprehensible "fees." Anecdotally, interest rates of double or even triple digits are fairly common among private parties, frequently with funds first cheaply obtained by SOEs from the state banks.[81] A vivid and illuminating example of how private lending works in the PRC is the so-called Nudity-Borrowing practice, where people with no assets borrow small amounts of money at short-term, loan-shark rates, with their fully identified nude and sexual pictures and videos as collateral. In one such case, exposed in 2016, hundreds of people, mostly college students, borrowed $40 to $1,000 at the rate of 50 percent or higher per week (roughly 2,700% annually), with over ten gigabytes of extremely compromising audio-video files held by one lender as collateral.[82] In a country that has the highest savings rate in the world, the dominant presence of the investment-destroying SOEs, the perverted stock market, the widespread financial fraud, the eerie private borrowing practices, and the unparalleled bubbles all evidence the deep and exorbitant dysfunctionality of the financial system under the CCP and the enormous and continued squandering of the Chinese wealth.

Extraction and Profligacy

The inherited and continuously refined Maoist state monopoly has enabled the incompetent micromanagement and outright mismanagement of the PRC fiscal system by the CCP rulers. The relative relaxation of that control over the past four decades has yet to fundamentally reduce the structural suboptimality of the PRC's economic development. Furthermore, the CCP-PRC is almost cursed to persist in its tradition of very high extraction of the Chinese economy, greatly concentrating and spending an increasing share of the fruits of the Chinese people's hard work for noneconomic and uneconomical purposes, resulting in chronical and massive irrationality and waste.

As a reincarnated Qin-Han polity struggling to thrive in the necessarily unfriendly world of the Westphalian System, the CCP-PRC has always had the incredible drive to exhaustively extract from the economy in order to safeguard and enrich itself. Accumulating and wielding evermore concentrated material power appears to be CCP's solution to its existential problems. Mao deliberately exaggerated the threat from internal and external enemies and endlessly wasted national resources to engage in a life-or-death war with both the world and the Chinese people. In addition to catastrophes like the Great Leap Forward to famine at home and the countless wasted ventures abroad, the CCP-PRC invested heavily in wasteful development of military-industrial complexes in remote and mountainous locations during the so-called Third Front Campaign in the 1960 and 1970s, a "militarization" of the PRC designed to fight a fantasized world war of revolution that was then profligately dismantled and abandoned in the 1980s.[83]

The post-Mao CCP-PRC state was compelled to scale back that kind of comical preparation for world war, which is still perceived as inevitable but somewhat less imminent. The same mandate or curse of high extraction and huge waste for the CCP's self-serving governance, however, continues and even intensifies, albeit with adjusted emphases. Beijing is as determined as ever to enrich itself and to ensure the authoritarian state has ever more power and influence in the world—its so-called aim of *fuguo qiangjun* (rich state and strong military).[84] Indeed, money and guns have always been the lifeblood for an autocracy like the CCP-PRC. This objective is literally identical to the Japanese call for *fukoku kyōhei* (rich state and strong military), made by Japanese nationalist and militarist leaders like Okubo Toshimichi and Ito Hirobumi, which inevitably led the Japanese Empire to march from the Meiji Restoration all the way to Pearl Harbor.[85]

Today's CCP-PRC lives with the same Maoist polity, worldviews, and fiscal objectives but has a much weaker claim to political legitimacy than Mao or the post-Meiji Japanese emperors, due to the evaporation of its top leaders' "charisma," the bankruptcy of its official ideology and dogma, and the persistent absence of even a Meiji (especially Taisho) style of limited constitutional democracy. Governing with guns and propaganda only, akin to sitting on a chair with just two legs, is perhaps still doable but certainly precarious, costly, and operose. The CCP needs other sources of legitimacy. An obvious choice is to rely on performative populism, material goodies, jobs, and income, to awe, pacify, and appease the people, especially the more politically potent urbanites. Buying political legitimacy, however, is inherently expensive and is a seemingly endless task since resources are always scarce and people's aggregate material desire is infinite. A centralized and bureaucratic way of purchasing political obedience results in even more short-term behavior and excessive Potemkin villages to show and regale the bosses, leading to inescapable inefficiency and a chronic dearth of innovation, both at a colossal scale.

In part because of its vast budget for military and police, and huge spending on misinformation and disinformation, the party-state is cursed to extract ever-more to spend and squander. Mega public projects for the sake of GDP growth numbers and vanity, wealth-destroying job programs, such as blindly subsidized export and the inefficient SOEs, and all sorts of bubbles everywhere are just some of the results of politicized short-term behaviors.[86] Reinforcing the CCP's state-capitalist or partocracy-capitalist, mercantilist, and militarist policies for regime security, the insatiable greed of the countless rent-seeking CCP cadres, and the boundless indulgence of the bloated PRC state apparatus further necessitate the strangling state monopoly and the extraordinarily high extraction of the Chinese economy. Playing a part in the boiling societal discontent reported in the previous chapter of this book, with the state getting two-thirds of the national income, "the Chinese people carry a heavy tax burden that is unfairly distributed," leading to riots and tax revolts.[87] Evidently, all this is still not enough to meet the enormous and ever-rising fiscal appetite of the party-state. Beijing has now sunk very deep in a sea of red ink, facilitated by its abuse of the imported technique of debt-financing in combination with the CCP-dictated monetary policy. By the mid-2010s, analysts had already noticed that "a credit-fueled expansion" under the ever-heavier mountains of public debts was casting a thick shadow on the sustainability of the Chinese economy.[88] The situation has become even worse since the COVID-19 pandemic in 2020–22.

PRC government revenue (excluding the significant income from the massive and monopolistic SOEs and land sales) was 35.3 percent of Chinese GDP in 2011, grew to 38.3 percent by 2019, and "has steadily risen to have a bigger share of the GDP in recent years." Excluding social security–equivalent funds, Beijing's take of the Chinese GDP by international criteria was 31.3 percent. Even by the more imprecise non-international criteria and standard, which hides government revenue, the state's share of the Chinese GDP has been growing rapidly every year for twenty years, faster than GDP growth, and has more than doubled from 1994 to 2013.[89] The PRC government at all levels collects nearly a thousand kinds of taxes and fees, including 47 percent on real estate purchases in Beijing. An average middle-class Chinese family typically paid about 51.6 percent of total income in numerous, mostly "hidden" taxes every year during the 2010s.[90] Some local governments even collect future years' taxes under creative names such as "preparing for fighting Japan soon."[91] By comparison, US government revenue (including social security funds) was only 15.4 percent of the GDP (and has been higher than 20% during only three years since the historically high point of 20.9% in 1945). If social security funds are excluded, then the US government's take of the GDP was only 9.9 percent in 2011.[92] Of course, the US Government is now increasingly funded by an ever-larger fiscal deficit. The PRC is moving in the same direction with significantly fewer checks and constraints, with its government debt ballooning up to 260 percent of Chinese GDP in 2016, and over 280 percent in 2021.[93] I will discuss the deficit and inflation in the PRC in more detail later in the chapter.

Of the estimated two-thirds of GDP extracted by the PRC state, the central government in Beijing receives a disproportionately large share. Senior CCP researchers concluded that the PRC central government routinely takes around 70 percent (68.2% in 2019) of the total tax revenue at "the world's highest" tax rate. This is in addition to its huge and opaque "auxiliary budgets" income (from the state monopoly of banking, sales of user's land rights, numerous fees, significant confiscations, and other "flexible sources") to almost double its total revenue in the 2010s to as much as 47 percent of China's GDP. The actual tax burden of Chinese firms (mostly the "hidden" indirect taxes and fees) was 67.3 percent in 2017, far above that in developed countries (37.6%), developing countries (38.5%), and the world's average (40.5%). As a result, extensive tax evasion is the norm in the PRC, since "if the [Chinese] enterprises all honestly paid their mandated taxes, then 80 percent of them would have gone broke."[94]

The PRC's state revenue has been growing much faster than the growth of China's economy, not to mention the much slower growth of per capita GDP, sometimes severalfold every year.[95] In the name of enriching the state and strengthening the military, Beijing has become an extractive and predatory state and is now one of the richest governments in the world. According to some Chinese economists, the PRC has become a polity of "strong state, rich central [government], and poor people" with three highly irrational and twisted forms of wealth transfer "that must be stopped": from the people to the government (through high and ever-rising taxation), from ordinary firms to the state monopolies, and from China to foreigners (through export subsidies and capital flight).[96] In 2018–21, in a move dubbed by some Chinese analysts as "all income goes to the Central,"[97] Beijing further centralized its fiscal extraction with the merger of all local taxes into the central government's taxation system and the full takeover of the previously locally run collection of the massive "fees for transfer of state land," or sale of user's land rights, which in 2019–20 accounted for 56 percent of total PRC government revenue, or over 94 percent of local governments' income.[98] While this massive recentralization may be rationalized as a desperate move to deflate the bubbles created by local governments, it reaffirms the authoritarian statist nature of the state–market and state–society relationships in the PRC.[99]

Irrational and suboptimal to the Chinese economy and the Chinese people, the extraordinary level of extraction by the PRC state has allowed it to pursue its ambitious policy goals of control at home and influence abroad, all while enriching the ruling elites. Just as in all governments, but especially those that are poorly monitored, the massive wealth of the nation is disproportionately accumulated by the leaders and ends up wasted and embezzled in many creative ways. The Chinese people, the wealth-creators, are poorly served. For example, the PRC government is reported to pay only about 17 percent of health-care costs in China, while the EU governments pay over 80 percent, the US government pays 46 percent, and the Thai government pays 56 percent. Worse, over 80 percent of this already inadequate government health-care funding for 1.4 billion people is reportedly earmarked for the 8.5 million senior officials only.[100] Beijing, as the politically all-important capital city, has been very inefficiently consuming great amounts of state funds, which may have some trickle-down benefits for the legal residents of the metropolis.[101] With its indulgent spending of huge amounts of public money to build up and beautify a few urban centers like Beijing, Shanghai, Guangzhou, and Shenzhen, the so-called first-tier cities (and, to a lesser extent, the second-tier "central cities"), the PRC has created and perpetuated countless bubbles, large and small, across the country. Essentially, to cite the analogy of the late economist Milton Freedman, the autocratic CCP manages the Chinese economy as if it were spending "somebody else's money" on itself, a situation where squandering is structurally inevitable.[102] Some senior PRC officials also seem to perceive the "serious quagmire" and depression that results. One PRC scholar openly asserted that a "guaranteed bubble" in the Chinese economy and its disastrous bust "is not a question of whether but when."[103]

To make the local and national GDP figures look palatable, many ghost towns and empty cities, including the now nearly deserted "China's future Manhattan," have popped up at the direction of the party leaders, funded with people's savings through the dysfunctional, state-controlled financial system with its poorly screened debt-financing.[104] Financially questionable, evidently wasteful, and even simply wealth-destroying mega projects include the excessive construction of high-speed railroads and highways,[105] the numerous airports ("new white elephants") of which "nearly 80 percent are losing money," the "insane" plans for rapid expansion of nuclear power plants, the hundreds of "tourism specialty towns" expensively built with artificial scenery and fake antiquity that quickly went broke and were demolished and thus "increased [local] GDP numbers twice,"[106] and scores of poorly deliberated dams on major rivers such as the Three Gorges Dam.[107] The ill-conceived and disaster-ridden political projects of diverting massive amounts of water from the Yangtze River valley to Beijing and northern China "are worse than the Three Gorges project" in terms of economic inefficiency and environmental consequences.[108] Examples of such wealth-destroying projects, large or small, to boost GDP figures seem countless: from a ¥335 million ($50 million) statuette standing only for a matter of months, to the mega plan for a 2,000-kilometer canal, with an "initial investment of ¥320 billion ($47.8 billion)," to connect the Yangtze and Pearl rivers.[109]

Outside of the PRC, the CCP spends the Chinese people's money without the people's input or consent on countless politicized projects—the enormously ambitious "One Belt One Road" program or Belt and Road Initiative (BRI), and talent-recruiting efforts as just two examples. With scantly studied and hastily assembled plans, Xi Jinping's signature BRI is reported to have now snowballed into one trillion US dollars of pledges and expenditures for mega projects that are utterly uneconomical if even technically feasible, including highways, pipelines, and high-speed rail lines going through the sparsely populated deserts of western China and central Asia and the harsh mountains of the troubled Tribal Region of Pakistan.[110] The "total mobilization of the country" (*juguo tizhi*) model imported from the Soviet Union for state investment without cost concerns for winning medals in international sporting events like the Olympic games, for example, has cost the Chinese people shocking amounts while impoverishing people's physical education and health and ruining the lives of countless young Chinese athletes, all for the glory of party-state's and bragging rights on the world stage.[111] With names like "Thousand Talents," Beijing actively "attracts" and recruits overseas Chinese and non-Chinese experts, especially the trophy kinds, with the hope they will bring real technological secrets, recognition, and glory to the CCP rulers. While the bubble of "recruiting talents" is inflated ever larger to benefit various vested interests and employ many substandard and even fake experts, "nearly 70 percent of Chinese intellectuals are already on the verge of death because of abusive working conditions" at home chiefly due to inadequate pay and medical care. In total, an official study concludes that "over 25 million human talents are wasted" in the PRC, at an annual opportunity cost of ¥900 billion or about 3 to 4 percent of China's GDP. An inexorable "age of involution" of "growth without development" is seen by Chinese observers in the 2020s as "the end of the Chinese model of growth."[112]

Quantitative Assessments of the Record

The economic calamity of the PRC under Mao during its first three decades of existence is readily apparent both qualitatively and quantitatively. Comparative quantitative analysis may further demonstrate the rather average, suboptimal performance of the PRC state over the past four decades, in order to contextualize the much-praised boom of GDP growth and the huge pile of foreign currency, among other remarkable accomplishments, commonly featured prominently in the PRC's economic record. Recent questions about the sustainability and reproductivity of a "China Model" of socioeconomic development are theoretically and practically meaningful, and they can be better addressed with facts.[113]

An interesting and revealing way to assess the PRC's record is to engage in a counterfactual analysis of relevant factors and alternative paths. Some have presented illuminating cases to show, qualitatively, the "forbidden fruit" of counterfactual analysis of human sociopolitical and military history in general, and of China in particular. Quantitative counterfactual analysis of economic history has also become more possible and useful with aid of fast computers, big data, and simulation through experimentation, as illustrated by the "impact valuations" of economic policies from the World Bank and Asian Development Bank.[114] Two such studies have separately concluded that the CCP-PRC appears to be an unnecessary detour, expensive distraction, and serious hindrance to Chinese economic development. One counterfactual study found that the Chinese GDP would have been 42 percent larger in 2010 had the Republic of China continued to rule the Chinese Mainland, and the Chinese people would have been spared the tens of millions of deaths and a long list of atrocities and sufferings. Another counterfactual estimate put the Chinese per capita GDP around $15,000 by 2011 if the CCP did not win the Chinese Civil War in 1949, on par with other East Asian nations, rather than just about $4,000 under the rule of the CCP.[115]

Quantitative works published on the PRC economy are abundant, though, as I mentioned in the introduction of this book, require very careful reading, verification, and authentication in their interpretation.[116] Here I will attempt to focus on an illustrative quantitative assessment of the PRC's socioeconomic record from three angles. First, I will show that Chinese economic growth is actually suboptimal and problematic with an international comparison of total factor productivity (TFP) and Incremental Capital-Output Ratios (ICOR). Second, I will explain how the rising irresponsibility of PRC fiscal and monetary policies has flooded the nation in a sea of red ink and inflated massive bubbles everywhere, with grave consequences right on the horizon for China and the world. Third, I will show that Chinese economic growth, in the aggregate, is inefficient and undesirable, with gauges like per-unit consumption of energy and a comparative profile of the largest and most profitable firms in the PRC.

Assessment One: GDP, the Factors, and Foreign Currency Reserve

Rivaling or even surpassing many other developmental states such as Japan and South Korea in the past, the PRC has officially reported a high rate of economic growth for many years—a breathtaking 9.8 percent annual rate on average from 1979 to 2012—to become the world's largest producer of 220 industrial products and the world's second largest economy as measured by GDP. The PRC has also accumulated the world's largest foreign exchange reserve for years, which peaked at almost $4 trillion in late 2014 and was still around $3.2 trillion in 2021.[117] The high growth has greatly contributed to the modernization of China's infrastructure, created millions of non-agriculture jobs, elevated hundreds of millions of people out of abject poverty, raised the standard of living visibly and absolutely (if not relatively when compared to other nations) for many if not most of the Chinese people, and enriched and strengthened the PRC state. The massive foreign currency reserve or surpluses of international economic transaction (trade surplus and inflows of foreign investment) in particular has given the Chinese greater access to the international market as consumers, students, tourists, emigrants, investors, and adventure seekers. The high growth rate and unprecedented piles of cash have generated significant new legitimacy and vast resources for the CCP at home and abroad. They give Beijing more diplomatic leverage and military power with higher stature on the international stage, constituting much of the discourse on the rise of China. The entire CCP-PRC officialdom has in fact developed an almost singular, decades-old GDP-centered system for evaluation and promotion. A "blind pursuit of GDP growth," which is one of the very few simple and quantifiable measurements in the opaque hierarchy of the party-state, has resulted in countless, creative, local schemes for expedient growth at the heavy expense of the environment and long-term sustainability, leading to widespread falsification of statistics.[118]

Economists, especially outside of the PRC, have raised serious questions about the data reliability, wisdom, and real impact of the continued high speed of GDP growth powered by massive, state-led investment and the unprecedented accumulation of foreign currencies. PRC GDP numbers supplied to IMF and World Bank are suspected of being inflated. Some studies have reduced the annual growth rate of the PRC's GDP by "at least 2 percentage points" or as much as half.[119] GDP itself quantitatively measures economic activities and transactions, the process of the economy, and not wealth creation and accumulation, which is after all the goal of the economy; it does not report or inform the prized efficiency and innovation. "GDP is a bad gauge of material well-being," "a deeply flawed gauge of prosperity," as it is a wildly inaccurate, grossly incomplete, and easily misleading measure of the economy. A leading Chinese economist called using GDP to gauge economic development "a mistake" since, in the 2010s, the PRC's second-place world ranking in GDP was only "at the same position as China's GDP in 1890."[120] To be sure, such a model of GDP growth through massive state investment, a supercharged version of Keynesian economics, creates jobs and uplifts many out of unemployment and poverty. But its overall effect and efficiency are dubious and often counterproductive. In fact, it is entirely possible for a large, active economy to burn or destroy rather than to create and retain wealth. While economic activities may have been growing quickly as measured by GDP, real wealth-building in the PRC has actually been slow and much less impressive, as a time-series study by Credit Suisse shows.[121] Moreover, since the mid-2010s, PRC GDP growth has been decelerating with further declining marginal gains, "coming down to earth" with the uncertainty of either a looming hard crash or a more desirable soft landing.[122] Slow or even stuck growth across the board, more than halved from that of a decade ago, seems to be brewing a "slow meltdown" to create "some of the biggest economic challenges" the CCP has faced in four decades. Some even predict the coming end of the entire Chinese economic rise in the 2020s.[123]

The single largest force driving the highspeed GDP growth in the PRC has been the state's extraordinarily large fixed-asset investment, powerfully impelled by the CCP's peculiar political needs, as outlined earlier. This is based on the state monopoly of the financial system, which appropriates the Chinese savings. The PRC savings rate has constantly been among the world's highest in the twenty-first century, following only Singapore and East Timor, putting away about half of the nation's total income, a ratio nearly ten times higher than in the United States or six times higher than in the Euro Zone.[124] It is twice as high as the peak savings rates reached in Japan and South Korea, in 1973 (23.1%) and 1988 (19%), respectively.[125] In 2019, the Chinese savings rate was still 44.9 percent.[126] The causes of the unusually high PRC savings are complex, including the lack of a social safety net via social security and pension programs; inadequate provision of health care, education, and other public services; high extraction by the state; peculiarly unsound demography shaped by birth-control policies; and the general sense of insecurity and uncertainty in the population.[127] In 2016, for example, PRC doctors openly argued that the decade-long health-care reform had "failed disastrously."[128] There has also been a massive inflow of foreign capital, mostly from Hong Kong, that laundered and disguised significant PRC capital as foreign investment back to the PRC.[129] As a result, fixed assets or capital investment accounted for 47 to 48 percent of China's GDP in 2009, ten points more than in Japan at its peak of growth, while the typical such ratio is around 20 percent in developed economies; it then climbed further to 49 percent in 2013 and was still at 43 percent in 2020, generating up to 72 percent of the annual GDP growth.[130]

This ratio, far too high even by the standard of a developing country in its stage of rapid growth, creates enormous dislocation and inefficiencies such as bad loans, excessive investments with low or no return, and wasteful bubbles. Judging by the Solow Residual, a measure of Total Factor Productivity (TFP), the PRC economy has had limited, declining, or even negative gains of TFP over the past two decades, signaling a systemic and massive inefficiency and misallocation with vast investment flowing to speculative and politicized projects. This is so because "genuine political or institutional reform has never been truly on the reform agenda."[131] The PRC officially acknowledged the very low ("below 6%") and declining profit margin of its crucial manufacturing industries, which produce 40 percent of GDP and 95 percent of exports.[132] As a comparison, the profit margin of the manufacturing industry was 13 to 19 percent in India and over 16 percent in the United States.[133] The poorly reasoned, opaquely managed, and excessive investment-driven growth may have already pushed the marginal return of capital to below the depreciation rate, literally destroying capital while starving long-term consumption.[134] Using the method of Incremental Capital-Output Ratio (ICOR), the GDP growth in the PRC is seen as increasingly inefficient when compared to other Asian economies during their periods of rapid growth, on par with or worse than that in India (see table 2.2). An

Table 2.2. Incremental Capital-Output Ratios in Asia
(Selected Countries)

Country		Investment (as % of GDP)	GDP growth (% annually)	ICOR
China	1991–2011	40.4	10.4	3.9
	(1991–1995)	39.6	11.6	3.4
	(1996–1999)	37.6	8.4	4.5
	(2001–2003)	40.5	8.0	5.06
	(2009–2011)	48.2	9.6	5.02
	2012	49.0	7.7	6.4
	2013	49.0	7.7	6.4 (7.1)*
Japan	1961–1970	32.6	10.2	3.2
Korea	1981–1990	29.6	9.2	3.2
Taiwan	1990–2012	21.9	8.0	2.7
India	1990–2012	28.8	6.6 (1995–2014)	4.2
	2013	30	5.0	6.0

Note: High ICOR figure indicates low productivity of investment: more units of capital to produce one unit of GDP.

*The New York–based CEIC Data Group estimate (ceicdata.com), 2014.

Sources: RIETI 2004; Kwan of Nomura's Institute of Capital Markets Research 2013. India figures calculated based on Krishnan 2013 and World Bank GDP growth and gross capital formation databases 2014.

OECD study on ICOR in Asia concluded that, during 1995–2011, China's ICOR was significantly worse than that in Thailand, Indonesia, and Malaysia.[135] The bad investments and wasted capital in the PRC are in the trillions; two Chinese state researchers found that a whopping $6.9 trillion in capital (37% of total investment) had "zero efficiency" and was wasted in 2009–13 alone.[136] The growing Chinese investment overseas seems equally inefficient, with huge losses caused by massive graft, theft, and ineptitude.[137]

The reliance on massive investment through the state-monopolized financial system for the politically driven high growth rate easily depletes China's world-class high savings with a low and declining ICOR. Once again, the capital-devouring SOEs are a key problem. Since the early 1990s, return on assets of private enterprises has been 13.2 percent versus

4.9 percent of the SOEs.[138] The massive wholly state-owned high-speed rail (HSR), for example, has been viewed as a shining project that gives affluent passengers comfort and convenience in rapid transportation, and the CCP good GDP numbers and bragging rights. But critics are right to question whether the shorter journey time between urban centers has really helped boost productivity and at what cost. The very expensive yet lightly used HSR lines (passenger trains only) accounted for an excessive one-fourth of the total PRC rail tracks (139,000 km) in 2019, with an estimated $7 to $8 trillion in debt. The total annual profit of the HSR does not cover the annual interest payment on its massive debt. Other than two (Beijing-Shanghai/Hangzhou and Beijing-Guangzhou/Shenzhen), the revenues of most of the more than thirty HSR lines cannot even cover their daily operational costs, much less the payment on the investment, which is refinanced with more debt and state appropriations. Yet, the clearly cost-ineffective HSR has expanded "full steam ahead" with new investment of around $120 billion every year during 2014–20.[139] It is a giant debt-crisis timebomb and already rapidly burning through capital. Other than the political rationales of high GDP and employment numbers, and more claims to the ranking of "number one in the world," which are indeed critically useful for the CCP regime, a leading reason behind the exorbitant, blind expansion of the HSR is probably the irresistible lure of excellent opportunities for officials and their buddies to massively enrich themselves through mega projects related to HSR construction. Indeed, the HSR projects have produced some of the largest cases of corruption and price-gouging ever revealed in PRC history, led by the cases of Railway Minister Liu Zhijun, who was sentenced to death with reprieve in 2013, and his successor Sheng Guangzhu, who was investigated in 2022, years after his retirement.[140]

Related to the inefficient and even wealth-destroying manner of GDP growth, the astronomical foreign exchange reserve in China, amounting to around $3 trillion for many years previous to 2023, appears to be a success story and does give the CCP a great war chest for ventures abroad. But it in fact reflects the deep flaws of runaway mercantilist, export-led growth and the state monopoly of the financial system—causes and symbols of excessive inefficiencies and dislocations, deprivation of human and labor rights, depressed standard of living, damaged environment, consequential global economic imbalances, and the stubborn low-value addition in the Chinese economy. Much of the PRC's massive foreign exchange reserve has become risky, unhedged, "hot" money for speculation. It is perhaps rational, even optimal for the CCP, however, to repress domestic consumption and withhold social welfare in order to finance ever-more export with more low-paying jobs. This way, Beijing may control the sociopolitical danger of mass unemployment and the risk of enriching people "unnecessarily" (and thus empowering them politically), while maximizing its spending power abroad with its monopoly over an increasing pile of hard currencies.[141] In its long tradition of control of foreign exchange, which concentrates all foreign currencies of the country in the hands of the party-state, Beijing reaffirmed in 2019 that any currency trade other than with the government was a crime.[142]

In the global production chain of the trendy iPhone, for example, the per-unit total cost can be $216 to $263, with a retail price of $649 to $849 (sold in China for up to $1,600) in the late 2010s. The Taiwanese firms Foxconn and Pegatron, which employ Chinese workers in the PRC to assemble the product for the California-based Apple, capture only $4 to $5.85 per unit.[143] Yet, craving ever more "real money," namely, hard currencies, and low-skilled jobs, the PRC state expensively subsidizes exports with draconian suppression of labor rights and environmental demands and, more directly, cash payments to exporters. The rebate of the value-added tax (commonly 16–25% of the total price), can be much higher in practice and "has been the only source of our profit" or "the only reason we still keep exporting" to just about all the Chinese exporters I interviewed from 2003 to 2021, thus making it much more important than currency manipulation. Unsurprisingly, export subsidy is also a major loophole for fraud and corruption.[144] State-subsidized exports have created increased international frictions: of the thirty-eight anti-dumping investigations by the European Union in 2016, twenty-eight involved China. Finally, in 2018, the most profitable market for PRC exports, the United States, took matters into its own hands and ditched the WTO to launch an epic trade war of tariffs with the PRC.[145]

The CCP's economic strategy has chiefly enriched the party-state as it now has massive purchasing power abroad through its monopoly of the financial sector and the foreign exchange reserve, but at a very high aggregated cost to the Chinese people.[146] The boom of labor-intensive processing industries made the PRC the "world's dumpsite" through the massive import of foreign refuse as raw material for years.[147] Moreover, nearly 69 percent of the foreign currency reserve has already been sunk into various PRC investments or capital-flight abroad. The disposable or "useable" PRC reserve (or "cash flow") therefore fell to around $1 trillion in 2020, the lowest in ten years (all in US treasury bonds, which was $60 billion in 2000).[148] Meanwhile, PRC analysts ominously reported "at least $1 trillion in economic dark matters" or hidden obligations of capital outflow that could wipe out the entire "useable" reserve and usher in a systemic shock. The big raises of interest rate by the US Federal Reserve (and the European Central Bank and other G7 countries) in 2022, colliding with Beijing's lax money supply to stimulate its sluggish economy, have led to significant decline of both the value of the RMB and the Chinese foreign currency reserve, despite the draconian PRC control of capital outflow. Overall, as a senior PRC economist concluded in May 2022, huge PRC holding of foreign currency and overseas assets have had "negative returns" for the past twenty years.[149]

The PRC's pile of foreign currency is even less a sign of economic success when considering the massive amount of imports needed to earn foreign currencies to sustain such an economy. In 2019, the PRC spent $2.1 trillion to import basic products and necessities, like microchips ($306 billion), oil and gas ($291 billion), electronics ($154 billion), iron ore ($101 billion), copper ($57 billion), and soy beans ($43 billion). At the same time, China's foreign debt grew massively from $146 billion in 2000 to $737 billion in 2012 (33% of foreign currency earnings that year) and $2.1 trillion in 2019 (77% of foreign currency earnings that year).[150] In the 2020s, while the PRC's foreign currency reserve remained largely stable, its foreign debt and capital outflow both kept growing (see table 2.3). To finance import, serve foreign obligations, and manage the "economic dark matter," China must earn, at minimum, more than $2.1 trillion in hard currency every year, or it must sell its US T-bills (which would be easy and the PRC did significantly in 2022) or overseas assets (which would be difficult and likely at a great loss, especially as some were financed with foreign borrowings). Other alternatives would be to cut critical imports and undermine hard currency-earning exports, reduce basic supplies at home to exacerbate the already serious inflation, negate spending promises like the BRI abroad, default on foreign debts and other obligations, or start currency devaluation—or some combination of all of these. The fragility of the Chinese economy, which is critically dependent on export chiefly to the United States, and subject to the CCP's politicized spending spree abroad, is obvious. Forced by the mounting external pressure of trade wars and reallocation of global supply chains, Beijing launched an "emphasis on internal economic circulation," or self-reliance to reduce and replace "global circulation" or foreign trade,

Table 2.3. Foreign Exchange Reserve, Assets, and Debt (in billions of US dollars)

Foreign Exchange Reserve		Foreign Debt	Investment Abroad	US T-bills
2004	619	263	53	223**
2005	826	297	65	310**
2006	1,081	339	91	397**
2007	1,547	389	116	477**
2008	1,966	390	186	727*
2009	2,453	429	246	895*
2010	2,914	549	317	1,160*
2011	3,256	695	425	1,152*
2012	3,388	737	532	1,220*
2013	3,880	863	661	1,270*
2014	3,899	1,780	881	1,244*
2015	3,406	1,383	1,096	1,246*
2016	3,098	1,416	1,357	1,058**
2017	3,236	1,758	1,809	1,185*
2018	3,168	1,983	1,982	1,124*
2019	3,263	2,057	2,095	1,070**
2020	3,216	2,401	2,199	1,072**
2021 (June)	3,214	2,527	2,300	1,078**

Note: End-of-year figures.

*China was the largest foreign holder of US Treasury Securities.

**China was the second largest (behind Japan) foreign holder of US Treasury Securities.

Source: PRC State Administration of Foreign Exchange (safe.gov.cn), 2021; US Department of the Treasury/Federal Reserve Board (ticdata.treasury.gov), 2021.

during the COVID-19 pandemic in 2020–22.[151] However, the apparent "inadequacy of domestic consumption" together with chronic structural problems are poised to significantly hamper that strategy of growth. As some PRC analysts put it, losing "the globalization dividend," an economy relying on internal circulation "of high investment and low efficiency" does not bode well.[152]

ASSESSMENT TWO: FISCAL AND MONETARY POLICIES

As twin policies, the PRC fiscal policy and monetary policy are both characterized by chronic irrationality and irresponsibility (though they are perhaps rational and optimal for the rulers). They are similarly unmonitored and unconstrained, ruler-centered with short-term remedies, and often suboptimal and problematic. Still insatiable in its extraordinarily high extraction of the Chinese economy, as discussed earlier, the post-Mao CCP has increasingly overlearned from politicians in places like Washington and Tokyo to borrow and spend, risking drowning the country in a sea of red ink. With the burning political desire to outsmart the so-called "middle-income trap" with crude monetary stimulation that flattens business cycles and ensures regime stability, plus its great spending spree on *weiwen* (internal security), the military and projects abroad, the CCP has, since 2008, adopted a series of outsized, lax, poorly designed and executed, and often irresponsible fiscal and monetary policies. It is *déjà vu* of the run-up to the ruinous inflation that occurred at least three times before, in the early 1950s, the early 1960s, and the late 1980s to early 1990s.[153] In the twenty-first century, the PRC central government has run a budget deficit every year, with the official deficit/income ratio skyrocketing from 7.8 percent in 2010 and 15.5 percent in 2015 to 25 percent in 2019 and then exploding to 43 percent in 2021.[154]

The intoxicatingly easy and quick fixes of deficit-spending and printing paper money, starting with over ¥4 trillion in 2008, have created a major "debt addiction" that is hard to break.[155] The PRC central government's direct debt to GDP ratio, as a result, shot up from 33 percent in 2010 to over 60 percent in 2020, and is projected to reach over 78 percent in another four years, according to foreign analysts. A more opaque and larger debt has been accumulated over the years by local governments. The CCP officials in the regions are unbounded by the kind of budget-balancing laws restraining US local governments, yet they are politically pressured and lured to pad their local GDP numbers with borrowed funds in many creative ways. Accordingly, the so-called "off-the-book" hidden local government debt alone was estimated to be at least $6 trillion in 2018.[156] Officially, as expected, Beijing only reported a much lower, approximately halved, local government debt (excluding the "hidden" local investment bonds) of $3.26 trillion in 2020 and $4.56 trillion in 2021.[157] The increasingly unbalanced local-central fiscal relationship in recent years, unsurprising given the persistent and aggravated regional disparity in economic development and state investment, indicates the dreadful shape of fiscal health at both levels of the PRC government. In the late 2010s, the fifty US states had to all balance their own budgets, with 22 percent (11) of them getting federal funds meaningfully more than their paid federal taxes.[158] In the PRC, official data indicated that 74 percent (23) of the thirty-one provincial units needed budgetary bailouts by the central government, which subsequently had to incur a large deficit—its fiscal payment to provincial governments exceeded the taxes all provinces paid in by more than 10 percent in 2020. That got even worse in 2021, when 84 percent (26) of the thirty-one provincial units had their debt–revenue ratio exceeding "the warning threshold" of 100 percent, with eleven of them over 200 percent and four of them above 300 percent (the highest was 506% in Qinghai); if the hidden debt of local investment bonds were included, then only two were below the threshold (Shanghai at 85% and Guangdong at 90%). By official data, the PRC pension system has also increasingly racked up huge deficits for nearly a decade, from 20 percent in 2013 to 28 percent in 2020, when the pension plans in twenty-five of the thirty-one provincial units required central government fiscal appropriations to stay solvent.[159]

In 2017, the PRC household debt to income ratio reached 100 percent and surpassed that of the United States; it continued to climb quickly to 128 percent by 2020, while the American ratio declined to below 100 percent.[160] According to *The Economist*, the whole PRC nation is deeply in debt, with a total debt to GDP ratio of 260 percent by 2016 (up from 150% in 2008), much higher than that of any other economy; this makes China the "People's Republic of Debt," with a staggering burst looming, demanding great reforms that are not on the horizon.[161] Relief is hard to find. To partially remedy the problem, local governments were allowed to issue their own bonds in May 2014 so as to "securitize" some state bank loans. However, Standard & Poor's quickly rated half of the provincial bonds as junk and only a quarter are considered investment grade. In just five months during the COVID-19 pandemic in 2020, "authorized" local government debt grew by up to ¥1 to ¥1.6 trillion ($140–224 billion or 30% of the total "on-the-book" debt). Almost as if in a feeding frenzy, one typical province, Anhui, reportedly borrowed $64 billion in just two weeks in April 2020 to add to its 2,583 stimulus projects costing $120 billion, with $762 billion more loans for 3,300 new projects lined up for approval. Others, like Fujian Province, have dived in deeper with even more red ink.[162]

Like so many other important statistics in the PRC, officially reported debt is murky and skewed due to secrecy rules and cooked books. Official PRC numbers show that the alarming "macro" (mainly government) debt-to-GDP ratio climbed to 245 percent in 2019 and to 280 percent in 2021 (or 273 percent by another official estimate in 2022), far higher than that in the United States (109% and 119%), with "annual interest payment twice the annual nominal increase of GDP." Non-PRC experts estimate the actual PRC debt-to-GDP ratio even higher, at 300 percent in 2019 and 317 percent in 2020.[163] This means the PRC has a sea of red ink about twice the size of that in the notoriously indebted United States, surpassing Japan, the second highest in the world, which had a peak debt-to-GDP ratio of 239 percent in 2020 (down to 221% in 2021).[164] To frame this picture, in the 2010s and 2020s, the IMF and World Bank have reported a range of government debt-to-GDP ratio between 35 and 70 percent for "low income countries," an average of that ratio at 55 to 110 percent for "advanced economies," and a preferred ceiling of that ratio at 60 percent for "emerging market" economies.[165]

Even for a mighty police state, taxes and loans can still be somewhat strenuous and inconvenient ways to extract and spend. When they are not enough, because Beijing lacks the credit rating and the functional market mechanism to effectively finance its deficit with domestic and international capital, the easiest way out is to simply print more paper money. Over the seven decades of its existence, the PRC has indeed massively overprinted its currency (the RMB, the people's money) quite a few times for pressing political necessities or expedient financial objectives. Each of those floods of money ended with serious inflation and painful crises of recession and depression, even political turmoil like the Tiananmen Uprising in 1989, which almost toppled the party-state.

In the twenty-first century, the PRC has resorted to printing unprecedented and unparalleled amounts of paper money. Official data show that Beijing printed money at a growth rate of 450 percent in 2000–10 (14.7 percent annually), much faster than the GDP growth rate, which averaged 9 percent. The RMB in circulation (M2 stock) reached ¥70 trillion ($10.62 trillion) in 2010, 1.74 times larger than the Chinese GDP and 18 percent more than the US Dollar M2 stock of $8.99 trillion (60% of the American GDP that year).[166] Four years later, M2 stock in the PRC ballooned to ¥120 trillion (about $19.7 trillion), or 1.89 times the Chinese GDP.[167] As a comparison, the total USD M2 stock in 2014 was $11.5 trillion, or about 68 percent of the

American GDP, over 71 percent smaller than the RMB. In 2020, the circulation of RMB exploded further to ¥209.4 trillion ($29.5 trillion), over 2.11 times larger than the size of the Chinese GDP, and $14.1 trillion (92%) larger than the total USD in circulation, which was $15.4 trillion or 72 percent of the American GDP (see table 2.4). By July 2021, that figure shot up further to ¥225.6 trillion ($33.76 trillion).[168] Apparently aiming to further ease the printing of RMB, among other purposes like increasing control over people's financial transactions, the PRC Central Bank launched a digital RMB of DCEP (Digital Currency Electronic Payment) in 2020.[169] Judging by the M2–GDP ratios in the two economies, a casual calculation circulated in Chinese cyberspace has gone so far as to worry that the "real RMB–USD exchange rate" might end up 19.97 to 1 instead of around 7 to 1.[170] The expansion of money printing remains relentless: in early 2022, the M2 stock of RMB increased 9.8 percent and the circulation of M0 (cash) exploded 18.5 percent, growing two to four times faster than the Chinese GDP. Months later, while being squeezed by the Western sanctions against Russia and the American interest rate hike, Beijing resorted to yet more printing of money—trillions of RMB—instead of loosening its control of the Chinese

Table 2.4. Two Economies, Two Currencies

Currencies		2010	2014	2020
PRC M2 (trillions)		¥70 ($10.62)	¥120 ($19.7)	¥209.4 ($29.5)
	As % of GDP	174	189	211.3
	% of circulating abroad	Almost none	Negligible	Miniscule
US M2 (trillions)		$8.99	$11.5	$15.4
	As % of GDP	60	68	72
	% of circulating abroad	40–70	40–70	40–70

Sources: US Federal Reserve, US Department of Commerce, People's Bank, State Statistical Bureau, 2012–2020.

capital market and/or letting its currency float, in an act some Chinese analysts described as simply "gambling with the fortune of the country."[171]

As a result, the purchasing power of people's money in the PRC fell like a rock. In 2021, an unofficial Chinese study on what one yuan of the RMB could buy over the past four decades, based on four methods, illustrated the wild trend of inflation, especially the out-of-control printing of paper currency in the PRC (summarized in table 2.5). It is illuminating to compare and contrast with that of one US dollar during the same time.

The astronomical amount of RMB printed is an astonishing result of irresponsible fiscal and monetary policies, which have become ever wilder. Additionally, the deeply entrenched overpromotion of export to satisfy Beijing's craving for foreign currency or "real money," which allows it to spend abroad, mightily drives the runaway PRC mint. Ever more RMB is needed to collect and hoard foreign currencies, particularly the US dollar, from the Chinese exporters. The problem of over-minting is gravely compounded by the fact that the RMB remains a soft currency, circulating basically only in the PRC despite Beijing's recent expensive push to "internationalize" it. The pressure of inflation thus becomes

Table 2.5. Purchasing Power of People's Money

Purchasing Power of ¥1	1978	1988	1998	2008	2013	2019
Weighed with GDP growth	1	0.39	0.16	0.07	0.04	0.03
Loss of value	—	–61%	–84%	–93%	–96%	–97%
By M2 supply	1	0.15	0.01	0.002	0.001	0.0007
Loss of value	—	–421%	–76%	–81%	–82%	–84%
By actual inflation rate	1	0.30	0.068	0.036	0.024	0.0198
Loss of value	—	–70%	–93%	–96%	–97.6%	–98.02%
Purchasing Power of $1*	1	0.55	0.40	0.30	0.28	0.26
Loss of value	—	–45%	–60%	–70%	–72%	–74%

*By actual inflation rate in the US. (*Source:* Chun Se 2020; Usinflationcalculator.com, February 8, 2022).

unbearably severe on the Chinese economy as well as the few small economies such as Cambodia and Zimbabwe that have been paid by Beijing to use the RMB to some extent.[172] By contrast, the US dollar has been widely accepted for many decades by nearly every country as a de facto world currency. An estimated 40 to 70 percent of US currency in circulation is held and permanently used outside of the issuing country as the main medium of exchange and a major storage of value. The increased supply of the US dollar thus generates only minimal pressure of inflation in the American economy, which is cushioned by the much larger world economy.[173]

With essentially no meaningful oversight, legal constraints, public scrutiny, or expert debate, the CCP-PRC party-state taxes, borrows, mints, and spends first and foremost to satisfy and please the rulers, with a gross suboptimality to the Chinese economy and the Chinese people. With such a combination of skewed fiscal policy, monetary policy, and industrial/export policy, the PRC keeps blowing bubbles of many kinds everywhere, with grave consequences for both the Chinese economy and the world economy. In 2014, Beijing "clandestinely" injected about ¥1 trillion through a new "midterm lending facility" to stimulate growth.[174] It then injected another ¥7 trillion in 2015 to "maintain economic growth," pushing the fixed investment–GDP ratio beyond the unprecedented height of 78.9 percent (it had been 26.4 percent in 2000, and 47.2 percent in 2008). In the standard CCP way, those stimulation funds basically all ended up going to the inefficient SOEs, the often wealth-destroying mega projects, the speculative boom of the real estate sector, countless financial speculations and schemes, and the offshore accounts of many cadres and their cronies. Chinese economists themselves warned in plain language years ago: "Only one thing is certain: people's money is becoming increasingly unsafe."[175]

In 2020, to counter the economic downturn caused by the SARS-COV-2 virus, the PRC launched yet more fiscal stimuli through deficit spending on literally thousands of mushrooming projects to be financed by printing more money at the central and local levels, making the already decade-old mega bubble even larger. PRC Premier Li Keqiang gave a rough figure of ¥2 trillion in new deficit spending and over ¥4 trillion in payroll tax relief for "new investment projects and preserving jobs." This round of stimulation may have been somewhat justified by the global pandemic, but the way it was carried out, with the traditional and total absence of scrutiny and debate, was typically suboptimal and problematic.[176] Nearly every other country launched similar efforts, but many, likely most, governments did it differently, with significant payments directly to the people, especially the poor. The US government, for example, directly dispersed funds to businesses and the people, with up to $5,400 for an average family of four in two direct payments in 2020, greatly enhanced unemployment benefits, and renters' relief. The direct payment by the Indian government was expectedly small, with $17 per person plus free grain and cooking gas for the needy in mid-2020.[177] Yet, very much as expected, the CCP acts again both as a fool, by repeating the same bubble-making mistake in trying to print money to get out the trouble, and as a miser, refusing to disperse funds directly to the people.[178] Most of the Chinese stimulus and relief funds, as usual, went to SOEs and construction projects. In over 120 days of quarantine, some PRC citizens received direct payments of a paltry ¥13 ($1.80) per person from the government, mostly as discount coupons for which they had to bid and grab at online stores.[179] This is perhaps a simple malevolence of the CCP Optimality and the China Suboptimality, very much in the tradition of the dark art of Legalism employed in the past centuries. The goal is to impoverish, weaken, and entangle the people through their submission to and dependence on the state, rather than giving out any "free" money to enrich and empower them. It is also a typical golden opportunity for many cadres in position of power and their cronies to make a killing through shady contracts, bribes, substandard work, and embezzlement associated with these dubious and unmonitored projects—all at the risk of exacerbated inflation as a form of inefficient and regressive taxation.

With all that paper money flooding out, the PRC has created and maintained epic bubbles everywhere, especially in real estate, that easily dwarf the hugely disastrous Japanese real estate bubble of the 1980s.[180] To observers, tolerance of a world-class real estate bubble is extremely foolish and dangerous in appearance. But it is entirely normal and expected in the PRC, as the rulers, instead of Chinese people or the market, dictate the flow of capital and other resources according to their wishes. Like the development of infrastructure such as the highspeed rail networks, the investment in housing projects is sensible and efficient in a developing country that chronically lacks adequate housing. Housing is a highly income-elastic and price-elastic product. Home construction and maintenance powerfully pulls industries like steel, concrete, energy, transportation, and domestic services, which all create plentiful low-tech and low-skilled jobs. For the justified goals of GDP growth and employment, real estate could be a method for sustainable growth. But, as in just about every area of the PRC political economy, particularly infrastructure development, the real estate sector is tightly controlled by the CCP autocracy with a disregard for and a distortion of the market mechanisms.[181] The PRC model of economic growth in general and the dysfunctional financial system in particular have turned real estate development into a deranged excess, chiefly serving the political needs of the CCP and the insatiable greed of the cadres and their cronies who monopolize the land and capital. The rapid boom of the real estate industry has quantitatively and qualitatively pleased many of the politically potent urban residents, as it has allowed for (limited) ownership of housing, employment of millions of low-skilled laborers, and a boost to GDP numbers. It has also raised hefty funds for local governments through auctions of the user's right (for 25 to 70 years) to the "people's" land, conveniently channeled public funds to the pockets of cadres and their developer buddies, and parked excess printed money in the sector so as to reduce inflationary pressure. Since the early 2010s, at the latest, the real estate market has become the only viable instrument of investment for the Chinese people under the dual jaws of inflation and capital control, accounting for 74.7 percent of Chinese family wealth (as compared to about 25 percent in the US), and providing 65 to 90 percent of the local government revenue. In the 2020s, of the thirty-seven large and medium cities in the PRC, only three had less than 50 percent of their local revenue from land sales (Beijing, Shanghai, and Shenzhen at 20 percent, 30 percent, and 40 percent, respectively); and thirteen of the cities relied on land sales for more than 100 percent of their local revenue.[182]

The construction, maintenance, and allocation of real estate, mostly apartment units, have all quickly become a giant bubble in the twenty-first century, showing clear suboptimality and irrationality. Official data shows that the housing market was saturated with 1.3 housing units per family by 2015, and that PRC residence-ownership was at 96 percent by 2020.[183] However, many of these units have been vacant for years, while many Chinese still have no affordable access to adequate housing. Prices have skyrocketed, chiefly driven by the speculation that resulted from greedy collusion between officials and developers. The allocation and ownership of housing units have been extremely uneven and unequal, as many of the subsidized, "free," and more desirable units are taken by the connected as perks and bribes, and a means to store value. Thus, the already very excessive real estate construction must continue to grow at a high speed for the ostensible purpose of housing people, and more concretely for tax revenue, GDP growth, and jobs numbers. The overall housing vacancy rate in urban China was 13 percent in 2013, climbing to 22.4 percent just over a year later, and remaining above 20 percent, in stark contrast to that of the United States (1.9–2.5%), the EU (9.5%), and Japan (13%).[184] The historically highest housing vacancy rate in the United States was only 2.9 percent, in 2008.[185] In Chinese cities, the unsold housing units at least doubled in 2012–14, putting the real estate market "way over the international warning line." The "greatest bubble by far" appears in major cities like Shanghai, where real estate prices jumped 525 percent in the 2010s. Beijing's housing vacancy rate was an incredible 28.9 percent in the late 2010s, 54.9 percent in the central district of Chaoyang, with 33 percent of new housing units in the mega city remaining empty.[186] Notwithstanding new housing construction that still outpaces housing demands, it would take forty-two years of population and economic growth to absorb the existing empty units in Beijing.[187] Even the habitually bullish Goldman Sachs analysts have long ranked PRC real estate bonds "the most risky in Asia."[188] The vacancy rate of commercial real estate in China surpassed its "historical peak in 2019" to reach 35 percent (30% for office space), "the worst in over a decade" for the country and also for the "first tier cities." Even with a 10 percent decrease in rental price, 19 percent of office space was reportedly vacant in Beijing; the rate was 40 percent in many parts of Shanghai and 28 percent in Shenzhen. In 2021, the office space vacancy rate in all of the thirty-eight major cities in the PRC was higher than 11 percent—over 30 percent in nineteen cities, and over one-third in twelve of them, despite the depressed and reduced rental prices, while the same rate was only 2 percent in Taipei and 9 percent in Hong Kong.[189]

The wild real estate bubble suggests incredible inflation and an inefficient distortion of the economy. In the mid-2010s, the real estate market in Beijing Metropolis alone equaled 120 percent of the entire US GDP, and the book value of real estate assets in the PRC already exceeded 300 percent of the Chinese GDP, on par with the historic bubble in 1989 when the Japanese real estate market peaked at 375 percent of its GDP and Tokyo's real estate value exceeded the US GDP before it quickly busted, resulting in a deep and long national recession for the next quarter-century.[190] The oversized Chinese real estate bubble has become ever larger as vast amounts of printed money keeps flowing in for quick profits. Of the fifty cities (from 22 countries) with the steepest rise in housing prices, twenty-seven are in China and none are in the United States.[191] By 2019, the total value of real estate in the PRC was estimated to be $65 trillion, or 480 percent of its GDP, or 109 percent of the combined real estate markets in the United States, the EU, and Japan. By contrast, the Chinese stock market was valued at only 10 percent of its real estate market, or 9 percent of the combined American, EU, and Japanese stock markets.[192] The value of real estate is about the same as stocks in the United States and EU (slightly higher in Japan), suggesting a far more balanced and efficient capital allocation.

The CCP-PRC party-state is now in fact caught between two rocks and a hard place: a hugely wasteful bubble ruins the Chinese economy but is "too big to burst," an insatiable appetite for more GDP growth and quick revenue by the central and local governments and connected interests such as developers and brokers, and a constant flood of newly printed RMB that needs a place to go. In the PRC, which is still a developing country, housing is now priced increasingly higher than in most developed countries, out of the reach of the common people, especially the young. As part of China's world-class socioeconomic inequality, real estate ownership is extremely unequal. In PRC cities in 2021, 2 percent of the families each owned three or more apartments, while over 30 percent of families had none, with 12 percent of households owning over 40 percent of all housing units. Many observers anticipate a national financial calamity as an inevitable outcome of the real estate bubble: "What looked like glittering success was in fact the iridescent patina on a rapidly expanding bubble [. . . that] would burst, and probably sooner rather than later." Many PRC experts seem only to disagree on the way in which this bubble, which per high estimates was larger than the world's total GDP by the end of 2010s, will burst. Some have dreaded the likely 50 percent decline of the housing market, others have speculated on the inflation-driven depreciation of the RMB = USD from $1 = ¥7 to $1 = ¥14, though "China's economy would totally collapse" at the exchange rate of $1 = ¥10.[193] In reality, double-digits declines of the real estate market were already reported in several regions in 2020 to 2022, while governments in many locales proclaiming "decrees inhibiting the lowering of price" (*xiandie ling*) to hopefully head off "something major that has happened in the real estate market."[194]

PRC experts also know that there are sensible and tested ways to reliably deflate the humongous real estate bubble and to correct the great distortion of the Chinese economy, to reduce the enormous waste of resources and capital reflected by the bizarre coexistence of a high vacancy rate and world-class housing prices, and to defuse a massive sociopolitical and economic time bomb.[195] Two methods stand out clearly: a real estate tax with a robust vacancy levy, and a transparency of ownership and transactions with, ideally, a legalization of private land ownership—to establish a functional and real market for real estate. But, once again, CCP politics are in the way, despite the countless vows by top leaders for over two decades to "avoid and reduce the real estate bubble/speculation."[196] Beijing appears unable and unwilling to implement any of the measures mentioned above due to enormous greed and deep fear. Too many leaders and senior cadres and their families own multiple high-priced housing units (sometimes hundreds) that they have obtained opaquely, probably unlawfully, and have kept "for free" and anonymously—thus, they strongly resist any disclosure of personal assets.[197] Too much of the politically critical GDP growth and employment has been depending on the speculative real estate sector—an addiction that grew even larger in the aftermath of the COVID-19 pandemic and amidst the trade war with the United States, judging by data from the PRC State Statistical Bureau in the 2020s. Too many Chinese, especially the elites, have sunk all they have into hype-priced concrete boxes as the last and only way to hang on to their wealth in a comprehensively inflationary economy with insecure property rights and a dysfunctional capital market. Thus, the real estate bubble has become simply too explosive a political bomb to defuse. So, other than a limited "experimental real estate tax," which has been "tested' on and off in places like Shanghai for over a decade,[198] all Beijing has are draconian moves of tug-of-war, implementing periodic administrative freezes on real estate transactions to maintain prices and "relaxing controls" soon afterward with ever-more new state funds pouring in along with bewildering propaganda. The wishful thinking of the party-state seems to be delaying the bursting of the bubble while continuously extracting from its expansion. One thing seems certain: Beijing keeps pressurizing the bubble in a manner that will only cause a bigger burst. Unless the CCP can rewrite the entire rules of economics or pull off miracles like the absolute control of everything and everyone in the PRC forever, the Chinese real estate bubble is destined for infamy and catastrophe. In late 2021, according to major PRC online news portals, the twenty-five largest real estate firms in the PRC were all facing insolvency, involving multi-trillions of RMB in bad loans and vanished capital.[199] The alleged frauds and failure of the largest firm, Evergrande, "caused financial distress" that was hard to control and sparked widespread street protests.[200] By the time this book went to print (end of 2022), the depression of the real estate market in the PRC appeared to have worsened.

Other than real estate, of course, massive and colorful bubbles have popped up in association with all kinds of assets, real or imagined, in the PRC. These range from (largely forged) antiques and arts, rare (often counterfeit) stamps and furniture, and a host of dubious and even noxious health products and services, to the endless and enormous investment scams and financial speculations on and off the internet that have led to the series of mega defaults of crazily over-leveraged debtors and creditors, many of which are state owned and guaranteed.[201]

ASSESSMENT THREE: ENERGY EFFICIENCY AND CORPORATE PROFITABILITY

The CCP-PRC's inefficient use of energy, about 70 percent of which derives from fossil fuels in 2021,[202] reveals the deep suboptimality of its socioeconomic development and raises questions about environmental cost and sustainability. The PRC yield of GDP per unit energy consumed is ranked as one of the lowest, worse than some of the world's poorest and most inefficient economies. By coal equivalent, energy consumption per unit of GDP is 2.5 times higher than the world average, 3.3 times that in the United States, and 7 times that in Japan, as well as significantly higher than in its fellow developing countries such as Brazil, India, and Mexico. By oil equivalent, the PRC fares worse than its peers by either HDI (Human Development Index) or per capita GDP, only slightly better than the least energy-efficient economies like Haiti and Tanzania (see table 3.6). In the 2010s to 2020s, the PRC produced 12 to 18 percent of the world's GDP but consumed over a quarter of the world's primary energy, including burning nearly half of the world's coal and emitting 30 percent of the world's carbon dioxide and other pollutants, more than the combined emission of the United States, the EU, and India, which together produce 43 percent of the world's GDP.[203] Moreover, the platitude absolving China due to its takeover of the "dirty factories from the West" seems embellished: China's critically important net exports are responsible for barely 10 percent of its carbon dioxide emissions.[204]

Table 2.6. GDP per Unit of Energy Used (Selected Countries)

Country	GDP (2011, PPP US$) per kg of oil equivalent	GDP (2017, PPP US$) per kg of oil equivalent
Tanzania	4.5	4.4 (2014)
Haiti	4.2	4.4 (2014)
China	**4.9**	**5.3 (2014)**
Kazakhstan	4.5	5.6 (2014)**
South Korea	6.1	6.8 (2015)
East Asia and Pacific	6.4	7.0 (2014)
India	7.8	8.0 (2014)
United States	7.2	8.6 (2014)
Vietnam	6.7	8.8 (2013)
World average	**7.4**	**8.2**
OECD	8.6	10.0 (2015)
Brazil	10.4	10.5 (2014)
Indonesia	9.5	11.1 (2014)
Japan	9.4	11.6 (2015)
Euro Zone	10.7	12.4 (2014)
Mexico	10.2	12.5 (2015)**
Ecuador	16.1	13.6 (2014)*
Peru	16.2	15.0 (2014)
Hong Kong	24.1	28.6 (2014)

Note: immediate peer countries of the PRC; *by HDI; **by per capita GDP.

Source: IEA statistics on World Bank database, accessed June 2, 2020.

A further quantitative assessment of the PRC's economic record can be attempted at the firm level. The number of Chinese companies listed among *Fortune* magazine's Global 500 Largest Firms increased from 96 in 2014 to 120 in 2019 (excluding four Hong Kong firms) while the US firms on the list decreased from 129 to 121. Ninety of the 120 Chinese behemoths were state owned, and none of them were convincingly not directly controlled by the CCP, with the largest "private" firms being Ping An Insurance (#21) and Huawei (#49). They were largely monopolies or oligopolies concentrated in oil (energy), banking, and construction. Some were formerly PRC central government ministries, and many still enjoy "ministry-level" status and privileges, such as the three entries in the top-ten list: Sinopec, State Power Grid Corporation, and China Petroleum.

These giants, however, are quite inferior with regard to efficiency and innovation. The PRC entries in the *Global 500* in 2020, for example, appeared to have only half the profit margin and less than 30 percent the return on assets as their peers from the United States; the ninety SOEs on the list performed even worse, with less than one-third the profit margin and half the return on assets as their thirty "private" peers on the list.[205] The largest PRC firms, as an official PRC study reported, tend to have "very low innovation ability and very low profitability," with on average only one-third the profitability as the largest American firms. The average per-worker productivity of the five hundred largest Chinese firms was only 30 percent of that of the five hundred largest US firms in the mid-2010s. They are "dependent on imported core technology," "with inferior quality," and "without major international brands." The PRC firms could turn only 10 percent of their innovation into products, far below the average rate of 40 percent in developed countries.[206] The big PRC firms "are poorly run" and breed corruption, embezzlement, and waste, according to a former top manager.[207]

Beijing's attempts to use government spending to create more mammoth companies in order to become a leader in the world market and a "great power of innovation" have often resulted in huge waste and inferior technologies. One example is the expensive but failed effort to establish Chinese TD (Time Division) standards of telecommunication (TD-SCDMA and TD-LTE) to oppose and replace the international standards (W-CDMA, CDMA 2000, and FDD-LTE).[208] The much-hyped 5G technology of the "private" firm Huawei appears to be repeating the same story, especially after the United States and many other nations started to sanction and strangle the firm. By late 2020, both the "immaturity" and the "unrecoverable investment of hundreds of billions" in the PRC's 5G technology started to get official affirmation in Beijing.[209]

In recent decades, the CCP has mobilized at home and abroad on a massive scale to chase the power and prestige of being the world leader in science and technology. The widely reported worldwide piracy of intellectual property and technology espionage aside, Beijing has overseen explosive growth in numbers, now firmly occupying the top or near-top position in the world with regard to government funding of

R&D, publication of academic papers, registration of patents, graduation rates of STEM (science, technology, engineering, and math) students, and employment of engineers and researchers.[210] However, a study by the Chinese Academy of Sciences concluded that the PRC is still significantly behind the United States, the EU, Japan, and South Korea in nine of the ten major technology clusters. At its speed of imitation and innovation and "assuming the US somehow stays still," the PRC might reach only 81 percent of the American level in 120 key technologies by 2050.[211] A US-trained senior PRC scholar concluded in 2021 in a politically permissible way that, to have a chance at becoming a leader of innovation in science and technology, China must first have "a fundamental and institutional reform" of its education system, priority list, and cultural environment.[212]

It is interesting to look at the major companies in the PRC. In 2021, the largest ten companies by market capitalization included two state-owned liquor makers (Maotai and Wuliangye), four internet-based e-commerce firms (Tencent, Alibaba, Meituan, and Pinduoduo), and four state-owned banks and insurers. The largest fifteen firms by revenue had one automaker, three in road and rail construction, two oil companies, and nine state-owned banks and insurers. The fifteen most profitable PRC firms included two IT firms (Tencent and Alibaba), the State Power Grid Corporation, eleven state-owned banks and insurers, plus the state-owned monopoly China Tobacco, which had a net profit equal to the net profits of all other fourteen firms combined.[213] Other than IT services plus the state monopolies of tobacco and oil, the largest PRC firms are all state-owned financial institutions. The peculiar fact that the state monopolies of alcohol and tobacco are so well-financed and profitable in the PRC appears to suggest a similar logic to the so-called "vodka politics" in Russia, which pursues state revenue and control at the expense of people's health.[214] In 2021–22, PRC IT firms all had a major (up to 39%) decline in profits, while their US counterparts all experienced a 12 to 21 percent of profit boom.[215] Perhaps related to this, PRC analysts concluded that, in terms of critical industrialization, China in the mid-2010s was still six to nine decades behind Europe, the United States, and Japan and four decades behind South Korea; China might complete "the first industrial modernization"—a level reached by developed countries in 1970—by 2030, reach the average 2010 level of the developed countries by perhaps 2050, and become one of the top ten by maybe 2100.[216]

What About India? A Note on Comparison

When assessing the PRC record in socioeconomic development with findings suggesting an inferiority, one often encounters the question, "What about India?" India has been frequently used as the country for comparison by many, with the notion that it showcases the superiority of the CCP-PRC system. This line of discourse has seemed to be one common example of using the so-called "whataboutism" or essentialism.[217] India, a neighboring democracy with one-third the territory and roughly the same population as the PRC (1.35 billion compared to 1.41 billion) has indeed seen slower economic growth during most of the recent decades. Measured by GDP figures, export, foreign exchange reserve, and state extraction and concentration of resources, the PRC is clearly ahead of India by a considerable margin. Such a contrast has often become a part of concerted and organized efforts to justify and promote a "China Model" or "Beijing Consensus," namely a one-party authoritarian state capitalism or partocracy capitalism. The invocation of India has become almost a kneejerk response (or the last fallback) for many Chinese inside and outside the PRC to argue that the CCP-PRC party-state "is not that bad," "democracy is just useless," and "it takes a leader (like the CCP or Deng or Xi or even Mao) rather than votes-chasing politicians to enrich a poor country."[218] Empirically, it is also common to find that many Chinese, officials, and the general public alike often display an outsized pride and sense of superiority against India, as illustrated by PRC social media postings about the spike of cases in India during the COVID-19 pandemic in spring 2021.[219]

However, India is not exactly a good comparison to China as there are so many uncontrolled but crucial variables, including India's multitude of racial, ethnic, linguistic, historic, and religious divisions and diversity. It is even more problematic to compare China to India in a selective, ahistorical, statist, and one-dimensional way. "What about India" in China studies often becomes an abuse and even repudiation rather than a support of whataboutism methodology. India started to abandon its state-planning socialistic economic policies only in the mid-1990s, more than ten years after the PRC. More importantly, perhaps, economic growth rate should not be the only measure of a state. For instance, India has never had the kinds of mass deaths or political persecutions that China has suffered numerous times over the past seven decades. India has a functional democracy with substantial freedom of speech, assembly, and migration, almost no "separatist" worries, and no expensive stability maintenance. India has never had extensive use of the death penalty, which remains a feature of today's PRC. If measured by a broader set of gauges, India's socioeconomic record is not that distinctively undesirable. Further, many observers have argued that the economic competition between Beijing and New Delhi is hardly over—it continues with fluid dynamics and is likely to have far-different results in the long term, not necessarily favoring the PRC. Since 2014, for example, India has overtaken the PRC in GDP annual growth rate, while a 2021 study found that the inflation of GDP numbers in the PRC is probably three times more serious than that in India.[220] As some have noted, the "runaway growth" of the PRC economy looked near its end if not already ended by late 2021.[221] In any event, the early reports about China's better-than-India economic growth does not affect the general observation presented in this chapter that the CCP-PRC has had an average, mostly suboptimal, and often disastrous record of socioeconomic development. The fact that Indian socioeconomic development still has much to be desired does not mean that the CCP party-state is superior or desirable; it does not affect the finding that the PRC is firmly in the ranks of average developing nations. Moreover, unlike the rise of China or, more precisely, the rising power of the CCP-PRC party-state, the rise of India or the rising power of the Indian state, which centralizes much less of the nation's wealth than does Beijing, hardly intends to be or is viewed as a systemic challenger, much less an existential threat, to the US-led West and the existing world order.[222]

3

Social Life

Bitterness, Happiness, and Resistance

This chapter takes a look at social life in China under the CCP-PRC party-state, especially the state–society relationship. It will assess the Chinese record of the quality of life, political and socioeconomic equality, social tranquility, mobility, and emigration. Issues to be examined in detail include disaster relief, public health, demographic changes and birth control, and war on poverty. It seeks to demonstrate the vastly different lives and life chances of the Chinese people and the PRC elites, both vertically (class division) and horizontally (spatial disparity). Through analyzing the phenomenon of so-called *chiku* (eating bitterness, a colloquial phrase for enduring hardships), surveys on people's sense of contentment and happiness, and the data on Chinese family life and migration patterns, this chapter will report on how the Chinese people feel about and respond to CCP governance in opinions and actions.

Over the decades, however suboptimal and cost-ineffective, the PRC has managed to achieve quite a few accomplishments that have significantly improved the quality of life in China, especially in the areas of extending life expectancy, reducing infant mortality, increasing literacy, and controlling infectious diseases. A massive increase in the number of non-agricultural jobs, great development of infrastructure (communications, transportation, and power grid), and a boom of the export sector and the real estate market, as I have reported earlier in this book, have contributed to an epic-sized alleviation of poverty. After decades of stagnation and decline under Mao, living standards in China have experienced profound improvement over the past three decades, especially in urban China. In the late 2010s and early 2020s, about 400 million Chinese people were officially estimated to be "middle class" with annual household incomes between ¥24,000 (US $3,540) and ¥250,000 (US $36,400), with the median at ¥29,975 (US $4,428); another roughly 30 million are in the "upper class" with household income above ¥250,000 (US $36,400). Though still just around 30 percent of the total population, a very large number of Chinese have now obtained disposable income and purchasing power approaching that of lower-middle class households in the West.[1] About 10 million Chinese or roughly 0.7 percent of the total population, mostly the ruling elites of the party-state and their associates (family members inclusive), have obtained an American- and world-class wealth, with household annual income over $79,760; the PRC also has over 1,000 billionaires, many more than any other country.[2] Numerous Chinese metropolises like Shanghai and Shenzhen have now attained world-class technological sophistication and cultural appeal. The PRC rulers and, to a lesser and rapidly decreasing extent, the upper and middle classes, apparently enjoy a modern, Western-style material life of comfort, convenience and luxury.

Yet, measured by their overall standard of living, quality of life, freedom of choice, and a host of comparative indexes of socioeconomic development, the PRC firmly remains a bona fide developing nation with world-record inequality. The party-state remains in a dominant position in the Chinese society and the Chinese sociocultural life. The overwhelming majority of the Chinese people, constantly inspired by what they see in the West, still dream of a better life with more rights and freedom.[3] As an illustration, the officially reported PRC median household income is only 7 percent of that in United States, under 10 percent of that in South Korea, 46 percent of that in the world, and 108 percent of that in India.[4] Even considering purchasing power parity and the fact that locally sourced and especially labor-intensive goods and services are indeed significantly cheaper in China, the majority of people in the PRC lead a life that is still typical and average for a developing nation. As I will detail later, by the international standard, nearly half of the Chinese population lives below the poverty line; by the US standard, that figure jumps to 85 percent with only 2 to 3 percent (maximum 8%) of the Chinese in the American "middle class" income bracket and fewer than 1 percent of the Chinese have household income above the US median household income. The brewing and sometimes boiling tensions between the PRC government of Qin-Han Legalism and the Chinese society—which has been transforming in the general direction of industrialization, urbanization, and Westernization, with a population that is rightfully wanting and highly restive—are a strong testimony about and also a clear indictment of the CCP party-state.

As I attempted to demonstrate earlier, Beijing has effectively and excessively appropriated the bounties of Chinese economic growth, made possible by the freer and hardworking Chinese people, in order to enrich, justify, strengthen, and beautify the regime. Yet, in an instance of fatal irony, Beijing now acts ever more powerfully to limit and reduce the freedom of the Chinese people with ever more means to control and indoctrinate. As the previous chapter of this book reported, the Chinese economy is on the path to slowing down or even stagnating in the 2020s. Social life for the Chinese people is therefore likely to become harder and more contentious. The China Suboptimality of the CCP-PRC party-state appears certain to protract the mediocrity and inferiority of its socioeconomic record at home. Externally, the Chinese wealth and capacity, disproportionately concentrated in the hands of the very few unmonitored and unconstrained but confident and indulgent autocrats and oligarchs, is inexorably turning the China Suboptimality, or the CCP Optimality, into a worldwide irritant, reshaping the world in a race to the bottom and conceivably ushering in a World Suboptimality for all of human civilization.

A Bona Fide Developing Country

The rapid growth of the GDP in the PRC has yet to change the fact that the Chinese people are still collectively stuck firmly in the ranks of developing countries. According to a senior PRC economist, the real story of economic development is the growth of per capita GDP rather than the growth of the size of national GDP.[5] In 2013, the PRC's share of the world economy was 11 percent (or 14% by PPP, purchasing power parity) larger than Japan's. But the PRC's per capita GDP (measured by current and PPP methods) was only 13 to 25 percent that in Japan, about the same as it was all the way back in 1950, which was 20 percent.[6] South Korean per capita GDP was about 40 percent higher than that in the PRC in 1950, but 2.4 times higher in 1973, and 3.5 times higher in 2012. In 1950, the Chinese people in Taiwan (ROC) were only slightly wealthier than the Chinese people on the Chinese Mainland (PRC), with a per capita GDP roughly 50 percent higher ($922 versus $624 by the PPP method). That gap increased to 3.1 times ($3,669 versus $1,186) by 1973, and further enlarged to over 4.2 times ($38,400 versus $9,100) in 2012. The other two non-PRC Chinese economies, Hong Kong and Macao, had a per capita GDP (by PPP) 5.6 and 9 times higher, respectively, than the PRC's in 2012.[7] In the 2020s, this comparative picture only improved slightly for the PRC (mostly in comparison to Taiwan), despite the continued growth of the Chinese economy. By conventional or PPP methods, per capita GDP of the PRC has always remained below the world's average. In 2013, the PRC's per capita GDP ranking among the nations was sandwiched between Turkmenistan–Thailand (by current USD) and Namibia–Jamaica (by PPP); in 2020, the immediate peering neighbors of the PRC by per capita GDP were Nauru–Malaysia (by current USD) and Venezuela–Botswana (by PPP) (see table 3.1).

Judging by the Human Development Index (HDI), a more comprehensive measure gauging economic, social, and cultural developments, devised by the United Nations Development Program (UNDP), the averageness and suboptimality of the PRC's socioeconomic performance are equally if not more evident. The massive GDP growth has not been matched by improvements of overall HDI in China,[8] perhaps because either the PRC's economic growth is ineffectual and exaggerated, or the gains have been allocated and utilized with significant inequity and irrationality. From 1980 to 2020, Chinese HDI scores improved but the PRC ranking actually stayed just below or at the world average: 81/124 in 1980, 101/187 in 2012, 85/189 in 2018, and 86/189 in 2020. By its HDI ranking, since 1980, the PRC has basically remained a developing country, sandwiched between peer countries of Jordan and Turkmenistan in 2012, Algeria–Peru and Ecuador–Azerbaijan in 2018, and Brazil and Ecuador in 2020 (see table 3.2).[9]

Bitterness Eaters and Luxury Indulgers

The historical and quantitative analyses presented so far point rather unambiguously to the fact that the Chinese people, including many if not most of the elites, endure the misfortunate of living under the China Suboptimality of the CCP-PRC party-state. People carry on the tradition of "eating bitterness" or *chiku, amor fati*, making a virtue out of

Table 3.1. Economies in Comparison (Selected Countries, 2019–2020)

| Country | % of World Population | % of World GDP | | Per Capita GDP | | |
		Current $	PPP	Current $	PPP	World Rank (n=200)
China	18.47	16.3	17.3	10,262	16,785	70–96
Taiwan	0.31	0.7	1.0	24,828	55,078	39–19
Hong Kong	0.10	0.4	0.4	48,756	62,375	15–11
Macao	0.01	0.01	0.01	84,096	129,103	3–2
South Korea	0.66	1.9	1.6	31,762	43,029	32–33
Japan	1.62	5.8	4.0	40,247	43,236	27–32
United States	4.25	24.4	15.8	65,281	65,281	7–14
World average	—	—	—	11,436	17,680	—

Sources: Chinese numbers are provided by the PRC government. IMF, World Bank, UNDP Databases, and CIA World Facts website.

Table 3.2. Human Development Index 1980–2020 (Selected Countries)

Country	HDI 1980 (n = 24)	HDI 1990 (n = 133)	HDI 2000 (n = 156)	HDI 2012 (n = 187)	HDI 2018 (n = 189)	HDI 2020 (n=189)
United States	2	2	3	3	15	17
Japan	10	7	11	10	19	19
South Korea	39	31	23	12	22	23
Hong Kong	27	19	28	13	4	4
Russia	—	30	55	55	49	52
Iran	73	85	75	76	65	70
Peer country	80 (Egypt)	81 (Samoa)	93 (Moldova)	100 (Jordan)	84 (Peru)	85 (Brazil)
China	81 (65%)	82 (69%)	94 (60%)	101 (54%)	85 (45%)	86 (46%)
Peer country	82 (Zambia)	83 (Jordan)	95 (Botswana)	102 (Turkmenistan)	86 (Ecuador)	87 (Ecuador)

Note: Taiwan is not counted for HDI due to the PRC influence in the UN. Chinese data, of course, is all officially provided by the PRC government. (Source: UNDP 2014–2021).

necessity, like their ancestors under the former imperial Qin-Han polity.[10] The small ruling class of the PRC, the party-state cadres, do have a much higher standard of living, enjoying social stature, power, financial stability, rationed prerogatives and luxuries, extra (often gray or dark) income, and the special provisions outlined earlier in this book. Yet, in exchange, they have to endure the China Suboptimality in a unique way. For one thing, simultaneously behaving as a mini-tyrant (to subordinates) and a sycophant (to superiors) seems to take a heavy psychological and physical toll. The CCP's Quixotic political campaigns and brutal power struggles, now mostly in the form of "anticorruption," grind mercilessly and endlessly. Traditionally, many if not the majority of the CCP-PRC cadres have reportedly relied heavily on sleeping aids and have suffered from various nerve and mental disorders associated with stress and fear. Mao Zedong himself and his top associates were all heavily addicted to strong doses of imported sleeping pills.[11] In the 2010s, "76% of civil servants" and "up to 98% of senior leading officials" were reported by the government to have physical and mental health problems including split personality (Dissociative Identity Disorder), anxiety, depression, and high rates of suicide.[12]

An average Chinese worker must face the bitterness of harsh working conditions and long hours, the so-called 996 (9 a.m. to 9 p.m., six days a week), and low (or in some cases delayed and denied) pay. Reflecting the fact that more family members need to work, the Chinese labor participation rate is by far the highest in the world at 76 percent, way ahead of the United States (65%), Japan (58%), and India (55%).[13] Work safety is widely lacking, exemplified by the blood-soaked coal industry, which provides more than 70 percent of China's energy supply.[14] The official figure of work-related casualties in coal mines in China ranged between 1.2 and 6 per every million tons of coal mined in the 2000s, which is twice that of India, three to fifteen times that of Poland, and 120 to 150 times that of the United States. The PRC is responsible for 37 percent of the world's coal production but 70 percent of world's coal mine deaths, in addition to the thousands of underreported cases of pneumoconiosis suffered by coal miners every year.[15] At the national production level of 3.7 billion tons,[16] thousands of Chinese coal miners are killed on the job every year.

Unsurprisingly, the real standard of living in the PRC remains low, as shown by an international comparison using the Engel Coefficient, which measures the portion of income spent on food. In 2011, the official Engel Coefficient in China was 0.38 for the urban sector and 0.43 for the rural sector; it actually rose by 3 to 6 percent over 2010 due to inflation.[17] At 0.4 nationally (0.29 for high income and 0.48 for low income),[18] the Chinese real living standard measured by the Engel Coefficient is that of a typical developing country, at roughly the same level as the American urban population all the way back in the 1890s, and would require forty-seven more years of "rapid economic growth" to just reach the average level (0.15) of the low income OECD (Organization of Economic Cooperation and Development) countries.[19]

An average Chinese worker faces world-class extraction by the PRC. In addition to the opaque and high indirect taxation like value-added tax and sales tax of 17 percent and higher, which contributes 60 percent of the government's total tax revenue, the income tax burden is higher than many countries. All personal income is taxed monthly starting at $455 with seven brackets including 30 percent for income over $5,384 and 45 percent for income over $12,307.[20] By comparison, personal income is taxed annually in Taiwan with five brackets including the highest rate of 40 percent for income over $162,857 (monthly equivalent of $13,451); in the United States, personal income is taxed annually with five brackets including the highest rate of 37 percent for income over $539,900 (monthly equivalent of $44,992); in India, personal income is also taxed annually with six brackets including the highest rate of just 30 percent.[21] With little pre-tax deducible, no inheritance/gift tax, and no real estate tax, the PRC tax burden is disproportionately heavier for working people. Furthermore, Chinese employees and employers shoulder the world's heaviest payroll taxes—six kinds of such taxes at a combined rate of 40 to 50 percent of wages (66% in some cities), "higher than that in Germany, Korea, Japan or the US." Yet the pension plans and health benefits cover only part of the population, with serious insufficiency and unevenness across regions, and about 10 to 20 million CCP-PRC cadres essentially paying no payroll taxes but enjoying twice the average pension and medical benefits. Reportedly, nearly 87 percent of the multi-trillion RMB social security funds had been expropriated or even embezzled by local officials by the mid-2010s.[22]

Predictably, the delivery of social security and social welfare assistance in the PRC seems to have been designed and implemented to "care for" the party-state rather than the needy. Health care in the PRC is similarly "shaped by the political calculations of the regime" as tools for political stability rather than social needs.[23] The majority of the population in rural areas have a government-sponsored medical insurance plan that looks like the worst kind of local-only HMO (health management organization) and pays "almost nothing." In 2019, the PRC government approved a total of 169,583 kinds of medicines (including 4,080 more expensive imported varieties). But only 1.6 percent of these were covered by the health plans, even just partially.[24] Chinese media reported that the state monopoly has "artificially kept" many insured patients away from the latest medication for seven or eight years or longer.[25] Labor with epidural to reduce pain, a widely used procedure in the West for many decades, only started its large-scale "trial use" in the PRC in 2019, according to official reports.[26] Studies report that the percentages of cancer patients and cancer deaths in the PRC are the highest in the world, with a cancer death rate 17 percent higher than the world's average.[27] The World Health Organization (WHO) reported that China, with 19 percent of the world's population, had 23.7 percent of new cancer cases (4.57 million) and 30 percent of cancer deaths (3 million) in the world in 2020; environment-related lung cancer and four cancers of the digestive system (liver, stomach, colon, esophagus) are the five most common cancers in China, while the most common cancer in the world remains breast cancer.[28] While "the cancer burden in the United States has decreased gradually [. . .] China [. . . has a] greater incidence of cancers," concluded a team of PRC researchers in 2022, reporting the growing annual number of cancer cases and deaths at 4.82 million and 3.21 million, respectively, with a death-to-case ratio of 67 percent in China versus 20 percent in the United States.[29] The lack of early detection and proper treatment seems much more serious in the countryside where the majority of the Chinese people live. In the 2010s, it was reported that the rural population had a life-expectancy twelve years shorter than the national average.[30]

Like the imperial rulers of the past, the CCP-PRC state has always worked hard to callously indoctrinate and internalize the value of eating bitterness as an officially praised and promoted form of stoicism with Chinese characteristics, or one of the "beautiful Chinese traditional norms and virtues," in its grand campaigns to control the people and their minds.[31] The CCP continues to propagate the bitterness-eating, hardworking, self-sacrificing "spirit of screws"—relishing as a screw on the party-state's "revolutionary engine" or the gratification of being a cog in the machine of socialism. This is apparent, for example, in the didactic (but largely apocryphal) stories of the model soldier Lei Feng

(1940–1962) who was first posthumously exalted by Mao Zedong in 1963 and has been continuously extolled by post-Mao CCP leaders.[32] Similarly, Mao promoted a "Mr. Fool" (*Yugong*), the character of an ancient fable-tale who committed his whole clan "of endless generations" to manually removing two massive mountains that blocked his way— that sheer determination then moved God to eventually haul away the mountains with divine force. This so-called "Yugong Spirit," glorifying bitterness-eating Voluntarism and inefficient endeavors of irrationality, has remained a staple in school textbooks from second grade to high school and an integral part of ethics education in the PRC.[33]

Meanwhile, the small group of the rich and powerful in the PRC, almost all of whom are, or are related to, "leading cadres" of the CCP, especially the senior leaders above the ministry-province level, have been enjoying world-class luxuries, wicked indulgences, and often excessive and iniquitous lifestyles, just like the imperial rulers in the past. For example, "global cognac sales depend on China's 'erotic sector,'" which is a major pastime for the nouveau riche. In 2017, China became the world's largest importer of luxury cars, sales of which (usually priced two to three times higher in China than in Europe or North America) grew nearly twice as fast as the total automobile market (36% annually in 2003–2013). Ferrari's sales boomed 155 percent in 2010 alone, and the PRC was the world's largest buyer of Bentleys and second largest of Lamborghinis for a number of years in the 2010s. On formal occasions, the top CCP leaders themselves now ride in the specially handcrafted *Hongqi* (Red Flag) Model L, "made in China" using imported technology and parts, and "as luxurious as Rolls-Royce."[34]

Inequality and Poverty

The bitterness of life for the Chinese people under the CCP-PRC party-state is more acrimonious than ever due to the combined and compounded impact of two great inequalities coexisting and growing today that makes Beijing's record of distributive justice among the worst in the world. First, there is the world-record vertical income inequality in a self-labeled class-less socialist country with a supposedly egalitarian economy, and then the peculiar horizontal and spatial inequalities and discriminations caused by the unique PRC internal-migration control of the *hukou* (household registration) system.[35] Stalinist state-socialism failed to really reduce inequality in other places, and the CCP's simulated pseudo-socialism has fared even worse.[36] A PRC study concluded in 2013 that the real Gini Coefficient, a measurement of inequality, was world-class already during the Mao era, at 0.61–0.7, twice the official number of 0.32.[37] An IMF study concluded in 2015 that China was "one of the most unequal countries in the world." The World Bank similarly concluded that the PRC Gini Coefficient has been among the uppermost in the world, much higher than its neighbors in East Asia and on par with world champions of inequality like Nicaragua.[38] From 2003 to 2019, the PRC income Gini Coefficient ranged between 0.472 and 0.491, with an average of 0.476, way above 0.4, the level "at which a society becomes vulnerable to social unrest" according to the United Nations.[39] Using different methods, US and PRC researchers separately reported that the PRC income Gini Coefficient shot up from 0.3 in 1980 to 0.55 in 2014, or from 0.45 in 1995 to 0.55 in 2002, and to 0.59 (even 0.61) in 2012, with confirmations by econometric analyses.[40] According to PRC Ministry of Treasury, only 65 million Chinese (fewer than 10% of the employed) earn enough to pay personal income tax that starts at the annual income of ¥60,000 ($8,900). In October 2021, a "leading authority on income distribution" in China put the PRC wealth and income Gini Coefficients at 0.704 and 0.52, respectively, both world-record high "for many years already and is still growing."[41]

In comparison, the US income Gini Coefficient (0.43 in 2018) is among the highest of the developed countries but remains considerably lower than that in the self-claimed "socialist" PRC. With a much lower Engel Coefficient and a much higher degree of both political equality and social mobility, the United States seems to have a problem more of relative poverty. By the World Bank's international poverty line (daily income of $5.5), there are basically no poor people in the United States, which has a national poverty line six times higher than the world poverty line.[42] Sociopolitical tensions caused by relative poverty certainly need remedies, yet the American inequality critically indicates a cost or side effect of competition that nonetheless does deliver economic efficiency and technological innovation. Further evidence of its systemic suboptimality, China has world-class inequality (and also a high Engel Coefficient), which is mostly created and continued by the CCP-PRC party-state, and still lacks both efficiency and innovation—thus, it suffers the cruel pains without the prized gains.

In the 2010s, the income of the top 5 percent in the PRC was thirty-four times higher than that of the bottom 10 percent, while the wealth of the top 10 percent was 160 times more than the bottom 10 percent.[43] In 2020, Premier Li Keqiang, the nominally number two man in the PRC, revealed in his annual press conference that "there are still 600 million people earning about ¥1,000 ($140) a month," even though the official PRC per capita monthly income was ¥2,558 ($358) with a median of ¥2,208 ($309). Soon enough, the PRC media and scholars felt safe enough to release and detail a truer picture of Chinese people's income: out of the 605 million Chinese with a monthly income at or below ¥1,090 ($152), 423 million people have a monthly income below ¥800 ($112) and 221 million people have a monthly income of ¥500 ($70). Only 16 percent of Chinese (229 million) have a monthly income at or above ¥3,000 ($420) and 5 percent of Chinese (72 million) at or above ¥5,000 ($699).[44] Combining the data from two other PRC ministries (Treasury and Labor), only 15 percent out of the 434 million workers in urban China (roughly 65 million) in 2018 had a monthly income above ¥5,000, the starting point for paying income tax.[45] The shocking but not uncommon discrepancy in the official data aside, it is sad that the overwhelming majority of Chinese people (85–95%) seem to live at or below the US poverty line, with at least 43 percent (605 million) Chinese under the international poverty line ($165 per month), and a frightful 16 percent (221 million) Chinese under the lines of deep and even abject poverty ($96 and $47 per month).[46]

Worse than income inequality, the wealth Gini Coefficient in the PRC grew from 0.45 in 1995 to the incredible height of 0.73 in 2012 (0.71 in 2020), with 1 percent of families owning one-third of China's assets, according to PRC economists. By the modest measure of having personal financial assets of $100,000, the PRC had only 12 to 14 million "middle-class and wealthy" people in mid-2010s, roughly 1 percent of the total population or about 2 percent of the working-age population. In 2020, the PRC Central Bank itself reported that 10 percent of households owned 48 percent of the national wealth, of which 70 percent was in real estate.[47] The PRC billionaires (many of whom are CCP-related oligarchs and live outside of China), estimated to number 16 in 2006, jumped to 373 in 2018, and 1,058 in 2021, owning $1 to $2 trillion in assets, while the world had a total of only 3,228 billionaires (the United States had 696).[48]

The world-record vertical inequality and widespread, relative and absolute, poverty in the PRC seem quite immovable, despite the much-propagated CCP anti-poverty campaigns over the years and Xi

Jinping's recent personal push,[49] powerfully proving the suboptimality of the CCP-PRC as well as its habitual duplicity and creative number games. The PRC has used its own legal poverty line of $0.95 daily income (probably the world's lowest, and only half of the World Bank's abject poverty line of $1.9 per day, or $57 per month) since late 2011; it was a paltry $0.51 before 2011 when the World Bank abject poverty line was $1.25.[50] By that extremely low standard of less than a dollar a day, over 100 million Chinese were officially "poor" in 2010, then down to 43 million in 2017 and 16.6 million (or 1.2% of the population) in 2019. However, by the World Bank's international standard of poverty (daily income of $5.5), the percentage of Chinese under the poverty line in the PRC was actually 43 percent in 2002, 34 percent in 2005, and 40 percent (or 500 million) in 2017. In 2020, as shown by Premier Li Keqiang's much-lauded "rare and brave" admission, it was back to 43 percent. Despite the nearly two decades of supposedly rapid growth and the many years of a hyperbolic "war to eliminate poverty by 2020," alas, there seems to be little progress, but rather, clear regression, with nearly half of the Chinese people still living in poverty by the international standard in the 2020s. Relative poverty in the rural areas actually increased from 12 percent in 1988 to 18 percent in 2021, according to PRC journalists.[51]

It seemed, therefore, comically and criminally deceptive for the CCP to declare at the end of 2020 that it had "miraculously and historically eliminated the thousand-year-old problem of abject poverty in China" in just five years under Xi Jinping. Just months later in April 2021, the CCP's own official media ran a rare but illuminating exposé on the blatant fraud and cover-up related to "poverty-eradication" in one county that had been personally honored by Xi on national TV just a few weeks before due to its stellar performance.[52] Furthermore, a profound twist in the CCP's much-propagated "war on poverty" seems to have quickly and conveniently revolved to serve the party-state's not so-hidden long-time political agenda for further state extraction and control of wealth, in the name of equality for the poor, anti-monopoly, and a "common prosperity" for all. In 2020–2021, the CCP began a new campaign to employ various harsh legal and extra-legal means to "clip the superrich [capitalists] and reallocate national wealth."[53] In addition to the targeted and purged superrich Chinese oligarchs I have discussed previously in this book, many fat cats, from real estate moguls like Feng Lun and Pan Shiyi to major bosses and stars in the massive industries of tutoring and entertainment, appeared to all suddenly face heavy levies, stern accusations, big fines, quick takeovers, forced foreclosures and liquidations, exiles, and even jail time.[54]

One additional reason for the deeply entrenched poverty in the PRC is the incapacity for upward social mobility through education. College education, with its seemingly fair and equal entrance exam (*gaokao*) and much elevated chance to live in the urban sector and join the CCP-PRC state payroll, functions as perhaps the most important avenue for both upward and horizontal social mobility in China.[55] Yet, from the mid-1990s onward, higher education in the PRC, especially the elite kind, has become increasingly exclusive, favoring the rich, urban, Han, male and privileged.[56] Massive expansion, rapid dilution and even erosion of college education, skyrocketing preparatory costs and tuition, admission biases, and especially the twisted post-graduation job market for the exploding number of graduates of non-elite colleges have rendered this narrow conveyer belt to success increasingly dysfunctional. Over 30 percent of PRC college students were from rural families in the 1980s with largely secure urban jobs awaiting them after graduation. This figure declined to only 15 percent by 2009 and ever lower since, with these graduates facing highly uncertain job prospects. Contrary to the government data that constantly portrays an 80 to 90 percent employment rate for college graduates, leaked numbers from a fairly prestigious university in 2022 showed that only 38.9 percent of its "normal" graduates got jobs; after accounting for the 22 percent who went to graduate school and the 4 percent who went abroad, the real unemployment rate was 35 percent. The anecdata about the many more "ordinary" colleges suggest a likely even higher unemployment rate after graduation, accompanied by a continued decline of starting salaries.[57] As part of voting with feet, therefore, it is no wonder that the elites in China now tend to simply send their children abroad to get a more valued education.

Accompanying the world-record vertical inequality, there is also the world-class horizontal inequality in China. The key PRC sociopolitical institution of the *hukou* (household registration) system, which restricts internal migration, has created and sustained the world's most extensive case of institutional exclusion with profound inequality and discrimination based on urban-rural and locational divides.[58] In the late 1990s, per capita government spending was ten times greater in some provinces than in others.[59] After three decades of adapting to a raw capitalist labor market to have substantial though still controlled labor mobility, increased localization of its implementation with useful flexibility and experimentation, and several rounds of cosmetic reconfiguration and relabeling, the *hukou* system continues to function as a legal Great Wall between the urban and the rural, and also countless legal "city walls" segregating regions, maintaining and even enlarging horizontal disparities.[60] In the 2010s and 2020s, official studies disclosed that urban dwellers on average had three times as much disposable income as rural residents. The PRC social security and pension plans cover two-thirds of urban *hukou* holders but only 4.6 percent of rural *hukou* holders, many of whom actually work and live in the cities and who still make up the majority of the Chinese people; the average gap of social security and pension payment between the two segments of society is 24-folds.[61] The same job in IT industry, for example, reported pays 73 percent lower in the seventy so-called "third-tier cities" (all provincial and prefectural capitals) than in the four "first-tier cities." Then there are still the ninety "fourth-tier" and 128 "fifth-tier" cities, plus the stacked hundreds of townships and thousands of villages.[62]

The peculiar *hukou*-based segregation and spatial inequality are particularly pronounced in the rural sector where the majority of the Chinese people still live.[63] A Chinese farming family now usually works a tiny piece of allotted land (less than 1.65 acres on average) but it takes "at least 16.5 acres" for a rural laborer to earn the same as an urban manual worker. In the late 2010s, the middle school dropout rate was as high as 63 percent in rural China. With the institutionalized political, socioeconomic, and cultural exclusion and marginalization, life in the rural and the lower-ranked cities resembles "a structured misfortune that is so hopeless and almost inescapable," wrote a PRC scholar in 2017. Rural women, unsurprisingly, seem to fare even worse than men across the board.[64]

Even the new, politically touted poverty relief is disbursed very differently across localities.[65] The horizontal stratification of the PRC and the interregional gap are obvious in so many ways that almost all of China's more than 220 million migrant workers want to settle in major urban centers, while fewer than 20 percent of them are willing to have their *hukou* relocated to the medium and small cities that are now decreed to be more accommodating to new immigrants.[66] Since 1992, the government has been developing a national highway system to link many small, peripheral cities and counties and supposedly develop the economy there. Yet without addressing the underlying sociopolitical problems, this agreeable and expensive effort seems to have been counterproductive: economic growth in the linked peripheral areas is 18 percent slower (and industrialization is 26% slower) than in the unlinked peripheral places, probably because the highways actually reinforce the concentration of production in the politically favored urban centers, exacerbating both capital flight and brain drain.[67]

Going by HDI (human development index), it could be said that there are actually many Chinas, at very different levels of socioeconomic and technological development, within the PRC. In the 2010s, the most developed provincial regions together with the three metro centers with HDI at the "high human development" tier had only 55.6 million people, or 3.2 percent of the total population of China.[68] The higher development level of the three metro centers has been critically financed and subsidized by the central government with national revenue (see table 3.3). By the mid-2010s, pensions for people in twenty-seven provinces had a provincial disparity as large as ten times, and the average household wealth can be over seven times greater in some regions than in others.[69] It is common for the per capita GDP/income in one city to be five to six times higher than that in another city in the same province. Even within the capital city of Beijing, in the mid-2010s, the gap in per capita GDP was 2.1 times among its four core districts (Xicheng versus Chaoyang), and 7.4 times among all of its sixteen subunits (Xicheng versus Yanqing). The average wage in Xicheng was 2.4 times that in Tongzhou, merely sixteen miles away.[70] In 2021, the capital city of Beijing had 104 top-ranked (3A) hospitals plus several top-ranked military hospitals, while the more populous city Shanghai had only sixty-six and the other two "first-tier" cities of Guangzhou and Shenzhen had only sixty-two and twenty-two, respectively, not to mention the hundreds of tier 2 to tier 5 cities and towns.[71]

The persistent and staggering vertical and horizontal socioeconomic inequalities and disparities, however, have thus far powerfully supported the CCP-PRC institutions and policies that created them. The better-off minority living in urban centers and the extraordinarily indulged ruling class and its cronies have been adamant and relentless in perpetuating those institutions, policies, distributions of gains, institutional exclusions and discrimination. Therefore, we have a seemingly "paradoxical" phenomenon in the PRC: Chinese elites and many of the middle to upper class appear strangely uninterested in political democratization.[72] An equal citizenship remains absent as a result of restricted internal

Table 3.3. Horizontal Inequality and Regional Disparity Measured by HDI

Region	HDI National (n = 31)		World (n = 189)	Peer/Reference Countries
—	0.934		3	United States
—	0.909		11	Japan
—	0.905		12	South Korea
—	**0.902**		—	**(Very high human development)**
—	0.9		14	Hong Kong
Beijing	0.821	1	38	Barbados; Poland
Shanghai	0.814	2	39	Poland; Chile
Tianjin	0.795	3	48	Bahrain; Bahamas
—	**0.753**	—	—	**(High human development)**
Jiangsu	0.748	4	69	Albania; Saint Kitts and Nevis
Zhejian	0.744	5	71	Venezuela; Kazakhstan
Liaoning	0.74	6	75	Iran; Macedonia
—	**0.736**	—	—	**(Latin American average)**
Guangdong	0.73	7	83	Saint Vincent and Grenadines; Oman
Inner	0.722	8	88	Armenia; Ecuador
Shandong	0.721	9	89	Ecuador; Turkey
Jilin	0.715	10	90	Turkey; Columbia
Fujian	0.714	11	91	Columbia; Tunisia
Heilongjiang	0.704	12	95	Sri Lanka; Belize
Hubei	0.696	13	99	Dominican Republic; China
Shaanxi	0.695	14	99	Dominican Republic; China
Shanxi	0.693	15	100	Dominican Republic; China
Hebei	0.691	16	100	Dominican Republic; China
—	**0.69**	—	—	**(World average)**
China	**0.689**	—	**101**	**Dominican Republic; Turkmenistan**

Table 3.3. Continued.

Region	HDI National (n = 31)		World (n = 189)	Peer/Reference Countries
Chongqing	0.689	17	101	China; Turkmenistan
Hunan	0.681	18	105	Maldives; Suriname
Hainan	0.68	19	106	Suriname; El Salvador
Henan	0.677	20	107	El Salvador; Gabon
—	**0.673**	—	—	**(East Asia average)**
Xinjiang	0.667	22	109	Bolivia; Palestinian Territory
Jiangxi	0.662	23	110	Palestinian Territory; Egypt
Sichuan	0.662	24	110	Palestinian Territory; Egypt
Anhui	0.66	25	111	Egypt; Mongolia
Guangxi	0.658	26	112	Mongolia; Moldova
Qinghai	0.638	27	114	Micronesia; Botswana
—	**0.631**	—	—	**(Medium human development)**
Gansu	0.63	28	120	Botswana; Honduras
Yunnan	0.609	29	130	Viet Nam; Namibia
Guizhou	0.598	30	131	Namibia; Nicaragua
Tibet	0.569	31	136	Iraq; Timor-Leste

Sources: UNDP 2013; UNDP & CASS, 2013. There has been no systematic report on the regional HDI in the PRC published since 2013.

migration and the steeply stratified income and wealth classes, both of which are key to the absolute and relative well-being and power of the privileged, the tiny "in" minority that is almost entirely composed of the party-state apparatus itself—as reported previously in this book, just about every CCP member is in that group. To be sure, the CCP under Mao and from Deng to Xi seems to know that rampant inequalities always critically undermine the political legitimacy of its "people's democratic dictatorship," and has always pledged loudly for a "common prosperity for everyone,"[73] despite its long record of quite the opposite. As this book has demonstrated, the PRC in its first thirty years achieved something of "common poverty" with neither prosperity nor equality; in the recent four decades, the party-state saw considerable prosperity with rampant inequality. However, as I have mentioned earlier in this book, the latest rhetoric and action since 2020 of "further promoting common prosperity" and "building an olive-shaped middle-class society" like that in the United States,[74] seem to consist of more schemes for controlling and extracting the rich than enriching and empowering the poor.

Disaster Relief

Comparatively, scholars have found that democracies have a distinctively better record of provision of public services, preservation of the environment, public safety, and protection of the population against natural or human-made disasters.[75] Not surprisingly, international comparison of the consequences of natural disasters vividly illustrates the clear suboptimality of the autocratic CCP-PRC party-state, despite its self-aggrandized "institutional superiority" in mobilizing and concentrating resources for urgent needs and big projects, such as disaster prevention and relief— the so-called ability "to concentrate force for big deeds."[76] For example, Mainland China has had its fair share of earthquakes given its size and geographic expanse but none that would be considered major (above magnitude 8). Yet, even with much less destructive power, earthquakes in Mainland China are somehow far deadlier than most, if not all, of the earthquakes in the world, ranking the PRC firmly in this regard among developing countries such as Haiti and Pakistan (table 3.4).

Similarly, road traffic-related deaths per capita in the PRC are 10 percent higher than the world's average and twice as high as in the United States, and more similar in fact to that in Botswana, Laos, and Cameroon. In the 2010s, with 16 percent of the world's automobiles, the PRC had 22 percent of the world's road deaths with a deaths per vehicle rate 40 percent higher than the world's average, ten times higher than in the United States, and higher than that in Tunisia, Laos, and Cambodia. The key reasons for so many road-related deaths in the PRC seem to be the poor regulation of road and vehicle safety and deficient driver's training.[77] All those terrible numbers appear to suggest the CCP's inattention to public safety, and incompetence in disaster prevention and relief due largely to the overly centralized, silo-like, maladroit bureaucracy with a very long chain of tight command that, according to scholars of public service, "may look majestic but shows all sorts of fumbles and stumbles

Table 3.4. Deadliest Earthquakes in the World (1964–2016)

Date	Location	Deaths	Magnitude
1976/07/27	**Tangshan, China**	**242,769–655,000***	**7.5**
2010/01/12	Haiti	316,000	7.0
2004/12/26	Indian Ocean Tsunami	227,898	9.1
2008/05/12	**Sichuan, China**	**87,287**	**7.9**
2005/10/08	Pakistan	86,000	7.6
1970/05/31	Chimbote, Peru	70,000	7.9
1990/06/20	Western Iran	50,000	7.4
2003/12/26	Southeastern Iran	31,000	6.6
1988/12/07	Spitak, Armenia	25,000	6.8
1976/02/04	Guatemala	23,000	7.5
2011/03/11	Tsunami in Japan	20,896	9.0
2001/01/26	Gujarat, India	20,085	7.6
1974/05/10	**Yunnan, China**	**20,000**	**6.8**
1999/08/17	Turkey	17,118	7.6
1978/09/16	Iran	15,000	7.8
1968/08/31	Dasht-e Bayaz, Iran	15,000	7.8
1970/01/04	**Tonghai, China**	**10,000**	**7.5**
1985/09/19	Mexico, Michoacan	9,500	8.0
1976/08/16	Mindanao, Philippines	8,000	7.9
2006/05/26	Indonesia	5,749	6.3
1995/01/16	Kobe, Japan	5,502	6.9
1972/04/10	Southern Iran	5,054	7.1
1976/11/24	Turkey-Iran	5,000	7.3
1980/10/10	El Asnam, Algeria	5,000	7.7
1998/05/30	Afghanistan-Tajikistan	4,000	6.6
1981/06/11	Southern Iran	3,000	6.9
1980/11/23	Southern Italy	2,735	6.5
1966/08/19	Varto, Turkey	2,529	6.8
1992/12/12	Flores, Indonesia	2,500	7.5
1999/09/20	Taiwan	2,400	7.6
1975/09/06	Turkey	2,300	6.7

Date	Location	Deaths	Magnitude
2003/05/21	Northern Algeria	2,266	6.8
2010/04/13	Qinghai, China	2,200	6.9
1998/07/17	Papua New Guinea	2,183	7.0
1975/07/17	Haicheng, China	2,000	7.0
1991/10/19	Northern India	2,000	7.0
In Comparison			
2013/10/14	Boho, Philippines	167	7.1
2016/04/16	Muisne, Ecuador	654	7.8
2016/04/14 and 16	Kumamoto, Japan	48	7.0
2014/04/01	Iquique, Chile	6	8.2
1964/03/28	Alaska, US	128	9.2
1971/01/17	San Fernando, CA, US	65	6.6
1994/01/17	Northridge, CA, US	60	6.7
1959/08/18	Montana, USA	28	7.3
1992/06/28	Landers, CA, US	3	7.3
1975/11/29	Hawaii, US	2	7.2
2003/12/22	Central California, US	2	6.6

*This is the second deadliest earthquake in world history; the PRC official figure of the death toll is 242,769, but experts' estimation is 655,000. The official fatality figures of other PRC earthquakes are believed to be underreported significantly as well. The deadliest ever earthquake in human history also happened in China—the magnitude 8 Shaanxi Earthquake in 1556 that killed 830,000 people. Of the top fifteen deadliest earthquakes ever, China had five. The deadliest earthquake in US history was the 1906 San Francisco Earthquake (magnitude 7.9), which killed 3,000 people. (*Sources:* U.S. Geological Survey data: accessed June 2021).

when in action."[78] In the PRC, according to its own experts, "inhuman and cruel" urban designs, public utilities, and social services seem commonplace.[79] Civic and private groups and efforts for disaster relief and emergency aid, such as the widely seen and praised Blue Sky Rescue teams, which meet a key demand, have unsurprisingly been greeted with suspicion by the CCP and often dismissed, discouraged, and even disallowed by the government.[80]

In addition to the poor management of natural disasters and accidents, the CCP-PRC party-state has caused many very deadly catastrophes, including the Great Famine (1958–1962), which starved over 37 million to death, and the numerous instances of political violence and purges that killed tens of millions more. Countless industrial and construction accidents, big and small, have led to massive death tolls, from the preventable collapse of the Banqiao Dam of Henan Province in 1975, which killed over 240,000 and is ranked the "world's deadliest man-made disaster ever," to the 2015 "super explosion" in Tianjin City, which killed and maimed many hundreds.[81] "Due to over deforestation" for timber, massive floods devastated a county in "the national natural preservation zone" many times in recent years; one such flood in 2002 "affected" all of the 35,000 residents and killed 237. In July 2021, mismanagement of flood discharge and collapse of reservoirs, even with advanced warning about torrential rain, appeared to be responsible for flooding Zhengzhou, a metropolis of 10 million in the central province of Henan, causing hundreds of deaths. Moreover, the fatality numbers were "indeed" underreported by at least one-third, according the government itself.[82] For years, many Chinese experts have worried about major manmade mega flood disasters waiting to happen every rainy season: China now has the world's largest number of reservoirs and high dams, including "the unprecedented and unparalleled concentration of many 200-meter high dams" of cascade reservoirs on rivers located in earthquake zones; 95 percent of all these dams "are built before the 1980s with the backward technology of earth-rock embankment rather than [more solid] concrete gravity" and are "highly dangerous." The most controversial and consequential of such concerns, other than about the cascade dams, which could fail in a devastating chain reaction, has been about the Three Gorges Dam, which could allegedly kill millions should it "very possibly" fail.[83]

In 2020–2022, to deal with the COVID-19 pandemic, which started in China in November–December 2019, exacerbated if not directly caused by the party-state's traditional policy of information control and suppression, Beijing relied on harsh lockdowns of numerous cities of multi-millions of residents including Shanghai, the largest metropolis with 25 million people, which is also China's financial and economic center and the only provincial unit that balanced its budget and did not need a fiscal bailout by the central government. Nationally, the CCP launched and sustained omnipresent and invasive surveillance, mandatory and exhaustive PCR (polymerase chain reaction) testing, extensive and even "preemptive" quarantines, a near-total ban of international travels, various games of numbers for the purpose of scoring points internationally, and meticulous censorship and propaganda. All this has fueled jingoism, social spasms and discords, truth- and data-oblivion, and anti-intellectualism, positioning the CCP-PRC a "leading role" in the world in spreading misinformation and disinformation about the virus, according to observers.[84]

The PRC's reaction to the pandemic since 2019 seems to confirm once again how suboptimal and even disastrous the party-state is in dealing with "natural" disasters, commonly aggravating the impact of destruction, injury and death. First, the CCP's second-nature suppression of the "bad" news of the virus enabled the outbreak of a global pandemic, as I have demonstrated earlier in the Introduction of this book; then the party-state resorted to panicky and draconian measures by creating the equivalent of a self-sustained national incarceration and international isolation, the world's longest in the global pandemic. It did so expectedly without much due process or public reasoning and resulted in dubious benefits to people's health and overall wellbeing. The rather familiar style of the "people's war on virus" demonstrates a "regardless of cost" expending of resources, manpower and government authority, seriously negative impact on the Chinese economy notwithstanding. These politics-driven draconian policies are backed with scant scientific discourse and using dated knowledge and inferior vaccines for an unrealistic and perhaps unnecessary aim of "zero-virus."[85] The methods used often appear to defy basic logic: to prevent the spread of a very contagious airborne virus, tens of thousands people (including the elderly and even infants) are made (sometimes by physical force) to congregate for hours, often repeatedly (anecdotally, for many hundreds or even over a thousand times in just two years), for PCR testing. Those deemed "close contacts" (at even hundreds of yards apart), along with symptomless people who have tested positive for the virus, are moved out of their homes to live collectively in congested makeshift quarantine camps, the so-called *fangchang* (mobile cabins) with abysmal conditions, where children and infants are sometimes separated from their parents.[86] Chemical disinfectants with unknown but likely serious side effects are dispersed on a massive scale throughout the cities and inside homes. Medical staff, police and "volunteers" are permitted to move around in white gowns that may or may not work, but countless homes, buildings and city blocks are locked and even welded shut for days and weeks like maximum security prisons, with often insufficient or even no supplies for basic sustenance. Many hospitals and even emergency rooms are closed, ignoring all other medical needs and resulting in many reported extra deaths—likely only the tip of the iceberg.

All this has demonstrated the CCP's awesome power of mobilization and social control but also revealed the regime's suboptimal governance in coping with disasters, and likely produced far more suffering and death than what the virus would have.[87] A team of PRC researchers found, for example, that overall mortality surged 56 percent in Wuhan city during its three-month lockdown in 2020, with over 68,000 "excess deaths"; for example, deaths from noninfectious diseases jumped 29 to 100 percent, and deaths from suicide and falls rose 66 percent and 43 percent, respectively.[88] Moreover, according to Chinese reporters, the party-state was responsible for "deliberate cover-ups and distortions, blind xenophobia, and baseless misinformation," with "very serious consequences" for the Chinese people and other nations using the inferior PRC-made vaccines, rather than the more effective mRNA vaccines.[89] As of this writing (fall 2022), China, the country where the pandemic started three years ago, is still enduring the longest and likely the heaviest impact of the virus in the world, unable to develop significant new and improved vaccines, medicines, or methods to manage the pandemic, while the pandemic has ended in nearly every other country.[90]

Another perhaps more insidious and long-lasting cause of death for the Chinese people as an indirect or even direct result of government policy is smoking. Tobacco use is socially, politically, and economically entrenched in the PRC. As such, the government has few incentives to reduce it. As mentioned earlier, the state tobacco monopoly is by far the largest single source of tax revenue. The state-owned China Tobacco directly employs over half a million people at a much higher than average wage and indirectly hires more than 20 million workers, including tobacco farmers. The PRC now has at least 300 million smokers, over one-third of the world's total, with over one million smoking-related deaths every year; 27 percent of all Chinese older than fifteen and 51 percent of all males are smokers with more than 68 percent of all Chinese regularly exposed to second-hand smoke.[91] The pervasive problems of unsafe consumer goods in general and the horrific safety of food and medicine in particular have led to untold pain, suffering and illness, and countless premature deaths in the PRC for many years, with seemingly little hope for relief as long as the CCP leaders enjoys their special provisions.[92] Despite the rising awareness of problems, and massive funds pouring in, garbage disposal and recycling are so poorly managed that even Beijing, the favored and showcased capital, has remained "a city besieged by waste" and toxins, according to foreign observers.[93]

More broadly, the energy and food security of the Chinese people, which was always insufficient and problematic from 1949 to the mid-1980s, have recently aroused renewed concern. Beijing has always called food security its "lifeline" and "top priority of governance." But the PRC was only 83 percent food self-sufficient in the 2010s and that percentage is declining, not quite constituting a crisis of food security but suggesting precariousness in the food supply. Moreover, the official statistics of grain production are likely to be significantly inflated at several levels.[94] Many anecdotal reports show the inflated numbers, inedible quality, and massive theft of grain stockpiles in state-owned warehouses, which are constantly plagued by corruption and mismanagement.[95] More than 80 to 85 percent (89 million tons in 2019) of soybeans, a staple of the Chinese diet and a critical feed for pig farms, is imported annually from faraway places like the United States, Brazil, and Argentina.[96] Though self-sufficient in petroleum before 1993, the PRC quickly developed a dependence on oil imports, becoming the world's largest oil importer in 2013 and importing 70 percent of its oil by 2018. The PRC's dependence on imported natural gas also jumped from zero in 2005 to over 40 percent in 2018.[97] Most of the imported oil travels from the Middle East and Africa, over long sea lanes through the Indian Ocean and the Malacca Strait.

The Elusive Happiness

Even with the world's second largest economy as measured by GDP, the PRC has a per capita GDP/income that is below the world average and an HDI score just around the world average; nearly half of the population is still living in poverty by international standards. These already very average numbers do not fully reveal the actual, even lower real living standard and the dismal quality of life under the China Suboptimality of the CCP-PRC. The world-record vertical and horizontal inequalities and the deficient governance in a host of areas from public security, personal safety, food and road safety to disaster relief are all profoundly detrimental and a source of widespread torment for the majority if not all of the Chinese people.

A PRC citizen, for example, must spend countless hours and enormous energy to apply for, obtain, carry, update, and produce a total of 400 (103 of which are considered "common") government permits, ID cards, and documentation ranging for basic ID to permission to give birth.[98] Chinese access to the boundless information and services in cyberspace is among the most restricted and censored in the world. Only China, Iran, and North Korea now fully block the world's top three social media platforms. About 20 percent of nearly 30,000 domains in the world (or 163 of the 1,016 Alexa Top 1,000 websites) are blocked in the PRC.[99] Chinese social media platforms such as WeChat, Microblog, and Tik Tok are routinely and heavily monitored and censored; content and user's accounts are often deleted with no notice or rationale. In the mid-2010s, Mainland Chinese paid more for internet access than all other East Asian countries, including the much richer Hong Kong and Japan (10 to 13.5% of total income on average, compared with 1 percent in OECD countries and 8 percent in East Asian-Pacific countries). Yet the PRC's WiFi broadband speed ranks eighty-second in the world, way below average. Web censorship is likely a key reason behind all of this. Even in the cosmopolitan city of Shanghai, access to the permitted foreign websites is slowed or blocked behind a paywall.[100] The censorship of the Great Firewall has created a parallel cyber universe for the Chinese people that often misinforms and misleads. Yet despite this high level of surveillance, cyberspace in the PRC, strangely enough, is rife with relentless crimes such as fraud and hacking. Baidu, the monopoly search engine, remains a poor substitute for Google, with a reportedly backward, overpriced, and substandard service.[101]

The US-based Freedom House constantly ranks the PRC as one of the least free countries in the world, together with North Korea and Somalia. The France-based Reporters Without Borders ranked the PRC 175 out of 180 in its World Press Freedom Index in 2014, and 177 out 180 in 2020. A Sweden- and Germany-led team of 2,000 international researchers ranked the PRC 162 out of 177 in its Academic Freedom Index in 2022, among the "least and declining" in the world, below Iran and Tajikistan.[102] The Swiss-based World Economic Forum ranked the PRC in its Global Gender Gap study at 87 out of 142 countries in 2014, and 107 out of 156 in 2021, sandwiched between Venezuela–Nepal and

Uganda–Myanmar. An IMF study concluded that "labor market barriers for women have increased over time" in the PRC. Despite the official slogans and gestures towards gender equality, as I reported earlier in this book, the CCP-PRC has never had any female top leaders (members of the Politburo Standing Committee) in its entire history. Only 3 to 8 percent of senior cadres have been females.[103]

The United Nations-sponsored World Happiness Index ranks the PRC at 93 out of 153 in 2013, and 84 out of 149 in 2020, considerably below the world average and sandwiched between the Philippines–Turkey and Mozambique–Turkmenistan, behind Ghana, Nepal, and Congo that are much poorer economically (see table 3.5).[104] Subjectively, the Chinese people seem to have a deep feeling of unhappiness, as seen in the few surveys and reports ever attempted. In September 2006, a major

Table 3.5. Happiness Ranking in Comparison

Country	Happiness Index 2012 (0–10)	World Ranking (n = 156)	Happiness Index 2020 (0–10)	World Ranking (n = 149)
United States	7.08	17	6.95	19
South Korea	6.27	41	5.85	62
Taiwan	6.22	42	6.58	24
Japan	6.06	43	5.94	56
Vietnam	5.53	63	5.41	79
Hong Kong	5.52	64	5.48	77
Russia	5.46	68	5.48	76
World Average	5.16	(84)	5.45	(80)
Turkey	5.35	77	4.99	104
Philippines	4.99	92	5.89	61
China	4.98	93	5.34	84
Mozambique	4.97	94	4.79	115
Turkmenistan	5.63	59	5.07	97

Note: The Happiness Index has been a team effort to quantify happiness since 2012. "Taiwan" and "Hong Kong" were changed in 2017 to "Taiwan Province of China" and "Hong Kong S.A.R. of China" in the reports, suggesting the effective influence of the PRC on the team. (Source: WHR 2013–2021).

PRC web portal, the Guangzhou-based *Wangyi*, was reported to have conducted a twelve-day opinion survey asking "if there is a next life, would you want to be born as a Chinese again," and found (before the survey was shut down by censors) that 64.7 percent of the 11,271 Chinese polled "do not want to be Chinese again in the next life," mostly for the reason that "a Chinese lacks human dignity in life." Almost ten years later, as many as 56.3 percent of Chinese surveyed simply wished "to be reborn in another place."[105] In 2014, a Peking University survey reported that 72.3 percent of lower-middle income youth in the PRC were "feeling unhappy" about their lives.[106] In 2018, the authorities had to formally denounce a rumor alleging that some monks in Kunming, the capital of Yunnan Province, would add a special prayer at Buddhist funeral ceremonies for "guaranteed reincarnation in the United States" for an extra ¥500 ($73).[107]

An important reason for this widespread discontent seems to be the serious gender imbalance in the PRC.[108] The imbalance is the result of the grand social engineering experiment of coerced birth-control implemented since the 1970s, which, in combination with an entrenched cultural preference for male offspring, led to selective abortions and female infanticides and abandonments, in addition to creating many other demographic problems like premature aging of the society.[109] The "abnormal" mortality rate of female infants, always high in the PRC, jumped from 10 percent in the 1970s to 60 percent in the 1990s as a direct result of the tightening of the birth control policy, according to a study by PRC scholars. China's gender ratio at birth "was within the normal range of between 103 to 107 [male per hundred female] throughout the 1960s and 1970s. But [. . .] climbed from 107.4 in 1980 to 116.9 by 2000 and has been around 120 since 2004."[110] Many "bachelors only" villages have emerged where large number of males simply have no prospect of finding mates, other than resorting to woman abduction and trafficking.[111]

Shortage of medical care has been another chronic problem. While the GDP has exploded from 1978 to 2014, per capita hospital beds and doctors have declined by one-third in Shanghai, one of the most developed regions in the PRC.[112] Perhaps due to improved reporting and general awareness, China's percentage of mentally ill citizens grew from 2.7 percent of the adult population in 1950s to over 17.5 percent in the mid-2010s, totaling 173 million people. However, there is reportedly an "outrageous lack" of psychiatric facilities and staff.[113] Additionally, perhaps because of environmental pollution and inadequate prenatal care, the "number of China's babies with congenital defects has soared over the past decade, with nearly 900,000 such cases reported each year" and "at least 100 thousand children are abandoned each year. Most are disabled and many are girls," as reported in a PRC newspaper.[114] In 2020, the official Chinese Academy of Sciences released research reporting that about a quarter of young Chinese have depression, and 40 percent of high schoolers are "depressed" (about 11 to 13% of them "have severe depression"); the national rate of depression was also reported by the Chinese researchers at 6.9 percent (with 65% being women), "increasing 120 times in the past 20 years"; all these figures seem higher than in the US and much higher than the world average.[115]

The suicide rate in China in the twenty-first century has been reported by researchers at twenty to twenty-three per 100,000, much "higher than the official [PRC, and hence the WHO] data" of eight to ten, twice the rate in the United States (11–14), and more than double the world average of nine to ten. Very unusually, the suicide rate of the rural population in China is three times higher than that of the urban population; the suicide rate of females is 25 percent higher than that of males while, in other countries, male rates are typically three to four times higher. In the late 2010s, a "shockingly high and rising suicide rate" of rural elders was reported by PRC scholars—in a rapidly aging society severely lacking financial support and medical care for seniors, many villagers simply told the fieldwork researchers that, "here, we don't have any elderly who died naturally."[116] In the West, more than 90 percent of people who commit suicide have mental illness; in China, that rate is "at most 63%."[117] The pattern of numbers game discussed earlier in this book aside, all these peculiarities seem to suggest certain special and strong socioeconomic and psychological duress felt acutely by the disadvantaged rural population, women, and the elderly.

In addition to the marginalized women, the ethnic minorities and the various lesser populations under the *hukou* system (which rigidly stratifies and excludes people), the mentally ill and the victims of natural or human-made disasters, the large number of people with physical disabilities (officially reported at 85 million while the real number "should" be as many as 210 million), have become mostly "invisible" in the PRC, hiding from hardships and prejudices that seem extensive and often deadly. Physically disabled people lack the visibility, opportunity, and connivences that many other societies commonly provide. Popular entertainers, literature and art, and the official cultural-entertainment industry are often seen exploiting people with physical disabilities and other disadvantages as an endless source of cheap laughter.[118]

It is not surprising, as a Chinese study concluded in the mid-2010s, that the PRC's "national image is declining," causing a chronic decrease in the numbers of foreign tourists, "due to the ever-serious pollution, growing inequality, corruption, and lack of security and safety."[119] As a reflection of foreigners' assessment of life in China, US military and diplomats get hazardous-duty or hardship-duty pay when stationed in the PRC, meaning that China is treated as equally dangerous to one's well-being as the world's poorest countries, active war zones, and harshest terrains.[120]

Voting with Feet

Chinese people, like all peoples, are not really hardwired to "eat bitterness" boundlessly and infinitely. Chinese private life and family values struggled to continue even during the Mao era.[121] When pushed to the limit, Chinese are also liable to quit, protest, or resist. The Chinese people in the PRC, even facing tight information control, draconian repression, and an unrelenting indoctrination of stoicism, have always attempted what Albert Hirschman has called to "voice and exit."[122] The nature and the power of the CCP-PRC party-state have rendered the voicing option costly and dangerous and with very limited effect; consequently, massive, creative, and ever-larger emigration waves well up whenever and wherever possible, to all places including "less developed" countries in Southeast Asia and Africa.[123] Even during the totalitarian Mao era, highly risky and often deadly "illegal" emigration and refugee waves occurred at a large scale, mostly destined for the nearby Hong Kong.[124]

In the present, illegal migration from the PRC has continued, but has now taken the form of well-organized, highly lucrative, but still deadly human trafficking. The yearly number of illegal emigrants is unknown but is probably significant.[125] In 2015 alone, Beijing reported that PRC citizens caught attempting to illegally emigrate to other countries jumped 165 percent.[126] Starting in the early post-Mao period, the PRC climbed to the position of the world's seventh largest source of international emigrants within the course of a decade. It was the fourth largest by 2013, with a total of over 11 million PRC citizens who permanently emigrated in the three decades prior to 2019.[127] Contrary to the general pattern of international emigration, rapid economic growth has actually sped up the massive emigration from the PRC. The PRC became the largest source of immigrants to the United States in the mid-2010s with 147,000 annually, outnumbering Mexico by 18 percent and the United Kingdom by 27 percent.[128] Nonimmigrant visitors from the PRC to the United States also grew rapidly, from 201,000 in 1999 to 528,000 in 2009, and 1.04 million in 2019, with about 15 to 24 percent more each year refused by US visa officers.[129]

Similar to emigrants from many developing countries, Chinese emigrants are often the brainiest and best educated. In late 1978, the PRC sent a vanguard group of fifty-two students to study in the United States.[130] Soon afterward, nearly every top university in the PRC became a preparatory school for foreign (especially American) graduate schools, with the unspoken understanding that "even the most enduring and bitterness-eating Chinese intellectuals cannot live [well] in China."[131] Peking and Tsinghua, the two best-known universities in the PRC, became the two largest feeders to PhD programs in the United States, surpassing the University of California at Berkeley in 2006.[132] In the 2010s and 2020s, about 20 percent of their graduates (or an incredible 76 to 80% of "high tech majors") study abroad each year.[133] In 2013 alone, over 413,000 Chinese students, including an increasingly number of college, high school and even primary school students, went abroad to study.[134] From 1997 to 2014, Chinese students studying in the United States increased sixfold, reaching more than a quarter of a million, more than the number of students from Europe, South America, Africa, Australia, and elsewhere in North America combined (or twice as many as from India), accounting for nearly one-third of all foreign students in the United States. The figure further increased to over 369,000 in 2020.[135] Pre-COVID pandemic, an estimated one million Chinese students were studying in the West.[136] In summer 2021, when the United States resumed issuance of student visas in China (still amidst the pandemic), over 57,000 were issued in the first two months, surpassing the pre-pandemic record despite the tenser relationship between Beijing and Washington.[137] Such a clear and massive *vote by feet* by the young represents a massive outflow of raw talent and educational investment.

Unlike many other sending nations, Chinese students tend to not return home after graduation. Official PRC figures have recorded a declining rate of students, mostly Masters and PhD degree earners, returning home after graduation, from 41.18 percent in 2000 to 27.98

percent globally in 2008.[138] This decline has stabilized and even reversed somewhat in recent years, as more Chinese students have gone abroad just to get a Bachelor's degree and return. By 2013, out of a total of 2.64 million PRC students who have studied abroad since the late 1970s, 1.09 million returned.[139] For those degree earners in countries that take in immigrants, the return rate of Chinese students remains very low, since "the main goal of most students studying abroad is to emigrate." In 2002 to 2007, only 3 to 6 percent of Chinese students with American doctorate degrees returned to the PRC, declining from 4 to 11 percent in the 1990s and far lower than the percentages of returning Indians (19%), Taiwanese (57%), Koreans (59%), Japanese (67%) and Mexicans (68%). In 2019–2020, 79 to 85 percent of PRC students with PhD degrees in STEM wanted to stay in the US. The same pattern remains that "Chinese students who receive their doctorate degrees in the United State are more likely than students from any other country to stay there," as reported by the journal *Nature*.[140]

To attract educated Chinese talent back to the PRC for a variety of purposes, including acquiring the latest technology and boosting the regime's political legitimacy, the PRC has devised and funded many elaborate recruitment schemes targeting the so-called returnees homophonically nicknamed in Chinese as the "sea turtles."[141] The most prestigious and expensive have been the Thousand Talents and Hundred Talents plans, orchestrated by the CCP's Central Organization Department since 2008. These plans aimed to reclaim top overseas talents, before they went into hiding in 2020 due to increased US scrutiny.[142] The significant fraud and corruption involved in these prestigious plans aside,[143] it seems that the efforts have lured mostly sojourning workers often cheating on and stealing from their foreign employers for easy and significant pay and perks offered by the PRC government.[144] The overwhelming majority (68.4% by 2012) of the "patriotic" returnees kept their foreign passports or green cards, and thus became known as "fishing seagulls."[145] Often viewed, not entirely unfairly, as contributing to academic corruption in the PRC, the much-showcased sea turtles and seagulls are dismissed by many natives I interviewed as "the leftovers" or "the eliminated" from the American-Western skilled-labor markets,[146] though the returnees may have in fact helped to transform and upgrade the PRC technologically in many important ways.[147]

Unlike most other countries with net emigration, China's emigrants include the rich, various established elites, and members of the urban middle class in addition to the more typical ambitious young students, poor and desperate laborers, and fortune seekers.[148] CCP officials have actually led the flight: Legal emigration aside, tens of thousands of party-state officials illegally "escaped or disappeared" into foreign countries with a reported ¥800 billion to ¥2 trillion ($118 to 290 billion) in funds during the period of 1993–2013 (6,694 cases in 2008 to 2013).[149] A shocking 60 to 74 percent of China's rich and upper-middle class, including the majority of China's super rich and often also CCP members, are reportedly seeking or have already obtained foreign residency or a non-PRC passport—a phenomenon that is unprecedented and unparalleled in human history. Perhaps only the exodus of Russian oligarchs under the reign of Vladimir Putin comes close. In some "hot" destinations like the United States, Canada, Australia, and New Zealand, rich Chinese now account for three-quarters to 90 percent of all applicants for immigration by investment.[150] Since 1992 when the US EB-5 Program started, PRC citizens have constituted 67 percent (86% in 2014) of all immigrants by investment under the program. This percentage grew 95 percent in 2008 to 2014, even though a PRC applicant has to wait six years for an available slot after paying from half to one million US dollars.[151] In 2014, when the Canadian government canceled its investment-immigration program, 57,000 rich Chinese (out of a total of 66,000 global applicants) were left out in the cold, and 1,355 filed lawsuits against Ottawa for damages.[152] In 2005 to 2014, babies deliberately birthed by affluent PRC mothers in the United States, a shortcut to emigration for the offspring taking advantage of American citizenship-by-birth laws, skyrocketed 100 times to reach 50,000 to 60,000 a year.[153] In 2014, a major designer of the CCP economic reform concluded that "two great exoduses" from the PRC have already taken place: a massive emigration of business and technological elites and a great capital flight.[154] Further, Chinese emigrants often seem willing to go just about anywhere, even places like Sub-Saharan Africa that are popularly viewed with stigma, condescension, and even racist stereotypes, but where 1 to 2 million PRC citizens now live (many illegally), reasoning that they "just want to get out of China."[155] In 2021, a Chinese essay on "why the rich choose to run away rather than reform [their own country]" concluded that "there are really no other safe choices."[156]

It is quite telling to consider how the PRC is viewed by foreign countries and by its own people. Many Chinese escaping from the PRC take the arduous, costly and uncertain road of seeking political asylum, not infrequently with exaggerated or bogus reasons and documents. Anecdotally, some PRC asylees seem to have the tacit approval of the CCP-PRC party-state, raising questions about what they really are.[157] Over the last quarter century (for which data is available), consistently one-third to 40 percent of all international asylum seekers in the US each year were citizens of the PRC, which has 19 to 20 percent of the world's total population. Out of the tens of thousands of seekers from the PRC each year in the twenty-first century, 3,000 to 10,000 were granted American asylum (over half of which were granted through court), more than any other country, including Venezuela, El Salvador, Egypt, Haiti and Ethiopia, and ten to twenty times more than its similarly populous but poorer neighbor India. The number of PRC citizens filing for political asylum in the United States has been steady with some slow annual growth, but the success rate has skyrocketed from less than 6 percent in 1997 to consistently over one-third in the 2010s, suggesting much improved utilization and manipulation of the US Asylum Program, especially through professionally prepared immigration litigations in local and rural American courts.[158]

PRC citizens also file for political asylum in large numbers in many other countries considered desirable destinations for emigration, like Australia, Canada, the European Union and New Zealand. Over 1,300 PRC citizens sought asylum in Canada in 2017, placing China among "the top five" origin countries. More than 9,000 cases in Australia in 2018 made the PRC by far the top origin country of asylees there. In 2019, over 6,000 cases of PRC asylum cases were pending in the EU. In 2018 to 2020, 69 to 117 PRC citizens each year filed asylum cases in New Zealand, accounting for 17 to 23 percent of all cases, with about half succeeding. Other than in New Zealand and the United States, the PRC political asylum seekers in countries around the world seem to have a less than 10 percent chance of success.[159] Sporadic press releases show that, in neighboring Japan, the number of PRC political asylum seekers placed China in the top five nations of origin in the 2000s along with Myanmar, Iran, Turkey, and Pakistan. In 2017, PRC asylees in Japan increased by 102 percent over the previous year to 315.[160]

For those without the means, opportunity or will to emigrate, short travels outside of the PRC (even just to Hong Kong, Macao, and the visa-free Jeju Island of Korea) offer attractive and rewarding chances to escape the higher-priced and substandard goods and services at home, especially for the Chinese people with rising disposable income.[161] While foreign tourists visiting the PRC peaked and started to decline after 2008, the number of Chinese tourists visiting other countries (60% of reportedly traveling for the purpose of shopping), jumped by double digits every year and is now three times greater than the number of foreign tourists visiting China.[162] Over 70 million citizens of the PRC went abroad annually in the 2010s, mostly tourists or students, while only one-third as many foreigners visited China. The PRC is the top origin country of students studying abroad worldwide, but the number of foreign students it hosts is only 10 percent of the world's average.[163] When unable to vote with their feet and physically exit their country, many PRC citizens then vote with their eyeballs to exit in spirit. In the 2010s, foreign films shown in theaters in China were typically limited by the government to only thirty-four a year; yet they earned about the same or more at the box office as the 600 or so movies made annually in the PRC.[164] The lottery may be another attractive psychedelic escapism: with an economy about 60 percent the size of that in the United States, the Chinese people spend about the same amount of money as Americans on lottery tickets every year.[165]

Watched, Worried, Wrathful

Needless to say, the overwhelming majority of Chinese people cannot escape their country through educational excellence, investment, illegal emigration, or asylum. Tight control of the press and the internet make opportunities to voice and vent very limited. Stoicism and cynicism can only do so much to calm the oppressed, the dissatisfied, and the unhappy.[166] Resistance through disloyalty and destruction become inevitable. Desperate resistance, revenge, and rebellion through violent, senseless and meaningless crimes and acts of sabotages seem to have become commonplace.[167] Therefore, as yet another key indicator of the China Suboptimality under the CCP-PRC party-state, Chinese domestic peace and social tranquility are evidently below average, even under the incredibly intrusive and forceful watch of the world's largest police-state.

As reported earlier in the book, the PRC maintains by far the largest police force in the world as well as numerous other security forces, spending more on domestic security than national defense since at the latest 2011. The police officers (all of whom are state employees and granted the prestigious urban residency) are assisted by the much larger contractual "police assistants" force.[168] Escapist social media like the popular WeChat have become powerful tools for the PRC police to surveil and control people and their minds. The police apparently even know and record the passwords of personal WeChat accounts, as evidenced by the fact that they permanently deleted a long-standing account in the United States "within 45 seconds" of the password being changed to "FxxkCCP89."[169] In 2014, the PRC formally launched "Sesame Credit," which was supposedly an imitation of the consumer credit records employed in the West, but was actually a system that applies a "Citizen Score" of trustworthiness, ranking everyone through an official, centralized blend of one's financial and spending history, political conduct, police records and reviews, and other "relevant factors."[170] This is akin to the personal dossier (*dangan*) system of the Mao era, which monitored and controlled everyone's life chances. Widespread surveillance cameras, with the latest facial-, body shape-, and walking-recognition technology, have made the horrific scenes of the novel *1984* into a reality in the PRC. With the "Brightening" Sky Net that runs one camera for every twenty Chinese to cover "completely every corner,"[171] the lives of one-fifth of humankind are ever more closely watched by the party-state. Life in a surveillance society akin to a fish tank may be something people can get used to, as different norms of privacy may be installed in people's mind over time; but, just like fish that still naturally enjoy small hiding spots and moment of solitude, it is hard for the people to acclimate to omnipresent, anonymous, weaponized tracking and recording technology. The toll on the Chinese mind, behavior, and health remains to be fully calculated and assessed, but is undoubtedly enormous, ravaging, and possibly even irreversible. As the late US Senator Frank Church famously said in 1975, a sophisticated and well-funded police-surveillance state with advanced technology makes "a tyranny total" and is "the abyss from which there is no return."[172]

Despite all the well-constructed, costly, highly lethal, and perhaps also the most elaborate and best equipped social control machinery deployed in the name of order and security, however, the Chinese people have to constantly worry about their lack of personal security and safety. As outlined in chapter 1 of this book, crime in the PRC, much of which is often senseless, brutal, vengeful and anti-social, is actually rampant and growing.[173] The people's sense of insecurity permeates Chinese society, with a strong sense of resignation to the lack of safety, peacefulness and social trust, which becomes especially notable when contrasted with broad attitudes in other Asian nations.[174] One PRC blogger asserted that "everyone feels like a victim, everyone victimizes others at the same time feeling fully justified."[175] In a 2015 study, out of fifty select mega cities in the world, the five PRC cities (Beijing, Shanghai, Tianjin, Shenzhen, Guangzhou) all ranked below average for safety and security, behind all six of the other East Asian cities (Tokyo, Singapore, Osaka, Hong Kong, Seoul, Taipei) and all the large metropolises in the United States (5), Canada (2), EU (6), and South America (2). In terms of livability, out of 140 rated cities, the PRC entries all ranked below average.[176]

Even politically ultra-sensitive "mass incidents" and riots happen at a world-class rate in the PRC, as I have reported in chapter 1 of this book. In addition to the jail-like metal bars and doors everywhere, almost every bank office, shop, and street corner displays large signs warning of fake bills, crimes, and conmen.[177] As long as they are "refraining from blocking the central work at the time" of the CCP, mafia-like gangs seem to thrive in the PRC.[178] Officials reported that e-fraud cases perpetrated through the phone and internet have exploded by 70 percent every year in the 2010s costing billions, with only a paltry 5 percent of cases ever solved. In 2013, cybercrime against consumers in China cost $37 billion, about the same as that in the United States ($38 billion) and thirty-seven times that in Japan, where up to 82 percent of cybercriminals caught in 2014 were PRC nationals.[179]

With perhaps the world's tightest control of firearms and sharp objects, including kitchen knives, the reported homicide rate in the PRC is lower than that in the United States but two to three times higher than that in Japan and South Korea: China reported 173,130 homicides from 2002 to 2012, more than the United States (144,599), where 60 percent of homicides involved private firearms.[180] With some of the harshest punishment against drug trafficking, often involving speedy and public executions, the PRC has a growing narcotics problem. The number of users of banned substances has been officially reported to have grown by double digits every year in the twenty-first century, with an increase of over 15 percent annually in 2007–2011, jumping to a 36 percent increase in 2015.[181]

Amidst sociopolitical control, population immobility, and limitations on individual privacy and choices, the instability of Chinese families and marriages has rapidly reached the levels of much richer and more open societies, with the national divorce rate growing nearly 40 percent within a five-year period. In 2019, the PRC national divorce rate climbed to the world-class height of 44 percent, with some provincial units registering divorce rates as high as 70 percent (see figure 3.1). However, studies found that Chinese women, unlike in many other countries with high divorce rates, are systemically disadvantaged and frequently mistreated in the divorce courts and litigations.[182]

Watched, worried, and wrathful, the bitterness-eating majority of the Chinese people simply have no way to change the PRC state's behavior politically (since meaningful elections, organization and assembly are prohibited) or legally (as an independent judiciary system is nonexistent). The PRC's much-touted education system has failed to provide sufficient upward mobility for the majority of the excluded.[183] There are few outlets (such as a free press or civil society) for meaningful venting and comforting. Under the CCP's suboptimal yet intrusive micromanagement of employment, income, promotion, and mobility, countless Chinese seem to have become exhausted or even crushed by the endless "bullshit jobs,"[184] especially the party-state's ever-changing and evermore political mandates, like the incessant quizzes based on memorizing the latest party lines.[185] The high-pressure boiler of PRC society naturally engenders persisting and deepening despair and desperation. It brews ever more hatred, along with irrational, unethical, and illegal acts including senseless crimes, destructive rampages, uncontrollable corruption and forgery by the government and the people, widespread distrust and

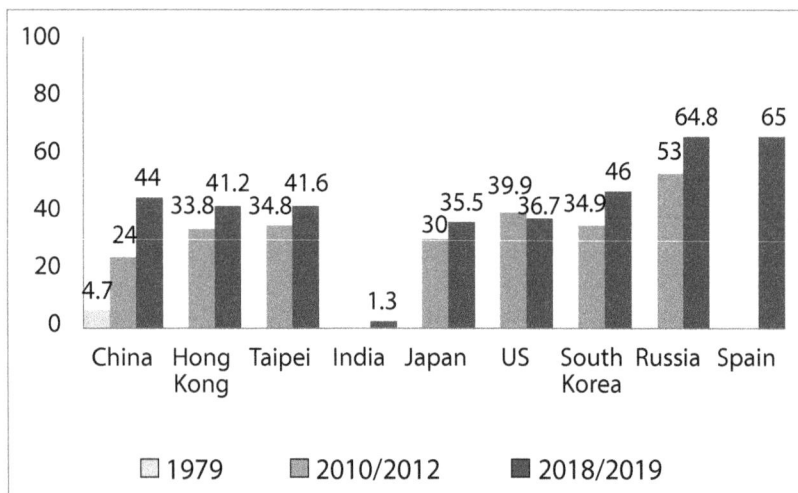

Figure 3.1. Divorce/marriage rates (percentage).

incivility, and opportunistic mob violence. Between the ruling elites and the people, a vicious but rather traditional loop appears to have formed, poisoning and corroding the Chinese society and mind with ever more real or perceived bitterness, injustice, rage, hostility, fear, and despair.[186] Even before the COVID-19 pandemic, the increasingly less favorable international environment prompted the CCP to demand yet more "longer, harder, and bitterer struggle" from the Chinese people.[187]

Since spring 2021, the phenomenon and philosophy of so-called *tangping* (lying flat or lying down, or nihilistic slackening), with its own "theory," has become very popular on PRC social media, despite the frantic censorship to erase the relevant postings, which resemble this: "since trying hard cannot get you what you want, it's better to just quit the rat race, which only rewards the power-holders, and to skate at the minimum to survive" as a couch potato and play possum. This seems to reflect and illustrate the depth and extent of passive resignation and resistance of many Chinese people,[188] akin to spontaneous strikes, withdrawal, disobedience, and noncooperation. Such a mentality of persistent despair and an attitude of passive resistance in open display found their early expression in the famous question "why my life is getting ever more hopeless?" which was first raised publicly in 1980. A subsequent nationwide "Pan Xiao discussion" about that question touched many nerves but was stopped by officials only a few months later, when the political utility of the discussion for top-level power struggles was over and the discussion started to query the rationality and legitimacy of the CCP-PRC regime itself.[189] Never fully explored and answered, such a sociopolitically loaded question has apparently persisted among many in the PRC ever since. In the 2010s and 2020s, various creative and colorful idioms and images tenaciously kept that soul-searching question alive in public discourse, especially in the cyberspace and among the youth, despite the CCP's tight censorship: from "wasted firewood," "Ge You/Beijing slouch," "Buddha-like slackness" and "Punk health" to "doom or bereavement culture."[190] Some PRC bloggers believed that "lying flat" was yet another "great awakening" of individual rights and freedom and "perhaps the most silent and most helpless [social] resistance in human history."[191] It is reported that many highly educated "sea turtles," returnees from studying abroad, have now increasingly felt frustrated by life back home and joined the *tangping* trend to become the so-called "sea trash."[192]

Such a sense of "loss" and resignation seemed to continue to permeate among the PRC elites in the 2020s, blending in with the trendy "run-study" (searching to emigrate), the so-called "petrel syndrome" (anticipating even wishing for ever-stronger gales, namely disastrous even catastrophic events) that reflects "the vacuum of faiths and despair of the masses," and the resolute attitude that "we are the last generation"—a calm but harrowing response to the police threat that "If you don't obey the orders [we will punish you and] three generations of your family"— during the lockdown of Shanghai in spring 2022.[193]

4

Spirit and Ecology

Culture, Ethics, and the Environment

After outlining Beijing's record of strong but suboptimal governance and impressive but inferior socioeconomic development, this chapter will continue to assess the CCP-PRC, with a focus on culture, spiritual life, and the environment in China. In addition to enduring a harsh dictatorship and perpetual bitterness-eating, the Chinese people have experienced the party-state's relentless effect on their rich culture and resplendent natural environment over the past seven decades.

From the very beginning, the CCP has attempted numerous and almost constant social- and mind-reengineering projects, attempting to remake not just the Chinese society and landscape but also the Chinese spirit and mind. Although the CCP-PRC party-state has been managed as a largely secular polity with populist impulses, it nonetheless resembles a powerful theocracy of Leninist–Stalinist atheism combined with Confucian-Legalism. Just like its overall performance in political governance and economic development, the CCP's projects involving the alteration of the Chinese culture and ecology have had a record of general suboptimality, frequent disasters, and much long-lasting desolation and devastation. The China Tragedy under Mao and the continued China Suboptimality have created and continued to have profound and adverse consequences, particularly on the minds of the Chinese people, including the elites. The vast impact of the party-state will reverberate socially, culturally, psychologically, and ecologically for generations. At its worst, as the daughter of a former CCP leader Luo Ruiqing concluded in her confessional, the PRC party-state professed to build a self-centered "eternal empire" but regressed to "animal instincts" and instead destroyed humanity and human dignity.[1]

With a performance not only average, suboptimal, and undesirable politically and socioeconomically for the Chinese people (but extraordinarily optimal for the regime's security and power), as the previous chapters of this book have attempted to show, the CCP-PRC party-state has also been quite damaging to the physical environment and spiritual life in China. Some of the injury and damage might still be treatable and reversible with a fundamental sociopolitical transformation and a thorough cultural detoxification, but sadly much of it is already incurable and irreversible, at least for the foreseeable future. Beyond the evident Westernization of many aspects of the Chinese culture over the past four decades—symbolized by the common lifestyle in the impressive urban centers, with their modern infrastructure and imported norms and ideas, including the Me Too campaign in the 2010s and 2020s[2]—there has been a deep and multifaceted state-caused destruction of the time-honored Chinese lifestyle, spirit, ecosystem, antiquities, social fabric, moral code, and intellectual creativity. Unfortunately, the Westernization of pop culture and lifestyle has so far accomplished little to establish the companion moral compass or value system, because the CCP has for political reasons fought mightily to resist and eradicate post-Enlightenment and post-Industrialization legal and ethical norms, such as respect for individual rights and contracts, equality and fair play, freedom of speech and faith, and cultural pluralism, which first emerged in the West.

Organized religions, ranging from the native Daoism and folk faiths to the imported Buddhism, Christianity (Catholicism and Protestantism), and Islam, all exist in the PRC with various degrees of Sinification, despite the almost constant political suppressions and persecutions, especially during the Mao era. In recent years, they have expanded considerably in the PRC as rising material wealth has led to and financed ever-more spiritual pursuits. The limited socioeconomic freedom that the CCP "returned" to the Chinese people in the post-Mao era has spilled over to allow more organized or self-organized religious activities, especially the less centralized and more egalitarian Protestantism. The PRC officially reported in the late 2010s that there were 200 million "religious" people in China, doubled the number in the 1950s; unofficially, that figure is estimated to be 300 to 350 million, or one-fifth to one-quarter of the total population.[3] Anecdotally, the so-called "hidden" and somewhat agnostic believers, even among the avowed "atheistic" CCP members, seem to be many more.

However, the CCP has continued its tradition of monitoring, infiltrating, marginalizing, subjugating, and "using" religious organizations. In a way akin to an imperial "atheist theocracy,"[4] the party-state forcefully registers all clergy and facilities, incorporates religious elites as state cadres at various ranks, and cracks down on "unlawful" or uncontrolled groups and practices, like the numerous Protestant "house churches" and the quasi-religious Falun Gong sect.[5] Beijing's policy of controlling the restive Muslin minorities with internment camps and repression of Islam in Xinjiang, in the name of anti-separatism and anti-terrorism, has been particularly extensive and harsh, drawing great international attention and indignation in recent years.[6] In 2016, Xi Jinping repeated the party line in openly calling for the tight control and extensive "use" of religion for the CCP's political objectives.[7] The powerful force of social norms and ethics generated by religion is systematically discredited and ridiculed, mostly in the name of science. And yet, the fundamental notion of science, independent inquiry and verification based on facts and logic, is diminished, as all PRC schools are directed by the CCP to teach no courses in logic and to tirelessly coerce conformity and obedience over individuality and innovation. With its omnipotent power and its omnipresent anti-Western politics, the CCP partocracy has caused many if not the majority of the Chinese people to lose the morality anchored in their traditional values based on an agrarian, paternalistic society, usually sustained by religious faith, while at the same time leaving them without the common sense and logic that constitute the basis for ethics in a secular and industrialized modern society. It has deformed the Chinese mind and environment, just as it has done to the Chinese economy and society, resulting in proliferating corruption, the obliteration of traditional morality, destruction of historical knowledge and relics, countless fake products and services, and appalling pollution of both the mind and the environment. In both the cities and the countryside, as foreign reporters have noted, "China's traditional social fabric has become shredded, [. . .] where families are falling apart, crime is soaring and the environment is killing people."[8]

To start, a form of cultural onanism, known as *zihai* or *yiyin* in Chinese, self-delusion and self-aggrandizement supported by fake history and pseudoscience, has considerably displaced the virtues of modesty, propriety, and reason, deeply corrupting both education and entertainment in the PRC. Some examples: Beijing officially boasts of "the four new great inventions" of high-speed trains, mobile payments, online shopping, and bike/car sharing. Senior official-scholars publish thick "discoveries" that Western peoples ranging from the ancient Egyptians, Greeks, and Romans to the modern English, French, and German all originated from central China. "Academic" conferences have been held to showcase the many "findings" about China as the "origin" of the entire Western culture, all the way from the Greek-Roman civilization, Judaism, the Christian Bible, and European languages, to the Enlightenment and modern science and medicine.[9] The PRC central government endorses the "science" that Chinese herbal medicine treats serious diseases better than allopathic medicine, including "curing COVID-19 with a 90 percent plus effectiveness."[10] The puerile fantasy tales of anti-Japanese TV soap operas, the so-called *kangri shenju*, which have dominated PRC screens since the 1990s, represent both an insult to people's intelligence and a lack of self-esteem coupled with an inferiority complex. In the 2020s, such stultification continued to producing farcical blockbuster, anti-American movies, regarding which a noted Chinese blogger, Luo Changping, who was mildly critical, was swiftly imprisoned.[11]

When pondering the rise of Chinese power and how to engage and manage it optimally, the world must consider the cultural and environmental impact of the CCP-PRC party-state, which behaves like a bull (or perhaps more precisely a ravaging ogre) with great ferocity in a china shop. The ruinous consequence of the CCP's model of governance and development on human minds and the environment is already felt far beyond Mainland China, affecting the entire planet and all of humankind.

The Officials-Standard and Society

Beyond physical and material assessments, it is challenging but imperative to gauge and compare the sociocultural impact of different governances vertically (time series) and horizontally (across nations) in our age of multiculturalism. As Jean-Jacques Rousseau classically argued long ago, "to form the most virtuous and enlightened, the wisest and best people" so as to ensure the "happiness of humankind" is "radically connected with politics, and that, upon whatever principles these were founded, a people would never be more than that which the nature of the government made them."[12] The history of culture, mindset, and ethics in the PRC, just as in the previous Chinese empires, has indeed been chiefly shaped, fundamentally determined, and powerfully sustained by the nature and operation of the government, a mighty authoritarian-totalitarian state that has inherited, regrouped, and magnified many of the traditional sociocultural features of a Qin-Han polity under the China Order.[13] "The new-normal of moral decay" in China today, argued a PRC scholar in 2022, is "the result of politics" and shaped mostly by "political institutions and government actions." The so-called "black box" power of culture in potently defining and confining human behavior is basically just the internalized sociopolitical and economic institutions through education, indoctrination, and socialization over time.[14]

Disguising their activities and intentions with imported jargons and symbols, the CCP's Qin-Han state has revived and sustained a dearth of individual character, moral compass, and truthfulness that was well observed in China before the twentieth century.[15] Many influential Chinese intellectuals have sharply criticized this cultural heritage and these norms as a so-called backward or corrupted "national character" (guomin xing), without an analysis of the peculiar Chinese sociopolitical system as the root cause of the spiritual and cultural decay and inertia.[16] They realize that the traditional Chinese moral codes, centered on the political norms of Confucian-Legalism rooted in a paternal-agrarian society, preserved or rejuvenated, are fundamentally and critically insufficient in China today.[17] To begin with, the deep moral problem of the absence of citizenship caused by the hukou (household registration) system has sustained an apartheid-like socioeconomic and cultural system in China, with a profound impact on people's norms and actions, perhaps less rigid but more omnipresent than the racially based apartheid in South Africa before the 1990s. The "moral qualities required in liberal, democratic societies," articulated by comparativists in ethics studies, have yet to take hold, while the traditional, native moral requirements are weak, abated, and even absent.[18]

The CCP autocracy, with its monopoly over all power and wealth, established from early on an officials-standard, using the rigid and bureaucratic ranks of the party-state as the standard for a centralized and hierarchical allocation of almost all resources, opportunities, and social stature. Nearly all successes, rights, and recognitions are measured and judged based on this standard. The unconstrained and unaccountable CCP rulers thus became the arbiters for all social norms and values, which have been subject to their often ad hoc and ever-changing wishes.[19] As expected, CCP-PRC officials, like the imperial officials before them, are inevitably and thoroughly selfish in maintaining and improving their positions based on the officials-standard. As I attempted to demonstrate in chapter 1, powerful state control and relentless "thought work" have long made the officials-standard along with its associated power fetishism the backbone of the PRC ethos.

To promote the ever-changing and often self-conflicting values and ethics at different times for its convenience and policy aims (mostly for the security and power of the regime), the CCP-PRC state constantly and unscrupulously rewrites history and moral codes. It produces countless illogical slogans and unabashed reversals, forces oblivion or amnesia through censorship and punishment, and propagates boundless misinformation and disinformation to justify and deceive—all truly making the PRC a gigantic and largely faithful copy of the fictional Oceania under Ingsoc as depicted by George Orwell in 1949.[20] The monopoly of the national "Network Newscast" (*xinwen lianbo*) by CCTV (China Central TV) traditionally and typically censors, distorts, and falsifies all sorts of news, even temperatures in its weather reporting so as to prevent work slowdowns on days that are too hot or too cold.[21] Third-party fact checkers like FactCheck.org, PolitiFact.com, and Snopes.com simply could not emerge, let alone survive, under the CCP censorship of the internet. Obscurantic fakery of history, as discussed in *The China Order*, the prequel to this book, unsurprisingly persists in China. For example, Xi Jinping openly declared in 2020 that China was "the home of oriental people, co-listed with Africa as the origin of humanity," directly contradicting the well-proven science on the origin of homo sapiens, which even PRC paleontologists and biologists have accepted for years.[22]

Everyone and everything in the PRC are converted or translated to and assessed or valued by official ranks and position; nothing is stable or permanent, or rewarding or socioeconomically meaningful without being well measured and recognized by the officials-standard. Political roles, social stature, information access, all sorts of perks and indulgences, and even basic rights and supplies are mostly if not all marked and rationed, often directly, by the officials-standard. Thus, every position with or without any real power or utility in the mammoth party-state apparatus has a clearly stipulated ranking or equivalent for "treatment" (*daiyu*). The entire society is stratified above the general masses with the likes of clerk level librarians or detectives, section-chief level surgeons or schoolteachers, deputy division-chief level monks or priests, bureau-chief level professors or CEOs, deputy-minister level biologists or bankers, and so on. The Party secretaries and presidents of all state-accredited universities have prefecture or deputy-prefecture ranks, with thirty-two of them ranked at the "deputy-ministry" level.[23] Self-employed businesspeople, artists, and performers, including martial artists, upon achieving success and drawing the notice of the party-state, are incorporated through the massive membership of the various layers of the rubber-stamp "people's congress" and "people's political consultation conference," to all have an appropriate and approved place and promotion according to the officials-standard. Favored singers and actors can be ranked as "major-generals" in the military, the equivalent of bureau-chiefs.[24]

As mentioned earlier in the book, the CCP-PRC has a world-leading-sized bureaucracy that monopolizes all the power, perks, and social stature in the country with additional, lucrative income from cronyism and nepotism. The PRC elites on the officials-standard live and behave like the nobles in the imperial time, yet only under the rule of their superiors and notably without the social norms and ethical constraints supposedly associated with the word nobility. The ruling elites in the PRC are every bit like the imperial ruling elites in the past but appear to be more corrupt and hypocritical, as the party-state officially pretends to believe in atheism, socialism-communism, egalitarianism, and "serving the people." They no longer justify their prerogatives through notions of heaven's will, religious morality, or patriarchal family values—these have long been the supposed and declared enemies of the CCP.[25] In people's minds, there inevitably grows the lack of a stable moral compass, ethical character, and introspection, all of which have been reduced or even decimated by vicious power struggles dressed as political campaigns, and the patchwork of official ideology that essentially worships only power and unscrupulous cynicism. Under a blanket moral relativism centered on the top leader of the party-state, legal and media scrutiny and constraints are generally missing, as are inner inhibitions based on faith, other than the politicized discipline inspectors and the unpredictable wrath of supervisors. The CCP-PRC ruling elites thus uniformly and consistently demonstrate how to act out of self-interest, while appearing to be obedient to superiors and ultimately the top ruler, however disingenuously and circumstantially.

Under such power fetishism, corruption, and unethical activities are both inevitable and necessary, perhaps at times and on issues constituting a flexibility even somewhat beneficial to raw capitalist economic development, featuring a seemingly paradoxical coexistence of "high corruption and high growth." This, however, is a costly externality of "exchanges of power for profit," and likely harms the economy overall, especially in the long run.[26] The fact that ostensibly every CCP-PRC official everywhere and at all ranks engages in endless corruption that is often "irrationally" outrageous and "inanely" oblivious in scale, methods, and length, according to a noted PRC sociologist, seems to suggest a mental sickness and a culture of "corruption for the sake of ever more corruption"—akin to a serious addiction to gambling or narcotics, as corruption and abuse of power and office have become "a spiritual life" in itself, and one of the few sources of "psychological ecstasy for the cadres" in the party-state. A "moral crisis" has thus colored both politics and social life in the PRC.[27] The China Tragedy under Mao, for example, forced millions of Chinese to openly and massively forge and deceive so as to avoid the unbearable political atrocity of being purged or "sent down." In the words of a PRC-based commentator who was later blacklisted, "the Chinese system since 1949 has been basically a system of bad coins driving out good coins," as described by Gresham's Law in economics, and has forced a national "competition to see who can be more idiotic" while remaining loyal to the ruler, thus creating perverse, race-to-the-bottom, social selections of ideas, actions, and policies, with grave consequences.[28]

Examples of personal betrayal, open deception and dishonesty, excessive exploitation and sexual harassment of subordinates and relatives, and insatiable greed have been set by the very top leaders throughout the Mao and post-Mao eras. The hallmark secrecy, deception, and hypocrisy of the many party leaders have delivered ever-more blows against social morals and common ethics, fundamentally causing "the failure of China's education [system]," according to a PRC writer.[29] A Taiwanese-American professor who lived in the PRC for decades concluded that "in 30 years [from 1982], all [I] saw on TV every day were lies," and the country "is governed by vicious cycles of violence and deception." Moral relativism and schizophrenic behavior appear commonplace in the PRC, especially among the elites.[30]

The rigid, unique, and centrally controlled officials-standard, as the only sociopolitical yardstick and ladder in a country where the state monopolizes just about all the resources, thus sanctions and promotes the same cultural and moral codes for the whole population beyond the officialdom. It may have been crucial in helping autocratic rulers remain in power and stabilize the party-state politically, but has unsurprisingly caused comprehensive corruption and moral decay throughout Chinese society. "Leading officials" of the CCP-PRC clearly have the most ability and fungibility to enrich and elevate their offspring, the so-called "Red (or Official) Generation II or III," in all careers in which they choose to prosper; other elites of various professions now also appear to unapologetically use blatant nepotism in their respective fields to give their offspring a shortcut to ascension into the so-called "Wealth (or Academia or Artisan) Generation II or III."[31] The scope and depth of corruption in the PRC appear to have far surpassed the legendary corruption of the imperial regimes in the past.[32] Even during the great spasms of the Cultural Revolution (1966–1976), when populist egalitarianism, puritanical communist rage, rationing of all daily necessitates, and political purges were taken to the extreme, various forms of fraud and corruption were still reportedly common among both officials and commoners.[33] In 2014, just one impromptu investigation of the real estate industry by the CCP's secretive discipline inspectors discovered serious corruption in 95 percent of localities under review.[34] The "exemplary" cases that the CCP's own media has endlessly paraded in the 2010s and 2020s to showcase its "great fruits of anti-corruption" only proved that shockingly boundless corruption of officials is everywhere and at all levels.[35] In 2022, a former "white glove"—a businessman running big businesses to enrich CCP leaders and officials as his cloaked patrons and even the "real" bosses—declared in an American TV interview that "Chinese businesspersons, big and small, all are and have to be white gloves for [CCP] officials"; the only difference is "the different rank of the officials" they serve and bribe.[36]

The undifferentiated, centralized, and total state monopoly of political power (with legislative, executive, and judicial powers fully centralized into one), social stratification, and unequal resource allocation have also caused the systematic suffocation of diversity, variety, and dissention, the foundation for meaningful competition and real innovation. The CCP polity thus appears to be the root and structural cause and the main mechanism for the deep and widespread cultural and moral degradation in the PRC, as well as the systemic lack of scientific and technological innovation among a huge population of otherwise highly creative human beings. One senior PRC scientist wrote in 2018 that, in China, "the fundamental obstacle to the development of science and technology is clear: ever since 1949, our state [government] from top to bottom has never understood science, especially engineering science (technology), has never respected science, and has never respected scientists. A series of political campaigns have aimed to hurt scientists, and extinguish the [individual] innovation of scientists."[37]

The CCP Pantheon of Demigods and Chiefs

As the self-labeled fearless and lawless rebel turned emperor, Mao Zedong perverted and destroyed classic Chinese culture and ethics in many ways. Under CCP rule, especially during Mao's reign, Chinese traditional institutions and norms of family, filial piety, and interpersonal fidelity were commonly maligned as evil "feudal values," while the imported Western values of citizenship, fraternity, and individuality were dismissed as rotten "bourgeoisie ideas." All of these values were to be mercilessly replaced by a complete sacrifice of *everyone* and *everything* for the leaders' momentary needs and policies, in the name of illusory and abstract communist ethics and the empty concept of "the people."[38] Fundamentally incapable of refuting the post–World War II ideas of democracy, freedom, rule of law, and individual rights, Mao and his successors have resorted to clever and extensive wordsmithery and legerdemains, with immeasurable and possibly irrevocable damage to integrity, logic, honesty, and truthfulness in China.

The CCP has traditionally labeled universal and traditional values with pejorative adjectives like "reactionary," "feudal," "bourgeois," "rightist," "Western," or "American," deeming them automatically evil and inapplicable in the PRC. At the same time, Mao justified every aspect of his incompetent and violent dictatorship through the empty terms "revolution," "the people," "proletarian," "leftist," "we Chinese," or "world communism."[39] Mao's successors inherited his unscrupulous obscurantism and sophistry, maintaining a "media schizophrenia," as an insider called it.[40] Even more impoverished in theory, the CCP now relies primarily on invoking "Chinese characteristics," "national rejuvenation," and "patriotism" to resist and discredit universal political and social values, continuing the trend of deep injury to integrity and morality in the PRC. A favorite tactic is to fight like Don Quixote against the windmill of a "Western" or "American" democracy, while pretending that the CCP's Qin-Han autocracy is a better, "Chinese-style" democracy, a "whole-process" democracy that is the real and the best democracy in the world.[41] Such a ploy manipulating nationalist emotions seems to be effective, as it is often echoed by many, even "liberal," Chinese scholars who seem to have stuck with their Sinocentric perspectives nourished by the traditional ideation of the China Order.[42]

Beyond the blind hierarchical loyalty and the total worship of and submission to political power based on force and ruse, nearly all of China's traditional social norms and values have been seriously insulted and damaged by the CCP's unrestricted actions. At times, such as during the Cultural Revolution (1966–1976), the paranoid Mao even denigrated the social norms of loyalty and obedience by manufacturing and manipulating the so-called "mass rebellion," smashing and displacing the state hierarchy, educational authority, and family bonds to safeguard and serve his personal dictatorship at all costs. Family members were often forced and incentivized to inform on and even publicly denounce each other for any perceived anti-Mao or anti-CCP acts or thoughts.[43] Education and enlightenment were systematically trashed and ridiculed so as to render the young ignorant, disrespectful, apathetic, and hateful—in order to cultivate the so-called "illiterate hooligans."[44] The CCP under Mao also systematically manufactured and propagated countless fictitious histories and phony models of both heroes and villains. Famous examples include the villain landlord Liu Wencai and the model soldiers Huang Jiguang and Lei Feng.[45] This obscurantism tenaciously continued after Mao's death. In 2019 and 2020, Beijing passed a series of rules banning any disrespect or defamation of the state-promoted "revolutionary heroes and patriots" or elements of "our national tradition," including Chinese herbal medicine. Fake "true stories" promoting the CCP's line and disparaging the United States that had been factually refuted long ago were still found in the officially mandated school textbooks in 2021.[46] In July 2021, for example, to fend off the pressure of an international inquiry, the CCP's media fabricated a fictitious "Swiss scientist critical of a COVID origins probe."[47]

Ethically challenged deeds, and even straightforward fakeries and grand plagiarism, are prominent among those in the CCP pantheon of demigods, starting with Mao himself. The widely circulated *Selected Works of Mao Zedong*, first published in the late 1940s, which collected Mao's essays in four volumes, has remained a ubiquitous and near-holy script in the PRC. Yet, it has been revealed by CCP archivists that the bulk of these essays are not Mao's work after all: of the 160 pieces, Mao is said to have only drafted twelve and revised thirteen, with the rest basically all written by Mao's comrades or secretaries. The same is true of many of Mao's widely circulated and praised poems. Mao's heavily doctored works and many other key CCP documents were commonly postdated or predated to propagate an unwarranted image of wisdom, vision, leadership, and talent.[48]

Mao's successors, perhaps personally pained by the total disregard of rules and morals, have attempted to restore some traditional Chinese cultural values and social norms, including a stable hierarchy and obedience, controlled meritocracy, and the Confucian-Legalist sense of predictability and fairness. However, the CCP continues to rule unscrupulously, as first evidenced by the 1976 palace coup d'état, which personally betrayed Mao only days after his death. Successive leaders have continued to discredit and dismiss law and ethics. The opaque and politicized use of the judicial system for extraction and suppression, the deliberate deception and imposed national amnesia about history and reality, and the endless concealment of countless state secrets have perhaps all simply showcased the lack of legitimacy of the regime as much as its lawlessness and unethicalness. Numerous Chinese (and occasionally official media) have concluded that it is impossible to enforce or abide by the law or promote social ethics as long as the lawmaker and enforcer, the CCP leadership, is above the law and ethics.[49]

In practice, today's CCP-PRC cadres appear to behave just like the imperial officials observed in the nineteenth century: "The governing class as a whole is not the best but the worst in the Empire. An intelligent Taotai [prefecture-level governor in the Qing empire] remarked to a foreigner 'the officials under the Emperor are all bad men and ought to be killed, but it would be of no use to kill us, as the next incumbents would be just as bad as we.'" More than a century later, one easily hears similar semi-confessionary and semi-rationalizing comments from CCP cadres at various ranks about their incompetency, corruption, lack of character, and abuses of power.[50] A hallmark corrupt practice in imperial China, the so-called "eating vacuous employment"—to inflate and fake the size of employment so as to pocket the pay for the nonexistent subordinates—for example, seems now widely in practice throughout the PRC government.[51] This habitual problem has evidently also permeated many state-owned entities from kindergartens, schools, colleges, hospitals, and enterprises to social service and welfare agencies.[52]

As has been amply revealed by countless books and articles often banned inside the PRC, just about every CCP-PRC leader and luminary, from Mao to his lieutenants, executioners, and even exonerated victims, including the officially enshrined and praised quasi-deities and demigods in the PRC pantheon like Chen Yi, Chen Yun, Deng Xiaoping, Li Xiannian, Liu Bocheng, Liu Shaoqi, Luo Ruiqing, Tao Zhu, Ye Jianying, and especially Zhou Enlai, all appear to have had serious character flaws and ethical deficiencies. They engaged in frequent betrayal, deception, pompousness, and concealment, and they harbored a deep sense of insecurity.[53] They, like Mao, have commonly disrespected life, dismissed both Chinese and Western moral codes, and exhibited unscrupulous selfishness. Traditionally, CCP leaders seemed to have almost all behaved like typical autocrats, passive-aggressive imperial servants, herdsmen, or head slaves. They themselves were also frequently reduced and brutally victimized by a system that offers them little personal independence or integrity; yet they often acted as Mao's willing and eager executioners in power struggles and purges.[54] Even the heavily censored or self-censored official or semi-official memoirs by the sociopolitical bigwigs, published or circulated since the 1980s in the PRC, have already yielded rich details about the corrupt, duplicitous, and unscrupulous lifestyle and behavior of the majority, if not all, of the CCP-PRC elites. These elites survived and thrived on double-talk and double dealing, with the commonly shared chronic symptoms of serious "nerve weaknesses."[55] Mao's personal physician and the former chief of the Zhongnanhai (CCP headquarters) medical bureau both recalled that "just about all of" the CCP leaders relied on heavy doses of sleeping pills.[56] Their personal and family lives were often understandably impaired: nearly all the marriages of the CCP leaders and cadres "I know are not good," recounted a nonagenarian insider in 2014, and spousal abuse and abandonment "are common phenomena."[57]

Of course, some of the CCP leaders, all unfortunately disgraced or purged, were clearly "better" even if still not quite "good enough." They had relatively more conscience and common sense, were less corrupt, more authentic and honest, capable of logical reasoning based on facts, with a sense of populist fairness and sharing considerable universal values and ideals. Some, like Hu Yaobang, Peng Dehuai, Zhang Wentian, and Zhao Ziyang, still clearly communist authoritarian leaders but not venerated at the highest altar of the CCP pantheon, have earned a good reputation and respect among the Chinese people (especially those who are informed) years after their purges and deaths, for their vision, open-mindedness, courage, and sacrifice in attempting political or policy changes and reforms.[58]

Perhaps as a sign of changing times, the systemic corruption of the CCP elites has evolved in recent decades toward the insatiable pursuit of wealth, in addition to power. Raw capitalism, naked materialism, and thorough cynicism have resulted in many officials running away to live comfortably in foreign (mostly Western) countries. Bribe taking, embezzlement, and direct power-money exchanges have become ubiquitous in the PRC. The highly disproportionate state concentration and monopoly of the PRC's economic gains and assets have greatly enabled unchecked political power-holders to legally, semi-legally (via so-called gray income), and illegally enrich themselves and their cronies, an ironic reversal of the CCP's nationalization of the Chinese economy under Mao. As a PRC dissident in exile accused: "In the first 30 years [of the PRC], the CCP used violence to confiscate every common folk's private property and turn that into so-called property of all people; in the 30 years after that, [the CCP] turned all people's assets into a very few officials' private property; two atrocities committed by the same party, unprecedented and unparalleled in human history." The degree and absurdity of the runaway greed and corruption of many CCP-PRC officials have indeed reached incredible levels; some have been revealed to hoard literally tons of cash and gold bars in their basements and secretly own "hundreds of housing units."[59] One already heavily censored "sample list of 120 corruption cases of senior officials during 1987–2010" shows that the post-Mao CCP-PRC leaders and officials have sunk deeply into the unethical abyss of corruption of various sorts, creatively and insatiably looting, embezzling, extorting, and conspiring to enrich and advance themselves and their families and associates, at the incredible expense of the people, the nation, and even the state and the ruling party itself.[60]

Recent years have seen frequent and expensive anti-corruption campaigns in the PRC. But they appear to have been selective and politicized, mostly in support of power struggles. In 2013 and 014, during the CCP's "rare storm" of anti-corruption, over forty-eight senior cadres of deputy-provincial or higher rank were purged. But those so-called "tigers" were all "from commoner families [with] none [. . .] identified as being members of what is known as the 'Red Second Generation' or 'Bureaucrat Second Generation,'" who have a political family background or links to the ruling elites. Such a burst of imperial rage, while effective for the purpose of terrifying, torturing, and abusing targeted officials, is inherently ineffective in controlling corruption.[61] As reported earlier, tens of thousands of CCP-PRC elites, from the very top down, continue to secretly hide billions of US dollars of opaque personal or family wealth offshore.[62] The ever-more numerous and harsher-sounding rules and decrees aiming at curbing corruption, such as the fourteen issued in 2013 alone, which, for the nth time, "seriously" ban the rather common practice of "purchasing offices and positions," and demand reporting the emigration status of the immediate family of senior officials (the so-called "naked officials," whose immediate family members have all emigrated), only reflect the hopeless depth and maddening scope of the corruption of the officialdom, which defy not just law or ethical codes but even basic common sense. A systemic "developmental corruption" and a "degenerative corruption" have now "paradoxically" and deeply intertwined with Chinese society, a scholarly study concluded.[63]

Corruption of the CCP-PRC cadres (including military officers) sometimes operates like a well-institutionalized and internalized "marketplace of graft." Offices and ranks are for sale as lucrative investments commonly financed through private lending, commercial loans, private business donations, and embezzled public funds. Many purchased offices quickly generate enough income to pay back the fee within the year and also yield handsome profits. Insiders have revealed that PLA-officer positions, from platoon leader to top commander, "all have price tags" for promotion, with over ¥20 million (US $3.2 million) required for a promotion to Lieutenant General.[64] Official media reported that for every million RMB in bribery received by the executive of a state-owned enterprise, over 100 million RMB in public funds are lost or wasted in addition to other incalculable damages and costs. Sporadic leaks from official sources show that 16,000 to 18,000 officials escaped abroad from the mid-1990s to 2011, taking with them at least ¥1 trillion in assets. Likely many more are stopped at the ports of exit. The record daily catch of fifty-one fleeing officials occurred during the twenty-four hours of September 30 to October 1, 2003. One insider estimated that each runaway official typically embezzles or takes bribes totaling $50 million, resulting in a total loss equivalent to 15 percent of China's GDP each year.[65]

Moral Vacuum, Amnesia, and the Mind

The CCP governance through force and ruse has resulted in and is nourished by the hypocrisy and schizophrenic behavior of just about every leader and senior cadre. A national decay of morality now appears to have affected both the elites and the masses. After generations of painful and deadly experience, the Chinese people have learned and internalized the CCP way of life, which has dismissed religion and religious morals, ruined the moral codes of China's traditional paternalistic agrarian society, and also rejected the rational morality of the modern, post-Industrial Revolution and post-Enlightenment West.[66] As self-professed atheists, the CCP leaders have adopted highly sinister and manipulative attitudes toward faith, inner morals, and sociocultural values. As reported earlier in this book, organized religions in the PRC have always been forcibly suppressed and subjugated or simply persecuted and eliminated, often physically. Individual rights, dignity, and independence are openly ridiculed and frequently decimated. In short, the CCP-PRC party-state has for decades scorned, muddied, and ruined both "Eastern" Confucian virtues and norms and "Western" liberal values and ethics. Tricks and deceptions for purposeful gains are often considered praiseworthy virtues and intellect. In 2007, for example, a former staff member publicly extolled how Zhou Enlai "wisely and skillfully" deceived the visiting Japanese Prime Minister Kakuei Tanaka in 1973, drinking lots of water from bottles of Maotai, a strong liquor, to demonstrate his "prodigious capacity for alcohol," in an attempt to literally intoxicate his guests of honor.[67]

Heavily censored and constantly rewritten official historical narratives are poor substitutes as sources of spiritual guidance and moral restraint. The CCP has attempted for over seven decades to replace traditional (Eastern) and modern (Western) morality and ethics, as well as faith-based socialization and norms, with the belief in a peculiar European radicalism, the "scientific, ultimate truth of the universe" of the Leninist–Stalinist version of Marxism imported from the Soviet Union.[68] The Chinese people have been brainwashed through the relentless "thought work" to become worker bees, or mindless screws in the socialist machine. Yet, as the China Tragedy and the China Suboptimality have amply proven, and the collapse of the Soviet Bloc has vividly illustrated, the imposed communist ethics are plainly phony and completely bankrupt, even to the uneducated masses. In this giant crisis and vacuum of faith and morality,[69] the CCP ends up ruling through coercion, inducing and indoctrinating the people to behave according to its Maoist version of naked Legalism through force and ruses. The dark side of traditional Chinese culture under a Qin-Han polity, which includes power worship, blatant manipulation, and duplicity, ends justifying means, bottomless and boundless selfishness, conformist and illogical herd mentality, and a master–slave split personality has swelled to a new height, now even without the limited constraints of Confucian rituals and norms or even Communist dogma.[70]

The Chinese billionaire auto-glass maker, Cao Dewang, famous for being featured in the award-winning 2019 documentary *American Factory*, while pledging "to obey the [PRC] government unconditionally," candidly asserted that, in the PRC, "intellectuals [when they have the pulpit or power] all tell lies [. . . as] many officials just want lies [. . .] and can't handle a word of truth, [. . .] because Chinese people lack faith and have no [moral] bottom lines."[71] The decorative ideological patchwork of pseudo-communism, pseudo-Confucianism, pseudo-populism, and pseudo-nationalism promoted by the leaders of the post-Mao PRC has little impact on people's behavior other than furthering cynicism, distrust, and debauchery.[72] Power and material wealth are the only certainties and values in life, for they seem permissible if one hides well and can get away with it, as the countless cases of cadres who have been caught have demonstrated. Therefore, as the Chinese poet Bei Dao famously wrote, in the PRC, "Debasement is the password of the base, Nobility the epitaph of the noble."[73] Another Chinese writer later furthered that lament: "[fake] nobility is the password of the base, [imposed] debasement the epitaph of the noble."[74]

In 2013–2014, the CCP-PRC party-state yet again officially redefined its "socialist core values" in twelve phrases and started to promote them through the state monopoly of the media, education, and entertainment apparatuses: [the state should be] rich and powerful, democratic, civilized, and harmonious; [society should be] free, equal, just, and ruled by law; [individuals should be]) patriotic, dedicated, trustworthy, and friendly. In juxtaposition with the actual behavior of party leaders, this hodgepodge of big words shows a statist ossification and the utter poverty of the minds of the CCP rulers, just like the Party's declared official ideology analyzed in chapter 1 of this book. The CCP further declared that these new values could be boiled down to "Marxism as the guiding ideals," "patriotism as the core national character," and "reform and innovation as the core spirits of the time."[75] Other than aiming to convince the people to obey in perpetuity, the bewildering and hollow nature of the CCP-PRC's faith-value system remains a root cause of China's woeful cultural and moral degradations.

For many decades, the CCP rulers, for their self-preservation and power, have forcibly and unrepentantly compelled the world's largest population to live with self-deceiving amnesia, forgetting or ignoring so many persecutions, disasters, famines, and mass murders, with the cover-up of the 1989 Tiananmen Uprising being especially flagrant.[76] In the CCP's version of history, the rulers (Mao and the Party) are always great and mostly right, while a handful of often-ludicrous scapegoats are responsible for the worst blunders and disasters.[77] A great contrast to such a cynical view of history and human life is the deep soul-searching and strong and massive repentance that people have experienced in many other countries for past injustices and atrocities, such as the truth and reconciliation programs in places like Germany, the United States, and South Africa.[78]

In order to enforce this tight control of people's minds and actions, the widespread culture of informants, bribery, perjury, and secret policing has become the necessary and accepted norm—deeply internalized in the PRC to sustain a culture of moral relativism, deceptive obedience, deliberate obscurantism, and worship of force and money.[79] Xi Jinping, for example, has resumed and intensified the Maoist practice of weekly or even daily "political study and self-criticism" for everyone, especially the cadres, requiring individuals to endlessly memorize party lines and analyze how to correct every "impure" thought or action. The ancient technique of "calling a stag a horse," as the Chinese idiom goes, forcing people to accept and cheer for things "that everyone knows full well" are wrong, foolish or useless, may indeed help to belittle and enslave people but also systematically brews and justifies duplicity.[80] An official study in 2012 found that 39 percent of all civil servants (75% of senior officials) had no problem with the legally and ethically questionable practices of "naked officials."[81] Many CCP-PRC officials have been caught falsifying their personal records, including "altering their age as many as 11 times" to meet various age requirements for appointment and promotion, so much so that, for some, "the information in their resumes is all fake other than their gender." Even the confessions written by some convicted officials turned out to be plagiarized.[82]

The systemic and systematic moral decay under the CCP appears to have become remarkably deep and extensive among both Chinese cultural elites and the general public.[83] Chinese society thus continues to spiritually cast out ideals of individuality, dignity, and morality, a leading PRC scientist lamented in 2014. Intellectuals in the PRC "have no independent position," a noted PRC writer commented: "Worse, they don't even have independent personalities."[84] Under Mao, there were countless but quickly silenced voices of protests; people who dared to articulate and pursue human rights, individuality, integrity, conscience, and critical thinking to resist the party-state were customarily persecuted, jailed, and executed. The brave Chinese intellectuals who dared to question and challenge have literarily vanished, with only very few of their names and their sketchy stories now known, including Lin Zhao, Liu Wenhui, Wang Shenyou, Zhang Chunyuan, Zhang Jiuneng, and Yu Luoke—all were predictably persecuted and executed in secrecy and forgotten even by their families.[85] The post-Mao PRC continues to jail political dissidents, with "at least 1,400" in 2016, including Liu Xiaobo, the first Nobel laureate (2010 Peace Prize) with PRC citizenship, who died in prison in 2017.[86]

Since 1949, the PRC intelligentsia has been full of opportunistic, ethically challenged characters like the servile talents and brazen apologists Guo Moruo, Qian Xuesen, Feng Youlan, Mao Dun, and Yu Qiuyu.[87] The non-PRC neo-Confucian scholar Mou Zhongsan openly called Guo, Feng, and several other leading intellectuals of the PRC "the most shameless people."[88] Indeed, the who's who list of the contemporary PRC literary and entertainment elite is laden with talented clowns slaving for the power-holders, egregiously lacking in independence, dignity, principles, and integrity.[89] Many PRC publications, often by the former party-state insiders, have documented that the majority of the PRC intelligentsia seems to have been largely diminished and molded into either executioners, followers, informants, passive accomplices, occasional whiners, or wasted talents, who are still frequently purged, victimized, and "destroyed" despite their servility.[90] Based on his extensive archival research, a PRC author concluded that intellectuals under the CCP, particularly during the Mao era, "all had dirty hands [as accomplices of the CCP's purges and thought reforms] for self-preservation [and] none of them were clean."[91] In the twenty-first century, many ranked PRC intellectuals are seen continuously acting as "shameless cheer-leading clowns" for party bigwigs like Bo Xilai and Xi Jinping.[92] A well-known historian based in Shanghai openly pledged in 2021 that to study history in the PRC "is to learn politics, to put the state's interest first and foremost [. . . and we] must hide away whatever findings that are not beneficial [to the state, so as] to guarantee the political legitimacy of the Chinese Communist Party."[93]

Chinese language, literature, and the fine arts themselves appear to have all been impoverished and profoundly twisted for political purposes, while many obsequious state-paid writers have behaved in ways "far more than disgusting," according to a PRC writer now living abroad.[94] Painters and performing artists, for example, have lined up to create endless fantastical Potemkin villages to adulate and worship the rulers, completely oblivious to the harsh reality, including national famine and political purges. A recent example is the giant painting by the top-ranked official painters titled *Constructing the Community of Common Human Destiny*, hanging in the People's Great Hall since 2017, which has drawn scathing ridicules from many Chinese artists.[95] Ba Jin, a renowned writer whose career was smothered under Mao, later recounted that PRC intellectuals had to adopt a "slave philosophy" and allow themselves to be enslaved not just in body but also in mind, or else they would not survive the CCP's political campaigns.[96] Though intellectuals suffered equally or worse under the CCP and Mao than their Soviet counterparts under Stalin, there has been no Chinese equivalent of the conscientious and monumental works of reflection that came out of the Soviet experience, such as *The Gulag Archipelago* by Aleksandr Solzhenitsyn.[97]

In short, the Chinese mind and conscience appear to have suffered severe damage under the CCP-PRC party-state. "It is an era of masking," declared the cover story of a PRC magazine in 2011, and "we have to fake it all the time."[98] Published reports in the PRC bemoan the fact that, today, a genuine cleansing of the Chinese mind and a full revival of the Chinese conscience are highly imperative and challenging but critically uncertain.[99] A Beijing-based philosopher openly decried in 2016 "the thorough decay of morality in China" due to "an inner cancer deep inside us" caused by "the political system which promotes lies and punishes truth-telling" and "the so-called public property rights."[100] PRC writers and scholars in exile have, perhaps somewhat hyperbolically, deemed most if not all PRC citizens, even those living abroad including many political dissidents in exile, "the unwelcome Chinese," who are profoundly inferior to other peoples, including non-PRC Chinese, because of their "ubiquitous lack" of a moral compass and compassion, courage and manners, integrity and dignity, and personal character. This lack is purportedly caused chiefly by three catastrophes in Chinese history: the Mongol and Manchu "exterminations of China" and "the plague of the Chinese Communist Party."[101]

Anecdata of Corruption

The cultural and ethical destruction and degradation in the PRC seems to have continued for decades after Mao's death but with greater variety and ubiquity. The boundless corruption of CCP-PRC officials has formed many tightly knitted vested-interest groups, the "semi-serfdom families" or "pyramids of cronyism," a system that now "trades power for money, sex, and more power" and aims to "use taxpayers' money against the taxpayers," as one PRC investigative journalist concluded in 2014.[102] Countless cases of "world-record" harems and the predatory sexual indulgences of officials, for example, show the abysmal ethics and strong misogyny among the CCP elites.[103] Despite extensive censorship, numerous reports have exposed serious allegations of corruption implicating the very top of the CCP-PRC including the family of Xi Jinping.[104] CCP officials, including senior military officers, when interviewed in private all concluded that "none of us can be clean of corruption" as it has become "the way to survive [in the officialdom] and [allows our families] to live a middle-class life."[105] Too many, however, have gone outrageously wild, totally unhinged from the law or morality. Between December 2012 and February 2015 alone, thirty-one senior officers at corps-commander rank or higher were purged for selling promotions: positions of commander of a company, battalion, and regiment were sold respectively for ¥ 200,000, ¥ 300,000, and ¥1million (roughly US $30,000, $45,000, and $147,000).[106]

Culturally and ethically customary and even accepted, deception and fakery appear to have thoroughly permeated Chinese society, producing massive "malinvestment" and "dodgy" conspicuous consumption.[107] To cope with the ever-changing government policies related to property rights and internal migration, many have had "Chinese style" fake marriages and phony divorces. The booming online dating scene is "infested" with massive and creative scams.[108] Customers have lost tens of millions to bogus bank clerks.[109] Numerous con artists hire foreign tourists as fake businessmen or even entertainment stars in order to dupe investors and customers. The COVID-19 pandemic in 2020–2022, as fully expected, saw countless "outrageously ugly acts" by corrupt officials and greedy crooks.[110] Amidst the overall decay of morals, a striking split between legal norms and reality has flourished nationwide. For example, prostitution is strictly illegal and harshly penalized in the PRC with hefty fines, public shaming, extralegal labor camp confinement, jail sentences, and even the death penalty. Yet the industry seems to thrive flamboyantly and creatively throughout the PRC.[111] The official CCP narrative called for an elimination of "vices" like prostitution under Mao's rule. But sex for goods, money, favors, and protection widely existed, especially among the "sent-down" youth in the 1950s through 1970s.[112] The hypocrisy surrounding the sex industry provides the police with a major source of power and revenue, as well as an effective means of "cleansing" cities and "trapping" opponents and dissidents on the orders from the top.[113] Harsh and selective police harassment and "strikes" seem to commonly exempt the high-class prostitution that caters to the rich and powerful.[114] In Dongguan, a prosperous city of eight million people (80% of whom are "migrants" with temporary residency permits), 6 to 10 percent of residents are estimated to be sex workers and generate 11 to 14 percent of the local GDP.[115] The police, long benefiting from its association with the fake illegalization of a massive sector of the economy, enforce the law with ridiculous deceit. In February 2014, under a direct order from Beijing, the Dongguan government sent out 6,525 police officers "to sweep" the thousands of suspected brothels, yet only "apprehended 67 suspects."[116]

Academia and Education

As some Chinese scholars have openly lamented, the worst kind of corruption in the PRC is probably the widespread "corruption of the intellectuals, which is the complete and final downfall of a society and a nation."[117] Unlike in the past under the imperial regimes, the deeply entrenched culture of plagiarism, falsification, and deception in the CCP-PRC has gone far beyond the officialdom (including judges and police) and has become common among educators (from kindergarten to university, with official recognition of "unbelievably serious" corruption),[118] scholars (even some of the highest ranked academicians at the best research institutions),[119] medical professionals,[120] state management of professional sports,[121] religious clergy,[122] artists and writers, academic and educational data services like CNKI (China National Knowledge Infrastructure),[123] and journalists.[124] The results of these corrupt behaviors are often costly and harmful, and even literally lethal. For example, the CCP's scientific "great leap forward" rush to build over 2,700 PS-2 level bio labs in 2019–2020, which involved the widespread corruption of medical administrators and professionals, has already caused some Chinese to openly worry about more leaks of deadly pathogens. The CCP's "COVID-19 tsar," the epidemiologist Zhong Nanshan who was decorated as a national hero by Xi Jinping on live TV in late 2020, has been peddling for years traditional herb medicines packaged by companies he has concealed "close ties" to as the officially approved and mandated remedies for infectious illnesses of SARS and COVID.[125] Allegations of ubiquitous plagiarism have implicated the highest level of the CCP-PRC leadership, and have even included questions about how Xi Jinping managed to get his PhD while working full time as a deputy provincial governor a thousand miles away from his university.[126]

The open purchase and publication of fabricated and plagiarized research papers and books seem to have become widespread. It amounts to institutionalized fraud at an industrial scale with "full customer service" in the PRC. The going rate for the easy online purchase of a plagiarized master's or doctoral thesis can be as low as $11.[127] Sales of fake academic papers and fraudulent publications is reportedly a billion-dollar industry in the PRC. Phony but "publishable" scientific papers cost only $250. On the other hand, "procuring" the top position of Academician at the Chinese Academy of Sciences would reportedly cost $3.8 million.[128] In 2014, official media reported that PRC citizens purchased 95 percent of the diplomas sold by the many US diploma mills.[129] The skyrocketing filing of patents in the PRC in recent years is evidently full of fakeries. A rogue senior policeman, for example, was granted 211 "patents" in 2011 alone.[130] In 2009, seventy falsified papers by the same two PRC researchers were retracted by just one British journal of crystallography. In 2010, in one Chinese government survey, a third of more than 6,000 scientific researchers at six leading institutions in the PRC admitted to plagiarism, falsification, or fabrication, compared to about 2 percent of the same number in the West.[131] In 2015, BioMed Central, a major bioscience publisher based in the United Kingdom, retracted forty-three "fabricated" or "compromised" papers, forty-one of which had been submitted by Chinese scholars, mostly from top PRC medical research institutions. In 2017, over 100 fake research papers from the PRC were withdrawn by just one journal, *Tumor Biology*. In 2020, it was discovered that about a dozen medical doctors and researchers based in leading PRC hospitals and institutes purchased over 400 fabricated research papers from just one "paper mill," and then published these papers in international journals as their academic accomplishments.[132] In 2020, of the total of 1,932 scientific papers published worldwide in English that were withdrawn for problems, 819 (published in 380 journals) were from PRC authors, 639 of which were demonstrably plagiarized or fabricated, making the PRC by far the world leader.[133] In 2021, *Nature* reported that hundreds of published "research papers" by PRC scholars contained telltale "tortured phrases," showing that they were sloppy fabrications. To perhaps document the academic fraud and plagiarism in the PRC, *Journal of Cellular Biochemistry* published a special supplement issue just to showcase the articles by Chinese medical researchers that the journal has retracted (178 in 2021 alone).[134] Sadly, many Chinese scientists, who are full of creative potential individually, seem to have collectively sunk deep into the moral vacuum, revealing a serious lack of "scientific integrity" in the CCP-PRC.[135]

Under the CCP, political pressure and control evidently misdirect research and corrupt researchers.[136] The country is now viewed by insiders as the world's number-one producer of "garbage academic papers" and countless "useless books"; this sad and "very shameful" situation is "extremely hard" to change. Some articles published in the officially ranked "core" academic journals in the PRC have been revealed to be simply farces.[137] Official presses have put out countless pompous "academic" books by often dubious "scholars," including a long treatise in 2020 that declared a "China solution [for the world] to bid farewell to Western economics," and a lengthier piece in 2021 that claimed that "the mainstream history textbooks in the West were all wrong" about the origin of human civilization.[138] Perhaps after having seen enough of such publications, a senior PRC scientist publicly asserted in 2021 that "90% of [China's] so-called academic research could be cut" as it "contributes basically nothing of value to human knowledge." This is especially troubling, as scholars, doctors, and educators were traditionally considered above corruption, with ethical standards higher than those of the officials, political elites, or the general public. Their corruption impairs the young, injures the weak and sick, devastates the mind and conscience of all the Chinese people, and distracts and pollutes scientific endeavors worldwide.[139]

Such behavior inevitably rubs off on the next generation; accordingly, rampant academic dishonesty is now present at essentially all academic levels. Many middle and high schools are thus praised for their extreme and "creative" method of curbing widespread cheating on tests: they put the students in an open field to take their written exams, to space them sufficiently apart from each other. Countless college students are reported to have hired people to take their classes and do their work.[140] One senior PRC educator mourned that school children are indoctrinated with duplicity and deception from kindergarten like "farmed hogs." In

2022, official "guidance of reading" for high schoolers still prominently promoted the "high ethics and great character" of a CCP operative for killing his wife—"my true love"—in order to protect some money raised for the party.[141] Noted Chinese intellectuals have openly accused colleges in the PRC of having degenerated into "chicken farms," claiming that the Chinese intelligentsias comprises "thoroughly bureaucratized and commercialized gangsters and plagiarists," who are "heartless and cynical," commonly engaging in "empty talk, sellout to rulers, plagiarism and shameless acts," with "little special merit other than eating bitterness and enduring hard work."[142] In 2013, the PRC Education Ministry posted a list of "100 fake universities" it had discovered. By 2021, that list grew to over 392, located in nearly all provinces, with 151 in the capital city of Beijing alone.[143]

Chinese academic corruption has prompted some CCP scholars to openly decry the situation as "far worse than malodourous."[144] This behavior has evidently gone global: many PRC students were found to have "seriously and extensively" cheated on American standardized tests such as the GRE, SAT, and TOEFL.[145] A "fraud frenzy" has led to a situation in which "as many as one in 10 applications to U.S. colleges by Chinese students may include fraudulent material, including phony essays and high-school transcripts." Chinese official media reported that a large number of PRC students in the United States have been found engaging in blatant and widespread academic fraud such as plagiarism, as evidenced by the 8,000 PRC students expelled by US colleges in 2014 alone.[146]

The decadence in academia and the deterioration in education in the PRC, featuring perhaps the worst kind of corruption and moral decay, appear to be the inevitable outcomes of CCP governance in general and its monopoly and tight control of the education system in particular. As one PRC education executive wrote in 2021, in the PRC, "education is [the CCP] state's grand course and it must obey the state's will."[147] The CCP's policy, as Xi Jinping reemphasized in 2021 in imperial-era language, is to control and "collect all talents under heaven [for the party] to use" in its ways for its missions.[148] Soon after their victory in 1949, the CCP forcefully took over and then wantonly decimated Chinese higher educational institutions that had been largely created and run by or modeled after Western institutions and educators. It closed, for example, at least "nine world-class universities" founded by religious organizations. Chinese academics and educators soon were abused, degraded, humiliated, enervated, tortured and even murdered during the countless campaigns of thought work and thought reform under Mao. The wholesale political hostility toward intellectuals lessened significantly after Mao but the educated in the PRC have never been truly dignified, much less free from the CCP autocracy. Adding to the onslaught on Chinese minds, the post-Mao CPP further orchestrated a nosedive into the swamp of officials-standard-defined materialism, expediency and corruption in the name of leading the world in academia and education. A Chinese study in the 2020s found that "scholars" with official positions openly engaged in widespread "legal corruption" to become "rule-makers, administrators, referees, and awardees" at the same time, with a probability thirty-three times higher than ordinary scholars of obtaining "academic resources" such as funds, ranks, and awards.[149] The government has massively and opaquely poured state funds into a plan to "create about 100 leading universities" (the 211 Project of 112 designated colleges) since 1995, and to "build some world-class research universities" (the 985 Project of thirty-nine elite colleges) since 1998.[150] Two of the universities, Peking and Tsinghua, each received over ¥4 billion (roughly US $650 million) in "the third round of fiscal appropriation" alone in 2013, and then ¥2.4 to ¥3.2 billion annually from 2013 to 2021, benefiting from the state's policy of "robbing the poor [schools] to pay the rich [schools]."[151] In 2021, in order to prevail in the "competition of the 21st century" or simply "the Sino-American technology war," the CCP ordered the first group of "12 top universities" to each set up a "college of future technology" with massive new funds to specifically focus on developing about a dozen "cutting-edge," "revolutionary," and "game changing" technologies (with a division of labor among the schools).[152]

Academics and professors in the PRC, all state employees, with the majority being CCP members, are ranked via the officials-standard. Scientists and educators became fed-by-rank pawns to be used at the ruler's pleasure for his political ambitions. College professors are divided into two tracks, permanent and contractual, and stratified into at least six formal layers (three for full professors), all tightly managed and controlled by the CCP committees at each school.[153] To lure, label, and control elite academicians with monetary rewards and honorary distinctions, the PRC has recruited 3,000 people annually since 1990 to receive a modest, tax-free but socially prestigious "special allowance," with the total number of such "special experts" exceeding 162,000 by 2010.[154] Other national plans with different degrees of financial incentives and perks include the Yangtze Scholars, Hundred Talents, Thousand

Talents, and numerous variants.[155] Just about all provincial governments use public funds to create their own (often multiple) special allowances and talent-attraction programs, such as the Huangpu River Scholars of Shanghai, Wan River Scholars of Anhui, Swan Plan of Guangdong, and Tai Mountain Scholars of Shandong.[156] All of these are under the direct management of the CCP's organizational departments in charge of all personnel at the various levels. To evade the critical and even prosecutorial attention from Western governments, most of these well-funded programs, especially the notorious Thousand Talents Plan, have literally gone "underground" as of 2021–2022.

Indeed, a CCP-led "great leap" in academia and higher education has been unfolding. First, the CCP poured in resources to bolster political indoctrination in higher education: from 2017 to 2021, the number of "colleges of Marxism" in universities (including medical schools) ballooned from 450 to over 1,400.[157] Since the late 1990s, the PRC has seen explosive growth in the numbers of colleges and think tanks, programs and degrees, titles and ranks, and papers and patents. For the sake of "leading the world" and relieving unemployment pressure, the government has pushed for an explosion in college admission each year for the last two decades, from 1.08 million admittances in 1998 to about 9 million in 2019. Graduate school admission has seen a similar boom, from 58,000 in 1998 to 850,000 in 2019.[158] And yet, like with the Great Leap under Mao four decades earlier, a serious, systemic deterioration in quality was inevitable. A member of the Chinese Academy of Sciences openly commented that "today, our graduate students are only as good as the associate or vocational school students of the past."[159] Just thirty years after 1982, when the first six PhDs students graduated, the PRC enrolled 300,000 PhD students and graduated about 60,000 PhDs in 2012, the largest numbers in the world, with a very low ("near-zero") attrition rate (commonly around 30% in the West). By the 2020s, the total enrollment of PhD students exceeded 420,000, with 100,000 being admitted and 65,000 graduating.[160] By contrast, after more than 250 years of development, nonprofit universities in the United States awarded about 51,000 PhD degrees in 2012 and 56,000 in 2019, 36 to 38 percent to foreigners.[161] In 2021, one top-ranked PRC university, Tsinghua, alone granted 3,168 PhDs, exceeding the total number of PhDs granted by the five top-ranked US universities combined.[162] But, "using just the standard of third-tier American universities," a senior Chinese scientist scathingly concluded, a shockingly 90 percent or even "99% of the [PRC] researchers, professors and PhDs are unqualified." A senior administrator at a top PRC university candidly told this author in private that "only one-third of our PhD students are real students."[163]

Similarly, Beijing has ordered more research output and particularly more thinktanks to befit its "leading of the world." In 2015, the CCP furthered efforts to "boost funding [. . .] to build a new type of think tanks with Chinese characteristics."[164] PRC-based research institutions, groups and centers of all stripes, all owned or controlled by the CCP, were created (or were often just reorganized or renamed), popping up everywhere like bamboo shoots. They truly exploded in numbers, from the world's twelfth in quantity to second in just a decade: from 74 in 2008, 429 in 2012, and 507 in 2018, to 1,413 in 2020. This represents a remarkable nineteen-fold increase in just eleven years, while the number of think tanks in just about every other country from India to the United States has remained basically stable.[165] The real performance of those think tanks, however, in the words of a senior Chinese scholar I interviewed in 2020, involves "lots of tanks but no think," let alone any thinking that may be useful.[166] In the end, the rampant corruption, politicized misallocation of massive resources and the great devaluation of academic titles and standards have led to the officially admitted "massive waste of talent" in China.[167]

In order to build some "world class" universities, the PRC spends 30 percent of its budget on a few colleges that enroll only 8 percent of college students, creating "world class inequality and polarization" in higher education, as openly noted by a senior PRC professor.[168] Moreover, the shower of massive public funds has provided ever-more incentives, stakes, opportunities, and mechanisms for extensive and persistent academic and educational corruption and fraud. Many forced mergers, senseless expansions, and additions of higher educational institutions, just like the mega construction projects analyzed in chapter 2 of this book, have become giant bubbles and fertile ground for shocking corruption and the massive squandering of resources.[169] In the first six months of 2014 alone, at least eighteen top leaders of PRC universities were purged for corruption. More senior academic leaders, like the president of Fudan University, managed to remain unscathed despite piles of allegations of plagiarism and corruption against them.[170] Without real freedom of speech and the press under the tight, centralized political and personal control of the CCP, widespread corruption seems to continue to plague education and research institutions, affecting nearly every faculty member.[171]

Other than successfully luring some foreign-trained and foreign-based scientists (often of dubious quality and usefulness) and legally or illegally acquiring new foreign technology (which has increasingly fueled US-PRC discord),[172] the great amount of resources spent on the PRC's R&D (research and development) program, the world's third largest in the mid-2010s (after the US and the EU), seems (as might have been expected) nonproductive. Much of the inadequately monitored funds is simply embezzled. In 2013, for example, more than fifty cadres in the Guangdong Science and Technology Bureau were indicted for corruption, including all the chiefs and deputy chiefs, and eight leading PRC academics were charged with fraud and embezzling tens of millions RMB of R&D funds in just one probe. One single project, to genetically modify seeds and spices, was awarded a whopping $2.9 billion in one decision in 2008, but its deputy-chief scientist was arrested in 2014 for embezzling much of the funds.[173] Even the anti-corruption in PRC colleges can be corrupt. Pan Suiming, a groundbreaking but unorthodox researcher of sexology based in Beijing, was reported to have been unjustly penalized by his detractors for trivial accounting errors.[174]

Driven by its burning desire for shortcuts to lead the world in science and technology, along with its propaganda needs, the CCP-PRC party-state, often in collusion with promotion-craving officials and greedy crooks, has poured billions into highly promoted projects with little review or evidence. The quantitative growth in the number of Chinese patents has been a "great leap" with 68.7 thousand patents filed in 2020 alone, a 16 percent annual increase, far more than the in the United States.[175] Many of these "breakthroughs," however, soon prove to be complete frauds and worthless, even pure fantasy. The 1992 formula for "turning water to oil," praised as the "fifth great invention" by both *People's Daily* and *Economic Daily*—the top newspapers of the Party and state—soon turned out to be a total fraud propagated by a driver-turned-engineer named Wang Hongcheng, who went to jail for his deceit. Yet the same type of "breakthroughs" has continued popping up over the past two decades. In 2003, an American-trained PhD named Chen Jin repackaged the Motorola microprocessor chip as his invention, aptly named the Hanxin (that is, the chip of the Han nation), wasting hundreds of millions in government funds and "ruining" the Chinese chip industry.[176] In 2020, amidst US export bans, Beijing announced the allocation of ¥9.5 trillion ($1.46 trillion) to develop a cutting-edge semiconductor industry. Within just eight months, nearly 10,000 firms, from cement factories to seafood farmers and real estate brokerages, jumped in suddenly in a "great leap for chips," which has already cost hundreds of billions in scandalous bankruptcies of mega projects.[177] More "innovative" still, a water-hydrogen car was "produced" in 2019 but soon proved to be just another scam by crooks colluding with local officials to swindle government funds.[178] Imported new concepts like nanotechnology, solar panels, and graphene layer have led to widespread schemes and frauds in the PRC in the 2010s and 2020s, such as "nano water," "solar trap," and "graphene underwear."[179] The ultra-expensive, "world's first," quantum satellite communication project led by foreign-trained physicist Pan Jianwei also seemed to be fizzling out in the 2020s amid serious allegations. Noticing the government-pushed Chinese efforts, a 2022 RAND report concluded that the United States remains "the current world leader in quantum technologies" and that "the eventual applications of quantum technology and their timelines remain highly uncertain."[180]

China clearly has much of the best raw student talent in the world, but they are subjected to the CCP's systemic propaganda and meticulous thought work through a monopoly on information, forceful indoctrination, and mind manipulation from very early on, with a high and often permanent cost to truth, taste, integrity, and independent thinking. Even the state-mandated Chinese language textbook in elementary schools is found to have "low and decaying" quality, plagued by illogical indoctrination, expedient censorship, politicized wordsmithery, and deceptive manipulation. Education in the PRC is viewed by many parents as nothing but a "tightly controlled pipeline producing scraps," with endless indoctrination of "phony ethics in elementary schools, empty ideals in middle–high schools, and tasteless aesthetics in colleges." Two PRC professors openly lament the state of the education system for producing students who "pretend to be obedient to power but harbor sinister motives" and "behave like voice recorders" with an inadequate cultivation of personality and intellectual capacity.[181] The few educators who have dared to deviate, even very slightly, from the CCP's guidelines and narratives, are commonly marginalized, dismissed, or even jailed. A large number of the thousands of people punished for "speech crime" in just eight years under Xi appeared to be educators at various levels.[182] The highest-rated universities in the PRC were considered by some insiders as academically at best third class globally in the 2010s, with only a "detectable" possibility of approaching second class in some specialized areas; the top three universities—Peking, Tsinghua, and Zhejiang—were at the level of the University of Alabama and the California State University System, and lower than the University of Florida or Michigan State University, according to an expert observer, because "the [PRC] government is too strong [in control], and the scholars are cut down and subdued." A leading internationally recognized mathematician dismissed the best PRC faculties and PhD programs in science as worse than undergraduate programs in the United States or Hong Kong.[183] PRC scholars concluded in the 2010s that, out of the five tiers of higher education in the world, the best Chinese universities were only in the fourth tier.[184] In 2022, several top PRC universities, likely fed up with their low rankings in the world, decided to "stop providing any information to [foreign] college ranking agencies" so to echo Xi Jinping's fresh call for "modeling after foreign universities no more" and "creating world-class universities with Chinese characteristics." Many Chinese educators soon dubbed such a move as "academic decoupling with the world" and "ranking our colleges with our own standard."[185]

An international team of researchers discovered in 2021 that both the critical thinking and academic skills of PRC students actually declined after their college education.[186] Many top Chinese college students seem to have creatively registered their verdict and voted with their feet by going abroad en masse (mainly to the West) to pursue further education since Beijing opened the door in the early 1980s. In the 2010s, elite PRC universities still often functioned like "prep schools" for foreign graduate programs. In 2018 and 2019, for example, one-fifth to nearly half of the graduates of the highest-ranked universities went to study overseas: 31 percent and 28 percent from the most prestigious Peking University and Tsinghua University, and 25 to 32 percent from other top schools like the University of Science and Technology, Fudan, Renmin, and Shanghai Jiaotong.[187] One report estimated that at least 37,000 graduates of the class of 2022 from 300 PRC high schools were accepted by 400 foreign (mostly Anglophone) colleges; and an annual list openly ranks the "best 100 high schools" in China by the number of their graduates accepted at the top eighty US colleges (especially the Ivy League), top ten UK colleges, and top three Canadian colleges.[188] The overwhelming majority of Chinese students who venture abroad to study have remained outside of the PRC after completion of their studies. In the two decades since 2000, over 85 percent of Chinese earners of American degrees (including 90% of PhD recipients) in STEM (science, technology, engineering and math), for example, have remained in the United States permanently after graduation.[189] In the 2020s, China provided 29 percent (the largest share) of the world's "top-tier AI researchers," yet only 11 percent are living and working at home in the PRC.[190]

According to some insiders, universities in the PRC have been "tormented" by officials and "degenerated intolerably." As some PRC scholars have vocally complained, the "big monster" of micro-management by the CCP has resulted in "nightmares" of waste, corruption, "suppression of innovation," "academic bubbles," and "chicken-farm-like universities."[191] The lack of university autonomy and faculty governance seems to have rendered PRC professors controlled, corrupt, and bitter "piece-wage workers" or "hourly laborers."[192] The PRC knockoff of the American tenure-track system, begun in 2007, seems, unsurprisingly, to have mutated into exploitation and enslavement of young academics, which sometimes literally kill them. The party bosses in colleges continue to herd the professors with institutionalized nepotism, irrationality and corruption in employment, promotion and resource allocation, similar to their overall suboptimal management of the country.[193] The secret informants widely planted in classes, the harsh living and working environment, the financial challenges and the micromanaging party bosses make the life of a PRC academic difficult and often miserable, especially for a no-star official-scholar or a serious intellectual trying to stay out the pigsty of moral degradation.[194]

The problem of fraud, which traditionally accompanied imperial exams in the past, has now morphed into widespread and industrialized cheating on the PRC's all-important college entrance exam, with the going rate of ¥3,000 to ¥25,000 ($485–$4,310) for a test score ensuring a college admission. In 2020, it was revealed that, for more than a decade officials in power in the two provinces of Shandong and Henan alone had had been stealing the passing college entrance exam scores of many hundreds of students—who lost their critical and life-changing chance at higher education—and selling them to others, who were then able to attend college with the fake, arrogated credentials.[195] In the twenty-first century, the "civil servant recruiting exam" has replaced the college entrance exam as the gateway to becoming a cadre and joining the ruling elites in the party-state. It is highly coveted and has a much lower rate of admission, even just for the lowest, entry-level positions. In fall 2021, for example, a twenty-seven-year-old, newly minted PhD in Planetary Geology from a top Chinese university, among many undergraduate and graduate degree holders, "happily" took such an exam to become an office-clerk "responsible for managing" 150–250 households in one of the eighty-two "neighborhood communities" of Donghu District of Wuhan city.[196] Anecdotal reports amply reveal that this prized exam is (unsurprisingly) filled with the same, if not worse, fraud and "built-in mechanisms" for cheating, nepotism, and political correctness during its written test and especially its second stage in-person interview.[197] Instead of creating a much-promoted "meritocracy," the college entrance exam simply "helps to justify and reproduce a highly unequal society" in the PRC.[198] The civil servant exam appears to do so even more.

"We All Fake It"

Related to the endless and countless games of numbers, deeply entrenched power-fetish-based cynicism, and omnipresent corruption already reported in this book, the attitude that "we all fake it" has become a dominant norm that has pervaded Chinese society at large. Even the astronomical and much-envied "net wealth" of many, if not all, PRC billionaires seems to be full of hot air.[199] This state of affair has led to all sorts of morally and legally questionable behavior by many if not the majority of ordinary Chinese in their daily lives—which may also be taken as a significant sign of widespread nonviolent social resistance, protest, and revolt against the authority of the party-state. Short-term behavior, ad hoc and nonstop bargaining, deceptive activities, fearful mistrust, disregard of rules and contracts, and unscrupulous selfishness seem to dominate many people's social and economic lives, with social trust in China "dropping to a record low," as proclaimed by the CCP's own mouthpiece.[200] A PRC sociologist went even further: "there is a huge problem of trust in China today, people have lost basic trust and the whole society is permeated with deception and fakery."[201] Fakery and deception in particular have reached the highest levels, as bemoaned by officials in front of the PRC Premier: "The village lies to the town, the town lies to the county, with lies all the ways to the State Council."[202] In 2015, a British researcher at the University of East Anglia found that citizens of the PRC were by far the most dishonest out of the 15,000 people from fifteen nations studied, with 70 percent of them found lying, and they, together with the Greeks, also evaluated their fellow countrymen as the least honest.[203]

Reflecting social ethics and perhaps partially responsible for the skyrocketing divorce rate in the PRC, as reported in the previous chapter,

Chinese people now have "the world's highest rate of infidelity," according to PRC sexologists, with 34 percent of men and 13 percent of women self-reporting extramarital affairs, while "70% of married couples are not in love at all." This places China next to Thailand and Western Europe for the world's highest rate of infidelity, while the infidelity rates for American men and women are reportedly 20 to 25 percent and 13 to 15 percent, respectively.[204] Two large online surveys in the PRC found in 2016 that 51 percent of the respondents (38% of women and 60% of men) had "cheated"; 88 percent of respondents approved of teacher–student relationships; and 69 percent of couples (77% of wives and 59% of husbands) regretted their marriages. Yet, 75 percent of PRC respondents still view infidelity as morally unacceptable, an attitude that is seemingly very mismatched with their actions, suggesting a widespread culture of deception and hypocrisy. By comparison, online surveys in 2019 found that 16 percent of US respondents had "cheated," basically in line with opinion survey findings that 85 percent of Americans view infidelity as morally unacceptable. Public attitudes also generally match actual acts of infidelity in just about all other countries surveyed.[205] Since 2002, DNA paternity testing has become increasingly popular in the PRC. In 2021, one-quarter of the tens of thousands of such tests were reportedly negative, thus "ruining countless families and marriages."[206]

Empirically, today's PRC is full of deliberately substandard products and services, intentionally fake and even poisonous food and medicine, and ever-more creative double-dealing and fraud online and offline. In the mid-2010s, PRC government inspectors concluded that 26 percent of all goods sold online were substandard or fake.[207] In fact, contrary to the feigned Maoist nostalgia, as a leading PRC intellectual reported, the same serious problem of food and pharmaceutical safety has always existed in the PRC. Dangerous products include baby formulas deliberately blended with melamine, recycled sewage grease that some have estimated to now account for 10 percent of all cooking oil sold in the PRC, all kinds of creatively poisoned rice, meat, and other foods, and ineffective or even toxic drugs and vaccines.[208] The Chinese supply chain of basic food and pet food is reportedly compromised and critically contaminated, often affecting foreign consumers as well.[209] An incredible 60 percent of Chinese vegetable growers, for example, sell heavily contaminated food that they never eat themselves, while 73 percent of their customers interviewed do not trust their products, according to official media. The fact that Chinese people do not dare to consume milk powder made in China, a

Hong Kong judge declared in 2015, "is truly a real national humiliation." Websites and search engines pay to forge eyeball counts and search results to mislead, deceive, hurt, and even kill consumers, so much so that the CCP's mouthpiece also complained about it openly.[210] One year after its 2014 world record IPO (initial public offering) on Wall Street, Alibaba, the Chinese equivalent of Amazon and eBay, was reported by the PRC government to be the worst e-marketer in China for peddling counterfeit products, which accounted for 63 percent of its total sales. By 2018, Alibaba was once again listed by the US government as a "notorious market for counterfeit goods."[211] All that while the ruling elites of the party-state, as I have discussed earlier in this book, live relatively safely on those "special provisions" (*tegong*) at taxpayers' expenses.

Around 2,000 cases involving counterfeit currency are officially reported annually, resulting in the production of a large quantity of foreign currency. In January 2020, for example, US Customs intercepted one shipment of nearly one million fake one-dollar bills made in China.[212] As much as eighty-three tons of gold, used by a major financial firm (listed on Nasdaq since 2010) as collateral for ¥20 billion in bank loans with certification and insurance from government agencies, turned out to all be bars of copper; this was only discovered in May 2020, months after the transaction. PRC reporters actually deemed this scam to be "not that unusual."[213] Fake identification cards and diplomas of all sorts are openly available on just about every city street corner in the PRC and have even been exported to flood US college campuses. Foreign experts, executives, and diplomats can also be faked for government loans and contracts, fooling even very senior PRC officials. Beijing is also alleged to have systematically staffed Buddhist temples in Tibet with "fake lamas."[214] In the 2020s, official media openly praised a village of thousands people in Henan Province, led by a fabled "godfather of counterfeiting," for prosperously "specializing" for decades in making "countless" bronze artifacts that "are exactly the same as the unearthed [pre-Qin] antiques." The explosive Chinese art auction market (incredibly 41% of the world's total in the 2010s) has been revealed to be thoroughly and creatively "fake and rigged."[215]

Excruciatingly painful examples published by official media have evidenced the deep wounds to the mind of the Chinese people under the CCP-PRC party-state. Surveillance videos have shown children hit by cars and then run over (or avoided) by several others without a single motorist or pedestrian stopping to check or help.[216] Many fraudulent accidents or *pengci* have been reported, influenced by the controversial case of Peng Yu in Nanjing, describing how people who helped the injured in public were at risk of frivolous lawsuits for medical expenses and damages; these might well have the support of the police and courts, based on the officially adjudicated but sickening "common sense" attitude that "if you were not responsible [for the fall or injury], why would you even try to help?"[217] In 2022, PRC bloggers wrote that, during the draconian quarantine attempts to achieve the political aim of "zero COVID," countless people, including those "at the very bottom of society," with even the smallest power over others (such as guarding a locked-down residential building or clinic) have blithely perpetuated many heartless and "boundlessly evil" acts that "are much worse than the virus," brutalizing, swindling and even slaying their fellow citizens.[218]

Publication, Antiquities, and Gastronomy

After the creation of the PRC, the CCP under Mao quickly stopped and reversed many of the sociocultural changes of the previous century. While today's PRC may appear visibly Westernized in social trends and pop culture, much like the pre-1949 ROC (Republic of China), it has stamped out the latter's considerable freedom of speech, publication, and assembly. Throughout the late-Qing and the ROC era, China had many hundreds of journals and presses, the overwhelming majority of which (including the openly rebellious publications by the CCP) were independent from the government and managed to evade state censors, thanks greatly to the existence of foreign concessions in many major cities.[219] In the PRC, out of the fairly large number of publishers (579 presses and 1,943 newspapers), few if any could survive long without the "approval" and "management" of the CCP under the world's most elaborate and effective censorship regime.[220]

In the 2010s, the CCP launched yet more national campaigns of rectification of "academic" journals to reorganize and eliminate those that "have had various problems."[221] Meanwhile, the PRC model of book publication is that authors who are not CCP leaders commonly pay press fees to publish books, especially academic monographs; they also have to pass at least two layers of censors, at the provincial and central levels. To perhaps help out the overworked censors, who bear "serious responsibility" for any approved book that is later discovered to be "bad" and eventually banned, the CCP in 2018 ordered a drastic one-third reduction in the number of books allowed to be published each year (from about 300,000 titles to 200,000). By 2020, the quantity control tightened by cutting the number of permitted titles by another 15 to 30 percent (down to 140,000 to 170,000), "making it now even more expensive to buy a quota" for book publication.[222] As a point of comparison, with a quarter of China's population, the United States had nearly twice as many newspapers and five times more book publishers, with two to three times more new books published each year in the 2010s.[223] In cyberspace, where the task of censorship has become ever heavier, PRC media firms, including Alibaba, Tencent (WeChat), and TikTok, have together created "a major industry" of online screening and deleting that costs billions and employs tens of thousands of censors working 24/7 in office complexes throughout the PRC.[224] In 2018 to 2021, the CCP decreed nine lists targeting 446 web hosts and broadcasters for "thorough and lasting banishment," so as to enhance its control of so-called "self-media" (*zimeiti*) in cyberspace.[225] CCP censorship of content has reportedly also reached foreign-based teachers hired as online English tutors.[226]

Beyond its monopoly in information and controlling of people's mind, the CCP, especially during Mao's "continued revolution," unleashed and magnified the traditionally periodic deluges of destruction at an unprecedented scale to create waves of obliteration of Chinese culture and antiquities. In fact, the CCP's deliberate demolition of cultural heritage and antiquities started from the very beginning, in the 1920s in Hunan and Jiangxi, where numerous religious structures and old buildings (as well as leading local gentry and scholars) were physically wiped out in the name of peasant revolution.[227] Then, after the creation of the PRC, and over the vocal objections of experts, historians and even Soviet advisors, Mao Zedong and Zhou Enlai directly ordered the destruction of most of the imperial buildings in Beijing. One particularly egregious target was Beijing City Wall, the largest and best-preserved ancient city wall in the world, which even the Japanese occupiers during World War II had carefully protected.[228] Around the country and for decades, especially during the "Cultural Revolution" (1966–1976), the CCP organized and encouraged mob destruction of countless irreplaceable antiquities and national treasures, including books, scrolls, manuscripts, sculptures, monuments, jewelry, porcelains, houses, tombs, religious shrines, and even whole city blocks. The Red Guards dug up and leveled the Confucius family compound, cemetery and shrines in Qufu, Nanjing and countless

other locations, which were considered holy and had previously survived wars, foreign invasions, and the elements for millennia.[229] At the
same time, fake "Tang poems," among others, were promoted with high
"authentication" to suit the momentary political needs for class struggle.[230]

After Mao, the CCP-PRC party-state seems to have continued to
destroy Chinese antiquities in various ways, sometimes arbitrarily tearing
down whole cities to build "modern" structures and fake antiquities,
motivated by the cadres' search for quick profits and demonstrable "development" measured by GDP growth and new buildings to promote their
careers in the officialdom. "The destruction of antiquity" since the 1980s,
concluded Chinese experts of antiquity, "has been worse than that during
the Cultural Revolution." In addition to the government's destruction
of antiquity in the name of economic development or political control
(such as the destruction of religious sites in Tibet and the old city of
Kashgar), the crazy pursuit of short-term profits in the absence of rule of
law, especially the lack of appropriate private property rights, combined
with the widespread moral vacuum and the suppression of free media,
has propelled people to literally raid uncountable tombs, build endlessly
fake antiquities, buildings, or even whole cities (often to "restore and
upgrade" long-gone ancient cities for the sake of tacky tourism), destroy
countless hometowns, and eradicate the traditional Chinese homeland.[231]
The ancient practice of editing local chorography (*difangzhi*) has been
widely hijacked by local CCP officials who spare no expense in writing
endless "fake and useless" local histories to glorify themselves.[232] "The
China of five thousand years," a Chinese poet lamented in 2015, "has
been completely demolished in the past thirty years." A PRC-based
senior philosopher echoed that "China's sociocultural inheritance is now
severed and traditions all destroyed."[233]

It also appears that the famously diverse and scrumptious Chinese
cuisines have significantly changed, if not degenerated, since the 1950s
to now narrowly focus on spicy, heavily flavored, and oily cooking, del-
icacies that in the past were often considered "low-end," at the expense
of marginalizing some "high-end" gastronomy. Chronic shortages of foods
including salt probably explains the popularity of the cheap but potent
hot chili pepper in China since its importation from the Western Hemi-
sphere in the late-Ming era (sixteenth century), most prominently in
the inland and more impoverished regions. The worsened economy and
the gastronomic preferences of CCP leaders from Mao to Deng (who
hailed from Hunan and Sichuan, respectively, provinces known for diets

heavy in chili and numbing peppers) and their eager followers apparently exalted the previously "unrefined" spicy foods, encouraging their adoption nationwide in the PRC.[234] In the 1950s, only around 2 percent of the dishes (3 of 143) offered at the top-class Sichuan Restaurant in The Beijing Hotel seemed spicy. Three decades later, nearly 11 percent of the same menu (36 of 328 dishes) appeared to be spicy, including entries like "spicy dog meat" and "spicy diced rabbit."[235] By the 2010s, according to food critics, numbing and spicy foods like red-oil hotpot, spicy pork, and chili fish head firmly dominated both the Sichuan and Hunan schools of cooking and Chinese eateries in general. Sichuan (66%), Guangdong (8%), and Hunan (5%) led the so-called eight Chinese culinary schools in popularity, with half of the top twenty most popular dishes in the PRC being spicy. In Taiwan, by comparison, the top forty dishes include only one spicy food (hot pot, at number thirty-six).[236]

The Environment and Ecology

Just as the rich and colorful Chinese culture and antiquities have been extensively contaminated, defiled and plundered, often irreplaceably and irreversibly, under the CCP-PRC party-state, the physical beauty and ecological health of the land, water, and air of Mainland China have also been gravely impacted and often damaged since 1949.[237] Some foreign observers have called the PRC "an environmental rogue state" and a "climate arsonist" with an "engine of environmental collapse." China's environment bore the brunt of economic failures and stagnation under Mao and has also suffered during the post-Mao era of economic growth and prosperity.[238] The Great Leap Forward, for example, is now considered a major cause of destruction of the Chinese ecosystem due to massive deforestation, losses of wetlands and waterways, and a rise in air and water pollution.[239] Over the past three decades, the same forces that have destroyed Chinese antiquities have also extensively damaged the Chinese environment: the absence of rule of law (especially private property rights) and free media, the lack of scientific and open studies and debates, the CCP's desperate populist urge to grow the economy and create jobs at all costs so as to legitimize its one-party dictatorship, and widespread corruption and the decay of morality and ethics, which promote short-term behaviors with little sense of long-term social responsibility.[240] The PRC has created a major environmental crisis, similar to but far more serious than those of peer countries, evidenced even by the likely skewed official data from the PRC Ministry of Environmental Protection itself.[241]

According to the PRC's own environmental scientists, nearly all of Mainland China experiences heavy acid rain, with more than half of all cities recording copious year-round acidic rainfall.[242] Countless fauna and at least 15 percent of flora species in China have already gone extinct in the past five decades. One-third of China Proper faces serious soil degradation and much of Chinese agricultural land has lost most of its bio-microorganisms and is thus "dead." Over 16 percent of the total territory and more than 20 percent of cultivated land in the PRC has been heavily polluted by heavy metals; the underground aquifers in two-thirds of Chinese cities have been badly polluted and depleted.[243] Consequently, as much as 10 percent of the rice produced in China contains an excessive amount of cadmium, a known carcinogen.[244] Groundwater levels in over fifty major cities including Beijing, Shanghai and 40 percent of the Northern China Plains (where 75–80% of the water supply is from wells), are literally sinking daily.[245]

Despite repeatedly lowering standards to cover up problems, the pollution of land, water and air in China has reached a level that is "unprecedented" in human history, according to PRC experts. Almost all rivers, lakes and reservoirs are contaminated, with two-thirds "seriously polluted." In 2014, 70 to 85 percent of the water in the seven largest river basins (where 80% of Chinese live) and two-thirds of underground aquifers in urban areas (up from 37% in 2000) were deemed too toxic for drinking even after treatment.[246] More than 20 percent of surface fresh water is ecologically "dead." Half of Beijing's surface water is "worse than Level V," the lowest level of water quality. Only 17 percent of urban tap water in China met the "international standard for drinking water" in the mid-2010s.[247] The massive overuse and abuse of antibiotics in medicine and agriculture, particularly in husbandry and fisheries, has led to a per capita consumption of antibiotics ten times that in the United States. Official media report that major rivers gush poisonous levels of antibiotics, and 40 percent of pregnant women and 80 percent of children who were tested in the most populous Lower Yangtze Valley were found to have toxic levels of twenty-one various antibiotics in their bodies (some of which were banned).[248] Years after coming to the United States, New Yorkers of Chinese heritage still have "the highest" concentration of three harmful heavy metals in their blood, with cadmium (174% and 135%), lead (148% and 124%), and mercury (266% and 177%) higher than New Yorkers and New Yorkers of non-Chinese Asian heritage, respectively.[249]

Nearly all of China's territorial ocean water is now polluted, with over half seriously contaminated and 90 percent having "no fish to catch," according to PRC reports. Nearly all of China's coastal seas "have been destroyed by greed and negligence," largely due to the world's largest and very poorly regulated seafood farming industry, which has boomed during recent decades.[250] Due to or exacerbated by the widespread collusion between officials and developers, over 1,000 freshwater lakes, the flood storage volume equivalent of China's largest five lakes, 83 percent of the Sanjiang Plains in Manchuria (one of the world's largest wetlands), 80 percent of coral reefs, 72 percent of mangrove forests, and 50 percent of coastal wetlands have all disappeared in the PRC over the past five decades. Furthermore, many lakes and rivers have suffered "grave destruction," including China's "mother river" itself, the Yellow River, which had had total dry-outs (sometimes affecting "up to 700 kilometers") for twenty-two years during 1972–1999 due to excessive damming and water diversion—it lost its water flow entirely for 226 days in 1997 alone. The ecosystem of the Yellow River basin, the cradle of ancient Chinese civilization, has thus suffered almost irreversible devastation.[251] Likewise, the Yangtze River, China's largest river by far, was reported by official media in 2021 to be almost "fishless."[252] The Qinghai-Tibetan Plateau, the "water tower" for 20 percent of humankind across many countries, is reportedly suffering "increasing" degradation and human disturbance of biodiversity and hydrogeology.[253]

As reported in chapter 2, the PRC is highly inefficient in its use of energy and raw materials. Its ecological footprint is already an unsustainable "2.5 times its own biocapacity," an international study concluded, and "China has relatively inefficient resource use compared with the US, UK. and South Africa. Every 1,000 USD of Chinese consumption generates about a four and a half times larger Ecological Footprint than the United States and UK, and over twice as much as in South Africa."[254] Unsurprisingly, biodiversity in the PRC has suffered significantly and perhaps irreversibly from the wasteful and predatory model of economic development, so much so that the World Wildlife Fund warns that China's environmental damage and loss of biodiversity are causing a "global disaster."[255] Chinese activities that devastate biodiversity have reached far abroad into places like Africa, where the presence of Chinese people and Chinese money reportedly has directly led to the depletion and extinction of many flora and fauna.[256] Despite Beijing's official participation in international bans on the ivory trade, for example, the PRC presidential delegation and the PLA flotilla were reported to have used diplomatic bags and navy ships to illegally ship "thousands of pounds of poached tusks" from Tanzania to China.[257]

Perhaps the most noticeable of all the environmental problems in the PRC is the almost constant smog that covers much of Mainland China with a toxic brew containing particulate matter (PM), especially PM2.5, affecting 800 million people or 62 percent of the total population. In 2014, out of 161 cities monitored, only sixteen met the PRC's official air quality standard, which is already much lower than the WHO (World Health Organization) standard.[258] Sixteen PRC cities, including mega cities like Beijing, are now ranked among the top twenty most polluted cities in the world with AQI (air quality index) readings routinely many to dozens of times worse than the WHO recommendation.[259] In 2015, more than 90 percent of 360 Chinese cities surveyed failed to meet the PRC's already-modest air quality standards.[260] Based on the WHO's AQI ranking of 1,082 cities in the mid-2010s, all thirty-one PRC cities ranked quite low—between number 814 (Haikou) and 1,056 (Lanzhou)—with Shanghai at 978 and Beijing at 1,035.[261]

Many have recently called Beijing, the crowded PRC capital, a giant "gas chamber."[262] An influential PRC education-entrepreneur asserted publicly in 2014 that, of the 500 cities in China, only five have air quality meeting international standards, and Beijing had only five days in 2013 without serious smog.[263] Outside of the big cities, half of China's prefectures have serious air pollution as well.[264] Chinese air pollution has now evidently affected air quality considerably in neighboring places like Japan, Korea, Taiwan, and even as far away as the United States.[265]

The PRC Minister of Health wrote in 2013 that, as China was the world's largest energy consumer, with a per-capita GDP energy consumption 1.4 times higher than the world average, heavy outdoor air pollution had caused a 465 percent jump in lung cancer cases in China since the mid-1970s, and half a million Chinese die prematurely every year.[266] A study by two University of California at Berkeley scientists in the mid-2010s concluded that a staggering 1.6 million people die every year (4,000 every day) due to PM2.5 pollutants in China, constituting 17 percent of all deaths in the country. PRC media reported that Chinese children have a cancer rate 2.5 times higher than the world's average, growing 18.8 percent from 2003 to 2008. And researchers have identified "startling connections between air pollution and decreased cognition and well-being," especially in young brains.[267]

Pain, suffering, death, and loss of biodiversity aside, the financial cost of the environmental degradation in the PRC is truly exorbitant. Multiple methods may be employed to calculate the economic costs. The PRC government itself has estimated that the serious pollution carries a shocking price-tag of 10 percent of its GDP.[268] The cost of mortality from air pollution in the PRC was estimated to be almost 12 percent of its GDP in 2010, compared to 7 percent in India, and 6 percent in South Korea.[269] A RAND study concluded in 2015 that China's air pollution cost 6.5 percent of its GDP in health impacts and loss of productivity each year "between 2000 and 2010"; this percentage has been rising since then, while water pollution and soil degradation cost an additional 2.1 and 1.1 percent of GDP respectively. The identifiable costs of just air and water pollution and soil degradation would add up to 9.7 percent of the GDP in the PRC, nullifying just about all (if not more than) the gains of its high and much-praised economic growth. By this analysis, PRC economic growth over the past four decades may have come to naught considering its ecologic problems. Treating the environmental problems is very costly: just one plan to modestly slow and reduce air pollution (by reducing coal use by half) would easily cost 2.2 percent of the GDP annually. In Linyi City of Shandong Province, a four-month "iron fist" campaign in 2015 reduced the air pollutant PM2.5 by 24 percent, but required the arrest of seventy-one people, closure of fifty-seven companies, and the loss of 60,000 industrial jobs, "threatening local financial and social stability."[270]

Contact with the outside world through trade and travel has noticeably raised environmental awareness in the PRC. Imported norms, technology, and images of other countries have had a positive impact.[271] PRC TV personality Chai Jing, for example, made an online documentary on air pollution that was a powerful and popular source of enlightenment.[272] As about half of Chinese surveyed think air pollution is a "big problem," the CCP has renewed its decades-old promises to treat pollution in Beijing through astronomical but opaque spending of the national treasury, as the pollution of the city has already made it "a city now almost uninhabitable for humans."[273] Since the privileged capital Beijing "does not have clean air, water, soil, and bright sunshine—the very essentials of life, [. . .] even ¥1 trillion ($166 billion, roughly Beijing's total GDP in 2012) in three years would be worth it," Beijing Mayor Wang Anshun vowed publicly in 2014, promising his head if the smog continued up until 2017. CCP leaders in other equally polluted regions have also competed with similarly gory but empty "vows." Of course, the smog continued and the mayor did not keep his promise, instead keeping his head and enjoying a cushy pre-retirement post.[274]

As part of Xi Jinping Thought, Xi created his so-called "two mountains theory," ostensibly calling for some rebalance between GDP growth and the environment by declaring that "clear water and green mountains are as good as mountains of gold and silver." He personally pushed to disperse and downsize the Beijing population and build a "grand city for the next millennium," the Xiong'an New District, to "undertake the noncapital functions of" the overly congested Beijing City.[275] This much-hyped Xiong'an New District, announced on April Fool's Day 2017, was to be a city of the future built around Beiyangdian Lake, sixty-five miles away from Beijing, the only (and already heavily polluted) wetland in Northern China. Only four years later, however, the "deputy capital of the nation" was unceremoniously downgraded to a mere prefecture seat under Hebei province, and now increasingly appears to be yet another of the bizarre, costly, and inadvisable projects undertaken and unfinished by the CCP.[276]

As fully expected, the CCP's decrees and slogans can hardly scrub pollution. With the expansive and expensive "special prevision" system for senior cadres, discussed earlier in this book, the CCP leaders and top lieutenants have selfishly protected themselves well from the polluted environment and the national problem of unsafe food and medicine; their exclusive special farms and hospitals, less polluted vacation resorts, and imported food, medicine, and filtration systems of air and water have allowed them to play the insincere game of state-dictated "anti-pollution," which have become mostly ineffective other than producing hefty profits for the officials-in-charge and their cronies. The "project of cleaning stinky and blackened rivers," for example, with an estimated cost of ¥7 trillion ($1.1 trillion), was reported six years later in 2021 as "incredibly wasteful," "totally wrong-headed," and "simply unfinishable."[277] Chai and her documentary on air pollution were both banished by Beijing scarcely two weeks after the film's premiere.[278] To improve the air quality for the 2014 APEC (Asia-Pacific Economic Cooperation) summit meeting held in Beijing, in order to save face in front of the foreign dignitaries and reporters, Beijing "tried multiple methods" with an "iron fist," in the tradition of the similar campaign that produced "Olympic blue" sky for the 2008 Olympic Games in Beijing. Countless people were mobilized to partially shut down the capital city of over 20 million residents for a whole week (November 5–12), furloughing with pay millions of workers for days; tens of thousands of factories and worksites in six provincial regions within a 600-kilometer (373 miles) radius (over 5,000 in Hebei Province alone) were ordered to temporarily close for ten days; dust- and smoke-producing activities were strictly forbidden in that vast area for the duration of the event. In a single week, the neighboring city of Shijiazhuang, twenty-nine officials were penalized for "not enforcing the special prohibition forcefully," and nine people were arrested for not obeying the strict ban. At a vast cost and considerable inconvenience and hardship to the estimated 50 to 100 million people affected, the expensive "APEC blue" sky in Beijing still appeared only briefly during the week of the event. Despite this, in September 2015, similarly massive, disruptive, and costly efforts were launched once again to create a few days of "parade blue" sky so that Xi Jinping could stage a grand military parade to commemorate the end of World War II.[279] For the 2022 Beijing Winter Olympic games, the CCP similarly ordered the economy in many parts of seven provincial units to shut down for more than two months. These short-term, quick fixes do little to avert the overall failure of environmental protection, which has been delivering heavy economic and sociopolitical costs in and beyond China.[280] In the 2020s, for example, annual carbon dioxide emissions in the PRC have been much greater than in the United States and the twenty-seven nations of the EU combined.[281]

Superpower of Imitation

Yet another profound indictment of the suboptimality of the CCP-PRC sociopolitical system has been the sustained lack of Chinese innovation and invention. This is, of course, unsurprising to observers who have studied the socioeconomic and cultural history of Imperial China, as I have attempted to do in this book's prequal, *The China Order*. The whole Chinese World had been basically un-innovative for many centuries, from the end of the Song Era in the late thirteenth century until the late nineteenth century.[282] Under the imposed Westphalian System, the Chinese people quickly learned from the West and started to produce their share of scientific discoveries and technological inventions. The brief three decades of the ROC era, despite never being free from highly destructive internal or external wars, produced many first-class Chinese students and scholars, who later accomplished impressive feats in many fields of science and technology. These scientists were mostly educated in Western ways (in China or overseas) and worked primarily in Western or Western-styled labs, universities, and factories. Nine ethnic Chinese have won a Nobel Prize in sciences since 1957—seven of whom grew up and were initially educated in the ROC, and only one of whom did the prize-winning work within the PRC.[283] Countless Chinese have made great contributions to science and technology outside of the PRC since the early twentieth century. Highlights include An Wang's pioneering work on personal computers, David Ho's innovative treatment of AIDS, and Jerry Yang's creative co-funding of Yahoo!. Given a suitable sociopolitical system under a conducive world order, it is clear that the Chinese are individually and culturally just as capable, creative, and innovative as any other people.

The development of Chinese creativity and innovation, however, was abruptly stopped by in the CCP-PRC, together with the derailment of China's sociopolitical progress and international integration. Chinese ingenuity has been systematically suppressed for seven decades on the Chinese Mainland, and the long drought of innovation of imperial times has resumed despite the great amount of money poured into endless CCP campaigns to "lead the world." China's traditional pseudo-scholarship and anti-intellectualism, controlled learning for the sake of the imperial exam only, and meticulous obscurantism peaked under Mao, as symbolized by the numerous political campaigns to "criticize Einstein," and class struggles against classical music and fine arts in the 1960s–1970s.[284] Such anti-science and anti-culture policies were only partially tempered in the post-Mao PRC. Predictably, the PRC has produced little scientific knowledge for humankind other than proving the complete idiosyncrasy and disastrous failure of Maoist economic policies and political governance through the loss of countless lives. Yet this precious and powerful lesson is still forcefully suppressed in the PRC.

As mentioned earlier, there has been just one PRC citizen awarded a Nobel Prize in sciences: Tu Youyou (born 1930), as a co-winner of the 2015 Nobel Prize in Medicine for her work performed four decades ago on the malaria-fighting compound artemisinin. Tu's formative years and basic education took place in the pre-PRC era, and she has been typically marginalized and unrecognized by the PRC authorities for her apolitical "honesty."[285] As reported in *The China Order*, PRC researchers have documented that, under the Qin-Han autocracy, the Chinese have been extremely uncreative in science and technology for millennia.[286] A PRC study of three major journal citation indexes, SSIE, SSCI, and AHCI, showed that highly cited journal papers published in Chinese have been very rare since 1900 (even fewer during the PRC era). Most recently, from 2006 to 2015, such articles produced in Chinese ranked third (0.59%) in natural sciences, behind English (96.9%) and German (0.61%); eighth (0.56%) in humanities and arts, behind English (73%) and seven other languages; and completely out of the top ten in social sciences, which included English (95%) and nine other languages including Spanish (1.42%), French (0.58%), Russian 0.37%), Turkish (0.16%), and Slovenian (0.06%).[287] The influence of the rich and long culture of the world's largest ethnolinguistic entity, the Han-Chinese, is low and withering. Studies show that, by the number of works translated into it, the Chinese language ranks only thirteenth in the world; by the number of works translated from it, the Chinese language ranks even lower at fourteenth. Chinese-using netizens exceed 760 million, second only to English-using netizens (950 million), but online (nonrepetitive) information in Chinese amounts to only 2 percent of the world's total, smaller than eight other languages including English (56%), Russian (6.5%), Japanese (5.6%), and Italian (2.4%).[288] It appears that the Chinese people, nearly one-fifth of humankind, create little valuable information for the world, while missing out on much of human knowledge.

The PRC's approach to science and technology has basically been based on adaptation and emulation of Western (and Russian) inventions and innovations, but often without acknowledgment much less proper compensation of the inventors. Given that it has access to one-fifth of humankind, with countless raw talent and the world's second largest R&D budget,[289] the PRC's extraordinarily low originality in science and technology, alone with social sciences and the humanities, has been truly remarkable. Real invention and innovation from the PRC for other peoples to learn, adopt and imitate remain extremely rare. Most of the latest laudatory reports or panicky warnings about China's prowess in innovation often tend to either confuse the admittedly impressive imitation and adaptation of imported ideas and technology with real invention and innovation, or conflate the massive number of funds, personnel, and labs and the raw quantity of papers and patents with genuine breakthroughs.[290]

As discussed earlier in the book, substandard and fraudulent works in PRC academic circles have become a chronic and cancerous epidemic, though quite expected considering the overall void of morality and ethics under the CCP, together with the utilitarian pressure for funding, promotion and recognition under the officials-standard of a developmental state. The PRC became the world's third largest producer of research papers by the mid-2010s, having grown quantitatively at the incredible annual rate of 15 percent from 2001 to 2011, although "China's increased research output is being used mostly within its borders," with "only South Korea and Taiwan citing Chinese research articles at the expected rate," according to an assessment in *Nature*.[291] Faring even worse than the former Soviet Union, which pioneered important advances in space travel and other fields of science and technology, the PRC has had no new scientific or technological breakthroughs to share, no original products or designs to sell, and almost no world-class brand names to show to date. The Chinese brands best known abroad, such as Haier home appliances, Huawei telecommunications equipment, Lenovo personal computers, and Xiaomi cell phones, have all relied on imported technology, design, and key components. The only noteworthy PRC-era technological invention, hybrid rice, is based on imported ideas, and its key research was started back in the 1930s, way before the PRC. Chiefly due to their lack of innovation, Chinese automobile makers (excluding joint ventures with foreign automakers) have only a paltry 18 percent and declining market share in the PRC, which is now the world's largest market for passenger cars.[292]

Reasons for the PRC's humiliating lack of invention and innovation are multiple, and many are the same as those responsible for the centuries-long stagnation of the imperial Chinese World as outlined in *The China Order*. Today, the CCP-PRC political system remains a key cause. "The problem," a Harvard University study concludes, "is not the innovative or intellectual capacity of the Chinese people, which is boundless, but the political world in which their schools, universities, and businesses need to operate, which is very much bounded." "Tensions between the old communist regime and modern market forces are hindering efforts" to increase innovation in China, another report published in *Nature* concludes.[293] The brutal purges of dissenting voices and the deliberate obscurantist acts by the CCP autocracy, the sociopolitical disincentives and punishments for diversity and deviance, the lack of freedom of speech and mobility, the twisted incentive structure under the state-monopolized officials-standard,[294] the state's monopoly and tight control of education and research institutions and resources, the lack of proper protection of property rights and especially intellectual property rights, and the widespread corruption and fraud resulting from the general decay of the work ethic and social morals have all mattered. Draconian censorship has decisively helped the bad coins drive out the good coins with regard to creative talent.[295] The continued dominance of highly centralized, imperial-exam-inspired test scores in PRC schools rewards rote memorization of officially sanctioned content and produces little true creativity.[296] The British journal *Nature* issued a special collection of works by Chinese scholars on how to improve PRC science and technology policy. The publication, however, was itself banned from distribution inside the PRC.[297]

Quite fitting the general pattern of the CCP's self-aggrandizement, official PRC researchers have indeed been making greater leaps in fakery and pseudo-science than those comical frauds of the imperial times for the entertainment of the rulers. A team at the Chinese Academy of Sciences, the highest organ of science in the country, issued its multi-hundred-page "scientific study on national wellbeing" annually in 2008–2013, ranking the PRC as the world's top (called a "healthy adolescent") out of 45 to 100 countries, followed by Mexico, Brazil, Thailand, and the Philippines, with the United States ranked last (and labeled a "menopausal oldie"), lower than Italy, Israel, and Singapore. It also "scientifically" predicted, just as the CCP has declared repeatedly since the 1990s, that the PRC would surpass the United States "in every category" by 2049 to realize "the China Dream." Similarly, the PRC State Research Institute of Social Development devised a "scientific index of rejuvenation of the Chinese nation" and declared it was 46.4 percent complete in 2005, 62.7 percent in 2010, and 65.3 percent in 2012, presumably accelerating to 100 percent before 2049, so as "to surpass the world power of the United States."[298]

A major twist in the story of the traditional Chinese lack of creativity is that the CCP-PRC, forced by international comparison and competition under the "un-Chinese" Westphalian System of world order, has systematically engaged in massive and sustained counterfeiting and piracy by any means necessary in order to stay in the power game of international politics. Since 2000, China has been named by the US Office of the National Counterintelligence Executive as "the top and the only separate country of industrial and technological espionage" against the United States.[299] "U.S. companies had suffered estimated losses in

2012 of more than $300 billion due to the theft of trade secrets, much of it the result of Chinese hacking," declared the US Trade Representative. The American Chamber of Commerce in China reported in 2013 that 26 percent of its members had trade secrets and proprietary information stolen in their Chinese operations; only 10 percent trusted Chinese cloud data service; 62 percent reported that PRC cyber control hurt their businesses; and 72 percent believed that the PRC was not effectively enforcing intellectual property rights.[300]

The state-sponsored reliance on piracy and counterfeiting may have compensated greatly for the economic and technological deficiencies and suboptimality inevitable under the CCP-PRC party-state, and had a crucial role in fueling the impressive economic growth and technological sophistication on the Chinese Mainland over the past three decades.[301] Comprehensive emulation and persistent piracy have given the party-state enormous financial benefits and a competitive edge. But the fact that "Beijing inhibits free and critical thinking," seems to also hamper what the CCP can muster for its external rivalry. The continued waste of the great talent of one-fifth of humankind in the PRC is itself a tragic loss for humanity.[302] As the West is becoming more aware and wary of Beijing and as Chinese labor costs rise, PRC's "days as a shameless copycat and sweatshop to the world" appear to be "numbered."[303] Since 2014, the United States in particular has accelerated its pushback against Beijing's piracy with legal means and an increasingly "whole of society" and "whole of government" approach.[304]

The PRC as a "superpower of counterfeiters" and haven for piracy,[305] necessitated by its sociopolitical institutions, norms, and pursuits, seems to have a more profound impact beyond reinforcing the general decay of morality, exacerbating the already inadequate property rights, and suffocating Chinese creativity and innovation. The PRC is now literally flooding the world market (especially China's own) with substandard and fake products and services, and was responsible for more than 70 percent of the total counterfeit goods traded in the world (or 87% of the seized fake goods in the US) consistently throughout the 2010s.[306] The US Chamber of Commerce concluded in a 2016 study that "nearly all global physical counterfeiting is from China and Hong Kong" with an estimated value of $461 billion each year, a verdict echoed by an OECD-European Union study in 2019. The German organization Aktion Plagiarius has issued an annual "Plagiarius Negative Award" since 1977, naming the top counterfeiters in the world. Unsurprisingly, the PRC has consistently taken all top "prizes" for plagiarism and counterfeiting in recent years.[307] More broadly, the real cost of those cheap knockoff goods on the environment, economic efficiency, and human and labor rights throughout the world is devastatingly large. Persistent and massive counterfeiting and piracy in the PRC intensely twist the incentive structures worldwide, making a yet-to-be fully appreciated but likely very negative impact on the innovation and invention of the whole of humankind—to drive everyone toward the bottom with regard to promoting innovation, protecting intellectual property rights, and facilitating positive competition.[308] This is, evidently, very much the essence of the overall challenge from the rising power of the CCP-PRC party-state, which clearly has the future of human civilization at stake.

Epilogue

From the Record

Fully mindful of the immodest ambitiousness of assessing an immense polity that has governed nearly one-fifth of humanity over seven decades in a single volume, and the challenge of analyzing the whole picture in a balanced way without becoming an "all-inclusive" blotter, I hope that I have presented a broad factual analysis and a holistic yet comparative assessment of the record of the CCP-PRC state. Overall, this book finds the party-state a genetically premodern (pre-Enlightenment) polity of authoritarianism and even totalitarianism, a reincarnation of the Chinese imperial Qin-Han polity with modifications. The CCP-PRC is a governance of Chinese Legalism wrapped in Confucian populism and Han-Chinese nationalism, together with imported ideologies, chiefly the Leninist–Stalinist version of Marxism or Communism, statist militarism, and imperialist globalism.[1] This mode of governance is adroit and resilient as an optimal model of government, having attained a remarkable longevity and power for the ruling CCP leaders, against all odds. It rules with unscrupulous use of force and ruse mainly for its own benefit, focusing on staying in power forever at all costs.[2] For the Chinese people, however, their government has had a mixed, mostly mediocre, largely suboptimal and undesirable, and often disastrous and even tragic record of performance. Upon closer look, the much-admired Chinese economic development in the decades since the 1990s, for instance, has been rather average, often underperforming with serious problems. The great resources and wealth provided by the hardworking Chinese people under an effective control and world-class extraction, however, have made the CCP-PRC party-state both increasingly assertive and very powerful. Unmonitored and unrestrained, the underperforming and undesirable CCP regime has controlled and used one-fifth of productive humankind to nonetheless become a suboptimal giant, a formidable contender for power and influence on the world stage, and a viable and even tempting substitute for the current world leadership. The rise of China, therefore, presents to the world a real choice for the competing vision and leadership Beijing represents, a suboptimal but feasible alternative for the political organization of human civilization.

The CCP party-state is a polity meant to be a world phenomenon, or a "world" polity by itself in isolation, in the awkward and agonizing disguise of the Chinese nation-state (in fact a remnant of a multi-nation empire). Like many of its predecessors, the party-state has been locked in a seemingly endless life-and-death struggle from day one, externally against the existing world order led by the West and internally against Chinese society, which has been strongly and continuously influenced by the outside world since the nineteenth century. With the so-called CCP Optimality, this party-state has illustrated the efficacy of authoritarianism and strengthened the allure of autocratic state-capitalism or partocracy-capitalism, despite its many blunders and horrific failures. It presents a model of governance that has been seductive and even addictive to ambitious leaders of various ethnicities because it has proven to be an optimal machine for safeguarding and enriching an autocracy. Simultaneously and symbiotically, the regime has produced the colossal China Tragedy and perpetuated the structural China Suboptimality for the Chinese people. This is seen in all four areas assessed in the pages of this book: political governance, socioeconomic development, people's lives, and culture and the environment.

With woefully inadequate political legitimacy after seventy-three years in power, the CCP-PRC remains a party-state autocracy that feels outdated and out of place in the post–World War II era, and especially in the post–Cold War world. With only force and ruse to rely on, and some populist appeal, the CCP rulers face constant insecurity and discontent. Facing the ever-acute "fundamental challenge [of] how to couple the Party's need for control at home with open markets abroad,"[3] the CCP must steer the PRC on its politically and ideologically predisposed or preordained road for ever more political control at home and abroad, driven or cursed by the ideation and tradition of the China Order of world empire and its professed official ideology of world communism. Increasing raw power and expanding centralized control are viewed and pursued as solutions and ultimate objectives. The CCP thus relentlessly struggles to recenter and reorder the world in its image, wherever and whenever it deems possible, attempting to replace the West and particularly the United States as the world leader. Its growing control of resources has, paradoxically, intensified rather than tempered the CCP's inherent urge for more power and control at home and abroad. Its grand mission is now in plain sight, redisplayed with a somewhat sophisticated liberal veneer and globalist guise, advocating as well an eventual world political unity under socialism and communism.[4]

The rise of China, or more precisely the rising power of the CCP-PRC party-state, is now impactfully mounting, rhetorically and also in action, a worldwide challenge for the vision and leadership that Beijing represents, an alternative mode of political organization and world order that this book and its prequel have examined. Human civilization is, therefore, facing a critical and lasting choice for drastically different futures. As demonstrated by history, and especially the history of the Sinic World, a malevolent and undesirable but determined and devious power can be surprisingly successful in its efforts to conquer, organize, and govern the entire known world, overpowering and outmaneuvering the stronger and the better, tragically and often irreversibly altering the direction of a human civilization. To repeat and reemphasize, a key conclusion of this book is that the CCP-PRC party-state represents an alternative political system that is suboptimal while formidable, undesirable yet feasible, derisory but serious, with many real and profound consequences for the world.

The above findings from the examination of the China Record in this book, together with those of its prequel, *The China Order*, I hope has set a solid foundation for further discussions in a subsequent volume on how to encounter and manage the rising PRC state power.

Notes

Introduction

1. F. Wang 2017; Wang Fei-Ling 2018.

2. *Carbis Bay G7 Summit Communiqué*, Cornwell, UK, June 13, 2021. *Brussels Summit Communiqué, Issued by the Heads of State and Government participating in the meeting of the North Atlantic Council*, Brussels, Belgium, June 14, 2021. G7 emphasized this more in *G7 Leaders' Communiqué*, Elmau, Germany, June 28, 2022. NATO for the first time targeted "the systemic challenges posed by the PRC to Euro-Atlantic security [. . . and to] our interests, security and values." *NATO 2022 Strategic Concept*, Madrid, Spain, June 29, 2022: 10 & 5.

3. For two recent sketches of the history of the CCP, see Editors 1991–2021 and Saich 2021.

4. Of course, even during the Mao era, the PRC governance was clearly not without some noteworthy achievements, which include enhanced national unity, development of infrastructure, and advances in literacy and life expectancy. These, however, should be contextualized akin to Mussolini "making" the trains in Italy run on time, Nazi Germany inventing missiles and jet planes, and the Soviet Union launching Sputnik and being the country of Dmitri Shostakovich. More on the PRC's accomplishments and costs later in this book.

5. For rich examples of the outrageous and catastrophic national forgery of statistics under Mao, see Li Rui 1999-II: 46–75. For vivid illustrations of "real" but misleading statistics in the PRC, see Qin Hui 2020. For manipulation of statistics in the Mao era, see Ghosh 2020. For a caution about PRC statistics today, see Crabbe 2014.

6. F. Wang 2017: 21–29; Ou 2021; *PRC Data Security Law* (数据安全法), Beijing, Sept. 1, 2021.

7. Psaki 2022.

8. Wang Hongru 2016; Ministry HRSS 2016–2022.

9. Jon Cohen 2022; Hathaway 2022; F. Wang 2017: 27; McGregor 2022.

10. Palmer 2015; Sisci 2015; Meng Fangui 2013; Neo Zion 2014.

11. Author's interviews in Southern and Eastern China, 1996–2004; Pei Pei 2005: 80–82; Stevenson and Wong, 2020: A20; Wallace 2014.

12. Balding 2013; Owyang and Shell 2017; Wei Chen et al. 2019; Martinez 2021.

13. Fang Yi 2014; Bird and Craymer 2019; Xinhua, Dec. 11, 2015.

14. Li Kejun 2014; Anderlini 2014; Xin Chao 2022.

15. Zhang Munan 2014.

16. Author's correspondence with Chinese scholars, 2015–2021. The reported PRC unemployment rate ranges wildly from 4.1 to 20 or even 30 percent. Li Xiaokun 2010; Zhang Da 2016.

17. Liu Gengyuan et al. 2020; Tan Hao Jun 2015: A02; Wu and Zhao 2015.

18. PRC SSB 2021.

19. Ying Yue 2021; *Kuai meiti* 2021; Suju Guijichu 2021; Ma Xioahua 2021; Xiao Hui 2021.

20. *Lianhe zaobao* 2021; Ministry of Public Security 2022.

21. 复耕; Tian Jianjun 2011; Yang and Qin 2014; Xu Peng 2022; Yi Qi Lai 2022.

22. Hu Rong 2010; *Wangyi*, June 9, 2020.

23. Sparshott 2015; WHO 2013: 244, 88; PRC MEM 2022.

24. Liu Yanwu 2014, 2018; Liu Yanwu et al. 2018.

25. J. Zhang et al. 2014; Leroy 2014; Follett 2018; Gulland 2019; US National Institute of Mental Health database, World Health Organization database, accessed June 16, 2021.

26. 优越性. For an official assertion of such "superiority," see Commentator 2013: 1. For PRC scholars' similar claims, see Hu Angang 2014.

27. The PRC is said to have a unique, optimal combination of traditional meritocratic bureaucracy with "strong state capacity of planned economy" that energized to achieve miracles with institutions of markets and globalization imported from the West. Zhou Li-An 2020.

28. Ravitch 2014; McKinsey Greater China 2020.

29. *The Economist*, "Keeping Watch," November 21, 2013. The actual non-PPP PRC GDP was 67 percent of the US GDP in 2019. World Bank database, 2021.

30. Levy and Peart 2011: 110–125; Allison 2022: 45.

31. Fuentes 2019; *Acta Scientia Circumstantiate*, Mar. 21, 2021; Qi Jun 2021.

32. 放卫星. Yang Jisheng 2012. The global deaths of the COVID-19 pandemic exceeded 400,000 in six months, with 6.9 million infected. Slotkin 2020. By January 2022, the global deaths attributed to the virus were at least 5.5 million, with more than 296 million infected. *WHO Coronavirus (COVID-19) Dashboard*, accessed Feb. 2022.

33. For problems of global health data, see Davis 2020. For the Chinese coverup, see Hill 2020.

34. The 10 percent rule seems also applicable to other PRC data reporting. Beijing reported, for example, spending $3.9 billion for hosting the 2022 Winter Olympics, only 10 percent of the actual cost of $38.5 billion. *Le Vent de la Chine*, Feb. 20, 2022.

35. Hollingsworth and Xiong 2021.

36. Liu Qin 2020. Wuhan population was 11.2 million. Wuhan Government 2020.

37. Mouton et al. 2020; E. Cheung 2020.

38. Scissors 2020; *The Economist*, "Covid-19 Death Tallies," May 13, 2021; Calhoun 2022.

39. PRC State Statistical Bureau 2006–2020 and 2021; Li Ting et al. 2021. In 2021, PRC official national death numbers and death ratio were again both higher than usual. Editors 2022.

40. M. Zhou et al. 2021; PRC CDC database, accessed Apr. 12, 2022.

41. AP: "China Delayed Releasing Coronavirus Info, Frustrating WHO," June 3, 2020.

42. Chinese people seem to have also endured the heaviest impact of the pandemic: the CCP imposed draconian lockdowns on almost all of the PRC mega-cities for weeks at a time, often repeatedly, from Wuhan in 2020, Xian in 2021–2022, to Shenzhen and Shanghai in 2022.

43. Yang and Zhong et al. 2020: 165–174. For modeling of the spread of the virus, see Martin Enserink and Kai Kupferschmidt, Blog on *Science*, Mar. 25, 2020; Adam 2020: 316–318.

44. Glanz and Robertson 2020: A1; Smout 2020. For an argument that blindly following the Wuhan lockdown may have been a major global blunder of overreaction, see Weiss 2020.

45. Without Beijing's full cooperation, the much belated international inquiry may or may never get to the truth; reports, though, have piled up to suggest a possibly unnatural origin of the virus in Wuhan. Hamilton 2020; Latham and Wilson 2020; Leitenberg 2020; Wade 2021; Bloom et al. 2021: 694; Jacobsen 2021; US DNI 2021; Chan and Ridley 2021; Felter 2021; Eban 2022.

46. *Bloomberg*: "China's Stats Accentuate Positive, Play Down Negatives," Dec. 11, 2021.

47. Northrop 2022; Parton 2022.

Chapter 1

1. As will be elaborated later in the book, in the PRC, the ideal of "rule of law" (the law governs all including the ruler) has always been substituted

with the ideal of "rule by law" (the ruler uses the law to govern and is above the law). Furthermore, the CCP, like many Chinese rulers before, seems to have the Xunzi version of rule by law—the ruler uses the law as he creates it (the law follows the current king or *fahouwang* 法后王), rather than the older Confucius notion of rule by law—the ruler uses law already created (king follows existing law or *faxianwang* 法先王). *Xunzi-Ruxiao* (荀子-儒效篇), third century BCE; *Analects-Taibo* (论语-泰伯篇), fifth century BCE; *Mengzi-Lilou Zhangju* Xia (孟子-离娄章句), fourth century BCE.

2. F. Wang 2017: 173–174. Freedom House 2021.

3. "Collective leadership shall be one of the supreme principles of the party." CCP Central 1980.

4. "CCP Central 2019; CDIC 2020; CCP Central 2021; Ren Lixuan 2022.

5. 述职. CCP Central-Politburo 2017; Xinhua March 1, 2021.

6. V. Shih 2008: 1177–92; Wen Shan 2018; Jili Tonshi 2022.

7. To be sure, while both Xi and the CCP Central may have bet since 2012 on a Mao-like strong dictator, the gamble appears to have faced challenges and uncertainties. The fact that Xi has to personally chair the "democratic life meetings" for top leaders, publicize the *shuzhi* mandate so as to belittle his "peers," and exhaustively promote himself as a super-prolific author, a global trekker, and a star of TV news every evening, instead of ruling confidently in comfort and leisure like Mao, may indicate that he has had to work harder and longer to achieve Mao's power and "freedom." His countless "important" articles and speeches to endlessly emphasize and demand the total obedience to "the authority and the centralized and uniform leadership of the Party Central" appears to reflect that struggle. Xi, Aug. 16, 2021.

8. Pompeo and Yu 2021; Naughton 2021: 190; M. Pei 2006.

9. 中国梦, 人类命运共同体. Xuan Yan June 7 and 8, 2021: 1. For the latest official take on its own history, see the three *Short History* books by CCP-Department of Propaganda 2021.

10. For how the CCP defeated its opponent, the softer authoritarian party-state of the KMT–ROC, to rule the Chinese Mainland, see F. Wang 2017: 159–181.

11. 伟大, 光荣, 正确 or 伟光正. This has been the official self-label of the CCP since Mao Zedong coined it in 1951. Han and Cao 2006. "Long Live the Great Chinese Communist Party" is carved on one side of the front entrance of Zhongnanhai, the CCP-PRC headquarters in Beijing. The other side has the slogan "Long Live the Invincible Mao Zedong Thought."

12. For a Chinese sketch of this polity, see Sheng Xuebin 2021. M. Chan Jan. 31, 2022.

13. As is the case with Aeschylus, Sophocles, and Shakespeare, "tragedy" indeed often results from "good intentions" and intense acts for some justified purposes and reasonable ideals.

14. 储安平. Cited in Qian Liqun (1998) 2002: 280–281. Also see Ye Fu 2010: 54.

15. Hu Songping 1993; Hu Ming 1996: 932; Hu Shi Jan. 9, 1950.

16. Qian Liqun (1998) 2002: 60; Zhang Zhongdong 1990; Bo Yang 2002; Li Ao 2004. Author's field notes in Taipei and the Green Island (绿岛), 2015.

17. Smarlo Ma 2004: 106.

18. For the massive unnatural deaths under Mao, see F. Wang 2017: 175–180. For thirty-six volumes of CCP records on mass deaths and politics-driven cannibalism in one province alone, see Song Yongyi 2016. For a case study of political campaigns from land reform to cultural revolution, see Wang Haiguang 2021.

19. Chen and Gao 1984: 161–162; Jin Zhong 2014.

20. A popular TV anchorman (Bi Fujian 毕福剑) was swiftly fired and silenced completely in 2015 for merely uttering a few disrespectful words about Mao at a private dinner party. Elementary school students in 2019 were videotaped openly and collectively pledging loyalty and professing love for Mao in their classrooms.

21. Editors, CCP history 1991, 2001, 2011, 2021; Wang Qishan 2020; Anna Bell 2022.

22. 休养生息. Shi Yuan 2008.

23. F. Wang 2017: 189; Chang and Halliday 2013; Malia 1994; Courtois (1997) 1999.

24. Appraisals here (and elsewhere in this book) about the CCP party-state may appear to some readers as trenchant and harsh, even unbalanced, as the PRC, even under Mao, has deeds that are positive and even estimable, which this book also discusses at length. Backed by a hopefully solid scholarship, my aggregate assessment strives to be a distinct conviction based on facts and reason with proper comparative and counterfactual framing, rather than simply a normative passion or a pedantic cataloging of "all" observable particulars.

25. Campbell and Lee 2011: 71–103; S. Wang 2014; D. Goodman 2014.

26. Xi Jinping Dec. 26, 2013; Yuan Jian 2008: 155; X. Guo 2019.

27. Plato (380 BCE) 1991; Aristotle (350 BCE) 1912; Locke (1690) 1980.

28. For the nature, continuity, and changes in Chinese politics in the post-Mao PRC, see Tsang and Men, eds. 2016; F. Wang 2017: 7, 181–188, 215.

29. F. Wang 2017: 161–168.

30. Benton and Lin, eds. 2010: 1. Benton and Lin, displeased by the Chang and Halliday book, argued for a "more balanced view" of Mao and defended Mao's record (pp. 6–11), in the same vein as Benton, ed., four volumes, 2007.

31. Xi Jinping December 26, 2013.

32. Pantsov and Levine 2012: 575; Song Yongyi 2008.

33. Glad 2002: 1–37.

34. Yang Tianshi 2013; Zhang Bojun in Smarlo Ma 2004: 94, 233–242; Yang Kuisong 2010.

35. Mao Zedong 1995: 119–263.

36. F. Wang 2017: 181.

37. For more on Mao and the "Mandate of the People," see F. Wang 2017: 167–182.

38. Zhang Lifan 2013. For a similar critique of Mao's record, see Yang Fei 2015.

39. Like Mao and Xi, Kim Jong-un, the North Korean dictator, apparently also substitutes the People for Heaven in regime justification. Voice of Korea 2021.

40. Mao Zedong Thought was coined by Wang Jiaxiang (王稼祥) in 1943 as a Sinicized Marxism-Leninism. It became the dogma supreme for the CCP with the key support of Mao's protégée and designated successor Liu Shaoqi (刘少奇) in 1945. Both Wang and Liu, however, were later cruelly purged by Mao in the 1960s. Jin Chongji 1998; Cheek 2010.

41. Ma Zedong (1939) 1991; Xi Jinping, May 20, 2015; Sha Yexin 2005. For how the local officials use a verity of ruses for the stability of the party-state, see Mattingly 2019.

42. 管子 (first century BCE), 商君书 (fourth century BCE), and 韩非子 (third century BCE).

43. "To uphold the leadership of the CCP, to uphold socialism, to uphold the people's democratic dictatorship, to uphold Marxism-Leninism." First proposed by Deng Xiaoping in 1979 in his speech titled "Uphold four cardinal principles" (坚持四项基本原则), Deng (1983)1994: 158–184. Later these four were declared to be the "fundamentals of the nation" in the CCP *Party Constitution* in 2007.

44. Wei Jingsheng 1978 and 1979; Liu Binyan et al. 1989; Okesenberg 1990; Bao Pu 2009: 1–88; Deng Xiaoping 1993: 370–371.

45. Wu Bangguo (Chief of the PRC National People's Congress and number three in the CCP leadership) 2011; Chen Yixin (Secretary General of the CCP's Central Commission on Politics and Law) 2020; Li Zhanshu 2021.

46. Xi Jinping 2020 and Aug. 17, 2022. For an outline of the "political reform" or the lack thereof in the post-Mao CCP–PRC, see Fewsmith 2021.

47. Y. Yu 2015; Blanchett 2019. For a long list of books Xi claims to have read, see Guo Jinlong 3022.

48. *Renmin ribao* March 23, 2021. For elaborations, see Lu and Liu 2020.

49. CCP Central, Nov. 11, 2021; Xinhua, Nov. 8, 2021.

50. CCP Central Academy of Party History and Documents, July 24, 2021. Xi's books, required reading for millions of cadres and students, seem quite pricey. One selection (dozens of volumes) of them, for example, was marketed at a "discounted rate" of ¥2,845 ($438 or the average monthly income) in a major online store. JD.com, accessed April 26, 2022.

51. Ministry of Education *Student Reader*, 2021.

52. For the rise of "Xiism," see Johnson 2017: 62–80.

53. CCP Central November 11, 2021; Song Yuntao 2016; Mao Jun 2017; Zhao Lin 2021.

54. Xinhua Oct. 23, 2022. Right up to the moment, there appeared to always be a possibility, however slim, that Xi might still fail. Many Chinese apparently wished that Xi not become another Mao-like emperor as he "does not deserve it" (or at least he should not be more than Deng who was "only" a paramount overlord or backstage ruler). Some even publicly called for deposing him as a "despotic thief of the state." Kubota et al. 2022; Tan Oct. 13, 2022. For the CCP, his step-down, a genuine retirement, or removal, given what has transpired over a decade, though, would surely signal the failure of the regime and ensure massive purges and serious and even fundamental shakeups of the party-state.

55. Marx (1852) 1907: 5.

56. Chen Jin 2019; Cai Li 2020.

57. Xi Jinping April 1, 2014. Xi's speech mixes and mismatches various forms of government with economic ideologies to paint the CCP autocracy as "socialism," reflecting a traditional narrative poorly articulated. Cao Guoxing 2013; Wu Yu 2013; Buckley 2013: A1; Meng 2014.

58. Xi Jinping Aug. 20, 2014.

59. 为中国人民谋幸福, 为中华民族谋复兴. Xi Jinping, Oct. 17, 2017; Xi, Mar. 2021.

60. Zheng Liping 2021; CCP Central-Department of Propaganda 2021; Ministry of Education *Student reader* 2021; Du Zhengyu 2020.

61. Wang Weiguang 2014; Willy Lam 2015.

62. Xi Jinping January 5, 2013, in CCP Central Document Bureau 2014.

63. NPC, July 2015, Articles 1, 2, and 4; Xie Maosong 2021.

64. Ministry of Civil Affairs 2021; Xinhua Oct. 15, 2021. The CCP's appropriation of "democracy" includes Mao's "people's democracy," "Chinese democracy," and numerous variants such as the often-used phrase "consultative democracy." Pan 2003: 3–43; Shi Ruijie 2018.

65. State Council 2021; Ministry of Foreign Affairs 2021.

66. 人民领袖. Xinhua, Oct. 20, 2017; Zhou Xinmin 2020, 2021; Wen Xing 2021; Su 2020.

67. CCP *Constitution* 2017 and 2022; PRC *Constitution* 2018.

68. 定于一尊. Li Zhanshu 2018. *Communiqué of the First Plenary Session of the 20th CCP Central* (中共二十届一中全会公报). Beijing: Xinhua, Oct. 23, 2022.

69. CCP *Constitution* 2017: 1; CCP Central-Department of Propaganda Sept. 29, 2021. Much of the CCP's ideological innovation and rebranding since the late 1990s appeared to have been largely concocted and later led by Wang Huning, a PRC-trained academic and wordsmith. I met Wang several times circa 1985–1995 (and showed him around Philadelphia when he was a visiting

scholar in the US in 1988) but lost contact since 2002 when he joined the CCP Central Commiittee. He became a full national-rank CCP leader (member of the Politburo Standing Committee) in 2017 and retained that position in 2022.

70. Zhou Xinmin 2020; State Council, Jan. 19, 2022; He Yiting 2020: 1.

71. 改天换地. Chui Lan 2013; Buckley 2020: A8; Cai Xia 2021.

72. CCP leaders including Mao, for example, are not nearly as dogmatic and rigid as their Soviet comrades about "allowing" capitalism and employing capitalists. J. Kelly 2021.

73. Editorial 2017; Xi Jinping Oct. 18, 2017, Sept. 16, 2021, and Oct. 16, 2022.

74. Chen Shenshen: "Political Logic of Zhongnanhai Empire" (陈申申: 中南海帝国的政治逻辑), online essay circulated in Shanghai, Nov. 16, 2020.

75. According to an observer, "CCP intelligence operations have always cooperated with secret societies, triads, and criminal gangs. The doyen of China Watchers, Pierre Ryckmans observed: the CCP 'is in essence a secret society. In its methods and mentality it presents a striking resemblance to an underworld mob.'" Brady 2020.

76. Jiang Hui 2020. For more about Xi's global solution, see Li and Fan 2018. Ju Chengwei 2019; Editorial 2017; Chen Shuguang 2018; Li Wei (State Council Director of Research) 2019; Feng and Chen 2017; Huang Ping 2019; Cheng Zhiqiang, 2020; F. Wang 2017: 198.

77. Doshi, July 1, 2021; C. Wong 2021; *The Economist*, "How Did Confucianism Win Back the Chinese Communist Party?" June 23, 2021.

78. *The Economist*, "Chinese Communist Party at 100," June 26, 2021; V. Shue 2022.

79. For a thoughtful take on Xi Jinping as Han Fei, see J. Zha 2020.

80. Wu Guoguang 2012: 7–8; Callick 2013; Bardhan 2020; X. Zhou 2022.

81. Morrow et al. 2003. For the relationship between socioeconomic performance and political system, see de Mesquita and Smith 2011; Koyama and Rubin 2022. The CCP appears to have also "retrofitted" its partocracy to give the local some instrumental but useful participation in governance. Gueorguiev 2021.

82. Bowie 2021; X. Yang 2021: 915–929; Bradsher 2022; Li Yuan, March 31, 2022.

83. S. Hsu et al., eds. 2021.

84. Except for two, all of those cases were "reversed" by the post–Mao CCP as "wrongful, fake, or mistaken." Guo Dehong 2019.

85. Walker 1955; Wittfogel 1964: 463–474; Teiwes 1979; Michael 1986: 175–277.

86. Chen Po 2016; Wei Yi 2011; Qian Liqun 2012: 314–315, vol. 2: 159–164, 287–289.

87. F. Wang 2017; F. Wang 2005.

88. For an insider's recount of CCP dictating judicial trials, see Li Jing 2011; Ng and He 2017.

89. Jing Yan 2019.

90. 双规. Zunyou Zhou 2021: 102–117; CCP Central 1956; NPC 1957.

91. PRC Supreme People's Procuratorate 2021.

92. Interviews and anecdata of various regions, 2010–2021. The PRC penal code defines 469 kinds of criminal offenses to include dozens of political offenses and "violations of regulations." NPC, Dec. 2020; Zhao Fuduo 2016; Ouyang Chenyu 2017; Supreme People's Procuratorate 2020.

93. Ramzy 2020: A6; Hernández and Bilefsky 2020: A17; BBC: "China Frees Canadians Michael Spavor and Michael Kovrig after Huawei Boss Released," Sept. 25, 2021.

94. Zhou Qiang (Chief of the Supreme People's Court) 2020 and 2021. The post-Mao CCP had rehabilitation campaigns in the late 1970s and early 1980s that overturned the majority of the political persecution cases during the Mao era. However, most victims of the "reversed" cases were dead, executed, or had had their (and their families') lives ruined long before.

95. Sapio 2008: 7–37. US statistics in uscourts.gov/statistics-reports, Jan. 10, 2021.

96. Wen Da 2013; Wen Ru 2014.

97. Wu Yue 2013.

98. Yang Shiba 2020. For examples of PRC lawyers mistreated and persecuted in recent years, see Human Rights Watch 2008; N. Gan 2017; E. Feng 2020; R. Perper 2020.

99. Wang Yanqing 2015; Wu Si 2016.

100. Zhao Yunheng 2015; Wu Youming 2016; Wang Yazhong 2022.

101. CDIC and CCTV 2022.

102. Author's interview with US, Hong Kong, and China researchers of the Chinese penal system, 2007–2021; Mumola and Karberg 2007: 1–4.

103. Jia Zhifang 2009: 214–302. For abuses of purged top CCP leaders, see Li Zuopeng vol. 2, 2011: 743–748; Luo Diandian 1999: 319–322; Luo Yu 2015. Even a former number four leader went "years" without a shower or bath in prison. Chen Xiaonong 2005: 426–427. For the hellish conditions of prisons in the PRC, see Gao Ertai 2009: 314–360; Liao Yiwu, vol. 2, 2002: 36–47, 213–220, and vol. 3, 2002: 40–51. For life in the most famous political prison, Qincheng (秦城), see Jin Jingmai 2002. For cases of many wrongfully jailed and executed in the PRC, see Liao Yiwu 2005. For reports about university graduates (social elites) wrongfully detained and tortured without a trial from eleven months to over ten years, see Gao Peng 2013 and Sun Xueyang 2014. For examples of police brutality, see He and Huang 2013 and V. Yu 2015. A "chief judge" could be wrongfully jailed and tortured; see Qi E Hao 2019. Officials

could also experience severe torture when just being investigated for corruption allegations; see Lu Huo 2021.

104. Zhao Chongqiang 2015. For a political dissident's eighty-one-day detention experience, see Y. Wang 2015. For an American's experience, see F. Langfitt 2014. For accounts of life inside prison in the 2020s, see *Zhihu:* "Stories of Brutality in Prison" (监狱残酷物语), April 30, 2020.

105. Zhang Peihong 2019.

106. Callick 2020; R. Fife 2020.

107. Reporters Nov. 28, 2014.

108. *PRC State Security Law*, Feb. 1993, and *PRC State Security Law-Details on Implementation*. June 4, 1994. For an incomplete but illustrative list of sentences under the crimes of endangering state security, see Biancheng Suixiang, Nov. 26, 2014.

109. 被精神病. Li Yan 2011. For monthly anecdata report on this police action, see *Mental Health and Human Rights in China Monthly*, July 2012–April 2018.

110. CCP Central (1922) 1989: 45; F. Wang 2017: 175–180. Only after 2007 was the final approval of executions "recentralized" to the Supreme People's Court in Beijing. Xiong Xuanguo 2008: 124–140; Duihua Foundation 2014.

111. Author's interviews with US and Chinese researchers of the Chinese penal system, 2007–2021.

112. Data Blog Dec. 13, 2013; Duihua Foundation 2021; Amnesty International 2020: 8–9.

113. Zhou and Guo 2011; Tiezzi 2014; For an insider's account on the implementation of capital punishment, see Qian Yang 2015.

114. Second People's Court of Tianjin 2021.

115. Xiao Hang 2014; Zhong Jian 2014; Robertson et al. 2019; Robertson 2020.

116. 严打. Ma Qibin (1989) 1991: 519. For anecdata on people (up to 1–5 percent of the population in some communities) arrested, jailed, and executed during these campaigns for trivial offenses and indiscretions, see Liao Yiwu 2002: 40–51 and Dong Jian 2013.

117. Chen Yixin April 29, 2021.

118. Wu Bo 2008; Wang and Xing 2014: A09. Based on such, the Supreme People's Court has periodically issued "adjudication explanations" and "guiding cases" to instruct the lower courts. For collections of both, see Supreme People's Court 2015 and 2022.

119. Supreme People's Court Jan. 19, 2021.

120. CCP Central (1964) 1998. Editors 1981. Mao admitted internally in 1969 that the 5 percent quota often became 10 percent or more, cited in Qiu Huizuo, vol. 2, 2011: 632.

121. For dark humor-like stories of how CCP officials at a major Chinese university tricked a professor into being a rightist "enemy" in order to fulfill the 5 percent quota at the time and how "activists against enemies" soon became enemies themselves in later rounds of Mao's campaigns, see Jia Zhifangn 2009: 56 and 218–242. For how ludicrous but deadly those political persecutions could be, see Wang Haiguang 2021.

122. 黑五类. For rich anecdata of the life of the persecuted people, see Jiao Guobiao 2010–12; Yang Xiguang and S. McFadden 1997; Mao Muqin 2012; Xie Yongn 2014.

123. Yang Kuisong vol. 1, 2009: 154; Ma Qibin (1989) 1991: 519.

124. For a representative autobiography of such a class enemy, see Kang Zhengguo 2004 (English edition, Z. Kang 2007). Du Xing 2010.

125. Political prisoners are often treated worse than common criminals. Jia Zhifang 2009: 288.

126. 重点人口. F. Wang, 2005: 44–46, 69, 103–112.

127. 刘晓波, 艾未未, 许志永, 浦志强, 高智晟, 法轮功. Liu Xiaobo 2012; Buckley Nov. 20, 2013: A11 and Dec. 7, 2013: A6; E. Wong 2013: C1; A. Jacobs, 2009: A4; Pils and Rosenzweig 2014; J. Tong 2009; Gao Zhisheng 2016; Rogers 2019.

128. 城管. Jacobs 2013: A4. 文字狱. @SpeechFreedomCN: *Chronicle of speech crimes in China* (中国文字狱事件盘点), Twitter, Oct. 2019–Jan. 14, 2022.

129. Ying Shusheng 2010: 10–13.

130. For one *laojiao* camp for juveniles that was "worse than Auschwitz" with thousands of extra-legal deaths, watch Zen Boyann2013. For brutality in a *laojiao* camp for women, watch Du Bin 2013. For personal accounts about labor camps, see Ningkun Wu and Yikai Li 1993; Wu Hongdan2003 (earlier English edition, Wu and Wakemann1995); Kong Lingping 2012. For a profile of "five notorious labor camps," see You Yi 2015. For labor camps in general, see Cohen and Lewis 2013 and laogai.org/page/bookstore-0, accessed Feb. 8, 2022.

131. Xinhua Dec. 28, 2013; Ai Mi 2013.

132. Wang Lin 2014: 2; Qun Shuo Feb. 2014; L. Lewis 2014: 36.

133. State Council (1993) 2011. Anecdotally, police are incentivized by quotas of fines (¥5,000 per case) to "hold and educate" people. Li Yinhe 2016; Li Chengpeng 2013: 123–134. For recollections by the political detainees who were "made-to-disappear" for long durations, Caster 2017.

134. Stavrou 2019.

135. Li Qiuxue 2009. 信访. Liu Zhenqiang 2021. CCP Central and State Council: various regulations and procedures on petition, National Public Complaints and Proposals Administration (国家信访局), www.gjxfj.gov.cn, last accessed Sept. 2022.

136. Liu Zhengqiang 2014; Ding Jiafa 2010. Many cases of the "intercepted" petitioners are listed by *Weiquan wang* (维权网) on Blogpost, last accessed Sept. 2022.

137. Segal 2016: 18–32; Roberts 2018; Li Rui 1999-I: 106.

138. 思想政治工作 or 思想改造. Schein 1971; Lifton 1989; Hu Ping 1999 and 2012; Zimbardo 2002; Taylor 2017. For anecdata, see Chen Tushou 2013 and Fu Zhibin, 2014.

139. Sha Yexin 2005.

140. Orwell 1949 (quotes on p. 178); Hendrix 2008; BBC: "China's 'Memory Holes' Swallow up Melissa Chan," May 9, 2012. *Rhodes* 2012, 2013; M. Rank 2014.

141. Mosse 1996: 245–252; Lacroix 2004; Cui Weiping 2015; Cai Xia et al. 2021.

142. Huxley 1932; Fic 2014.

143. For more on the CCP imposter bloggers and posters, see F. Wang 2017: 186, 239. For an exposé of how brazen and greedy "big" agents of misinformation and disinformation work and profit in PRC cyberspace, see Jia Ye 2021.

144. "Names of 2,650 web commentators for 2015 in Fudan University leaked" (2015年复旦大学2650名网评员名单泄漏), last accessed Feb. 2022. dongyangjing.com/bbs_disp.cgi?zno=80409&kno=001&no=0410.

145. CCP Central Feb. 4, 2021.

146. Li Bin 2020. Ministry of Education, Press Conference, Beijing, Dec. 7, 2021.

147. 素质教育. Han Xiyan 2021; Bai Qingyuan 2021; Bai Xiaosheng 2021; Zhao Wanwei 2021; Yu Weiyue 2022.

148. Guoqiao Tudou 2021; Ministry of Education *Student Reader* 2021.

149. State Council Information Office 2021.

150. Shi Po 2010; author's interviews, 2001–2022; SpeechFreedomCN, 209–222.

151. Osnos 2014: 30–35.

152. 三个至上. Hu Jintao 2007; reiterated by Xi Jinping in Huang Liang 2014.

153. Xi Jinping Oct. 14, 2021 and Aug. 17, 2022.

154. A. Nathan 2014: 1–6; Buckley and Jacobs 2015: A1.

155. CCP Central-Organization Department 2014.

156. CCP Central Oct. 23, 2014; E. Wong Dec. 30, 2014.

157. Zhang Qianfan 2020.

158. Haraszti 1987; Y. Cheng, Dec. 15, 2020.

159. Han Deqiang 2013; Ni Guanghui 2013: 1; Qi Zhifeng 2013.

160. Author's interviews with PRC citizens in the 2010s–2020s. For findings of the shocking lack of basic facts about Chinese history among 6,000 respondents in three major cities, see Xing Zhuo 2006, 2016.

161. Chen and Dickson 2010; J. Chen 2014; F. Wang 2005; Wallace, June 2014.

162. "False/spurious consciousness" was discussed by Friedrich Engels (1895) 2010: 164.

163. 驭民术. *Book of Lord Shang* (fourth century BCE) 2009; De La Boétieor (1574) 2022.

164. Such as the Shanghai-based and US-educated venture capitalist Eric X. Li (李世默) 2012, 2013. For exposé of Li, see D. Ma 2012 and G. Rachman 2020.

165. Yao Yang 2013; D. Bell 2015.

166. 人治, 依法治国 and 由法治国, 法治. CCP Central Oct. 23, 2014. The official English translation is deliberately misleading: Xinhua Oct. 28, 2014.

167. 依(领导的想)法治国, 靠武力 and 权术治国. Liu Dao 2021.

168. From 法制to 法治. Sheng Ping 2020.

169. Xi Jinping April 2015; CCP Oct. 2019.

170. To be sure, US-based Sinologists can also confuse their readers (and perhaps themselves as well) about "rule of law" in China. Y. Wang 2015.

171. 官本位. Kong Deyong 2016: 16.

172. Qidian Renwen 2020.

173. 权力拜物教. Xu Yaotong 2006; Zhuang Shengdie 2007; Mu Ran, Nov. 29, 2014.

174. For an interesting example of this, see Zhang and Zhu 2011: 1601–1615.

175. The CCP controls and monopolizes the national digital database, CNKI, and profits enormously with heavy user fees levied on Chinese researchers and students who have to use it. Liu Li Feb. 25, 2019.

176. Brandt and Schafer 2020; Guo Yuhua 2009; Zhu Xueqin 2014. *China Digital Space*: "Little pinks" (小粉红), Jan. 20, 2021; Yu Liang, 2021; Hai Shang Ke 2022.

177. Smyth 2019; Luedi 2020; Gershaneck 2020.

178. Li Yuan 2020: B1.

179. Examples are Liu Yu 2009, Zhang Qianfan 2012, Qin Hui 2015, and Xu Zhangrun 2018, 2021.

180. Hollingsworth and Xiong 2021. Two representative prolific online authors defying the CCP in recent years are Biancheng Suixiang (编程随想), program-think. blogspot.com, active Jan. 2009–May 2021 with a sharp voice, rumored to have been secretly jailed or suddenly deceased; and Hulan Panzi (呼兰胖子) or Tian You (天佑), real name Yang Ming (杨明), with dozens of online accounts deleted in a few years, last seen as hulanpangzi59@WeChat.com/weibo.cn, in Sept. 2022.

181. Yu Xiaoji 2011. 19.3 percent were "party-state cadres and managers," 16 percent professionals, 3 percent students, 7.6 percent "other employed," and 20 percent retirees. Central-Organization Department 2021.

182. *NPC Delegates Roster* (全国人大代表名单), Beijing: NPC, released March 2021. Press Release by CCP Central Department of Organization, Beijing, Sept. 26, 2022.

183. "CCP Central-Politburo Standing Committee members in history" (历届中国共产党中央政治局常委), *Wangyi* (网易), Guangzhou; "19th Central Leadership" and "20th Central Leadership (十九届, 二十届中央领导机构), *Xinhua* (新华), Beijing. For an interactive database on the bio-sketches of the CCP Central Committee members, see macropolo.org/digital-projects/the-committee, all last accessed October 2022.

184. CCPnews: "Rank of the 31 Deputy-Ministry Level Universities in China" (中国31所副部级大学排名), accessed July 15, 2021.

185. *The Times of India*: "BJP Membership Near 18 Crore," New Delhi, India, Aug. 29, 2019.

186. Keythman 2021 and Hamel 2021; Zweig 2002; Groot 2003; Xie Maosong 2021.

187. 中国共产党是中国工人阶级的先锋队, 同时是中国人民和中华民族的先锋队; 幸福, 好日子, 共同富裕. CCP Central-Department of Propaganda March 24, 2021. Xi Jinping July 1, 2021. The elaborate version of the Party's nature and mission is in CCP Central-Department of Propaganda, Aug. 26, 2021.

188. *CCP Constitution*, Chapter 1, Article 6 (1982) 2022; Xinhua July 2, 2021.

189. CCP Central-Organization Department, June 30, 2021.

190. For a glimpse of the CCP's tradition of tight secrecy, see CCP Central Party History Bureau 1994. The CCP-PRC started to replace life-time tenure with age-specific retirement for its cadres only in 1982. However, retired cadres, especially senior officials, get to enjoy complete pay and many perks for life. Ma Qibin (1989) 1991: 179.

191. McGregor 2011: 1–33; Morrow et al. 2003.

192. 领导小组. CCP Central March 2018.

193. The longest serving (1954–2020) "People's Delegate" to the NPC, nicknamed the "living fossil delegate" was a local CCP cadre, who proudly declared herself to have "always voted yes and never voted no" in the NPC. Yin Wei 2008; Zhang Bin 2012; Shen Hua 2020.

194. A noted case was the execution of Priest Wang Zhiming (王志明 1907–1973), commemorated in 1998 with a statue at Westminster Abbey in London as one of the ten twentieth-century martyrs. westminster-abbey.org/our-history/people/wang-zhiming, accessed July 20, 2021. For more about Wang and the suppressed but tenacious independent Christians in Southwest China, see Liao Yiwu, vol. 2, 2008: 48–73. For the recent CCP acts of "regulating religion in China," see Berkley Forum: "Regulating Religion in China," Washington, DC: GU, March 16, 2020.

195. The eight so-called "democratic parties" (*minzhu dangpai*民主党派) in the PRC, with a total of 1.12 million members (many of them are actually "underground" CCP members) in the 2020s, are ministry-ranking PRC agencies for united front policy and propaganda. "Eight Democratic Parties" (八大民主

党派), PRC Central Government website, www.gov.cn, accessed Jan. 13, 2022. For field study of the CCP governance at and below the township level, see He Xuefeng 2021.

196. Baidu blog (百度贴吧) tieba.baidu.com/p/3422163689, accessed Aug. 16, 2015. For firsthand experiences of CCP governance at the county level, see Li Kejun 2014.

197. Deng Zhaowen 2011.

198. Zhang Haiyang 2013. *PRC Law on the Protection of Military Stature and Rights* (中华人民共和国军人地位和权益保障法) 2021: Article 12; Xi Jinping, July 1, 2021, and Aug. 1, 2021.

199. Wang Ping 1992: 584; author's interviews with senior PLA officers, 2014–2018. Under Mao, the cutoff was a platoon. Wu Faxian 2006: 731. For an insider's exposé of the PLA under the CCP, see Liu Jiaju 2020.

200. IISS 2018. State Council July 24, 2019. The budget and even the personnel of the Chinese military and police are likely underreported.

201. Yu Xiang 2021.

202. China's urban police density was internally reported in the late 1990s as more than twice that of the United States. Li Zhongxin 1999.

203. The CCP created its secret police, the State Political Protection Bureau (国家政治保卫局), in the 1920s for regime protection and intelligence. Gong Chu 1978: 569–579. Then it was expanded in the late 1930s to become the CCP's Department of Society (社会部), Department of Intelligence (情报部), and Department of (underground) Urban Works (城工部)—all were renamed, reorganized, and expanded after 1949. CCP Central Party History Bureau 1994: 119–125, 139, 162. Academic works on the Chinese secret police are rare. For a recent effort, see X. Guo 2012: 300–373.

204. The PRC and the PLA intelligence networks often spy internally to detect dissention and opposition or for power struggles. CCP officials themselves are also frequent targets. Lin Shanshan 2012. For the world's most sophisticated web policing, see Tao Xizhe 2007; Chambers 2012: 31–46.

205. 内参 and 机要邮局. *Dianji* 2013; Hai Yuncang 2014; Ma Xiangping 2001. Mao and Deng relied on internal reporting, Liu Xiange 2017; Yin Yungong 2012; Yu Keping 2014: 5–6 and 9.

206. 中央警卫局 and 特勤局. The latter was set up in 2019 as a national force to monitor and protect active and retired senior leaders. Xu Tengfei 2019.

207. He and Huang 2013: 91–92.

208. Ministry of Public Security-Personnel Training Bureau 1999: 234–252. For examples of famous artists/scholars recruited and used for many years as informants such as Ying Ruocheng (英若诚), Wen Huaisha (文怀沙), Huang Miaozi (黄苗子), and Feng Yidai (冯亦代), see Ying and Conceison 2009 and Gu Weihua 2009: C15. For how a promising physicist worked as an informant and failed academic for decades, see Liu Xiaosheng 2021.

209. Cao Jinqing 2000: 464–465; Li Fucheng 2021.

210. 信息员. The classroom informants are used to ensure that teachers follow the Party lines. Author's interviews with PRC college administrators and faculty, 2010–2021.

211. Hannah Beech, "The Other Side of the Great Firewall," *Time*, June 22, 2015: 50.

212. CIIC 2021. The so-called "youth web civilization volunteers" are mandated to be 10.08 million strong, or 10 percent of the CYL members. CYL Central 2015: 8. In just two months, the CYL recruited 157.6 thousand in Fujian, including 92,359 boys aged fourteen to eighteen and 3,870 girls younger than fourteen, to meet the mandated size of 330,000 for that province. CYL Fujian Provincial Committee 2015.

213. G. King et al. 2016.

214. Zhao and Xu 2014; Chang Xiaobin 2014; author's interviews, 2010–2021.

215. 干部. *Renmin Ribao* Chief Editor, April 15, 1998.

216. Song Wu, March 14, 2005; Yang Jisheng 2006: 284–287.

217. Wang Hongru 2016; Liu Sunan 2016; Ministry of HRSS 2016–2022; Chen Jian 2022.

218. Zhang and Yan 2021: 14–32.

219. Jiang Xiaotian 2021; Lao Xu 2016; Ma Jichao 2021; Lu Yu 2022.

220. A. Wu 2014: 97, 197.

221. Sun Liangquan 2021; Jin Nian 2021.

222. 吃空饷. Wang Xuanhui 2014; Sha Xueliang 2019; Chen Qiao 2019; Xu Ran 2020; Guan Cha Yuan 2021; Cao Hou 2022.

223. Mo Zhengxin 2005; Zhou Tianyong (professor of Central CCP Party School) 2010.

224. Li Chengpeng 2014; Wang Shu 2014.

225. Feng Junqi 2010; Ming and Li 2015.

226. Lao Man 2019. "Resident Income and Consumption in 2018" (2018 年居民收入和消费支出情况), State Statistical Bureau, Jan. 21, 2019. Facing financial hardship, the government started to freeze and reduce cadre pay. *Zhihu* Dec. 13, 2021.

227. 公务员考试. Sun Yu 2020; Yang Chengpai 2021.

228. *Tsinghua University* 2020, 2021.

229. 城管. Chaoyang Government 2022; Nan Shen 2022.

230. Xin Ziling 2009: 538–542; 2012. Chen Yingchao 2008; *Douban* 2008; Teng Biao 2021.

231. For a recent case of assimilation or elimination, see Chen Xingjia 2021.

232. Peng Xizhi 2014; S. Wee 2018: B5; Wu Shenbiao 2020.

233. 公务员, 领导干部, 一般干部, 官 and 吏. State cadres include those in the state "non-profit" units (事业单位) and state-owned enterprises. For a fictional

portrait of the cadres, see Zhang Ping 2009. For an autobiography of "leading cadres," see Pu Yang 2011. For an analysis of the role and power of the cadres, see J. Fitzgerald 2022.

234. For an insider's memoir about the organization department, see Yan Huai 2017.

235. A. Wu 2014: 155; State Council, March 19, 2019.

236. State Council, March 19, 2019.

237. F. Wang 2017: 183–188. In 2018, the CCP-PRC renamed ten ranks of "full and deputy leading cadres" at the five levels as "cadres with positions" (职务), and many more "civil servants" as twelve "cadres with ranks" (职级) at the five levels. NPC (2005) 2018.

238. 高干: 厅局级, 副省部级, 省部级, 副国级 and 正国级. Liang Zi 2018; Xinhua database, Beijing, accessed Feb. 14, 2022; author's interviews, 2018–2022.

239. Gong Wen 2021.

240. For anecdata of formal salary and bonuses of mid- and low-rank cadres and PLA officers in the 2020s, see FJBM 2022, *Zhicheng caijing* 2022, and Changsha City 2022.

241. Even during the chaotic 1960s and 1970s, the gap was still twenty times. Yang Kuisong vol. 1, 2009: 433–452; 2007. In 2014, salary gap of US federal employees was 11.7 times. US OPM 2014.

242. 特供. An Moluo 2015. For the elitist lifestyle of CCP leaders even before 1949, see Cai Xiaoqian 1970. For a glimpse of the special provision system of the Soviet Union by a CCP envoy in Moscow, which the CCP modeled after, see Li Jingxian 2021.

243. Gao Zhiyong 2007: 17–18. Yang Kuisong, vol. 1, 2009: 456–457. For a rare, detailed expose of the special provision, see Lu Zongshu 2011 (soon censored out but recirculated and updated, like Ri Du 2021); Xiao Qiang 2011; Sun Zhongyuan 2011: 3.

244. Shuai Hao 2011.

245. The "981 首长健康工程," RFA September 16, 2019; detailed reports about this "scientific project" were on the Beijing-based *Interactive Encyclopedia* (互动百科) and the PLA General Hospital website, until abruptly removed in late September 2019.

246. 待遇. Ye Zhuyi 2011.

247. Author's interviews, 2010–2021. For an anecdote of the meticulous but consequential changes of "treatment" demoted leader Ji Dengkui (纪登奎) experienced, see Zhao Shukai 2021.

248. Barboza 2012; Forsythe 2014; Demick 2015.

249. Stevenson and Forsythe 2020: A1. Reuters: "Three Listed Units of China's HNA Disclose Embezzlements of Nearly $10 billion," Beijing, January 31, 2021.

250. Yao Dongqin 2015. CCTV: *Xinwen lianbo* (新闻联播), Beijing, Feb. 24, 2021.

251. Forsythe and Ramzy 2016; A. Olesen 2016. *Offshore Leaks Database*, offshoreleaks.icij.org, searched June 11, 2020. Wilson-Chapman et al. 2019; Fitzgibbon 2020; Tokar 2020.

252. D. Bell 2015; Meng Yaping 2019; Wooldridge 2021.

253. Q. Zhang 2020: 213–247. Italics original.

254. Huang Yushun 2017. A PRC scientist deems many PRC officials "eunuchs." Rao Yi 2014.

255. At one online forum in 2021, the many participants from the Chinese business community all asserted, based on their "decades of experience," that PRC officials "are anything but meritocrats." *Zhongguo moshi II* (中国模式 II), Sept. 21, 2021.

256. 逆淘汰. *Lilun* 2014; Yao Heng 2014; Zhou Jianhong 2015; Yuan Chao 2017; Guo Xue 2021.

257. 维稳. Xu Kai 2011; Buckley, March 5, 2011.

258. Zenz 2018; X. Guo 2012.

259. Wu Si 2006.

260. For a recount of CCP power politics by a legendary figure, see Schwarcz 1992.

261. F. Wang 2017: 178–183.

262. He and Huang 2013; L. Li 2020; CCP Central, Dec. 24, 2021.

263. Zhu and Zhang 2020: 1–17.

264. *Hotan ribao* (和田日报), April 10, 2017; CCTV April 2, 2021.

265. Legalist classics from *Guan Zi* (管子), *Shangjun Shu* (商君书) to *Han Fei Zi* (韩非子) all contained such insights. Morrow et al. 2003; Broadhurst and Wang 2014: 157–178.

266. Garside 2021.

267. Bajohr 2001; Kroeze et al. 2018.

268. This verdict, of course, allows Xi to purge and replace cadres anywhere he wants for power and control. CDIC April 10, 2016; Editorial April 11, 2016: 1.

269. CDIC June 28, 2021. Supreme People's Procuratorate June 2, 2020; CDIC and CCTV 2022; Wang Xiaodong 2021.

270. Xinhua November 8, 2021; CDIC ccdi.gov.cn/scdc, accessed Feb. 2022.

271. Chen Huijuan 2021; BBC *News in Chinese*, Sept. 27, 2022.

272. 娃娃巨贪. Wang Mingyuan 2021.

273. Wang Shaowei 2016: 1; F. Wang 2017: 182–183.

274. Gu Yi 2017.

275. Link 2021.

276. Li Yancheng 2011; Wang Ruohan 2013; *The Economist*, "China's Rich List," Sept. 29, 2012.

277. Bai Jianjun 2010: 147; Supreme People's Procuratorate 2020.

278. *Sina caijing* (新浪财经), "Hurun richest Chinese" (胡润百富榜), Beijing, Sept. 23, 2014.

279. Wang Xiaoqing 2015; Shou Ye 2017; Zhou Songtao 2020.

280. UBC and Price Waterhouse 2019: 11; Zhang Yingjian 2020.

281. Xiao Shan 2020; Zhihu (知乎): "Who's Ye Jianming" (叶简明是谁), August 7, 2020; Ng and Xie 2018; *Caixin*, May 10, 2018; Tai Le 2020; Cooper and Russell 2022.

282. Zhou Qunfeng 2020. Gaobeidian People's Court verdict on July 28, 2021. Li Yuan July 28, 2021. For Sun's political and ideological dissent, see Cheng Tiejun 2021. Niu Ye 2022.

283. D. Shum 2021; Inskeep 2021.

284. 马云 and 马化腾. Shang Guoqiang 2019; Deng Xinhua 2022.

285. Dong Langxing, December 30, 2019.

286. State Administration for Market Regulation 2020; Si Yang 2021.

287. Wei and Yang 2020; Cai Pengcheng 2020; author's interviews, 2018–2021.

288. 泰山会, 西山会, 湖畔大学. Zhou Yuanzheng 2021. *Sohu* (搜狐): "Ling Jihua Secret Society Xishan Hui" (令计划秘密组织西山会), Dec. 24, 2014. Jin Rongdao 2020; Hu Tou 2021.

289. 赵本山, 毕福剑, 芮成钢, 叶迎春, 沈冰, 贾晓晔; Du Enhu 2014; Chang An Jian 2018.

290. Many influential (and often lucrative) PRC internet personalities, the so-called Big VIPs (大V), are frequently cut down with their online presence suddenly banned or even deleted all together. Author's research notes, 2010–2022. *Safeguard Defenders* 2020; Carter 2021.

291. Klein 2008.

292. Radio Free Asia, Sept. 26, 2017; R. Chun 2018; Schiefelbein 2018; E. Feng 2019.

293. Chen Yixin June 21, 2018; Mitchell and Diamond 2018; M. Jude 2020.

294. Y. Chen et al. 2018; Xu and Xiao 2018.

295. A quick search on Chinese economic-financial news sites such as *Caixin*, *Sina Caijing*, *Sohu Cajing*, and *Tencent* yields countless cases of such in the 2020s.

296. Author's interviews 2003–2022. For police brutality and systemic coverup, see Tatlow 2016.

297. 立案. Liu 2008: 131–147; Bai Jianjun 2010: 144–159; Supreme People's Procuratorate 2020.

298. Hu Lianhe 2006.

299. Xinhua May 15, 2020; NPC Dec. 26, 2020; Supreme People's Procuratorate, March 8, 2021.

300. Ransmeier 2017; Wu Qinying 1988; Xie and Jia 1989; Zhuang Ping 1991; *Jiancha ribao*, Aug. 14, 2000; Ministry of Public Security 2003; Wang Qiliang 2010; J. Wang 2014; Liu Wei 2017; Wang Jingling et al. 2018; W. Zhen et al. 2018; Y. Xia et al. 2020: 238–252; *Zhihu* May 21, 2020; Wang and Dong 2022: A1; Lu Si 2022.

301. Luscombe 2014: 32–33.

302. Zhongmin Social Assistance Institute 2021. For samples of missing children cases, see www.baobeihuijia.com, accessed Feb. 20, 2022. Goldberg 2012; Pang and Zhang 2019: 8.

303. Scoggins 2021; Wang and Zheng 2015.

304. Li Yuan, Feb. 15, 2022.

305. Author's survey of WeChat and Weibo blogs and chat rooms, January–March 2022. Quote is from Michel Bonnin, email correspondence, Feb. 18, 2022.

306. Anshi Sizhi (暗室四知), *Weibo-guoji* (微博国际版), Feb. 23, 2020.

307. Tacitus (109) 2004: 3.19. For official CCP reports, see Zhao Changmao 2007; *Banyuetan* (半月谈): "Credibility Problem of Government Officials Has Become the Focus of Attention" (政府官员诚信问题成关注焦点), no. 7, 2007; Cui and Wei 2013.

308. Xu Yanhong et al. 2014.

309. Zhengzhi Shitan 2022; Cong Yi 2022; Sun Liping 2009; Li Yaping 2022.

310. Zhu Jicha 2021; Lam, July 23, 2021.

311. F. Wang 2017: 176–181. For this in the late-Mao era, see Walder 2014: 513–539.

312. *The Economist*, "Labour Unrest: Out Brothers, Out!" Jan. 31, 2015: 37–38.

313. Zeng Peng et al. 2006; Keidel 2006; Minzner 2009: 93. For hydro-projects that ignited grassroots social protests, see Mertha 2010.

314. Page 2011; Forsythe 2011; Zhu Li 2012; Yu Keping 2014: 9. Many of these incidents, upon closer look, are often senseless and random but bloody acts venting deep grievances and revenges. Author's research notes, 2001–2021.

315. Tanner 2004; *The Economist*, "Protest in China," Sept. 29, 2005; Freeman 2010; Forsythe, March 6, 2011; Ringen 2015.

316. Li and Tian 2014: 270–288.

317. Liu and Mozur 2022; Gan April 2022; Kuo 2022; Li Yuan, May 6, 2022. For a collection of essays of exposés, denunciation and defiance, see Jia Lin 2022. For a Shanghai-based rapper's fiery call to "fxxk the state, fxxk the government," see Astro 2022. For the blank white paper-holding protesters, see AP News, "China lockdown protests pause as police flood city streets," Nov. 29, 2022.

318. Lao Dongyan Oct. 31, 2019.

319. In 2010, with 4 percent of the population and about four hundred riots, South Korea was fourteen times more tranquil per capita than the PRC. Author's interviews in Seoul, July 2011. In the United States, reports on peaceful/lawful protests are often mixed with reports on violent or unlawful riots. In 2017, there were a total of 4,296 mass protests (of ten or more attendees), some of which turned violent, giving American society roughly the same level of social tranquility per capita as South Korea. Tommy Leung and Nathan Perkins on countlove.org, searched July 2021.

Chapter 2

1. Walder 2015: 315–346.

2. PRC officially reported in 2019–21 that up to 400 million people had a "middle class" household annual income between ¥24,000 ($3,540) and ¥250,000 ($36,400), with the median at ¥29,975 ($4,428), and another 30 million had an "upper class" household annual income above ¥250,000 ($36,400). Cyrill 2019; State Statistical Bureau 2021.

3. For PRC advocates of this China Model for sustained high economic growth, see Justin Yifu Lin 1999 and 2012. For PRC rebuttals of Lin, see the essays by Wei Sen, Yu Yongding, and Zhang Shuguang et al. 2013: 1051–1094. For more on the PRC's institutional "superiority" and economic "miracle," see Zhou Li-An (2008) 2017.

4. For "moral economy of empire" in China, see Laliberté 2016. For developmental state, see Evans 1995; Woo-Cumings 1999; Kohli 2004; M. Wan 2008; Greene, 2008; and Walter and Zhang 2012. For the role by Taiwan, see Rigger 2021.

5. H. Wu 2019: 1–22.

6. Reardon 2021; Zuo Fang 2014: 214.

7. Sachs et al. 2003: 983; Xu Chenggang 2017; Sun Laibin 2019; Li Xaiodan 2020.

8. Ang 2016; Zhang Qi 2021.

9. Vu 2010; F. Wang 2005: 117–127; Xu Xiaonian May 10, 2013.

10. Ozawa 2004: 379–388.

11. S. Li 2022.

12. For a partial self-assessment, see Wang Hongguang 2018; Ang 2020.

13. Tao Ran, 2021; Tao and Su 2021.

14. Myrdal 1968; North 1990; Sen 2003; Acemoglu and Robinson 2012.

15. Acemoglu et al. 2019: 47–100. Quotes on pp. 47–48 and 96–97.

16. S. Tang 2022; Zhou Wen 2021.

17. *Index of Economic Freedom*, Washington, DC: Heritage Foundation, 2021.

18. Telep and Lutz 2018: 693–708; CRS 2019; Baschuk 2020; Mishra 2020.

19. Pearson et al. 2020.

20. Ross 1999: 297–322 and 2015: 239–259; Smith and Waldner 2021.

21. Gill and Kharas 2015; Wang Renbo 2021.

22. Yang Xiaokai 2000; Yang Li May 8, 2004; Jiang Zong 2020.

23. Thaxton 2008; Kung and Chen 2011: 27–45; Yang et al. 2014: 864–883.

24. Xue Muqiao 1996: 197, 203.

25. Mao's speech to top CCP cadres, April 5, 1959, in Li Rui, vol. 2, 1999-II: 465–466.

26. Lu Shuzheng 2003.

27. US State Department 1954.

28. Wang and Liu 2012: 68–87. The tragic fate of the idealistic but deceived and abused returnees is powerfully embodied by Ningkun Wu (巫宁坤 1920–2019), who I personally had the fortune to have as a teacher indirectly in my undergraduate school in Anhui and directly in my master's program in Beijing. Wu and Li 1993.

29. Zhao Shuli (赵树理), in Qian Liqun (1998) 2002: 238–239.

30. F. Wang 2004: 115–132. For visual evidence of rations, see Yang Fei 2014.

31. *Tencent* January 2, 2014; Zhu Pule 2014 and 2022; Cairang 2007; Cao Yunwu 2006.

32. Zhao Dexin 1999: 42; *Tencent* Jan. 2, 2014; Zeng Peiyan 1999: 897–898.

33. Meng Fangui 2013; Neo Zion 2014. More of this in the next chapter of this book.

34. Such as the justification by Song Jian 1980.

35. He Jiyuan 1998. Mao ordered "to have more population" and defended "the price of work-death for industrialization" in 1958. In Li Rui 1999: 209.

36. Bonnin (2004) 2013. An earlier work on this subject is Bernstein, 1977. For the sad fate of the sent-down youth and their offspring decades later in the twenty-first century, see Sun Peidong 2012; Wang and Zhou 2015.

37. 国策. Greenhalgh 2005: 253–276. For PRC rationalization of population control, see He Qinglian 1988 and Chen Xiaonan 2013.

38. Ministry of Health 2010.

39. Commission of Health 2020; Wu Bin 2020.

40. Wang Feng 2016. The CCP, however, still pledges to enforce family planning and the modified birth quota. CCP Central Oct. 29, 2015.

41. Wang Ling 2016; An Bang 2014; Hesketh 2005: 1171–1176; Hofman 2021: 3–7.

42. Population Training Center 1991; Greenhalgh 2003; Laogai Foundation 2004; Potts 2006.

43. S. Lin 2014; Cai Xia 2015; Qiu Feng 2015; Xue 2015; Lin Shijue 2021.

44. *The Economist*, "Tales of the Unexpected," July 11, 2015; Whyte 2015: 144–159.

45. Xinhua May 31, 2021; Goldman 2021: A10; Zhao Tong June 2, 2021.

46. Research Center of Hukou Management, PRC Ministry of Public Security (公安部户政管理研究中心); Johnston 2021: 91–111.

47. Liang Jianzhang 2022.

48. Lin Xiaozhao 2022; OECD database, worldpopulationreview.com, both accessed March 2022.

49. Ministry of Public Security Jan. 24, 2022.

50. Twitter.com/JunZhan12743255/, May 31 and June 2, 2021. Likely to evade censors, sharp political commentaries and reportage are posted here with soft-erotica images.

51. Wu Jinglian 2008; Li Yining 2011: 102–163; Wu Kaizhi 2012.

52. Rodrik 2008 and 2009; Zhou Hong 2007.

53. Y. Huang 2008.

54. IMF Data 2021 and World Bank Data 2021. *The Economist*, "The Dragon Takes Wing," May 3, 2014. For a debate of the problematic comparison of GDPs in PPP, see the commentaries at chinafile.com/will-chinas-economy-be-1-dec-31-and-does-it-matter, accessed Jan. 13, 2021.

55. Pan Hongmin 2001; CICA 2005–13.

56. Lardy 2014: ix; Ge Long 2016.

57. Pantsov and Levine 2015: 325–376, 395–434.

58. Zhou Qiren 2014.

59. Qin Hui 2008; Chancellor 2013.

60. Sirkin et al. 2014; Tabuchiaug 2015: A1.

61. World Bank database, accessed March 2021. Reuters: "China's 2020 GDP Growth Set to Sink to 44-Year Low," April 14, 2020. In 2020, the PRC Premier for the first time in decades stopped projecting the annual growth target. Li Keqiang 2020; Press Release by PRC State Statistical Bureau, Beijing, February 28, 2021. Li returned to the traditional practice of projecting GDP growth of 6 percent for 2021 and 5.5 percent for 2022. Li Keqiang 2021, 2022.

62. He Qinlian 2005; Wang and Wang 2007: 30–37.

63. 九龙治水, 央妈; Nie Riming 2021.

64. *The Economist*, "Investing in Chinese Shares" Sept. 27, 2014: 71.

65. Qiu Lin 2014; Wu Xiaobo 2014.

66. L. Wei 2015; D. Barboza 2015.

67. Bank of America Merrill Lynch calculated that the total capitalization of the PRC equity market was 4.5 percent of that in the United States or one-third of that in Japan. Kawa 2015.

68. Xi Jinping, Sept. 2, 2021.

69. The lack of private land rights has locked the village that pioneered the 1978 spontaneous decollectivization into poverty and stagnation. Chen and Chun 2008.

70. Xu Chenggang (许成钢), *Sina blog*, Sept. 18, 2014. Vietnam luickly established a "land user right certificate" of "50 years to indefinite," as de facto land ownership. Author's interviews in Vietnam 2008; Shira 2019. For a veiled take on land rights in the PRC, see Tan Rong 2021.

71. *The Economist*, "China's Financial System" and "Big but Brittle," May 7, 2016.

72. Shenzhen Bureau of Justice 2020; Meng Qingguo 2021; NISSTC 2021.

73. *Zhihu*: "Why P2P Only Became Fraud in China?" (为何全世界的P2P仅中国出现骗局), Jan. 22, 2016; Zheng Hedao 2019; Ba Jiuling 2019; Deng and Yu 2020; Yao Chanjun 2021.

74. Official PRC inflation figures exclude the highly inflationary items like housing and health care. www.91rate.com, State Bureau of Statistics, and US Bureau of Labor Statistics websites, accessed Jan. 11, 2022.

75. Gruin and Knaack 2019.

76. Yi Gang (Governor of the Chinese People's Bank) 2021; Ge Long 2016.

77. Four giant state banks contributed 73 percent of all SOE profits in 2018. Da Xueshi 2019.

78. 民有, 国营, 党管. Dong Wenbiao quoted in Zhou Yuanzheng 2021.

79. *Zhihu:* "Latest list of the central SOEs" (最新中央企业名单), May 2020; Li Jing 2020.

80. 支付宝 and 白条. The popular WeChat Pay by Tencent is essentially an online debit card. For a survey of financial technology in the PRC, see Hsu and Li 2020.

81. "Legal ceiling" for business lending in 2020 was 39 percent. Author's interviews 2021.

82. Shuai Bang 2016. This practice apparently continues throughout the PRC and "has become a whole chain of industry" that often turns the defaulting borrowers (mostly young women) into forced pornography and prostitution work. Ou La 2019.

83. Naughton 1988: 351–386; Meyskens 2020. The CPP later referred to this strategy as "huge economic waste and loss of time." Liu Huaqing 2004: 288. For an example of such wastes, see Fu Tianming 2011: 75–76. For PRC academic works on the Third Front that include many revisionist and even apologist efforts, see Zhou Xiaohong 2020: 17–25; Xu and Zhang 2021. For a collection of vivid anecdotes about life in the Third Front, see Y. Wang et al. 2022.

84. 富国强军. Hu Jintao July 1, 2011. The theme has been repeated by the CCP ever since.

85. 富國強兵. Reischauer 1986.

86. Xinhua April 8, 2013; Sharma 2013; Pettis 2013.

87. Ringen 2015. For taxation and PRC politics, see C. Zhang 2021.

88. Kynge 2014.

89. Table 3.3, Ministry of Treasury 2012; Ministry of Treasury 2020; Xinhua Jan. 23, 2013.

90. Xuan Feng et al. 2010: 24–28, 29–40.

91. For over-taxation, see opinion.china.com.cn/event_1805_1.html, Jan. 2021.

92. US OMB 2021: table 2.3.

93. *The Economist,* "The 15-Year Hitch," May 7, 2016; IIF 2020; Yi Gang *Speech* 2021.

94. Zhou Tianyong (professor of Central CCP Party School) 2010, 2018.

95. In 2013, at a "much reduced pace," the PRC central government fiscal revenue still grew 10 percent, about 1.4 times the growth rate of the GDP. *Jinghua shibao* (京华时报) Dec. 12, 2013: A01.

96. Zhang Shuguang (Chairman of Tianze Institute) 2011.

97. Deng Yuanjie 2021.

98. CCP Central and State Council 2018, 2021; Ministry of Treasury 2021; Li Xuhong 2021.

99. This could be a "special deal" to give private firms some breathing room. Bai 2019.

100. Dao Ke 2006; Wang Yaofeng 2013. The Chinese Academy of Sciences issued a one-sentence denial of a "research report" on that figure attributed to it. CAS 2013. The figure, however, appeared later in other reports like this, such as Wei Jiaqi 2020. For more on the evolution, problems, and lessons of the PRC health care system, see Blumenthal and Hsiao 2005: 1165–1170 and 2015: 1281–1285.

101. *Zhihu* Dec. 11, 2014.

102. The better scenarios are to "spend your own money" on yourself or on somebody else, where much higher degrees of efficiency are ensured. Freedman 1980: 116–117.

103. Xia Bin 2014: 10–15; N. Zhu 2016.

104. Li Guang 2013; Liu Liping 2014; Feng Huiling 2014. For a $100-billion ghost city, see Zaho Jiwei 2014; Sabrie 2014; Li Tiemin 2020; *Nikkei Asia*: "Concrete 'Ghost Towns,'" Feb. 9, 2022.

105. Bradsher 2013: B1; Kam Wing Chan: "China's High-Speed Trains," *China Focus*, Mar. 28, 2011. Michael Pettis highlighted to me the excessive irrationality of HSR railroad projects in 2013. For highways losing money on a massive scale, see Chen Fang 2014: 2.

106. Su Xiaozhou 2014; *Reuters*: "Lovely Airport, Where Are the Planes?" April 10, 2015. Graham-Harrison 2015; Zhi Zhu 2021.

107. For the "disasters" of the PRC's politicized damming projects started in the 1950s, see Li Rui vol. 2, 1999-II: 242–256; Guo Yushan 2011; Wines May 20, 2011: A4; Khetani, 2012.

108. Qiu Baoxing 2013: 1–11. *Jinghua shibao* (京华时报), "Move Southern Water to the North" (南水北调), Oct. 13, 2014: A06–7; *The Economist*, "A Canal Too Far," Sept. 27, 2014: 18, 44–35; Yi Ju 2014; Wang Weiluo 2015: 58–59.

109. *Sohu*: "Jingzhou Guangong Statuette" (荆州关公像), Jan. 9, 2021; Zhang Jing 2021.

110. Chatzky et al. 2020; *Nikkei*: "Deadly IS Attack Threatens China's Belt and Road in Pakistan," Jan. 10, 2021.

111. 举国体制. Beech 2021. One Chinese analyst estimated that "the cost of an Olympic gold medal for China is ¥600 million" (中国一枚奥运金牌的成本是6亿), or "the same as the total revenue of 9 poor counties." *Caijing toutiao* (财经头条), Beijing, Aug. 17, 2016.

112. Pan and Wang 2006; Huang Jing-Yang 2021.

113. Ringen 2016: 16–26.

114. Lebow 2010; Waldron 1999; Gertler 2016; White and Raitzer 2017.

115. *The Economist*, "Post-war China," Oct. 11, 2014; Zhang Qi 2011.

116. For overviews of China's economy, see Naughton 2006; Lardy 2012; Chow and Perkins 2014; Kroeber 2020.

117. State Statistical Bureau 2013; Li and Kim 2014; IMF: "China: International Reserves and Foreign Currency Liquidity," Oct. 31, 2014; Xinhua 2020; Safe.gov.cn, accessed Jan. 2022.

118. Li Jinlei 2014; Pan Qi 2014.

119. *Scissors* Oct. 28, 2014. *Bloomberg*: "China's GDP Growth Pace Was Inflated for Nine Years," Mar. 7, 2019; Wildau 2019; Chen et al; 2019; Niyazov 2019; Bird and Craymer 2019.

120. Stiglitz et al. 2010. *The Economist*, "How to Measure Prosperity" and "The Trouble with GDP," April 30, 2016; Xu Chenggang 2014.

121. Credit Suisse Research Institute 2014. Many Chinese netizens sarcastically call GDP homophonically *jidepi* (鸡的屁 chicken fart). Cao Jianjun 2013; Yu Zou, "Building a High-Rise Is Chicken Fart, Demolishing It Is Also Chicken Fart, Building It Again Is Chicken Fart Once More" (建楼是鸡的屁，炸楼又是鸡的屁，再建还是鸡的屁), @zouyuqhd, Twitter, Dec. 14, 2020.

122. *The Economist*, "China's Economy: Coming Down to Earth," April 18, 2015.

123. Duesterberg 2021; Bradsher January 17, 2022; *Scissors* Nov. 12, 2014; Rosen 2021.

124. World Bank Gross Savings database, OECD data base, PRC stats.gov.cn, accessed June 2021.

125. Yueh 2014; *The Economist*, "Hole in Won," May 31, 2014.

126. Jahn 2020.

127. Kazarosian 1997: 241–247; Callen and Thimann 1997; Barnett and Brooks 2010; Baldacci et al. 2010; Ma and Yi 2010; *The Economist*, "Dipping into the Kitty," May 26, 2012; Bonham and Wiemer 2012; Curtis et al. 2015: 58–94; L. Zhang et al. 2018.

128. Chen Yanping 2016.

129. OECD 2000; Graham and Wada 2001; Das 2007: 285–301; World Bank April 18, 2015; BBC News: "China Overtakes US for Foreign Direct Investment," Jan. 30, 2015.

130. *The Economist*, "China's Economy," January 14, 2010; Zhang Monan 2013; Lahart 2014; "Gross Fixed Capital Formation" *data.worldbank.org*, accessed Jan. 24, 2021.

131. *The Economist*, "Unproductive Production," Oct. 11, 2014. Quote in H. Wu 2019: 9.

132. Miao Wei 2015.

133. India Brand Equity Foundation 2013: 2–3; US Census Bureau 2014: 4.

134. For a theoretical discussion of the destruction of capital, see Solow 1956: 65–94. For an analysis of the Chinese data suggesting a large "hidden transfer of resources" caused by the over reliance on investment, see Lee et al. 2012.

135. OECD Development Centre 2013: 280–281. A different study holds that China's ICOR was just at the average level in the region. Carbon 2012.

136. *Reuters*: "China Wasted $6.9 Trillion on Bad Investment Post 2009," Nov. 20, 2014. A critique of this study is *The Economist*, "Wasted Investment" Nov. 28, 2014.

137. For a $10 billion loss by the PRC state-owned oil companies in Angola, see Huang Kaiqian 2015; *AFN Daily*: "Scary Losses: Chinese Investment Halved," Sydney, Jan. 18, 2021.

138. Lardy 2014: 97–99.

139. Walter and Howie 2012; Davies 2019; Zhou Ying 2019; F. Tang 2020-I. Information on HSR lines from crh.gaotie.cn, last accessed July 2, 2022. Another estimate believes six short (in fact four different) lines are profitable (*Wangyi* 网易, Oct. 10, 2020).

140. Bei Yi 2012; Hille 2013; Kong Deqian 2015; Dong Xizhong 2022. For how the CCP cadres and their buddies collude to siphon public funds, see Lu and Wang 2022.

141. Pettis 2013, 2014; Oster and Lee 2014; US Commercial Service 2019; Krugman 2022.

142. Supreme People's Court and Supreme People's Procuratorate 2019.

143. 鸿海 and 和硕. Author's calculation based on interviews, 2019.

144. H. Hung 2021; Chen Xiaoying 2013.

145. *The Economist*, "The 15-Year Hitch," May 7, 2016; Setser 2018, 2020.

146. The PRC requires that all hard currency income from export must be sold to state banks for RMB; for "legit" needs, people can purchase only approved amount of hard currency from state banks. For PRC economists' hesitant critique of this, see Lu Feng 2014. Leftist officials worry about politically loss of the "top-level control" of the Chinese economy to "forces of international capital," Yu Yunhui 2013.

147. Wang Xuejin 2015.

148. *Wangyi* (网易): "Foreign Exchange Reserve Dropped below $1 trillion" (外汇储备净额跌破1万亿美元), Aug. 17, 2020; Fan Li 2020. Database at safe.gov. cn; US Department of the Treasury/Federal Reserve (ticdata.treasury.gov), both accessed Dec. 2021.

149. Zhao Jian 2015; Yu Yongding, 2022.

150. PRC Customs 2020; SAFE 2021.

151. Duan and Huang 2020; *The Economist*, "China's 'Dual-Circulation' Strategy Means Relying Less on Foreigners," Nov. 7, 2020.

152. Tang Ji 2020; Shi Zhichang 2020; Yuan Jian 2020.

153. Arnold 2015.

154. It was 8.1 percent in 2013, 15.5 percent in 2015, 17.7 percent in 2016, and 17.8 percent in 2017 and 2018. PRC budgetary figures are expectedly sketchy and deliberately inconsistent. Data here are based on the analyzed

government data. Zhong and Li 2018; Ceicdata.com and Evergrande Institute Data, searched June 10, 2020; Lin Caiyi 2021.

155. *Bloomberg*, "China Finds Debt Addiction Hard to Break in Growth Quest," July 17, 2014.

156. Textor 2020; Liu et al. 2022: 40–71; Khan 2018; X. Yu 2020.

157. Xinhua: "China's Outstanding Local Gov't Debt Rises in April," May 11, 2020; Lin Caiyi 2021.

158. Tierney 2017.

159. Zheng Jie Ju 2020; *Wangyi*: "Provincial Tax Payments to the Central" (各省市净上缴中央税收), July 14, 2021; Lin Caiyi 2021, 2022.

160. Wright and Feng 2020.

161. *The Economist*, "China's Financial System" and "Big but Brittle," May 7, 2016.

162. Wildau 2014; A. Lee 2020; F. Tang 2020-II.

163. Zhang Xiaojing 2020; Gang 2020; Tiftik 2021; Zhang Ming 2021; Liu Guoqiang 2022.

164. IMF database, accessed February 8, 2022.

165. Saxegaard 2014; Pienkowski 2017; IMF Policy Paper 2020, 2021.

166. *Chinese securities news* (中国证券报): "Chinese Money Supply Expanded 450 Percent in Ten Years" (中国货币供应量十年扩大450%), Beijing, Oct. 18, 2010.

167. Liu Zheng 2014; State Statistical Bureau at stats.gov.cn, accessed Nov. 2, 2014.

168. US Federal Reserve, US Department of Commerce, People's Bank of China, databases, accessed Nov. 2014, May 2020, and Sept. 2022.

169. Tang Jing 2020.

170. O. Wang 2018.

171. People's Bank of China Feb. 10, 2022; Wen Lin 2022.

172. Niu Baiyu 2014.

173. Porter and Judson 1996: 899; Feige et al. 2001; Judson 2012.

174. Qian Qiujun 2014; Jiang Chao 2014.

175. Yang Zhijin 2015; Wu Xiaobo 2014.

176. Li Keqiang, Press Conference, Beijing, May 28, 2020; Mallaby 2020.

177. USDT 2021; *Reuters*: "India Outlines $23 Billion Stimulus to Help Poor," March 26, 2020.

178. Maizland 2020; Su Xiaozhang 2020. For an apology for the CCP, see Zhang Deyong 2020.

179. Many could not "grab" the pennies while others resold the coupons for profit. *Xinjing* (新京报), "Why Can't Grab the Consumer Coupons?" (消费券为什么抢不到), May 24, 2020.

180. Noguchi and Poterba 1994: 11–28; Okina et al. 2001: 395–450.

181. For inefficiency of infrastructure development in general, see Shi and Huang 2014.

182. Dong Fan 2014; Tie Jun 2014; Kai Feng 2022.

183. Mao Daqing 2015; People's Bank of China April 25, 2020.

184. Cui Lili 2013; Wang Jingwen 2014; Gu Zhijuan 2018; *Bloomberg*: "A Fifth of China's Homes Are Empty. That's 50 Million Apartments," Nov. 8, 2018.

185. US Census Bureau data of 1956–2014. Accessed Nov. 2014.

186. Zhang Min 2014; Dent 2012; *21st Century Business Herald*, Beijing, June 17, 2013. Officially, the vacancy rate in Beijing was 20 percent in 2018. *Sohu caijing* Oct. 13, 2018.

187. Feng Haining 2012: 2.

188. Jin Ze 2014.

189. Wang Xiaohui 2020; Zhong Min 2021; Mi Yang 2021.

190. Liu Binde 2013.

191. Hurun Feb. 20, 2020.

192. Su Ju Bao 2018; Ren Zeping 2019. Another estimate put that figure at $100 trillion, "larger than the total GDP of the world." Zhang Dawei 2018; Tao Zhugong 2019.

193. Nie and Guo 2021; Orlik 2020: 118. Figures from "Forum of Forty in Chinese Finance" (中国金融四十人论坛) in 2017; Zhang Dawei 2018; *Sohu* (搜狐): "How Big Is the Chinese Real Estate Market?" (中国楼市总市值到底有多大?), Sept. 3, 2020.

194. Xie Zhongxiu 2020. 限跌令, Chen Yushu 2021; Lin Xiaozhao 2021; Zhen Sujing 2022.

195. Author's interviews with PRC officials and scholars, 2004–2021.

196. Hu Jintao July 25, 2011; Ji Simin 2015; He Xiaotao 2020.

197. Gui Tiantian 2014.

198. Zhang Yi 2021; *Huaxia shibao* (华夏时报), Aug. 19, 2021; NPC Oct. 2021.

199. Xie and Bird 2020; "List of Real Estate Companies Facing Bankruptcy" (房地产公司暴雷排行榜), *Tencent news*, *Wangyi news*, and *WeChat Blog*, Sept. 17–18, 2021.

200. Pettis Sept. 20, 2021; A. Su 2021; Wang Jing 2021: 29–45.

201. Ma Xiaolong 2020; Siwei Jinrong 2020.

202. *Electricity Market Report*, Paris: IEA, 2022. However, Beijing's (hence IEA's) renewable energy figure, especially regarding solar and wind, is overstated as it is about "capacity built" rather than real output. The "actual" percentage of fossil fuel used in China could be as high as over 90 percent. Author's interviews of PRC scholars, 2021–22.

203. Wang Xiuqiang 2013; IMF 2014; Ritchie and Roser 2020; World Bank, *World Integrated Trade Solution Database* and US EPA, *Global Greenhouse Gas Emissions*, March 15, 2022.

204. Kahn 2007; "CO2 Emissions Embodied in Trade-China," OurWorld InData.org, March 2022.

205. *Global 500; Fortune* 2014, 2020.

206. Chinese Enterprise Association and Chinese Businessmen Association 2014.

207. Li Chengyou 2011.

208. Lewis 2013; Kan Kaili 2014.

209. FNIC 2019; Haselton 2020; Ranger 2020; Yuan Du 2020; Lou Jiwei 2020.

210. Ren Zeping Feb. 16, 2020.

211. Leng Fuhai 2019.

212. Lu Bai 2021.

213. *China Daily:* "Top 10 Chinese Listed Companies by Market Value," Jan. 8, 2021. *Fortune-Chinese* (财富中文), Beijing, June 9, 2020.

214. Schrad 2014.

215. *Sina Caijing* (新浪财经): "The Gap between Sino-American Internet Giants Is Further Enlarging" (中美两国互联网巨头的差距正在进一步拉大), Beijing, Jan. 28, 2022.

216. He Chuanqi 2015.

217. K. Chen 2019; Franceschini and Loubere 2020; Szarejko 2021.

218. Zhao Jianjun 2003: 28–31; Ying Qian 2010; author's interviews and field notes, 2002–21.

219. Oshin 2021.

220. Li and Sharma 2019; Iqbal 2019; Dreze and Sen 1995: 27–86; Massing 2003; Y. Huang 2006: 117–122 and 2010; Huang and Khanna 2010; Sen 2013: A27; Martinez 2021.

221. Chang Che: "The End of China's Runaway Growth," *SupChina*, Oct. 4, 2021.

222. Turner 2013; Arora and Miglani 2020; US DOS 2021; US DNI 2021: 6–8, 25.

Chapter 3

1. At the exchange rate of ¥6.77 = $1. The US middle class (household income $45,000 to $135,000, with the median at $67,521) is 52 percent of the population; the South Korean middle class (household income $23,568 to $70,704, with the median at $47,136) is two-thirds of the population. Another calculation puts the size of Chinese middle and upper classes at 109 million (or 8% of the total population) with household income above $50,000. Cyrill 2019; Wan and Meng 2020; Pew Research Center, 2020; State Statistical Bureau Feb. 2021.

2. UBC and Price Waterhouse 2019; Wan and Meng 2020; Hurun 2021.

3. Li Yuan Feb. 15, 2022.

4. Results of cross-national comparisons of quantitative data such as income often vary with imprecisions due to the different methods and criteria used by the various data collectors, deliberate numbers games notwithstanding. It is necessary to have a triangulation of various sources and an attempt to minimize the uncorroborated or overcritical figures. Phelps and Crabtree 2013; Cyrill 2019; Wan and Meng 2020; Pew Research Center 2020; State Statistical Bureau 2021; WPR 2022.

5. Liang Hong 2014.

6. The ratio was 24.9 percent in 2018. World Bank website, accessed June 1, 2020. For why PRC has been performing much worse by a senior Chinese scholar, see Cai Dingjian 2007. For a comparison between China and Japan that illustrates the PEC's suboptimal performance, see Zhao Xiao 2014. For a similar comparison by the Bureau Chief of Research at the PRC State Council, see Liu Yingjie 2018.

7. Nationmaster.com, Jan. 2, 2014; CIA 2013–2022; IMF, *Economy & Growth*, Aug. 21, 2014; *The Economist*, "The Dragon Takes Wing," May 3, 2014.

8. UNDP 2010 and 2014. It must be noted that UNDP, like all UN agencies, has been the target of increased influence by the PRC and fed with Beijing's numbers in recent years. *The Economist*, "China Uses Threats and Cajolery to Promote Its Worldview," Dec. 7, 2019; K. Lee 2020.

9. UNDP 2013: 148–149; 2019: 304–307; 2021: 343–346.

10. 吃苦. F. Wang 2017: 126–133. For an early portrayal of this "Chinese characteristic," see Smith 1894: 19–34, 144–170. For a report about it today, see Cody 2008: A1.

11. Li Zhi-Sui (1994) 2011. Lower officials too need sleeping aid. Li Rui 1999-I: 205.

12. Jing Jun 2012; Zhou Liping 2014.

13. US Bureau of Labor Statistics 2012: 15–21.

14. Chan and Gao 2012: 355–377; Wright 2012; Peng Yi 2013; CCTV: *Xinwen lianbo* (新闻联播), Sept. 3, 2012.

15. PRC Coal Ministry figures; Lin Yanxing 2009.

16. Yang Siyang 2014. *The Economist*, "Black Death," July 18, 2015: 37.

17. Statistical Bureau 2012: table 10. The chief of the Statistical Bureau, however, wrote in a CCP journal with slightly different figures of 0.36 and 0.40. Ma Jiantang 2012.

18. *The Economist*, "China's Hidden Wealth," August 13, 2010. US national Engle Coefficient in 2010 was 0.1 (0.07 for the high income and 0.145 for the low income). US Department of Labor 2012: 8.

19. Pritchett and Spivack 2013: 15–19.

20. NPC (1993) 2017. Monthly tax brackets are ¥3,000 at 3 percent, 20 percent for income over ¥12,000, 30 percent for income over ¥35,000, 35

percent for income over ¥55,000, and 45 percent for income over ¥80,000. NPC (1980) 2018.

21. US IRS 2021. National Taxation Bureau 2021. Indian Ministry of Finance 2020.

22. Of the total 125 countries, only ten other counties have China's high payroll tax rate. Qi Yanbin 2015; Fang Yi 2013.

23. J. Pan 2020; X. Huang 2020: 199.

24. PRC Medical Products Administration, nmpa.gov.cn, accessed July 9, 2020.

25. Yuan Duanduan 2015. A box-office hit in 2018–19, *Dying to Survive* (我不是药神), and a TV docuseries *This is Life* (生门) broadcasted in 2017–2019 were rarely allowed to powerfully show the pain, misery, and abuse endured by the sick in the PRC.

26. Guo Yujie 2022.

27. Five-year survival rate of colon-cancer patients in China was 30 percent (as compared to 70% in the US). Bray 2018: 394–424.

28. Database of the International Agency for Research on Cancer (IARC), World Health Organization, accessed Feb. 19, 2021. In 2022, PRC researchers predicted the total annual cases of cancer grew to 4.82 million with 3.21 million deaths,

29. W. Chen et al. 2022: 584–590.

30. Xiong Peiyun 2011; Fu Yongjun 2020. For family life in the rural, see G. Santos 2021.

31. Luo Guoji 1995: 3–4, 74–75, 163, 395–406; Liu Changjin 1997: 101–107; Wang Bixue 2011; *Chengshi wanbao* (城市晚报): "Traditional Virtues in Local Communities (传统美德进基层), Changchun, Dec. 10, 2013. *Model Lecture* (国旗下讲话稿): "Struggle arduously, eat bitterness and endure hard work (艰苦奋斗吃苦耐劳), Beijing, Feb. 15, 2014.

32. For Lei Feng's "communist ethics of screws," that is, being content as just a small screw on the revolution machine, see Xinhua Dec. 6, 2014, and *Renmin ribao* Mar. 4, 2022.

33. 愚公. *Lie Zi-Tangwen* (列子·汤问), third century; Mao Zedong (1945): 1101–1104; Xi Jinping Aug. 22, 2019; Ministry of Education 2020–2022.

34. Osburg 2013. For the ubiquity of sexual indulgence by PRC officials, see Palmer 2013 and Zhang Weibin 2014; Kuo 2014; Chinese Automobile 2013; Luo Xiaojun 2013.

35. Khan and Riskin 2001; Knight 2013; F. Wang 2005: 124–149. For scholarship and data on this PRC institution, see F. Wang 2014. For the urban-rural division, see Rozelle and Hell 2020.

36. Djilas 1957; Szelenyi 1983; Bian 1994.

37. Meng Fangui 2013; Neo Zion April 13 and May 16, 2014.

38. Cevik and Correa-Caro 2015: 3; Sicular 2013: 1–5.

39. Guo and Sun 2012; Ceicdata.com, accessed June 4, 2020. The sporadically released PRC official data shows the same: State Statistical Bureau, 2015.

40. Swanbrow 2014; Xie Yu et al. 2014; S. Hu Dec. 21, 2012; J. Chen 2015.

41. Liu and Zhou 2021; Li Shi 2021.

42. Schaeffer 2020; World Bank 2020. US poverty line was $12,760 (one person) to $26,200 (family of four). ASPE: *2020 Poverty Guidelines*, Washington, DC: DHHS, 2020.

43. Li and Sicular 2014: 1–41; ISSS 2013; Li Shi 2021.

44. Based on the then exchange rate: ¥7.15 = $1. Statistical Bureau 2020; Li Keqiang, Press Conference, Beijing, May 29, 2020; Wan and Meng 2020.

45. Deputy Minister of Finance Cheng Lihua (程丽华): press conference, Beijing, Aug. 31, 2018. Ministry of HRSS 2019.

46. World Bank establishes three lines of daily income to measure poverty ($5.5), deep poverty ($3.3), and abject poverty ($1.9). World Bank 2020. ASPE 2020 (see note 42 above).

47. Xie Yu 2014; Sun Yinni 2021; Forbes 2014; People's Bank of China April 25, 2020.

48. UBC and Price Waterhouse 2019; Hurun 2021.

49. Li and Sicular 2014: 1–41. Xi decreed in 2015 to "eradicate poverty" by 2020, Zhang Ruimin 2019. He then declared in 2020 the "mission completed," Xi Jinping April 30, 2020.

50. PRC official poverty lines were always incredibly low: $0.08 (1986–2006) and $0.30 (since 2007) daily income as its "abject poverty line"; $0.34 (2000–2007), $0.42 (2007–2010), $0.51 (2011), and $0.95 (since 2011) as its "poverty line." "China's Poverty Line" (中国贫困标准), Baidu Baike (百度百科), June 2020. All at the then exchange rate.

51. Bbs.pku.edu.cn: "Li Keqiang's Bravery" (北大未名: 李克强的勇敢), May 20, 2021; Hernández 2017; Tan Xinyu 2020. With official PRC numbers and the problem-laden PPP method, the World Bank records a decline of Chinese poverty rate from 43 percent in 2002 to 6.5 percent in 2016. World Bank data, June 2, 2020. Officially, PRC had 5.5 million poor people needing assistance in 2020 (State Statistical, Bureau communique, Jan. 2020); Sun Yinni 2021.

52. Yuan Yilin 2020. CCTV: "Elimination of Poverty with Fakery" (掺假的脱贫摘帽), Beijing, April 23, 2021; Wu Xing Ji 2021.

53. Xinhua August 17, 2021; Zhi Gu 2021.

54. 冯仑, 潘石屹; Zhou Zhiyu 2021; Wu Zepeng 2021; Zhao Dongshan 2021; Lai Jinhong 2021.

55. 高考. For history of the exam and the CCP's politicization of it, see Yu Jie 1999 and Liu Haifeng 2019. For an anthropological study of the exam and its impact, see Howlett 2021.

56. X. Wang et al. 2013: 456–470; Chen Guang 2021.

57. Qiu Ruixian 2009; Shi Shusi 2013; Zhilian Zhaopin, April 27, 2022.

58. S. Potter 1993: 465–499; K. Chan 1994; F. Wang 2005.

59. It was ¥2,348 in Shanghai but ¥278 in Henan. State Reform Commission 1998: 22.

60. F. Wang 2009: 335–364. The CCP launched in 2014 yet another "major" reform of the *hukou* system including disusing the unsightly rural versus urban labels. Branigan 2014. Yet, the new reform has been slow and inconsequential for the 245 million migrant population. Fang Lie 2014; Lu Yijie 2015: 5. In the 2020s, the system continues to perpetuate both vertical and horizontal inequalities, while being effectively used by the party-state for a variety of policy objectives such as minimizing urban slums and responding to pandemics.

61. Li Peilin 2013; Cai Fang 2022. In the 2020s, the rural residents became eligible for the national pension-insurance plan, but their retirement benefit, from ¥70 ($10) to ¥110 ($15) a month (after15 years of mandatory, nonstop contribution), appeared symbolic and negligible. cpic.com.cn/baike/323.html

62. Wang and Li 2017. *Zhuhu*: "Tiers of Chinese Cities" (2020中国城市等级划分), July 2021.

63. For anecdotal reports about human tolls of the *hukou* system, see Liao Yiwu 2002: 95–117. For the significant benefits associated with urban *hukou*, see M. Akgüç 2014. For a study of "the rural problem" by PRC sociologist, see He Xuefeng 2019. For stories of rural poverty and decay in the 2010s–2020s, see Gao Shenke 2016; Xiyuan Qiu 2016; Xiao Huilong 2016; Xiao Song 2020.

64. Liu Yonghao 2014; Shi Yaojiang 2016; Huang Deng 2017; Xu Lingxiao 2022,

65. Solinger and Hu 2012: 741–764; Lu Qian 2019; Zhang Meng 2019.

66. F. Wang 2005: 127–147; Li Peilin 2013.

67. $10.2 billion (¥66 billion) in 2013, PRC Ministry of Transportation 2014. Faber 2015.

68. State Statistical Bureau 2011.

69. Li Tangning 2014. For how people keep congregating into major urban centers, see Guan Dian 2015. People's Bank of China 2020.

70. Jiang and Li 2013: A08; Zhang Xin 2015.

71. Dashan Shuofang 2021.

72. J. Chen 2014.

73. Mao Zedong (1955) 1977: 168–191; Yu and Wang 2013; Xinhua Aug. 17, 2021.

74. Hua Xia Nov. 3, 2020; Jiang Mengyin 2021.

75. Lake and Baum 2001: 587–621; Ward 2014: 309–343; Blimpoa 2013: ii57–ii83; Strömberg 2007: 199–222.

76. 集中力量办大事; Fang N 2013; Tao Wenzhao 2011.

77. WHO 2013; Du Shi 2020.

78. Zhang Liang Aug. 17, 2015. For comparison, see Brusentsev and Vroman 2016.

79. Zhu Xuedong 2021.

80. Tangshan Government 2021. GTV @ YouTube: "Henan Blue Sky Rescue team disbanded" (河南蓝天救援队解散), July 21, 2021.

81. F. Wang 2017: 176–180; Cai Jun 2018; Xinhua Feb. 5, 2016.

82. Ma Jichao 2021; Shen Moke 2021; PRC MEM 2022; Fan Zhi 2022.

83. Cui Li 2017; *Kwongwah* 2020; VOA Aug. 11, 2020.

84. AP: "Anatomy of a Conspiracy," Feb. 15, 2021. Dubow 2021; IFJ 2022.

85. Normile 2021; *The Economist*, "Shanghai's Lockdowns Will Rock China's Economy," March 29, 2022; CCP Central May 5, 2022.

86. Wei Zhou 2022. 方舱. For lockdowns and square cabins in Shanghai, PRC's most advanced city, see Fang Zhouzi 2022; Chen Xueping 2022; Culver 2022.

87. For anecdotes of life, death, and suffering during the lockdowns of three metropolises of Wuhan (2020), Xian (2021–2022), and Shanghai (2022) reported by Chinese, each with over 10 to 20 million population, see Fang Fang 2020; G. Yang 2022; Jiang Xue 2022; Wang Ji 2022; Xu Jin 2022; Ruan Tang 2022; Zhao Qiliu 2022; and Cong Yi 2022.

88. M. Zhou et al. 2021. For an anecdotal listing of such "excess death" in Shanghai, by anonymous netizens, see "Passed in Shanghai" (上海逝者) on airtable.com. April 19, 2022.

89. Cheng Mo 2021. For the low effect of PRC vaccines, see Premikha et al. 2022.

90. The CCP refused to allow the Western mRNA vaccines beyond allegedly using it for only a few top elites, mandated the less effective PRC vaccines and a "zero-virus" goal that ignore science about the virus and its evolution, and imposed mass lockdowns repetitively. All that seems sensible only for the ruler's control and power and a jingoistic vanity. Before the dust of power transition and struggle settled at the twentieth CCP national congress, there was little chance for changes, as Xi Jinping is personally and fully staked in those policies. Author's interviews of PRC officials, scholars, and medical executives 2020–2022. For mismanagement and "involution" of the massive PRC vaccine program, see Zhao and Xing 2022. In May 2022, Anthony Fauci, the US expert, simply called CCP's COVID "a disaster." Agrawal 2022.

91. Figures from Xinhua, WHO, and PRC Health Ministry in Tai Le 2021.

92. Only when the CCP leaders all start to eat the same food from the ordinary stores, food safety problem in the PRC may then have a real chance of abatement. Author's interviews with Xinhua and *Renmin Ribao* reporters, 2003 and 2009.

93. Landsberger 2019.

94. Wang Libin 2020. A visible sign showing this is that the best provided and protected capital city Beijing in fall 2020 publicly tried to secure its

food supply from eight major grain production provinces. Sun Jie 2020; G. Liu 2020: 25434–25444.

95. Guo Jiuhui 2013; Ge Xiuyu 2017; CCTV: "9,000 Tons of State Grains Stolen" (9000多吨国粮被盗), June 14, 2019; Chen Jian 2020; Huang Qiuxia 2021.

96. Xibu Zhengquan 2020.

97. Kroeber 2020: 85, 196.

98. Xinhua: "People on the Way to Get Permits" (人在证途), Feb. 24, 2014.

99. Dugan 2014. "Online Censorship in China," en.greatfire.org, Dec. 17, 2014.

100. Fu Weigang 2015; *Caijing* (财经), Aug. 10, 2015.

101. Zhou Bojue 2014. *Zhihu* May 10, 2016. For official PRC reports on the internet, see Yu Guoming 2010–2020.

102. Freedomhouse.org, 2020, 2021; Reporters Without Borders 2020; Kinzelbach 2022.

103. World Economic Forum 2014, 2021. For women's low status in corporate China, see Tatlow and Forsythe 2015: A1; Brussevich 2021; Ma Junmao 2015.

104. Helliwell et al. 2013, 2022.

105. Zhong Zukang 2007; Zhang Zhuan 2009. For a Chinese musician's take of this, hear Zhou Yunpeng 2009; for background of the lyrics, see bbs. tianya.cn/post-free-2886976-1.shtml, posted Nov. 12, 2012. Zhang Yuan 2015.

106. Han Xiaorong 2014.

107. Yunnan Buddhist Association "sternly" called this a rumor on Aug. 9, 2018. However, the rumor still circulated in the PRC cyber space years later in 2020–2021.

108. V. Hudson 2004. Even though this imbalance may help to make people "work harder" so to increase GDP, Wei Shangjin (Chief Economist of Asian Development Bank) quoted in Wang Jifei 2014. PRC official data reports that the gender ratio of Chinese birth is 116–118 males for 100 females. Huang and Liang 2015. PRC gender imbalance at birth is much higher than all sizable nations—all non-PRC Chinese populations have the normal ratio of 102. CIA 2015.

109. Zeng Liming 2004; Zhao Baige 2007: 7–8; Song Quancheng 2014: 115–122. About 2.4 girls "disappeared [unborn] every minute due to gender discrimination in China," Yao and Shi 2015.

110. Cao Meng 2013: 162–166; Zhao and Chen 2011.

111. 光棍村. Yan Ruyi 2019; Xi Xifei 2021; *Wangyi* Jan. 3, 2022.

112. From thirty to twenty per 10,000 people. Fu Weigang 2014.

113. Li Yan 2011. The low figure of the 1950s is probably an underreporting. Editorial of *Lancet* 2015: 2548. For a survey of mental health in the PRC, see J. Yang 2018. For a study of social anxiety, mental distress, and psychotherapeutic culture in the PRC, see L. Zhang 2020.

114. Wang Jing Jan. 6, 2015.

115. Fu Xiaolan 2020; *Baidu wenku* (百度文库), *White paper on depression figures in China* (中国抑郁症人数白皮书), Mar. 2020; Wu Xiaobo 2021; "The State of Mental Health in America: 2022," Mental Health America; National Institute of Mental Health, both accessed Feb. 2022. WHO 2022 (the "official" WHO figures are lower than that of PRC researchers).

116. Liu Yanwu 2014, 2018; Liu Yanwu et al. 2018; Liu and Cook 2020: 378–391.

117. J. Zhang 2002: 167–184; Phillips 2003: 22–24; Wu Fei 2007, 2009; US National Institute of Mental Health database, WHO database, accessed June 16, 2021.

118. Xie Renci 2021; Yu Haikuo 2015; Xi Congqing 2018.

119. Sheng and Chen 2015.

120. Comptroller 2021, see figure on 17-9.

121. Y. Yan 2003.

122. Hirschman 1970, 1978: 90–107.

123. Shen Yanhui 2007; Browne 2014. For an analysis of PRC emigration patterns in recent years, see Chen Hongyu 2012.

124. Exoduses to Hong Kong started right after 1949 and continued for many decades, with at least three major waves of hundreds of thousands of refugees in 1957, 1962, and 1972–1974. "Countless people" were killed or drowned trying. Chen Shuo 2015; Chen Bingan 2011; Lin Tianhong 2010; *Fenghuang lishi* April 25, 2011.

125. An Nan et al. 2013; Wu Yong 2020. Like the imperial rulers in the past and unlike more other countries, the PRC controls emigration with various restrictions.

126. PRC Ministry of Foreign Affairs 2016.

127. Zhang Ke 2014; *World Migration Report 2020*, UN: IOM, 2020.

128. Dominiczak 2013; Shah 2015.

129. US Department of State, Bureau of Consular Affairs database, accessed July 22, 2021.

130. Qian Jiang 2015: 5.

131. *Wangyi* (网易): "Why Students of Peking and Tsinghua Universities Compete for Going Abroad?" (为什么北大清华的学生争着出国), Guangzhou, Oct. 22, 2014.

132. Mervis 2008: 185; Xue Yong 2010: 294–297.

133. Zi You 2014; Tsinghua University 2020, 2021; Peking University 2020, 2021,

134. China EOL: *Report on Study Abroad* (中国教育在线: 出国留学报告), Beijing, 2014.

135. Newman 2014. "Number of Chinese Students in the US," statista. com, June 2020.

136. *World Education News and Reviews*, "Education in China," Dec. 17, 2019.

137. US Department of State, Bureau of Consular Affairs database, accessed July 22, 2021.

138. *OxResearch Daily Brief*: "China: Returnees Are Critical in Innovation Push," UK, July 2009.

139. Xinhua Oct. 14, 2013.

140. Zi You 2014; NCSES 2020; Zweig and Kang 2020; J. Qiu 2009.

141. 海龟(归). For the role and fate of returnees in the PRC, see G. Peterson 2014.

142. Wang Xiaobo 2010. For this "Recruitment Program of Global Experts" and its recruits, see the official 1000plan.org that went off line after 2020. *United daily* (联合早报): "'Thousand Talent' disappeared" ("千人计划" 消失), Singapore, Nov. 14, 2020.

143. For Chinese critique of the plan, see Xiao Rewu Yi 2014. For a non-Chinese review, see Sharma 2013. For its frauds and abuses, see Hvistendahl 2014: 411–415.

144. Many were later caught with their careers ruined; Barry and Kolata 2020: A12.

145. 海鸥; Zhang Dongdong 2012.

146. Ji Wei 2014; author's interviews of PRC educators 2010–2018 and 2021–2022.

147. Wang Huiyao 2012; Zweig and Wang 2011: 413–431.

148. For example, the offspring of a well-known CCP "martyr" became naturalized US citizens. Yao Hongen 2015.

149. Chen Feng 2014; Yao Dongqin 2015.

150. Erling 2014; Zhang Ke 2014; R. Wang 2013; Frank 2013; Zhang Bin 2014; VanderKlippe 2014; *The Economist*, "Middle Class Flight: Yearning to Breathe Free," April 26, 2014: 42–43.

151. IIUSA, *EB-5 Investor Markets Report*, Washington, DC: IIUSA, 2016: 11, 19.

152. Tao Duanfang 2014.

153. Tong Mu 2014.

154. Gao Shangquan 2014.

155. Wang and Elliot 2014. For Chinese emigration to Africa, see H. French 2014.

156. Wanli Yuntian 2021.

157. Goldstein and Semple 2012: A28. Semple et al. 2014: A1. For former PRC police officer failed to get US political asylum, see Liu Daqi 2014. Author's interviews, 2015–21.

158. In fiscal years 2004–2018, for example, many tens of thousands of PRC citizens filed for asylum each year, up from around 10,000 five years ago, with 4,495 to 8,585 cases granted each year. DOJ-INS 1999–2013; Mossaad 2005–2019.

159. Refugee Council 2020. IRCC 2019. EUSO 2020. New Zealand Immigration 2020.

160. Immigration Bureau 2005 and 2018.

161. Author's interviews in Hong Kong, Macao, Taiwan, and Korea, 2007–2016.

162. *Qianjiang wanbao* (钱江晚报): "Hundred Billion Tourist Deficit Is Alarming" (千亿美元旅游逆差令人警醒), Hangzhou, Sept. 28, 2014: A24.

163. Wang Huiyao 2014: 18, 47, 66. Many of the foreign students in the PRC have been the so-called "purchased" students from low-income countries lured by funding many times higher than what native students get.

164. Frater 2015; Mo Xiaoxia 2017.

165. Naspl.org. PRC lottery appears rigged with revenue misused and embezzled, *Fenghuang jinrong* (鳳凰金融): "Ten Dark Shots of Chinese Lottery" (中国彩票十大黑镜头), June 2, 2020.

166. For a folklore artist spastically displaying some symbols of sociopolitical ills in the PRC, mocking the famous twelfth-century Song-era painting, "Along the River during the Qingming Festival" (清明上河圖), see Wu Xuefeng 2014.

167. Author's research notes, 2010–2021. For a general discussion about social resistance in the PRC, see Perry and Selden 2010.

168. 辅警. AFP: "China Spends $125 Billion Per Year on Riot Gear and 'Stability Maintenance,'" May 19, 2013; Chen Zhifeng 2014.

169. McDonell 2019; B. Allen-Ebrahimian (of *Axios*) @BethanyAllenEbr, June 5, 2020.

170. Daum 2017. The completion of the system is behind the schedule. Run by the PRC agency of State Information Center, a Credit China (中国信用) net already provides online searchable blacklists of seven kinds "targeted people" and various entities. creditchina.gov.cn or www.zgxyw.gov.cn, last accessed on Oct. 1, 2022.

171. Chen Yixin 2018.

172. Frank Church, On *Meet the Press*, NBC, Washington, DC, Aug. 17, 1975.

173. For graphic anecdata on serial murder, woman trafficking, senseless killing, and cannibalism, see Mo Zou 2021; Xi Minghua 2022; Lao Fu 2022; *Zhihu*, March 10, 2022.

174. Si Gong 2006. Author's interviews in eleven Asian countries, 1993–2019.

175. Hu Jiujiu 2014.

176. EIU 2015: 33–35.

177. Author's observation in dozens of Chinese locations, 2000–2004, 2010, 2013.

178. Lü Dewen 2015. For more on organized crime in the PRC, see P. Wang 2017.

179. Reng Pengfei 2014; Symantec 2014.

180. UNODC: *Global Study on Homicides* 2013, Vienna, 2013: 126–127, 141.

181. PRC National Commission on Drug Prohibition database, posted May 11, 2015.

182. Cui Jing 2013; Wang Jinhua 2020; X. He 2021.

183. Y. Xiong 2015: 161–184.

184. Graeber 2018.

185. Students and state employees in particular are required to constantly update their scores of online learning of Xi Thought through platforms like *Xuexi Qiangguo* (学习强国) at www.xuexi.cn, last accessed October 2022.

186. For a revealing albeit cursory report on the complicated and suffering life of individuals in China (its Chinese version censored in the PRC), see Osnos 2014. For social decay, see Wang Jinwen 2013; Huang Zhizhong 2013; and Zhai Richang 2019.

187. Chang An Jian (2019) 2021.

188. 躺平, 躺平学, and 躺平主义; Lu Xing Jia 2021; Si Weijiang 2021; Zhi Guzi 2021; Shi Hanbin 2021; Liu Run June 1, 2021; Dai Jianye 2021; L. Kuo 2021.

189. Pan Xiao 1980; *Fenghuang zixun* 2009; Pan Yi (one of the original questioners) 2020.

190. 废柴, 葛优/北京躺, 佛系, 朋克养生, and 丧文化. Yu Leyin 2016; Xiao Ziyang 2017; Editor February 9, 2018; Jin Hui 2019; CNSA 2019.

191. Li Zife (李子佛) @lizife, Twitter, May 16 and 30, 2021.

192. 海龟 and 海废; Lian Qingchuan 2021.

193. Lao Dongyan 2022; 润学, 海燕综合症; A Min 2022; Dong Yizhi 2020; Xi Po 2022. The video of "last generation" response quickly went viral, defying censors, N. Gan May 2022. In the summer and fall of 2022, for example, seemingly endless posts circulated on PRC social media despite censorship to rumor, beckon, and even cheer for a full war over Taiwan or a violent coup overthrowing Xi Jinping so "to end it all." Author's notes, June–October, 2022.

Chapter 4

1. 罗瑞卿. Luo Diandian 1999: 103–104, 124.

2. Quite a few rich and famous have been exposed for their alleged offences of sexual harassment. L. Ma 2022; Metoochina.me, last accessed Oct. 6, 2022.

3. SCIO 2018; LLC; Cook 2017.

4. For the concept of "atheist theocracy," see Heimann 1953: 311–331.

5. Koesel 2013: 572–589; Taji 2019; Lim 2021; Ownby 2008; J. Tong 2009; Shea 2022.

6. Basu 2020; Tobin 2020; Weiss 2021; Maizland 2021; G7 2021; NATO 2021.

7. Xi Jinping April 23, 2016.

8. Joe Zhang 2014.

9. 自嗨 and 意淫; Chen Fang 2017; Du Gangjian 2017; Huang Heqing 2021.

10. Wang Junping 2020. For the brazen absurdity of numerous "master doctors of Chinese medicine," see Kexue Gongyuan 2022.

11. 抗日神剧; Ueki Iwata 2018; Wang and Chew 2021; Dante Lam 2021; *Renmin ribao*: "Luo Changping Arrested" (罗昌平被逮捕), October 22, 2021.

12. Rousseau (1782) 2000: 395.

13. Li Chengpeng 2013: 39–40; F. Wang 2017: 101–126.

14. Bao Gangsheng 2022; F. Wang 1998: 10, 18–19.

15. Smith 1894: 186–286. Over a century later, a PRC scholar openly moaned the absence of a moral "bottom line." Yi Zhongtian 2002.

16. 国民性; Zhang Xuezhong 2016 (soon deleted by censors).

17. Deng Xiaomang 2014. For a discussion of the traditional twist of "human nature" in Chinese culture, see Chang Hao 1989.

18. Alexander and Chan 2004: 609–629; Marchal 2022: 227–243.

19. For complex ranks of CCP-PRC officials-standard, see Nie Huihua 2015.

20. G. Orwell 1949.

21. 新闻联播; Sha Yexin 2005.

22. F. Wang 2017: 21–29; Xi, Nov. 30, 2020; HUGO 2009: 1541–1545; Xu Minghui 2016.

23. Fitzgerald 2022; Tencent: "What Is the Officials-Rank of University President" (大学校长是什么行政级别), Oct. 30, 2019.

24. Zhong Jian 2010.

25. Wang Xiao 2012. Social capital like clan networks, relentlessly smashed by the party-state, actually saved many lives during the great famine under Mao. J. Cao et al. 2020.

26. Rock and Bonnett 2004: 999–1017; Y. Ang 2020.

27. Sun Liping, September 4, 2021; Ci Jiwei 2009: 19–25; Y. Yan 2021: 96–120.

28. Wang Jian, July 12, 2021; Ran Yunfei 2007.

29. For shocking anecdotes of the hidden but rotten lifestyle and violent behaviors of Mao and his top lieutenants as well as their offspring, see Li Zhi-Sui 1996; Chang and Halliday 2006; Luo Diandian 1999: 46, 74, 153; Feng Jicai 2014.

30. Chi-wen Lee 2014; Ma Jian 2015; 156–158.

31. 红二/三代 or 官二/三代 and 富二代/三代, 学二代/三代 and 文二代/三代. Zhu Bin 2017: 193–216. Author's interviews in and out of the PRC, 2003–2021.

32. For one telling example, see Hai Yun 2001 and Sheng Xue 2001. For CCP supporters conceding the incurability of the party's corruption, see Song Zhaolai 2014.

33. Jin Dalu 2011.

34. *Jinghua shibao* (京华时报), Beijing, Oct. 13, 2014: A01, A10.

35. CDIC and CCTV 2016, 2020, 2021, 2022.

36. Shum Feb. 4, 2022.

37. Schmid and Wang 2017; Tan Qingming 2018.

38. Liu Shaoqi (1962) 2002; Philosophy Editors 2019.

39. Mao's speeches to top CCP cadres, in Li Rui 1999-I: 225, 254, 279.

40. Moser Aug. 7, 2006.

41. Fang Ning 2013; Su Changhe 2014; Ministry of Foreign Affairs 2021; State Council 2021 and 2022.

42. Li and Gan 2014.

43. 造反. This included family members of even the Chairman of the PRC and Mao's designated successor Liu Shaoqi. Kan Jinzhao 1967.

44. "Illiterates and Hooligans" (文盲加流氓), as worded by Deng Xiaoping in 1978 to criticize Mao's "Gang of Four." Deng Xiaoping (1983) 1994: 103–110.

45. Xiao Shu 1999; Mo Zhengxin 2007; Xiao Bazhu 2013.

46. Ran Yunfei 2007; Lin Weiqi 2020; Zhang Min 2021.

47. Taylor 2021.

48. Hu Xingdou 2015.

49. Yi Quan 2008; Commentator Feb. 27, 2013; Wang Xiaoming 2014. *CCP Constitution*, Beijing, 2017 and *PRC Constitution-Preamble*, Beijing, 2018.

50. Smith 1894: 285. Author's interviews of officials in China, 1990s–2010s. For examples of the common view that "officials are all bad apples" (当官的没一个好东西), see Xiao Renfu 2009 and Dao Boman 2014.

51. 吃空饷. Qun Shuo Oct. 2014; Chen Qiao 2019; Xu Ran 2020; Guan Cha Yuan 2021.

52. PRC State Council 2014; Ministry of Education 2015, 2018.

53. 陈毅、陈云、邓小平、李先念、刘伯承、刘少奇、罗瑞卿、彭德怀、陶铸、叶剑英and周恩来. For the repulsive acts by those leaders in the Gao Gang (高岗) case, see Chen and Liu 2010: 61–82, 131–242; Luo Diandian 1999. For Tao Zhu's bloody rule in Southern China, see Yang Li 1997. For Liu Shaoqi as Mao's top executioner until he was purged, see Song Yongyi 2006. For Zhou Enlai as Mao's leading accomplice, see Gao Wenqian 2003/2007, Sima and Ouyang 2009, Wang Rui 2010: 2–18, and Sima Qingyang 2012. For the treacheries, iniquities, and indignities of other CCP heroes, see Chi Houze 2006, Shuo Liweng 2008, and Li Datong 2019. For an ingenue's account of Mao and his reign, see Y. Chen 2022.

54. For the bloody struggles and betrayals inside the CCP before 1949, see Gong Chu 1978; Braun 1982; Zhang Guotao 1974; Wang Ming (1975) 2009. For the thick and deadly conspiracies surrounding the pivotal Lin Biao case, see Shu Yun 2011; Li Zuopeng 2011: 765–798. For the cruel power struggles under Deng Xiaoping, see Hu Jiwei 1996 and Wu Jiaxiang 2002. For snap-shots of the near total absence of decent people at the top of CCP leadership, see Zhu Heping 2006; Zhang Sheng 2008; Zhong Qiguang 1995: 257–264; Xiao and Jiang 2005: 26–32. For an insider's account about the intricacies of the

CCP leadership during the Cultural Revolution, see Wang Li 1993. For an exemplary penance by a senior CCP official, see Wei Junyi 1998. For examples of corruption of senior CCP leaders in the twenty-first century, see CDIC 2006; Jiang Weiping 2010; Xinhua: "Bo Xilai Sentenced to Life in Prison" (薄熙来被判无期徒刑), Sept. 22, 2013; Chang Yan 2012. For corruption of senior military commanders, see Zhang Jinchang 2015; Yan and J. Cao 2015.

55. 神经衰弱. See the voluminous memoirs with greatly varied quality and truthfulness by Ba Jin (巴金), Bo Yibo (薄一波), Chen Boda (陈伯达), Chen Yonggui (陈永贵), Chen Xilian (陈锡联), Chen Zaidao (陈再道), Deng Liqun (邓力群), Ding Sheng (丁盛), Gu Mu (谷牧), Hu Jiwei (胡绩伟), Hu Qiaomu (胡乔木), Huang Yongsheng (黄永胜), Ji Xianlin (季羡林), Jia Zhifang (贾植芳), Jiang Weiqing (江渭清), Jin Yuelin (金岳霖), Kuai Dafu (蒯大富), Li Lanqing (李岚清), Li Peng (李鹏), Li Rui (李锐), Li Xiannian (李先念), Li Zupeng (李作鹏), Liu Bocheng (刘伯承), Liu Huaqing (刘华清), Lv Zhengcao (吕正操), Nie Rongzhen (聂荣臻), Nie Yuanzi (聂元梓), Qian Weichang (钱伟长), Qiu Huizuo (邱会作), Su Yu (粟裕), Wei Junyi (韦君宜), Wu De (吴德), Wang Dongxing (汪东兴), Wang Fang (王芳), Wang Ping (王平), Wang Shoudao (王首道), Wang Zhen (王震), Wu Faxian (吴法宪), Wu Xiuquan (伍修权), Xiao Jun (萧军), Xiao Ke (肖克), Xiong Xianghui (熊向晖), Xu Jiatun (许家屯), Xu Jingxian (徐景贤), Xu Shiyou (许世友), Xue Muqiao (薛暮桥), Yang Chengwu (杨成武), Yang Dezhi (杨得志), Yang Jiang (杨绛), Yang Shangkun (杨尚昆), Yang Xianyi (杨宪益), Yao Wenyuan (姚文元), Yu Guangyuan (于光远), Zhang Aiping (张爱萍), Zhang Zongxun (张宗逊), Zhao Ziyang (赵紫阳), Zhong Qiguang (钟期光), and Zhou Yiliang (周一良). For an official profile of 100 PRC leaders, see Zheng Gang 2000.

56. Li Zhi-Sui (1994) 2011; Wang Minqing 2011: A44.

57. Yuan Ling 2014: 62–75.

58. 胡耀邦, 彭德怀, 张闻天, and 赵紫阳.

59. Hu Ping 2014. In just one month, PRC media openly reported three "big cases" illustrating the outrageousness of official corruption: when the second highest military commander was purged right after his retirement, investigators discovered in just one of his many houses in Beijing briberies piled up in the basement including over a ton of cash in many currencies and a dozen truckloads of jade, emeralds, antiques, and paintings. Zhong Jian 2014. One middle-level official in Beijing was discovered hoarding 200 million RMB cash of bribery. Supreme Procuratorate 2014. A much lower ranked official in the neighboring Hebei Province stockpiled 120 million RMB cash, 37 kg gold, and the deeds of sixty-eight housing units in his home (*Jinghua shibao* 京华时报, Beijing, Nov. 13, 2014: 14). Zou Le 2014. For more "small" officials took huge briberies, see Li Wenji 2014: A19.

60. Chen and Xu 2010. For the endless anecdotes of official corruption approved by the censors to publish, see the only PRC journal (run by the CCP

Sichuan provincial committee) devoted to covering corruption cases, *Lianzheng liaowang* (廉政瞭望), Chengdu, 1989–2022.

61. Barmé 2014. For a revealing expose on CCP's anti-corruption efforts and methods of its Discipline Inspection as secret police, see Luo Changping 2014: 67–90.

62. Guevara et al. 2014; J. Lee 2015.

63. CDIC decrees, in *Jinghua shibao* (京华时报), Beijing, Jan. 16, 2014: A04; Jan. 26, 2014: A04–A05. Zhao Qiang 2014. For the price tag of offices "purchased" by thirty-one cadres in one prefecture, see Shen Du 2019. Wademan 2012.

64. C. Huang 2014-I; Chu Chaoxin 2015. A rare official exposé of this market is Liang Aiping 2014. Yang Chunchang 2015. The return on office-purchasing "investment" can be 300 percent or higher. Xu Yaotong 2006.

65. Yang Ye 2014; Yao Dongqing 2012.

66. X. Wang 2002: 1–17; A. Kleinman 2011.

67. Zhou Bin 2007.

68. F. Wang 2017: 21–29; Sun Linping 2013; Yang Hanqin 2019.

69. H. Restall 2003; Lim and Blanchard 2013; L. Murray 2015.

70. For a synopsis of those traditional Chinese norms, see F. Wang 2017: 101–114.

71. Zhong Weizhi 2018.

72. For a CCP version of the history of Chinese ideology, see Cai Xiao 2021.

73. 卑鄙是卑鄙者的通行证, 高尚是高尚者的墓志铭; Bei Dao 1979, 1991.

74. 高尚是卑鄙者的通行证, 卑鄙是高尚者的墓志铭; Yu Jie 2014: 13.

75. 富强, 民主, 文明, 和谐, 自由, 平等, 公正, 法治, 爱国, 敬业, 诚信, 友善. *Renmin ribao* "Socialist Core Values" (社会主义核心价值观), Feb. 12, 2014: 1; Commentator 2011.

76. L. Lim 2014.

77. A latest example of such effort is the heavily promoted 2014 movie by Zhang Yimou (张艺谋), PRC's leading court artisan, *Coming home* (归来).

78. Goldhagen 1997; Hayner 2001; Hazan 2010; Sitze 2013.

79. For how the CCP recruited and wasted "talents" to work secretly for decades to spy on fellow scientists, see *Tencent jiaodian renwu* (腾讯焦点人物), Mar. 31, 2015.

80. 指鹿为马. Sima Qian (second century BCE) 2013. For the ludicrous but earnest national campaign to "study Xi," see Carrico 2018.

81. Legal Institute 2012. Two years later, the CCP started to bar naked officials being promoted to be chiefs above county/division levels. Article 24–4, CCP Central, Jan. 15, 2014: 16.

82. Zhang Manshuang 2016; Qiu Rui 2015.

83. For crushed conscience and human dignity in the PRC, see Ye Fu 2010. For how the 2008 Olympic Games reflected the inferiority complex and

deceptive CCP showmanship, see Guan Jun 2009: 57–77, 148–168; Price and Dayan 2008.

84. Rao Yi 2014: 28–30; Zong Pu 2010: 107.

85. 林昭 (1932–1968), 刘文辉 (1937–1967), 王申酉(1945–1977), 张春元 (1932–1970), 张九能(1939–1970), 遇罗克(1942–1970). Gu Zhun (顾准 1915– 1974), a senior and able CCP financial cadre who was brutally persecuted, was a rare case of a thoughtful critic of the Maoist regime with his writings fairly well preserved. Gu Zhun 2007; Luo Yinsheng 2005; Wang Shenyou 2002; Hu Jie 2005; Hoover Institution 2009; Chen Binqi 2013. For more on these and other rare, brave but "vanished thinkers" in the PRC, see Qian Liqun 2012 (quote in vol. 2, p. 148); Yang Xiguang (Xiaokai) 1994; Liu Wenzhong 2004; Ying Hongbiao 2009.

86. 刘晓波 (1955–2017). Wong and Chen 2017.

87. 郭沫若, 钱学森, 冯友兰, 茅盾, and 余秋雨; You and Lin 1998; Liu Zhong-jing 2015; Liang Musheng 2015; Hua Xinmin 2010; Cai, Xie and Guo 2015; Zhou Yan 2011: 113–158; Yu Jie 2014; Zhang Hong 2004; Yi Zhongtian 2011.

88. Mou Zhongsan 1991: Preface.

89. Wang and Lao 2000. In 2015, the then only PRC Nobel Laureate who is not jailed or in exile, the novelist Mo Yan (莫言), publicly heeds the Party line and flatters the CCP leaders with duplicity. Jing Yanan 2015; Jiang Zuquan 2016.

90. For leading intellectuals tormented, emasculated, and ruined by Mao and the CCP, see Chen Tushou 2000. For intellectuals' misfortune in PRC, see Zi Zhongyun 2011. Established scholars and artists like Feng Yidai (冯亦代) and Huang Miaozi (黄苗子) became CCP's secret informants. Zhou Yan 2011: 133–143. A noted historian who, after sufferings of decades under CCP, forged history maliciously for self-serving, see Han Shishan 2005. For how generations of Chinese intellectuals were brutalized and "destroyed" by the CCP, see Xie Yong (1999) 2013.

91. Li Xiaoting 2013; Chen Tushou (2000) 2013; Li Xiaoting 2013.

92. Cheng Enfu (程恩富), Cui Zhiyuan (崔之元), Hu Angang (胡鞍钢), Li Xiguang (李希光), Wang Shaoguang (王绍光), Wen Tiejun (温铁军), Zhang Weiwei (张维为), Ge Bichao 2018.

93. Ge Jianxiong 2021.

94. Yu Hua 2011. A party boss of a writers guild in Shandong published poems to adulate the CCP in the name of earthquake victims of substandard buildings, declaring "even though dead, we are still happy as the Party cares for us" and wanted to watch from the grave and "cheer together for the Beijing Olympic games" on TV. Ying Zi 2008. For recent examples of cadres corrupting Chinese language, see Xin Qing Nian 2022. For similar corruption of German language in Nazi Germany, see Grunberger 1971: 285–434 and Klemperer (1975) 2006.

95. Shuai Hao (2013) 2021;Wang Jun 2017; Hong Qiaojun 2021.

96. 身奴 and心奴; Ba Jin 2000: 322–328.

97. Solzhenitsyn 1973. For an imitation by victim of the CCP in exile, see Zhang Xianchi 2012.

98. Team Reporters 2011: 1.

99. Wang Yi 2005; Wu Qiantao 2010; Chen Yanbin 2013.

100. He Guanghu 2016.

101. Chen Pokong 2015. For a critique of Chen, see Xia Ming 2015. Chao Changqing 2015.

102. Luo Changping 2014: 89–90, 98–109, 124. Luo was jailed later in 2021 for questioning CCP's anti-American movies.

103. Shao Daosheng 2007; Gao Fusheng 2014. For how CCP leaders including Mao victimized female dancers and singers of the PLA "art troupes" (文工团), watch Wang Yunlong 2016.

104. *Bloomberg*, "Xi Jinping Millionaire Relations Reveal Fortunes of Elite," June 29, 2012. Barboza 2012: A1. Forsythe 2014: A1. International Consortium of Investigative Journalists revealed multitrillion dollar PRC wealth hidden away offshore, offshoreleaks.icij.org, 2022.

105. Author's interviews in Beijing, Chongqing, Hefei, Hong Kong, Shanghai, Shenzhen, Xian, and outside of the PRC, 2000–2021.

106. *Sohu junshi* (搜狐军事), March 4, 2015. *Mingbao* (明報): "PLA Regiment Commander Worth a Million" (軍中團長價值百萬), Hong Kong, March 4, 2015.

107. *The Economist*, "Fakes and Status in China," Jan. 3, 2012.

108. Dai Xiting 2015; J. Huang et al. 2015, May 2021.

109. Xiao Guangming 2015.

110. Hattamn2014; Dong Xin 2022; Sun Yian 2022.

111. For sex industry, see T. Zheng 2009, 2012. For sex workers, see Huang and Pan 2004.

112. Qin Quanyao 2012; Lan Tai 2014.

113. Author's interviews of police in Anhui, Guangdong, Jiangsu, and Shanghai, 2004, 2010; AP: "Sex Tape Used to Bribe Chinese Official Goes Viral," Nov. 27, 2012; Zhang Qianfan 2013.

114. Kang Chenwei 2016.

115. Dongguan Statistical Bureau: *Demographic data of Dongguan* (东莞人口数据报告), 2011; *Caijing* (财经): "Peeking Dongguan" (窥视东莞), Feb. 10, 2014; C. Huang 2014-II.

116. CCTV: *Xinwen Lianbo* (新闻联播), Feb. 10, 2014.

117. He Yuxing 2015.

118. *Banyuetan*: "Shocking Educational Corruption" (惊心怵目的教育腐败), Oct. 11, 2003; Qun Shuo 2013. For examples of teachers' corruption and their abuse of test regimes, see *The Economist*, "Chinese Schools," Jan. 21, 2014. For senior professors as xenophobic and narcissistic "patriots," watch Zheng Qiang 2014, 2020.

119. For cases of plagiarism and falsifications by PRC scholars, see the collection on www.xys.org, an overseas Chinese website dedicated to exposés of PRC academic corruption since 1996 and a Beijing-based collection "Say No to Academic Falsification" (向学术造假说不), *Renmin wang* (人民网), both last accessed 2022.

120. For official PRC inaction and reaction to the disastrous SARS epidemic in 2003, see *Chinese Law and Government* collecting China's SARS-related documents, UCLA, vols. 36–4, 36–6, and 37–1, 2003–2004. For how the Chinese doctors and hospitals continued to cover up epidemics one decade after SARS, see Cai Rupeng 2013. For corruption in the Chinese medical profession, see Zhang Ping 2013. For medical administrators colluded with the CCP authority to cover up the COVID-19 pandemic in 2019–2020, see Gong Qinqi 2020 and watch N. Wang 2021.

121. Supreme People's Procuratorate, Dec. 3, 2017; Xiao Tian 2019. For illustration of state medal-machine in sports impairing people's minds and lives, see Qin Banliang 2021. For Chinese national soccer program plagued by corruption, see Liu Jianhong 2022.

122. Liu Chang 2012. For tales of monks in Shaolin Temple, see Polly 2007.

123. Lu Lilong 2013; 中国知网. Wang Kaidong 2022.

124. Liu and Yang 2014; Ma Kai 2015; Guo Yukuan 2016; Yuan Zhixiao 2019.

125. Sun Aimin 2020; Riordan et al. 2022.

126. Thompson 2013; Hancock and Liu 2019.

127. Fang Zhouzi 2005; Hvistendahl 2013: 1035–1039; Schneider 2020; Li Yubo 2007.

128. Y. Zhao 2014: 94, 99; Fang Jing 2006; Ye and Lu 2013: 7.

129. Zhong Xin 2014.

130. Meng Zhaoli 2014: A14. For a Kafkaesque story about PRC prisoners purchasing fake inventions to get early parole, see Ramzy 2015. Editors Aug. 28, 2014.

131. *The Economist*, "Scientific Research, Looks Good on Paper," Sept. 28, 2013.

132. Barbash 2015; S. Chen 2017; F. Ching 2017; Chawla 2020; Else and Noorden 2021.

133. Lei Lei 2021.

134. Else 2021; *Journal of Cellular Biochemistry* 122-S1: S1–S136, Oct. 2021.

135. Krimsky 2019: 351–368; E. Xiao 2020.

136. Acemoglu et al. 2021.

137. Li Bozhong 2005; Mu Ran Oct. 24, 2014; Liu Mingyang 2020; Zhu Weijing 2020.

138. Ouyang Junshan 2020; Guo Rongxing 2021.

139. Qin Siqing 2021; Jia Ye 2014.

140. Li Zhiqiang 2014; Zhang Wen 2014; Rauhala 2015: 36–41; Wang Jing 2015.

141. Kan Kaili 2012; Yu Xianbin 2022.

142. Xiao Han 2006; Xin Ke 2013, 2014; Qin Hui Dec. 1, 2014.

143. Wang Xiaoyang 2013; Xin Dongfang 2021.

144. Wang Haiguang (professor of history at CCP Central Party School) 2020.

145. Yu Minhong 2015.

146. Pratt 2014; Lu and Hunt 2015; Global Net 2016.

147. Liu Run, June 7, 2021.

148. 聚天下英才而用之. Xi Jinping, May 28, 2021.

149. Ning Lizhong 2014; Deng Xize 2021.

150. Rhoads and Wang 2014; PRC Ministry of Education 2014.

151. Dai Xiting 2014; Editorial, Nov. 24, 2014; Chen Zhiwen 2021.

152. PRC Ministry of Education, May 26, 2021; Xiao Mu 2021.

153. Xi Jinping Dec. 29, 2014. For how the scholars are tightly restricted in interaction with foreign peers especially since 2007, see Jia Qingguo 2021.

154. 155. CCP Central-Organization Department et al., www.1000plan. org, accessed July 1, 2019. Permanent Subcommittee on Investigations 2019.

156. "Local Talent-Attractions Programs" (地方引才计划), 1000plan.org/ qrjh/section/4, accessed Nov. 27, 2014; Anhui Provincial Government 2012.

157. Ministry of Education, Press Conference, Beijing, Dec. 7, 2021.

158. Li Keqiang 2014; Ministry of Education, www.eol.cn, accessed July 1, 2020.

159. Yang Wanguo 2014.

160. Chen Pingyuan 2014; Lu Yuanqiang 2013: 2; Ministry of Education data, July 23, 2021.

161. *Graduate Enrollment and Degrees*, Washington: CGS, 2014: 15–16; NSF 2014, 2020.

162. Yuan Xiaohua 2021; NSF 2020; *US News & World Report* July 1, 2021.

163. Wang Hongfei 2007. Similar but more comprehensive critics can be seen in Xue Yong 2010: 225–237, 270–302, and Zhou Guangli 2010. For a much rosier assessment by the government, see Ministry of Education, May 10, 2011: 15. Author's interview in Shanghai, 2010.

164. CCP Central and State Council Jan. 21, 2015: 1.

165. Data from TTCSP 2008–2021.

166. For how thinktanks are poorly utilized according to one insider, see Wang Wen 2021. For how some of the tanks self-congratulate themselves with "studies" that dismiss democracy and pandemic control in the United States, see Renda Chongyang 2021.

167. Peng Chenguang 2013. For one effort for a "genuine" think tank modeled after US institutions, Institute for Advanced Study in Humanities at Zhejiang University since 2014, see Zhao Dingxin 2022.

168. Wang Rong 2021.

169. Author's interviews with faculty and administrators of about two dozen 211 and 985 schools, 2000–2021. Basic information about the two projects is on PRC Ministry of Education website. For Chinese exposes and critiques, see Wang Zeng 2004 and Ding Dong 2009. For a "leftist" critique of the "corruption and decay" of top PRC universities, see Gan and Liu 2014.

170. Xu Jing 2014: A6; Yang Yuliang (杨玉良), xys.org/dajia/yangyuliang.html, accessed 2021.

171. For anecdotes of corruption among college faculty in the PRC, see zhihu.com/question/20362737, accessed July 23, 2021; Qiao Jialan 2022.

172. US Senate 2019; Barry and Kolata 2020: A12.

173. Lan Zhixin 2014; CCTV: "Evening News" (晚间新闻), Oct. 11, 2014; Du and Wang 2014.

174. 潘绥铭; Mao Kaiyun 2014.

175. World Intellectual Property Organization database, accessed March 3, 2021.

176. Wu Zhanqiao 2017; Jia Zheng 2019.

177. Jiang Jun 2020; Peng Xin 2020; Su and Qiu 2021. Zhang Erchi et al. 2022.

178. Guo Linlin 2019.

179. Yang Dezhi 2001; Liu and Liao 2021; Jing Lai 2021; Tan Suo 2021.

180. X. Pang 2019. For its defense, see Wu Changfeng 2019. CCP top leaders had a special session to promote "quantum technology" as the "critically important cutting-edge breakthrough." Xi Jinping Oct. 17, 2020. The quantum "revolution" project seemed indeed personally blessed by "the top" so the multibillion RMB waste, increasingly seen in plain sight, continues. Author's interviews, May 2021; Parker 2022.

181. Guo Chuyang 2010, 2021; Ye Kai 2018; Ling Juelin 2015.

182. Shi Po 2010; Ming Shi Shuo 2022; *Chronicle of Speech Crimes in China* (中国文字狱事件盘点), @SpeechFreedomCN, Twitter, last accessed October 2022.

183. C. Lee 2012. Comparative studies reveal less shocking but similar findings. Mohrman 2013: 727–743; Yang Meng 2005. An insider's exposé of Peking University is Xie Ning 2014.

184. Sheng and Wang 2014: 1–10.

185. Xinhua April 25, 2022. Author's correspondence with PRC educators, May 2022.

186. Loyalka 2021.

187. *Boya shuju* (博雅数据) database on study overseas, Beijing, accessed Feb. 8, 2021.

188. *Sohu news* (搜狐新闻), Beijing, Dec. 14, 2021.

189. Zweig and Kang 2020; Corrigan et al. 2022.

190. *The Global AI Talent Tracker*, Macro Polo Institute, searched April 13, 2022.

191. Zhang Kaiyuan 2009; Shan and Li 2014: 6–10; Jiang Yin 2014: 2–3.

192. Gong Renren 2005; Tian and Lu 2016.

193. *Wangyi*: "Full Analysis of the Fudan Incident" (复旦事件全分析), June 6, 2021. Liu Zheng 2021. For defense of tenure-track system in the PRC, see Rao Yi 2021.

194. Xu Xiao: *Half Life as Human* (徐晓: 半生为人), Beijing: Tongxin, 2005.

195. Lei Lei 2006; *Tencent xinwen*: "Cases of College Entrance Stolen" (高考顶替专题), June 29, 2020; Tong Xia 2020.

196. Hao Tianjiao 2021.

197. Lan Tian 2010; Leng Haoyang 2019; Xue Peng 2020; Lan Linzong 2021.

198. Howlett 2021: 9.

199. *Sina cajjing* (新浪财经): "The Puffed-Up Rich in China" (虚胖的中国富豪), May 31, 2021.

200. Zhu and Zhao 1994; Xiao Jinbo 2016; Zhong Bai 2010; Tianjin Government 2020; State Anti-Fraud Center 2021; He Dan 2013.

201. Li Yinhe 2012.

202. 村骗乡、乡骗县、一直骗到国务院; Primer Wen Jiabao heard at the 2007 annual meeting of the PRC People's Political Consultative Conference, Ma Diming 2012.

203. Hugh-Jones 2016: 99–114.

204. Pan and Huang 2013; Pan Suiming 2020; W. Wang 2018; L. Brown 2020.

205. "2016 Investigative Report on Marriage and Love in China" (2016年中国婚恋调查报告), *Redian diaocha* (热点调查), Tencent, Aug. 10, 2016; "2016 Investigative Report on Chinese Attitude toward Infidelity" (2016中国人出轨态度调查报告), *Shishi shuo* (事实说), Tencent News, Aug. 15, 2016. Both have 50,000 to 70,000 effective respondents. Zuckerman 2020.

206. Qin Lian: "One in Four Is Not One's Own" (勤廉: 每4个有1个非亲生), *Wangyi*, April 2021.

207. Team Reporters 2011; Liu Moxian 2009: 77–95; Nong Yibang 2020; Sun Bo 2014.

208. Qin Hui February 28, 2014; Sheridan 2008; Yardley and Barboza 2008: A1; *Routers*: "China Milk Banned in Asia, Africa, Europe Union," Sept. 26, 2008; Wines 2010: A5; Wan Jinhui 2011; Sheng Xiang 2014: 3; Liu Wei 2014; *China Digital Times*: "Tag: Food Safety," Jan. 30, 2014; Waldmeir 2013; Liu Gang 2013; Cao Er 2020.

209. NHK: *China's Dangerous Food* (中国の危険な食品), Tokyo: Nov. 8, 2014; Nazeer 2015.

210. Zhang Haibo 2014; Zheng Baowei 2015; Luan Yushi 2018.

211. L. Chen et al. 2014; Yuan Guoli 2015: 3; Shepard 2018.

212. *China Statistical Yearbook*, 2015–2019. itslaw.com, searched June 8, 2020. Guzman and Ries 2020. The dollar bills could be for the benign use as sacrifice for deceased ancestors.

213. Wu Yujian 2020.

214. Author's field notes in China, 2000–2004, 2010; Fliegelmanfeb 2015: ED7; P. T. Black: "How to Be a Rent-a-Foreigner in China," *Adage Blog*, Nov. 30, 2010; Chodorow 2014; Tsering 2015.

215. Shengshi Guxiang 2021; Jiang Zheng 2012: A5.

216. Moore 2011; Wines Oct. 19, 2011: A8.

217. 碰瓷. Zhang Yue 2008; Liu Zhiwei 2012. Such a decay of social morality seems widespread enough for it be portrayed by a skit in the official CCTV's annual Spring Festival Gala Show, *Assist or Not?* (扶不扶), Beijing, Jan. 30, 2014. For more cases of such in the 2020s, see Zhuo Zi 2021.

218. Hai Mang 2022; Su Yian 2022.

219. Xin Lijian 2012.

220. News and Publication General Bureau 2009; Zhao Weifeng 2003. For an example of media control by decree, see CCP Central-Propaganda Deportment 2007.

221. For the campaign in one major province, see Guangdong Government 2015.

222. Editor June 3, 2020.

223. If "on-demand," self-publishers," and "micro-niche publications" are included, the US annul new book publication was fifteen times more, around 3 million. UNESCO and PulishersGlobal.com, accessed March 2021.

224. One YouTube-like company, Kuaishou (快手), had half of its 8,000 employees working on content censoring in 2019. Xu Hong 2021.

225. 自媒体. *Xinjing bao* (新京报): "The 9th Banishing List of Web-Broadcasters Published" (第九批网络主播警示名单公布), Beijing, Nov. 23, 2021.

226. Steinberg and Li 2019.

227. As reported by Mao himself. Mao Zedong (1927) 1991: 12–44.

228. Shen Yurong 1999; Li Fei 2012. Mao in fact personally ordered the demolishment of "old buildings and cities" in other ancient cities such as Nanjing, Kaifeng, Changsha, and Jinan. Chen Xiaonong 2005: 153.

229. For very incomplete lists of major destructions of the antiquity after 1949, see Guo Ke 2008: 52–54; 2020. For the total destruction of Confucius relics in 1966–1967, see Liu Yanxun 2010; Zhang Shunqing No. 2, 2015: 23–26 and No. 7, 2015: 37–41. For samples of destroyed famous graves, see Mao Jianjie 2012: 5; Song Dailun 2013. For burning of irreplaceable scrolls and books, see Hei Tu 2018.

230. Yan Jiulin 2021.

231. Xie Chensheng 2013; Anderlini 2011; Hammer 2010; Johnson 2014: A1.

232. 地方志; Zou Yilin 2015.

233. Yu Jian 2015; 文脉已断, 传统毁弃; Liu Dong 2016.

234. Guo Yiwen 2017; Cao Yu 2019.

235. Beijing Hotel 1959; Cheng Qingxiang 1987.

236. Caijing APP 2017; M. Wong 2015.

237. For environmental problems in Chinese history, see Elvin 2004. For environmental degradation in the PRC, see Economy 2010; Shapiro 2012.

238. Smith 2020-I, 2020-II; Shapiro 2001.

239. Li Rui 1999-II: 237–240; He Liangliang 2010; Gai Kaicheng 2008: chapter 3.

240. For pollution by China's steel industry, see AAM 2009, and more generally, Rosen 2007.

241. MEP 2003–2021. For CCP's troubled "war on pollution," see Economy 2019: 152–185.

242. Serious acid rain already covered 40 percent of the PRC in 1997. Chief Editor 1998.

243. Earth Village 2014; Liu Wei 2006: 2; MEP 2014.

244. *Dongfang ribao*, "Cadmium Rice All over Country" (鎘大米遍布全國), March 31, 2015: 2.

245. Su Yan: *Shangahi Sinking* (苏言: 上海沉没), Nanjing: Jiangsu renmin, 2010. CCTV: "Land Sinking" (地面沉降), Feb. 20, 2012; Wang Baocun 2020: 143–148.

246. Li Shangyong 2014: 96–100; *The Economist*, "Green Teeth," May 17, 2014: 44.

247. Sheng Keyi 2014: SR4; Beijing EPB 2015: 10–15; Zhuang Yixie 2018.

248. Feng and Du Ximeng 2015; Sheng Yun 2014; Ling Junhui 2020.

249. Cadmium (0.69 ug/l and 0.60 ug/l higher), lead (0.81 ug/dl and 0.44 ug/dl higher), mercury (5.73ug/l and 4.11 ug/l higher). D. Yin 2013; McKelvey 2007, 2018: 813–825.

250. Xiao Shibai 2015; Zhen Jian 2019.

251. Li Changan 2004: 24–26; Sun Zhigao 2006: 83–87; Hornby 2014; Wang Xiangwei 2021. According to official media, Yellow River has resumed "year-round water flow" since 1999 due to "strict water regulation and massive water injection." Wang Hao 2022. Anecdata on PRC social media tend to show that the mighty river now often appears as long stretches of desert with a small stream and seasonal floods.

252. Mu Hai 2021.

253. Withnall 2015; Wilson and Smith 2015: 16–22.

254. China-ASEAN Environmental Cooperation Centre and WWF 2014: 4.

255. WWF. "Environmental Problems in China," wwf.panda.org, accessed Nov. 6. 2014.

256. Simpson 2012; Rweyemamu 2013; Levin 2013: A1; Fiskesjö 2014.

257. Levin 2014: A14; EIA (Environmental Investigation Agency) 2014.

258. P. Xu 2013: 2067; PRC standard for PM2.5 is 100 v. WHO's of 25 or less. Over 250 other "less important cities" were not monitored but also heavily polluted. MEP 2015.

259. Coonan 2013. AFP: "China Pollution Levels Hit 20 times Safe Limit," Oct. 10, 2014.

260. E. Wong, April 22, 2015: A6.

261. WHO 2014. Intriguingly, after the official "updates" in 2016 and 2018, the global ranking data disappeared. Searched March 2015, May 2019, and June 2021.

262. Chen An 2012. For the impact of heavy smog on civil aviation, see Mi Ge 2014: 1.

263. Yu Minhong 2014. For time-series data of air quality in five PRC cities, compiled by the US Embassy to China since 2008, see stateair.net/web/historical/1/1.html, accessed June 8, 2020.

264. L. Han et al. 2015.

265. *The Chosunilbo*: "China to Share Pollution Data with Korea," Seoul, Feb. 27, 2004. *Mainichi*: "Air Pollution PM2.5 Levels Rise across Japan, 10 Prefectures Issue Warnings," Tokyo, Feb. 27, 2014. Central News Agency: "Pollution Control Not Part of Cross-Strait Meteorological Pact," Taipei, Feb. 28, 2014; J. Lin 2014: 5–6.

266. Zhu Chen 2013: 1959. In the thirty-one large cities, a quarter-million "extra" deaths (or 0.1% of the population) occur every year due to air pollution. Greenpeace and Peking University 2015. Lung cancer cases grew 4.5 percent every year in China (43% over one decade in Beijing). Li Bin 2015.

267. Rohde and Muller 2015; Yuan Duanduan 2014; Weir 2012: 32.

268. Xinhua: "Pollution costs US$ 200b each year," Beijing, June 5, 2006; Palit 2013. For a non-PRC academic discourse on China's serious pollution, see the eight articles in "Special Section on Dying for Development," *The China Quarterly* 214 (June) 2013: 243–393.

269. World Bank and PRC State EPA 2007. *The Economist*, "Big Burden," Sept. 20, 2014.

270. Watts 2010; Crane and Mao 2015: 3, 18–21; Luo and Pan 2015; Li Jing July 2, 2015.

271. Zeng and Eastin 2011.

272. Chai Jing: *Under the Dome* (柴静: 穹顶之下), documentary, Beijing, 2015.

273. Desilver 2013; Su and Zhang 2014.

274. Huang Haixin 2014; Feng Yongqiang 2018; Zhang Moling 2014.

275. 绿水青山就是金山银山. CCP Central March 24, 2015 and April 1, 2017; State Council 2019.

276. Wen Long 2020; Uuakii 2020; Hebei Government 2021.

277. Shuili Jiayuan 2021.

278. E. Wong March 7, 2015: A6.

279. Beijing City Government: *Letter to Residents of the Capital city* (告市民书), Nov. 3, 2014; Zou Chunxia 2014: A09. Author's interviews, Nov. 2014;

L. Kuo 2014; Li Zheng 2014: 9; Tatlow 2014; US Embassy 2014; Xie Wei 2015.

280. CCTV: *Xinwen Lianbo* (新闻联播), Nov. 24, 2021; Y. Huang 2020.

281. Ourworldindata.org/co2-emissions, accessed March 15, 2022.

282. C. Singer 1954–1984. More concisely, Derry and Williams 1993.

283. Nobelprize.org, last accessed October 2022. The scholar Zhou Youguang (周有光 1906–2017) commented that of the late-Qing, ROC, Mao, and Deng eras, the ROC had "the best" culture and education. t.qq.com/p/t/462969048420132, posted March 6, 2015.

284. Chen Xiaonong 2005: 367–368; Li Hui 2010; Chu Lan 1974; Liu Jingzhi 2009: 515–518; D. Hu 2005: 130–151.

285. 屠呦呦. *Sina xinwen*, Oct. 5, 2015; Rao Yi 2015. Two PRC writers have won the Nobel Prize in Literature: Gao Xingjian (高行健 2000), in exile since the 1980s, and Mo Yan (莫言 2012). The first PRC Nobel laureate is Liu Xiaobo (刘晓波 Peace Prize 2010) who was jailed as a political prisoner in 2009 and died in jail in 2017. The Dalai Lama won the Nobel Peace Prize (1989) as a political exile from Tibet since 1959. Nobelprize.org, accessed October 2022.

286. F. Wang, 2017: 125–126.

287. W. Liu 2017: 115–123. The three indexes, Sections Science Citation Index Expanded, Social Sciences Citation Index, and Arts and Humanities Citation Index, to be sure, may have some bias favoring English journals. Didegah and Gazni 2011: 303–310.

288. Ronen 2014: E5616–E5622; Wei Mi 2017.

289. Thibodeau 2012.

290. Osawa and Mozur 2014; Wertime 2014; Yip 2014; Stassopoulos 2015.

291. Morrison 2014.

292. Dong Jieling 2015. Data from PRC Automobile Industry Association, Aug. 2014.

293. Xu Xiaonian 2012; Abrami, Kirby, and McFarlan 2014: 107–111; P. Tian 2015.

294. Schmid and Wang 2016.

295. During 2004–2011, for example, Beijing reportedly banned as many as 6,000 movies (many were Chinese made). Li Chengpeng 2013: 24.

296. Y. Zhao 2014: 121–125.

297. Editorial, "Diversionary Tactics," *Nature* 436, 152 (July 14) 2005.

298. Yang Duogui 2008–2013; Li Jinlei 2013; J. Chin 2013. To promote its documentaries, the CCP simply created fictitious international film festivals and awards. Schoenmakers 2022.

299. Hannas, Mulvenon, and Puglisi 2013: 3.

300. Reuters, "Survey Details Data Theft Concerns for U.S. Firms in China," Mar. 30, 2013.

301. Breznitz and Murphree 2011.

302. Feigenbaum 2003; Fitzgerald 2013. Author's interviews with US experts studying China's ventures regarding key military technologies such as hypersonic and hybrid missiles, jet engines, stealthy planes, submarines, and aircraft carriers, 2013–2021.

303. *The Economist*, "Soaring Ambition," May 12, 2012: 89.

304. Wan and Nakashima 2014; Giglio 2019. NBC: "American Universities Are a Soft Target for China's Spies," Feb. 2, 2020; Wray (FBI) 2020; Abdelhady 2019; White House May 20, 2020.

305. Han Han 2009; Hu Xingdou 2008.

306. Wei Chunzhao 2008; M. Turnage 2013; Sauer 2013; Levin 2013.

307. GIPC 2016; OECD and EUIPO 2019; Plagiarius 2020.

308. Harney 2008; Powell 2007; Rapoza 2012; Abbey 2018; OECD June 2019.

Epilogue

1. For more about these Chinese and imported ideologies, see F. Wang 2017.

2. The CCP repeated in the 2020s that the unchallenged CCP party-state is Beijing's first and foremost "bottom line" in the US–China relationship. Wang Yi 2021.

3. Kelly 2021: 211.

4. For the official fusing of the "rejuvenation" of the Chinese world order with the course of world communism, see Xi Jinping July 1, 2021. For the wrapping of Beijing's ambition with liberal internationalist phraseology, see Da Wei 2021: 99–109; Xi Jinping Jan. 17 and Oct. 16, 2022.

Works and Sources Cited

AAM. *An Assessment of Environmental Regulation of the Steel Industry in China*. Washington, DC: Alliance for American Manufacturing, 2009.

Abbey, Matthew. "Counterfeiters Will Win the Trade War," *Foreign Policy*, Aug. 10, 2018.

Abdelhady, Hdeel. "Tech War: The United States' Whole-of-Government Approach to China Is a Force Multiplier," *Mass Piont*, May 7, 2019.

Abrami, Regina, William Kirby, and F. Warren McFarlan. "Why China Can't Innovate," *Harvard Business Review* 92–93 (Mar. 2014): 107–111.

Acemoglu, Daron et al. "Democracy Does Cause Growth," *Journal of Political Economy* 127(1), 2019.

Acemoglu, Daron et al. "Political Pressure and the Direction of Research: Evidence from China's Academia," paper of "SI 2021 Science of Science Funding," July 22, 2021.

Acemoglu, Daron, and James Robinson. *Why Nations Fail: The Origins of Power, Prosperity, and Poverty*. New York: Crown, 2012.

Adam Sitze. *The Impossible Machine: A Genealogy of South Africa's Truth and Reconciliation Commission*. Ann Arbor: University of Michigan Press, 2013.

Adam, David. "The Simulations Driving the World's Response to COVID-19," *Nature* 586, 2020.

Agrawal, Ravi. "Fauci: China's COVID-19 Situation a 'Disaster,'" *Foreign Policy*, May 4, 2022.

Ai Mi. "A Dark Page of China's *Laojiao*" (艾米: 中国劳教黑暗的一页), RFI, Nov. 24, 2013.

Akgüç, Mehtap et al. "Expropriation with Hukou Change: Evidence from a Quasi-Natural Experiment," IZA Paper 8689, Bonn, Germany: Institute for the Study of Labor, 2014.

Alexander, Peter, and Anita Chan. "Does China Have an Apartheid Pass System?" *Journal of Ethnic and Migration Studies* 30, 2004: 609–629.

Allison, Graham et al. *The Great Economic Rivalry: China vs the U.S.* Cambridge, MA: Belfer Center, Harvard University, Mar. 2022.

Amartya Sen, "Why India Trails China?" *The New York Times*, June 19, 2013: A27.

Amnesty International. *Death Sentences and Executions 2019*. New York, 2020. www.amnesty.org/en/documents/act50/1847/2020/en

An Bang. "Population Pressure Suppresses China's Economic Reorientation and Elevation" (安邦: 人口压力施压中国经济转型升级), *Caijing xinwen* (财经新闻), Beijing Nov. 24, 2014.

An Nan et al. *American Dream*—documentary on illegal emigration to US by the post-90 generation (安南等: 美国梦-90后美国偷渡客纪录片), YouTube, May 14, 2013. youtube.com/watch?v=UJh0Nq2ovxY

Anderlini, Jamil. "'Keqiang Index'" *Financial times blog*, Oct. 21, 2014. ft.com/content/25bf14dc-0cec-35ef-872b-e29803fa88e5.

Anderlini, Jamil. "Dalai Lama Accuses China of 'Cultural Genocide,'" *Financial Times*, Nov. 7, 2011.

Ang, Yuen Yuen. *How China Escaped the Poverty Trap*. Ithaca, NY: Cornell University Press, 2016.

Ang, Yuen Yuen. *China's Gilded Age*. New York: Cambridge University Press, 2020.

Anhui Provincial Government. "Notice on Implementing the Selection of 2012 Personnel to Receive the State Council and Provincial Government Special Allowances" (安徽省政府: 关于开展2012年享受国务院和省政府特殊津贴人员选拔工作的通知), Hefei, Anhui, Apr, 2012.

Aristotle. *Politics*. New York: Dutton, 1912.

Arnold, Wayne. "China Hits Panic Button: Beijing's Latest Rate Cut May Not Be Enough to Revive Growth in the Debt-Laden Economy," *Barron's*, May 11, 2015.

Arora, Neha, and Sanjeev Miglani. "U.S. Warns of Threat Posed by China, Signs Military Pact with India," Reuters, Oct. 27, 2020.

Ba Jin. *Random Thoughts* (巴金: 随想录). Beijing: Renmin Wenxue, 2000: 322–328.

Ba Jiuling. "Chinese P2P Died at Age 13" (巴九灵: 中国P2P卒, 享年13岁), *Sina caijing*, Oct. 14, 2019.

Bai Jianjun. "Causes, Acts and Punishment of Crime Based on Crime Data in China" (白建军: 从中国犯罪率数据看罪因,罪行与刑罚的关系), *Chinese Social Sciences*, No. 2, 2010: 144–159.

Bai Jianjun. "Chinese Crime Rate Figures" (白建军: 中国犯罪率数据), *Chinese Social Sciences*, Beijing, No. 2, 2010.

Bai Qingyuan. "[Test Prep Centers] Finally Banned" (白清源: [辅导中心]终于禁了), *Caijing* (财经), June 17, 2021.

Bai Xiaosheng. "300 Billion Evaporated" (百晓生: 3000亿灰飞烟灭), *Mingjin wang* (鸣金网), June 25, 2021.

Bai, Chong-En. "Special Deals with Chinese Characteristics," Working Paper, Cambridge, MA: NBER, May 2019.

Bajohr, Frank. *Parvenus and Profiteers: Corruption during the Nazi Era*. Frankford: Fischer, 2001.

Baldacci, Emanuele et al. "Public Expenditures on Social Programs and Household Consumption in China," *IMF Working Paper*, No. 10–69, Washington, DC: IMF, 2010.

Balding, Christopher. "How Badly Flawed Is Chinese Economic Data? The Opening Bid is $1 Trillion," Rochester: *SSRN Working Paper*, Aug. 14, 2013.

Bao Gangsheng. "Slide of Morality Is Absolutely Not Caused by Reform and Open" (包刚升: 道德滑坡绝不是改革开放造成的), *Sina caijing toutiao* (新浪财经头条), Beijing, Jan. 25, 2022.

Barbash, Fred. "Major Publisher Retracts 43 Scientific Papers amid Wider Fake Peer-Review Scandal," *The Washington Post*, Mar. 27, 2015.

Barboza, David. "Billions in Hidden Riches for Family of Chinese Leader: Many Relatives of Mr. Wen Became Wealthy during his Leadership." *The New York Times*, Oct. 26, 2012.

Barboza, David. "Stock Sell-Off Is Unabated in China," *The New York Times*, July 8, 2015.

Bardhan, Pranab. "The Chinese Governance System: Its Strengths and Weaknesses in a Comparative Development Perspective," *China Economic Review* 61, June 2020.

Barmé, Geremie. "Tyger! Tyger! A Fearful Symmetry," *The China Story*, Australian Center on China, Oct. 16, 2014.

Barnett, Steven, and Ray Brooks. "China: Does Government Health and Education Spending Boost Consumption?" *IMF Working Paper*, No. 10–16, Washington, DC: IMF, 2010.

Barry, Ellen, and Gina Kolata. "China's Lavish Funds Lured U.S. Scientists," *The New York Times*, Feb. 8, 2020.

Baschuk, Bryce. "China Loses Landmark WTO Dispute over Status as Non-Market Economy," *Bloomberg News*, June 17, 2020.

Basu, Zachary. "Biden Campaign Says China's Treatment of Uighur Muslims is 'Genocide,'" *Axios*, Aug. 25, 2020.

Beech, Hannah. "The Other Side of the Great Firewall," *Time*, June 22, 2015.

Bei Dao. *Answering* (北岛: 回答), *Shikan* (诗刊), Beijing, No. 3, 1979. Beijing. (English in *Aug Sleepwalker*, Cambridge, MA: New Directions, 1991.)

Bei Yi. "Grey Money HSR" (北烨: 灰金动车), *Tencent-Shijie* (腾讯-视界), Mar. 4, 2012.

Beijing EPB. *Beijing Environmental Statement 2014* (北京市环保局: 北京环境状况公报 2014), Apr. 16, 2015.

Beijing Hotel. *Famous Dishes in Beijing Hotel* (北京饭店名菜谱). Beijing: Qinggongye, 1959.

Bell, Anna Scott, ed. "Past as Prologue: Studying Party History for Xi's New Era," Washington, DC, Center For Advanced China Research, 2021.

Bell, Daniel. *The China Model: Political Meritocracy and the Limits of Democracy*. Princeton, NJ: Princeton University Press, 2015.

Benton, Gregor, and Lin Chun, eds. *Was Mao Really a Monster? The Academic Response to Jung Chang & Jon Halliday's Mao: The Unknown Story*. London: Routledge, 2010.

Benton, Gregor, ed. *Mao Zedong and the Chinese Revolution*, 4 vols. London: Routledge, 2007.

Bernstein, Thomas. *Up to the Mountains and Down to the Villages: The Transfer of Youth from Urban to Rural China*. New Haven, CT: Yale University Press, 1977.

Bert Hofman et al. "The Economic and Social Impacts of Population Ageing: China in a Global Perspective," *China: An International Journal*, Singapore 19.

Bian, Yanjie. *Work and Inequality in Urban China*. Albany, NY: SUNY Press, 1994.

Biancheng Suixiang. "Who Are the People Sentenced under 'Crimes of Rebellion'?" (编程随想: 被判"谋反罪"的都是哪些人), program-think.blogspot.com/2014/11/political-offences-in-china.html, Nov. 26, 2014.

Bird, Mike, and Lucy Craymer. "China Says Growth Is Fine. Private Data Show a Sharper Slowdown," *Wall Street Journal*, Sept. 8, 2019.

Blanchette, Jude. *China's New Red Guards: The Return of Radicalism and the Rebirth of Mao Zedong*. New York: Oxford University Press, 2019.

Blimpoa, Moussa et al. "Public Investment in Rural Infrastructure: Some Political Economy Considerations," *Journal of African Economies* 22(suppl 2), 2013: ii57–ii83.

Blumenthal, David, and William Hsiao. "Lessons from East China's Rapidly Evolving Health Care System," *The New England Journal of Medicine*, Apr. 2, 2015: 372–314.

Blumenthal, David, and William Hsiao. "Privatization and Its Discontents—The Evolving Chinese Health Care System," *The New England Journal of Medicine*, Sept. 2005: 353.

Bo Yang. *Bo Yang memoirs* (柏杨回忆录), Shengyang: Chunfeng wenyi, 2002.

Bonham, Carl, and Calla Wiemer. "Chinese Saving Dynamics: The Impact of GDP Growth and the Dependent Share," Working Paper, No. 2010–11R, Manoa, HI: UHERO, 2012.

Bonnin, Michel. *The Lost Generation: The Rustification of China's Educated Youth (1968–1980)*. Translated by Krystyna Horko. Hong Kong: Chinese University Press (2004) 2013.

Bowie, Julia. *COVID-19 and Chinese Communist Party Resilience*, CACR, Jan. 25, 2021.

Bradsher, Keith. "China's Economy Is Slowing, a Worrying Sign for the World," *The New York Times*, Jan. 17, 2022.

Bradsher, Keith. "Shenzhen Imposes a Lockdown and Shanghai Restricts Nonessential Travel as China's New Cases Jump," *The New York Times*, Mar. 21, 2022.

Bradsher, Keith. "Speedy Trains Transform China," *The New York Times*, Sept. 24, 2013.

Brady, Anne-Marie. threadreaderapp.com/thread/1285127701091606529.html, July 20, 2020.

Brandt, Jessica, and Bret Schafer. "How China's 'Wolf Warrior' Diplomats Use and Abuse Twitter," Brookings Institution, Oct. 28, 2020.

Branigan, Tania. "China Reforms *Hukou* System to Improve Migrant Workers' Rights," *The Guardian*, July 31, 2014.

Braun, Otto. *A Comintern Agent in China 1932–1939*. Stanford, CA: Stanford University Press, 1982;

Bray, Freddie et al. "Global Cancer Statistics 2018," *CA: Cancer Journal for Clinicians*, American Cancer Society, 68, 2018: 394–424.

Breznitz, Dan, and Michael Murphree. *Run of the Red Queen: Government, Innovation, Globalization, and Economic Growth in China*. New Haven, CT: Yale University Press, 2011.

Broadhurst, Roderic, and Peng Wang. "After the Bo Xilai Trial: Does Corruption Threaten China's Future?" *Survival* 56(3), 2014: 157–178.

Brody, Jane. "When a Partner Cheats," *The New York Times*, Jan. 22, 2018.

Brown, Lachlan. "Infidelity Statistics," *Hack Spirit*, June 16, 2020.

Browne, Andrew. "The Great Chinese Exodus," *Wall Street Journal*, Aug. 15, 2014.

Brusentsev, Vera, and Wayne Vroman. *Disasters in the United States: Frequency, Costs, and Compensation*. Kalamazoo, MI: Upjohn Institute, 2016.

Brussevich, Mariya et al. *China's Rebalancing and Gender Inequality*, Washington, DC, IMF Working Paper WP21–138, May 2021.

Buckley, Chris. "'Big Cannon' Blasted Xi. Now He's Been Sentenced to 18 Years," *The New York Times*, Sept. 23, 2020.

Buckley, Chris. "China Takes Aim at Western Ideas," *The New York Times*, Aug. 20, 2013.

Buckley, Chris. "Chinese Nobel Winner Appealing Subversion Conviction," *The New York Times*, Nov. 20, 2013.

Buckley, Chris. "Chinese Police Recommend Trial for Rights Advocate," *The New York Times*, Dec. 7, 2013.

Buckley, Chris, and Andrew Jacobs. "Maoists in China, Given New Life, Attack Dissent," *The New York Times*, Jan. 5, 2015.

Cai Decheng. "Expose Qian Xuesen Who Suppressed 'Science Herald' Four Times" (蔡德诚: 揭秘钱学森四次打压<科技导报>). blog.sciencenet.cn

Cai Dingjian. "Why China Has Not Become a Developed Country Like Japan" (蔡定剑: 中国为什么没有像日本一样成为发达国家), *Guangming wang* (光明网), Beijing, Mar. 2, 2007.

Cai Fang. "Seize the Window of Opportunity for Breaking the Duality Structure" (蔡昉: 抓住破除二元结构的窗口期), *Aisixiang* (爱思想), Beijing, Jan. 17, 2022.

Cai Jun. "Deadliest Human Technology Error–Caused Disaster in the World" (蔡骏: 世界史上人为技术错误造成的灾害TOP1), *Zhihu* (知乎), Aug. 28, 2018.

Cai Li. "Need Third Cultural Revolution" (蔡历: 需要第三次文化革命), *WeChat Blog*, May 14 2020.

Cai Pengcheng. "Ant Group under Siege" (蔡鹏程: 蚂蚁金服, 四面楚歌), *Sina* (新浪), Nov. 3, 2020.

Cai Rupeng. "Ten Years of SARS" (萨斯十年), *Zhongguo xinwen* (中国新闻), Mar. 1, 2013.

Cai Shenkun. "Who Should Tighten Belt" (蔡慎坤: 谁更应该过紧日子), *CXYInfo* (产学研信息港), Changsha, Jan. 3, 2022.

Cai Xia. "Party Celebration of Fascist Aesthetics" (蔡霞: 法西斯美学党庆), *RFA*, July 9, 2021.

Cai Xia. "How Helpless and Embarrassing: My Experience of Birth Planning" (蔡霞: 几多无奈与不堪: 我的计划生育经历), *Minjian lishi* (民間歷史), Hong Kong, May 12, 2015.

Cai Xia. "The Party That Failed: An Insider Breaks with Beijing," *Foreign Affairs*, Jan. 2021.

Cai Xiao. *On the Chinese Way* (蔡晓: 中国道统论). Beijing: Zhongguo shehui kexue, 2021.

Caijing APP. "Big Data on the Eight Culinary Schools in China" (财经APP: 大数据看中国八大菜系), *Sina xinwen* (新浪新闻), Beijing, Nov. 11, 2017.

Cairang Duoji. "Food Supply in Beijing during the Great Famine, 1959–1962" (才让多吉: 1959–1962年大饥荒期间北京的食品供应), *Yanhuang chunqiu* (炎黄春秋), Beijing, No. 8, 2007.

Calhoun, George. "Beijing Is Intentionally Underreporting China's Covid Death Rate," *Forbes*, Jan. 2 and Jan. 5, 2022.

Callen, Tim, and Christian Thimann. "Empirical Determinants of Household Saving," IMF *Working Paper*, No. 97-181, Washington, DC, IMF, 1997.

Callick, Rowan. "Kafkaesque Philosophy Exacerbates China's Opaque Legal System," *The Australian*, Surry Hills, Australia, June 22, 2020.

Callick, Rowan. *The Party Forever*. New York: St. Martin's, 2013.

Campbell, Cameron, and James Z. Lee. "Kinship and the Long-Term Persistence of Inequality in Liaoning, China, 1749–2005." *Chinese Sociological Review* 44(1), 2011: 71–103.

Cao Er. "Fake Chinese Herbal Medicine Has Gone Crazy" (草儿: 中药造假, 已经疯狂), *Tencent News* (腾讯新闻), Apr. 10, 2020.

Cao Guoxing. "Authorities Require College Teachers 'Don't Talk about Seven Things'" (曹国星: 官方要求高校教师"七个不要讲"), *Radio France International in Chinese*, May 10, 2013.

Cao Hou. "Shocking, Massive Phantoms Suddenly Emerged in Shanghai" (曹侯: 震惊, 上海突现大规模灵魂出窍), *WeChat Blog* (微信公众号), Apr. 22, 2022.

Cao Jianjun. "Naked GDP Is Just Chicken Fart" (曹建军: 扒个精光的GDP, 就是鸡的屁), *ScienceNet.cn*, July 22, 2013.

Cao Jinqing. *China by the Yellow River: A Scholar's Observation and Reflection of Rural Society* (曹锦清: 黄河边的中国-一个学者对乡村社会的观察与思考). Shanghai: Wenyi, 2000.

Cao Meng. "Gender and Regional Variation of Infant Mortality in China" (曹萌: 中国婴儿死亡率性别比的地域差异), *Zhongguo weisheng tongji* (中国卫生统计), Beijing, No. 2, 2013.

Cao Yu. *History of Chili Pepper-Eating in China* (曹雨: 中国食辣史). Beijing: Lianhe, 2019.

Cao Yunwu. "Only Move North Could They Survive" (曹筠武: 只有北向才是生路), *Nanfang zhoumo* (南方周末), Guangzhou, Mar. 30, 2006.

Cao, Jiarui et al. "Clans and Calamity: How Social Capital Saved Lives during China's Great Famine," King Center on Global Development, Stanford University, May 2020.

Carbon, David. *How Inefficient Is China's Investment?* Singapore, DBS report, Nov. 12, 2012.

Carothers, Christopher. "Taking Authoritarian Anti-Corruption Reform Seriously," *Perspectives on Politics, First View*, July 15, 2020: 1–17.

Carrico, Kevin. "I Mastered Xi Jinping Thought, and I Have the Certificate to Prove It," *Foreign Policy*, Oct. 2018.

Carter, Elizabeth. "Streamed Trials and Televised Confessions," PhD Dissertation, UCLA, Los Angeles, California, 2021.

Caster, Michael. *People's Republic of Disappearance: Stories from China's forced disappeasrnce system* (失踪人民共和国: 来自中国强迫失踪体系的故事), Safeguard Derfenders, 2017.

CAS (Chinese Academy of Sciences). "Report of '80% Government Health Spending for Cadres' Was Inaccurate" ("政府投入医疗费80%为干部"报道失实), *Renmin wang* (人民网), Beijing, Aug. 28, 2013.

CCP Central and State Council. *On Further Deepening the Reform of the Collection and Management of Taxes* (关于进一步深化税收征管改革的意见), Beijing, Mar. 24, 2021.

CCP Central and State Council. "Plan of Reform of the Collection and Management of National and Local Taxes" (中共中央国务院: 国税地税征管体制改革方案), Beijing, July 20, 2018.

CCP Central and State Council. "Notice on Continuing Governmental Special Allowance for the Experts, Scholars and Professionals Who Made Outstanding Contributions" (中共中央 国务院关于对做出突出贡献的专家、学者、技术人员继续实行政府特殊津贴制度的通知), Beijing, Decree No. 2001-10, 2001.

CCP Central and State Council. *Opinion on Strengthening New Type of Think Tanks with Chinese Characters* (中共中央办公厅,国务院办公厅: 关于加强中国特色新型智库建设的意见), *Renmin ribao* (人民日报), Jan. 21, 2015.

CCP Central-Politburo. "Certain Rules for Strengthening and Protecting the Centralized Leadership of the Party Central" (关于加强和维护党中央集中统一领导的若干规定), Oct. 30, 2017.

CCP Central-Academy of Party History and Documents. *Total Records of Publication* (中共中央党史和文献研究院成果总库), ebook.dswxyjy.org.cn/list/64.

CCP Central-Department of Propaganda. "First Group of Great Spirits of the CCP Spiritual Lineage" (中国共产党人精神谱系第一批伟大精神), Beijing, Sept. 29, 2021.

CCP Central-Department of Propaganda. "Logo for the 100th Birthday Celebration of the CCP" (中国共产党成立100周年庆祝活动标识), Xinhua, Beijing, Mar. 24, 2021.

CCP Central-Department of Propaganda. *The Historical Mission and Value of the CCP* (中宣部: 中国共产党的历史使命与行动价值), Beijing, Aug. 26, 2021.

CCP Central-Department of Propaganda. *Short History of the PRC, Short History of Reform and Open,* and *Short History of Socialist Development* (中华人民共和国简史, 改革开放简史, 社会主义发展简史), Beijing: Renmin, Sept. 2021.

CCP Central Department of Propaganda. "Banned Words in News Reporting" (新闻报道中的禁用词<第一批>), *Xinwen yueping dongtai* (新闻阅评动态), Beijing: Xinhua, Internal publication, No. 315, circa 2007.

CCP Central-Document Bureau, ed. *Important Documents since the 18th Party Congress* (中央文献研究室: 十八大以来重要文献选编). Beijing: Zhongyang Wenxian, 2014.

CCP Central-Document Bureau, ed. *Selected Important Documents since the Creation of the State* (中共中央文献研究室: 建国以来重要文献选编). Beijing: Zhongyang Wenxian 19, 1998.

CCP Central-Organization Department. *Internal Statistical Report of the CCP* (中国共产党党内统计公报), Beijing: Xinhua, June 30, 2021.

CCP Central-Organization Department. "Notice on Enhancing Ideals, Belief, and Ethics in Educating and Training Cadres" (中共中央组织部, 关于在干部教育培训中加强理想信念和道德品行教育的通知), Beijing, July 20, 2014.

CCP Central-Party History Bureau. *Short History of CCP's Secrets Keeping Work* (中共保密工作简史). Beijing: Jincheng, 1994.

CCP Central. "On Enhancing the Party's Political Construction" (中共中央关于加强党的政治建设的意见), Beijing, Jan. 31, 2019.

CCP Central. "On Comprehensively Enhancing Youth Pioneer Work in the New Era" (中共中央: 关于全面加强新时代少先队工作的意见), Beijing, Feb. 4, 2021.

CCP Central. "Plans on Deepening the Reform of the Party and State Institutions" (中共中央: 深化党和国家机构改革方案), Beijing, Mar. 2018.

CCP Central. "Rules on Some Detailed Polices in Rural Socialism Education Campaign" (关于农村社会主义教育运动中的一些具体政策的规定), Beijing, Sept. 18, 1964.

CCP Central. "Xi Jinping Chaired Meeting of CCP Central Politburo Standing Committee, Analyzing the Covid-Control Situation" (习近平主持中共中央政治局常务委员会会议，分析当前新冠肺炎疫情防控形势)," Beijing, Xinhua, May 5, 2022.

CCP Central. "CCP Central Decision on Some Major Issues of Comprehensively Advancing the Governing of the Country According to Law" (中共中央关于全面推进依法治国若干重大问题的决定), Oct. 23, 2014.

CCP Central. *CCP Central Resolution on the Major Achievements and Historical Experience of the Party's 100 Years of Endeavors*, Beijing: Xinhua English, Nov. 11, 2021.

CCP Central. *CCP's Position on Current Affairs* (中国共产党对于时局的主张), in *Selected CCP Central documents* (中共中央文件选集), Beijing: Renmin 1 (1922) 1989.

CCP Central. "Certain Rules on Political Life Inside the Party" (关于党内政治生活的若干准则), 5th Plenum of the 11th Committee, Beijing, Mar. 4, 1980.

CCP Central. *Communique of the 6th Plenum of the 19th Party Congress* (中国共产党第十九届中央委员会第六次全体会议公报), Beijing, Nov. 11, 2021.

CCP Central. *Communiqué of the Fifth Plenum of the 18th CCP Central Committee* (中国共产党第十八届中央委员会第五次全体会议公报), Beijing, Oct. 29, 2015.

CCP Central. *Instruction to All Provinces to Immediately Set Up Agencies for Education through Labor* (中共中央：关于各省市立即筹办劳动教养机构的指示), Beijing, Jan. 10, 1956.

CCP Central. *Resolution on Certain Key Issues about Adhering and Perfecting Socialist System with Chinese Characteristics to Promote Modernization of the Structure and Ability of State Governance* (关于坚持和完善中国特色社会主义制度推进国家治理体系和治理能力现代化若干重大问题的决定), Beijing, Oct. 2019.

CCP Central. *Rules on Ensuring CCP Members' Rights* (中共中央：中国共产党党员权利保障条例), Jan. 5, 2021.

CCP Central. *Working Rules of CCP Discipline Inspection Committees* (中国共产党纪律检查委员会工作条例), Beijing, Dec. 24, 2021.

CCP Central. *Decision on Building Xiongan New District in Hebei* (中央决定设立河北雄安新区). Apr. 1, 2017.

CCP Central. *Views on Accelerating Eco-Civilization* (关于加快推进生态文明建设的意见), Beijing, CCP Politburo, Mar. 24, 2015.

CCP Central. *Working Regulations on Promoting and Appointing Leading Party and Government Officials* (中共中央：党政领导干部选拔任用工作条例), Beijing, Jan. 15, 2014.

CCP Central. *CCP Constitution* (中国共产党章程), 1922–2017.

CCTV. *The Challenge of China's Anti-terrorism in Xinjiang* (中国新疆反恐挑战), Documentary, Apr. 2021. youtube.com/watch?v=WlDWYg91ANI

CDIC (Central Discipline Inspection Commission). "Press Conference on the Celebrations of the Centennial of the CCP," Beijing, June 28, 2021.

CDIC (Central Discipline Inspection Commission) and CCTV. *Always on the Road* (中央纪委与中央广播电视总台: 永远在路上), eight-episode documentary, 2016; *State Monitoring* (国家监察) five-episode documentary, 2020; *Rectifying Trend and Anti-corruption Right with You* (正风反腐就在身边), four-episode documentary, 2021; *Zero Tolerance* (零容忍), five-episode documentary, Beijing, 2022.

CDIC (Central Discipline Inspection Commission). "'Four Obeys' Principle Must Be Enforced Unconditionally" ("四个服从"的原则, 必须无条件地执行), Beijing, June 30, 2020.

CDIC (Central Discipline Inspection Commission). "No Region or Agency Is Problem Free" (没有没问题的地区或部门), Beijing, Apr. 10, 2016.

CDIC. *Report on Investigation in Shanghai* (关于上海调查工作报告), Beijing, No. 4, 2006.

Cevik, Serhan, and Carolina Correa-Caro. *Growing (Un)equal: Fiscal Policy and Income Inequality in China and BRIC+.* Washington, DC: IMF Working Papers, 2015.

Chambers, David. "The Past and Present State of Chinese Intelligence Historiography," *Studies in Intelligence* 56(3), Sept. 2012: 31–46.

Chan, Alina, and Matt Ridley. *Viral: The Search for the Origin of COVID-19.* New York: HarperCollins, Nov. 2021.

Chan, Hon, and Jie Gao. "Death versus GDP! Decoding the Fatality Indicators on Work Safety Regulation in Post-Deng China," *The China Quarterly* 210 (June 2012): 355–377.

Chan, Kam Wing. *Cities with Invisible Walls.* New York: Oxford University Press, 1994.

Chan, Melissa, "China Is Regularly Called 'Authoritarian.' That Doesn't Feel Like Enough," *The Washington Post*, Jan. 31, 2022.

Chancellor, Edward, "China: The Graveyard for Investment White Elephants," *Financial Times*, Aug. 4, 2013.

Chang An Jian (CCP Central WeChat Blogger on law and politics). "Debate Water-Hydrogen Cars" (长安剑: 争议水氢车), Beijing, May 26, 2019, reposted Feb. 15, 2021.

Chang An Jian. "Over 800 Million—Fan Binbin Fined Heavily for Tax Evasion" (长安剑: "超8亿! 范冰冰逃税被重罚"), ent.sina.com.cn/s/m/2018-10-03/doc-ihkvrhps1746080.shtml, Oct. 3, 2018.

Chang Hao. *Sense of Dark Evil and Tradition of Democracy* (張灝: 幽暗意識與民主傳統), Taipei: Lianjing, 1989.

Chang Xiaobin. "Solidify the Defense Line of Our Country's Big Data Management" (常小兵: 筑牢我国大数据管理的安全防线), *Qiushi* (求是), Beijing, Dec. 15, 2014.

Chang Yan. *Story of the Translation-editing Bureau: True Record of Yi Junqing's nth Mistress* (常艳: 编译局的故事: 衣俊卿小n 实录), web book, Beijing, 2012. chinadigitaltimes.net/chinese/268978.html

Chang, Jung, and Jon Halliday. *Mao: The Unknown Story*. New York: Anchor, 2006.

Changsha City. "Rules on Regularize Bonus for Civil Servants in the Whole City" (全市规范公务员绩效奖金实施办法), Hunan, Jan. 15, 2022.

Chao Changqing. "Yuan Zhiming or Cai Ling, Who Should Go to Hell?" (曹長青: 遠志明柴玲, 誰該下地獄), caochangqing.com, Apr. 20, 2015.

Chaoyang Government. *Finalists of Civil Servants Hiring*, batches I and II (朝阳区2022年考试录用公务员拟录用人员公示, 第一批 and 第二批), Beijing, Apr. 8 and 12, 2022.

Chatzky, Andrew, and James McBride. *China's Massive Belt and Road Initiative*, CFR Backgrounder, New York: CFR, Jan. 28, 2020.

Chawla, Dalmeet. "A Single 'Paper Mill' Appears to Have Churned Out 400 papers," *Science*, Feb. 27, 2020.

Chen An. "Beijing Already a Gas Chamber?" (陈安: 北京已成为毒气城?) *Kexue wang*, Jan. 22, 2012.

Chen Bingan. *Great Escape to Hong Kong* (陈秉安: 大逃港). Hong Kong: Zhonghe, 2011.

Chen Binqi. *After Graduation: Experience of a "Reactionary Student" in the 1960s* (陈秉祺: 毕业之后: 上世纪六十年代一个"反动学生"的经历). Hong Kong: Jiujiang wenhua, 2013.

Chen Dameng, and Liu Shi. *Frame-up: Re-investigating Gao Gang Case* (陳大蒙, 劉史: 落井下石-重查高崗案). Hong Kong: Mingjing, 2010.

Chen Fang et al. "New Four Great Inventions: Mark China and Inspire the World" (陈芳等: 新四大发明: 标注中国, 启示世界), *Xinhua*, Beijing, Aug. 11, 2017.

Chen Fang. "Why Doubts Exist about the 'Losses' of Highways" (陈方: 高速公路存在"亏损"为何被质疑), *Guangming ribao* (光明日报), Beijing, Dec. 24, 2014.

Chen Feng. "China's Run-Away Officials over Ten Thousand" (陈锋: 中国外逃官员等1万多人), *Huaxia shibao* (华夏时报), Beijing, Nov. 7, 2014.

Chen Guang. "Who's Attending the Top Schools in China?" (陈光: 谁在上中国顶尖名校) *Tencent* (腾讯), June 2, 2021.

Chen Guili, and Chun Tao. "Story of Xiaogang Village" (陈桂棣, 春桃: 小岗村的故事), Beijing, 2008.

Chen Hongyu. "Causes and Implications of the Chinese Mainland Emigration in Recent 20 Years" (陳鴻瑜: 近20年中國大陸移民潮的原因及影響), Taipei, 華僑協會總會, 2012.

Chen Huijuan. "12,576 Law-Enforcement Officers Surrendered to the Discipline and Monitory Commissions" (陈慧娟: 12576名干警主动向纪委监委投案), *Guangming ribao* (光明日报), Beijing, June 10, 2021.

Chen Jian. "China's State Payroll Already More than 80 Million" (陈剑: 中国财政供养人口已超8000万), *The Paper* (澎湃), Shanghai, Feb. 4, 2022.

Chen Jian. "State Grain Warehouse Empty Unnoticed for a Year" (陈健: 国有粮库空仓近一年无人发现), *Liaowang zhoukan* (瞭望周刊), Beijing, Aug. 1, 2020.

Chen Jin. "Mao Zedong and the Original Mission of Chinese Communists" (陈晋: 毛泽东与中国共产党人的初心使命), *CCP Party History and Archives*, Sept. 10, 2019.

Chen Pingyuan. *Small Words on Universities* (陈平原: 大学小言). Beijing: Sanlian, 2014.

Chen Po, "On the History Prior to Cultural Revolution" (陈坡: 文革前史刍议), *Aisixiang* (爱思想), Apr. 10, 2016.

Chen Pokong. *Unwelcome Chinese* (陳破空: 不受歡迎的中國人). Hong Kong: Kaifang, 2015.

Chen Qiao. "Let 'Vacuous-Employment Eaters' Have No Place to Hide" (陈乔: 让"吃空饷"者难以遁形), *Zhongguo jijian jiancha bao* (中国纪检监察报), Beijing, Sept. 13, 2019.

Chen Shuguang. "China Solution for the World" (陈曙光: 向世界贡献中国方案), *Guangming ribao* (光明日报), Oct. 10, 2018.

Chen Shuo et al. *After Escaping to Hong Kong* (陈烁等: 逃港之后), Shenzhen University research reported in *Shenzhen wanbao* (深圳晚报), Apr. 23, 2015.

Chen Tushou. *People of the Old Country Have Some Thoughts* (故国人民有所思). Beijing: Sanlian, 2013.

Chen Tushou. *Men Are Sick, Does Heaven Know? Reports on the Chinese Literary Circles after 1949* (陈徒手: 人有病, 天知否: 一九四九年后中国文坛纪实). Beijing: Renmin wenxue, 2000.

Chen Wanqing et al. "Cancer Statistics in China and United States, 2022," *Chinese Medical Journal* (中华医学杂志英文版), Beijing 135(5), Mar. 5, 2022: 584–590.

Chen Xiaonan. "Mao Zedong Inclined for Birth Control in the 50s, Changed Direction for the Urge of Surpassing the UK and Catching Up to the US" (陈晓楠: 50年代毛泽东已明确节制生育, 后因急于超英赶美转向), *Phoenix TV*, Hong Kong, Dec. 16, 2013.

Chen Xiaonong, ed. *Final Oral Memoirs of Chen Boda* (陳曉農: 陳伯達最後口述回憶). Hong Kong: Yangguang huangqiu, 2005.

Chen Xiaoshu, and Xu Kai. "Records of Corruption of Senior Officials" (陈晓舒, 徐凯: 高官贪腐录), *Caijing* (财经), Beijing, No. 22 (Oct. 25), 2010.

Chen Xiaoying. "Big Business to Fraud the Country" (陈小瑛: 诈骗国家的大买卖), *Huaxia shibao* (华夏时报), Beijing, July 5, 2013.

Chen Xingjia. *On the Curve of the Gorge River* (陈行甲: 在峡江的转弯处). Beijing: RMRB, 2021.

Chen Xueping. "Doubts, Reasons and Suggestions about the Pandemic in Shanghai" (陈雪频: 关于上海疫情的疑惑，原因和建议), *Wechat Blog* (微信公众号), Apr. 14, 2022.

Chen Yanbin. "Evaluate and Improve the Current Moral Situations in China" (陈延斌: 当前中国社会道德状况的评价与治理对策), *Zhongzhou Journal* (中州学刊), Zhengzhou, No. 5, 2013.

Chen Yanping. "The Failure of Health Care Reform Is Disastrous" (陈砚平: 医改的失败是劫难性的), *Sciencenet.cn blog*, Beijing, Jan. 31, 2016.

Chen Yingchao. "500 Privileged Families Monopolize China" (陈泱潮: 500个特权家庭垄断中国), *Boxun* (博讯), US, Apr. 20, 2008 & *Douban* (豆瓣), July 28, 2008.

Chen Yixin. "Brightening Project: The Long Eyes Protecting the People" (陈一新: "守护人民安宁的'千里眼'-'雪亮工程,'" Supreme People's Court, Beijing, June 21, 2018.

Chen Yixin. "First Year of Normalizing Sweeping the Dark and Elimination of the Bad" (陈一新: 扫黑除恶常态化第一年), speech at the Central Politics and Law Commission, Apr. 29, 2021.

Chen Yixin. "Xi Jinping Thought on Rule by Law Is the Latest Fruit of Sinification of Marxism" (陈一新: 习近平法治思想是马克思主义中国化最新成果), *Renmin ribao*, Dec. 30, 2020.

Chen Yuqiong, and Gao Jianaguo. "Time Characteristics of Major Climate Disaster Killing More than 10 Thousand in Chinese History" (陈玉琼, 高建国: 中国历史上死亡一万人以上的重大气候灾害的时间特征), *Daziran tansu* (大自然探索), Beijing, no. 10, 1984: 161–162.

Chen Yushu. "Stop the Decline of Housing Prices" (陈玉书: 房价别跌了), *Zhongguo xinwen* (中国新闻), Beijing, Sept. 13, 2021.

Chen Zhifeng. "China's Military Budget and 'Stability-Maintenance' Cost" (陈志芬: 中国军费和"维稳"开支), *BBC in Chinese*, Mar. 5, 2014.

Chen Zhiwen. "Who Actually Gives Tsinghua 317 Million" (陈志文: 清华的317亿经费到底是谁给的), *Kexue wang* (科学网), Beijing, Apr. 4, 2021.

Chen, Jiandong et al. "Chinese Gini Coefficient from 2005 to 2012, Based on 20 Grouped Income Data Sets of Urban and Rural Residents," *Journal of Applied Mathematics*, 2015.

Chen, Jie, and Bruce Dickson. *Allies of the State: China's Private Entrepreneurs and Democratic Change*. Cambridge, MA: Harvard University Press, 2010.

Chen, Jie. *A Middle Class without Democracy: Economic Growth and the Prospects for Democratization in China*. New York: Oxford University Press, 2014.

Chen, Keyu. "The Fallacy in Chinese 'Whataboutism,'" *The Geopolitics*, Nov. 14, 2019.

Chen, Liyan et al. "Alibaba Claims Title for Largest Global IPO Ever with Extra Share Sales," *Forbes*, Sept. 2014.

Chen, Stephen. "Science Journal Retracts 107 Research Papers by Chinese Authors," *South China Morning Post*, Apr. 23, 2017.

Chen, Wei et al, "A Forensic Examination of China's National Accounts," Brookings, Mar. 7, 2019.

Chen, Yu-Jie et al. "'Rule of Trust': The Power and Perils of China's Social Credit Megaproject," *Columbia Journal of Asian Law* 32, Fall 2018.

Chen, Yuan-tsung. *The Secret Listener: An Ingenue in Mao's Court*, New York, NY: Oxford U Press, 2022.

Cheng Mo. "Why the Record-High New Cases and Deaths in Some Countries with High Rates of Vaccination" (程墨: 为何一些疫苗高接种率国家新增病例和死亡创记录), *China Digital Times*, June 30, 2021.

Cheng Qingxiang. *Sichuan Dishes in Beijing Hotel* (程清祥: 北京饭店的四川菜), Beijing, 1987.

Cheng Tiejun. *Sun Dawu's Dream for Capital-Socialism* (程铁军: 孙大午的资本社会主义梦). New York: Gongmin she, Aug, 2021.

Cheng Zhiqiang. "The China Solution Promotes World Peace and Development" (程志强: 促进世界和平与发展的中国方案), *Renmin ribao* (人民日报), Apr. 2, 2020.

Cheng, Yangyang. "The Battlefield of Memory," *Los Angles Review of Books*, Dec. 15, 2020.

Cheung, Elizabeth. "Coronavirus: Testing in Pandemic's Early Stages Showed No Immunity among Hong Kong Residents," *South China Morning Post*, Hong Kong, June 10, 2020.

Chi Houze. "Question the 'Criticizing Lin' Speech by Marshal Liu Bocheng" (迟厚泽: 质疑刘伯承元帅"批林"谈话), *Wangshi* (往事), No. 14, 2006.

Chief Editor. *Internal Reference* (总编室: 内部参阅), *Renmin ribao* (人民日报), Beijing, Nos. 394 and 409, classified weekly for bureau chief and higher, Jan. 14, 1998 and Apr. 15, 1998.

Chin, Josh. "China's National Rejuvenation Now 65.3% Complete, Index Says," *Wall Street Journal*, Nov. 22, 2013.

China-ASEAN Environmental Cooperation Centre and WWF. *Ecological Footprint and Sustainable Consumption in China 2014*. Beijing, 2014.

Chinese Automobile Trade Corporation. *China's Imported Auto Market 2013* (中国进口汽车市场 2013). Beijing: CATC, 2013.

Chinese Enterprise Association, and Chinese Businessmen Association. *Trends, Problems, and Recommendations about the Development of Chinese Large Companies 2014* (中国企业联合会与中国企业家协会: 2014年中国大企业发展的趋势,问题和建议), Beijing, Sept. 2014.

Ching, Frank. "China's Problem with Fake Research Papers," *The Globe and Mail*, Aug. 11, 2017.

Chodorow, Gary. "Scientist Alleges Fraud in China's 'Thousand Talent' Foreign Expert Program," *Law and Border*, Oct. 26, 2014.

Chow, Gregory, and Dwight Perkins, eds. *Routledge Handbook of the Chinese Economy*. London: Routledge, 2014.

Chu Chaoxin. "Guidelines on the Price Tag of Buying and Selling Offices in China" (褚朝新: 中国官场买官卖官价格指南), *Gongshi wang* (共识网), Sept. 24, 2015.

Chu Lan et al. *Critique the Revisionist Reviews on Untitled Music* (初澜等: 批判关于无标题音乐的修正主义观点). Guangzhou: Guangdong Renmin, 1974.

Chui Lan. "Why Mao Zedong Enchanted the World?" (萃岚: 毛泽东缘何让世界为之倾倒), CCP News Net (中国共产党新闻网), Beijing, Dec. 9, 2013.

Chun Se. "Ten Thousand RMB 40 Years Ago" (春色: 40年前的万元户), *Wangyi* (网易), Dec. 23, 2020.

Chun, Rene. "Facial-Recognition Technologies Are Proliferating, from Airports to Bathrooms," *The Atlantic*, Apr. 2018.

Ci Jiwei. "The Moral Crisis in Post-Mao China: Prolegomenon to a Philosophical Analysis," *Diogenes*, 56(1), Feb. 2009: 19–25.

CIA. *The World Factbook* and "World Factbook" website, Washington, DC, 2013–2022.

CICA (Chinese Industrial and Commercial Association). *Report on the Development of Chinese Non-state Economy* (工商联: 中国民营经济发展报告), Beijing, 10 annual volumes, 2005–2013.

CIIC (China Internet information center 中国互联网络信息中心). *Statistical Report on Internet Development in China—2020* (2020中国互联网络发展状况统计报告), Apr. 2021.

CNSA (China Netcasting Services Association). "Ban the Promotion of Doom Culture and One Night Stand" (禁止宣传丧文化, 一夜情), *Beijing qingnianbao* (北京青年报), Jan. 10, 2019.

Cody, Edward. "In China's Quake Zone, Aftershocks of the Spirit: Hardy Optimism Likely to Mask Despair," *The Washington Post*, June 25, 2008: A1.

Cohen, Jerome, and Margaret Lewis. "Plenum Pledge Won't Make Scrapping China's Labour Camps Any Easier," *South China Morning Post*, Hong Kong, Nov. 19, 2013.

Cohen, Jon. "COVID-19 May Have Killed Nearly 3 Million in India, Far More than Official Counts Show," *Science*, Jan. 6, 2022.

Commentator. "Firmly Grab the Key of the Construction of Socialist Core Values" (紧紧抓住社会主义核心价值体系建设这个根本), *Qiushi* (求是), Beijing, Dec. 1, 2011.

Commentator. "To Construct the Supremacy of Law for Rule by Law" (评论员: 营造法律至上的法治环境), *Renmin ribao* (人民日报), Beijing, Feb. 27, 2013.

Commission of Health. *China Health Statistical Yearbook* (卫健委: 中国卫生健康统计年鉴), 2020.

Comptroller. *Department of Defense Financial Management Regulation. Volume 7a: Military Pay Policy. Active Duty and Reserve Pay*, Washington, DC, DOD, 2021.

Cong Yi. "My Worldviews Reconstruct When All Five in My family Had Covid" (从一: 当我们一家5口都感染了新冠 我的三观重组了), *WeChat Blog* (微信公众号), May 4, 2022.

Cook, Sarah. "Falun Gong's Secrets for Surviving in China," *Union of Catholic Asian News*, July 19, 2019.

Cook, Sarah. *The Battle for China's Spirit: Religious Revival, Repression, and Resistance under Xi Jinping*, Special Report, Freedom House, 2017.

Coonan, Clifford. "Beijing Is Left Fighting for Breath as Pollution Goes Off the Scale," *The Independent*, Jan. 29, 2013.

Cooper, Sam, and Andrew Russell. "Over $154M Tied to Detained Chinese-Canadian Oligarch Invested in GTA Real Estate," *Global News*, Feb. 28, 2022.

Corrigan, Jack et al. *The Long-Term Stay Rates of International STEM PhD Graduates*, Center for Security and Emerging Technology, Georgetown University, Apr. 2022.

Courtois, Stéphane et al. *The Black Book of Communism: Crimes, Terror, Repression*. Translated by Jonathan Murphy. Cambridge, MA: Harvard University Press (1997) 1999.

Crabbe, Matthew. *Myth-Busting China's Numbers: Understanding and Using China's Statistics*. Basingstoke, UK: Palgrave, 2014.

Crane, Keith, and Zhimin Mao. *Costs of Selected Policies to Address Air Pollution in China*. Santa Monica, CA: RAND, 2015.

Credit Suisse Research Institute. *Global Wealth Databook 2014*. Zurich, Switzerland, 2014.

Creek, Timothy. *A Critical Introduction to Mao*. New York: Cambridge University Press, 2010.

CRS (Congressional Research Service). "China's Status as a Nonmarket Economy," Washington, DC, Jan. 10, 2019.

Cui Jing et al. "Chinese Divorce Rate Grew Nearly 40% in the Past Five Years" (崔静 等: 中国离婚率近5年增长近40%), chinanews.com.cn/sh/2013/11-15/5509637.shtml, Nov. 15, 2013.

Cui Li. "China Has the Most Reservoir Dams" (崔丽: 中国水库大坝数量最多), *Zhongguo qingnianbao* (中国青年报), Beijing, Nov. 10, 2017.

Cui Lili. " 'High Housing Price Is Harmless,' a Preposterous Logic" (崔李李: "高房价无害," 荒谬的逻辑), *Huanqiu renwu* (环球人物), Beijing, No. 17, 2013.

Cui Weiping. "Fascist Esthetics" (崔卫平: 法西斯的美学), *Fenghuang wang* (凤凰网), Hong Kong, Aug. 11, 2015.

Cui Yongguan, and Wei Hui. " 'Blind Spots' of Government Credibility Need to be Cleared Up" (翟永冠&韦慧: 政府诚信"盲点"待消), *Liaowang* (瞭望), Beijing, July 15, 2013.

Culver, David. "'We Are Starving': Shanghai Residents Protest Largest Lockdown in the World," CNN, Apr. 11, 2022.

Curtis, Chadwick et al., "Demographic Patterns and Household Saving in China." *American Economic Journal: Macroeconomics* 7(2), 2015: 58–94.

CYL Central. *Notice on Broadly Organizing Youth Web Civilization Volunteers Army, Deeply Promoting Youth Web Civilization Volunteer Activities* (共青团中央: 关于广泛组建青年网络文明志愿者队伍、深入推进青年网络文明志愿行动的通知), #2015-5, Beijing, Feb. 16, 2015.

CYL Fujian Provincial Committee. Summary table on the information of youth web civilization volunteers (共青团福建省委: 青年网络文明志愿者信息汇总表), Fuzhou, Apr. 29, 2015.

Cyrill, Melissa. "China's Middle Class in 5 Simple Questions," *China Briefing*, Feb. 13, 2019.

Da Wei. "Direction of the Evolution of Current International Order and China's Choices" (达巍: 现行国际秩序演变的方向与中国的选择), *Guoji wenti yanjiu* (国际问题研究), Beijing, No. 1, 2021: 99–109.

Da Xueshi, "SOEs Were Only Half as Efficient as Non–SOEs in 2018" (大学仕: 2018 年国企经营效率是民企的一半), *Sohu News*, Beijing, Mar. 27, 2019.

Dai Jianye. "On Lying Flat" (戴建业: 闲扯'躺平'), *Aisixiang* (爱思想), June 4, 2021.

Dai Xiting, "How Many Chinese-Style Fake Divorces Are There? (戴熙婷: 中国式假离婚知多少?), *Xinjing bao* (新京报), Beijing, Apr. 17, 2015.

Dai Xiting. "Abolish 985 and 211?" (戴熙婷: 废除"985" "211"?), *Xinjing bao* (新京报), Nov. 14, 2014.

Dante Lam et al. *Changjin Lake* (长津湖Chosen Reservoir). Beijing: Aug First studios, Oct. 2021.

Dao Boman. "'Stuffed Tiger' and 'Hungry Tiger'" (道伯曼: "饱虎"与"饿虎"), *Renmin wang* (人民网), Beijing, Oct. 12, 2014.

Dao Ke. "China's Healthcare Funds Used Unfairly" (刀客: 中国医疗经费使用不公), *Xin kuai bao* (新快报), Guangzhou, June 9, 2006.

Das, Dilip. "Foreign Direct Investment in China," *Asian Business & Management* 6, 2007.

Dashan Shuofang. "'No More New Hospitals' inside of the Fifth Ring" (大山说房: 五环内"禁止新医院"), *Wangyi* (网易), Beijing, Sept. 13, 2021.

Data Blog, "Death Penalty Statistics, Country by Country," *The Guardian*, Dec. 13, 2013.

Daum, Jeremy. "China through a Glass, Darkly: What Foreign Media Misses in China's Social Credit," *China Law Translate*, December 12, 2017.

Davies, Ross. "High-Speed Rail: Should the World Be Following China's Example?" *Railway Technology*, Sept. 24, 2019.

Davis, Sarah. *The Uncounted: Politics of Data in Global Health*. New York: Cambridge University Press, 2020.

De La Boétieor, Étienne. *On Voluntary Servitude* (Discours de la servitude volontaire), singulier.eu (1574) 2022.

De Mesquita, Bueno, and Alastair Smith. *The Dictator's Handbook: Why Bad Behavior is Almost Always Good Politics*. New York: Public Affairs, 2011.

Demick, Barbara. "The Times, Bloomberg News, and the Richest Man in China," *The New Yorker*, May 5, 2015.

Deng Xiaomang. "The Bottom-Line of Chinese Morality" (邓晓芒: 中国道德的底线), *Huazhong kejidaxue xuebao* (华中科技大学学报), Wuhan, No. 1, 2014.

Deng Xiaoping. "Speeches in the South" (南方谈话) in Feb. 1992. *Selected Works of Deng Xiaoping* (邓小平文选) 2, Beijing: Renmin, 1993.

Deng Xiaoping. "Uphold Four Cardinal Principles" (坚持四项基本原则), *Selected Works of Deng Xiaoping* (邓小平文选) 2, Beijing: Renmin (1983) 1994.

Deng Xinhua. "Ma Huateng's Desire to Stay Alive" (邓新华: 马化腾的求生欲), *Sina caijing* (新浪财经), Beijing, Jan. 14, 2022.

Deng Xize. "Cannot Ignore 'Legal Corruption' When Improv[ing] Academic Environment in China" (邓曦泽: 中国改善学术环境不能回避"合法"腐败), *Lianhe zaobao* (联合早报), July 8, 2021.

Deng Yuanjie. "All Income Goes to the Central" (邓元杰: 一切收入都归中央), *Zhihu* (知乎), Beijing, June 7, 2021.

Deng Zhaowen. "Who Are the Real Vested-Interest Holders?" (邓聿文: 真正的既得利益者是谁?), *Aisixiang* (爱思想), Beijing, Dec. 23, 2011.

Deng, Chao, and Xie Yu. "China's Once-Hot Peer-to-Peer Lending Business is Withering," *Wall Street Journal*, Feb. 2, 2020.

Dent, Harry. "Greatest Real Estate Bubble in Modern History not Done Bursting," *Forbes*, Oct. 3, 2012.

Derry, T. K., and Trevor Williams. *A Short History of Technology*. New York: Dover, 1993.

Desilver, Chen Drew. "As China Coughs and Chokes, Public Concern about Air Pollution Rises," *The Pew Research Center*, Oct. 22, 2013.

Dianji jinri (点击今日). "'Rule the Country with Internal Reference' Becomes Chinese Character" ("内参治国"成中国特色), Beijing 1083, *Sohu* (搜狐), Jan. 23, 2013.

Didegah, Fereshteh, and Ali Gazni. "The Extent of Concentration in Journal Publishing," *Learned Publishing* 24(4), 2011: 303–310.

Dikötter, Frank. *The Tragedy of Liberation: A History of the Chinese Revolution 1945–1957*. New York: Bloomsbury Press, 2013.

Ding Dong. "We Should Resolve the Problems of the 211 Project" (丁东: 211工程中的问题该解决了) *Xinjing bao* (新京报), Beijing, June 29, 2009.

Ding Jiafa, "Security Firm Set 'Black Prison for Petitioner Interception' in Beijing" (丁家发: 保安公司在京建"截访黑监狱"), *Shichang xingbao* (市场星报), Hefei, Sept. 26, 2010.

Djilas, Milovan. *The New Class*. New York: Praeger, 1957.

DOJ-INS. *Annual Report—Asylees*, 1997–2013, Washington, DC, DOJ, 1999–2013.

Dominiczak, Peter. "Most Immigrants to the UK Now Come from China," *The Telegraphy*, Nov. 28, 2013.

Dong Fan. "Real Estate Is an Industry That Sun Never Sets" (董藩: 房地产是"日不落"行业), *Wangyi caijing* (网易财经), Tianjin, Sept. 11, 2014.

Dong Jian. "Rare Photos from the 1983 'Hard Strike' Surfaced" (洞见: 1983年"严打"的罕见照片曝光), *My China News*, Dec. 1, 2013.

Dong Jieling. "How Really Is Innovation in China?" (董洁林: 中国创新到底怎么样?), *Financial Times* (in Chinese), Jan. 6, 2015.

Dong Langxing, "41 Private Enterprises Nationalized" (董郎行: 41家民企收归国有), *Ten Cent Kuaibao* (腾讯快报), Dec. 30, 2019.

Doshi, Rush. "The Chinese Communist Party Has Always Been Nationalist," *Foreign Policy*, July 1, 2021.

Doshi, Rush. *The Long Game: China's Grand Strategy to Displace American Order.* New York: Oxford University Press, 2021.

Dreze, Jean, and Amartya Sen. *India: Economic Development and Social Opportunity.* Oxford, UK: Oxford University Press, 1995.

Du Bin. *Above the Ghosts' Heads: The Women of Masanjia Labor Camp* (杜斌: 小鬼头上的女人), documentary film, youtube.com/watch?v=sFEl7oophB0, Hong Kong, 2013.

Du Enhu. "Zhang Yimu Accepts the 7.48 Million Fine for Over-Quota Births" (杜恩湖: 张艺谋接受 748万超生罚款), *West China Metro News* (华夏都市报), Chengdu, Jan. 12, 2014.

Du Fang, and Wang Chunfu. "The Trail of Corruption of 'China's Youngest Academician'" (杜放 王存福: "中国最年轻院士"的腐败轨迹), *Xinhua Daily Telegraph*, Beijing, Oct. 15, 2014.

Du Gangjian. *Origin of Civilization and the Harmonious world* (杜钢建: 文明源头与大同世界). Beijing: Guangming, 2017.

Du Shi. "Why So Many Car Accidents in China?" (读史: 中国车祸为什么这么多), *Sohu xinwen* (搜狐新闻), Mar. 12, 2020.

Du Xing. "45 Codes for 'Family Background'" (杜兴: 45个"家庭出身"代码), *Kan lishi* (看历史), Beijing, No. 2, 2010.

Du Zhengyu. *Guide on Political Thought Education in Biology* (杜震宇: 生物科学思政教学指南). Shanghai: Huadong shida, 2020.

Duan Siyu, and Huang Siyu. "Liu He: A New State of Two-Circular Economy Is Forming in China" (段思宇, 黄思瑜: 中国双循环发展新格局正在形成), *Yicai* (一财), Shanghai, June 18, 2020.

Dubow, Ben et al. "Jabbed in the Back: Mapping Russian and Chinese Information Operations during COVID-19," Washington, DC: Center for European Policy Analysis, Dec. 2, 2021.

IFJ. *Research Report on China and Its Impact on Media 2021*, Brussels, Belgium: International Federation of Journalists, Feb. 8, 2022.

Duesterberg, Thomas. "The Slow Meltdown of the Chinese Economy: Beijing's Troubles Are an Opportunity for the U.S.," *Wall Street Journal*, Dec. 20, 2021.

Dugan, Lauren. "The Countries That Block Twitter, Facebook and YouTube," *Media Bistro*, Mar. 31, 2014.

Duihua Foundation. *Death Penalty Reform*, San Francisco, duihua.org/resources/death-penalty-reform/, Jan. 2021.

Duihua Foundation. "Deciding Death: How Chinese Judges Review Capital Punishment Cases," *Human Rights Journal*, New York, Nov. 18, 2014.

Earth Village. "Situation of Eco Damages in Our Country (我国生态环境破坏状况), earth365.com, Feb. 3, 2014.

Eban, Katherine. " 'This Shouldn't Happen': Inside the Virus-Hunting Nonprofit at the Center of the Lab-Leak Controversy," *Vanity Affairs*, Mar. 31, 2022.

Economy, Elizabeth. *The River Runs Black: The Environmental Challenge to China's Future*, 2nd edition. Ithaca, NY: Cornell University Press, 2010.

Editor. "Buddha-like Slackness: New Trend of Mentality in Chinese Society" (佛系-中国社会心态新动向), *Tansuo yu zhengming* (探索与争鸣), Shanghai, Feb. 9, 2018.

Editor. "Heavier Blow, Tighter Control of Quality" (再出重拳, 严控出版质量), *Zhongzhou qikan* (中州期刊), Zhengzhou, Henan, June 3, 2020.

Editorial, "Keep Velocity and Pace" (力度不减节奏不变), *Zhongguo jijian jiancha bao* (中国纪检监察报), Beijing, Apr. 11, 2016.

Editorial. "What's the Relationship between Eight Points of Clarification and Fourteen Points of Perseverance?" (八个明确"和"十四个坚持"是什么关系), CCTV, Beijing, Oct. 28, 2017.

Editorial. "Mental Health in China: What Will Be Achieved by 2020?" *The Lancet* 385, No. 9987 (June 27) 2015.

Editorial. "Where Is the Route to Reforming Colleges after Goodbye to 985?" (告别"985"之后, 高校改革路在何方), *Nanfang dushi bao* (南方都市报), Guangzhou, Nov. 24, 2014.

Editorial, "Chinese Wisdom and China Solution Influences the World" (中国智慧中国方案影响世界), *Renmin ribao* (人民日报), Oct. 24, 2017.

Editors. "Wang Lijun's Sea-Sized Patents Are Not 'Inventions' " (王立军的海量专利不是"发明"), *Xinijing bao* (新京报), Aug. 28, 2014.

Editors. "Is the Slogan of Uniting Two 95%s Correct?" (团结两个百分之九十五的口号对吗?), *Shanxi shengwei dangxiao xuebao* (山西省委党校学报), Taiyuan, no. Z1, 1981.

Editors. *Short History of the CCP* (中国共产党简史). Beijing: Renmin, 1991, 2001, 2011, 2021.

Editors. "Main Economic Data 2021" (2021年全年主要经济数据), *Jingji ribao* (经济日报), Jan. 18, 2022.

EIA (Environmental Investigation Agency). "Crime and Corruption behind Tanzania's Elephant Meltdown," London: EIA, Nov. 6, 2014.

EIU. *The Safe Cities Index 2015*. London: Economist Intelligence Unit, 2015.

Else, Holly, and Richard Van Noorden. "The Fight against Fake-Paper Factories that Churn out Sham Science," *Nature*, Mar. 23, 2021.

Else, Holly. 'Tortured Phrases' Give Away Fabricated Research Papers," *Nature*, Aug. 5, 2021.

Elvin, Mark. *The Retreat of the Elephants: An Environmental History of China*. New Haven, CT: Yale University Press, 2004.

Erling, Johnny. "Chinas Superreiche flüchten in Scharen ins Ausland" (China's Super-rich Flee in Droves Abroad), *Die Welt*, Feb. 7, 2014.

EUSO. *Asylum Quarterly Report*, EU Commission, June 2020.

Evans, Peter. *Embedded Autonomy: States and Industrial Transformation*. Princeton, NJ: Princeton University Press, 1995.

Faber, Benjamin. "Trade Integration, Market Size, and Industrialization: Evidence from China's National Trunk Highway System," *Review of Economic Studies*, 2015.

Fan Li. "How Much of Our Country's Foreign Exchange Reserve Is Useable?" (范棣: 我国外汇储备还有多少可用？), *Maocaijing* (蠡财经), Beijing, Oct11, 2020.

Fan Zhi. "Indeed Underreported" (范之: 果然瞒报), *WeChat Blog* (微信公众号), Jan. 21, 2022.

Fang Fang. *Wuhan Diary: Dispatches from a Quarantined City* (方方: 方方日记), translated by Michael Berry. New York: HarperVia, 2020.

Fang Jing. "Online Black Market for Papers" (互联网上的论文黑市), CCTV *Jiaodian fangtan* (焦点访谈), Beijing, Jan. 14, 2006.

Fang Lie et al. "Some Regions *hukou* Reform Encounter 'Deurbanization'" (方列等: 部分地区户改遭遇"逆城镇化"), *Jingji cankao* (经济参考), Beijing, Nov. 4, 2014.

Fang Ning. *Chinese Experience of Democracy* (房宁: 民主的中国经验). Beijing: Zhongguo sheke, 2013.

Fang Yi. "Three Quarters GDP figures of 23 Provinces Exceed National Total" (方烨: 26省统计前三季度GDP之和超全国), *Economic Reference News* (经济参考报), Beijing, Nov. 4, 2014.

Fang Yi. "State of the Reform of China's Social Security" (方烨: 中国社保改革的现状), *Jingji cankao bao* (经济参考报), Beijing, July 2, 2013.

Fang Zhouzi (Shimin). "Happy Life in Shanghai Concentration Camp" (方舟子/方世民: 上海集中营的幸福生活) @fangshimin, Twitter, Apr. 10, 2022.

Fang Zhouzi. "Building World-Class University and Academic Standard (方舟子: 世界一流大学建设与学术规范), Speech at Zhejiang University, Nov. 27, 2005.

Feige, Edgar et al. "Currency Substitution, Unofficial Dollarization and Estimates of Foreign Currency Held Abroad," *EconWPA-International Finance*, June 6, 2001.

Feigenbaum, Evan. *China's Techno-Warriors: National Security and Strategic Competition from the Nuclear to the Information Age*. Stanford, CA: Stanford University Press, 2003.

Felter, Claire. "Will the World Ever Solve the Mystery of COVID-19's Origin?" *CFR Backgrounder*, New York, Nov. 2021.

Feng Haining. "Panicky Grab of Housing Is Exaggerated Individual Case" (冯海宁: 恐慌性抢房是被夸大的个案), *Zhongguo qingnian bao* (中国青年报), Beijing, Dec. 14, 2012: 2.

Feng Huiling. "China Has about 50 'Ghost Cities'" (冯会玲: 中国将现近50座"鬼城"), *Touzi shibao* (投资时报), Wuhan, Oct. 14, 2014.

Feng Jicai. "Deception Is the Reason for the Failure of China's Education." (冯骥才: 中国教育的失败源于欺骗), *Gongshi wang* (共识网), Beijing, Mar. 12, 2014.

Feng Junqi. "Cadres of Zhong Xian" (冯军旗: 中县干部), PhD thesis, Peking University, 2010.

Feng Lei, and Chen Hen. "Chinese Wisdom Shins the Road to Global Governance" (冯蕾, 陈恒: 照亮全球治理之路的中国智慧), *Guangming ribao* (光明日报), May 9, 2017.

Feng Yongqiang. "Shaanxi Provincial Secretary: Use Iron Fist to Treat Smog" (冯永强: 陕西: 铁腕治霾), *Zhongguo huanjing bao* (China Environmental News), Beijing, Feb. 28, 2018.

Feng Yue, and Du Ximeng. "Over One Thousand Children in Jiang-Zhe-Hu Tested, 60% Positive for Antibiotics" (冯悦, 杜希萌: 江浙沪逾千儿童尿检近6成检出抗生素), Xinhua, Apr. 19, 2015.

Feng, Emily. "How China Is Using Facial Recognition Technology," NPR, Dec. 16, 2019.

Feng, Emily. "Rights Activist Xu Zhiyong Arrested in China amid Crackdown on Dissent," NPR, Feb. 17, 2020.

Fenghuang lishi (鳳凰歷史). "People Voted with Feet: The 'Major Escape to Hong Kong' in the 1960s" (人民选择用脚投票: 1960年代"大逃港"实录), Hong Kong, Apr. 25, 2011.

Fenghuang zixun (凤凰资讯). "The 1980 'Pan Xiao Discussion' that Drew National Attention (1980年引发全国关注的"潘晓讨论"), Hong Kong, Aug. 31, 2009.

Fewsmith, Joseph. *Rethinking Chinese Politics*. New York: Cambridge University Press, 2021.

Fic, Victor. "Huxley vs. Orwell: China Today," *Asia Sentinel*, Mar. 18, 2014.

Fife, Robert. "'Something Has to Change': Michael Kovrig's Letters Detail Life in a Beijing Jail Cell," *The Global and Mail*, Ottawa, Canada, June 23, 2020.

Fiskesjö, Magnus. "The Chinese Elephant Massacre in Africa: Extinction Looms," *H-Net: Network on Asian Studies and History*, Nov. 6, 2014.

Fitzgerald, John. *Cadre Country: How China became the Chinese Communist Party.* Sydney, Australia: UNSW Press, 2022.

Fitzgerald, John. "China's Scientists Trapped," *The Australian Financial Review*, Melbourne, Oct. 4, 2013.

Fitzgibbon, Will. "U.S. Poised to Celebrate Its First Panama Papers Tax Conviction," ICIJ.org, Feb. 11, 2020.

FJBM (福建便民网), "Salary of Township Cadres" (乡镇干部工资待遇标准如何), Fuzhou, Fujian, Jan. 12, 2022.

Fliegelmanfeb, Oren. "Made in China: Fake IDs," *The New York Times*, Feb. 8, 2015: ED7.

FNIC. "Still 'Crazily Hyping' 5G" (还在"狂吹" 5G), *Zhihu* (知乎), Jan. 29, 2019.

Follett, Chelsea. "The Remarkable Fall in China's Suicide Rate," Cato Institute, May 17, 2018.

Forbes. *2014 White Paper on the Wealth of China's Affluent Population* (2014 中国富裕阶层财富白皮书) Forbes, Beijing, Apr. 16, 2014.

Forsythe, Michael. "Investigating Family's Wealth, China's Leader Signals a Change," *The New York Times*, Apr. 19, 2014.

Forsythe, Michael. "China's Spending on Internal Police Force in 2010 Outstrips Defense Budget," *Bloomberg News*. Mar. 6, 2011.

Forsythe, Michael. "As China's Leader Fights Graft, His Relatives Shed Assets," *The New York Times*, June 17, 2014.

Forsythe, Michael. *China Cracks Down in Wake of Riots, Bombings*, Bloomberg, June 13, 2011.

Forsythe, Michael, and Austin Ramzy. "China Censors Mentions of 'Panama Papers' Leaks," *The New York Times*, Apr. 5, 2016.

Franceschini, Ivan et al. "What about Whataboutism?" *Made in China*, July 7 2020.

Frank, Robert. "China's Rich Fleeing the Country—with Their Fortunes," CNBC, Nov. 25, 2013.

Frater, Patrick. "China Surges 36% in Total Box Office Revenue," *Variety*, Jan. 4, 2015.

Freedman, Milton. *Free to Choose*, New York: Harcourt, 1980.

Freeman, Will. "The Accuracy of China's 'Mass Incidents,'" *Financial Times*, Mar. 2, 2010.

French, Howard. *China's Second Continent: How a Million Migrants Are Building a New Empire in Africa*. New York: Knopf, 2014.

Fu Tianming. "Not Fully Declassified 'Underground Great Wall'" (傅天明: 未完全解密的'中国地下长城'), *Baokan huicui* (报刊荟萃), Xian, No. 10, 2011: 75–76.

Fu Weigang. "The Cost of Urbanization from the Perspective of Public Services" (傅蔚冈: 从公共服务看城市化成本), *Nanfang dushi bao* (南方都市报), Guangzhou, Aug. 17, 2014.

Fu Weigang. "Why the Internet Is So Expensive in China" (傅蔚冈: 中国上网贵到底贵在哪儿), *Nanfang dushi bao s* (南方都市报), Guangzhou, Apr. 21, 2015.

Fu Xiaolan et al., eds. *Report on Chinese National Mental Health Development* (傅小兰等: 中国国民心理健康发展报告). Beijing: Shehui kexue wenxian, 2020.

Fu Yongjun. "The Real Chinese Countryside" (付永军: 真实的中国农村), *Jinri toutiao* (今日头条), Dec. 18, 2020.

Fu Zhibin. *History of Brain Washing* (傅志彬: 洗脑的歷史). Taipei: Daguan, 2014.

Gai Kaicheng. "Study on Western (China) Eco-condition and Balanced Economic Development" (盖凯程: 西部生态环境与经济协调发展研究), PhD thesis, Chongqing: Xinan Caijing, 2008.

Gan Yang, and Liu Xiaofeng. "How Has Peking University Degenerated So Much Today?" (甘阳,刘小枫: 今日北大怎么会沦落至此?), opinion.dwnews.com, July 25, 2014.

Gan, Nectar. "'We Are the Last Generation': China's Harsh Lockdowns Could Exacerbate Population Crisis," CNN, May 16, 2022.

Gan, Nectar. "'Voices of April': China's Internet Erupts in Protest against Censorship of Shanghai Lockdown Video," CNN, Apr. 25, 2022.

Gan, Nectar. "Isolated, Tortured and Mentally Scarred . . . the Plight of China's Persecuted Human Rights Lawyers," *South China Morning Post*, Hong Kong, July 9, 2017.

Gao Ertai. Looking for Home (高爾泰: 尋找家園), 3 vols, Taipei: Yinke, 2009.

Gao Fusheng. "The Guinness Record of Official's Keeping of Mistresses" (高福生: 看官员包养情妇等吉尼斯记录), *Guangming wang* (光明网), Beijing, Apr. 4, 2014.

Gao Peng. "College Girl Jailed Wrongfully by Out of Town Police for 10 Months (高鹏: 女大学生被异地警方错抓羁押10个月), *Nanfang wang* (南方网), Aug. 22, 2013.

Gao Shangquan. "Two Great Exoduses and One Major Destruction" (高尚全: 两个大逃亡, 一个大破坏), *Aisixiang* (爱思想), Beijing, Oct. 26, 2014.

Gao Shenke. "Impression of Home Villages during Spring Festival" (高胜科: 春节返乡见闻), *Caijing* (财经), Beijing, Feb. 14, 2016.

Gao Wenqian. *Zhou Enlai in His Last Years* (高文謙: 晚年周恩來). Hong Kong: Mingjing, 2003.

Gao Wenqian. *Zhou Enlai: The Last Perfect Revolutionary*. New York: Public Affairs, 2007.

Gao Zhisheng. *Rise up China in 2017* (高智晟: 2017年, 起來中國), Taipei: Lianmeng, 2016.

Gao Zhiyong. "Recall the Goods Supply in Beijing during the Hard Time" (高智勇: 北京市困难时期商品供应追记), *Yanhuang chunqiu* (炎黄春秋), Beijing, No. 8, 2007: 17–18.

Garside, Roger. "Regime Change in China Is Not Only Possible, It Is Imperative," *The Globe and Mail*, Apr. 30, 2021.

Ge Bichao. "Bo Xilai's Cheer-Leading Clowns" (戈壁草: 薄熙来的吹鼓手), *WeChat Blog*, Aug. 19, 2018.

Ge Jianxiong. "How Should We View History?" (葛剑雄: 我们应该怎样看待历史), Open lecture, Xian, Jan. 4, 2021.

Ge Long. "SOEs: the Achilles' Heel of the Chinese Giant" (格隆: 国企-中国巨人的阿喀琉斯之踵), *Sina caijing* (新浪财经), Beijing, Apr. 30, 2016.

Ge Xiuyu et al. "Investigation of a Grain Bureau Chief Found a Nest of 'Big Rats'" (葛秀钰等: 查个粮食局长挖出一窝"硕鼠"), *Zigong wang* (自贡网), Zigong, Sichuan, Nov. 27, 2017.

Gershaneck, Kerry. *Political Warfare: Strategies for Combating China's Plan to "Win without Fighting."* Quantico, VA: Marine Corps University Press, 2020.

Gertler, Paul. *Impact Evaluation in Practice*, 2nd edition. Washington, DC: World Bank, 2016.

Ghosh, Arunabh. *Making It Count: Statistics and Statecraft in the Early People's Republic of China*. Princeton: Princeton University Press, 2020.

Giglio, Mike. "China's Spies Are on the Offensive," *The Atlantic*, Aug. 28, 2019.

Gill, Indermit, and Homi Kharas. "The Middle-Income Trap Turns Ten," World Bank Policy Research Working Paper 7403, Aug. 2015.

GIPC. *Measuring the Magnitude of Global Counterfeiting*. Washington, DC: US Chamber of Commerce, June 2016.

Glad, Betty. "Why Tyrants Go Too Far: Malignant Narcissism and Absolute Power," *Political Psychology* 23-1, 2002: 1–37.

Glanz, James, and Campbell Robertson. "Lockdown Delays Cost at Least 36,000 Lives, Data Show," *The New York Times*, May 21, 2020.

Global Net. "Ghost-Writing Becomes an Industry" (环球网: 代写成产业), *Huanqiu* (环球), Jan. 8, 2016.

Goldberg, Barbara. "Missing Children in U.S. Nearly Always Make It Home Alive," Reuters, New York, Apr. 26, 2012.

Goldhagen, Daniel. *Hitler's Willing Executioners: Ordinary Germans and the Holocaust*. New York: Vintage, 1997.

Goldman, Russell. "From One Child to Three: How China's Family Planning Policies Have Evolved," *The New York Times*, June 1, 2021.

Goldstein, Joseph, and Kirk Semple. "Law Firms Are Accused of Aiding Chinese Immigrants' False Asylum Claims," *The New York Times*, Dec. 19, 2012.

Gong Chu. *Gong Chu Memoirs* (龔楚回憶錄). Hong Kong: Mingbao, 1978.

Gong Qinqi. "The Whistle Giver" (龚菁琦: 发哨子的人), *People* (人物), Mar. 10, 2020.

Gong Renren. "Professor, Piece-wage Worker and Academic Freedom" (龚刃韧: 大学教授, 计件工与学术自由), *21ˢᵗ shiji* (二十一世纪), Hong Kong, No. 38 (May) 2005.

Gong Wen. "What's the Odds for a Staff Member Being Promoted to Provincial Governor or Minister?" (公文: 科员升到省长部长, 概率有多大), *Zhihu* (知乎), Beijing, Jan. 19, 2021.

Goodman, David. *Class in Contemporary China*. Malden, MA: Polity, 2014.

Graeber, David. *Bullshit Jobs: A Theory*. New York: Simon & Schuster, 2018.

Graham, Edward, and Erika Wada. "Foreign Direct Investment in China: Effects on Growth and Economic Performance," *IIE Working Paper*, No. 01-03, Washington, DC: IIE, 2001.

Graham-Harrison, Emma. "China Warned over 'Insane' Plans for New Nuclear Power Plants," *The Guardian*, May 25, 2015.

Greene, Megan. *The Origins of the Developmental State in Taiwan*. Cambridge, MA: Harvard University Press, 2008.

Greenhalgh, Susan. "Missile Science, Population Science: The Origins of China's One-Child Policy," *The China Quarterly* 182, June 2005: 253–276.

Greenhalgh, Susan. "Planned Births, Unplanned Persons: 'Population' in the Making of Chinese Modernity," *American Ethnologist* 30(2), May 2003.

Greenpeace, and Peking University. *Dangerous Breath II* (危险的呼吸2), Beijing, Feb. 4, 2015.

Groot, Gerry. *Managing Transitions: The Chinese Communist Party, United Front Work, Corporatism and Hegemony*. London, UK: Routledge, 2003.

Gruin, Julian, and Peter Knaack. "Not Just Another Shadow Bank," *New Political Economy*, Jan. 2019.

Grunberger, Richard. *The 12-Year Reich: A Social History of Nazi Germany 1933–1945*. New York: Da Capo, 1971.

Gu Feng. "How Many Political Tycoons in the CCP?" (谷风: 中共腐败权贵家族知多少), *Beijing spring* (北京之春), Flushing, New York, May 17, 2014.

Gu Weihua. "Zhang Yihe: Sad Long Road, Sprints Back" (顾维华: 章诒和: 悲兮远道,魂兮归来), Shanghai: *Oriental Morning News* (东方早报), Apr. 10, 2009: C15.

Gu Yi. "Super Fraud Led to Case in Case of SOE Corruption" (顾亦: 超级骗局牵出国企腐败案中案), shjcy.gov.cn/jcfy/lsgc/32588.jhtml, Shanghai, Nov. 27, 2017.

Gu Zhijuan. "Vacancy Tax Is Coming?" (顾志娟: 空置税要来了?), *Xinjing bao* (新京报), Oct. 26, 2018.

Gu Zhun. *Collected Works of Gu Zhun* (顾准文集). Beijing: Zhongguo shichang 2007.

Guan Cha Yuan. "More Urgent to Solve Vacuous Employment of Leading Cadres" (观察员: 解决领导干部"吃空饷"更紧迫), *Zhongcheng wang* (中城网), Beijing, Mar. 13, 2021.

Guan Dian. "Waves of Chinese Migrants" (观点: 中国人口迁徙浪潮), *Sohu* (搜狐), Oct. 12, 2015.

Guan Jun. *Big Foot Prints: Witnessing 2008 under the Olympic Shadows* (关军: 大脚印儿: 见证奥运阴影下的2008), Beijing, e-book monograph, readmoo.com/book/2100259670001, 2009.

Guangdong Government. *On the Rectification of the First Batch of Academic Journals in Guangdong Province* (关于广东省首批学术期刊认定及整改意见的公告), Nov. 19, 2015.

Gueorguiev, Dimitar. *Retrofitting Leninism: Participation without Democracy in China*. New York: Oxford University Press, 2021.

Guevara, Marina Walker et al. "Leaked Records Reveal Offshore Holdings of China's Elite," Washington, DC: International Consortium of Investigative Journalists, Jan. 21, 2014.

Gui Tiantian. "Liu Zhijun Gu Junshan Have Hundreds of Real Estate Assets" (桂田田: 刘志军谷俊山拥数百套房产), *Renmin wang* (人民网), Beijing, Nov. 23, 2014.

Gulland, Anne. "Drop in Suicide Rate in China Fuels Global Fall in Deaths," *The Telegraph*. June 6, 2019.

Guo Chuyang. *Save the Kids: Critique of Elementary Chinese Textbook* (郭初阳: 救救孩子-小学语文教材批判). Wuhan: Changjiang Wenyi, 2010.

Guo Chuyang. "Learning Chinese Language, Don't Need Textbook" (郭初阳: 学语文, 不需要语文书). *Yixi Talk* (一席), Hangzhou, May 23, 2021.

Guo Dehong. "Anti-Party Cliques" (郭德宏: 反党集团), *Weibo* (微博), Beijing. Apr. 22, 2019.

Guo Jinlong. "Books Supreme Leader Has Read" (郭晋龙: 最高领导人读过的书). *WeChat Blog* (微信公众号), Jan. 23, 3022.

Guo Jiuhui. "Several Central Grain Warehouses in Henan Embezzled ¥700 Million" (郭久辉: 中储粮河南多个粮库骗7亿资金) *Liaowang zhoukan* (瞭望周刊), Beijing, Aug. 17, 2013.

Guo Ke. "Incomplete List of Precious Antiquities Destroyed during the Cultural Revolution" (过客: 文革中被破坏的珍贵文物不完全清单), *Dushu wenzhai* (读书文摘), Wuhan, No. 12, 2008.

Guo Ke. "What Famous Buildings Demolished after the Founding of the PRC "(过客: 建国至今有哪些被拆掉的著名建筑), zhihu.com/question/248 57760.

Guo Linlin et al. "Inventor of Water-Hydrogen Engine Is a Big Scammer" (郭琳琳等: 发明水氢发动机的庞青年是大忽悠), *Beijing qingnian bao*, Beijing, May 25, 2019.

Guo Ping. "Zhao Jiuzhang's Great Misfortune as Qian Xuesen's Colleague" (过平: 赵九章极大不幸与钱学森同事), my.cnd.org; Apr. 26, 2015.

Guo Rongxing. *New History on World's Civilizations: Mainstream Textbooks in the West Were Wrong* (郭荣星: 世界文明新史-西方主流教科书错了). Beijing: Guojia Xingzheng, 2021.

Guo Xue. "China's Officialdom 'Reserve-Elimination' Will Threaten National Security" (国学: 中国官场"逆淘汰"将危及国家安全), *Wangyi* (网易), Beijing, Apr. 18, 2021.

Guo Xuezhi. *The Politics of the Core Leader in China*. New York: Cambridge University Press, 2019.

Guo Yiwen. "How Chili Peppers Conquered People's Stomach," (郭晔雯: 辣椒如何征服国人的胃), *The Paper* (澎湃), Shanghai, Oct. 11, 2017.

Guo Yuhua. "Sociological Imagination on 'Wolf Milk'" (郭于华: 关于"狼奶"的社会学想象), *China In Perspective*, Feb. 10, 2009.

Guo Yujie. "Labor Wards Very Quiet in 2022" (郭玉洁: 2022年的产房静悄悄), *Zhongguo qingnian bao* (中国青年报), Beijing, May 2, 2022.

Guo Yukuan. "Reporters Should Be Responsible to History—Dialogue with Yang Jisheng" (郭宇宽: 记者要对历史负责-对话杨继绳), *Jinyang wang* (金羊网), Guangzhou, Aug. 14, 2016.

Guo Yushan. "Cost of the Three Gorges Project" (郭玉闪: 三峡工程的代价), *Zhongguo baodao zhoukan* (中国报道周刊), May 25, 2011.

Guo, Xuezhi. *China's Security State: Philosophy, Evolution, and Politics*. New York: Cambridge: Cambridge University Press, 2012.

Guo, Yingjie, and Wanning Sun, eds. *Unequal China The Political Economy and Cultural Politics of Inequality*. London: Routledge, 2012.

Guoqiao Tudou. "Daxiang Gonghui Ended" (过桥土豆: 大象公会落幕), *Wangyi* (网易), July 15, 2021.

Guzman, Francisco, and Brian Ries. "Customs Police Seized $900,000 in Counterfeit Money from a Shipping Container," CNN, Jan. 28, 2020.

Hai Mang. "You Did What the Virus Can't" (海虻: 病毒做不到的, 你们做到了), *WeChat Blog* (微信公号), Jan. 7, 2022.

Hai Shang Ke. "So Many 'Putin Fans'" (海上客: 有那么多"普京粉"), *Sohu* (搜狐), Feb. 24, 2022.

Hai Yun. *The Major Case of Yuanhua in Xiamen* (海韵: 厦门远华大案). Beijing: Haiguan, 2001.

Hai Yuncang. "The Secretive 'Internal Reference' That Reaches Zhongnanhai Directly" (海运仓: 那些直达中南海的神秘"内参"), *Ta Kung Pao* (大公报), Hong Kong, Dec. 28, 2014.

Hamel, Gregory. "Problems with a Long Chain of Command," *Azcentral*. https://yourbusiness.azcentral.com/problems-long-chain-command-17294.html

Hamilton, Clive. "It Would Be Unwise to Dismiss Donald Trump's Wuhan Lab Leak Theory," *Sydney Morning Herald*, Sydney, Australia, May 9, 2020.

Hammer, Joshua. "Demolishing Kashgar's History," *Smithsonian Magazine*, Mar. 2010.

Han Deqiang. "Chairman Is Actually a God" (韩德强: 毛主席就是一个神), BBC in Chinese, Beijing, Dec. 19, 2013.

Han Han. "No Counterfeit, No New China" (韩寒: 没有山寨, 就没有新中国). *Sina* (新浪). Mar. 3, 2009.

Han Shishan. "Retrial of the Yang Lien-sheng Zhao Lisheng Confrontation on the Phone" (韩石山: 重审杨联陞赵俪生电话冲突案), chinawriter.com (中国作家网), Mar. 27, 2005.

Han Xiaorong. "Peking University Releases First National Report on the State of Life of the *Losers*" (韩晓蓉: 北大发布全国首份"屌丝生存状况报告), *The Paper* (澎拜), Oct. 29, 2014.

Han Xiyan. "Great Adjustment of K–12 education—No Exception" (韩希言: K12教育大调整开启-无一幸免), *Wadun Business* (沃顿商业), Beijing, June 15, 2021.

Han Guangfu, and Cao Xiling, eds. *One Thousand Whys in the CCP History* (韩广富, 曹希岭: 中国共产党历史上的1000个为什么). Beijing: Dangshi, 2006.

Han, Lijian et al. "Increasing Impact of Urban Fine Particles (PM2.5) on Areas Surrounding Chinese Cities," *Scientific Reports* 5, No. 12467, July 29, 2015.

Hancock, Tom, and Nicolle Liu. "Top Chinese Officials Plagiarised Doctoral Dissertations," *Financial Times*, Feb. 26, 2019.

Hannas, William, James Mulvenon, and Anna Puglisi. *Chinese Industrial Espionage: Technology Acquisition and Military Modernisation*. London, UK: Routledge, 2013.

Hao Tianjiao. "Behind the Recruitment of PhD" (郝天娇: 博士应聘背后), *Changjiang ribao* (长江日报), Wuhan, Sept. 17, 2021.

Haraszti, Miklos. *The Velvet Prison.* New York: Basic Books, 1987.

Harney, Alexandra. *The China Price: The True Cost of Chinese Competitive Advantage.* New York: Penguin, 2008.

Haselton, Todd. "I just tried the first mainstream 5G phone, and so far 5G isn't all it's cracked up to be," CNBC, Mar. 2, 2020.

Hathaway, Oona. "Keeping the Wrong Secrets: How Washington Misses the Real Security Threat," *Foreign Affairs,* Jan–Feb, 2022.

Hattam, Meredith. "Life as a Fake Beauty Queen in Small-Town China," *The Atlantic,* Nov. 8, 2014.

Hayner, Priscilla. *Unspeakable Truths: Transitional Justice and the Challenge of Truth Commission,* London, UK: Routledge, 2001.

Hazan, Pierre. *Judging War, Judging History: Behind Truth and Reconciliation,* translated by Sarah de Stadelhofen. Stanford, CA: Stanford University Press, 2010.

He Chuanqi. *Report on Chinese Modernization 2015: Studies of Industrialization* (何传启: 中国现代化报告2015—工业现代化研究), Beijing: Beida, June 2015.

He Dan. "Trust among Chinese 'Drops to Record Low,'" *China Daily,* Beijing, Feb. 18, 2013.

He Guanghu. "What's the Root Cause of China's Moral Decay?" (何光沪: 中国道德腐烂的病根是什么), *Gongshi wang* (共识网), Beijing, May 23, 2016.

He Jiyuan. "Argument on Population between Ma Yinchu and Mao Zedong" (贺吉元: 马寅初与毛泽东人口问题的一场论争), *Zhongguo dangan bao* (中国档案报), Beijing, Oct. 15, 1998.

He Liangliang. "Great Leap Forward Led to Huge Destruction of the Eco System" (何亮亮: 大跃进造成巨大的生态破坏), Hong Kong: Phoenix TV, Dec. 29, 2010.

He Ping, and Huang Wenguang. *A Death in the Lucky Holiday Hotel.* New York: Public Affairs, 2013. (何频,黄聞光: 中國權貴的死亡遊戲), Hong Kong: Lingxiu, 2013.

He Qinglia. *Population: China's Hanging Sword* (何清涟: 人口-中国的悬剑). Chengdu: renmin, 1988.

He Qinlian. "Economic Oligopoly Economy and Political Monopoly" (何清涟: 寡头经济与政治垄断), *Huaxia wenzhai* (华夏文摘), May 2005.

He Xiaotao. "The Central Decided on the Economy Next Year" (何小桃: 中央定调明年经济), *Xinhua,* Dec. 18, 2020.

He Xuefeng. "Grasp the 25 Laws of Chinese Politics at the Bottom" (贺雪峰: 扼住中国底层政治的25个定律), *Wenhua zongheng* (文化纵横), Beijing, No. 10, 2021.

He Xuefeng. *Foundation of Great Power* (贺雪峰: 大国之基). Shanghai: Dongfang, 2019.

He Yiting. "Xi Jinping Thought Is Marxism in the 21st century" (何毅亭: 习近平新时代中国特色社会主义思想是21世纪马克思主义), *Xuexi shibao* (学习时报), Beijing, June 15, 2020.

He Yuxing. "Most Hopeless Downfall: To the Chinese Intellectuals" (何玉兴: 最绝望的堕落-写给中国知识分子), *Fenghuang xinwen* (凤凰新闻), Hong Kong, Feb. 28, 2015.

He, Xin. *Divorce in China: Institutional Constraints and Gendered Outcomes.* New York: NYU, 2021.

Hebei Government. *Regulations on Xiongan New District* (河北雄安新区条例), July 29, 2021.

Hei Tu. "How Many Books/Scrolls Burned during the Cultural Revolution?" (黑土: 文革到底毁了多少文物字画?) *Sohu xinwen* (搜狐新闻), Aug. 21, 2018.

Heimann, Eduard. "Atheist Theocracy," *Social Research* 20(3), Autumn 1953: 311–331.

Helliwell, John et al. *World Happiness Report.* New York: UN, 2013, 2020.

Hendrix, Steve. "Chinese 'Truth'—Take Two," *The Washington Post Blog*, Aug. 14, 2008.

Hernández, Javier, and Dan Bilefsky. "For Canadians Held in China, Two Years of Isolation and Uncertainty," *The New York Times*, Dec. 10, 2020.

Hernández, Javier. "Xi Jinping Vows No Poverty in China by 2020. That Could Be Hard." *The New York Times*, Nov. 1, 2017.

Hesketh, Therese, Li Lu, and Zhu Wei Xing. "The Effect of China's One-Child Family Policy after 25 Years," *The New England Journal of Medicine* 353, Sept. 2005: 1171–1176.

Hille, Kathrin. "China Ex-Rail Chief Given Suspended Death Sentence for Corruption," *Financial Times*, June 8, 2013.

Hirschman, Albert. "Exit, Voice, and the State," *World Politics* 31-1, Oct. 1978.

Hirschman, Albert. *Exit, Voice, and Loyalty.* Cambridge, MA: Harvard University Press, 1970.

Hollingsworth, Julia, and Yong Xiong. "The Truthtellers: China Created a Story of the Pandemic. These People Revealed Details Beijing Left Out," CNN, Feb. 2021.

Hong Qiaojun. "This Painting Pins Chinese Fine Arts Association to the Pole of Shame" (洪巧俊: 这幅画把中国美协钉在耻辱柱上), *Tongdao zhiyou* (同道之友), Jilin, Mar. 15, 2021.

Hoover Institution. *The Lin Zhao Papers*, Collection, Stanford University, Stanford, California, 2009.

Hornby, Lucy. "The Fight for 'China's Sorrow,'" *Financial Times*, Sept. 1, 2014.

Howlett, Zachary. *Meritocracy and Its Discontents: Anxiety and the National College Entrance Exam in China.* Ithaca, NY: Cornell University Press, 2021.

Hsu, Sara, and Jianjun Li. *China's Fintech Explosion: Disruption, Innovation, and Survival*. New York: Columbia University Press, 2020.

Hsu, Szu-chien, Kellee Tsai, and Chun-chih Chang, eds. *Evolutionary Governance in China: State-Society Relations under Authoritarianism*, Cambridge, MA: Harvard Asian Center, 2021.

Hu Jie. *Searching Lin Zhao's Soul* (胡杰: 寻找林昭的灵魂), Documentary, Hong Kong, 2005. youtube.com/watch?v=G3FJWh3qSKk

Hu Jintao. Speech at the Celebrating the 90th Birthday of the CCP Meeting (胡锦涛: 在庆祝建党90周年大会上的讲话), Beijing: Xinhua, July 1, 2011.

Hu Jintao. "Firmly Regulate Real Estate Sector" (胡锦涛: 房地产调控决心不动摇), CCTV, Beijing, July 25, 2011.

Hu Jintao. Speech at the National Work Conference on Politics and Law (胡锦涛: 在全国政法工作会议上的讲话), Beijing, Dec. 26, 2007.

Hu Jiujiu. "Shameless Chinese" (胡赳赳: 无耻的中国人), *Baidu* (百度) Blog, Jan. 3, 2014.

Hu Jiwei. *Hu Jiwei Memoirs* (胡绩伟回忆录), unpublished monograph, 1996.

Hu Lianhe. *Transition and Crime* (胡联合: 转型与犯罪), Beijing: Zhongyang dangxiao, 2006.

Hu Ping. *People's Domestication, Avoidance, and Rebellion* (胡平: 人的驯化、躲避與反叛), Hong Kong: Asian Science, 1999; in English: *The Thought Remolding Campaign of the Chinese Communist Party-State*, Amsterdam: Amsterdam University Press, 2012.

Hu Rong. "Our Country's Poverty Line Too Low (胡蓉: 我国贫困线标准过低), *Shenzhen business news* (深圳商报), Oct. 29, 2010.

Hu Shi. "There Can Never Be Freedom under the rule of the Communist Party" (胡適: 共產黨統治下決沒有 '自由'), *Ziyou zhongguo* (自由中國), Taipei, Jan. 9, 1950.

Hu Songping. *Records of Conversations with Mr. Hu Shi* (胡颂平: 胡适之先生晚年谈话录), Beijing: Youyi, 1993.

Hu Tou. "Why Lakeside University Is Stopped" (虎头: 湖畔大学为何被叫停), *Sohu*, June 1, 2021.

Hu Xingdou. "How Sad My China: China Has Become a Country with Fakes Everywhere (胡星斗: 哀我中华: 中国已经沦为无处不造假的国家), *Zhongguo baogao* (中国报道), Aug. 12, 2008.

Hu Xingdou. "*Selected Works of Mao Zedong* Should Be Renamed "Selected works of CCP's First Generation Leaders" (胡星斗:《毛泽东选集》应更名为《中共第一代领导人选集》), *Sina* (新浪), July 9, 2015.

Hu, Danian. *China and Albert Einstein*. Cambridge, MA: Harvard University Press, 2005.

Hu, Ming. *Annotated Biography of Hu Shi* (胡明: 胡适传论). Beijing: Renmin wenxue, 1996.

Hu, Shen. "China's Gini Index at 0.61, University Report Says," *Caixin*, Beijing, Dec. 21, 2012.

Hua Xia. "Xi Says China to Further Promote Common Prosperity," Beijing: Xinhua, Nov. 3, 2020.

Hua Xinmin. "Qian Xuesen in Cultural Revolution" (华新民: 文革中的钱学森), *Remembrance* (记忆), 43, 2010.

Huang Deng. *Family on the Great Earth: The Countryside in the Eyes of a Peasant's Daughter-in-Law* (黄灯: 大地上的亲人: 一个农村儿媳眼中的乡村图景). Beijing: Taihai, 2017.

Huang Haixin. "Come for Beheading If Cannot Treat Air Pollution by 2017" (王海欣: 2017年不能实现空气治理就提头来见), *Jinghua shibao* (京华时报), Beijing, Jan. 19, 2014.

Huang Heqing. *Dubious History of European Civilization* (黄河清: 欧洲文明史察疑). Beijing: Dabaike, 2021.

Huang Jing-Yang. "Age of Involution: Uncontrolled Investment, Redundant Competition, and the End of Chinese Model of Growth" (黄靖洋: 內卷時代: 無節制的投入、同質化的競爭, 與中國增長模式的極限), *Initium* (端傳媒), Hong Kong, Jan. 7, 2021.

Huang Kaiqian et al. "The Ten Billion USD Oil Trap" (黄凯茜: 百亿美元石油陷阱), *Financial news weekly* (财新周刊), Beijing, No. 30 (Aug. 3) 2015.

Huang Liang. "Stick to 'Three Supremacies' Forever" (黄亮: 始终坚持"三个至上"), *Renmin ribao* (人民日报), Beijing, Jan. 10, 2014.

Huang Ping. "Community of Common Destiny for Humanity Provides 'the China Solution' for Global Governance (黄平: 人类命运共同体为全球治理提供"中国方案"), *Hongqi wengao* (红旗文稿), No. 20, Oct. 24, 2019.

Huang Qiuxia. "Clean Out the 'Bugs' in the Grain Warehouses" (黄秋霞: 清理粮仓"蠹虫"), *Beijing ribao* (北京日报), Beijing, July 23, 2021.

Huang Wenzheng, and Liang Jianzhang. "No More Misinterpretation of Demographic Data" (黄文政, 梁建章: 不要再曲解人口数据), *Caixin* (财新), Beijing, Feb. 15, 2015.

Huang Yushun. "Where Will 'Political Meritocracy' Lead To?" (黄玉顺: "贤能政治"将走向何方), *Wenshizhe* (文史哲), Jinan, Shandong, No. 5, 2017.

Huang Zhizhong. "I Don't Want to Carry Hostility Standing Next to You" (黄执中: 我不想带着戾气站在你身边), *New Observer* (新观察), no. 310, Beijing, Aug. 2013.

Huang, Cary. "Deleted Xinhua Report Gives Rare Insight into China Corruption," *The South China Morning Post*, Hong Kong, Nov. 30, 2014-I.

Huang, Cary. "Prostitution Thrives as Officials Say One Thing and Do Another," *South China Morning Post*, Hong Kong, Aug. 10, 2014-II.

Huang, Jing Min et al. "Quit Playing Games with My Heart: Understanding Online Dating Scams," Working Paper, University College, London, 2015.

Huang, Xian. *Social Protection under Authoritarianism: Health Politics and Policy in China.* New York: Oxford University Press, 2020.

Huang, Yanzhong. *Toxic Politics: China's Environmental Health Crisis and Its Challenge to the Chinese State.* New York: Cambridge University Press, 2020.

Huang, Yasheng, and Tarun Khanna. "Can India Overtake China?" *Foreign Policy,* July 10, 2010.

Huang, Yasheng. "Growth and Freedom," *Forbes,* June 15, 2010.

Huang, Yasheng. *Capitalism with Chinese Characteristics: Entrepreneurship and the State.* New York: Cambridge University Press, 2008.

Huang, Yingying, and Suiming Pan. "Job Mobility of Brothel-Based Female Sex Workers in Current Northeast China," An ISG paper, Beijing: Renmin University, 2004.

Hudson, Valerie. *Bare Branches: The Security Implications of Asia's Surplus Male Population.* Cambridge, MA: MIT press, 2004.

Hugh-Jones, David. "Honesty, Beliefs about Honesty, and Economic Growth in 15 countries," *Journal of Economic Behavior & Organization* 127, 2016: 99–114.

HUGO Pan-Asian SNP Consortium et al. "Mapping Human Genetic Diversity in Asia," *Science* 326, 2009: 1541–1545.

Human Rights Watch. *Walking on Thin Ice: Control, Intimidation and Harassment of Lawyers in China,* New York, Apr. 28, 2008.

Hung, Ho-fung. "Repressing Labor, Empowering China," *Phenomenal World,* July 2, 2021.

Hu Angang. "China's Governance Superior to That in the West" (胡鞍钢: 中国国家治理优于西方), *Chinese Social Sciences Today* (中国社会科学报), Beijing, no. 665, Nov. 5, 2014.

Hurun. *Hurun Global Housing index 2019,* Shanghai, Feb. 20, 2020.

Hurun. *Hurun Global Rich List 2021,* Beijing and Mumbai, Mar. 2, 2021.

Huxley, Aldous. *Brave New World.* London: Chatto & Windus, 1932.

Hvistendahl, Mara. "Show Me the Money," *Science* 346, Oct. 24, 2014.

Hvistendahl, Mara. "China's Publication Bazaar," *Science* 342(29), 2013.

IMF. "World Bank-IMF Debt Sustainability Framework for Low-Income Countries," Mar. 17, 2021.

IMF. "The Evolution of Public Debt Vulnerabilities in Lower Income Economies," Feb. 10, 2020.

IMF. *World Economic Outlook Oct. 2014,* Washington, DC: IMF, 2014.

Immigration Bureau University Press. *Release on Asylum.* Tokyo: Ministry of Justice, 2005 and 2018.

India Brand Equity Foundation. *Indian Manufacturing: Profit Potential and Opportunities.* New Delhi, India, 2013.

Indian Ministry of Finance. *Income Tax Slabs & Rates 2020–2021,* New Delhi, India, 2020.

Inskeep, Stee. "'Red Roulette' Reveals the Inside of China's Wealth-Making Machine," *Morning Edition*, NPR News, Sept. 6, 2021.

IISS (International Institute for Strategic Studies). *The Military Balance 2018*, Sweden, 2018.

Iqbal, Zain. "China vs. India: Economic Growth Comparison Across Various Data Points," *Alpha Invesco*, 2019.

IRCC. *Asylum Claimants*, Ottawa, Canada, May 17, 2019.

ISSS. *China Family Panel Studies* (中国社会科学调查中心: 中国家庭追踪调查). Beijing: Beida, 2013.

Iwata, Ueki. *Readings on Anti-Japan fantasy TV series* (岩田宇伯: 中国抗日ドラマ読本). Tokyo, Japan: Publib (パブリブ), 2018.

Jacobs, Andrew. "Death of Watermelon Vendor Sets off Outcry in China" & "China Still Presses Crusade against Falun Gong," *The New York Times*, Apr. 28, 2009; July 21, 2013.

Jacobsen, Rowan. "How Amateur Sleuths Broke the Wuhan Lab Story and Embarrassed the Media," *Newsweek*, June 2, 2021.

Jahn, Mark. "10 Countries with the Highest Savings Rates," *Investopedia*, Oct. 24, 2020.

Ji Simin. "Xi Jinping 18 Words Set Real Estate" (计思敏: 习近平18字定调房地产), *The Paper* (澎湃), Nov. 10, 2015.

Ji Wei et al. "Reports Says China Faces Serious Migration Deficit (纪伟等: 报告称中国面临严重移民赤字), *Huanqiu shibao* (环球时报), Beijing, Jan. 22, 2014.

Jia Qingguo. "On Improving the Management of Sino-foreign Scholar Exchange" (贾庆国: 关于改进专家学者对外交流管理工作), Beijing: Charhar Institute, Mar. 5, 2021.

Jia Ye. "'Handler' Rao Jin: The Man behind Jin Canrong, Sima Nan, and Li Yi" (贾也: "操盘手"饶谨, 金灿荣, 司马南, 李毅背后的男人), *Baidu-guan shixiang* (百度-观世相), July 30, 2021.

Jia Ye. "Why Educational Corruption Is the More Serious Corruption (贾也: 教育腐败为何是最严重的腐败), *Fenghuang xinwen* (凤凰新闻), Hong Kong, Jan. 28, 2014.

Jia Zheng. "The Whole Story of the Hanxin Fraud of Billions" (贾征: 汉芯造假骗亿万经费始末), *Kuai keji* (快科技), Beijing, Feb. 22, 2019.

Jia Zhifang. *My Life's Dossier* (贾植芳: 我的人生档案), Nanjing: Jiangsu wenyi, 2009.

Jiancha ribao (检察日报). "Visit the 'Number One Village of Woman Trafficking' in Siyang of Jiangsu" (探访江苏泗阳"拐卖妇女第一村"), Beijing, Aug. 14, 2000.

Jiang Chao et al. "Haitong's Macro-Analysis on Central Bank's Operation of MLF" (姜超等: 海通宏观评央行MLF操作), *Sina caijing* (新浪财经), Beijing, Nov. 7, 2014.

Jiang Hui. *Yellow Book of International Communist Movement* (姜辉: 国际共产主义运动发展报告黄皮书). Beijing: CASS, 2020.

Jiang Jun. "After ¥9.5 Trillion Investment, Ten Thousand Firms Switch to Make Chips" (蒋军: 9.5万亿投入造芯片之后, 万家企业开始转型造芯), *Tencent* (腾讯), Sept. 25, 3020.

Peng Xin. "Hundred-Billion Chip Project Crashed" (彭新: 千亿投资的芯片项目陷入停摆), *Wangyi* (网易), Sept. 1, 2020.

Jiang Mengyin. "Seek Common Prosperity: Eight Key Points and Five Proposals for Understanding and Promoting Common Prosperity" (蒋梦莹: 求解共富-理解共同富裕的八个要点与促进共同富裕的五条建议), *The Paper* (澎湃新闻), Shanghai, Aug. 25, 2021.

Jiang Weiping. *Biography of Bo Xilai* (姜维平: 薄熙来传). Hong Kong: Xiafeier, 2010.

Jiang Xiaotian. "Yongshun Civil Servants Hair-Checked for Narcotics" (蒋小天: 永顺公职人员毛发验毒), *Nanfang dushibao* (南方都市报), Guangzhou, Mar. 31, 2021.

Jiang Xue. "Ten Days in Changan" (江雪: 长安十日), *WeChat Blog* (微信公号), Jan. 4, 2022.

Jiang Yanxin, and Li Dandan. "Beijing's Temporary Residents Reduced 416 Thousand Last Year" (蒋彦鑫, 李丹丹: 去年北京暂住人口减少41.6万), *Xinjing bao* (新京报), Sept. 8, 2013.

Jiang Yin. "Nightmare of Reimbursement: Dialogue on Funding Management" (蒋寅: 报销恶梦! 关于科研经费的对话), *Wenhui xueren* (文汇学人), Shanghai, Dec. 19, 2014: 2–3.

Jiang Zheng. "Fake Auctions, Auctions of Fakes" (蒋铮: 假拍, 拍假), *Yangcheng wanbao* (羊城晚报), Guangzhou, June 25, 2012: A5.

Jiang Zong. "Must Guard against the Latecomer Disadvantage" (江宗: 后发劣势不可不防), *Jiefangjun bao* (解放军报), May 12, 2020.

Jiang Zuquan. "Pre- and Post-Wenge" (蒋祖权: 文革前后), *HXZQ* (华夏知青), Feb. 14, 2016.

Jiao Guobiao, ed. *Recollections by the Five Black Kinds* (焦国标: 黑五类忆旧), online series on *Sina* (新浪), 17 volumes, 2010–2012.

Jili Tonshi. "Six Disciplines and 149 Negative Times Listed" (纪律通识: 六项纪律149条负面清单), *Wangyi* (网易), Beijing, Mar. 17, 2022.

Jin Chongji. *Biography of Liu Shaoqi* (金冲及: 刘少奇传). Beijing: Zhongyang wenxian, 1998.

Jin Dalu. *Normal and Abnormal: Social Life in Shanghai during "Cultural Revolution"* (金大陆: 非常与正常: 上海"文革"时期的社会生活). Shanghai: Cishu, 2011.

Jin Hui. "Is Punk Health Really for Health?" (靳慧: 朋克养生真的是在养生吗), *Xinhua*, Apr. 24, 2019.

Jin Jingmai. *What a Big Moon, What a Huge Sky* (金敬迈: 好大的月亮好大的天). Beijing: Dianying, 2002.

Jin Nian. "A Glance at the Fines in Provinces" (锦年: 各省市罚款收入排名一览), *Sohu xinwen* (搜狐新闻), Mar. 16, 2021.

Jin Rongdao. "Lakeside University: An Extremely Dangerous Signal" (今融道: 湖畔大学, 一个极其危险的信号), *Zhihu* (知乎), Beijing, Oct. 2020.

Jin Ze. "Goldman Sachs: Chinese Real Estate Bonds the Riskiest in Asia" (金泽: 高盛: 中国房地产开发商债券风险亚洲最高), wallstreetcn.com, Oct. 29, 2014.

Jin Zhong. "Ten Great Crimes of Mao Zedong (金鐘: 毛澤東十大罪), *Open* (開放), Hong Kong, No. 326, Feb. 2014.

Jing Jun et al. *2012 Green Book on the Health of Civil Servants in China* (景军等: 2012中国公务员健康绿皮书). Beijing: Tsinghua University, 2012.

Jing Lai. "Chinese Academician Reveals the Scheme of Graphene" (景来: 中科院院士揭露石墨烯骗局), *Wangyi* (网易), Oct. 10, 2021.

Jing Yan. "New Police Law: Police Can Shoot without Warning" (警眼: 新警察法, 警察可以直接开枪). *Sohu wang* (搜狐网), Beijing, Aug. 15, 2019.

Jing Yanan. "CIDC Interview of Mo Yan" (景延安: 中纪委专访莫言), ccdi.gov.cn, Jan. 1, 2015.

Lin, Jintai et al. "China's International Trade and Air Pollution in the United States," *Proceedings of the National Academy of Sciences of the United States of America*, Jan. 16, 2014: 5–6.

Johnson, Ian. "In China, 'Once the Villages Are Gone, the Culture Is Gone,'" *The New York Times*, Feb. 1, 2014.

Johnson, Matthew. "Securitizing Culture in Post-Deng China: 1994–2014," *Propaganda in the World and Local Conflicts*, Slovakia 4(1), 2017: 62–80.

Johnston, Lauren. "Getting Old Before Getting Rich," *China: An International Journal*, Singapore 19(3) Aug. 2021: 91–111.

Ju Chengwei. "Chinese Road to Modernization of Governance" (鞠成伟: 国家治理现代化的中国道路), *Zhongguo jijian bao* (中国纪检监察报), Dec. 26, 2019.

Jude, Mike. *Worldwide Video Surveillance Camera Forecast, 2020–2025.* Framingham, MA: IDC, 2020.

Judson, Ruth. "Crisis and Calm: Demand for U.S. Currency at Home and Abroad from the Fall of the Berlin Wall to 2011," *International Finance Discussion Paper 1058*, Washington, DC: U.S. Federal Reserve, Nov. 2012.

Kahn, Joseph, and Mark Landler. "China Grabs West's Smoke-Spewing Factories," *The New York Times*, Dec. 21, 2007.

Kai Feng. "Ranking of Land Sales in the Country" (凯风: 全国卖地收入排行), *The Paper* (澎湃), Jan. 16, 2022.

Kan Jinzhao. *Completely Smash the Reactionary Line of the Bourgeoisie Class* (看今朝: 彻底砸烂资产阶级反动路线-打到刘少奇). Nanning: Red Guards publication, 1967.

Kan Kaili. "China Must Reflect the Institutional Roots for the Wrong Decisions on TD" (阚凯力: 中国须反思TD决策错误的制度根源), *Financial Times in Chinese*, Dec. 17, 2014.

Kan Kaili. "Chinese Colleges Have Become Hog Farms" (阚凯力: 中国的大学已经变成了养猪场), *Sina Blog*, July 13, 2012.

Kang Chenwei. "Her Country" (康宸玮: 她的国), *Qiguo wenxue* (契阔文学), Feb. 22, 2016.

Kang Zhengguo. *My Reactionary Confession* (康正果: 我的反动自述). Hong Kong: Mingbao, 2004. In English: *Confessions: An Innocent Life in Communist China*. New York: Norton, 2007.

Kawa, Luke. "Bank of America: These Five Maps Show the Major Global Trends Investors Need to Know." *Bloomberg Business*, Aug. 15, 2015.

Kazarosian, Mark. "Precautionary Savings—A Panel Study," *The Review of Economics and Statistics* 79(2), May 1997: 241–247.

Keidel, Albert. "China's Social Unrest: The Story behind the Stories," *Policy Brief*, Washington, DC: Carnegie Endowment for International Peace, 48-2006.

Kelly, Jason. *Market Maoists: The Communist Origins of China's Capitalist Ascent.* Cambridge, MA: Harvard University Press, 2021.

Kexue Gongyuan. "Listen to the Diagnosis of COVID by Masters of Chinese Medicine" (科学公园: 听中医大师们诊断新冠), *Sina weibo* (新浪微博), Beijing, Jan. 13, 2022.

Keythman, Bryan. "Problems with a Long Chain of Command," *Chron.* https://smallbusiness.chron.com/problems-long-chain-command-39155.html

Khan, Azizur, and Carl Riskin. *Inequality and Poverty in China in the Age of Globalization*, New York: Oxford University Press, 2001.

Khan, Zia. "Chinese Local Governments' Hidden Debt Could Be as High as US\$6 Trillion," *S&P Global Ratings*, Oct. 16, 2018.

Khetani, Sanya. "China's Enormous Three Gorges Dam Could End Up Being A Huge Mistake," *Business Insider*, Apr. 23, 2012.

Klein, Naomi. "China Unveils Frightening Futuristic Police State at Olympics," *The Huffington Post*, Aug. 8, 2008.

Kleinman, Arthur. *Deep China: The Moral Life of the Person.* Berkeley: University of California Press, 2011.

Klemperer, Victor. *Language of the Third Reich* (LTI: Lingua Tertii Imperii), translated by Martin Brady. London: Continuum (1975) 2006.

Knight, John. "Inequality in China: An Overview," *World Bank Research Observer Advance Access*, July 18, 2013.

Koesel, Karrie. "The Rise of a Chinese House Church," *The China Quarterly*, 215, 2013.

Kohli, Atul. *State-Directed Development: Political Power and Industrialization in the Global Periphery.* New York: Cambridge University Press, 2004.

Kong Deqian. "Liu Zhijun, Gu Kailai Suspended Death Commuted to Life in Prison" (孔德婧: 刘志军、薄谷开来死缓减为无期), *Beijing qingnianbao* (北京青年报), Dec. 14, 2015.

Kong Deyong. "We Need Troops Mastering Both Marxism and Confucianism" (孔德永: 我们需要一支兼通马克思主义与儒学的队伍), *Guangming daily* (光明日报), Beijing, Apr. 11, 2016.

Kong Lingping. *Records in Blood* (孔令平: 血紀), Taipei: Xinrui Wenchuan, 2012.

Koyama, Mark, and Jared Rubin. *How the World Became Rich: The Historical Origins of Economic Growth*. Cambridge, UK: Polity, 2022.

Krimsky, Sheldon. "Breaking the Germline Barrier in a Moral Vacuum," *Accountability in Research*, July 15, 2019: 351–368.

Krishnan, Ravi. "Rising ICOR and Poor Growth," *Live Mint*, Mumbai, Feb. 25, 2013.

Kroeber, Arthur. *China's Economy*. New York: Oxford University Press, 2020.

Krugman, Paul. "Of Dictators and Trade Surpluses," *The New York Times*, Aug. 22, 2022.

Kubota, Yoko et al. "Rare Beijing Protest Channels Covid Frustrations before Communist Party Meeting," *Wall Street Journal*, Oct. 13, 2022.

Kung, James, and S. Chen. "The Tragedy of the *Nomenklatura*: Career Incentives and Political Radicalism during China's Great Leap Famine," *American Political Science Review* 105(1): 2011.

Kuo, Lily. "Student Poetry Contest in China Becomes Unexpected Outlet for Dissent," *The Washington Post*, Apr. 24, 2022.

Kuo, Lily. "Young Chinese Take a Stand against Pressures of Modern Life—by Lying Down," *The Washington Post*, June 5, 2021.

Kuo, Lily. "Beijing's Attempt to Scrub the Air before APEC Is Shaping Up to Be a Huge Fiasco," *Quartz*, Nov. 5, 2014.

Kuo, Lily. "Global Cognac Sales Depend on the Health of China's 'Erotic Sector,'" *Quartz*, Apr. 21, 2014.

Kwan, C.H. Nomura's Institute of Capital Markets Research, *Financial Times* blog, Feb. 16, 2013.

Kwongwah (光華). "Downpour Starts Worry over Three Gorges Dam" (暴雨引三峽大坝溃堤忧虑), Malaysia, June 24, 2020.

Kynge, James. "The Journey from Luxury to Thrift Will Test Beijing's Mettle: China's Ballooning Debt and Slowing Growth Will Be Tough to Manage," *Financial times*, Oct. 24, 2014.

Lacroix, Michel. *Violence as Beauty: Esthetics of Fascism in France, 1919–1939* (De la beaute comme violence—l'esthetique du fascisme francais 1919–1939). Canada: PU Montréal, 2004.

Lahart, Justin. "With Less Chinese Support, BRICs Tumble," *Wall Street Journal*, Dec. 30, 2014.

Lai Jinhong. "Wind of Rectification Blowing in China's Entertainment Circles" (赖锦宏: 中国娱乐圈吹整顿风), *World Journal* (世界日報), New York, Aug. 17, 2021.

Lake, David, and Matthew A. Baum. "The Invisible Hand of Democracy: Political Control and the Provision of Public Services," *Comparative Political Studies* 34(6), Aug. 2001: 587–621.

Laliberté, André. "China: The Moral Economy of Empire," in *Ethnic Claims and Moral Economies*, edited by André Laliberté et al. Vancouver: UBC Press, 2016: 123–147.

Lam, Willy Wo-Lap. "Early Warning Brief: Xi Jinping Issues Tough Warnings to Enemies within the Party," Washington, DC: Jamestown Foundation, July 23, 2021.

Lam, Willy Wo-Lap. *Chinese Politics in the Era of Xi Jinping: Renaissance, Reform, or Retrogression?* London: Routledge, 2015.

Lan Linzong. "Hunan Provincial Civil-Servant Exam Caught 83 Cheaters" (兰琳宗: 湖南省考83人作弊被通报), *Zhongyang jiwei wang* (中央纪委网), Apr. 20, 2021.

Lan Tai. "Sex Crimes during Wenge and Sex Trade in Dongguan: Which Is Worse?" (兰台: 文革中性犯罪与东莞性交易谁更恶劣?) *Fenghuang wang* (凤凰网), Feb. 14, 2014.

Lan Tian. "The Corruptive Practice of Civil-Servant Exam" (蓝天: 公务员考试制度的弊端), *Sina* (新浪), Dec. 7, 2010.

Lan Zhixin. "Systemic Corruption of Guangdong Science and Technology Administration" (蓝之馨: 广东科技行政系统腐败), *Diyi caijing ribao* (第一财经日报), Shanghai, Feb. 17, 2014.

Landsberger, Stefan. *Beijing Garbage: A City Besieged by Waste*. Amsterdam: Netherlands: Amsterdam University Press, 2019.

Langfit, Frank. "I Did 7 Months of Forced Labor in a Chinese Jail," NPR, May 29, 2014.

Lao Dongyan. "Legal Concerns over Facial-Recognition at Subway Stations" (劳东燕: 地铁使用人脸识别的法律隐忧), *Caixin* (财新), Beijing, Oct. 31, 2019.

Lao Dongyan. "Facing the Real World" (劳东燕: 直面真实的世界), *China Digital Times*, Jan. 29, 2022.

Lao Fu. "The Guilty" (劳夫: 罪人), *WeChat Blog*, Xian, Feb. 8, 2022.

Lao Man. "Exorbitant Civil Servants" (老峦: 养不起的公务员), *China Digital Times*, Berkeley, CA, Apr. 1, 2019.

Lao Xu. "Downsize Bureaucracy Is Real Way to Reduce over Capacity" (老徐: 精简机构和官员,才是真正的去过剩产能和库存), *Kunlunce* (昆仑策), Beijing, Apr. 18, 2016.

Laogai Foundation. *Better Ten Graves Than One Extra Birth: China's Systemic Use of Coercion to Meet Population Quotas*. New York, 2004.

Lardy, Nicholas. *Markets over Mao: The Rise of Private Business in China*. Washington, DC: IIE, 2014.

Lardy, Nicholas. *Sustaining China's Economic Growth after the Global Financial Crisis*. Washington, DC: Peterson Institute, 2012.

Latham, Jonathan, and Allison Wilson. "The Case Is Building That COVID-19 Had a Lab Origin," *Independent Science News*, June 2, 2020.

Lebow, Richard Ned. *Forbidden Fruit: Counterfactuals and International Relations.* Princeton, NJ: Princeton University Press, 2010.

Lee, Amanda. "Coronavirus: China local Government Debt Could Hit Record High as Beijing Front-Loads More Bonds," *South China Morning Post,* Hong Kong, May 14, 2020.

Lee, Chi-wen Jevons. "Cursory Comments on Second Class Universities" (李志文: 漫谈二流大学), wenku.baidu.com/view/7e1f9fe2524de518964b7dc3.html, Feb. 2, 2012.

Lee, Chi-wen Jevons. "Propaganda, Lies, Dictatorship, Autocracy, and Tyranny (李志文: 宣传, 谎言, 独裁, 专制, 与暴政), *Sina* (新浪) *Blog,* Oct. 15, 2014.

Lee, Il Houng et al. "Is China Over-Investing and Does it Matter?" *IMF Working Paper* No. 12-277, Washington, DC: IMF, 2012.

Lee, Kristine. "It's Not Just the WHO: How China Is Moving on the Whole U.N.," *Politico,* Apr. 15, 2020.

Legal Institute. "Report on Monitoring and Managing 'Naked Officials'" ("裸官"监管调研报告) in *Blue book on legal governance 2012* (法治蓝皮书 2012), Beijing: CASS, Feb. 20, 2012.

Lei Lei. "Buy 'Guns': 25 Thousand Goes to First-tier College" (雷磊, 买"枪": 两万五,上一本), *Nanfang zhoumo* (南方周末), Guangzhou, June 19, 2006.

Lei Lei. "Chinese Scholars Withdrew 819 papers" (蕾蕾: 中国学者819篇撤稿), *Iplagiarism,* Beijing, Jan. 4, 2021.

Leitenberg, Milton. "Did the SARS-CoV-2 Virus Arise from a Bat Coronavirus Research Program in a Chinese Laboratory? Very Possibly," *Bulletin of Atomic Scientists,* June 4, 2020.

Leng Fuhai, ed. *Assessing the Chinese and American Levels of Science and Technology* (冷伏海: 中美科技水平评估). Beijing: Chinese Academy of Sciences, Jan. 18, 2019.

Leng Haoyang. "Many Places Revealed Cases of Cheating at Civil Service Exam" (冷昊阳: 多地通报公务员考试违纪情况) *Zhongguo xinwen* (中国新闻), June 14, 2019.

Leroy, Aliaume. "China's Suicide Rate Has Dramatically Declined in Recent Years: Report," *Shanghaiist,* June 27, 2014.

Levin, Dan. "Chinese President's Delegation Tied to Illegal Ivory Purchases during Africa Visit," *The New York Times,* Nov. 6, 2014: A14.

Levin, Dan. "From Elephants' Mouths, an Illicit Trail to China," *The New York Times,* Mar. 2, 2013.

Levin, Ned. "China's Counterfeits in the Spotlight," *Financial Times,* Nov. 26, 2013.

Levy, David, and Sandra Peart. "Soviet Growth & American Textbooks: An Endogenous Past," *Journal of Economic Behavior & Organization* 78(1/2) 2011: 110–125.

Lewis, Leo. "Chinese Open New Secret Jails to Bully Critics into Silence," *The Times,* London, Feb. 15, 2014.

Lewis, William. "4G in China: FDD LTE v. TD-LTE v. 3G," *The Global Law & Business Perspective*, May 8, 2013.

Li Ao. *Li Ao Memoirs* (李敖回忆录). Beijing: Zhongguo youyi, 2004.

Li Bin. "Situation of Cancer Ferocious" (李斌: 癌情凶猛), Beijing: Xinhua, Feb. 3, 2015.

Li Bin. "Our Province Improves the Promotion for Young Pioneer Advisors" (李斌: 我省完善少先队辅导员职称晋升), *Sichuan Ribao* (四川日报), Chengdu, Dec18, 2020.

Li Bozhong. "We Chinese Scholars Are Really Shameful for Our Era" (李伯重: 我们中国学者实在有愧于我们的时代), *Shehuikexue luntan* (社会科学论坛), Shijiazhuang, No. 3, 2005.

Li Changan. "The State of Chinese Wetland Environment and Protection Measures" (中国湿地环境现状与保护措施), *Zhongguo shuili* (中国水利 Chinese irrigation), Beijing, No. 3, 2004.

Li Chengpeng. "Reading History But Don't Believe Love Anymore (李承鹏: 看着历史书却不相信爱情了), *Sina* (新浪), Feb. 8, 2014.

Li Chengpeng. *All in the World Knows* (李承鹏: 全世界人民都知道). Beijing: Xinxing, 2013.

Li Chengyou. "Confession of a SOE Chief" (李承友: 一位国企老总自白), *Sina*, Mar. 15, 2011.

Li Datong. "How to Assess Deng Xiaoping" (李大同: 如何评邓小平), *Wanwei* (万维), New York, Sept. 23, 2019.

Li Fei. "Changes of City Gates" (李飞: 城门的变迁), *Zhongguo zhoukan* (中国周刊), May 23, 2012.

Li Fucheng. "Discussion on the Practice of Police Shooting" (李富成: 警察开枪之实践检讨), *Dongfang fayan* (东方法眼), Beijing, July 12, 2021.

Li Guang. "Counting the 12 Already Known Ghost Cities in China" (黎广: 盘点中国已知12座"鬼城"), *Shidai zhoubao* (时代周报), Beijing, July 18, 2013.

Li Hai, and Fan Shucheng. "China's Supirio Governance" (李海, 范树成: 中国治理优势), *Beijing ribao* (北京日报), Dec. 3, 2018.

Li Hui. "Truth of the 1974 Black Painting Incident (李辉: 1974 年黑画事件真相), *Yanhuang shijie* (炎黄世界), Guangzhou, No. 1, 2010.

Li Jing. "A Forcefully Promoted New Theory of SOEs" (李锦: 一个正在大树特树的国企理论), PRC State Asset Commission, public speech, Beijing, Dec. 27, 2020.

Li Jing. "Eyewitness of the Pan Hannian Trial" (李菁: 潘汉年案审判亲历), *Sanlian shenghuo zhoukan* (三联生活周刊), Beijing, No. 19 (May 11), 2011.

Li Jing. "60,000 jobs: The Cost of One Chinese City's Cleaner Air," *South China Morning Post*, July 2, 2015.

Li Jingxian. "Impression of the Special Provision Stores in USSR" (李景贤: 苏联特供商店印象), *Haiwai wenzhai* (海外文摘), Beijing, May 12, 2021.

Li Jinlei. "China Says Goodbye to 'All about GDP'" (李金磊: 中国告别"唯GDP论"), *Zhongguo xinwen* (中国新闻), Beijing, Aug. 13, 2014.

Li Jinlei. "'Chinese Nation Rejuvenation Index' Said to Rise to 65.3% Last Year (李金磊: "中华民族复兴指数"称去年增至65.3%), *Zhongguo xinwen* (中国新闻), Beijing, Nov. 21, 2013.

Li Kejun. *Governance Ruse of County Secretaries* (李克军: 县委书记们的主政谋略). Guangzhou: Renmin, 2014.

Li Keqiang. *Report on Government Work* (李克强: 政府工作报告), Beijing, 2020, 20121, 2022.

Li Lin, and Tian He. *Bluebook of China's Rule of Law 2014* (李林,田禾: 中国法治发展报告 No. 12-2014). Beijing: Shehui kexue wenxian, 2014.

Li Peilin et al. *2014 Bluebook on Society* (李培林等: 2014 社会发展蓝皮书), Beijing, Chinese Academy of Social Sciences, Dec. 26, 2013.

Li Qiuxue. *On the History of Chinese Appeal System* (李秋学: 中国信访史论). Beijing: Shehui kexue, 2009.

Li Rui. *Real Records of Lushan Conference* (李锐: 庐山会议实录). Zhengzhou: Renmin, 1999(I).

Li Rui. *Witness Account of the Great Leap Forward* (李锐: 大跃进亲历记). Haikou: Nanfang, 1999(II).

Li Shangyong. "How Serious Is the Chinese Environmental Situation" (李尚勇: 中国环境现实有多严峻), *Zhongguo gaige* (中国改革), Beijing, No. 4, 2014: 96–100.

Li Shaomin. *The Rise of China, Inc.* New York: Cambridge University Press, 2022.

Li Shi. "Common Prosperity: The Hard Thing Is 'Income Higher, Inequality Lower'" (李实: 共同富裕, 难在"收入要高、差距要小"), *Nandu guancha* (南都观察), Beijing, Oct. 19, 2021.

Li Tangning. "Difference in Basic Pension Grows Gradually in China's Provinces" (李唐宁: 中国各省基础养老金差距正逐渐拉大), *Jingji cankao bao* (经济参考报), Beijing, Nov. 28, 2014.

Li Tiemin. "Dushan County 'Burnt 40 Billion' Is Only Tip of the Iceberg" (李铁军: 独山县"烧掉400亿"只是冰山一角), *Sina caijing* (新浪财经), Beijing, July 14, 2020.

Li Wei. "Give the World More Chinese Wisdom, China Solution and China Power" (李伟: 为世界贡献更多中国智慧中国方案中国力量) *Dangjian yanjiu* (党建研究), No. 1, 2019.

Li Wenji et al. "Section-Level Mega Corruptions" (李文姬等: 科级巨贪), *Fazhi wanbao* (法制晚报), Nov. 24, 2014.

Li Xaiodan. "Innovation and Macro Policy in New Situation" (李晓丹: 新格局下的创新与宏观政策), *EEO* (经济观察网), Beijing, Dec. 25, 2020.

Li Xiaokun. "Wen Upbeat on US Relations Despite Strains," *China Daily*, Mar. 23, 2010.

Li Xiaoting. "Scholars Remember Thought Reform," (李晓婷: 学者忆思想改造), *Nanfang zhoumu* (南方周末), Guangzhou, Aug. 9, 2013.

Li Xuhong. "What Does It Mean to Relocate State Land Transfer Fees?" (李旭红: 国有土地出让金划转意味着什么), *Liaowang* (瞭望) No. 24, June 16, 2021.

Li Yan. "Report on China's Mentally Ill" (李妍: 中国精神病患者报告), *Chinese Economic Weekly* (中国经济周刊), Beijing, No. 28, July 18, 2011.

Li Yancheng. "China Has 72 billionaires Die in Eight Years, Mostly Unnaturally" (李雁程: 8年来国内有72名亿万富豪死于非命), *Xin Wenhuabao* (新文化报), Changchun, July 22, 2011.

Li Yaping (李亚平). "Woman in Iron Chain" (铁链女), *Wechat Blog*, Feb. 15, 2022.

Li Yinhe. "About the Death of Lei Yang" (李银河: 从雷洋之死说开去), *Sina*, May 13, 2016.

Li Yinhe. "Why Crisis of Trust Could Happen in China" (李银河: 中国为什么会出现信任危机), *Dongfang nvxing* (东方女性), Shanghai, No. 12 (Dec), 2012.

Li Yining. *The Road of Chinese Economic Reform and Development* (厉以宁: 中国经济改革发展之路). Beijing: Waiyu jiaoxue yu yanjiu, 2011.

Li Yuan. "Covid, Russia and Economy Put the 'China Model' to the Test," *The New York Times*, Mar. 31, 2022.

Li Yuan. "Has Shanghai Been Xinjianged?" *The New York Times*, May 6, 2022.

Li Yuan. "Trapped Abroad, China's 'Little Pinks' Rethink Their Country," *The New York Times*, June 30, 2020.

Li Yuan. "Two Arrests, Two Outcomes Tell a Tale of Xi Jinping's China," *The New York Times*, Feb. 15, 2021.

Li Yuan. "Who Is the Real China? Eileen Gu or the Chained Woman?" *The New York Times*, Feb. 15, 2022.

Li Yubo. "Master's Thesis Costs Only 70 RMB" (硕士论文只要70 元), Beijing, *Zhongguo qingnian bao* (Chinese Youth Daily), Mar. 15, 2007.

Li Zehou, and Gan Chunsong. "'Chinese Style of Liberalism' Is the Political Future" (李泽厚, 干春松: "中国式自由主义"是未来政治走向), *Nanguo xueshu* (南国学术), Macao, No. 1, 2014.

Li Zhanshu. Closing speech at the 31st meeting of the Standing Committee of the 13th NPC (栗战书: 十三届全国人大常委会第三十一次会议闭幕讲话), Beijing, Oct. 23, 2021.

Li Zhanshu. Speech at the NPC Party Group (栗战书: 在全国人大常委会党组的讲话), Xinhua, July 16, 2018.

Li Zheng. "Let the APEC Blue Stay in the Sky Permanently" (李拯: 让"APEC蓝"永驻天空), *Renmin ribao* (人民日报), Beijing, Nov. 7, 2014.

Li Zhi-Sui. *The Private Life of Chairman Mao*. New York: Random House, 2011.

Li Zhiqiang. "A School in Hubei Moved Test to the Forests" (李志强: 湖北一学校为防作弊将考场搬进树林), *Xinhua wang* (新华网), May 4, 2014.

Li Zhongxin. *Study on China's Community Policing* (李忠信: 中国社区警务研究). Beijing: Qunzhong, 1999.

Li Zuopeng. *Li Zuopeng Memoirs* (李作鹏回憶錄). Hong Kong: Beixing, 2 vols, 2011.

Li, Eric X. "The Life of the Party," *Foreign Affairs*, Jan/Feb, 2013.

Li, Eric X. "Why China's Political Model Is Superior," *The New York Times*, Feb. 16, 2012.

Li, Fion, and Kyoungwha Kim. "China's Reserves Retreat from $4 Trillion Mark as Outflows Seen," *Bloomberg News*, Oct. 16, 2014.

Li, Jerry, and Amit Sharma. "Dragon vs. Elephant: The Elephant May Grow Slower than the Dragon, but That Does Not Mean That It Is Unsatisfactory," *Your Story*, Sept. 11, 2019.

Li, Ling. "The 'Organisational Weapon' of the Chinese Communist Party China's—Disciplinary Regime from Mao to Xi Jinping," in Creemers and Trevaskes, eds., *Law and the Party in China: Ideology and Organisation*. Cambridge, UK: Cambridge University Press, 2020.

Li, Shi, and Terry Sicular. "The Distribution of Household Income in China: Inequality, Poverty and Policies," *The China Quarterly* 217, Mar. 2014: 1–41.

Lian Qingchuan. "Returnees Become Waste" (连清川: 海归变废物), *WeChat Blog*, Dec. 6, 2021.

Liang Aiping. "Some Get Loans to Buy Official Positions, Some Get Private Business to Sponsor It" (梁爱平: 有人贷款买官有人由民企赞助), *Xinhua*, Nov. 16, 2014.

Liang Hong. "Per Capita GDP in Our Country is 12% of the U.S." (中金首席经济学家梁红: 我国人均GDP相当于美国12%), *Sina caijing* (新浪财经), Beijing, Nov. 1, 2014.

Liang Jianzhang et al. *Report of Child-Rearing Cost in China—2022* (梁建章等: 中国生育成本报告2022版). Beijing: Yuwa renkou, 2022.

Liang Musheng. "The Despicable Guo Moruo and the Noble Hu Shi" (梁木生: 郭沫若的卑劣与胡适之的高尚), *Gongshi wang* (共识网), May 7, 2015.

Liang Zi. "How Many Cadres China Really Has at Minister/Province Level?" (梁子: 中国省部级干部到底有多少), *Ten Cent News*, Sept. 17, 2018.

Liao Yiwu. *Chats with Lowest Social Strata in China* (廖亦武: 中国底层访谈录). Taipei: Maitian, 2002.

Liao Yiwu, *Collection of Wronged Cases in China* (廖亦武: 中国冤案录). Washington, DC: Laogai Foundation, 2005.

Liao Yiwu. *Last Landlords: Interviews of the Survivors of the Land Reform* (廖亦武: 最后的地主: 土改幸存者采访录). New York: Mingjing, 2 vols, 2008.

Lifton, Robert Jay. *Thought Reform and the Psychology of Totalism: A Study of 'Brainwashing' in China*. Chapel Hill: University of North Carolina Press, 1989.

Lilun xuexi (理论学习). "Six Major Weird Phenomena of Officialdom Reserve-Elimination" (官场逆淘汰六大怪象), Jinan, Shandong, No. 11, 2014.

Lim, Benjamin, and Ben Blanchard. "Xi Jinping Hopes Traditional Faiths Can Fill Moral Void in China," Reuters, Sept. 29, 2013.

Lim, Louisa. *The People's Republic of Amnesia*. New York: Oxford University Press, 2014.

Lim, Steve. "The Future of the House Church," *China Source*, June 18, 2021.

Lin Caiyi. "Debt Atlas of Chinese Local Governments" (林采宜: 中国各地政府的债务地图), *Sina*, Dec. 21, 2021.

Lin Caiyi. "How Big Is the Gap of Social Security in Various Places" (林采宜: 各地社保缺口究竟有多大), *Caixin* (财新), Beijing, Jan. 5, 2022.

Lin Shanshan. "Man Self-reports Stories of Dismantling Listening Devices" (林珊珊: 男子自述为官员拆窃听器经历), *Nanfang renwu zhoukan* (南方人物周刊), Guangzhou, Dec. 6, 2012.

Lin Shijue. "A Rural Cadre's Experience of the Birth Control Era" (林世钰: 一个乡村基层干部亲历的计划生育时代), Personal blog, Apr. 19, 2021.

Lin Tianhong. "30 Years of Refugee-Run to Hong Kong from Shenzhen" (林天宏: 深圳30年大逃港), *Zhongguo qingnian bao* (中国青年报), Beijing, Dec. 8, 2010.

Lin Weiqi. "No Defaming of Chinese Traditional Medicine" (林玮琪: 不得诋毁污蔑中医药) *Xinjing bao* (新京报), Beijing, June 2, 2020.

Lin Xiaozhao. "21 Cities Ordered to Stop Real Estate Price Cut" (21城发布房价限跌令), *Diyi caijing* (第一财经), Shanghai, Nov. 13, 2021.

Lin Xiaozhao. "Chinese Birth Rate Lower than 1% Two Years in the Row" (林小昭: 中国人口出生率连续两年跌破1%), *Diyi caijing* (第一财经), Shanghai, Jan. 17, 2022.

Lin Yanxing. "Accidents and Death Toll of Chinese Coal Industry Declined by Big Margin" (林艳兴: 中国煤矿事故数及死亡人数大幅下降), Xinhua, Sept. 5, 2009.

Lin Yifu. *China's Miraculous Development Strategy and Economic Reform* (林毅夫: 中国的奇迹发展战略与经济改革). Shanghai: Renmin, 1999.

Lin, Justin Yifu. *New Structural Economics* (新结构经济学). Beijing: Beida, 2012.

Lin, Sophia. "China's Population-Control Machine Churns On," *Freedom House*, Jan. 13, 2014.

Ling Juelin. "'Why Schooling?' Interview with Deng Xiaomang and Xiang Xianming" (凌绝岭: 读书到底为了什么-采访邓晓芒、项贤明), *Tongzhou gongji* (同舟共进), No. 3, 2015.

Ling Junhui et al. "Report on the Pollution of Antibiotics in Yangtze Valley" (凌军辉等: 长江流域抗生素污染调查), *Liaowang zhoukan* (瞭望周刊), Beijing, Apr. 25, 2020.

Lingling Wei. "Chinese Government Struggles in Attempt to Stem Distress in Stock Market," *Wall Street Journal*, July 8, 2015.

Link, Perry. "The CCP's Culture of Fear," *The New York Review*, Oct. 21, 2021.

Liu Binde. "Real Estate Price Is Crazy in Beijing: Far Larger than US GDP" (刘德炳, 北京地价已疯狂: 土地总市值远超美国GDP), *Zhongguo jingji zhoukan* (中国经济周刊), Aug. 27, 2013.

Liu Binyan (刘宾雁) et al. *Tell the World: What Happened in China and Why*, translated by Henry Epstein. New York: Patheon, 1989.

Liu Chang. "Anti-Corruption in Buddhism: Punishing Abbot Monks (刘长: 佛门反腐-刑上住持), *Nanfang zhoumo* (南方周末), Guangzhou, Dec. 15, 2012.

Liu Changjin. "The World Influence of the Beautiful Chinese Virtues" (刘苍劲: 中华民族传统美德对世界的影响), *Beijing daxue xuebao* (北京大学学报), Beijing, No. 1, 1997: 101–107.

Liu Dao. "The Ghosts of the Sacrificed in the July 20 Zhengzhou Flood" (流岛: 720郑州水灾中被献祭的亡灵), *Wanwei blog* (万维博客), July 24, 2021.

Liu Daqi. "Former Chinese Policewoman Denied Asylum" (劉大琪: 前中國女警申請庇護駁回), *World Journal* (世界日報), New York, Nov. 5, 2014.

Liu Dong. "Reconstruct the Chinese Cultural Tradition" (刘东: 重建中国社会的文化传统), *Tongzhou gongjin* (同舟共进), No. 2, Feb. 23, 2016.

Liu Gang. "Investigate the Out-of-Control Fake Medicine (刘刚: 假药泛滥乱像调查), *Xinjing bao*, Nov. 18, 2013.

Liu, Gengyuan et al. "On the Accuracy of Official Chinese Crop Production Data," *PNAS* (Proceedings of National Academy of Sciences), 117(41), 2020: 25434–25444.

Liu Guoqiang (Deputy Governor of the People's Bank). "China's Macro Debt Ratio Is 272.5%" (刘国强: 中国的宏观杠杆率为272.5%), *Tencent News* (网易新闻), May 5, 2022.

Liu Haifeng. "Ups and Downs: 70 Years of China's College Admission Exams" (刘海峰: 跌宕起伏: 中国高校招生考试70年), *Studies of Higher Education* (高等教育研究), No. 11, 2019.

Liu Huaqing. *Liu Huaqing Memoirs* (刘华清回忆录). Beijing: PLA Press, 2004.

Liu Jiaju. *Behind the Glory: My Observation inside the PLA* (刘家驹: 光荣的背后-我的军旅见闻). Austin, TX: Huayi Press, 2020.

Liu Jianhong. "Soccer Youth Training Requires Backdooring and Gifting" (刘建宏: 足球青训要走后门, 送红包), *Sohu xinwen* (搜狐新闻), Beijing, Feb. 2, 2022.

Liu Jing, and Zhou Lian. "How to View the Recent 'Decline' of the West" (刘擎, 周濂: 如何看待西方近年来的"衰落"), *Xinjing bao-shupin zhoukan* (新京报书评周刊), Beijing, Apr. 4, 2021.

Liu Jingzhi. *On Chinese History of New Music* (劉靖之: 中國新音樂史論). Hong Kong: Chinese University Press, 2009.

Liu Li. "CNKI Taxes to Get Rich from Exploiting Chinese Students" (琉璃: 靠盘剥中国学生发财的知网税), *Zhihu* (知乎), Beijing, Feb. 25, 2019.

Liu Liping. "Series on Chinese Empty Cities I: Crashed in Xiangluo Bay" (刘利平: "中国空城"系列调查之一: 折戟响螺湾), *Fenghuang caijing* (凤凰财经), Hong Kong, Apr. 4, 2014.

Liu Mingyang. "Core Journal *Glaciology and Geocryology* Is Suspended for Rectification" (刘名洋: 核心期刊《冰川冻土》被停刊整顿), *Xinjing bao*(新京报), Beijing, Jan. 26, 2020.

Liu Moxian. "Annotated Review of the Study of False Advertisements in China (刘莫鲜: 中国虚假广告研究述评), *Modern China Studies*, Princeton, 16(4), 2009: 77–95.

Liu Pei, and Liao Yue. "Peasants Trapped by Solar Panels" (刘培, 廖越: 困在光伏里的农民), *Fenghuang caijing* (凤凰财经), Nov. 9, 2021.

Liu Qin. "Antibody among 4.43% of Wuhan Population" (柳青: 武汉人群抗体阳性率4.43%), *IT Times*, Beijing, Dec. 29, 2020.

Liu Run. "Is the Education-training Industry Dying" (刘润: 教培行业是要黄了吗), *Zhihu*, June 7, 2021.

Liu Run. "Long Live Struggle, Lying Flat Is No Crime" (刘润: 奋斗万岁, 躺平无罪), *Sina Tech*, June 1, 2021.

Liu Shaoqi. *On the Cultivation of the Communist Party Member* (论共产党员的修养). Beijing: Renmin (1962) 2002.

Liu Sunan. "The Total Size of Chinese Civil Servants" (刘素楠: 中国公务员总数), *Jiemian xinwen* (界面新闻), Shanghai, June 21, 2016.

Liu Wei et al. "Fake and Bad Food: Unbearable for the People" (伪劣食品: 百姓不能承受之重), *Renmin zhengxie bao* (人民政协报), Beijing, Jan. 28, 2014.

Liu Wei. *Human Mourning: Crime of Human Trafficking in Full Perspective* (刘伟: 人之殇 全景透视下的拐卖人口犯罪). Jinan: Shandong renmin, 2017.

Liu Wei. "Investigating Pollution of Underground Water" (刘维: 全国地下水污染调查), *Herald of Geological Survey* (地质勘查导报), Beijing, June 17, 2006: 2.

Liu Wenzhong. *Stormy Road of Life* (劉文忠: 風雨人生路). Macau: Chongshi wenhua, 2004.

Liu Xiange. "How Mao Zedong 'Rules the Country with *Neican*'" (刘宪阁: 毛泽东是怎样以"内参治国"的), *Xiangchao* (湘潮), Changsha, Hunan, Mar. 2017.

Liu Xiaobo. *No Enemies, No Hatred*. Cambridge, MA: Harvard University Press, 2012.

Liu Xiaosheng. "The Story of an Associate Professor as Secret Informant" (刘小生: 一位副教授的告密往事), *Zhihu* (知乎), Beijing, July 11, 2021.

Liu Yanwu et al. *Studies on Rural Suicide Issues—Huazhong Rural Governance* (刘燕舞等: 农民自杀问题研究-华中村治研究). Beijing: Sheke wenxian, 2018.

Liu Yanwu. *Sociological Study of the Life Conditions of Rural Elderly* (农村老年人生活状况的社会学研究). Beijing: Zhongguo shehui kexue, 2018.

Liu Yanwu. *Studies on Rural Suicide* (刘燕舞: 农民自杀研究). Beijing: Sheke wnxian, 2014.

Liu Yanxun. "Story on the Devastation of Confucius' Tomb" (刘炎迅: 孔子墓蒙难记), *Zhongguo xinwen zhoukan* (中国新闻周刊), Beijing, Mar. 18, 2010.

Liu Yingjie. "Fully Appreciate the Gap of Development between China and Japan" (刘应杰, 深刻认识中国与日本发展的差距), *Qunzhong* (群众), Nanjing, May 21, 2018.

Liu Yonghao. "Rural Life Situation Still Needs Big Lift" (刘永好: 农村生活状态仍需很大提升), speech at the Sanya International Economic Forum, Sanya, Dec. 14, 2014.

Liu Yu. *Details of Democracy* (刘瑜: 民主的细节). Beijing: Sanlian, 2009.

Liu Zheng et al. "Our Country's M2 Money Supply Exceeds 120 Trillion" (刘铮等: 我国广义货币供应量破120万亿) Beijing: Xinhua, July 15, 2014.

Liu Zheng. "What's Wrong Is the Rule of Veto Power of the [CCP] Secretary" (刘正: 错的是书记的一票否决制), *Wanwei* (万维), June 8, 2021.

Liu Zhengqiang. "The Dilemma and Reconstruction of China's Management of Petition System" (刘正强: 中国信访治理的困境及其重构), PhD thesis, Aichi University, Japan, Sept. 2014.

Liu Zhenqiang. "Deep Planting and Aiding the Strong: The Logic of Petition Linking the Governance of an Ultra-large Country" (刘正强: 厚植与补强: 信访制度链接超大型国家治理的政治逻辑), *Sixiang zhanxian* (思想战线), Kunming, Yunnan, No. 4, 2021.

Liu Zhiwei. "Reinvestigate the Truth of Peng Yu Case (刘志伟: 彭宇案真相再调查) *Liaowang dongfang zhoukan* (瞭望东方周刊), Shanghai, Jan. 16, 2012.

Liu Zhongjing. "Guo Muruo Proliferated" (刘仲敬: 泛滥的郭沫若), *Gongshi* (共识网), May 7, 2015.

Liu, Adam et al. "China's Local Government Debt," *The China Journal* 87(1), Jan. 2022: 40–71.

Liu, J., "Data Sources in Chinese Crime and Criminal Justice Research," *Crime* 50(3), 2008.

Liu, Jieyu, and Joanne Cook. "Aging and Intergenerational Care in Rural China: A Qualitative Study of Policy Development," *Contemporary Social Science* 15(3), 2020: 378–391.

Liu, John, and Paul Mozur. " 'Totally Inhumane': Child Separations Feed Anger in a Locked-Down Shanghai," *The New York Times*, Apr. 3, 2022.

Liu, Weishu. "The Changing Role of Non-English Papers in Scholarly Communication," *Learned Publishing* 30(2), 2017: 115–123.

LLC. *China: Religion and Chinese Law.* Washington, DC: Law Library of Congress, June 2018.

Locke, John. *The Second Treatise of Government.* Indianapolis, IN: Hackett (1690) 1980.

Lou Jiwei. "Current 5G Technology Is Very Immature" (楼继伟: 现有5G技术很不成熟), *Sina caijing* (新浪财经), Beijing, Sept. 23, 2020.

Loyalka, Prashant et al. "Skill Levels and Gains in University STEM Education in China, India, Russia and the United States," *Nature Human Behaviour*, Mar. 1, 2021.

Lu Bai. "How China Possibly Become a Strong Power of Science and Technology" (鲁白: 中国怎么可能成为科学强国), *Zhishi fenzi* (知识分子), Beijing, Mar. 4, 2021.

Lü Dewen. "The Landscape of Black Society in Chinese Small County Towns" (吕德文: 中国小县城里的黑社会江湖), *Wenhua zhongheng* (文化纵横), Beijing, May 22, 2015.

Lu Feng. "The Puzzle of RMB Appreciation" (卢锋: 人民币的升值之惑), *Phoenix TV* (凤凰卫视), Oct. 22, 2014.

Lu Hongbo, and Liu Yujin. *One Hundred Famous Quotes Party Members Should All Know, 1921–2021* (吕红波, 刘宇晴: 党员应知的百年百句名言1921–2021). Beijing: Remin ribao, Nov. 2020.

Lu Huo. "Former Deputy-Mayor of Shahe in Hebei Was Tortured" (陆火: 河北沙河前副市长称遭刑讯逼供), *WeChat Blog* (微信公众号), Oct. 6, 2021.

Lu Lilong. "19 Signs of Darkness in the Literary Circles of Chinese Mainland" (鲁李龙: 中国大陆文坛厚黑录之一十九种现象), *Zhongguo nanfang yisu* (中国南方艺术), June 24, 2013.

Liu Haiying, and Yang Chao. "Media Monitoring Has Problems of Fakery" (刘海燕杨超: 媒体监督存在不实问题), *Jin chuangmei* (今传媒), Beijing, Jan. 3, 2014.

Lu Qian. Chronology of Hukou Reform (卢谦: 户籍改革时间轴), *Jingji guancha* (经济观察), Beijing, Dec. 25, 2019.

Lu Shuzheng. "International Comparison of China's Socioeconomic Development, 1956–1978" (吕书正: 1956–1978年中国社会经济发展的国际比较), *Shoudu shifan daxue xuebao* (首都师范大学学报), Beijing, No. 1, 2003.

Lu Si. "The Actions of Chinese Government on Human Trafficking" (卢斯: 中国政府在人口贩卖上的作为), *China Digital Times*, Feb. 3, 2022.

Lu Xing Jia. "Lying Flat Is Justice" (旅行家: 躺平即是正义), *Zhongguo renkou* (中国人口), Apr. 17, 2021.

Lu Yijie. "New Residential Permit System 'Waiting for Birth' amidst Controversies" (卢义杰等: 新居住证制度争议声中"待产"), *Zhongguo qingnian bao* (中国青年报), Beijing, Jan. 5, 2015.

Lu Yuanqiang. "Chinese Production of PhDs World's Largest Five Years in a Row" (卢元强: 中国博士产量全球5连冠). *Guoji jinrong bao* (国际金融报), Beijing, May 8, 2013.

Lu Zongshu et al. "Low Key Growing Food (吕宗恕等: 低调种菜), *Nanfang zhoumo* (南方周末), May 6, 2011.

Lu, Shen, and Katie Hunt. "Fraud Frenzy? Chinese Seek U.S. College Admission at Any Price," CNN, July 12, 2015.

Luan Yushi. "Don't Let Fake Data Damage the Internet" (栾雨石: 莫让虚假数据祸害网络), *Renmin ribao-haiwaiban* (人民日报·海外版), Beijing, Oct. 29, 2018.

Luedi, Jeremy. "Beijing-Linked Student Groups Threaten Academic Freedom in Canada," *True North Far East*, Jan. 19, 2020.

Luo Bo, and Pan Linqing. "Linyi Comprehensive Treatment of Air Pollution Has Solid Achievement" (罗博, 潘林青: 临沂大气污染综合整治取得扎实成效), Xinhua, Linyi, July 3, 2015.

Luo Changping. *On Striking Iron* (罗昌平: 打铁记). Beijing: Caijingxi, 2014.

Luo Diandian. *Archives of Red Families* (罗点点: 红色家族档案). Haikou: Nanhai, 1999.

Luo Guoji. *Chinese Traditional Virtues* (罗国杰: 中国传统道德). Beijing: Renmin daxue, 1995.

Luo Xiaojun. "Luxury Cars Fight the 'Policy Market'" (骆晓昀: 豪车博弈"政策市"), *Liaowang dongfang* (瞭望东方), Shanghai, No. 40 (Oct. 20), 2013.

Luo Yinsheng. *The Last 25 Years of Gu Zhun* (罗胜银: 顾准的最后25年). Beijing: Wenshi, 2005.

Luo Yu. *Farewell to General Staff* (羅宇: 告別總參謀部). Hong Kong: Jinzhong, 2015.

Luscombe, Belinda. "Bring Back All Girls," *Time*, May 26, 2014: 32–33.

Ma Diming. "A Real Case of 'Lying All the Way to the State Council'" (马涤明: 现实版的"一直骗到国务院"), *Qianlong wang* (千龙网), Beijing, Mar. 26, 2012.

Ma Jian. "Cultural Rule-ism and Social Decay Phenomenon" (马健: 文化规制主义与社会溃败现象?), *Lingdaozhe* (领导者), Beijing, No. 63, Apr. 2015: 156–158.

Ma Jiantang. "Scientific Development Forges Glory" (马建堂: 科学发展铸就辉煌), *Qiushi* (求是), June 18, 2012.

Ma Jichao. "Abolish or Not: What to Do with 'Pocket County' of Only 30,000" (马纪朝: 存废之争: 仅3万人的"袖珍"小县出路在哪), *Diyi caijing* (第一财经), Shanghai, May 6, 2021.

Ma Junmao. "Female Officials in China" (馬俊茂: 中國女官), *Takung pao* (大公報), Hong Kong, Mar. 8, 2015.

Ma Kai. "To Treat Corruption in Journalism" (马凯: 新闻腐败的治理路径), *Qinnian jizhe* (青年记者), No. 2, 2015.

Ma Qibin. *The 40-Year Rule of the CCP* (马齐彬: 中国共产党执政四十年). Beijing: Zhanggong dangshi ziliao, 1991.

Ma Xiangping. "Before and After the Making of One Xinhua Internal Reporting That Shock the Country" (马祥平: 一篇震动全国的新华社内参的产生前后), *Xinhua* (新华), July 9, 2001.

Ma Xiaohua. "Demographic Experts Explain the Doubts" (马晓华: 人口专家释疑), *Diyi caijing* (第一财经), Shanghai, May 11, 2021.

Ma Xiaolong. "The Precarious Tencent Financial" (马晓龙: 腾讯金服如履薄冰), *Sina* (新浪), Nov. 5, 2020.

Ma, Damien. "What It Means to Be a Rising Public Intellectual in China," *The Atlantic*, Feb. 28, 2012.

Ma, Guonan, and Wang Yi. "China's High Saving Rate: Myth and Reality," *BIS Working Papers*, No 312, Basel, Switzerland: Bank for International Settlement, 2010.

Ma, Li. *#MeToo and Cyber Activism in China*. London, UK: Routledge, 2022.

Maizland, Lindsay. "China's Repression of Uyghurs in Xinjiang," New York: CFR, Mar. 2021.

Maizland, Lindsay. "Why Countries Are Giving People Cash Amid the Pandemic," New York: CFR, May 5, 2020.

Malia, Martin. *The Soviet Tragedy: A History of Socialism in Russia, 1917–1991*. New York: Free Press, 1994.

Mallaby, Sebastian. "The Age of Magic Money: Can Endless Spending Prevent Economic Calamity?" *Foreign Affairs*, May–June, 2020.

Mao Daqing. "Real Estate Market Can Escape from Three Things" (毛大庆: 房地产市场三件事逃不过), *Cajing* (财经), Beijing, Jan. 21, 2015.

Mao Jianjie. "Devastation of Famous Tombs in West Lake" (毛剑杰: 西湖名人墓地之劫), *Wenzhai bao* (文摘报), Feb. 4, 2012: 5.

Mao Jun. *Following You Is Following the Sun* (毛军: 跟着你就是跟着那太阳), youtube.com/watch?v=CK_1tYyJ-aE, 2017.

Mao Kaiyun. "Sexology Professor Forced to Retire, a Punishment a Bit Unjust" (毛开云: 性学教授被退休, 这个处分有点冤), star.news.sohu.com/20141028/n405545134.shtml, Oct. 28, 2014.

Mao Muqin. "'Five Black Kinds,' 'Seven Black Kinds' to 'Nine Black Kinds'" (毛牧青: "黑五类" "黑七类" 到"黑九类"), *Phoenix Blog*, Hong Kong, Aug. 3, 2012.

Mao Zedong. "Yugong Moving Mountains" (愚公移山), *Selected Works of Mao Zedong* (毛泽东选集) 3, Beijing: Remin (1945) 1991: 1101–4.

Mao Zedong. "On Agricultural Collectivization" (毛泽东: 关于农业合作化问题), *Selected works of Mao Zedong* (毛泽东选集) 5, Beijing: Remin (1955) 1977: 168–191.

Mao Zedong. "Report on the Peasant Movement in Hunan" (湖南农民运动考察报告), *Selected Works of Mao Zedong* (毛泽东选集), Beijing: Renmin 1 (1927) 1991: 12–44.

Mao, Zedong. "Forewords of *Communists*" (毛泽东: 《共产党人》发刊词), *Selected Works of Mao Zedong* (毛泽东选集) 2, Beijing: Renmin (1939) 1991.

Mao, Zedong. *Mao Zedong Early Works 1912–20* (毛泽东早期文稿 1912–20). Changsha: Hunan, 1995.

Maral, Kai. "Forgiveness in Neo-Confucianism," in M. Lotter and S. Fischer, eds., *Guilt, Forgiveness, and Moral Repair: A Cross-Cultural Comparison*. London, UK: Palgrave Macmillan, 2022.

Martínez, Luis. "How Much Should We Trust the Dictator's GDP Growth Estimates?" BFI Working Paper, University of Chicago, July 2021.

Marx, Karl, and Frederick Engels. *Selected Works 50, Letters (1892–95)*. London, UK: Lawrence, 2010.

Marx, Karl. *The Eighteenth Brumaire of Louis Bonaparte*. Chicago: Kerr, 1907.

Massing, Michael. "Does Democracy Avert Famine?" *The New York Times*, Mar. 1, 2003.

Huang, Yasheng. "Are China and India Performing Well Relative to Their Competitive Potential?" in Schwab & Porter, *Global Competitiveness Report*. New York: Palgrave, 2006.

Mattingly, Daniel. *The Art of Political Control in China*. Cambridge, UK: Cambridge University Press, 2019.

May. "Eyewitness of Elite Dating Plays in Shanghai" (May: 上海精英相亲局实录), *Wangyi* (网易), July 5, 2021.

McDonell, Stephen. "China Social Media: WeChat and the Surveillance State," *BBC*, Beijing, June 7, 2019.

McGregor, Richard. *The Party: The Secret World of China's Communist Rulers.* New York: HarperCollins, 2011.

McGregor, Richard. "Xi Jinping's Radical Secrecy," *The Atlantic*, Aug. 21, 2022.

McKelvey, Wendy et al. "A Biomonitoring Study of Lead, Cadmium, and Mercury in the Blood of New York City Adults," *Environmental Health Perspectives*, Oct. 1, 2007.

McKelvey, Wendy et al. "Tracking Declines in Mercury Exposure in the New York City Adult Population, 2004–2014," *Journal of Urban Health*, 95(6), Dec. 2018: 813–25.

Meng Fangui. "On the 'Polarization' in the Mao Zedong Era" (孟凡贵: 论毛泽东时代的"两极分化"), *Baidu wenku* (百度文库), Dec. 26, 2013.

Meng Qingguo. "Study of Capitalization of Government Data" (孟庆国: 政府数据资产化探究), *Guomai dianzi zhengwu* (国脉电子政务网), Beijing, Jan. 15, 2021.

Meng Yaping. "China's Meritocracy: Selection and Election of Officials." *CGTN*, Beijing, Dec. 26, 2019.

Meng Zhaoli et al. "Corrupted Officials Doing Innovation, Using Patents for Selfish Gains" (孟昭丽等: 贪官搞发明 借专利牟私利), *Beijing qingnian bao* (北京青年报), Aug. 27, 2014.

Meng, Angela. "Xi Jinping Rules Out Western-style Political Reform for China," *South China Morning Post*, Hong Kong, Sept. 6, 2014.

MEP (Ministry of Environment Protection). *Communiqué on China's environmental situation* (环境保护部: 中国环境状况公报), Beijing: MEP, annually, 2003–2021.

Mertha, Andrew C. *China's Water Warriors: Citizen Action and Policy Change.* Ithaca, NY: Cornell University Press, 2010.

Mervis, Jeffrey. "Top PhD Feeder Schools Are Now Chinese," *Science* 321 (July 11, 2008).

Meyskens, Covell. *Mao's Third Front: The Militarization of Cold War China.* New York: Cambridge University Press, 2020.

Mi Ge. "China Eastern Flight Refused Diverted Landing Twice, Almost Led to Air Disaster" (米格: 东航客机备降两遭拒险酿空难), *Yangtze shangbao* (长江商报), Oct. 26, 2014.

Mi Yang. *White Paper on Office Building Market in China 2021* (米阳: 2021中国办公楼市场白皮书), Jones Lang LaSalle, Beijing, Sept. 14, 2021.

Miao Wei (PRC Minister of Industry and Informationization). "Build to Upgrade the Industries in the New Normal" (苗圩: 打造新常态下工业升级版), *Qiushi* (求是), Beijing, No. 1, 2015.

Micheal, Franz. *China through the Ages: History of a Civilization.* Boulder, CO: Westview, 1986.

Ming Liang, and Li Zheng. "673 Units of a County" (明亮,李政: 县里的673个事业单位), ylch377.com, Dec. 24, 2015.

Ming Shi Shuo. "Most Controversial Principal Dismissed" (名师说: 最富争议的校长[王铮]被免职), *Jinri toutiao* (今日头条), Beijing, Jan. 12, 2022.

Ming Wan. *The Political Economy of East Asia: Striving for Wealth and Power*. Washington, DC: CQ Press, 2008.

Ministry of Civil Affairs. "On the Eradicating Breeding Ground of Illegal Social Organizations" (铲除非法社会组织滋生土壤), Beijing: Circular Minfa (民发文件) # 25, Mar. 23, 2021.

Ministry of Education et al. "How Exactly Is the Quality of Chinese PhDs," (中国博士质量究竟如何?), *Guangming ribao* (光明日报), Beijing, May 10, 2011.

Ministry of Education. "College Counselor," gxfdy.edu.cn, Feb. 21, 2022.

Ministry of Education. "Yugong Moving Mountains" (愚公移山), *Language Textbook* (语文教材), various editions for grades 2, 4, 8, and 9. Beijing: Jiaoyu, 2020–22.

Ministry of Education. *Student Reader of Xi Jinping Thought in the New Era of Socialism with Chinese Characters* (习近平新时代中国特色社会主义思想学生读本), Beijing, Sept. 2021.

Ministry of Education. "First Group of Colleges of Future Technologies in 12 Top Universities" (第一批12所顶级大学成立未来技术学院), Beijing, May 26, 2021.

Ministry of Education. "No Abolishment of 985 and 211 Projects" (教育部: 不存在废除"211""985"情况), *Xinjing bao* (新京报), Nov. 14, 2014.

Ministry of Education. *Circular on Concerted Rectification of Vacuous Employment Problem* (关于开展"吃空饷"问题集中治理工作的通知), Beijing, No. 1, 2015; No. 479, 2018.

Ministry of Emergency Management. "Report on the 7/20 Mega Rainfall Disaster in Zhengzhou, Henan" (河南郑州7·20特大暴雨灾害调查报告), Beijing, Jan. 2022.

Ministry of Foreign Affairs. *Consular Protection and Assistance Cases Abroad in 2015* (外交部: 境外领事保护与协助案件总体情况), Beijing, May 5, 2016.

Ministry of Foreign Affairs. *The State of Democracy in the United States* (美国民主情况), Beijing, Dec. 5, 2021.

Ministry of Health. *China Health Statistical Year Book* (中国卫生统计年鉴), Beijing, 2010.

Ministry of HRSS. *Annual Statistical Report on Human Resources and Social Security* (年度人力资源和社会保障事业发展统计公报), Beijing, 2016–2022.

Ministry of Public Security-Personnel Training Bureau. *Basic Textbook on Public Security in the Local Communities* (治安基层基础教程). Beijing: Qunzhong, 1999.

Ministry of Public Security. *Nightmare: Cases of Woman and Child Trafficking* (公安部: 噩梦-拐卖妇女儿童案件实录), Beijing, 2003.

Ministry of Public Security: "National Newborns by Hukou Were 8.87 million" (公安部: 全国户籍新生儿887.3万), *Jinri toutiao* (今日头条), Beijing, Jan. 24, 2022.

Ministry of Transportation. *2013 Statistical Communiqué of National Toll Highways* (交通运输部: 2013年全国收费公路统计公报), Beijing, Dec. 23, 2014.

Ministry of Treasury. *Basic Information about Chinese Treasury 2011* (2011中国财政基本情况), 2012.

Ministry of Treasury. *Final Account of 2018 and Budget of 2019 for Central and Local* (2018年中央和地方预算执行情况与2019年中央和地方预算草案的报告), Mar. 17, 2019.

Ministry of Treasury. *Fiscal State 2019* (2019年财政收支情况), Beijing: Feb. 10. 2020.

Ministry of Treasury. *General Notice 2021-19* (财综2021-19号), Beijing, June 4, 2021.

Minzner, Carl F. *Riots and Cover-Ups: Counterproductive Control of Local Agents in China.* St. Louis, MO: Washington University School of Law, 2009.

Mishra, Asit R. "India Rejects Market Economy Tag for China," *Live Mint*, New Delhi, June 18, 2020.

Mitchell, Anna, and Larry Diamond. "China's Surveillance State Should Scare Everyone," *The Atlantic*, Feb. 2, 2018.

Mo Xiaoxia. "How to Import Hollywood Blockbusters" (莫小夏: 好莱坞大片如何被引进?) *Zhihu* (知乎), Beijing, Nov. 29, 2017.

Mo Zhengxin. "The Most Expensive Party Is the Chinese Communist Party (穆正新: 最昂贵的政党是中国共产党), *Beijing zhichun* (北京之春), New York, No. 10, 2005.

Mo Zhengxin. "The Fairytale of Huang Jiguang's Turret Blocking" (穆正新: 成人不宜的黄继光堵枪眼), *Boxun* (博讯), Feb. 21, 2007.

Mo Zou. *Archives of Nightwalking* (魔宙: 夜行档案), *WeChat blog* (微信公众号), 2021.

Mohrman, Kathryn. "Are Chinese Universities Globally Competitive?" *The China Quarterly*, 215, Sept. 2013: 727–743.

Moluo, An. "Are There 'Specially Provided Foods'?" (庵摩罗: 到底有没有"特供食品"?), sina.com.cn/s/blog_e5a275240101m6ie

Moore, Malcolm. "As Chinese Hit-and-Run Girl Dies, Passersby Claim They Did Not See Her," *The Telegraphy*, Oct. 21, 2011.

Morrison, Jessica. "China Becomes World's Third-Largest Producer of Research Articles, but Quantity Is Being Favoured Over Quality," *Nature* 506, Feb. 6, 2014.

Morrow, James D., Bruce Bueno de Mesquita, Randolph M. Siverson, and Alastair Smith. *The Logic of Political Survival.* Cambridge, MA: MIT Press, 2003.

Moser, David. "Media Schizophrenia in China," danwei.org, Aug. 7, 2006.

Mossaad, Nadwa. *Annual Flow Report, Refugees and Asylees 2005–2020*, Washington, DC, DHS, 2005–2019.

Mosse, George. "Fascist Aesthetics and Society: Some Considerations," *Journal of Contemporary History* 31(2), Apr. 1996: 245–252.

Mou Zhongsan. *Way of Politics and Way of Governance* (牟中三: 政道與治道). Taipei: Xuesheng, 1991.

Mouto, Christopher. "19 Air Traffic Visualization: COVID-19 Cases in China Were Likely 37 Times Higher Than Reported in Jan. 2020," *Research Reports* A-248-3, RAND, June 2020.

Mu Hai. "Yangtze River 'Has No Fish to Catch'" (牧海: 长江 "无鱼可捕"), *Liaowang* (瞭望), Beijing, Jan. 6, 2021.

Mu Ran. "Power Fetishism Is the Largest Cult" (木然: 权力拜物教是最大的邪教), *Dong Wang* (東網), Hong Kong, Nov. 29, 2014.

Mu Ran. "A Panorama of the Corruption of Chinese Academic Papers" (木然: 中国学术论文腐败全景图), *Caijing* (财经), Beijing, Oct. 24, 2014.

Mumola, Christopher, and Jennifer Karberg. "Drug Use and Dependence, State and Federal Prisoners, 2004," Washington, DC: U.S. Department of Justice, NCJ 213530, Jan. 2007.

Murray, Lisa. "Xi Rounds on China's Moral Vacuum," *Financial Review*, Feb. 24, 2015.

Mydral, Gunnar. *Asian Drama*. Oxford, UK: Oxford University Press, 1968.

Nan Shen. "PhDs from Peking University Applying for Jobs as Street Patrol" (南深: 北京大学博士考街道办城管), *Zhongguo jijin bao* (中国基金报), Apr. 13, 2022.

Nathan VanderKlippe. "Rich Chinese Angry over Cancelled Canadian Immigrant Program," *The Globe and Mail*, Mar. 4, 2014.

Nathan, Andrew. "Modern China's Original Sin: Tiananmen Square's Legacy of Repression," in Gideon Rose, ed. *Tiananmen and After*. New York: *Foreign Affairs* Ebook, 2014.

National Taxation Bureau. *Income Tax Formula for 2020–2021* (台北國稅局: 107 至109年度綜合所得稅速算公式), Taipei, 2021.

Naughton, Barry. "The Third Front: Defence Industrialization in the Chinese Interior," *The China Quarterly*, 115, 1988.

Naughton, Barry. *The Chinese Economy: Transitions and Growth*. Cambridge, MA: MIT Press, 2006.

Naughton, Berry. "A Perspective on Chinese Economics," in Anne Thurston, ed., *Engaging China: Fifty Years of Sino-American Relations*. New York: Columbia University Press, 2021.

NCSES. *Survey of Earned Doctorates 2019*, US National Science Foundation, 2020.

Neo Zion. "Supplement of the Meng Article" (补遗) and "Rejoinder of the Meng Article" (再论), cinacn.blogspot.com (经济金融人文群博客), Apr. 13 and May 16, 2014.

New Zealand Immigration. *Statistics & Research*, Wilmington, New Zealand, 2020.

Newman, Jonah. "Almost One-Third of All Foreign Students in U.S. Are from China," *The Chronicle of Higher Education*, Feb. 7, 2014.

News & Publication General Bureau. "Reform of China's Newspapers and Magazines Will Complete in 3 Years" (中国报纸期刊改革将在3年内完成), Beijing: Xinhua, Oct. 31, 2009.

Ng, Eric, and Xie Yu. "Xi Orders Arrest of CEFC Founder, Ending Entrepreneur's Stellar Rise," *South China Morning Post*, Hong Kong, Mar. 1, 2018.

Ng, Kwai Hang, and Xin He. *Embedded Courts: Judicial Decision-Making in China*. New York: Cambridge University Press, 2017.

Ni Guanghui. "CCP Central Committee Holds Meeting Celebrating the 120th Birthday of Comrade Mao Zedong" (倪光辉: 中共中央举行纪念毛泽东同志诞辰120周年座谈会), *Renmin ribao* (人民日报), Beijing, Dec. 27, 2013.

Nie Huihua. "The Political Logic of the Administrative Ranks of Chinese Officials" (聂辉华: 中国官员级别的政治逻辑), *The Financial Times in Chinese*, Sept. 8, 2015.

Nie Rimin, and Guo Xiaojing. "How Much Housing a Chinese Family Really Has" (聂日明, 郭晓菁: 中国家庭究竟有几套房), *Lujiazui pinlun* (陆家嘴评论), Shanghai, Nov. 10, 2021.

Nie Riming. *Who Controls China's Financial System* (聂日明: 谁掌控中国金融系统), SILF, 2021.

Ning Lizhong. "Nine World-Class Universities That Have Disappeared on Chinese Mainland" (宁利忠: 在中国大陆已经消失的9所世界级大学), *ScienceNet. cn* blog, June 8, 2014.

NISSTC. *Rules on Information Security of Data Collected by Connected Vehicles* (信安标委: 信息安全技术网联汽车采集数据的安全要求), National Information Security Standardization Technical Committee 全国信息安全标准化技术委员会, Beijing: Apr. 29, 2021.

Niu Baiyu. "US Stops the Medicine, China Still Can't Help It" (牛白羽: 美國已經停止吃藥,中國依舊藥不能停), *Dong wang* (東網), Hong Kong, Nov. 2, 2014.

Niyazov, Sukhayl. "China's Real GDP Growth Is Half the Reported Number," *Medium*, Sept. 23, 2019.

Noguchi, Yukio, and James M. Poterba. *Housing Markets in the United States and Japan*. Chicago: University of Chicago Press, 1994.

Nong Yibang. "Map of the Fraud Industry in China" (农一帮: 中国诈骗产业地图), *Tencent* (腾讯), Jan. 16, 2020.

North, Douglass C. *Institutions, Institutional Change and Economic Performance*. New York: Cambridge University Press,1990.

Northrop, Katrina. "Open Source: Despite Popular Perceptions That China Is a Black Box, Creative New Research Methods Are Shining a Light In," *The Wire-China*, Jan. 16, 2022.

NPC. "Authorizing Testing of Real Estate Tax Reform in Some Areas" (全国人大常委会授权国务院在部分地区开展房地产税改革试点工作), Beijing, Oct. 23, 2021.

NPC. *PRC Criminal Code* ((中华人民共和国刑法), Amended Version 10, Beijing, 2017.

NPC. *Amendment to the PRC Criminal Code*, Beijing, Dec. 26, 2020.

NPC. *Law on Personal Income Tax in the People's Republic of China* (中华人民共和国个人所得税法), Beijing (1980) 2018.

NPC. *Methods of Holding and Educating People of Prostitution and Whoring* (卖淫嫖娼收容教育办法), Beijing, 1993, revised 2011.

NPC. *PRC Law on Civil Servants* (中华人民共和国公务员法), Beijing (2005) Dec. 29, 2018.

NPC. *PRC National Security Law* (中华人民共和国国家安全法), enacted July 1, 2015.

NPC. *Resolution on Education through Labor* (关于劳动教养问题的决定), Beijing, Aug. 1957.

NPC. *Provisional Rules on Value-Added Tax in the People's Republic of China* (中华人民共和国增值税暂行条例) (1993) 2017.

NSF. *Doctorate Recipients from U.S. Universities.* Washington, DC: National Science Foundation, 2014 and 2020.

OECD and EUIPO. *Trends in Trade in Counterfeit and Pirated Goods*, Paris, France, 2019.

OECD Development Centre. *Economic Outlook for Southeast Asia, China and India 2014*, Paris: Nov. 2013.

OECD. "Main Determinants and Impacts of Foreign Direct Investment on China's Economy," *Working Papers on International Investment*, Paris: OECD, 2000.

OECD. "Trade in Fake Goods Is Now 3.3% of World Trade and Rising," Mar. 18, 2019.

Okina, Kunio. "The Asset Price Bubble and Monetary Policy: Japan's Experience in the Late 1980s and the Lessons." *Monetary and Economic Studies.* Tokyo: Bank of Japan, 19–21, 2001.

Oksenberg, Michel et al. *Beijing Spring, 1989: Confrontation and Conflict.* Armonk: Me Sharp, 1990.

Olsen, Alexa. "Leaked Files Offer Many Clues to Offshore Dealings by Top Chinese," ICIJ.org, Apr. 6, 2016.

Orlik, Thomas. *China: The Bubble That Never Pops.* New York: Oxford University Press, 2020.

Orwell, George. *1984.* London: Secker & Warburg, 1949.

Osawa, Juro, and Paul Mozur. "The Rise of China's Innovation Machine," *Wall Street Journal*, Jan. 16, 2014.

Osburg, John. *Anxious Wealth: Money and Morality among China's New Rich.* Stanford, CA: Stanford University Press, 2013.

Oshin, Olafimihan. "China Mocks India in Social Media Posts, Prompting Backlash," *The Hill*, May 3, 2021.

Osnos, Evan. "Confucius Comes Home: Move Over, Mao," *The New Yorker*, Jan. 13, 2014.

Osnos, Evan. *Age of Ambition: Chasing Fortune, Truth, and Faith in the New China*. New York: Farrar, 2014.

Oster, Shai, and Justina Lee. "UBS Raises Flag on China's $1 Trillion Overseas Debt Pile," *Bloomberg*, Dec. 23, 2014.

Ou La. " 'Nudity Loans' Revived: Lure Female Colleges Students" (欧拉: "裸贷" 复活: 诱惑女大学生), *Sina Tech News*, Beijing, Oct. 31, 2019.

Ou Li. "Insists on Party Manages Data, Ensures Data Security" (欧黎: 坚持党管 数据, 保障数据安全), *Qizhi* (旗帜), Aug. 2021.

Ouyang Chenyu. "Not Guilty Verdict Rate Has Lots of Room for Improvement" (欧阳晨雨: 无罪判决率还有不少提升空间), *Zhongguo qingnianbao* (中国青年 报), Beijing, Jan. 12, 2017.

Owyang, Michael, and Hannah Shell. "China's Economic Data: An Accurate Reflection, or Just Smoke and Mirrors?" Federal Reserve Bank of St. Louis, July 25, 2017.

Ouyang Junshan. *Farewell to Western Economics: The China Solution to the Construction of Community of Common Destiny* (欧阳君山: 别了, 西方经济学-构 建命运共同体中国方案). Beijing: Hualing, 2020.

Ownby, David. *Falun Gong and the Future of China*. New York: Oxford University Press, 2008.

Ozawa, Terutomo. "Veblen's Theories of 'Latecomer Advantage' and 'The Machine Process,'" *Journal of Economic Issues* 38(2), Jan. 2004: 379–388.

Page, Jeremy. "Wave of Unrest Rocks China: Threats to Social Order Increasingly Hit Cities," *Wall Street Journal*, June 15, 2011.

Palit, Amitendu. "Renewed Effort to Curb Pollution," *China Daily*, Beijing, Dec. 19, 2013.

Palmer, James. "For American Pundits, China Isn't a Country. It's a Fantasyland." *The Washington Post*, May 29, 2015.

Palmer, James. "Kept Women," *Aeon*, Oct. 10, 2013.

Pan Chenguang, and Wang Xianlei, eds. *Report on Human Talent Development in China—No. 3* (潘晨光 & 王宪磊: 中国人才发展报告 No. 3). Beijing: CASS, 2006.

Pan Hongmin. "Study on the Development and State of China's Private Enterprises" (潘宏铭: 中国私营企业发展和现状调查), *Zhonghuo shichang jingji* (中 国市场经济), Beijing, Feb. 2001.

Pan Qi. "Story of Metamorphosis of Ways to Evaluate Officials" (潘琦: 官员政 绩考核变形记), *Fazhi zhoumo* (法制周末), Beijing, Oct. 22, 2014.

Pan Suiming, and Huang Yingying. *Changes of Sex: Chinese Sexual Life in the 21st Century* (潘绥铭 & 黄盈盈: 性之变: 21世纪中国人的性生活). Beijing: Renmin daxue, 2013.

Pan Suiming. "Why Sexual Revolution Always Precedes Political Revolution" (潘绥铭: 为什么性革命总是发生在政治革命之前), *Sohu* (搜狐) *Blog*, Beijing, May 13, 2020.

Pan Xiao. "Oh My Life, Why Is It Getting Evermore Hopeless?" (潘晓: 人生的路啊, 怎么越走越窄?), *Zhongguo qingnian* (中国青年), Beijing, May 1980.

Pan Yi. "After 40 Years, Pan Xiao Discussion Is Not Obsolete" (潘祎: 四十年过去了, 潘晓讨论还没有过时), Personal Blog, May 28, 2020.

Pan, Jennifer. *Welfare for Autocrats: How Social Assistance in China Cares for Its Rulers*. New York: Oxford University Press, 2020.

Pan, Wei. "Toward a Consultative Rule of Law Regime in China," *Journal of Contemporary China* 12(34), 2003: 3–43.

Pang Chen, and Zhang Hanyue. "Smart Police to Get Lost Children Home Fast" (庞晟, 张瀚月: 智慧警务, 让失踪儿童快回家), *Renmin ribao-haiwaiban* (人民日报-海外版), Aug. 5, 2019.

Pang, Xiao-Ling et al. "Hacking Quantum Key Distribution via Injection Locking," *Quantum Physics*, Cornell University, arXiv: 1902.10423v3, Mar. 4, 2019.

Pantsov, Alexander, and Steven Levine. *Deng Xiaoping: A Revolutionary Life*. New York: Oxford University, 2015.

Pantsov, Alexander, and Steven Levine. *Mao: The Real Story*. New York: Simon & Schuster, 2012.

Parker, Edward et al. *An Assessment of the U.S. and Chinese Industrial Bases in Quantum Technology*. Santa Monica, CA: RAND, 2022.

Parton, Charles. "China Watching in the 'New Era': A Guide," *Explainer* No. GPE05, Council on Geostrategy, London, UK, Feb. 2022.

Pearson, Margaret, Meg Rithmire, and Kellee Tsai. "Party-State Capitalism in China," *Harvard Business School Working Paper*, No. 21-065, Nov. 2020.

Pei, Minxin. *China's Trapped Transition: The Limits of Developmental Autocracy*. Cambridge, MA: Harvard University Press, 2006.

Pei Pei. "Public Companies: Books Are Cooked This Way" (裴培: 上市公司-假账就是这样做出来的), *Asset Management* (理财), Shanghai, No. 12, 2005: 80–82.

Peking University. *Report on Graduates' Employment Quality* (北京大学毕业生就业质量报告), 2020 and 2021, Beijing, Dec. 2020 and Dec. 2021.

Peng Chenguang, ed. *2013 Annual Report on the Development of Chinese Talent* (潘晨光: 中国人才发展报告 2013). Beijing: Zhongguo shehui kexue, 2013.

Peng Tian. "A Tale of Two Systems," *Nature*, 520, S28–S30 (Apr. 30) 2015.

Peng Xizhi et al. *Results of Study on Social Changes in the Yangtze Delta* (彭希哲等: 长三角社会变迁调查结果), Shanghai: Fudan daxue, 2014.

Peng Xu. "Haze, Air Pollution, and Health in China," *The Lancet* 382(9910), Dec. 21, 2013.

Peng Yi et al. "'The Chinese Pain' of the Coalminers" (潘毅等: 煤矿工人的"中国痛"), *Nanfeng chuan* (南风窗), Guangzhou, Sept. 2, 2013.

People's Bank of China. *Report of Financial Data of Jan.* 2022 (中国人民银行: 2022年1月金融统计数据报告), Beijing, Feb. 10, 2022.

People's Bank of China. *Report on China's Urban Residents' Family Assets and Debt in 2019* (2019年中国城镇居民家庭资产负债情况调查), Beijing, Apr. 25, 2020.

Permanent Subcommittee on Investigations. *Threats to the U.S. Research Enterprise: China's Talent Recruitment Plans*, US Senate, Nov. 8, 2019.

Perper, Rosie. "Chinese Human Rights Lawyer Disappears after Posting a Letter on WeChat Criticizing the Government's Response to COVID-19," *Business Insider*, May 11, 2020.

Perry, Elizabeth, and Mark Selden, eds. *Chinese Society: Change, Conflict and Resistance*, 3rd edition, London: Routledge, 2010.

Peterson, Glen. *Overseas Chinese in the People's Republic of China*. London: Routledge, 2014.

Pettis, Michael. "What Does Evergrande Meltdown Mean for China?" Carnegie Endowment, Sept. 20, 2021.

Pettis, Michael. "China Does Not Need to Grow at 7.5%," Carnegie Endowment, July 18, 2013.

Pettis, Michael. *Avoiding the Fall: China's Economic Restructuring*, Carnegie Endowment, 2013.

Pettis, Michael. *The Great Rebalancing: Trade, Conflict, and the Perilous Road Ahead for the World Economy*. Princeton, NJ: University Press, 2014.

Phelps, Glenn, and Steve Crabtree. "Worldwide, Median Household Income about $10,000," Gallup, Dec. 13, 2013.

Phillips, Michael. "Overview of Suicide in China," *Psychiatric Times* 20(11), Jan. 2003.

Philosophy Editors. "Basic Features of Socialist and Communist Ethics" (社会主义和共产主义道德的基本特征), CSSN (中国社会科学网), Beijing, Apr. 15, 2019.

Pienkowski, Alex. "Debt Limits and the Structure of Public Debt," IMF, May 2017.

Pils, Eva, and Joshua Rosenzweig. "Beijing Confronts a New Kind of Dissident, The New Citizen Movement Can Continue Even as Xu Zhiyong Sits in Jail," *Wall Street Journal*, Jan. 26, 2014.

Plagiarius, Aktion. "Negative Award Plagiarius 2020: The Boldest Counterfeit Products of the Year," Frankfurt, Germany, Feb. 7, 2020.

Plato. *The Republic*. New York: Basic Books, 1991.

Polly, Matthew. *American Shaolin*. New York: Gotham, 2007.

Pompeo, Mike, and Miles Yu. "The Triumph and Tragedy of 1989," *The Hill*, June 4, 2021.

Population Training Center. *Demographics Theory, National Condition, and the Practice of Birth-planning* (人口理论, 国情, 计划生育实践), Beijing: Zhongguo renkou, 1991.

Porter, Richard, and Ruth Judson. "The Location of US Currency: How Much Is Abroad?" *Federal Reserve Bulletin*, Oct. 1996.

Potter, Sulamith. "The Position of Peasants in Modern China's Social Order," *Modern China*, 9, 1993.

Potts, Malcolm. "China's One Child Policy: The Policy That Changed the World," *British Medical Journal* 333, Aug. 2006.

Powell, Bill. "A Losing Battle against Chinese Piracy," *Time*, Apr. 10, 2007.

Pratt, Timothy. "Chinese Students Found Cheating to Get into U.S. Colleges," CNN, July 1, 2014.

PRC Constitution (中华人民共和国宪法), Beijing: NPC, 1956–2018.

PRC Customs. *Import-Export of China 2019* (2019年度中国进出口情况报告), Beijing, 2020.

Premikha, M. et al. "Comparative Effectiveness of mRNA and Inactivated Whole Virus Vaccines against COVID-19 Infection and Severe Disease in Singapore," *Clinical Infectious Diseases*, Apr. 12, 2022.

Price, Monroe, and Daniel Dayan, eds., *Owning the Olympics: Narratives of the New China*. Ann Arbor: University of Michigan Press, 2008.

Pritchett, Lant, and Marla Spivack. *Estimating Income/Expenditure Differences across Populations: New Fun with Old Engel's Law*, Center for Global Development, 2013.

Psaki, Jen. "Press Briefing by Press Secretary," Washington, DC: White House, Mar. 18, 2022.

Pu Yang (Jiang Zongfu). *Way of Officials* (普扬/姜宗福: 官路). Beijing: Wenyi, 2011.

Publius Cornelius Tacitus. *The Annals of Tacitus-Book 3*, translated by A. J. Woodman and R. H. Martin. New York: Cambridge University Press, 2004.

Qi E Hao. "Judge Liu Deshan Found Innocent after 15 Months in Jail" (企鹅号: 刘德山法官被关押15个月后被判无罪), *Tencent xinwen* (腾讯新闻), Dec. 14, 2019.

Qi Yanbin. "Five Insurances and One Fund Accounts for Nearly Half of Wages" (齐雁冰: "五险一金"占工资额近半), *Beijing qingnian bao* (北京青年报), Jan. 5, 2015.

Qi Zhifeng. "World Media Views China: The Absurdity of Mao's Birthday" (齐之丰: 世界媒体看中国-毛诞的荒诞), *VOA in Chinese*, Washington, DC, Dec. 25, 2013.

Qian Jiang. "37 Years Ago, the People Who Opened the Door to Study Abroad" (钱江: 37年前, 推开留学之门的那些人), *Zhonghua dushu bao* (中华读书报), Beijing, July 22, 2015.

Qian Liqun. *1948: Chaos of the Heaven and Earth* (钱理群: 1948 天地玄黄). Jinan: Jiaoyu (1998) 2002.

Qian Liqun. *Mao Zedong Era and Post–Mao Zedong Era 1949–2009* (钱理群: 毛泽东时代和后毛泽东时代), two volumes. Taipei: Lianjing Press, 2012.

Qian Qiujun. "New Normal of Central Bank's Release of Water" (钱秋君: 央行放水新常态), *Huaxia shibao* (华夏时报), Beijing, Oct. 22, 2014.

Qian Yang. "Signing Off Death Penalties, Torture of the Soul" (钱杨: 死刑复核, 灵魂折磨), *Personalities* (人物), Beijing, No. 1, 2015.

Qiao Jialan. "Why I Resigned Professor Job in Shanghai after Ten Years" (乔葭兰: 十年后, 我为什么要辞掉上海的大学教职), *China Digital Times*, Jan. 27, 2022.

Qidian Renwen. "Why Chinse Want to Be Officials" (起点人文: 中国人为什么想当官), WEMP Blog, Oct. 23, 2020.

Qin Banliang. "After Quan Hongchan Earned Championship" (秦半两: 全红婵夺冠之后), *Huxiu wang* (虎嗅网), Beijing, Aug. 10, 2021.

Qin Hui. "The Division and the State of the Right and Left in China" (秦晖: 中国左右派的区分与现状), *Zhengshang neican* (政商内参), Dec. 1, 2014.

Qin Hui. "The Past and Present of Food Safety" (秦晖: 食品安全的过去与现在), *Nanfang zhoumo* (南方周末), Guangzhou, Feb. 28, 2014.

Qin Hui. "The Road of Chemical Fertilizers with Chinese Characteristics" (秦晖: 有中国特色的化肥之路), *Aisixiang* (爱思想), Aug. 10, 2020.

Qin Hui. *Out of the Imperial System* (秦晖: 走出帝制). Beijing: Qunyan, 2015.

Qin Hui. "China Uses Its 'Low Human Rights Advantage' to Forge Shocking Competitiveness" (秦晖: 中国以 "低人权优势" 造就惊人竞争力), *EEO* (经济观察网), Beijing, July 10, 2008.

Qin Quanyao. "How Much Did It Cost Sleeping with a Woman during Three-Year-Disaster? (秦全耀: 三年灾害时睡一次女人多少钱?), blog.sina.com.cn/laotuzaizi, Dec. 21, 2012.

Qin Siqing. "Cut 90% of China's Academic Research Would Affect Nothing" (秦四清: 砍掉中国90%的学术研究什么也不影响), *Wangyi* (网易), Beijing, July 16, 2021.

Qiu Baoxing. "State of Water Security and Policies in the Cities of Our Country" (仇保兴: 我国城市水安全现状与对策), *Urban Development Studies* (城市发展研究), Beijing, 20(12), 2013.

Qiu Feng. "Rethink the Damage of Humanity by the Birth Planning" (秋风: 反思计划生育对人性的破坏), *Financial Times in Chinese*, Jan. 16, 2015.

Qiu Huizuo. *Qiu Huizuo Memoirs* (邱會作回憶錄). Hong Kong: Xin shiji, 2011.

Qiu Lin. "Chinese Stock Market Already Has Kundalini Syndrome" (邱林: 中国股市已走火入魔), *Dongfang caifu* (东方财富), Jan. 15, 2014.

Qiu Rui. "Decode the Confessions of Senior Mainland Officials" (邱锐: 解密大陆高官忏悔录), *Fenghuang zhoukan* (鳳凰週刊), Hong Kong, No. 27 (Sept. 2), 2015.

Qiu Ruixian. "College Students from the Rural Decline in Proportion Every Year" (邱瑞贤: 农村大学生比例逐年降低), *Guangzhou ribao* (广州日报), Jan. 23, 2009.

Qiu, Jane. "China Targets Top Talent from Overseas: Package Aims to Entice High-Flyers Back Home," *Nature* 457(522), Jan. 29, 2009.

Qun Shuo. "Seek Full Accountability on Vacuous Employment" (群硕: 将吃空饷问责到底), *Diyi caijing ribao* (第一财经日报), Shanghai, Oct. 8, 2014.

Qun Shuo. "Two Locals in Henan Respond to 'Mutated Education Camps'" (群硕: 河南两地回应"变异劳教"), *Legal Evening News* (法制晚报), Beijing, Feb. 13, 2014.

Qun Shuo. "The Embarrassment of Self-Admission" (群硕: 自主招生的尴尬), *Diyi caijing ribao* (第一财经日报), Beijing, Dec. 25, 2013.

Rachman, Gideon. "Eric Li: 'How Do You Block a Country of 1.4bn People?'" *Financial Times*, Feb. 7, 2020.

Ramzy, Austin. "China Sentences Hong Kong Bookseller Gui Minhai to 10 Years in Prison," *The New York Times*, Feb. 26, 2020.

Ramzy, Austin. "In China, an Ingenious Scheme for Getting Out of Jail Early," *The New York Times*, Jan. 20, 2015.

Ran Yunfei. *Leading to Empire of Competing for Idiocy* (冉云飞: 通往比傻帝国). Guangzhou: Huacheng, 2007.

Ranger, Steve. "Huawei, 5G Networks and Security: How Did We End Up Here?" ZD Net, July 14, 2020.

Rank, Michael. "Orwell's 1984 in China: Big Brother in Every Bookshop," *The Asia-Pacific Journal* 11(23.2), June 9, 2014.

Ransmeier, Johanna. *Sold People: Traffickers and Family Life in North China.* Cambridge, MA: Harvard University Press, 2017.

Rao Yi. "China's Trend of Making Eunuchs Not Yet Ended" (饶毅: 中国的太监化现象尚未终结), *Lingdao wencui* (领导文萃), Fuzhou, No. 17, 2014: 28–30.

Rao Yi. "Personnel System in Chinese Colleges" (饶毅: 中国高校人事制度), *Caixin*, June 11, 2021.

Rao Yi. "What Is behind the Long Ignorance of Tu Youyou Is the Obstacle of Innovation" (饶毅: 长期忽略屠呦呦背后因素是创新发展的阻力), *Kexue wang* (科学网), Oct. 7, 2015.

Rapoza, Kenneth. "In China, Why Piracy Is Here to Stay," *Forbes*, July 22, 2012.

Rauhala, Emily. "China's Big Test," *Time*, Apr. 13, 2015: 36–41.

Ravitch, Diane. "The Myth of Chinese Super Schools," *The New York Review of Books*, Nov. 20, 2014.

Reardon, Lawrence. *A Third Way: The Origins of China's Current Economic Development Strategy.* Cambridge, MA: Harvard University Asia Center, 2021.

Refugee Council. "Statistics on People Seeking Asylum in the Community," Canberra, Australia, May 8, 2020.

Reischauer, Haru Matsukata. *Samurai and Silk: A Japanese and American Heritage.* Cambridge, MA: Belknap Press of Harvard University Press, 1986.

Ren Zeping et al. *Report on Chinese Residential Real Estate Market 2019* (任泽平, 中国住房市值报告2019), Beijing, Oct. 23, 2019.

Ren Zeping. "Comparison of S&T Power in China and the US" (任泽平: 中美科技实力对比), Beijing, Hengda Institute, Feb. 16, 2020.

Renda Chongyang. "The Works by Renda Chongyang in 2021" (人大重阳2021年工作), Beijing, Dec. 30, 2021.

Reng Pengfei et al. "E-fraud" (任鹏飞等: 电信诈骗), *Jingji cankao bao* (经济参考报), Beijing, Oct. 27 and 28, 2014.

Reporters Without Borders. *World Press Freedom Index*. Paris: Reporters sans frontières, 2020.

Restall, Hugo. "China's Crisis of Morality," *Wall Street Journal*, Aug. 22–24, 2003.

RFA (Radio Free Asia). The "981 首长健康工程," "Health-Care of CCP Leaders Aims at 150 Years of Life" (中共领导人保健以150岁为目标), Radio Free Asia. Sept. 16, 2019.

Rhoads, Robert, Xiaoyang Wang, et al. *China's Rising Research Universities: A New Era of Global Ambition*. Baltimore, MD: Johns Hopkins University Press, 2014.

Rhodes, Emily. "China Bans Haruki Murakami's '1984': George Orwell Would Have Seen the Irony," *The Spectator*, Sept. 27, 2012.

Rhodes, Emily. "How '1984' Is China? Complexities of Censorship in the People's Republic," *The Chinese Nightingale*, Apr. 3, 2013.

Ri Du. "'Special Provision' for Senior Officials—from Yanan to Zhongnanhai" (热度: 高官"特供"-从延安到中南海), *Wechat Blog* (微信公众号), Oct. 16, 2021.

RIETI. "Why China's Investment Efficiency is Low," Tokyo: Research Institute of Economy, June 18, 2004.

Rigger, Shelley. *The Tiger Leading the Dragon: How Taiwan Propelled China's Economic Rise*. Lanham, MD: Rowman & Littlefield, 2021.

Ringen, Stein. "China's Heavy Tax Burden Heightens Risk of Worker Revolt and More Repression," *South China Morning Post*, Hong Kong, May 4, 2015.

Ringen, Stein. *The Perfect Dictatorship: China in the 21st Century*. Hong Kong: Hong Kong University Press, 2016.

Riordan, Primrose et al. "China Covid-19 Tsar Pushed Treatments without Revealing Business Ties." *Financial Times*, Apr. 24, 2022.

Ritchie, Hannah, and Max Roser. "CO_2 and Greenhouse Gas Emissions," *OurWorldInData*, 2020.

Roberts, Margaret E. *Censored: Distraction and Diversion Inside China's Great Firewall*. Princeton, NJ: Princeton University Press, 2018.

Robertson, Matthew et al. "Analysis of Official Deceased Organ Donation Data Casts Doubt on the Credibility of China's Organ Transplant Reform," *BMC Medical Ethics* 20(79), Nov. 2019.

Robertson, Matthew. *Organ Procurement and Extrajudicial Execution in China*. Washington, DC: Victims of Communism Memorial Foundation, Mar. 10, 2020.

Rock, Michael, and Heidi Bonnett. "The Comparative Politics of Corruption," *World Development* 32(6), June 2004: 999–1017.

Rodrik, Dani. "Second-Best Institutions," *American Economic Review: Papers & Proceedings* 98(2), 2008.

Rodrik, Dani. *One Economics, Many Recipes: Globalization, Institutions, and Economic Growth*. Princeton, NJ: Princeton University Press, 2009.

Rogers, Benedict. "Where Is Gao Zhisheng?" *UCA News*, Apr. 30, 2019.

Rohde, Robert, and Richard Muller. "Air Pollution in China: Mapping of Concentrations and Sources," San Francisco, CA: *PLOS One*, 2015.

Ronald Kroeze et al. *Anticorruption in History: From Antiquity to the Modern Era.* Oxford, UK: Oxford University Press, 2018.

Ronen, Shahar et al. "Links That Speak: The Global Language Network and Its Association with Global Fame," *Proceedings of National Academy of Science* 111(52), 2014: E5616–E5622.

Rosen, Daniel. "China's Economic Reckoning: The Price of Failed Reforms," *Foreign Affairs*, July/Aug. 2021.

Rosen, Gary. "My Short March through China," *Commentary*, December 2007.

Ross, Michael. "The Political Economy of the Resource Curse," *World Politics*, 51–52, 1999.

Ross, Michael. "What Have We Learned about the Resource Curse?" *Annual Review of Political Science* 18, 2015: 239–259.

Rousseau, Jean-Jacques. *The Confessions*, translated by Angela Scholar. New York: Oxford University Press, Book 9 (1782) 2000.

Rozelle, Scott, and Natalie Hell. *Invisible China: How the Urban-Rural Divide Threatens China's Rise.* Chicago: University of Chicago Press, 2020.

Ruan Tang. "Yes, I'm Running Out of Food" (阮唐: 是的, 我快断粮了) and "Yes, I'm Not Dead Yet" (是的, 我还没死), *Wechat Blog* (微信公众号), Apr. 8, 2022; Apr. 11, 2022.

Ruslan, Medzhitov et al. "Investigate the origins of COVID-19," *Science* 372, May 14, 2021.

Rweyemamu, Aisia. "Kagasheki Unveils Chinese Ivory Haul in Dar es Salaam," *IPP Media*, Nov. 5, 2013.

Sabrie, Gilles. "Caofeidian, the Chinese Eco-city that Became a Ghost Town," *The Guardian*, July 23, 2014.

Sachs, Jeffery, Hu Yongtai, and Yang Xiaokai. "Economic Reform and Constitutional Reorientation" (J. Sachs, 胡永泰, 杨小凯: 经济改革和宪政转轨), *Jingjixue jikan* (经济学季刊), Beijing, 2(4), July 2003.

SAFE. "Chinese Foreign Debt and National Economy and Foreign Currency Income, 1985–2019," (1985–2019年中国外债与国民经济外汇收入), Beijing: SAFE, 2021.

Safeguard Defenders. "China Unleashes Forced Confessions to Control Coronavirus Rumours," Spain, Jan. 29 2020.

Saich, Tony. *From Rebel to Ruler: One Hundred Years of the Chinese Communist Party.* Cambridge, MA: Harvard University Press, 2021.

Santos, Gonçalo. *Chinese Village Life Today: Building Families in an Age of Transition.* Seattle: University of Washington Press, 2021.

Sapio, Flora. "Shuanggui and Extralegal Detention in China," *China Information* 22(1), 2008.

Sauer, Abe. "Supply and Demand: China's Counterfeit Market Is Booming," *Brand Channel*, Oct. 2 2013.

Saxegaard, Magnus. "Safe Debt and Uncertainty in Emerging Markets," IMF, Dec. 2014.

Schaeffer, Katherine. "6 Facts about Economic Inequality in the U.S.," *Pew*, Feb. 7, 2020.

Schein, Edgar. *Coercive Persuasion: A Socio-psychological Analysis of the "Brainwashing" of American Civilian Prisoners by the Chinese Communists.* New York: Norton, 1971.

Schiefelbein, Mark. "Chinese Authorities Use 'Gait' Surveillance to Identify People by Their Body Shape and Walk," *AP News*, Beijing, Nov. 6, 2018.

Schmid, Jon, and Fei-Ling Wang. "Beyond National Innovation Systems: Incentives, Politics, Culture, and China's Innovation Performance," *Journal of Contemporary China* 26 (104), 2017.

Schneider, Leonid. "The Full-Service Paper Mill and Its Chinese Customers," *For Better Science*, Jan. 24, 2020.

Schrad, Mark Lawrence. *Vodka Politics: Alcohol, Autocracy, and the Secret History of the Russian State.* New York: Oxford University Press, 2014.

Schoenmakers, Kevin. "Telling China's Story, Poorly," *China Media Project*, Aug. 15, 2022.

Schwarcz, Vera. *Time for Telling Truth is Running Out: Conversations with Zhang Shenfu.* New Haven, CT: Yale University Press, 1992.

Scissors, Derek. "Estimating the True Number of China's COVID-19 Cases," American Enterprise Institute, Apr. 7, 2020.

Scissors, Derek. "GDP Misleads on China and the US," *China-US Focus*, Oct. 28, 2014.

Scissors, Derek. "The Great Fall from Grace: Is China's Rise Over?" *The National Interest*, Nov. 12, 2014.

Second People's Court of Tianjin. "First Verdict on the Lai Xiaomin Case of Bribery, Embezzlement, and Polygamy" (赖小民受贿、贪污、重婚案一审宣判), Jan. 5, 2021.

Segal, Adam. *The Hacked World Order: How Nations Fight, Trade, Maneuver, and Manipulate in the Digital Age.* New York: Public Affairs, 2016.

Semple, Kirk, Joseph Goldstein, and Jeffrey E. Singer. "Asylum Fraud in Chinatown: An Industry of Lies," *The New York Times*, Feb. 23, 2014.

Sen, Amartya. *Inequality Reexamined.* Oxford, UK: Oxford University Press, 2003.

Setser, Brad. "Lessons from Phase One of the Trade War with China." New York: CFR, Jan. 31, 2020.

Setser, Brad. "U.S.-China Trade War: How We Got Here." New York: CFR, July 9, 2018.

Sha Xueliang. "Multiple Districts in Beijing Rectify 'Vacuous-Employment'" (沙雪良: 北京多区整治"吃空饷"), *Beijing zhidao* (北京知道), July 30, 2019.

Sha Yexin. "Culture of 'Propaganda'" (沙叶新: "宣传"文化), *Aisixiang* (爱思想), Beijing, Sept. 5, 2005.

Shah, Neil. "Immigrants to U.S. from China Top Those from Mexico," *Wall Street Journal*, May 3, 2015.

Shan Yinwen, and Li Chunyi. "Big Monster Got Me" (单颖文, 李纯一: 有大怪兽 缠着我), *Wenhui xueren* (文汇学人), Shanghai, Dec. 5, 2014: 6–10.

Shang Guoqiang. "Three Richest Chinese Made to Retire" (尚國強: 中國三大首 富被退休), *Up Media* (上報), Taipei, Sept. 25, 2019.

Shao Daosheng. "Corrupted Officials All Oversexed" (邵道生: 自古贪官多好色), *Xinhua*, Apr. 4, 2007.

Shapiro, Judith. *China's Environmental Challenges*. Malden, MA: Polity Press, 2012.

Shapiro, Judith. *Mao's War against Nature: Politics and the Environment in Revolutionary China*. New York: Cambridge University Press, 2001.

Sharma, Ruchir. "China's Illusory Growth Numbers," *Wall Street Journal*, Oct. 20, 2013.

Sharma, Yojana. "'Thousand Talents' Academic Return Scheme under Review," *University World News*, No. 273, May 25, 2013.

Shea, Nina. "The CCP Wages a Second Genocide—against Falun Gong," *National Review*, Feb. 4, 2022.

Shen Du. "Story of Sale of Offices by Xinyang Public Security Chief" (沈度: 信 阳原公安局长), *The Paper* (澎拜), Shanghai, Oct. 19, 2019.

Shen Hua. "On the Passing of China's People's Congress 'Voting Machine'" (申华: 中国人大"举手机器"申纪兰身后的话题), VOA, Washington, DC, July 6, 2020.

Shen Moke. "Zhengzhou Flood, Reservoirs Collapse: We Want Truth, Not Murky Narratives" (沈默克: 郑州洪灾, 水库溃坝: 我们要真相, 不要糊涂账), *China Digital Times*, July 20, 2021.

Shen Yanhui. "100 Thousand Emigrate to Vietnam, Myanmar, Cambodia, Laos, and Thailand" (谌彦辉: 云南十万边民移居越老東泰缅), *Fenghuang zhoukan* (凤凰周刊), No. 19, 2007.

Shen Yurong. "The Protection and Destruction of Beijing City" (申予荣: 北 京城垣的保护与拆除), *Beijing guihua jianshi* (北京规划建设), No. 2, 1999.

Sheng Keyi. "China's Poisonous Waterways," *The New York Times*, Apr. 6, 2014: SR4.

Sheng Ping. "'Fazhi' Media Renamed to Show the Progress of Fazhi Propaganda" (昇平: "法制"媒体更名彰显法治宣传进步), *Renmin wang* (人民网), Beijing, July 30, 2020.

Sheng Wenqian, and Wang Dongfang. "Five Tiers of Higher Education in the World" (沈文钦, 王东芳: 世界高等教育体系的五大梯队), *Gaodeng jiaoyu yanjiu* (高等教育研究), No. 1, 2014.

Sheng Xiang. "Out of Control Counterfeit and Bad Goods in the Rural Caused by Missing Regulation (盛翔: 农村假冒伪劣泛滥源于监管缺失), *Fazhi ribao* (法制日报), Beijing, Jan. 26, 2014.

Sheng Xue. *Dark Inside of Yuanhua Case* (盛雪: 远华案黑幕). Hong Kong: Minjing, 2001.

Sheng Xuebin. *Two Thousand Years of Qin System* (谌旭彬: 秦制两千年). Hangzhou: Renmin, 2021.

Sheng Yang, and Chen Yushan. "Investigation Says Foreign Tourists Continuously Decrease" (沈洋, 陈毓珊: 调查称中国入境游人数持续下降), Beijing: Xinhua, Jan. 14, 2015.

Sheng Yun. "Antibiotics Found in Rivers Like Yangtze" (盛云: 长江等河流检出抗生素), CCTV, Dec. 25, 2014.

Shenghua Lu, and Hui Wang. "How Political Connections Exploit Loopholes in Procurement Institutions for Government Contracts: Evidence from China," *Governance*, Sept. 22, 2022.

Shenzhen Bureau of Justice. *Rules on Digital Data in Shenzhen* (深圳司法局: 深圳经济特区数据条例), Shenzhen, July 15, 2020.

Shepard, Wade. "Alibaba's Taobao Is Once Again Branded A 'Notorious Market' For Counterfeit Goods," *Forbes*, Jan. 26, 2018.

Sheridan, Michael. "China's Elite Eat Pure Food as Babies Die," *Sunday Times*, London, Sept. 28, 2008.

Shi Hanbin. "My Take on Views of Injustice and Lying-Flat" (时寒冰: 我来评评不平躺平之评), *Sina* (新浪) *Blog*, May 30, 2021.

Shi Po. "Liu Daoyu: 22 Years after Being Fired as President of Wuhan University" (石破: 刘道玉: 被免除武大校长22年), *Nanfeng chuan* (南风窗), Guangzhou, Jan. 21, 2010.

Shi Ruijie. "Consultative Democracy Is the Unique Form and Special Advantage of Our Socialist Democratic Polity" (史瑞杰: 协商民主是我国社会主义民主政治的特有形式和独特优势), *Guangming ribao* (光明日报), Mar. 23, 2018.

Shi Shusi. "Rural Ap Is Hard to Get to College, Even Harder to Find a Job" (石述思: 农村孩子上大学难就业更难), *Sina News* (新浪新闻), Dec. 29, 2013.

Shi Yaojiang et al., "Drop-outs of Middle School in Rural China" (史耀疆: 中国农村中学辍学调查), *Zhongguo gaige* (中国改革), No. 2, 2016.

Shi Yuan. "Han Dynasty's Recuperating and Recovery Policy" (史源: 汉朝的休养生息政策), *Zhengce liaowang* (政策瞭望), No. 12, 2008.

Shi Zhichang. "This Round of Internal Circulation Will Change Everyone's Wealth" (势之场: 这轮经济内循环, 将改变所有人的财富) *Xintiandi Caijing* (新天地财经), Oct. 18, 2020.

Shi, Hao, and Shaoqing Huang. "How Much Infrastructure Is Too Much? A New Approach and Evidence from China," *World Development* 56, 2014: 272–286.

Shira, Dezan. "Land Rights in Vietnam," *Vietnam Briefing*, June 25, 2019.

Shou Ye. "Wang Jianlin's Waterloo" (兽爷: 王健林的滑铁卢), *Huxiu* (虎嗅), Dec. 11, 2017.

Shu Yun. *One Hundred Questions about 9/13* (舒云: 百问九一三). Hong Kong: Mingjing, 2011.

Shuai Bang. "10G Photos of Shocking Nudity Loans" (率邦: 10G裸贷照片触目惊心), *Sohu* (搜狐), Dec. 6, 2016.

Shuai Hao. "'Great Leap Forward' of Maotai Production in Three years of Difficulty" (帅好: 三年困难时期"茅台酒生产大跃进"), *Wenhui dushu* (文汇读书), Shanghai, Nov. 8, 2011.

Shuai Hao. "Chinese Painters during the Years of Famine" (帅好: 饥饿年代的中国画家), *Sina shoucang* (新浪收藏), Beijing, Mar. 20, 2013. Updated as "飢荒年代的中國畫家" in *Open* (開放), Hong Kong, Feb. 3, 2021.

Shue, Vivienne. "Regimes of Resonance: Cosmos, Empire, and Changing Technologies of CCP Rule," *Modern China*, Jan. 11, 2022.

Shuili Jiayuan. "¥7 trillion Market for Cleaning Blackened Stinky Rivers" (水利家园: 7000亿黑臭河整治市场), *Sohu xinwen* (搜狐新闻), Nov. 10, 2021.

Shum, Desmond. "Every Chinese Merchant Is a White Glove" (沈栋: 每个中国商人都是白手套), RFA (Radio Free Asia), Feb. 4, 2022.

Shum, Desmond. *Red Roulette: An Insider's Story of Wealth, Power, Corruption, and Vengeance in Today's China*. New York: Simon & Schuster, 2021.

Shuo Liweng. "Ye Jianying Is the Vanguard of Attacking Luo Ruiqin" (蓑笠翁: 叶剑英—批判罗瑞卿的急先锋), *China News Digest* (华夏文摘), Gaithersburg, MD, No. 652, June 10, 2008.

Si Gong. "Chinese Credibility Has Incredibly Deteriorated" (思公: 中国诚信竟然如此恶化), CRI on Line (国际在线), Nov. 29, 2006.

Si Weijiang. "Era of Lying Flat" (斯伟江: 躺平时代), *Tencent* (腾讯) *Blog*, May 23, 2021.

Si Yang. "Any Group to Be Reorganized as a Financial Stock Company under Central Bank" (思洋: 蚂蚁集团将重组为央行监管的金融控股公司), *Sohu* (搜狐), Beijing, Jan. 19, 2021.

Sicular, Terry. "The Challenge of High Inequality in China," *Inequality in Focus*, Washington, DC: World Bank 2(2), Aug. 2013.

Sima Qian. *Records of the Grand Historian-Qin Shi Huang* (司马迁: 史记-秦始皇本纪). Beijing: Zhonghua shuju (2nd century BCE), 2013.

Sima Qingyang, and Ouyang Longmen. *Newly Discovered Zhou Enlai* (司馬清揚 & 歐陽龍門: 新發現的周恩來), 2 volumes. Hong Kong: Mingjing, 2009.

Sima Qingyang. *Zhou Enlai and Lin Biao* (司马清扬: 周恩来与林彪). Hong Kong: Mingjing, 2012.

Simpson, Peter. "Chinese Expats Caught Eating Endangered Zimbabwe Tortoises," *The Telegraph*, London, Feb. 19, 2012.

Singer, Charles et al., eds. *A History of Technology*. 8 volumes. New York: Oxford University Press, 1954–1984.

Sirkin, Harold et al. *The Shifting Economics of Global Manufacturing: How Cost Competitiveness Is Changing Worldwide*. Boston: Boston Consulting Group, 2014.

Sisci, Francesco. "What Are China's Top Economic Weaknesses?" *Asia Times*, May 27, 2015.

Siwei Jinrong. "A New De-leveraging Campaign May Have Already Started (四维金融: 新一轮去杠杆运动可能已经开始了), *Sohu caijing* (搜狐财经), Nov. 14, 2020.

Slotkin, Jason. "Global COVID-19 Deaths Surpass 400,000," *NPR News*, June 7, 2020.

Smarlo, Ma. *Witness the Secret History of the CCP* (司马璐: 中共历史的见证). New York: Mirror, 2004.

Smith, Arthur. *Chinese Characteristics*. 5th edition. New York: Fleming H. Revell, 1894.

Smith, Benjamin, and David Waldner, eds., *Rethinking the Resource Curse*. New York: Cambridge University Press, 2021.

Smith, Richard. "Climate Arsonist Xi Jinping: A Carbon-Neutral China with a 6% Growth Rate?" *Real-world Economics Review*, No. 94, 2020(I).

Smith, Richard. *China's Engine of Environmental Collapse*. London, UK: Pluto, 2020(II).

Smout, Alistair. "UK Lockdown a Week Earlier Could Have Halved COVID-19 Death Toll, Scientist Says," Reuters, June 10, 2020.

Smyth, Jamie. "Australia: The Campus Fight over Beijing's Influence," *Financial Times*, Nov. 12, 2019.

Solinger, Dorothy, and Yiyang Hu. "Welfare, Wealth and Poverty in Urban China: The *Dibao* and Its Differential Disbursement," *The China Quarterly* 211, Sept. 2012: 741–764.

Solow, Robert. "A Contribution to the Theory of Economic Growth," *The Quarterly Journal of Economics* 70(1), Feb. 1956: 65–94.

Solzhenitsyn, Aleksandr. *The Gulag Archipelago, 1918–1956*. New York: Harper, 1973.

Song Dailun. "Famous Graves Destroyed during Wenge: From Confucius to Li Hongzhang (宋代伦: 文革時期被挖墳的歷史名人: 從孔夫子到李鴻章), *Takungpao* (大公報), July 16, 2013.

Song Quancheng. "Sociological Analysis on Gender Imbalance at Birth" (宋全成: 出生性别比偏高的人口社会学分析), *Shandong daxue xuebao* (山东大学学报), Jinan, No. 2, 2014.

Song Wu. "To Break the Chinese Quagmire of 26 People Feeding One Official (宋勿: 破解26人养1名官员的中国困局), *Guoji xianqu daobao* (国际先驱导报), Beijing, Mar. 14, 2005.

Song Yongyi, ed. *Classified Archives of Guangxi during Wenge* (宋永毅: 广西文革机密档案资料), Mingjing, 2016.

Song Yongyi. "'Cultural Revolution' and the Irrational Mao Zedong" (宋永毅: "文化大革命"和非理性的毛泽东), *Dangdai zhongguo yanjiu* (当代中国研究), 4, 2008.

Song Yongyi. "Hidden History: Liu Shaoqi's Special Contribution to 'Wenge'" (宋永毅: 被掩藏的历史: 刘少奇对"文革"的独特贡献), *Dangdai zhongguo yanjiu* (当代中国研究), 94, 2006.

Song Yuntao. "East is Red Again" (宋云涛: 东方又红), *Tencent shipin* (腾讯视频), 2016. youtube.com/watch?v=8krIYuJ0pwA

Song Zhaolai. *China's Big Game of Anti-corruption in China* (宋赵来: 中国反腐大棋局), monograph, Beijing, 2014.

Sparshott, Jeffrey. "WSJ Survey: China's Growth Statements Make U.S. Economists Skeptical," *Wall Street Journal*, Sept. 11, 2015.

Stassopoulos, Tassos. "China Emerges as a Global Innovator," *Financial Times*, Apr. 30, 2015.

State Administration for Market Regulation. "Investigation of Alibaba's Case of Monopoly" (对阿里巴巴集团涉嫌垄断立案调查), Beijing, Dec. 24, 2020.

State Anti-Fraud Center. *Propaganda Handbook on Anti-fraud via Phone and Internet* (国家反诈中心: 防范电信网络诈骗宣传手册). Beijing: Ministry of Public Security, 2021.

State Council Information Office. *China's Policies and Practices on Protecting Freedom of Religious* (国务院新闻办公室: 中国保障宗教信仰自由的政策和实践), Beijing, Apr. 2018.

State Council Information Office. *List of News Providers on the Internet* (国务院网信办: 互联网新闻信息稿源单位名单), Beijing, Oct. 2021.

State Council. "Research Center on Xi Jinping Economic Thought Formally Launched" (国务院: 习近平经济思想研究中心正式挂牌), gov.cn/xinwen (中央政府新闻), Jan. 19, 2022.

State Council. *Chinese National Defense in New Era* (新时代的中国国防), Beijing, July 2019.

State Council. *China's Democracy* (国务院: 中国的民主), Beijing, Dec. 4, 2021.

State Council. *Actively Develop Whole-Process Democracy* (国务院: 积极发展全过程人民民主), Beijing, Sept. 20, 2022.

State Council. *Circular on Concerted Rectification of Vacuous Employment in Government Entities* (关于开展机关事业单位"吃空饷"问题集中治理工作意见的通知), Beijing, No 65, 2014.

State Council. *Notice on Reforming the Salary System of Civil Servants* (国务院: 关于改革公务员工资制度的通知), Beijing, Mar. 19, 2019.

State Council. *Methods of Holding and Educating People of Prostitution and Whoring* (国务院: 卖淫嫖娼收容教育办法), Beijing, 1993, revised 2011.

State Council. *2018–2035 Master Plan for Xiongan New District* (国务院: 河北雄安新区总体规划2018–2035年), Beijing, Jan. 2, 2019.

State Reform Commission. *Inside Information on Economic Reform* (国家体改委: 改革内参), Beijing, No. 273 (Sept) 1998.

State Statistical Bureau. "Reform and Open Forged Glory, Economic Development Wrote New Chapter (改革开放铸辉煌, 经济发展谱新篇), Beijing, Nov. 6, 2013.

State Statistical Bureau. "2018 Resident Income and Consumption" (2018年居民收入和消费支出情况), Beijing, Jan. 2019.

State Statistical Bureau. "Annual Statistical Report" (年度统计报告), Beijing, yearly 2006–2020.

State Statistical Bureau. *Communique of the 7th Census* (第七次人口普查公报), Beijing, 2021.

State Statistical Bureau. Press Release, Beijing, Feb. 28, 2021.

State Statistical Bureau. *Xinwen gongbao* (新闻公报), Jan. 20, 2015.

State Statistical Bureau. *Data of the 2010 Census* (2010人口普查资料), Beijing, 2011.

State Statistical Bureau. *Residential Income and Consumption*, Beijing, Jan. 7, 2020.

State Statistical Bureau. *Chinese Statistical Abstract 2012* (中国统计年鉴 2012), Beijing, 2012.

Stavrou, David. "A Million People Are Jailed at China's Gulags," *Haaretz*, Tel Aviv, Israel, Oct. 17, 2019.

Steinberg, Julie, and Shan Li. "Chinese Education Startup Puts Western Teachers on Notice," *Wall Street Journal*, Mar. 21, 2019.

Stevenson, Alexandra, and Edward Wong. "Chinese Coffee Chain's Scandal Renews U.S. Calls for Oversight," *The New York Times*, May 1, 2020.

Stevenson, Alexandra, and Michael Forsythe. "Luxury Homes Tie Chinese Communist Elite to Hong Kong's Fate," *The New York Times*, Aug. 13, 2020.

Stiglitz, Joseph, Amartya Sen, and Jean Paul Fitoussi. *Mismeasuring Our Lives: Why GDP Doesn't Add Up*. New York: New Press, 2010.

Strömberg, David. "Natural Disasters, Economic Development, and Humanitarian Aid," *The Journal of Economic Perspectives* 21(3), 2007: 199–222.

Su Changhe. "Comparing Chinese Style Democracy with American Style Democracy" (苏长和: 中国式民主与美国式民主之比较), *Renmin ribao* (人民日报), Beijing, Sept. 5–6, 2014.

Su Jianxun, and Qiu Xiaofeng. "Hundred-billion Fraud of Chips" (苏建勋, 邱晓芬: 千亿芯片大骗局), *Sina caijing* (新浪财经), Beijing, Jan. 28, 2021.

Su Ju Bao. "450 Trillion, Chinese Real Estate Larger than US, EU, and Japan Combined" (数据宝, 450万亿, 中国房产市值超美欧日总和)I *Sina caijing* (新浪财经), Nov. 19, 2018.

Su Ning, and Zhang Jiantao, eds. *Report on International Urban Development 2014* (苏宁, 张剑涛: 国际城市发展报告2014), Shanghai: Shanghai Social Science Academy, 2014.

Su Xiaozhang. "China, Why Not Disperse Money" (苏小张: 中国为什么不撒钱), *Jingji guancha bao* (经济观察报), Apr. 23, 2020.

Su Xiaozhou. "Nearly 80% of Small Airports Losing Money Yet Cannot Stop the Construction" (苏晓洲: 小机场近八成亏损难抵建设潮), *Jingji cankao bao* (经济参考报), Beijing, Oct. 29, 2014.

Su Yian. "The Evil during the Pandemic is Just Boundless and Endless" (孙毅安: 疫情期间, 那种恶, 无边无际), *Sohu News* (搜狐新闻), Jan. 9, 2022.

Su, Alice. "As China's Property Giant Evergrande Veers toward Collapse, Its Unpaid Debts Spark Protests," *Los Angeles Times*, Sept. 18, 2021.

Sun Aimin. "Great Leap Forward of P2 Labs in China" (孙爱民: 中国P2实验室大跃进), *Caijing* (财经), Beijing, May 16, 2020.

Sun Bo. "Substandard Online Goods are 26%" (孙博: 电商产品质量不合格率达到26%), Xinhua, Nov. 21, 2014.

Sun Jie. "Beijing, Tainjin, Hebei Sign Mutual Grain-Security Assistance Agreement in Case of Critical Crisis" (京津冀签署重大危机粮食安全互助协议), *Beijing wanbao* (北京晚报), Sept. 8, 2020.

Sun Laibin. "The Way of Institutional Protection and Innovation in China" (孙来斌: 中国制度守正创新之道), *Renmin ribao* (人民日报), Feb. 13, 2019.

Sun Liangquan. "One-Third of the Budget Relies on Fines" (孙亮全: 靠罚款撑起1/3财力), *Banyuetan* (半月谈), Beijing, Apr. 17, 2021.

Sun Linping. "Where Is the Confidence of the China Dream?" (孙临平: 中国梦的自信在哪里), *Jiefangjun Bao* (解放军报), Beijing, May 22, 2013.

Sun Liping. "Biggest Threat Is Not Social Instability but Social Decay" (孙立平: 最大的威胁不是社会动荡而是社会溃败), *Nanfang ribao wang* (南方日报网), Guangzhou, Mar. 5, 2009.

Sun Liping. "Sometimes Corruption Is Perhaps a Spiritual Life" (孙立平: 有时, 腐败也许是一种精神生活), *Wechat Blog* (微信公号), Beijing, Sept. 4, 2021.

Sun Peidong. *Who'd Marry My Daughter?* (孙沛东: 谁来娶我的女儿). Beijing: Shehui kexue, 2012.

Sun Xueyang. "College Graduate Jailed Wrongfully for Ten Years" (孙旭阳: 大学生含冤入狱十年), *Nanfang dushibao* (南方都市报), Guangzhou, Feb. 26, 2014.

Sun Yinni. "How to Reduce Inequality in China" (孙颖妮: 中国如何缩小贫富差距), *Caijing* (财经), Nov. 2021.

Sun Yu. "Chinese Graduates Seek Shelter in Civil Service," *Financial Times*, Oct. 27, 2020.

Sun Zhigao et al. "The State and Problems of Wetland Resources in China" (中国湿地资源保护现状与存在等问题), *Journal of Arid Land Resources and Environment* 20(2), Mar. 2006.

Sun Zhongyuan. "How Food Special Provision System for Central Leaders Was Established (孙中原: 中央首长特供食品制度是怎样建立起来的), *Zhongguo laonian bao* (中国老年报), Beijing, Sept. 12, 2011.

Supreme People's Court. *Collection of Supreme People's Court Adjudication Explanations 1949–2013* (最高人民法院司法解释汇编1949–2013), Beijing, 2015.

Supreme People's Court. "Guidelines on Further Promoting Socialist Core Values in Adjudication Documents" (关于深入推进社会主义核心价值观融入裁判文书), Beijing, No. 21, Jan. 19, 2021.

Supreme People's Court. *Collection of Supreme People's Court Guiding Cases* (最高人民法院指导性案例汇编), Beijing, 2022.

Supreme People's Court and Supreme People's Procuratorate. *Rules on Illegal Currency Exchange* (最高人民法院、最高人民检察院: 非法买卖外汇认定标准), Feb. 9, 2019.

Supreme People's Procuratorate. "Shocking Corruption at the Top of Chinese Sports" (中国体坛高层触目惊心的腐败), *Fangyuan* (方圆), Beijing, Dec. 3, 2017.

Supreme People's Procuratorate. *Main Data on Procuratorates Work* (全国检察机关主要办案数据), Beijing, annually, 2019–2022.

Supreme People's Procuratorate. "Shocking Corruption at the Top of Chinese Sports" (中国体坛高层触目惊心的腐败), Beijing, Dec. 3, 2017.

Supreme People's Procuratorate. "200 Million in Cash Found in the Home of Wei Pengyuan" (最高检: 魏鹏远家中搜出2亿余元), *Zhongguo xinwen wang* (中国新闻网), Beijing, Oct. 31, 2014.

Swanbrow, Diane. "Income Inequality Now Greater in China than in US," *Michigan News*, Apr. 28, 2014.

Symantec. *2013 Norton Report*, cited in Monami Yui and Shingo Kawamoto, "Chinese Criminals Blamed for Record Japan Bank Cybertheft," *Bloomberg*, Dec. 17, 2014.

Szarejko, Andrew. "China Whataboutism," *The Diplomat*, Feb. 3, 2021.

Szelenyi, Ivan. *Urban Inequalities under State Socialism*. New York: Oxford University Press 1983.

Tabuchiaug, Hiroko. "Chinese Textile Mills Are Now Hiring in Places Where Cotton Was King," *The New York Times*, Aug. 3, 2015.

Tai Le. "Anbang Insurance Group Dissolves and Is Liquidated" (泰勒: 安邦保险集团将申请解散并清算), *Zhongguo Jijin Bao* (中国基金报), Beijing, Sept. 15, 2020.

Tai Le. "Wages of China Tobacco Revealed" (泰勒: 中国烟草总公司工资曝光), *Zhongguo jijin bao* (中国基金报), Beijing, Jan. 10, 2021.

Taji, Wael. "Inside the House Church Movement in China," *Palladium*, Aug. 19, 2019.

Tan Haojun. "Two Sets of Data Submitted" (谭浩俊: 两套数据上报), *Beijing news* (新京报), Jan. 6, 2015.

Tan Qingming. "How Do 'Core Technologies' Come? How to Have Innovation?" (谈庆明: "核心技术"何来? 创新何来), *Tencent* (腾讯), Aug. 7, 2018.

Tan Rong. *Introduction to Land System in China* (谭荣: 中国土地制度导论). Beijing: Kexue, 2021.

Tan Suo. "After the Revelation of Quantum Fraud, Graphene Fraud Emerged" (探索: 量子骗局被揭开后, 石墨烯骗局也浮出水面), *Wangyi* (网易), Dec. 28, 2021.

Tan Xinyu. "War on Poverty Continues in 2019," *China Daily*, Beijing, Feb. 2, 2020.

Tan, Yvette. "China Protest: Mystery Beijing Demonstrator Sparks Online Hunt and Tributes," BBC News, Oct. 13, 2022.

Tang Ji. "Internal Economic Circulation Must Consider the Inadequacy of Domestic Consumption" (唐杰: 经济内循环要高度关注国内消费需求不足问题), *Sohu* (搜狐), Sept. 3, 2020.

Tang Jing. "Central Bank's Digital Currency Has Come" (唐婧: 央行数字货币 DCEP来了), *Sina caijing* (新浪财经), Beijing, Aug. 17, 2020.

Tang, Frank. "China's High-speed Railway Network Advances Full Steam Ahead, Despite 'Grey Rhino' Financial Risk," *South China Morning Post*, Hong Kong, Jan. 21, 2020(I).

Tang, Frank. "Coronavirus: China Risks Local Government Debt Surge as Beijing Tries to Spur Economic Growth," *South China Morning Post*, Apr. 29, 2020(II).

Tang, Shiping. *The Institutional Foundation of Economic Development*. Princeton, NJ: Princeton University, 2022.

Tangshan Government. "Tangshan Civil Affairs Bureau Requested Illegal Social Group Tangshan Blue Sky Rescue to Disband" (唐山民政局劝散唐山蓝天救援队), Hebei, July 13, 2021.

Tanner, Murray Scot. "China Rethinks Unrest," *The Washington Quarterly*, Summer 2004.

Tao Duanfang. "1355 Rich Chinese Sued Canada for Canceling Investment Immigration" (陶短房: 1335名中国富翁起诉加拿大取消投资移民), *Huanqiu shibao* (环球时报), June 4, 2014.

Tao Ran. "Chinese Model for Reform and Development" (陶然: 转型发展的中国模式), *Daxue shalong* (大学沙龙), online, Sept. 18, 2021.

Tao Ran, and Su Fubing. "A 'China Model' of Economic Growth" (陶然, 苏福兵: 经济增长的"中国模式"), *Bijiao* (比较), Beijing, No. 2, June 2021.

Tao Wenzhao. "Dialectic Views on Concentrate Resources to Do Big Things" (陶文钊: 辩证看待集中力量办大事), *Beijing ribao* (北京日报), Nov. 14, 2011.

Tao Xizhe. *Expose the Inside of China's Internet Control* (陶西喆: 揭开中国网络监控机制的内幕), New York: Reporters without Borders, 2007.

Tao Zhugong. "Current Chinese Real Estate Worth ¥450 Trillion, 5 times the GDP" (陶朱公, "目前中国房地产总市值450万亿人民币 5倍于GDP), *Zhihu cajing* (知乎财经), Aug. 8, 2019.

Tatlow, Didi Kirsten, and Michael Forsythe. "In China's Modern Economy, a Retro Push against Women," *The New York Times*, Feb. 20, 2015.

Tatlow, Didi Kirsten. "Chinese Man's Death in Custody Prompts Suspicion of Police Brutality," *The New York Times*, May 12, 2016.

Tatlow, Didi Kirsten. "In Beijing, Clearer Views Hide Real Life," *The New York Times*, Nov. 7, 2014.

Taylor, Adam. "Chinese State Media Has Seized on a Swiss Scientist Critical of a Covid Origins Probe. The One Problem: He Might Not Exist." *The Washington Post*, Aug. 10, 2021, 2021.

Taylor, Kathleen. *Brainwashing: The Science of Thought Control*. New York: Oxford University Press, 2017.

Team Reporters. "Masking Era: Why We All Must Fake It (假面时代: 为什么我们都要装), *Zhongguo zhoukan* (中国周刊), Beijing, No. 8, 2011.

Teiwes, Frederick. *Politics and Purges in China: Rectification and the Decline of Party Norms 1950–1965*. Armonk, NY: M.E. Sharpe, 1979.

Telep, Jeffrey, and Richard Lutz. "China's Long Road to Market Economy Status," *Georgetown Journal of International Law* 49 (Aug. 2018): 693–708.

Tencent (腾讯). "How to Assess Economic Accomplishments in the Mao Era" (该怎样评价毛时代的经济成就), Guangzhou, Jan. 2, 2014.

Teng Biao. "China's Politics Needs the Death Penalty as Its Partner" (滕彪: 中国政治需要死刑作伴), *Deutsche Welle News* (in Chinese), June 19, 2013.

Teng Biao. "China Ready for Democracy?" (滕彪: 中国准备好迎接民主了吗), *TengBiao Blog*, June 9, 2021.

Textor, C. "National Debt of China in Relation to GDP 2012–25," Statista.com, Oct. 22, 2020.

Thaxton, Ralph. *Catastrophe and Contention in Rural China: Mao's Great Leap Forward*. Cambridge, UK: Cambridge University Press, 2008.

US Department of Labor. *Consumer Expenditures in 2010*, Report 1037, Washington, DC, 2012.

Thibodeau, Patrick. "China Set to Surpass U.S. in R&D Spending in 10 years," *Computerworld.com*, Dec. 24, 2012.

Thompson, Stephen. "Plagiarism and Xi Jinping," asiasentinel.com, Sept. 24, 2013.

Tian Jianjun. "To Evade Land Inspection, Grow Vegetables on Cement Road" (田建军: 为逃土地检查水泥路上种菜), *Zhongguo qinnianbao* (中国青年报), Beijing, July 2011.

Tian Mei, and Lu Genshu. "Publish or Out" (田美, 陆根书: 发表还是出局), *Fudan jiaoyu luntan* (复旦教育论坛), Shanghai, No. 5, 2016.

Tianjin Government. "Expose 47 Common Ways of Electronic Fraud" (曝光47种常见电信网络诈骗手法), gyxxh.tj.gov.cn, Apr. 7, 2020.

Tie Jun. "Huge Difference in the Composition of Family Assets in China and the U.S." (铁军: 中美家庭资产构成的巨大差别), *Sina caijing* (新浪财经), Beijing, Sept. 19, 2014.

Tierney, John. "Which States Are Givers and Which Are Takers?" *The Atlantic*, Mar. 8, 2017.

Tiezzi, Shannon. "Is China Rethinking the Death Penalty?" *The Diplomat*, Nov. 26, 2014.

Tiftik, Emre et al. "Debt Clouds Over the Post-COVID Recovery," Washington, DC: Institute of International Finance, Jan. 7, 2021.

Ting Li et al. "'Detailed Analysis of the Communique of Seventh Census'" (七普公报'详细解读: 特别回应数据之惑)," *Sina caijing* (新浪财经), May 12, 2021.

Tobin, David. *Securing China's Northwest Frontier: Identity and Insecurity in Xinjiang*. Cambridge, UK: Cambridge University Press, 2020.

Tokar, Dylan. "Accountant Pleads Guilty Ahead of Trial in Panama Papers Case," *Wall Street Journal*, Feb. 28, 2020.

Tong Mu. "To Give Birth in the US Jumped 100 times in 10 years" (童木: 赴美生子人数10年翻百倍), *Shidai zhoubao* (时代周报), Beijing, Oct. 14, 2014.

Tong Xia. "Stories of Assumed Identity" (童夏: 说说冒名顶替的那些事), *Sohu caijing* (搜狐财经), July 4, 2020.

Tong, James W. *Revenge of the Forbidden City: The Suppression of the Falungong in China*. New York: Oxford University Press, 2009.

Tsering Woeser. "Lama Jiumei's Oral Statement" (唯色: 喇嘛久美的口述记录), woeser.middle-way.net/2015/02/blog-post_15.html, Feb. 2015.

Tsinghua University. "Report on Graduates' Employment Quality 2020 and 2021" (清华大学毕业生就业质量报告), Beijing, Dec. 2020 and Dec. 2021.

TTCSP. *Global Go to Think Tank Index Reports*. Philadelphia: University of Pennsylvania, annually, 2008–2021.

Turnage, Mark. "A Mind-Blowing Number of Counterfeit Goods Come from China," *Business Insider*, June 25, 2013.

Turner, Oliver. "West Fears the Rise of Some countries More than Others," *The Conversation*, Dec. 9, 2013.

US Census Bureau. *U.S. Manufacturing, Mining, Wholesale Trade, and Selected Service Industries*. Washington, DC: USCB, 2014.

UBC and Price Waterhouse. *Billionaires Insights 2018: New Visionaries and the Chinese Century*. Switzerland, 2019.

UNDP and Chinese Academy of Social Sciences. *Chinese Human Development Report 2013*. Beijing: CASS, 2013.

UNDP. *Human Development Report*. New York: United Nations Development Program, 2010, 2013, 2014, 2020, 2021.

UNODC. *Global Study on Homicides 2013*. Vienna: UNODC, 2013.

US Bureau of Labor Statistics. *Charting International Labor Comparisons*. Washington, DC: US Department of Labor. Sept. 2012.

US Commercial Service. "China-Foreign Exchange Controls," Washington: DC, July 30, 2019.

US Director of National Intelligence (DNI). *Unclassified Summary of the Intelligence Community Assessment on COVID-19 Origins*, Washington, DC, ODNI, 2021.

US DNI. *Annual Threat Assessment*, Washington, DC, Director of National Intelligence, Apr. 9, 2021.

US DNI. *Unclassified Summary of Scientists*, May 5, 2021.

US DOS. "U.S. Relations with India," Washington, DC, Department of State, Jan. 20, 2021.

US Embassy. "Beijing Weather during APEC" (APEC北京天气). tianqi.com/news/52704.html, also aqicn.org/city/beijing/us-embassy

US IRS. "Revenue Procedure 2021-45," Washington, DC, Nov. 10, 2021.

US Office of Management and Budget (OMB). Receipts by source as percentages of GDP: 1934–2018, Table 2.3. whitehouse.gov/omb/budget/historicals, Jan. 12, 2021.

US OPM, *Pay & Leave*. Washington, DC, Office of Personnel Management, 2014.

US Senate. *Threats to the U.S. Research Enterprise: China's Talent Recruitment Plans*. Washington, DC, Senate, Nov. 18, 2019.

US State Department. *Implementation of Refugee Relief Act of 1953*, Washington, DC, May 18, 1954.

USDT. *Disaster Financial Assistance with Food, Housing, and Bills*, Washington, DC, Department of Treasure, usa.gov, Jan. 2021.

Uuakii. "Xiongan New District, the Most Likely Future of Northern China" (Uuakii: 雄安新区, 推演华北最富可能的未来), zhuanlan.zhihu.com/p/106580331, Mar. 14, 2020.

VOA. "Flood Tests Three Gorges Dam, a 'Time Bomb' over the Heads of 600 Million People?" (洪水考验三峡大坝, 六亿人头顶"定时炸弹"), Washington, DC, Aug. 11, 2020.

Voice of Korea. "Kim Jong-un Says People Is Heaven" (金正恩说人民就是天), *Pyongyang News*, May 31, 2021.

Vu, Tuong. *Paths to Development in Asia: South Korea, Vietnam, China, and Indonesia*. New York: Cambridge University Press, 2010.

Wade, Nicholas. "The Origin of COVID: Did People or Nature Open Pandora's Box at Wuhan?" *Bulletin of the Atomic Scientists*, May 5, 2021.

Wademan, Andrew. *Double Paradox: Rapid Growth and Rising Corruption in China*. Ithaca, NY: Cornell University Press, 2012.

Walder, Andrew. *China Under Mao: A Revolution Derailed*. Cambridge, MA: Harvard University Press, 2015.

Waldmeir, Patti et al. "China Widens Probe into Drug Pricing and Corruption," *Financial Times*, Aug. 15, 2013.

Waldron, Arthur, "China without Tears," in Robert Cowley, ed., *What If?: The World's Foremost Historians Imagine What Might Have Been*. New York: Berkley Books, 1999.

Walker, Richard. *China under Communism, the First Five Years*. New Haven, CT: Yale, 1955.

Wallace, Jeremy. "Juking the Stats? Authoritarian Information Problems in China," *British Journal of Political Science*, June, 2014.

Wallace, Jeremy. *Cities and Stability: Urbanization, Redistribution, and Regime Survival in China*. New York: Oxford University Press, 2014.

Walter, Andrew, and Xiaoke Zhang, eds. *East Asian Capitalism: Diversity, Continuity, and Change*. Oxford, UK: Oxford University Press, 2012.

Walter, Carl, and Fraser Howie. *Red Capitalism: The Fragile Financial Foundations of China's Extraordinary Rise*. Singapore: Wiley, 2012.

Wan Haiyuan, and Meng Fanqiang. "964 Million People Have Monthly Income below ¥2,00S" (万海远, 孟凡强: 月收入2000元以下有9.64亿人), *Caixin* (财新), June 3, 2020.

Wan Jinhui. "Experts Say Two Million Tons of Sewage Grease Returned to Dining Tables in China" (万建辉: 专家称中国每年有200万吨地沟油返回餐桌), *Changjiang ribao* (长江日报), Wuhan, Sept. 15, 2011.

Wan, William, and Ellen Nakashima. "U.S. Announces First Charges against Foreign Country in Connection with Cyberspying," *The Washington Post*, May 19, 2014.

Wang Baocun. "Study of the Evolving Pattern of Ground Sinking in Zhengzhou" (汪宝存等: 郑州市地面沉降时空演变规律研究). *Guotu ziyuan yaogan* (国土资源遥感), Beijing, 32(3), 2020.

Wang Bixue. "On Eating Bitterness" (王比学: 谈吃苦), *Renmin ribao* (人民日报), June 7, 2011.

Wang Delu, and Liu Zhiguang. "Scientists Returned from US in the 1950s and Their Fate" (王德禄, 刘志光: 1950年代归国留美科学家的归程及命运), *Kexue wenhua pinglun* (科学文化评论), Beijing, 9(1), 2012.

Wang Fei-Ling. 王飛凌: 中華秩序-中原, 世界帝國與中國力量的本質. Taipei: Baqi, 2018.

Wang Feng. "Two Kids Policy Already Too Late" (王丰: 二孩政策, 为时已晚), Beijing: Tsinghua-Brookings Center Blog, Apr. 13, 2016.

Wang Haiguang [CCP Central Party School]. "Chinese Academic Circles Is Worse than Malodourous" (王海光: 臭不可闻的中国学术江湖), *Sohu* (搜狐), Beijing, Feb. 26, 2020.

Wang Haiguang. *Manufacturing Counter-Revolutionaries* (王海光: 制造反革命). Hong Kong: Chinese University Press, 2021.

Wang Hao. "Yellow River Accomplishes Continous Water Flow for 23 Years" (王浩: 黄河实现连续二十三年不断流), *Renmin ribao* (人民日报), Beijing, Sept. 19, 2022.

Wang Hongfei. "Nine of Ten PhDs and PhD Advisors Are Unqualified" (王鸿飞: 十有八九的博士和博导不合格," *Kexue shibao* (科学时报), Beijing, Oct. 2, 2007.

Wang Hongguang. *To Fill the Trap of the Second Largest Economy: Gaps between China and the US and Its Trends* (王宏广等: 填平第二经济大国陷阱-中美差距及走向), Beijing: Huaxia, 2018.

Wang Hongru. "China Publishes Its Total of Civil Servants for the First Time Ever" (王红茹: 中国公务员总数首次披露), *Zhongguo jingji zhoukan* (中国经济周刊), Beijing, June 21, 2016.

Wang Huiyao et al., eds. *Report on China's International Migration 2014* (王辉耀等: 中国国际移民报告 *2014*), Beijing: Shehui kexue wenxian, 2014.

Wang Huiyao. *Globalizing China: The Influence, Strategies and Successes of Chinese Returnees*. Bradford, UK: Emerald Group, 2012.

Wang Ji. "Facing a Pandemic, What the Shanghainese Really Worry About" (汪诘: 面对疫情，上海人真正怕的是什么), *Kexue yougushi* (科学有故事), Apr. 2, 2022.

Wang Jian. "Rethinking the Campaign of Sending-Down Youth" (王健: 对知青运动的重新思考), WeChat Blog (微信公号), Shanghai, July 12, 2021.

Wang Jifei. "1/9 Men Could Not Find a Wife" (王继飞: 1/9男人找不到老婆), *Chengdu shangbao* (成都商报), Oct. 28, 2014.

Wang Jing et al. "How Did Evergrande Get to This?" (王婧等: 恒大何以至此), *Caixin zhoukan* (财新周刊), Beijing, Sept. 20, 2021: 29–45.

Wang Jing. "The Chaos of 'Renting People to Take Classes' in Some Colleges" (王靖: 部分大学校园出现"租人上课"乱象), *Xinhua* (新华), Beijing, Apr. 1, 2015.

Wang Jing. "Baby Hatch Programs Struggle to Cope with Number of Infants with Birth Defects," *Caixin English*, Guangzhou, Jan. 6, 2015.

Wang Jingling et al. *Interviews with Woman Trafficked* (王金玲等: 被拐卖婚迁妇女访谈实录). Beijing: Kexue wenxian, 2018.

Wang Jingling. *Study of Human Trafficking in China* (王金玲: 中国拐卖拐骗人口问题研究). Beijing: Kexue Wenxian, 2014.

Wang Jingwen. "Lift Buy-Control Can Hardly Save Housing Market" (王静文: 解除限购难救楼市), *Meizhou caijing guancha* (每周财经观察), Beijing, Aug. 11, 2014.

Wang Jinhua (王金华). Press Conference, Ministry of Civil Affairs, Beijing, Jan. 18, 2020.

Wang Jinwen. "Why the Chinese Society Is Permeated by Hostility" (王进文: 中国社会为何戾气弥漫), *New York Times in Chinese*, Aug. 16, 2013.

Wang Jun. "Ode to Peace in the New Era" (王俊: 新时代和平颂), *The Paper*, Shanghai, Dec. 3, 2017.

Wang Junhao, and Wang Jianming. "Administrative Monopoly in China's Monopoly Industries and Its Control Policy" (王俊豪，王建明: 中国垄断性产业的行政垄断及其管制政策), *Zhongguo gongye jingji* (中国工业经济), Beijing, No. 12, 2007: 30–37.

Wang Junping. "Chinese Medicine Treats COVID with 90% Plus Effectiveness" (王君平: 中医药治疗新冠肺炎总有效率达百分之九十以上), *Renmin Ribao* (人民日报) Apr. 26, 2020.

Wang Li, and Zheng Zhixiong. "Price of Hukou-Less" (王丽，郑智维: 没有户口的代价), *Minsheng zhoukan* (民生周刊), Beijing, No. 7, 2015.

Wang Li. *Wang Li fansi lu* (*Wang Li reflections* (王力反思録). Hong Kong: Beichen, 1993.

Wang Libin. "Safeguard the Lifeline of Food Security" (王立彬: 守住粮食安全的命根子), *Xinhua wang* (新华网), Beijing, Aug. 7, 2020.

Wang Lin. "Prevent Expended Detention Alienate to Be Another Education through Labor" (王琳: 谨防扩大拘役异化成另一种劳教), *Jinghua shibao* (京华时报), Beijing, Jan. 25, 2014.

Wang Ling. "Real Portrait of China's Sibling-less Children" (王羚: 中国独生子女的真实写照), *Diyi caijing ribao* (第一财经日报), Beijing, Apr. 2, 2016.

Wang Lixin, and Li Weiwei. *Where Does the Money Come From?* (王立新, 李为为: 钱从哪里来). Beijing: Huaxia, 2017.

Wang Ming. *Fifty Years of the CCP* (王明: 中共五十年). Hong Kong: Haye (1975) 2009.

Wang Mingyuan. "90s-Born Mega Corruptors Are Endless" (王明远: 90后巨贪层出不穷), *WeChat Blog* (微信公众号), July 20, 2021.

Wang Minqing. "Key to Lonigviity Is No Indulgence" (王敏清: 长寿的秘诀是不享福), *Jinling wanbao* (金陵晚报), Nanjing, Dec. 19, 2011.

Wang Ning. "Chinese Renmin University Withdraw from International College Ranking" (汪宁: 中国人民大学退出国际大学排名), CCTV, Beijing, May 9, 2022.

Wang Ping. *Wang Ping Memoirs* (王平回忆录). Beijing: PLA, 1992.

Wang Qiliang. "China's 30 Years of 'Anti-trafficking'" (王启梁: 中国"反拐"三十年), in *Towards Law Deeply Imbedded in Society and Culture* (迈向深嵌在社会与文化中的法律). Beijing: Fazhi, 2010.

Wang Qishan. "Chairmen Mao Era Was a Great Benevolent Governance" (王岐山: 毛主席时代是大仁政), *Wangyi* (网易), Guangzhou, Apr. 16, 2020.

Wang Renbo. "Modern China and the Psychological Trauma of the Intellectuals" (王人博: 近代中国与知识分子的心灵创伤), *Aisixiang* (爱思想), Beijing, May 28, 2021.

Wang Rong. "How Can China's Higher Education Tolerate Such a Huge Inequality" (王蓉: 中国高等教育为什么能容忍如此巨大的分化), Peking University, *Sohu* (搜狐), Apr. 4, 2021.

Wang Rui. "Zhou Enlai and the One Strike Three Anti-Campaign" (王锐: 周恩来与"一打三反"运动), *Remembance* (記憶), Beijing, No. 16, Sept. 13, 2010: 2–18.

Wang Ruohan. "Death of Zeng Chengjie: Behind the Secret Execution (王若翰: 曾成杰之死-秘密处决背后). *Xinmin zhoukan* (新民周刊), Shanghai, No. 29, July 2013.

Wang Shaowei. "Keep Velocity and Pace" (王少伟: 力度不减节奏不变) *Zhongguo jijian jiancha bao* (中国纪检监察报), Beijing, June 16, 2016.

Wang Shenyou. *Selected Works of Wang Shenyou* (王申酉文集). Hong Kong: Gaowen, 2002.

Wang Shu. "First Exposé of Staff at the CDIC" (王姝: 中纪委编制首度揭秘), *Xinjng bao* (新京报), Dec. 10, 2014.

Wang Shu, and Xing Shiwei. "People Wants Justice, Court Backs Him Up" (王姝,邢世伟: 百姓要公道,法院为他撑腰), *New Beijing news* (新京报), Beijing, Mar. 12, 2014: A09.

Wang Shuo, and Lao Xia. *Beauty Presents Me Drugged* (王朔, 老侠: 美人赠我蒙汗药). Wuhan: Changjiang wenyi, 2000.

Wang Weiguang. "Upholding People's Democratic Dictatorship Does Not Lose Argument" (王伟光: 坚持人民民主专政, 并不输理), *Red Flag Drafts* (红旗文稿), Beijing, Sept. 23, 2014.

Wang Weiluo. "Collective Silence of the Intellectuals and the Failure of South–North Water Diversion Project" (王維洛: 知識分子集體失聲與南水北調中線工程失敗), *Dongxiang* (動向), Hong Kong, Dec. 2015: 58–59.

Wang Wen. "To Mobilize the Million-Soldiers" (王文: 调动百万大军), *Zhiku lilun yu shijian* (智库理论与实践), Beijing, No. 1, 2021.

Wang Xiangwei. "Ahead of COP15 Summit, China Cracks Whip on Environmental Corruption in Kunming," *South China Morning Post*, Hong Kong, May 15, 2021.

Wang Xiao. "The Revival of Bureaucratic System in New China, 1949–1976" (王霄: 官僚制在新中国的复活1949–1976). *Aisixiang* (爱思想) July 24, 2012.

Wang Xiaobo. "'Thousand Persons Plan' Practiced for One Year" (王晓波: "千人计划"实施一年), *Shanghai qiaobao* (上海侨报), Feb. 21, 2010.

Wang Xiaodong. "To Punish Corruption Harsher by Law" (王晓东: 依法从严惩治腐败犯罪), *Renmin fayuan bao* (人民法院报), Beijing, Oct. 14, 2021.

Wang Xiaohui. "First-Tier City Vacancy of Office Highest in Ten Years" (王晓慧: 一线城市写字楼空置率创十年新高), *Huaxia shibao* (华夏时报), Beijing, Dec. 27, 2020.

Wang Xiaoming. "Hard to Think about Abide the Law" (王晓明: 想守法地生活?难!), *Dangdai wenhua yanjiu* (当代文化研究), Shanghai, Oct. 26, 2014.

Wang Xiaoyang. "Warning List of Hundred Fake Universities in China" (王晓阳: 百所中国虚假大学警示榜), Beijing; Xinhua, July 3, 2013.

Wang Xiuqiang. "China's Per Unit GDP Energy Consumption 2.5 Times World's Average" (王秀强: 中国单位GDP能耗达世界均值2.5倍), *21 shiji jingji baodao* (21世纪经济报道), Beijing, Nov. 30, 2013.

Wang Xuanhui. "Report Card on Rectifying Vacuous Employment in 30 Provinces" (王选辉: 30省份公布清退吃空饷成绩单), *Fazhi wanbao* (法制晚报), Beijing, Oct. 6, 2014.

Wang Xiaoqing. "Chairman of Fuxing Guo Guangchan in Fact Disappeared" (王晓庆: 复星集团董事长郭广昌确已失联), *Caixin* (财新), Dec. 10, 2015.

Wang Xuejin. "'Native Trash Already a Headache, How to House 'Foreign Garbage'?" (王学进: "土垃圾"已头疼,哪还容得下"洋垃圾"), Beijing: Xinhua, Jan. 5, 2015.

Wang Yanqing. "How the Rich Serve Time" (王燕青: 富人怎么坐牢), *Southern Weekend* (南方周末), Aug. 25, 2015.

Wang Yaofeng. "Difficulty of Seeing Doctor by Officials Shows the Entanglement of Self-Interest" (王垚烽: 官员体验看病难更显自身利益羁绊), *Fazhi ribao* (法制日报), Beijing, Aug. 15, 2013.

Wang Yi. "Meet US Deputy Secretary of State Sherman" (王毅会见美国常务副国务卿舍曼), PRC Foreign Ministry, Tianjin, July 26, 2021.

Wang Yi. *So Beautiful It Has Shocked the Central* (王怡: 美得惊动了中央). Chengdu, 2005.

Wang Yunlong. *Dancing Companion* (王云龙: 陪舞者), documentary, Hong Kong, 2016. neodb.social/movies/82837.

Wang Zeng. "Two Critiques of 985 Project" (王铮: 对"985工程"的两个批评), *Kexue dui shehui yingxiang* (科学对社会影响), Beijing, No. 3, 2004.

Wang, Fei-Ling, and Esi A. Elliot. "China in Africa: Presence, Perceptions and Prospects," *Journal of Contemporary China* 23: 90, Nov. 2014.

Wang, Fei-Ling. "Reformed Migration Control and New List of the Targeted People: China's *Hukou* System in the 2000s," *The China Quarterly* 177, Mar. 2004, 115–132.

Wang, Fei-Ling. *Organization through Division and Exclusion: China's Hukou System.* Stanford CA: Stanford University Press, 2005.

Wang, Fei-Ling. *The China Order: Centralia, World Empire, and the Nature of Chinese Power.* Albany, NY: SUNY Press, 2017.

Wang, Fei-Ling. "Renovating the Great Floodgate: The Reform of China's Hukou System," in Martin King Whyte, ed., *One Country, Two Societies: Rural–Urban Inequality in Contemporary China.* Cambridge, MA: Harvard University Press, 2009: 335–364.

Wang, Fei-Ling. "The *Hukou* (Household Registration) System," in Timothy Wright, ed., *Oxford Bibliography in Chinese Studies.* New York: Oxford University Press, 2014.

Wang, Fei-Ling. *Institutions and Institutional Change in China: Premodernity and Modernization.* London & New York: Macmillan & St Martin's, 1998.

Wang, Nanfu. *In the Same Breath*, HBO Documentary, 2021. youtube.com/watch?v=HXgPNA19YKo

Wang, Orange. "US$1 for 19.77 Yuan? How a Bogus Social Media Rumour Reveals Fear That China Is Printing Money," *South China Morning Post*, Hong Kong, Oct. 16, 2018.

Wang, Peng. *The Chinese Mafia: Organized Crime, Corruption, and Extra-legal Protection.* Oxford, UK: Oxford University Press, 2017.

Wang, Rachel. "Why China's Rich Want to Leave," *The Atlantic*, 4, 2013.

Wang, Shun, and Weina Zhou. "The Unintended Long-Term Consequences of Mao's Mass Send-Down Movement: Marriage, Social Network, and Happiness," Seoul, Korea: KDI Paper No. 15-03, July 30, 2015.

Wang, Shun. "The Long-Term Consequences of Family Class Origins in Urban China," Seoul, Korea: *KDI Research Paper Series*, No. 14(12), 2014.

Wang, Vivian, and Joy Dong. "Anger Erupts in China Over Video of Mentally Ill Woman Chained in Shack," *The New York Times*, Feb. 1, 2022.

Wang, Wendy. "Who Cheats More?" *Institute for Family Studies*, Jan. 10, 2018.

Wang, Xiaobing et al. "College Is a Rich, Han, Urban, Male Club: Research Notes from a Census Survey of Four Tier One Colleges in China," *The China Quarterly* 214, June 2013.

Wang, Xiaoying. "The Post-Communist Personality: The Spectre of China's Capitalist Market Reforms," *The China Journal* 47, 2002: 1–17.

Wang, Y. Yvon et al., eds. *"Back Then Everyone Had It Tough": Everyday Lives in China's Rural "Small Third Front Factories, 1964–1988.* New York: Palgrave, 2022.

Wang, Yaqiu. "What You Need to Know about China's 'Residential Surveillance at a Designated Place,'" *China Change*, Aug. 2, 2015.

Wang, Yi, and Matthew Chew. "State, Market, and the Manufacturing of War Memory: China's Television Dramas on the War of Resistance against Japan," *Memory Studies*, June 23, 2021.

Wang, Yuhua. *Tying the Autocrat's Hands: The Rise of The Rule of Law in China.* New York: Cambridge University Press, 2015.

Wang, Zhen. "Child Trafficking Networks of Illegal Adoption in China," *Nature Sustainability*, UK, May 2018.

Wangyi (网易). "Poverty Covered by the Poverty Line" (被贫困线掩盖的贫穷), June 9, 2020.

Wangyi (网易). "Rural Bachelors Buy Wives Regardless Where They Are From" (农村光棍男人买媳妇不问来历), Jan. 3, 2022.

Wanli Yuntian. "Why the Rich Chose to Run Away Rather Than Reform" (万里云天: 为什么富人不选择改良, 而是选择逃离), *Kaidi* (凯迪), Haikou, Hainan, Aug. 15, 2021.

Ward, Hugh et al. "State Capacity and the Environmental Investment Gap in Authoritarian States," *Comparative Political Studies* 47(3), Mar. 2014: 309–343.

Watts, Jonathan. *When a Billion Chinese Jump: How China Will Save Mankind—Or Destroy It.* New York: Scribners, 2010.

Wechat Blog (微信公众号). "Names of Over 2,000 Web-Commentators for 2015 in Fudan University Leaked" (2015年复旦大学2000多名网评员名单泄漏), Nov. 22, 2021.

Wee, Sui-Lee. "China's Parliament Is a Growing Billionaires' Club," *The New York Times*, Mar. 3, 2018.

Wei Chunzhao. *Studies of Counterfeits* (韦春昭: 假货研究). Beijing, Gongshang, 2008.

Wei Jiaqi. "CAS Reports 80% of Health Spending Are Only for Party Members and Cadres" (伟家齐: 中科院报告称医疗投入的80%专为党员干部服务), *Wangyti* (网易), Oct. 9, 2020.

Wei Jingsheng. *Tansuo* (探索), Beijing, Jan. 1979.

Wei Junyi. *Thinking the Pain* (韦君宜: 思痛录). Beijing: Shiyue Wenyi, 1998.

Wei Lingling, and Jing Yang. "Ant Founder Jack Ma Faces Backlash from Regulators," *Wall Street Journal*, Nov. 3, 2020.

Wei Mi. "Don't Know English Led to Information Island for 1.3 Billion People" (魏称: 不懂英语, 造就了13亿人的信息孤岛), *Zhongguo xinwen* (中国新闻), Beijing, June 4, 2017.

Wei Sen (韦森), Yu Yongding (余永定), Zhang Shuguang (张曙光), et al. Debate in *Economics Quarterly* (经济学季刊), Beijing 12(3), Apr. 2013: 1051–1094.

Wei Yi. "Dialogue with Du Daozheng" (卫毅: 对话杜导正), *Southern People* (南方人物), Nov. 4, 2011.

Wei Zhou. "Why PCR [Test] for All Never Ends" (维舟: 全员核酸为何没完没了), *Zhihu*, Apr. 10, 2022.

Wei, Jingsheng. "The Fifth Modernization: Democracy and Others" (魏京生: 第五个现代化-民主与其它), Big poster (大字报), Xidan, Beijing, Dec. 5, 1978.

Weir, Kirsten. "Smog in Our Brains," *Monitor on Psychology* 43(7), July/Aug. 2012.

Weiss, Jessica Chen. "Mike Pompeo Accused China of Committing 'Genocide,' an International Crime. Biden's Team Agrees," *The Washington Post*, Jan. 23, 2021.

Weiss, Yinon. "How Fear, Groupthink Drove Unnecessary Global Lockdowns," *RealClear Politics*, May 21, 2020.

Wen Da, "How to Execute the Confiscation of Total Personal Assets" (问答: 没收个人全部财产如何执行), *Sohu xinwen* (搜狐新闻), Beijing, July 9, 2013.

Wen Lin. "Come On, Let's Bet the Fortune of the Country" (温林: 来呀! 赌国运呀!) *WeChat Blog* (微信公众号), Mar. 23, 2022.

Wen Long. "What Happened to Xiongan New District" (文龍: 北京視為「千年大計」的雄安新區怎麼樣了), *Secret China*, Apr. 22, 2020.

Wen Ru. "Is It Fair to Both Get about 10 years for Embezzling 100 Thousand and 5 Million" (温薷: 贪10万和500万都判10年左右公平吗?), *Xinijing bao* (新京报), Beijing, Mar. 12, 2014.

Wen Shan. "149 List of Negative Items Draw the Red Line Again" (文山: 149条"负面清单"再划行为"红线"), *Sina xinwen* (新浪新闻), Beijing, July 15, 2018.

Wen Xing et al. "Point Out the Direction for Global Cooperation and Development" (温馨等: 为推动全球合作发展指明方向), Beijing: Xinhua, Dec. 6, 2021.

Wertime, David. "It's Official: China Is Becoming a New Innovation Powerhouse," *Foreign Policy*, Feb. 7, 2014.

White House. *United States Strategic Approach to The People's Republic of China*, report to Congress, Washington, DC, May 20, 2020.

White, Howard, and David Raitzer. *Impact Evaluation of Development Interventions*. Manila: Asian Development Bank, 2017.

WHO. "Depression," and "Depression Rates by Country 2021," Geneva, Switzerland, 2022.

WHO. *Ambient (Outdoor) Air Pollution Database, by Country and City*, Geneva, 2014–2018.

WHO. *Global Status Report on Road Safety 2013*, Geneva, Switzerland, 2013.

WHR. *World Happiness Report*. New York: UN, 2013–2021.

Whyte, Martin King et al. "Challenging the Myths about China's One-Child Policy," *The China Journal* 74, July 2015: 144–159.

Wildau, Gabriel. "China's Economy Is 12% Smaller than Official Data Say, Study Finds," *The Financial Times*, Mar. 6 2019.

Wildau, Gabriel, "Half of Chinese Provinces Deserve Junk Ratings, S&P Warns," *The Financial Times*, Nov. 20, 2014.

Wilson-Chapman, Amy et al. "What Happened after the Panama Papers?" ICIJ. org, Apr. 2019.

Wilson, Maxwell, and Andrew Smith. "The Peak and the Watershed: The Impact of Small Mammal Poisoning on the Ecohydrology of the Qinghai-Tibetan Plateau," *AMBIO* 44(1), Feb. 2015.

Wines, Michael. "China Admits Problems with Three Gorges Dam," *The New York Times*, May 20, 2011.

Wines, Michael. "Bystanders' Neglect of Injured Toddler Sets Off Soul-Searching on Web Sites in China," *The New York Times*, Oct. 19, 2011.

Wines, Michael. "More Tainted Dairy Products Are Found in Chinese Stores," *The New York Times*, Jan. 26, 2010.

Withnall, Adam. "China Faces Criticism from Conservation Scientists for Attempts to Exterminate Real-Life 'Pikachu' with Mass Poisoning," *The Independent*, Jan. 21, 2015.

Wittfogel, Karl. "The Historical Position of Communist China: Doctrine and Reality," *The Review of Politics* 16(4) Oct. 1964: 463–474.

Wong, Chun Han. "Is China's Communist Party Still Communist?" *Wall Street Journal*, June 30, 2021.

Wong, Chun Han, and Te-Ping Chen. "China Sentences Activist to Prison for 'Picking Quarrels,'" *Wall Street Journal*, Aug. 3, 2017.

Wong, Edward. "An Artist Depicts His Demons," *The New York Times*, May 27, 2013.

Wong, Edward. "Prison Sentence for Maker of Documentary on Chinese Constitutional Rule," *The New York Times* blog, Dec. 30, 2014.

Wong, Edward. "China Blocks Web Access to 'Under the Dome' Documentary on Pollution," *New York Times*, Mar. 7, 2015.

Wong, Edward. "Hundreds of Chinese Cities Don't Meet Air Standards, Report Finds," *The New York Times*, Apr. 22, 2015.

Wong, Maggie Hiufu. "40 of the Best Taiwanese Foods and Drinks," CNN, July 25, 2015.

Woo-Cumings, Meredith. *The Developmental State*. Ithaca, NY: Cornell University Press, 1999.

Wooldridge, Adrian. "Meritocracy, not Democracy, Is the Golden Ticket to Growth," *Bloomberg*, May 16, 2021.

World Bank and PRC State EPA. *Cost of Pollution in China: Economic Estimates of Physical Damages*, Washington, DC, 2007.

World Bank. "Foreign Direct Investment—the China Story," Washington, DC, Apr. 18, 2015.

World Bank. *Poverty*, Washington, DC, Apr. 16, 2020.

World Economic Forum. *Global Gender Gap Report*, Switzerland, 2014 and 2021.

WPR. *Median Income by Country*, worldpopulationreview.com/country-rankings/median-income-by-country, *World Population Review*, 2022.

Wray, Christopher [FBI Director]. "Wray Says Whole-of-Society Response Necessary to Confront China Threat," *Homeland Security Today*, Feb. 6, 2020.

Wright, Logan, and Allen Feng. "COVID-19 and China's Household Debt Dilemma," Rhodium Group, May 12, 2020.

Wright, Tim. *The Political Economy of the Chinese Coal Industry: Black Gold and Blood-Stained Coal*. London: Routledge, 2012.

Wu Bangguo [Chief of the PRC National People's Congress]. Speech to the 4th meeting of the 11th PRC NPC (吴邦国: 在11届人大四次会议上的讲话), Beijing: Xinhua, Mar. 10, 2011.

Wu Bin. "Why Abortion Numbers Stay High" (吴斌: 为何人工流产数量居高不下), *Nanfang dushibao* (南方都市报), Guangzhou, Jan. 9, 2020.

Wu Bo. "Death Penalty or Not Should Base on People's Feelings" (吴渤: 判不判死刑要以人民感觉为依据), *Xinhua News Dispatch*, Zhuhai, Apr. 11, 2008.

Wu Changfeng. "Quantum Encryption Show Problems?" (吴长锋: 量子加密惊现破绽?), *Keji ribao* (科技日报), Beijing, Mar. 16, 2019.

Wu Faxian. *Hard Times—Wu Faxian Memoirs* (歲月艱難-吴法憲回憶録). Hong Kong: Beixing, 2006.

Wu Fei. *Meaning of the Simple Life—Cultural Analysis of Suicide in One County of Northern China* (吴飞: 浮生取义-对华北某县自杀现象的文化解读). Beijing: Renmin daxue, 2009.

Wu Fei. *Suicide as a China Issue* (吴飞: 自杀作为中国问题). Beijing: Sanlian, 2007.

Wu Guoguang. "Preface to Chen Xitong says by Yao Jianfu" (吴国光: 姚监复-陈希同亲述). Hong Kong: Xin Shiji, 2012.

Wu Hongda. *Stormy Rains Last Night* (吴弘达: 昨夜雨骤风狂). Washington, DC: Laogai, 2003.

Wu Jianhua, and Zhao Shiyong. "The Trickeries of China's Local Debts" (吴建华 and 赵士勇: 中国地方债玄机), *China Times* (华夏时报), Beijing, Jan. 7, 2015.

Wu Jiaxiang. *Diaries in the Zhongnanhai* (吴稼祥: 中南海日記). New York: Mingjing, 2002.

Wu Jinglian. "Thinking Institutions of the 30-Year Economic Reform in China" (吴敬琏: 中国经济改革30年的制度思考), *21st shiji shijie jingyi baodao* (21世纪世界经济报道), Beijing, Sept. 23, 2008.

Wu Kaizhi. "On the Political and Economic Origins of the Chinese Rural Reform" (吴凯之: 论中国农村改革的政治与经济起源), *Shehui kexue luntan* (社会科学论坛), Beijing, 9, 2012.

Wu Qiantao. *Investigating Contemporary Chinese Citizens' Moral State* (吴潜涛: 当代中国公民道德状况调查). Beijing: Renmin, 2010.

Wu Qinying. "Heavy Thoughts—Track Report on the 11 Graduate Students Trafficked" (武勤英: 沉重的思考-对11位女研究生被骗案的追踪采访), *Guangming ribao* (光明日报), Beijing, Sept. 3, 1988.

Wu Shenbiao. "Our NPC Deputies Probably Knocked Out US Congressmen with Per Capita Wealth" (吴胜彪: 我国全国人大代表, 人均财富恐已秒杀美国国会议员), *Wangyi* (网易), Dec. 5, 2020.

Wu Si. "Business of Selling Justice" (吴思: 出售公正的生意), *Gongshi wang* (共识网), Apr. 10, 2016.

Wu Si. "Doctored History Does Not End Well" (吴思: 被打扮的历史没有好下场), *Xin Zhoukan* (新周刊), Nov. 8, 2006.

Wu Xiaobo. "'Bubbles' Coming Back" (吴晓波: 卷土重来的"泡沫") and "Why I Never Play Stocks" (我为什么从来不炒股), *Caijing* (财经), Beijing, Dec. 3 and 10, 2014.

Wu Xiaobo. "Depression Cases Exploded 120 Times in 20 Years" (吴晓波: 抑郁症发病率20年暴涨120倍), *Sohu xinwen* (搜狐新闻), Sept. 28, 2021.

Wu Xing Ji. "Not Worry about Fake Assistance to the Poor in Shangxi" (無星记: 陕西扶贫造假不可怕), *Wangyi* (网易), Guangzhou, Apr. 25, 2021.

Wu Xuefeng. "Netzen Publish New Along the River during the Qingming Festival" (吴雪峰: 网友发布新清明上河图), *Nanfang dushi bao* (南方都市报), Guangzhou, Nov. 24, 2014.

Wu Yong. "The American Dream of the Illegal Emigrants" (吴用: 偷渡客的美国梦), shuku.net/novels/stowaway.html, Dec. 2020.

Wu Youming. *Police of 13 Years* (吴幼明: 从警13年), *Tianya Blog* (天涯), May 13, 2016.

Wu Yu. "Upgrading the Theme Melody: 'Five 'Don't Dos' Followed by 'Seven Don't Talks'"? (吴雨: 主旋律升级: "五不搞"后迎来"七不讲"?), *Deutsche Welle in Chinese*, posted May 10, 2013.

Wu Yue. "31 Court Chiefs, Only One Passed the Legal Exam" (吴越: 31名法院院长,仅一人通过司法考试), *Sina* (新浪), Aug. 13, 2013.

Wu Yujian et al. "¥20 Billion Fake Gold Collateral Exposed" (吴雨俭等: 两百亿元假黄金质押案暴露), *Caixing zhoukan* (财新周刊), Beijing, no. 25 (June 29) 2020.

Wu Zepeng. "Behind the Suspicious Case of Feng Lun's 'Misappropriating Funds'" (吴泽鹏: 冯仑"挪用资金疑案"背后), *Meiri jingin xinwen* (每日经济新闻), Chengdu, Aug. 18, 2021.

Wu Zhanqiao. "Shocking Fraud of 'Water to Oil' 20 Years Ago Happened Again" (吴展桥: 20年前的"水变油"惊天骗局), *Nanfang wang* (南方网), Guangzhou, Aug. 24, 2017.

Wu, Alfred. *Governing Civil Service: Pay in China*. Copenhagen, Denmark: NIAS Press, 2014.

Wu, Harry, and Carolyn Wakeman. *Bitter Winds*. Hoboken, NJ: Wiley, 1995.

Wu, Harry X. "In Quest of Institutional Interpretation of TFP Change—The Case of China," *Man and the Economy*. Berlin: De Gruyter 6(2), Dec. 2019: 1–22.

Wu, Ningkun (巫宁坤), and Li Yikai (李怡楷). *A Single Tear: A Family's Persecution, Love, and Endurance in Communist China*. Boston: Little Brown, 1993.

Xi Congqing. *Humanism and the Cause for People with Disabilities in China* (奚从清: 人道主义与中国残疾人事业). Hangzhou: Zhejiang daxue, 2018.

Xi Jinping. "CCP Leadership Is the Most Essential Nature of Socialism with Chinese Characteristics" (习近平: 中国共产党领导是中国特色社会主义最本质的特征), *Qiushi* (求是), Beijing, No. 14, 2020.

Xi Jinping. "Consolidate and Develop the Broadest Patriotic United Front" (习近平: 巩固发展最广泛的爱国统一战线), Beijing: Xinhua, May 20, 2015.

Xi Jinping. "Ensure the Military Always Listens to the Party and Follows the Party" (习近平: 确保官兵永远听党话、跟党走), *Qiushi* (求是), Beijing, Aug. 1, 2021.

Xi Jinping. "Establish Beijing Stock Exchange" (习近平: 设立北京证券交易所), Xinhua, Sept. 2, 2021.

Xi Jinping. "Insisting Sinicization of Religions in Our Country" (习近平: 坚持我国宗教中国化方向), Xinhua, Dec. 4, 2021.

Xi Jinping. "Report to the 19th CCP National Congress" (习近平: 在中国共产党第十九次全国代表大会上的报告), Beijing, Oct. 17, 2017.

Xi Jinping. "Report to the 20th CCP National Congress" (习近平: 在中国共产党第二十次全国代表大会上的报告), Beijing, Oct. 16, 2022.

Xi Jinping. Speech at the CCP Central's meeting on People's Congress work (习近平: 在中央人大工作会议上的讲话). Beijing: Xinhua, Oct. 14, 2021.

Xi Jinping. Speech at the conference on the elimination of poverty (习近平: 在打好精准脱贫攻坚战座谈会上的讲话), *Qiushi* (求是), Apr. 30, 2020.

Xi Jinping. Speech at the meeting celebrating the centenary of the CCP (习近平: 在庆祝中国共产党成立一百周年大会上的讲话), Beijing, July 1, 2021.

Xi Jinping. "Summarize the Party's Historical Experience, Enhance Party's Political Construction" (习近平: 总结党的历史经验 加强党的政治建设), *Qiushi* (求是), Beijing, Aug. 16, 2021.

Xi Jinping. "To Construct an Archeology with Chinese Characters, Styles, and Manners" (习近平: 建设中国.色中国风格中国气派的考古学), *Qiushi* (求是), Beijing, Nov. 30, 2020.

Xi Jinping. "Unshakably Adhere and Enhance the Party's Comprehensive Leadership" (习近平: 毫不动摇坚持和加强党的全面领导), *Qiushi* (求是), Beijing, No. 18, Sept. 16, 2021.

Xi Jinping. "New-Era Yugong Spirit" (新时代愚公精神), *China wang* (中国网), Aug. 22, 2019.

Xi Jinping. *Selected Views on Comprehensive Use of Law to Govern* (习近平: 关于全面依法治国论述摘编), Beijing: CCP Central, Apr. 2015.

Xi Jinping. Speech at College of Europe at Bruges (习近平: 在布鲁日欧洲学院的演讲), Apr. 1, 2014.

Xi Jinping. Speech at the forum commemorating the 110th birthday of Deng Xiaoping (习近平, 在纪念邓小平同志诞辰110周年座谈会上的讲话), Beijing, Aug. 20, 2014.

Xi Jinping. Speech at the symposium commemorating the 120th birthday of Comrade Mao Zedong (习近平: 在纪念毛泽东同志诞辰120周年座谈会上的讲话), Beijing, Dec. 26, 2013.

Xi Jinping. "Important Decrees on Party-Construction in Colleges" (习近平就高校党建工作作出重要指示), Beijing: Xinhua, Dec. 29, 2014.

Xi Jinping. Speech at CCP Politburo No. 24 Group Study Session on quantum technology (习近平: 在中央政治局第二十四次集体学习量子科技), Beijing: Xinhua, Oct. 17, 2020.

Xi Jinping. Speech at the 20th Meeting of Chinese Academicians (习近平: 在中国科学院第二十次院士大会上的讲话), Beijing: Xinhua, May 28, 2021.

Xi Jinping. Speech at the National Conference on Religious Work (习近平: 在全国宗教工作会议上讲话), Beijing: Xinhua, Apr. 23, 2016.

Xi Jinping. Speech at the virtual 2022 World Economic Forum (习近平在2022年世界经济论坛视频会议的演讲), Beijing, Jan. 17, 2022.

Xi Jinping. "We Will Never Allow Our Rule Change Color" (习近平: 我们决不允许江山变色), Liaoning: Xinhua, Aug. 17, 2022.

Xi Jinping. *On CCP's History* (习近平: 论中国共产党历史). Beijing: Wenxian, Mar. 2021.

Xi Minghua. "What I Know about Women Trafficked in Feng County" (谢明华: 我所了解的丰县拐卖妇女), *China Digital Times*, Feb. 4, 2022.

Xi Xifei. "Rural Bachelors: To Where They Are From" (西西废: 农村光棍: 从哪里来, 到哪里去), *The Paper* (澎湃), Shanghai, Oct. 23, 2021.

Xia Bin. "Unusual Policy Is Needed for Unusual Time" (夏斌: 非常时期必须采取非常政策), *Tansuo yu zhengming* (探索与争鸣), Shanghai, No. 11, 2014: 10–15.

Xia Ming. "Ferry Self and Others in the Sea of Fear" (夏明: 恐惧之海中渡己渡人), *Zonglan zhongguo* (纵览中国), Apr. 5, 2015.

Xia, Yiwei et al. "Mapping Trafficking of Women in China: Evidence from Court Sentences," *Journal of Contemporary China* 29(122), 2020: 238–252.

Xiao Bazhu. "Lei Feng-Moral Model Made with Lies" (小吧主: 雷锋-谎言编织的道德楷模), *Baidu* (百度), Oct. 26, 2013.

Xiao Guangming et al. "Tens of Millions Deposits 'Disappeared' in Hebei ICBC Bank" (肖光明等: 工商银行河北储户数千万存款"失踪"), *Zhongguo xinwen* (中国新闻), May18, 2015.

Xiao Han. "Strange Phenomenon in the Academia and the Dignity of Scholars" (萧翰: 学界怪状与学者尊严), *Zhongguo qingnian bao* (中国青年报), Jan. 18, 2006.

Xiao Hang. "What to Do about Insufficient Organs after Organ Donation from the Executed Is Halted?" (晓航: 死囚器官捐献叫停后器官不够用咋办?), *Sina* (新浪), Dec. 4, 2014.

Xiao Hui. "Three Essays Unsettled the SSB" (小晖: 蛮三篇横空出世, 统计局坐不住了), i.ifeng.com/c/86GLavDrkYu, May 14, 2021.

Xiao Huilong. "Impression of Visiting Hometown During Spring Festival" (肖辉龙: 春节返乡见闻录), *Caijing* (财经), Beijing, Feb. 15, 2016.

Xiao Jinbo. "Watch Out, Ten New Ways of Fraud Exposed" (孝金波: 小心上当! 十种新型诈骗骗术曝光), *Renmin wang* (人民网), Sept. 8, 2016.

Xiao Long, and Jiang Wen. "Misunderstanding and Conflicts between Peng Dehuai and Liu Bocheng" (晓农, 疆文: 彭德怀刘伯承的误会与纠葛), *Dangshi wenyuan* (党史文苑), Nanchang, No. 1, 2005: 26–32.

Xiao Mu. "Sino-American Technology War" (小木: 中美科技战), *Dongxi zhiku* (东西智库), Beijing, Sept. 8, 2021.

Xiao Qiang. "China's 'Customs Special Supply Food'" (萧强: 中国的"海关特供菜"), RFA, May 18, 2011.

Xiao Renfu. *Leaders Are Human Too* (肖仁福: 领导也是人). Beijing: Qunyan, 2009.

Xiao Rewu Yi. "Exposé of the Thousand Talents Scholars" (小人物乙: 晒晒千人计划学者们), xys.org, Oct. 24, 2014.

Xiao Shan. "Three Years Later, Xiao Jianhua Is Said to Be Still Alive" (小山: 3年记, 传肖建华还活着), Radio France International, Jan. 27, 2020.

Xiao Shibai. "China's Coastal Seas Destroyed by Greed" (肖诗白: 被贪婪毁掉的中国近海), *Guojia dili* (国家地理), Beijing, Dec. 19, 2015.

Xiao Shu. *Truth about Liu Wencai* (笑蜀: 刘文彩真相). Xian: Shangxi shida, 1999.

Xiao Song. "The Crying Village" (小松: 哭泣的村庄), *Toutiao* (头条), Beijing, June 25, 2020.

Xiao Tian. "How Shocking Is the Corruption in Chinese Sports?" (肖天: 中国体坛腐败有多触目惊心?), *Liaowang zhiku* (瞭望智库), Beijing, Jan. 1, 2019.

Xiao Ziyang. "From Wasted Wood to Ge You Slouch: A Study on the "Doom Culture" of Online Youth from Socio-psychological Perspectives" (萧子扬: 从"废柴"到"葛优躺": 社会心理学视野下的网络青年"丧文化"研究), *Qingshaonian xuekani* (青少年学刊), Jinan, No. 3, 2017.

Xiao, Eva. "Chinese Research Papers Raise Doubts, Fueling Global Questions about Scientific Integrity," *Wall Street Journal*, July 5, 2020.

Xibu Zhengquan. "Will the Global Price of Soybeans Rise Still Further?" (西部证券: 全球大豆价格还能一路上涨吗), *Zhengquan yanjiu baogao* (证券研究报告), Beijing, Apr. 11, 2020.

Xie Chensheng. "Antiquity-Destruction in Our Country over the Past 20 Years Has Been Worse than Cultural Revolution" (谢辰生: 我国近20年文物破坏甚于文革), *Nanfang dushi bao* (南方都市报), Oct. 23, 2013.

Xie Maosong. "CCP is a New Civilization" (谢茂松: 中国共产党是一种新文明), keynote speech, Shanghai: Fudan University, Mar. 23, 2021.

Xie Maosong. "China in 2021: Melt the Old to Forge the New Pulse of Civilization" (谢茂松: 展望2021年的中国: 熔旧铸新的文明脉动), *Zhongguo pinglun* (中国评论), Hong Kong, Jan. 2021.

Xie Ning. *My 30 Years in Peking University* (谢宁: 我在北京大学的三十年), book manuscript, 2014.

Xie Renci. "In China, 85 Million People Dare Not to Go Out of Their Home" (谢仁慈: 在中国, 8500万人不敢出门), *Dingxiang yuan* (丁香园), Dec. 3, 2021.

Xie Wei. "Story behind the 'Parade Blue'" (谢玮: "阅兵蓝"背后的故事), *Zhongguo xinwen zhoukan* (中国经济周刊), Beijing, Sept. 5, 2015.

Xie Yong. "The Impact of Family Background and Categorization since 1949" (谢泳: 四九以后出身成分的影响), *Gongshi wang* (共识网), Apr. 11, 2014.

Xie Yong. *Ages Passed: The Fate of Liberal Intellectuals in China* (谢泳: 逝去的年代: 中国自由知识分子的命运). Fuzhou: Fujian jiaoyu (1999) 2013.

Xie Yong. "Qian Xuesen and His Classmate Xu Zhangben" (谢泳: 钱学森和他的同学徐璋本). mjlsh.usc.cuhk.edu.hk

Xie Yu et al. *Report on the Development of Livelihood in Chinese 2014* (谢宇等: 中国民生发展报告 2014), Beijing: Peking University, July 25, 2014.

Xie Zhihong, and Jia Lusheng. *Ancient Crime: Reports on Woman Trafficking* (谢致红, 贾鲁生: 古老的罪恶-拐卖妇女纪实), Hnagzhou: Zhejiang wenyi, 1989.

Xie Zhongxiu. "Tug of War to Save the Market" (谢中秀: 救市拉锯战), *Shidai Zhoubao* (时代周报), Mar. 31, 2020.

Xie, Stella Yifan, and Mike Bird. "The $52 Trillion Bubble: China Grapples With Epic Property Boom," *Wall Street Journal*, July 16, 2020.

Xin Chao. "The Data-Revise of Fixed Asset Investment and Its Influence" (辛超: 固定资产投资数据的修订及影响), *Zhengquan shichang zhoukan* (证券市场周刊), Beijing, Feb. 10, 2022.

Xin Dongfang. "*People's Daily* Exposed 392 Fake Universities" (新东方: 人民日报曝光392所 野鸡大学), *Tencent xinwen* (腾讯新闻), June 7, 2021.

Xin Ke. "Chinese Intelligentsias Are Already Gangsters and Cult-Members" (辛可: 中国知识分子已经黑帮化,邪教化), public lecture at Beijing Normal University, 2014.

Xin Ke. *No More Decency* (辛可: 斯文扫地). Beijing: Jiuzhou, 2013.

Xin Lijian. "Press Freedom in the ROC Era" (信力建: 民国时期的新闻自由), *Zhongguo baodao zhoukan* (中国报道周刊), Beijing, May 2012.

Xin Qing Nian. "Real Buddha Says Only Common Words, Monster Often Talks in Couplet Sentences" (新青年: 真佛只说家常话, 妖怪常说对仗句), Weibo (微博), May 6, 2022.

Xin Ziling (Song Ke). "Situation and Future" (辛子陵/宋科: 形势与未来), speech to the retirees of PRC Ministry of Science and Technology, Beijing, Feb. 10, 2012.

Xin Ziling (Song Ke). *Concerns about the Rise and Fall of the CCP* (辛子陵/宋科: 中共興亡憂思錄). Hong Kong: Tianxingjian, 2009.

Xing Zhuo. "Chinese Civil Survey" (邢卓: 中国民间民情调查), *Zhongguo minjian minqin diaochasuo* (中国民间民情调查所), 2006, repeated in 2016.

Xing Zuo. "Survey on Civic Conditions in China" (邢卓: 中国民间民情调查), online published by Institute of Chinese Civic Survey (中国民间民情调查所), 2006 and 2016.

Xinhua. "Full-Process People's Democracy: Xi Jinping's Deep Analysis" (全过程人民民主: 习近平深刻论述), Beijing: Xinhua, Oct. 15, 2021.

Xinhua. "Job Reports to the Party Central and General Secretary Xi Jinping" (向党中央和习近平总书记述职), Beijing, Mar. 1, 2021.

Xinhua. "Leaders Discuss the 19th Party Congress Report" (领导讨论19大报告), Oct. 20, 2017.

Xinhua. "Many Localities in the Northeast Fabricate GDP, County Economies Larger than Hong Kong" (东北多地GDP造假, 县域经济规模超香港), Dec. 11, 2015.

Xinhua. "NPC Standing Committee's Resolution to Abolish the Legal Regulation of Education by Labor" (全国人大常委会关于废止劳动教养法律规定的决定), Beijing, Dec. 28, 2013.

Xinhua. "Report on Tiantin Harbor 8/12 Super Fire and Explosion" (天津港"8·12"特别重大火灾爆炸事故调查报告), Beijing, Feb. 5, 2016.

Xinhua. "The Decision on Major Issues Concerning Comprehensively Advancing the Rule of Law," Oct. 28, 2014.

Xinhua. "The Irreversible Course of History" (新华社: 不可逆转的历史进程), Beijing, Nov. 8, 2021.

Xinhua. "Three Children Birth Policy Is Here" (三孩生育政策来了), Beijing, May 31, 2021.

Xinhua. "Total National Fiscal Revenue 11.7 Trillion Last Year, Share of GDP Reached a New Record," Jan. 23, 2013.

Xinhua. "Vows for Joining the CCP at Different Eras" (中国共产党各时期的入党誓词), July 2, 2021.

Xinhua. "Xi Jinping Inspects Chinese Renmin University" (习近平在中国人民大学考察), Beijing, Apr. 25, 2022.

Xinhua. "Xi says China to Sustain 'Relatively High' Growth," Boao, Hainan, Apr. 8, 2013.

Xinhua. "Over 2.64 Million Chinese Students Abroad by the End of Last Year, over 1.5 Million Not Returned" (去年底中国累计留学者达264万 逾150万未归国), Beijing, Oct. 14, 2013.

Xinhua. "Xi Jinping Chaired the Tenth Meeting of the Central Finance and Economy Commission" (习近平主持召开中央财经委员会第十次会议), Beijing, Aug. 17, 2021.

Xinhua. *Learning Lei Feng Spirit* (学习雷锋精神), Beijing, Dec. 6, 2014.

Xiong Peiyun. *China Inside a Village* (熊培云: 一个村庄里的中国). Beijing: Xinxing, 2011.

Xiong Xuanguo. "Reform and Perfection of China's Approval System for Capital Punishment" (熊选国: 中国死刑核准制度改革与完善), in Li Lin, ed. *China Report on the Development of Rule of Law* (6) (李林: 中国法治发展报告No.6), Beijing: Shehui kexue wenxian, 2008: 124–140.

Xiong, Yihan. "The Broken Ladder: Why Education Provides No Upward Mobility for Migrant Children in China," *The China Quarterly* 221, Mar. 2015: 161–184.

Xiyuan Qiu. "The Rural Has No Idyllic" (西原秋: 农村没有田园牧歌), *Guancha* (观察), Feb. 14, 2016.

Xu Chenggang. "Institutional Innovation Is More Important to China" (许成钢: 制度创新对中国更重要), *Sina caijing* (新浪财经), June 13, 2017.

Xu Chenggang. Speech at Moganshan Forum 2014 (许成钢: 2014莫干山论坛讲话), *Sina caijing* (新浪财经), Beijing, Sept. 18, 2014.

Xu Hong. "Salute to the Censor Industry in the Great country" (许宏: 向大国审稿产业致敬), *Minguo wang* (民国网), Aug. 29, 2021.

Xu Jin. "Shanghai in Pandemic and the Light of Humanity" (徐瑾: 疫情中的上海与人性之光), *FT in Chinese* (FT 中文网), Apr. 3, 2022.

Xu Jing. "Eighteen University Leaders Investigated in 2014" (徐静: 2014年全国18名高校领导被调查), *Guangzhou ribao* (广州日报), Aug. 27, 2014.

Xu Kai et al. "Bill of Public Security" (徐凯等: 公共安全账单) *Caijing* (财经), No. 11, 2011.

Xu Lingxiao. "See Them, Hear Them, Care about Them" (许玲晓: 看见她们, 听见她们,关注她们), *WeChat Blog* (微信公众号), Feb. 21, 2022,

Xu Minghui. "How Modern Molecular Biology Prove 'African Origin' of Humankind" (徐明徽: 现代分子生物学如何力证人类"非洲起源说"), *The Paper* (澎湃), Shanghai, Aug. 23, 2016.

Xu Peng. "To Deal with Grain-Farming, How Ridiculous Are the Local Counterefforts" (徐鹏: The Counter 为了应付复耕, 下面的对策有多荒唐), *WeChat Blog* (微信公众号), Mar. 25, 2022.

Xu Ran. "What Happened to the Cadres Eating Vacuous Employment" (许然: 那些"吃空饷"的干部, 最后都咋样了), *Lianzheng liaowang* (廉政瞭望), Beijing, No. 6, 2020.

Xu Tengfei. "Wang Xiaohong Became the Party Secretary and Director of the Special Service Bureau" (许腾飞: 王小洪已任特勤局党委书记, 局长), *Xinjingbao* (新京报), Nov. 4, 2019.

Xu Xiaonian (许小年). *Sina caijing* (新浪财经), Beijing, May 10, 2013.

Xu Xiaonian. "Who Suppresses the Nation's Innovation Ability?" (许小年: 谁压制了民族的创造力?) *IT shidai zhoukan* (IT 时代周刊), Beijing, No. 8, Apr. 20, 2012.

Xu Yanhong et al. "Analysis of Ten Social Diseases in Today's China" (徐艳红等: 当前中国十大社会病态分析报告), *Renmin luntan* (人民论坛), Beijing, No. 9, Sept. 15, 2014.

Xu Yaotong. "Break 'Power Fetishism'" (许耀桐: 破解"权力拜物教"), *People's Forum* (人民论坛), Beijing, Sept. 18, 2006.

Xu Youwei, and Zhang Chengcheng. "Overview of Studies on Third Front in 2020" (徐有威, 张程程: 2020年三线建设研究述评), *Sanxia daxue xuebao* (三峡大学学报), Yicang, No. 4, 2021.

Xu Zhangrun. "Imminent Fears, Immediate Hopes," open letter, Beijing, 2018.

Xu Zhangrun. *Ten Letters in the Year of Gengzi* (许章润: 庚子十劄). New York: Bouden, 2021.

Xu, Vicky Xiuzhong, and Bang Xiao. "China's Social Credit System Seeks to Assign Citizens Scores, Engineer Social Behaviour," ABC News Australia, Mar. 30, 2018.

Xuan Feng. "Ten of Thousands in Taxes for Middle Class" (炫风: 中产万税) and Shen Ding "Who Moved Mr. A's Tax Bill" (沈玎: 谁动了Mr. A的税单), *Nandu zhoukan* (南都周刊), Guangzhou, Dec. 13, 2010.

Xuan Yan. "Socialism Has Not Let China Down;" "China Has Not Let Socialism Down" (宣言: 社会主义没有辜负中国;中国没有辜负社会主义), *Renmin ribao* (人民日报), June 7 and 8, 2021.

Xue Muqiao. *Xue Muqiao Memoirs* (薛暮桥回忆录). Tianjin: Tianjin Renmin, 1996.

Xue Peng. "Provincial Exams Coming: Cases to Show the Prohibited" (薛鹏: 省考在即: 从案例看哪些行为不可为), *Zhongyang jiwei wang* (中央纪委网), July 15, 2020.

Xue Yong. *Critique of Peking University: Chinese Higher Education Is Sick* (薛涌: 北大批判: 中国高等教育有病). Nanjing: Jiangsu wenyi, 2010.

Xue, Xinran (薛欣然). *Buy Me the Sky: The Remarkable Truth of China's One-Child Generations*. London: Ebury Digital, 2015.

Yan Huai. *In and Out of the Central Organization Department* (閻淮: 進出中組部). Hong Kong: Mingjing, 2017.

Yan Jiaqi, and Cao Kun. "16 PLA Commanders above Corps Level Have Been Caught" (闫嘉琪 &曹昆: 解放军16名军级以上干部被查处), *Xinhua*, Beijing, Jan. 16, 2015.

Yan Jiulin. "Three Silly Fake Tang Poems" (言九林: 三首拙劣的假唐诗), *Duan-shiji-Tencent* (短史记-腾讯), Feb. 22, 2021.

Yan Ruyi. "China's 'Bachelor Crisis'" (闫如意: 中国的"光棍危机"), *Phoenix Weekly*, Apr. 5, 2019.

Yan, Yunxiang. "The Politics of Moral Crisis in Contemporary China," *The China Journal* 85, Jan. 2021.

Yan, Yunxiang. *Private Life under Socialism: Love, Intimacy, and Family Change in a Chinese Village, 1949–1999*. Stanford, CA: Stanford University Press, 2003.

Yang Chengpai. "2022 State Exam Opens, Applicants Exceed 2 million for the First Time" (羊城派: 2022国考开考! 报考首破200万人), *Cajing toutiao* (财经头条), Nov. 28, 2021.

Yang Chunchang. "Major Generals Expose the Inside of Xu Caihou Selling Offices" (杨春长等: 少将曝徐才厚卖官内幕), Beijing: Xinhua, Mar. 10, 2015.

Yang Dezhi. "The Hubbub of 'Nano Water' Folly" (杨得志: 鼓噪—时的"纳米水"闹剧), *Zhongguo qinnianbao* (中国青年报), Beijing, Apr. 6, 2001.

Yang Duogui et al. *National Health Report* (杨多贵: 国家健康报告). Beijing: Science Press, 5 annual volumes, 2008–2013.

Yang Fei. "Sharing with College Student Friends My Personal Views about Chairman Mao" (杨非: 和大学生朋友谈谈我对毛主席的个人看法), *Sina Blog* (新浪), Aug. 19, 2015.

Yang Guobin. *The Wuhan Lockdown*. New York: Columbia University Press, 2022.

Yang Hanqin. "Stick to the Original Mission of Communists" (杨汉卿: 坚守共产党人的初心和使命), *Nanfang zhazhi* (南方杂志), Guangzhou, No. 14, July 2019.

Yang Jisheng. *Analysis of the Social Strata in Contemporary China* (杨继绳: 中国当代社会各阶层分析). Lanzhou: Gansu Renmin, 2006.

Yang Kuisong. "Comparative Study of Mao Zedong and Chiang Kai-shek" (杨奎松: 毛泽东与蒋介石的比较研究), Lecture at Peking University, Beijing, Apr. 2010.

Yang Kuisong. "Q&A on the Income of Party-State Cadres since the Founding of the Nation (杨奎松: 关于建国以来党政干部收入的问答), *Southern Weekend* (南方周末), Aug. 29, 2007.

Yang Kuisong. *Study of the History of Building the PRC* (杨奎松: 中华人民共和国建国史研究). Nanchang, Jiangxi Renmin, 2 vols., 2009.

Yang Li. "Economic Latecomer Confronted with Curses," *China Daily*, May 8, 2004.

Yang Li. *Red Rose with Thorns* (杨立: 带刺的红玫瑰). Guangzhou: Dangshibang, 1997.

Yang Meng. "Master Mathematician Shing-Tung Yau Severely Critical of Chinese Academic Corruption" (杨猛: 数学大师丘成桐痛击中国学术腐败), *Haixia Dushibao* (海峡都市报), Fuzhou, July 11, 2005.

Yang Shaogong, and Qin Huajiang. "Shuqian in Jiangsu Responses to Growing Beans on Road" (杨绍功, 秦华江: 江苏宿迁回应铺路种豆), *Xinhua News*, Beijing, July 26, 2014.

Yang Shiba. "Life inside the Detention Center" (杨十八: 看守所里的生活), *Zhihu*, July 16, 2020.

Yang Siyang. "The Whole Country Produced 3.7 Billion Tons of Coal in 2013" (杨斯阳: 2013年全国煤炭产量达37亿吨), *Zhongguo jingji wang* (中国经济网) Beijing, Jan. 16, 2014.

Yang Tianshi. "Mao Zedong Called Chiang Kai-shek a 'Great Leader'" (楊天石: 毛澤東曾稱蔣介石是 "偉大領袖"), *Fenghuang zixun* (鳳凰資訊), Hong Kong, 23, Apr. 4, 2013.

Yang Wanguo et al. "NPC Delegates Suggest Abolishing the Third-Level bachelor Education" (杨万国等: 人大代表建议取消三本), *Xinjing bao*, Beijing, Mar. 9, 2014.

Yang Xiangfeng. "Domestic Contestation, International Backlash, and Authoritarian Resilience: How Did the Chinese Party-state Weather the COVID-19 Crisis?" *Journal of Contemporary China* 30(132), 2021.

Yang Xiaokai. "China's Latecomer Disadvantage" (杨小凯: 中国的后发劣势), Lecture at Unirule Institute of Economics, Beijing, Dec. 1, 2000.

Yang Xiguang (Xiaokai). *Records of Ghosts and Monsters: Spirits Jailed during the Cultural Revolution* (杨曦光/小凯: 牛鬼蛇神录: 文革囚禁中的精灵). Hong Kong: Oxford University Press, 1994.

Yang Ye. "SOE Executives Give 100 Million away for 1 million Corruption" (杨烨: 国企高管腐败100万要输送1亿元交易额), *Jingji cankao* (经济参考), 北京, Nov. 13, 2014.

Yang Zhijin. "Investment 'Breaks through' in 2015" (杨志锦: 2015年投资"闯关"), *21 shiji jingji baodao* (21世纪经济报道), Guangzhou, Feb. 2, 2015.

Yang, Zifeng, and Nanshan Zhong. "Modified SEIR and AI Prediction of the Epidemics Trend of COVID-19 in China under Public Health Interventions," *Journal of Thoracic Disease* 12(3), Mar. 2020.

Yang, Dali et al. "A Tragedy of the *Nomenklatura*? Career Incentives, Political Loyalty and Political Radicalism during China's Great Leap Forward," *Journal of Contemporary China* 23(89), 2014: 864–883.

Yang, Fenggang. "Will Chinese House Churches Survive the Latest Government Crackdown?" *Christianity Today*, Dec. 31, 2019.

Yang, Jie. *Mental Health in China*. New York: Polity, 2018.

Yang, Jisheng. *Tombstone: The Great Chinese Famine, 1958–1962*. New York: Farrar 2012.

Yang, Xiguang, and Susan McFadden. *Captive Spirits: Prisoners of the Cultural Revolution Hardcover*. Hong Kong: Oxford University Press 1997.

Yao Chanjun. "Another 100 Billion Case Busted" (要参君: 又一千亿大骗局案发了), *Caiwen yaochan* (财闻要参), Jan. 16, 2021.

Yao Dongqin. "100 Thousands Corrupt Officials Fled China with $2 Trillion" (姚冬琴: 中国外逃贪官10多万人, 卷款逾2万亿美元), *Zhongguo jingji zhoukan* (中国经济周刊), Beijing, June 14, 2015.

Yao Dongqing. "Corrupted Officials Ran Away with Assets Exceeding a Trillion" (姚冬琴: 贪官外逃携带资金超万亿), *Zhongguo jingji zhoukan* (中国经济周刊), Beijing, June 5, 2012.

Yao Heng. "Sweep 'Reserve-Elimination' in the Officialdom" (姚桓: 扫除官场"逆淘汰"), *Zhongguo dangzheng ganbu luntan* (中国党政干部论坛), Beijing, No. 11, 2014.

Yao Hongen. "Why Jiang Jie's Only Son Gave Up Chinese Citizenship" (姚鸿恩: 江姐独子为何弃中国国籍), *Sohu* (搜狐) and *Sina* (新浪), Feb. 18, 2015.

Yao Jiayi, and Shi Rui. "China's Gender Imbalance the Worst in the World" (姚家怡 & 石睿: 中国性别失衡全球最严重), *Caixin* (财新), Beijing, Jan. 21, 2015.

Yao Yang. "Where is Chinese Government's Motivation of Reform?" (姚洋: 中国政府改革的动力在何处), *Gongshi wang* (共识网), July 18, 2013.

Yardley, Jim, and David Barboza. "Despite Warnings, China's Regulators Failed to Stop Tainted Milk," *The New York Times*, Sept. 27, 2008: A1.

Ye Fu. *Where Is Home?* (野夫: 乡关何处). Beijing: Zhongxin, 2010.

Ye Kai. "From Phony Ethics in Elementary School, Empty Ideals in Middle School, to Tasteless Aesthetics in College" (叶开: 从小学的虚假道德, 中学的空洞理想到大学的无趣审美), *Wangyi*, Apr. 13, 2018.

Ye Tieqiao, and Lu Yijie. "Reconstruct the Process of Zhang Shuguang's Addition as Academician (叶铁桥, 卢义杰: 张曙光增选院士过程还原), *Zhongguo qingnian bao*, Beijing, Sept. 13, 2013.

Ye Zhuyi. "How Can Official Fed on *Tegong* Food Feel the Sharp Pain of Food Safety? (叶祝颐: 吃特供的官员对食品安全何来切肤之痛?), *Sichuan xinwen wang* (四川新闻网), Chengdu, Sept. 17, 2011.

Yi Gang [People's Bank Governor]. Speech at the Lámfalussy Lectures, Beijing, Jan. 25, 2021.

Yi Gong. "Weekly Insight: Surging Global Debt," Institute of Intel Finance, Washington, May 14, 2020.

Yi Gang. "China's System of Interest Rates and Market-Oriented Reform of Interest Rate" (易纲: 中国的利率体系与利率市场化改革), *Jinrong yanjiu* (金融研究), Beijing, No. 9, 2021.

Yi Ju. "South-North Water Diversion Is More Horrible than Three Gorges Project" (殷炬: 比三峡工程更可怕的"南水北调"), *Sina* (新浪), July 6, 2014.

Yi Qi Lai. "Chaotic Return to Farming on the Net" (—起来: 网上反映的复耕乱象) *Sohu* (搜狐), Mar. 30, 2022.

Yi Quan. "Hard to Enforce Law, Hard to Abide Law Too" (烨泉: 执法难 守法也难), *Fazhi ribao* (法制日报), Beijing, Apr. 7, 2008.

Yi Zhongtian. "Don't Be as Shameless as Yu Qiuyu" (易中天: 不要像余秋雨那样无耻), lecture, Xiamen University, Apr. 4, 2011.

Yi Zhongtian. "Now China Lacks the Bottom Line the Most" (易中天: 当下中国最缺底线), *Aisixiang* (爱思想), Beijing, Feb. 7, 2002.

Yin Wei. "Shen Jilan: 'Living Fossil' of the People's Congress Institution" (尹薇: 申纪兰: 人大制度"活化石"), CCTV, Beijing, Mar. 10, 2008.

Yin Yungong. "Deng Xiaoping and 'Internal Reference'" (尹韵公: 邓小平与 "内参"), *Dangde wenxian* (党的文献), Beijing, No. 6, Nov. 2012.

Yin, David. "Chinese Still Affected by Mainland Pollution, Even after Moving to New York," *Forbes Asia*, June 21, 2013.

Ying Hongbiao. *Traces of the Vanished* (印红標: 失踪者的足跡). Hong Kong: Chinese University, 2009.

Ying Qian. "Comparing China Model and India Model" (尹倩: 中国模式与印度模式之比较), in Zhao Jianying and Wu Bo, eds. *On China Model* (赵剑英, 吴波: 论中国模式), Beijing, 2010.

Ying Shusheng. "Education through Labor and Anti-Rightist Struggle" (尹曙生: 劳动教养和反右斗争), *Yanhuang chunqiu* (炎黄春秋), Beijing, No. 4, 2010: 10–13.

Ying Yue. "Seventh Census Overturns Five Main Understandings" (尹悦: 七普人口数据颠覆五大认知), *Sina caijing* (新浪财经), Beijing, May 11, 2021.

Ying Zi. "Wang Zhaoshan 'Happy Even as Ghosts' Ashamed Literature" (隐之: 王兆山 "做鬼也幸福"令文学蒙羞), *Yangzi wanbao* (扬子晚报), Nanjing, June 17, 2008.

Ying, Ruocheng, and Claire Conceison. *Voices Carry: Behind Bars and Backstage during China's Revolution and Reform.* Lanham, MD: Rowman Littlefield, 2009.

Yip, George. "China's Many Types of Innovation," *Forbes Asia*, Sept. 19, 2014.

You Jiuzhou, and Lin Yimei. "Guo Moruo's Personality Problem" (尤九州, 林亦梅: 郭沫若的人格问题), *Xuzhou jiaoyu xueyuan xuebao* (徐州教育学院学报), Xuzhou, No. 3, 1998.

You Yi. "Snap Shots of the Past of China's Five Labor Camps" (友忆: 中国五大劳改营的往事掠影), *China in Perspective* (纵览中国), Princeton, NJ, Feb. 1, 2015.

Yu Guoming et al., eds. *Annual Report on Social and Media Situations in China* (喻国明等编: 中国社会舆情年度报告), Beijing, Renmin ribao, 2010–2020.

Yu Haikuo. "How to Understand Disabled People in Literature and Art Works" (于海阔: 怎样看文艺作品中的残疾人问题), *Zhongguo yishu bao* (中国艺术报), Beijing, Feb. 11, 2015.

Yu Hua. *China in Ten Words.* New York: Pantheon Books, 2011.

Yu Jian. "The China of Five Thousand Years Has Been Completely Demolished in the Past Thirty Years" (于坚: 五千年的中国在最近三十年被完全的拆迁了), *Sohu* (搜狐), July 22, 2015.

Yu Jie. *Fire and Ice* (余杰: 火与冰). Hong Kong: Jiujiang, 2014.

Yu Jie. *Inside Reference on Furthering Education* (余杰: 升学内参). Beijing: Wenlian, 1999.

Yu Jie. "Yu Qiuyu: Why Don't You Repent?" (余杰: 余秋雨: 你为什么还不忏悔), 2000. people.com.cn

Yu Keping. "Democracy or Populism" (俞可平: 民主还是民粹), *China Governance Review* (中国治理评论), Beijing, No. 5, Oct. 2014: 5–6 and 9.

Yu Leyin. "Ge You Slouch Suddenly Become Hot" (鱼乐颖: 葛优躺突然火了), *Sina* (新浪), Beijing, July 8, 2016.

Yu Liang. "Genealogy and Ecology of 'Little Pinks' and the Future of Chinese Youth" (余亮: "小粉红"的系谱、生态与中国青年的未来), *Wenhua zongheng* (文化纵横), Oct. 10, 2021.

Yu Minhong. "Bad Apples Hurt All Chinese Students Overseas" (俞敏洪: 害群之马伤害整个中国留学群体), *Yangguang wang* (央广网), Beijing, Mar. 10, 2015.

Yu Minhong. "On Smog in Beijing" (俞敏洪谈北京雾霾), *China Daily*, Apr. 21, 2014.

Yu Xianbin. "Red Head Cover" (余显斌: 红盖头), *Xinkechengbao-yuwendaokan* (新课程报-语文导刊), Xian, Apr. 15, 2022.

Yu Xiang. "Newest Ranking of Iron Rice Bowls" (雨巷: 最新的铁饭碗排名), *Sohu* (搜狐), June 18, 2021.

Yu Xiaoji et al. "From Two Digits to 80 Million" (余晓洁: 从两位数到八千万), *Xinhua News Dispatch*, Beijing, June 25, 2011.

Yu Ying-shih. "Xi Jinping Wants to Be Mao Zedong the Second" (余英时: 习近平要做毛泽东第二), *RFA Commentary*, Feb. 24, 2015.

Yu Yongding. "World Economy, Finance, and Outlook of World Order" (余永定: 世界经济、金融与全球秩序展望), speech at Tsinghua Wudaokou Forum of Chief Economists (清华五道口首席经济学家论坛), Beijing, May 14, 2022.

Yu Yongyue, and Wang Shiming. "On the Theoretical Origin and Development of Deng Xiaoping's Common Prosperity Thought" (余永跃、王世明: 论邓小平共同富裕思想的理论来源及其发展), *Kexue shehui zhuyi* (科学社会主义), Beijing, Nov. 26, 2013.

Yu Yunhui. "Who Controls the 'Top Decision Power' of the Chinese Economy?" (余云辉: 谁掌控了中国经济的"顶层权力"?), *Seeking Truth Theory Net* (求是理论网), Beijing, May 31, 2013.

Yu Weiyue. "Always Remember 'the Principle of the State' to Govern Out-School Educatiuonal Institutions" (俞伟跃: 始终牢记"国之大者" 规范校外教育培训机构), *Zhongguo jichu jiaoyue* (中国基础教育), Beijing, Sept. 2022.

Yu, Verna. "Tales of Torture: Time Spent in Chinese Police Custody Leaves Victims Permanently Scarred," *South China Morning Post*, June 27, 2015.

Yu, Xie. "China's Local Governments Binge on Off-the-Books Debt," *Wall Street Journal*, May 11, 2020.

Yuan Chao. "'Guanxi' Entanglement, Layers Malfunction and Officialdom Reverse Elimination" (袁超"关系"裹挟, 科层失灵与官场逆淘汰), *Lilun tantao* (理论探讨), Shanghai, No. 3, 2017.

Yuan Du. "5G, Nothing More than a Common Fairytale for the World" (远读: 5G, 不过是世界人民共同的神话), *Wangyi* (网易), Guangzhou, Aug. 4, 2020.

Yuan Duanduan. "Hidden Tumor: The Ignored Child Cancer" (袁端端: 暗瘤-被忽视的儿童癌症), *Nanfang zhoumo* (南方周末), Guangzhou, Oct. 9, 2014.

Yuan Duanduan. "It Delayed the Time for Chinese to Take New Medications" (袁端端: 它延缓了中国人吃上新药的时间), *Nanfang zhoumo* (南方周末), Guangzhou, Dec. 11, 2015.

Yuan Guoli. "Authentic Goods Less than Six-Tenths on the Web-Commerce, Taobao Scored the Lowest" (袁国礼: 网购商品抽检正品不足六成, 淘宝网正品率最低), *Jinghua shibao* (京华时报), Jan. 24, 2015.

Yuan Jian. "High Investment, Low Efficiency, Internal Circulation: Where Will Chinese Economy Go after Losing Globalization Dividend?" (袁剑: 高投资、低效率、内循环, 失去全球体系红利的中国经济何去何从), *Bancheng hui* (半城会), Nanjing, 2020.

Yuan Jian. *China: The End of a Miracle* (袁剑: 中国,奇迹的黄昏). Hong Kong: Wenhua yishu, 2008.

Yuan Ling. "Shi Qiulang: Me and My father Shi Zhe" (袁凌: 师秋朗: 我与父亲师哲), *Boke tianxia* (博客天下), Yinchuan, Ningxia 165 (July) 2014: 62–75.

Yuan Xiaohua. "PhDs from Tsinghua in One Year" (袁小华: 清华一年博士毕业生), *Kexue wang*(科学网), Beijing, June 29, 2021.

Yuan Yilin. "Complete Farewell to Abject Poverty" (阮煜琳: 彻底告别绝对贫困), China News Agency, Beijing, Nov. 23, 2020.

Yuan Zhixiao. "News Corruption and Suggested Ways to Address It" (袁之霄: 新闻腐败及其对策浅议), *Renmin wang* (人民网), Beijing, Dec. 5, 2019.

Yueh, Linda. "Japan's Savings Rate Turns Negative for First Time," *BBC News*, Dec. 26, 2014.

Zaho Jiwei. "Caofeidian Redemption" (赵记伟: 曹妃甸的救赎), *Faren* (法人), June 2014.

Zen Boyan. *Dabao Camp of Little Education though Labor* (曾伯炎: 大堡小劳教), documentary, Hong Kong, 2013. youtube.com/watch?v=CCkIrMhbGN0&t=1s.

Zeng Liming. "Society Concerns the Rising Gender Imbalance" (曾利明: 社会关注性别比升高), *Renmin luntan* (人民论坛), Beijing, No. 9, 2004.

Zeng Peiyan. *Economy in the 50 Years of New China* (曾培炎: 新中国经济50年). Beijing: Jihua, 1999.

Zeng Peng et al., "Behind the Collective Protests" (曾鹏: 在集體抗議的背後), *Modern China Studies*, Issue 2, 2006.

Zeng, Ka, and Joshua Eastin. *Greening China: The Benefits of Trade and Foreign Direct Investment*. Ann Arbor: University of Michigan Press, 2011.

Zenz, Adrian. "China's Domestic Security Spending: An Analysis of Available Data," *China Brief* 18(4), Washington, DC: Jamestown Foundation, Mar. 12, 2018.

Zha, Jianying. "China's Heart of Darkness-Prince Han Fei and Chairman Xi Jinping," *China Heritage*, July 22, 2020.

Zhai Richang. "Why the Hostility among People Gets Ever Worse in Recent Years" (宅日常: 为什么近年来国人的戾气越来越重), *Sohu News* (搜狐新闻), Aug. 5, 2019.

Zhang Bin et al. "Why People Emigrate More as They Become Richer?" (张斌等: 国人为什么越富越移民), *Jingji guancha bao* (经济观察报), Beijing, Feb. 21, 2014.

Zhang Bin. "Shen Jilan Response to the Report on Never Vote No" (张斌: 申纪兰回应从未投反对票报道), *Jinghua shibao* (京华时报), Beijing, Mar. 5, 2012.

Zhang Da. "How Serious Is China's Employment Situation?" (张达: 中国就业形势有多严峻?), money.163.com, May 13, 2016.

Zhang Dawei. "China's Real Estate Value Exceeds World's GDP" (张大伟: 中国房产市值超过全球GDP总和) and "Chinese Real Estate Market Values about $100 trillion" (中国房产市值约100万亿美元), *Sina caijing* (新浪财经), Beijing, Nov. 20, 2018.

Zhang Deyong. "Why China Is Not Like the US to 'Give People Money'" (张德勇: 中国为什么不像美国那样给民众"发钱"), *Shangguan xinwen* (上观新闻), Shanghai, Apr. 1, 2020.

Zhang Dongdong. "Report Says More than 40% Chinese Returnee Talents Have Foreign Citizenship or Green card" (张冬冬: 调查称逾四成中国海归人才拥有外国国籍或绿卡), *Zhongguo xinwen* (中国新闻), Beijing, July 23, 2012.

Zhang Erchi. "Storm of Grand Chip-Fund" (张而驰: 芯片大基金风暴), *Caixin* (财新), Aug. 8, 2022.

Zhang Guotao. *Zhang Guotao Memoirs* (張國燾回憶錄). Hong Kong: Mingbao, 1974.

Zhang Haibo. "Nearly Six-Tenths of Peasants Admit One Family Two Systems for Agricultural Products (张海波: 近六成中国农民承认农产品一家两制), *Cankao xiaoxi* (参考消息), Feb. 18, 2014.

Zhang Haiyang. "Unwavering Sticking to the Party Absolute Leadership of the Military" (张海阳: 毫不动摇坚持党对军队的绝对领导), *Jiefangjun bao* (解放军报), Beijing, Dec. 4, 2013.

Zhang Hong. "Why Do I Criticize Yu Qiuyu?" (张闳: 我为什么批评余秋雨), *Xinjing bao* (新京报), Aug. 19, 2004.

Zhang Jinchang. "The Corrupted Officer Wang Shouye I Knew" (张金昌: 我认识的贪官王守业), *Yanhuang chunqiu* (炎黄春秋), Beijing, No. 1, 2015.

Zhang Jing. "Dig a Canal of Two Thousand Li" (张静: 挖两千里运河), *Liaowang dongfang* (瞭望东方周刊), Shanghai, Apr. 4, 2021.

Zhang Kaiyuan. "Who's 'Tormenting' China's Universities?" (章开沅: 谁在"折腾"中国的大学), *Tongzhou gongji* (同舟共进), Guangzhou, No. 6, 2009.

Zhang Ke. "Nearly 10 Million Chinese Emigrated in 23 years" (章轲: 中国23年移民近千万人), *First Financial Daily* (第一财经日报), Beijing, Jan. 22, 2014.

Zhang Liang. "Mysterious Command Center" (张良: 神秘的指挥部), *Vision Times*, New York, Aug. 17, 2015.

Zhang Manshuang. "The Myth of Age in Officials' Resumes" (张曼双: 官员履历里的年龄之谜), *Chongqing chenbao* (重庆晨报), May 29, 2016.

Zhang Meng. "Thirty-One Provinces Enter Key Stage of Hukou Reform" (张猛: 31省份户籍制度改革进入关键期), *Zhongguo xinwen wang* (中国新闻网), Beijing, Nov. 11, 2019.

Zhang Min. "Housing Inventory Doubled in Two Years" (张敏: 楼市库存近两年来近翻倍), *Zhongguo zhengquan bao* (中国证券报), Beijing, Sept. 16, 2014.

Zhang Min. "How Many Fake Texts Are Still Fooling Our Pupils' Intelligence?" (张敏: 还有多少假课文在侮辱孩子的智商), *Sina xinwen* (新浪新闻), Beijing, Apr. 18, 2021.

Zhang Ming. "China's Residual Debt Is 2.7 Times of GDP" (张明: 中国存量债务达GDP的2.7倍), *Caijing* (财经), Beijing, May 18, 2021.

Zhang Moling. "Tangshan Case under the Storm of Treating Smog" (张墨宁: 治霾风暴下的唐山样本), *Nanfeng chuang* (Southern winds), Guangzhou, Jan. 16, 2014.

Zhang Munan. "China as World's Largest Trading Country Is a 'Mirage'" (张茉楠: 中国世界第一贸易大国是幻觉), *Financial and Economic Net* (财经网), Beijing, Aug. 11, 2014.

Zhang Peihong. "100 Observations of Jails" (张培鸿: 律师看守所见闻100条), *Zhifei falu* (智飞法律), ishare.ifeng.com/c/s/7poANsiscZD, Sept. 9, 2019.

Zhang Ping. *State Cadres* (张平: 国家干部). Beijing: Renmin wenxue, 2009.

Zhang Ping. "Chinese Medial System Becomes Spring Bed for Corruption" (中国医疗体制成为腐败温床), *Deutsche Welle News* in Chinese, Aug. 2, 2013.

Zhang Qi. Interview of Huang Yasheng (张琪: 采访黄亚生), *Jingji guancha* (经济观察), July 4, 2011.

Zhang Qi. "The Evolution of Macroeconomic Thoughts in Contemporary China" (张琦: 当代中国宏观经济思想的变迁), *Zhongguo Gaige* (中国改革), Beijing, No. 4, Aug. 2021.

Zhang Qianfan. *For Human Dignity* (张千帆: 为了人的尊严). Beijing, Minzhu Fazhi, 2012.

Zhang Qianfan. "Debating Public Power behind the Xue Manzi Case" (张千帆: 薛蛮子事件背后的公权之辨), *Financial Times* (in Chinese), Sept. 6, 2013.

Zhang Qinafan. *Constitutional Politics in China* (张千帆: 宪政中国). New York: Boden, 2020.

Zhang Ruimin. *Study of the CCP's Practice of Anti-Poverty* (张瑞敏: 中国共产党反贫困实践研究). Beijing: Renmin, 2019.

Zhang Sheng. *Coming from War—Record of the Life of Zhang Aiping* (张胜: 从战争中走来: 张爱萍人生记录). Beijing: Zhongguo qingnian, 2008.

Zhang Shuguang [Chairman of Tianze Institute]. *Chinese Opinions: Interviews with Economists* (张曙光: 意见中国: 经济学家访谈录) 41, Mar. 2011.

Zhang Shunqing. "Records of 'Crusade against Confucius' in Qufu by Tang Houlan" (张顺清: 谭厚兰曲阜"讨孔"纪实), *Yanghuang chunqiu* (炎黄春秋) No. 2, 2015: 23–26.

Zhang Shunqing. "The Tragedy of Turning Confucius' Cemetery into Farm" (张顺清: 孔林变农场的悲剧), *Yanghuang chunqiu* (炎黄春秋) No. 7, 2015: 37–41.

Zhang Weibin. "Why Corrupt Officials Can't Pass the Hurdle of Lovers" (张卫斌: 贪腐官员缘何难过情人关?), *Fazhi wanbao* (法制晚报), Beijing, Feb. 18, 2014.

Zhang Wen. "Shaanxi School Organizes Thousand Students Taking Test Outdoor" (张闻: 陕西一学校组织千余学生户外考试), *Yangguang wang* (央广网), Beijing, Nov. 17, 2014.

Zhang Xianchi. *Gelagu Stories* (张先痴: 格拉古轶事). Keller, TX: Fellows (溪流), 2012.

Zhang Xiaojing. "Quarterly Report on China's Macro Leverage Ratio, Q2 2020," National Institution for Financial and Development, Beijing, Sept. 9, 2020.

Zhang Xin. "Which District in Beijing Is the Richest?" (张昕: 北京哪个区最富?), weizhishu.com/posts/bendi/201504/6828479494145.html, Apr. 16, 2015.

Zhang Xuezhong. "What's Wrong with the Critique of National Characters by Lu Xun, Bo Yang, and Long Yintai et al." (张雪忠: 鲁迅, 柏杨和龙应台等人的国民性批判错在哪里), *WeChat Blog*, Sept. 2016.

Zhang Yi. "Shanghai to Collect Real Estate Tax on Jan. 28?" (张煜: 上海个人房产税1月28日起征收?), *Sina caijing* (新浪财经), Jan. 29, 2021.

Zhang Yingjian. "What Happened to the Chinese Entrepreneurs Collectively?" (张英健: 中国企业家群体怎么了), *Fenghuang xinwen* (凤凰新闻), Hong Kong, Dec. 17, 2020.

Zhang Yuan. "Image Map of the 34 Provinces" (张媛: 全国34省形象地图). horizonkey.com/c/cn/news/2015-03/26/news_2651.html, Mar. 3, 2015.

Zhang Yue. "Only the Truth Can't Be Mediated" (张悦: 唯有真相不可调解), *Nanfang zhoumo* (南方周末), Guangzhou, May 1, 2008.

Zhang Zhongdong. *Hu Shi, Lei Zhen, Yin Haigunag: Portraits of Liberal Figures* (張忠棟: 胡適, 雷震, 殷海光-自由主義人物畫像). Taipei, Zili Wanbao, 1990.

Zhang Zhuan. "Top Banned Book and Its Brother" (張專: 頭號禁書及其兄弟), *Singtao daily* (星島日報), Hong Kong, Apr. 3, 2009.

Zhang, Changdong. *Governing and Ruling: The Political Logic of Taxation in China.* Ann Arbor: University of Michigan Press, 2021.

Zhang, Jie et al. "The Change in Suicide Rates between 2002 and 2011 in China," *Wiley Online Library*, Apr. 2014.

Zhang, Jie et al. "An Overview of Suicide Research in China," *Archives of Suicide Research* 6(2), 2002.

Zhang, Joe. "The Disintegration of Rural China," *The New York Times*, Nov. 28, 2014.

Zhang, Li. *Anxious China: Inner Revolution and Politics of Psychotherapy.* Berkeley, CA: University of California Press, 2020.

Zhang, Longmei et al. "China's High Savings: Drivers, Prospects, and Policies," *IMF Working Paper*, Dec. 2018.

Zhang, Monan. "Breaking China's Investment Addiction," *Project Syndicated*, Feb. 14, 2013.

Zhang, Qianfan. "Democracy and Meritocracy: A False Dichotomy," *Journal of Chinese Philosophy* 47(3/4), Sept–Dec. 2020: 213–247.

Zhang, Xiaoquan, and Feng Zhu. "Group Size and Incentives to Contribute: A Natural Experiment at Chinese Wikipedia," *American Economic Review* 101(4), June 2011: 1601–1615.

Zhao Baige. "Gender Balance and Harmonious Society" (赵白鸽: 性别比平衡与和谐社会), *Zhongguo dangzheng banbu luntan* (中国党政干部论坛), Beijing, No. 9, 2007: 7–8.

Zhao Changmao. "Raise Government's Credibility and Enforcing Ability" (赵长茂: 提高政府公信力和执行力), *Liaowang* (瞭望), Beijing, May 7, 2007.

Zhao Chao, and Xu Bo. "162,000 Experts Enjoying State Council Special Government Allowance" (赵超, 徐博: 我国累计评出享受国务院政府特殊津贴专家16.2万人), Beijing: Xinhua, May 23, 2011.

Zhao Chongqiang. "Shanxi Man Used Cartoons to Describe His Experience of Being Tortured to Confess" (赵崇强: 山西男子用漫画描绘被刑讯经过), *The Paper* (澎湃新闻), Aug. 9, 2015.

Zhao Dexin. "Route, Stages, and Basic Lessons of China's 50-Year Economic Development (赵德馨: 中国经济50年发展的路径, 阶段与基本经验), *Zhongguo jingjisgu yanjiu* (中国经济史研究) 5(6), 1999.

Zhao Dingxin. "On the Experience and Pursuit of IAS at Zheda" (赵鼎新: 谈浙大人文高等研究院的历程与追求), *The Paper* (澎湃), Shanghai, Jan. 18, 2022.

Zhao Dongshan. "Tutoring Industry Is Dead" (赵东山: 教培已死), *Zhongguo qiyejia* (中国企业家杂志), Beijing, July 26, 2021.

Zhao Fuduo. "Not Guilty Verdicts Have Been 0.016% since 2013" (赵复多: 2013年来无罪判决率为0.016%), *Caixing* (财新), Beijing, Nov. 5, 2016.

Zhao Jian. "Guard against the Economic Dark Matters behind the RMB" (赵建: 警惕人民币背后的经济暗物质), *Yanghang guancha* (央行观察), June 6, 2015.

Zhao Jianjun. "Comparing Economic Development in China and India (赵建军: 中国与印度经济发展比较), *Chinese National Conditions and Strength* (中国国情国力), Beijing, No. 4, 2003.

Zhao Lin. *Billions of People Following You* (亿万人民跟着您), Youku video (优酷视频), 2021. youtube.com/watch?v=OwSGzaMuiqA

Zhao Qiang. "Purging 'Naked Officials'" (赵强: 清理"裸官"), CCTV, Beijing, May 29, 2014.

Zhao Qiliu. "Shanghai Doctors on the Front Line of Anti-Pandemic: More Patients Likely Die from the Lockdown than from the Virus" (赵其流: 上海一線抗疫醫生: 因封控去世的患者可能比病毒致死的更多), *Initium Media* (端傳媒), Singapore Apr. 4, 2022.

Zhao Shukai. "Vice-Premier with 'Minister-Rank'" (赵树凯: "正部级"的副总理), *WeChat Blog* (微信公众号), Aug. 14, 2021.

Zhao Tianyu, and Xing Ying. "Who Got the ¥120 Billion Funds for Covid Vaccines" (赵天宇 辛颖: 1200亿元新冠疫苗钱, 谁拿到了) *Caijing zhazhi* (财经杂志), Apr. 4, 2022.

Zhao Tong. "State Allows Three kids, I Laughed My Head Off" (昭通: 国家放开三孩, 我已笑死), *Tencent* (腾讯), June 2, 2021.

Zhao Wanwei et al. "State-Run Care Centers Are Coming" (赵琬微等: 公办托管班来了), Xinhua, July 8, 2021.

Zhao Weifeng. "To Understand the Phenomenon of Chinese Independent Poetic Journals" (赵卫峰: 中国诗歌民办报刊现象认识), *Sina* (新浪), 2003.

Zhao Xiao. "Why We Still Should Learn from Japan" (我们为什么还要向日本学习), *Sohu Finance-Economics* (搜狐财经), June 2, 2014.

Zhao Yunheng. "Where Exactly Did the Proceeds of Crime Go" (赵运恒: 赃款赃物到底都去哪儿了), *Sina* (新浪), Mar. 6, 2015.

Zhao Zhouxian, and Xu Zhidong. "Trend of IT Technology and Ideological Security" (赵周贤, 徐志栋: 信息技术发展趋势与意识形态安全), *Red Flag Draft* (红旗文稿), Beijing, Dec. 5, 2014.

Zhao Ziyang et al. *Prisoner of the State: The Secret Journal of Zhao Ziyang*. New York: Simon, 2009.

Zhao, Yong. *Who's Afraid of the Big Bad Dragon? Why China Has the Best (and Worst) Education System in the World*. San Francisco: Jossey-Bass, 2014.

Zhao, Zhongwei, and Wei Chen. "China's Rising Sex Ratio at Birth," *East Asian Forum*, June 2011.

Zhen Jian. "90% of China's Coastal Seas Have No Fish to Catch" (针见: 中国 90%近海已无鱼可捕), *Tencent xinwen* (腾讯新闻), Nov. 30, 2019.

Zhen Sujing. "Decrees Inhibiting Price Decrease Again" (甄素静: 限跌令又现), *Meiri jingji xiwen* (每日经济新闻), Sichuan, June 23, 2022.

Zheng Baowei. "People Don't Dare to Eat Chinese Milk Powder—a National Humiliation" (郑宝炜: 国民不敢吃中国奶粉是国耻), *United Daily* (联合早报), Singapore, Feb. 7, 2015.

Zheng Gang. *Red Summaries—the Ups and Downs of CCP Senior Leaders* (郑刚: 红色纪要-中共高层要员沉浮录), 3 volumes. Beijing: Xiyuan, 2000.

Zheng Hedao. "80 Thousand People Have No Escape, Lost 18 Billion" (正和岛: 8万人无一幸免欠了180亿), *Sohu* (搜狐), June 26, 2019.

Zheng Jie Ju. "Eight Provinces Feed the Whole Country" (正解局: 8个省份税收养活全国), *Jiemian* (界面), July 3, 2020.

Zheng Liping. "Great Rejuvenation of Chinese Nation Entered Irreversible Stage of History" (郑丽平: 实现中华民族伟大复兴进入了不可逆转的历史进程), *Guangming ribao* (光明日报), Aug. 26, 2021.

Zheng Qiang. Speech by Zhejiang University Zheng Qiang (浙大郑强演讲), Hangzhou, 2014 and 2020.

Zheng, Tiantian. *Red Ethnographies of Prostitution in Contemporary China: Gender Relations, HIV/AIDS, and Nationalism*. New York: Palgrave Macmillan, 2012.

Zheng, Tiantian. *Red Lights: The Lives of Sex Workers in Postsocialist*. Minneapolis: University of Minnesota Press, 2009.

Zhengshi Shitan. "I Will Never Trust Even a Single Word in the Official Statement about Shanghai" (政知时谈: 对上海的通报, 我一个字都不会再信), *WeChat Blog* (微信公众号), Apr. 22, 2022.

Zhi Gu. "Tolerance for Inequality has Reached the Limit, the Third Reallocation Is Coming" (智谷: 对贫富差距容忍到了极限, 第三次分配来了), *Wangyi* (网易), Beijing, Aug. 19, 2021.

Zhi Guzi. "Why China Is Just Rising Up but the Young Have Lain Flat" (智谷子: 为什么中国刚刚崛起, 青年却躺平了) *WeChat Blog*, May 28, 2021.

Zhi Zhu. "Specialty Towns Went Bankruptcy Wholesale" (智筑: 特色小镇, 批量倒闭了), *Tencent* (腾讯), Apr. 28, 2021.

Zhicheng caijing (至诚财经). "Latest News on 2022 Military Pay Raise" (2022军人涨工资最新消息), Beijing, Jan. 7, 2022.

Zhihu (知乎). "Civil Servant Salary Seen Reduced 15% in Many Localities" (多地公务员曝减薪25%), news.creaders.net/china/2021/12/12/2429615.html, Dec. 13, 2021.

Zhihu (知乎). "Why 'Shanghai Enriched Neighbors and Beijing Impoverished Neighbors'" (为什么说"上海富了周围,北京坑了周围"?), Beijing, zhuanlan. zhihu.com/p/103183053, Dec. 11, 2014.

Zhihu (知乎). "What Are Horrific or Little-Known Homicide Cases in China?" (中国有哪些恐怖或鲜为人知的杀人案件), Beijing. zhihu.com/question/26686292.

Zhihu (知乎). "Where Is Google Better than Baidu?" (Google 搜索比百度搜索好在哪些地方). zhihu.com/question/20140749, May 2016.

Zhihu (知乎). "Behind Rampant Human Trafficking" (拐卖人口现象猖獗的背后), zhuanlan.zhihu.com/p/142785160, May 21, 2020.

Zhilian Zhaopin. *Report on Employment Power of College Graduates 2022* (智联招聘: 2022大学生就业力调研报告), Beijing, Apr. 27, 2022.

Zhong Bai. "Thirteen People Swindled 130 Million" (终白: 13人骗了30亿), *Zhengquan shibao* (证券时报), Jan. 3, 2010.

Zhong Jian. "Inside Organ Transplanting from the Executed on the Mainland" (钟坚: 大陆死刑犯器官移植内幕), *Phoenix Weekly* (凤凰周刊), Hong Kong, Nov. 11, 2014.

Zhong Jian. "Analyzing the 'Civilian Major Generals' in Mainland Military" (钟坚: 解析大陆军方"文职少将"群体), *Fenghuang zhoukan* (凤凰周刊), No. 26, Hong Kong, Sept. 16, 2010.

Zhong Jian. "Inside Story of Seizing Xu Caihou the Traitor" (钟坚: 国贼徐才厚查抄内幕), *Fenghuang zhoukan* (凤凰周刊), Hong Kong, No. 52, Nov. 20, 2014.

Zhong Min. "Behind the Worst Numbers in Beijing, Shanghai, and Shenzhen" (中民: 京沪深十年来最差统计数据背后), Peking University Alumni Forum, Jan. 17, 2021.

Zhong Qiguang. *Zhong Qiguang Memoirs* (钟期光回忆录). Beijing: PLA, 1995.

Zhong Weizhi. "Cao Dewang: Chinese People Are Not Bad, It Is the Elites Who Are Bad" (仲伟志: 曹德旺-中国民众不坏,中国坏就坏在精英), *Huxiu* (虎嗅), Beijing, Sept. 29, 2018.

Zhong Xin. "U.S. Degree Mills Out of Control, 95% Diplomas Given to Chinese" (钟欣: 美国"野鸡大学"泛滥, 证书95%给了中国人), *Beijing qingnian bao* (北京青年报), Feb. 24, 2014.

Zhong Zhengsheng, and Li Huiquan. "Deficit Ratio Analysis" (钟正生 & 李蕙荃: 赤字率分析), *Caixin zhiku* (财新智库), Mar. 22, 2018.

Zhong Zukang. *Don't Want to Be Chinese in Next Life* (鐘祖康: 來生不做中國人). Taipei: Yunchen, 2007.

Zhongmin Social Assistance Institute. White Paper on Missing People in China (中民社会救助研究院: 中国走失人口白皮书), Beijing, Feb. 2021.

Zhou Bin. "I Eye-Witnessed the Inside of Sino-Japanese Negotiation for Diplomatic Relations" (周斌: 我亲历的中日邦交谈判内幕), *Xinmin zhoukan* (新民周刊), Shanghai, No. 15, 2007.

Zhou Bojue. "Analysis of China's Internet Black Market—Baidu's Price-Bidding Page" (周伯爵: 中国互联网黑市分析-百度竞价单页), *Huxiu* (虎嗅), Aug. 27, 2014.

Zhou Guangli. *Investigating the Quality of Chinese PhDs* (周光礼: 中国博士质量调查). Wuhan: Huazhong keji daxue, 2010.

Zhou Hong. "Foreign Aid and Contemporary International Relations" (周弘: 对外援助与当代国际关系), CASS Journal (中国社会科学院院报), Feb. 1, 2007.

Zhou Jianhong. "The Mechanism of Reverse-Elimination in Officialdom and Ideas for its Treatment" (周建红: 官场逆淘汰的形成机制及治理思路), *Lingdao kexue* (领导科学), Zhengzhou, Henan, No. 6, 2015.

Zhou Li-An. "Institutional Model and the Chinese Experience" (周黎安: 经济学的制度范式与中国经验), *Tsinghua Social Science*, Beijing 1–2, 2020.

Zhou Li-An. *Local Governments in Transformation* (周黎安: 转型中的地方政府). Shanghai: Renmin (2008) 2017.

Zhou Liping et al. "Report on Health of Civil Servants" (周丽萍等: 公务员健康报告), *Anti-Corruption Outlook* (廉政瞭望), Chengdu, no. 22, Nov. 2014.

Zhou Qiang. *Working Report of Supreme People's Court* (周强: 最高人民法院工作报告 2020), Beijing, 2020 and 2021.

Zhou Qiren. "Plan and Strategize for Investment in 'the Winter'" (周其仁: 在"冬天"谋划布局投资), Lecture at Chinese Keystone Forum on Management, Beijing, Oct. 30, 2014.

Zhou Qunfeng. "28 People Including Su Dawu and Wife Arrested" (周群峰: 孙大午夫妇等28人被抓), *China News Weekly* (中国新闻周刊), Beijing, Nov. 13, 2020.

Zhou Songtao. "Towards Zero Completely: Wanda Sold All Overseas Assets" (周松涛全部归零: 万达卖光海外资产), *Sohu* (搜狐), Nov. 27, 2020.

Zhou Tianyong [professor of Central CCP Party School]. *Chinese Opinions: Interviews with Economists* (周天勇: 意见中国: 经济学家访谈录), No. 13, July 2010.

Zhou Tianyong. "How Heavy Is the Actual Tax Burden in China?" (周天勇: 中国税收负担究竟有多重), *Financial Times in Chinese*, Dec. 18, 2018.

Zhou Wen. *Why States Rise and Fall* (周文: 国家何以兴衰). Beijing: Renmin daxue, 2021.

Zhou Xiaohong. "Oral History, Collective Memory and Narratives of Industrialization (口述史、集体记忆与新中国的工业化叙事), *Xuexi yu tansuo* (学习与探索), Haerbing, No. 7, 2020.

Zhou Xinmin. "The Era of Great Change Calls for World Political Leader" (周新民: 大变局时代呼唤世界政治领袖), *Jinri Toutiao* (今天头条), Beijing, June 9, 2020.

Zhou Yan. *Elite's Decay: Intellectuals in the Evolutionary Era* (周言: 士林的沒落: 革命時代的知識人), Taipei: Xiuwei zixun, 2011.

Zhou Ying. "China's Railroad Exceeds 139,000 km," *China News Agency*, Beijing, Nov. 22, 2019.

Zhou Yuanzheng. "The Mysterious Organization Taishan Society Is Disbanded" (周远征: 神秘组织泰山会已解散), *Tencent Xinwen* (腾讯新闻), Guangzhou, Jan. 21, 2021.

Zhou Yunpeng. "Chinese Children" (周云蓬: 中国人的孩子), youtube.com/watch?v=UDSk_4l1vOg, June 9, 2009.

Zhou Zhaojun, and Guo Jinchao. "China Amends Criminal Code" (周兆军, 郭金超: 中国修改刑法), *Xinhua News Dispatch*, Beijing, Feb. 25, 2011.

Zhou Zhiyu. "Can Pan Shiyi Sell SOHO as Wished?" (周智宇: 潘石屹能如愿卖掉SOHO吗?), *Huaerjie jianwen* (华尔街见闻), Shanghai, Aug. 7, 2021.

Zhou, Maigeng et al. "Excess Mortality in Wuhan City and Other Parts of China during the Three Months of the COVID-19 Outbreak." London, *BMJ*, Feb. 2021, 327n415.

Zhou, Xueguang. *The Logic of Governance in China: An Organizational Approach.* New York: Cambridge University Press, 2022.

Zhou, Zunyou. " 'Residential Surveillance at a Designated Residence': A Special Form of Pre-trial Detention in China's Criminal Procedure," *Journal of Contemporary China*, 30(127), 2021.

Zhu Bin. "Effects of Spouse's Family Background on Elite Status Attainment in Urban China" (朱斌: 中国城市居民的配偶家庭与精英地位获得), *Shehui* (社会), Beijing, 37(5), 2017.

Zhu Chen et al. "China Tackles the Health Effects of Air Pollution," *The Lancet* 382(9909), Dec. 14, 2013.

Zhu Heping. "Marshal Zhu De during the Cultural Revolution (朱和平: 朱德元帅的文革岁月), *Dangshi bochai jishi* (党史博采纪实), Beijing, No. 12, 2006.

Zhu Jicha. "Xi Jinping on 'Three Political Abilities' Three Times in One Month" (朱基钗: 习近平一个月内三提"政治三力"), Beijing: Xinhua, Jan. 23, 2021.

Zhu Li, and Zhao Hong. *Big Fake: Survey of the Counterfeiting Industry* (朱力, 赵红: 大作假-伪造业扫描). Guiyang: Guizhou Renmin, 1994.

Zhu Li. *Out of the Whirlpool of Social Contradictions and Conflicts* (朱力: 走出社会矛盾冲突的漩涡). Beijing: Shehui kexue wenxian, 2012.

Zhu Pule. "Daily Life in Mao Era" (朱普乐: 毛时代的衣食住行), *Aisixiang* (爱思想), Oct. 1, 2014, *Weibo* (微博), Jan. 3, 2022.

Zhu Weijing. "Core Journal Publish the Essay by the Chief Editor's Ten-Year-Old Son" (诸未静: 核心期刊发主编十岁儿子散文), *Nanfang dushi bao* (南方都市报), Feb. 10, 2020.

Zhu Xuedong. "A Perspective on Design by a Non-Professional" (朱学东: 一个非专业人员的设计观), *Jinri toutiao* (今日头条), Beijing, July 21, 2021.

Zhu Xueqin. "Spit Out Wolf Milk" (朱学勤: 吐尽狼奶), *Xin Shiji*, Shanghai, Feb. 15, 2014.

Zhu, Jiangnan, and Dong Zhang. "Weapons of the Powerful: Authoritarian Elite Competition and Politicized Anticorruption in China," *Comparative Political Studies* 50(9), 2017.

Zhu, Ning. *China's Guaranteed Bubble.* New York: McGraw-Hill, 2016.

Zhuang Ping. "Analysis of the Social Phenomenon of Women Trafficking in Our Country" (庄平: 关于我国买卖妇女社会现象的分析), *Shehuixue yanjiu* (社会学研究) 5, 1991.

Zhuang Shengdie. "The Historic-Cultural Foundation for the Power Fetishist Society" (庄生蝶: 权力拜物教社会的历史文化基础), *Sina* (新浪), Oct. 13, 2007.

Zhuang Yixie. "Why China's Tap Water Is Not Drinkable?" (庄亦谐: 为什么中国的自来水不能直接喝), *Wangyi xinwen* (网易新闻), Beijing, Jan. 6, 2018.

Zhuo Zi. "I'll Kill Him When I'm Better" (桌子: 病好了我要杀他), Blog, youwuqiong.top/492021.html, Oct. 16, 2021.

Zi You. "The Cream of the Crop of Chinese Students Who Went Abroad All Ended Up in the U.S." (子侑: 中国留学精英, 尽入美国怀抱), *Wangyi* (网易), Oct. 22, 2014.

Zi Zhongyun. *Backbones of Intellectuals* (资中筠: 士人风骨). Nanning: Guangxi shida, 2011.

Zimbardo, Philip. "Mind Control: Psychological Reality or Mindless Rhetoric?" *Monitor on Psychology* 33(10), 2002.

Zong Pu. *Old Things and New Tales* (宗璞: 旧事与新说). Beijing: Xinxing, 2010.

Zou Chunxia. "How Was APEC Blue Maintained?" (邹春霞: "APEC蓝"是如何保障的?), *Beijing qingnian bao* (北京青年报), Nov. 13, 2014.

Zou Le. "Liu Zhijun, Gu Junshan et al. Own Hundreds of Housing Properties" (邹乐: 刘志军,谷俊山等坐拥数百套房产), *Beijing chenbao* (北京晨报), Nov. 23, 2014.

Zou Yilin. "Interviews on Thoughts on Chorography" (邹逸麟: 方志思想采访录), *Shizhi yanjiu* (史志研究), Ningbo, No. 1, 2015.

Zubaidah, Nazeer. "Indonesia Gripped by Plastic Rice Scare," *The Strait Times*, Singapore, May 26, 2015.

Zuckerman, Arthur. "50 Cheating Statistics: 2019/2020 Demographics, Reasons & Who Cheats More," *Compare Camp*, May 29, 2020.

Zuo Fang. *How Steel Could Not Be Made* (左方: 鋼鐵是怎樣煉不成的). Hong Kong: Tiandi, 2014.

Zweig, David, *Internationalizing China: Domestic Interests and Global Linkages*. Ithaca, NY: Cornell University Press, 2002.

Zweig, David, and Huiyao Wang. "Returnee Entrepreneurs: Impact on China's Globalization Process," *Journal of Contemporary China* 20(70), 2011: 413–431.

Zweig, David, and Siqin Kang. "America Challenges China's National Talent Programs," *Occasional Paper* No. 4, CSIS, May 2020.

Index

10 percent rule, 10, 233n34

211 Project, 200

5G, 131

981 Project 981 首长健康工程, 68, 247n245

985 Project, 200

acid rain, 214

AI (artificial intelligence), 79, 206

air pollution & quality, 213–14, 216–19

Alibaba 阿里巴巴, 77, 102, 132, 209, 211

Anhui 安徽, 119, 152, 201, 252n28

anti-corruption, 17, 37, 71–74, 141, 183, 188, 203, 274n61

anti-Japanese TV soap opera, 抗日神剧, 178

anti-pollution, 218–19

Anti-Rightist 反右, 19, 44, 241n121

antiquity, 2, 4, 21, 176, 107, 210–13, 281n229

APEC, 218–19

art troupes 文工团, 276n103

asylum, 167–68, 268n157 & n158

atheist/atheism, 58, 67, 175, 181, 190

atheist theocracy, 177

Australia, 165, 167, 168

authoritarianism, 15–18, 26–27, 34, 50, 57–58, 69–70, 83, 87–88, 100, 104, 106, 133, 179, 187, 227–28

baby mega-corruptor 娃娃巨贪, 73

bachelors village 光棍村, 162

Baidu 百度, 160

Banqiao Dam 板桥水库, collapse of, 156

Basic Party Line, 36, 127, 177

Beijing City 北京, 62, 63–64, 93, 107, 150, 159, 199, 214, 217–19, 265n94

real estate of, 126; Wall of, 211

Beijing Hotel, 213

Beijing Stock Exchange, 100

Belt and Road Initiative 一带一路, 108, 116

Biden, Joe, 5

billionaires, in China, 75–78, 136, 146, 147

birth control, *also see* demography, 77, 93–95, 112, 135, 162, 266n108

bitterness, eater of, eating 吃苦, 89, 97, 135, 138, 141–44, 164, 165, 172, 175, 199

BJP (Bharatiya Janata Party), 56

Blue Sky Rescue 蓝天救援队, 155

body slave, mind slave 身奴心奴, 194, 276n96

Book of Guan Zi 管子, 26, 248n265
Book of Han Fei 韩非子, 26, 238n79, 248n265
Book of Lord Shang 商君书, 26, 248n265
bubbles, in the economy, 107–108, 123–29, 202
Buddhism, 162, 176, 209

Cadre 干部, 17, 26, 40–41, 50, 53, 55–57, 60–69, 72–75, 77–78, 92, 104, 123–25, 141–42, 161, 177, 180–82, 185–89, 191–92, 203, 206–207, 218, 243n181, 244n190, 246n233, 247n237
calling a stag a horse 指鹿为马, 192
Canada, 167, 168, 171
cancer, case and death, 143, 216, 262n27 & n28, 283n266
CCP (Chinese Communist Party) 中国共产党, 1–5, 15–22, 33
    20th Party Congress 20 大, 28, 55, 237n54; Central Committee, 55, 73, 244n183; *Constitution* of, 31–32; DNA, 17, 22–34, 88; "great, glorious and correct," 18, 234n11; ideology of, 24–33; magic weapons, 26; mission of, 18, 20, 29–30, 51, 229, 244n187; not dogmatic, 104, 191, 238n72; pantheon of, 184–89; Politburo, 55, 73; Politburo Standing Committee, 55, 71, 73, 161, 238n69; size of, 55–56; spiritual lineage, 32, 190; tycoon relations, 74–78, 102
CCP leaders, 20–21, 26–28, 43, 52, 57, 66–69, 73, 78, 87, 93, 144, 183, 187, 190, 210, 212–13, 218, 239n103, 272n53 & n54
CCP Optimality, 34–35, 70, 81, 124, 137, 228

CCP-PRC, *see* party-state
CCTV 央视, 78, 180
censorship, *also see* misinformation, disinformation, Great Fire Wall, 81–82, 157, 160, 173, 180, 195, 204, 210–11, 223, 246n212
census, 7, 81
Central Military Commission 中央军委, 58
Central Security Bureau 中央警卫局, 59, 245n206
chained mother of 8, 81
Chiang Kai-shek 蒋介石, 24
China Dream 中国梦, 17–18, 33, 223, 234n9
China, international comparison of, 2, 88, 109–17, 120–22, 133–34, 136, 138–43, 145–47, 153–56, 160–64, 178, 208, 211, 213, 235n24, 253n54, 261n6
China Model, 86–91, 109, 133, 251n3
China Order 中华秩序, 1, 2, 21, 25, 33, 39, 53, 179, 185, 228
China Suboptimality, 34–37, 78, 81, 88, 124, 137–38, 141, 159, 169, 175, 190, 228
China Tobacco, 59, 132, 158
China Tragedy, 18–22, 25, 34, 35–36, 85, 90, 175, 182, 190, 228
Chinese Academy of Sciences 中国科学院, 132, 163, 197, 201, 223
Chinese Civil War, 16, 18–19, 66, 91, 109
Chinese Exclusion Act of 1882, 92
Chinese Revolution, 29, 33, 36, 85, 211
chorography 地方志, 212
Christianity, 24, 58, 176–77, 178, 244n194
circulation, global and internal, 116–17

cities, tier of, 107, 126, 149, 250
Citizen Score/Sesame Credit 社会信
  用/芝麻分, 170
civil rights, in China, 29, 37
civil servant 公务员, *see* cadre
civil servant exam 公务员考试, 63,
  206–207
class, 3, 45, 49, 55, 56, 58, 136, 152,
  260n1
  enemies of, 44–45, 92, 220,
    241n124; middle, 51, 105, 136,
    146, 153, 167, 195, 251n2,
    260n1; ruling/upper, 64–68, 136,
    141, 144, 150, 152, 167, 186,
    212, 251n2, 260n1
Classified Post System 机要邮局, 59
CNKI (China National Knowledge
  Infrastructure) 中国知网, 196,
  243n175
coal industry, 102, 141
Cold War, 50, 54, 228
collective leadership, 16–17
college entrance exam 高考, 148,
  206–207, 263n55
Comintern (Communist International),
  23, 56
common prosperity, 29–30, 56, 147,
  152–53
communes 公社, 21, 92, 93
Communism, 17, 18, 23, 29, 33, 49,
  50, 56, 66, 181, 184, 191, 227,
  228–29, 285n4
Communist Youth League 共青团,
  58, 60
community of common destiny for
  humanity 人类命运共同体, 17,
  32, 33, 234n9
Confucianism 儒家, 22, 24, 33, 46,
  49–50, 52, 69, 70, 175, 179,
  186, 190, 191, 193, 227
Confucius 孔子, 30, 211–12, 234n1,
  281n229

corporate profitability, 129, 132
corruption, 41, 51, 52, 68–69, 71–74,
  89, 96, 98, 114, 115, 131, 159,
  164, 172, 177, 181–83, 188–89,
  207, 213, 223, 271n32, 272n54,
  273n59 & n60
  anecdata of, 194–96; in academia
    and education, 166, 196–203,
    206–207, 275n90 & n94,
    276n118, 277n119, 279n169 &
    n180
counterfactual analysis, 209, 235n24
counterfeit 山寨, 79, 129, 208–209,
  223–25
county, size of government, 58,
  62–63
COVID-19, 10–11, 35, 80, 98, 105,
  117, 119, 128, 133, 173, 178,
  195, 197, 210
  cases and deaths, 10–11, 232n32;
    lockdown, 79, 82, 156–58,
    233n42 & n44, 265n87; mobile
    cabin 方舱, 157, 265n86; origin,
    10–11, 185, 233n45; vaccine,
    157–58, 265n89 & n90; zero-
    virus/COVID policy, 157, 210,
    265n90
crime, 42–43, 75–76, 80, 170–71,
  177, 269n178
  offenses, 115, 204, 239n92,
    269n173; rate, of cadres, 72–74
Cultural Revolution 文革, 19, 20, 21,
  29, 183, 185, 211, 212, 272n54
cynicism, 54, 72, 169, 181, 188, 191,
  207

Dalai Lama 达赖喇嘛, 284n285
danwei (work units) 单位, 21
DCEP (Digital RMB), 212
death penalty, capital punishment,
  19, 40, 42–43, 58, 67, 72–73,
  74–76, 82, 101, 102, 114, 134,

death penalty, capital punishment
(*continued*)
154–56, 158, 171, 193, 195,
239n103, 240n110 & 116
death toll, 7–8, 19–20, 23, 41, 46,
74, 80, 95, 108, 109, 141, 143,
153, 156, 158–59, 216, 235n18,
241n130, 252n35, 265n88
debt, debt ratio, 89, 105, 110, 114,
116–20
decree inhibiting price drop 限跌令,
127
deficit, 91, 105, 118–20, 123
of environment/human rights 环境/
人权赤字, 90–91, 97
democracy, Chinese kind of, 30–31,
49–51, 57, 69, 184, 237n64
"democratic parties" 民主党派,
244n195
demography, 6–7, 94–95, 112, 162
Deng Xiaoping 邓小平, 20, 27–28,
30–32, 71, 76, 88, 133, 152,
187, 212, 236n43, 272n54
developmental state, 86, 87–88, 110,
222, 251n4
DIC (discipline inspection
committee) 纪检委, 39, 58, 59,
63, 71, 181, 183, 274n61
disaster relief, 2, 135, 153–59, 160
disinformation, *see also* censorship,
16, 26, 36, 48, 53–54, 104, 157,
180, 242n143
divorce rate, 171–72, 207
dossier 档案, 170
Dongguan 东莞, 196
Dow Jones Index, 99
drug trafficking, 171

earthquake, 154–55, 156, 275n94
EB-5 Program, 167
ecological footprint, 215

economic dark matters, 116
economic distortion, 98–103, 125–
29
economic extraction, by the state, 3,
17, 21, 33, 37, 86, 88, 91, 93,
96, 98, 103–108, 112, 118, 133,
142, 147, 186, 227
economic growth, *see* GDP
emigration, 82, 135, 164–69, 189,
267n124 & n125, 286n155
energy, 37, 89, 124, 130, 141
efficiency of, 93, 110, 129–30,
215, 216; renewable, 259n202;
security of, 159
Engel Coefficient, 141–42, 261n18
environment, problems of, 3, 22, 68,
108, 110, 114, 129, 143, 162,
175–78, 213–29, 225, 282n237
& 251, 283n263 & n266
epidemic, 11, 277n120
ethics, *also see* moral code/morality,
2, 4, 21, 24, 44, 73, 144,
175–78, 180–82, 184, 186–87,
189–90, 194–95, 198–99, 204,
205, 213, 222, 262n32
European Union, 86, 100, 115, 116,
168, 224
Evergrande 恒大, 129
extralegal, 39, 44–47, 71, 74, 76, 78,
79, 147, 195, 241n130

fake, fakery, 7, 26, 107, 108, 171,
177, 180, 185, 191–92, 194–96,
197, 199, 206, 207–10, 212,
223–24, 238n84, 277n130
false/spurious consciousness, 51,
243n162
fahouwang 法后王 & *faxianwang* 法先
王, *also see* rule by law, 233n1
Falun Gong 法轮功, 45, 177
Fascist aesthetics, 48

fazi 法治/法制, *see* rule of law and rule by law

feudal ("Eastern") values, 177, 179, 184, 190

fifty-cents party 五毛党, 48, 60

fiscal policy, 12, 63, 86, 89, 103–108, 110, 118–20, 123, 156, 200, 254n95, 257n154

Five Black Kinds 黑五类, 44–45

food, 67, 85, 92, 101, 141–42, 212–13

  safety, 68, 79, 158–59, 160, 208–209, 218, 265n92; security, 6–7, 159, 265n94

foreign currency reserve, 86, 89, 96, 110, 114–17, 133, 257n146

Four Cardinal Principles 四项基本原则, 27, 236n43

Foxconn 鸿海, 115

France, 178, 221

fraudulent accident 碰瓷, 210, 281n217

Fudan University 复旦大学, 48, 202, 205

G7, 116

games of numbers, 4–12, 70, 111, 118, 134, 156, 157, 159, 163, 207, 218, 261n4

ganbu 干部, *see* cadre

gaogan (senior official) 高干, *also see* cadre, 26, 59, 66–69, 73–75, 102, 107, 128, 141, 144, 161, 188–90, 192, 195, 218, 244n190, 272n54

gastronomy, 212–13

GDP, as "chicken fart," 256n121; growth of, 7, 96–98, 99–100, 110–14, 123, 134, 253n61; size of, 6, 89, 91, 109, 110, 121, 137–39, 232n29, 253n54; per capita, 63, 91, 95, 106, 109, 129, 137–39, 150, 159

gender, equality and gap/ratio of, 49, 55, 94, 160–61, 162, 266n108

Generation II or III, of red and official or wealth, 红(官/富)二/三代, 183, 188

Germany, 72, 142, 178, 192, 221, 231n4, 275n94

Gini Coefficient, 5–6, 93, 145–46

globalism, 1, 18, 34, 227

government of PRC, levels of, 58, 65–66

GPS, GCJ-02 v. WGS-84, 9

Green Island 绿岛, 235n16

Great Famine 大饥荒, 6, 9, 19, 67, 91, 93, 94, 95, 103, 156, 271n25

Great Firewall, *also see* censorship, 47, 160

great leap backward, 18, 70

Great Leap Forward 大跃进, 9, 11, 21, 103, 201, 213

Guangdong 广东, 82, 119, 151, 201, 203, 213

Guangzhou 广州, 107, 114, 150, 171

Haier 海尔, 222

Happiness Index, 160–62

harsh strike 严打, 43, 147, 177, 196, 240n116

hazardous-duty or hardship-duty pay, 164

healthcare, 10–11, 63, 65, 67, 68, 74, 107, 108, 112, 142–43, 162–63, 187, 196, 210, 255n100

Hebei 河北, 62, 76, 151, 218, 219

Henan 河南, 152, 156, 206, 209

Hitler, Adolf, 19, 23, 28

HNA Group (Hainan Airline) 海航集团, 68

Holocaust, 20

homicide rate, 171

Hong Kong, 6, 54, 69, 76, 77, 87, 90, 112, 126, 130, 138, 160–61, 164, 168, 171, 205, 224, 267n124

house church, 177

household income, 3, 119, 136, 150

housing, *see also* real estate, occupancy, 65, 67, 79, 92, 124–28

HSR (high-speed rail) 高铁, 108, 114, 124, 255n105, 257n139

Hu Jingtao 胡锦涛, 50, 71, 88

Hu Yaobang 胡耀邦, 187

Huawei 华为, 40, 130, 131, 222

hukou (household registration) 户口, 37, 51, 81, 93, 95, 144, 148–50, 163, 179, 264n60 & n63

Human Development Index (HDI), 129–31, 138, 140, 150, 159

"many Chinas" by HDI, 150–52

human origin, 180

human rights, 4, 16, 21, 38, 71, 85, 88, 97, 192

human trafficking, 80–81, 162, 164, 269n172

Hunan 湖南, 62, 152, 211, 212–13

Huxley, Aldous, 48

illiterate and hooligan 文盲加流氓, 185, 272n44

IMF, 111, 120, 145, 161

Imitation 山寨, 21, 85, 132, 219, 221–25

superpower of, 219–25

imperial exam 科举, 55, 220, 223

Incremental Capital-Output Ratios, 109, 112–13

India, 5, 56, 95, 112–13, 129–30, 133–34, 136, 141, 142, 165, 168, 202, 217

inequality, 16, 64, 66, 86, 153, 164, 202

horizontal, 148–53; vertical, 136, 144–48

infidelity, 208

inflation, 7, 9, 91, 101, 116, 118, 120, 122–25, 126, 127–28, 134, 142, 254n74

informant, 60, 245n208, 274n79, 275n90

innovation, 16, 37, 56, 85, 111, 177, 220–22

lack of, 12, 86, 87, 89, 100, 104, 131–32, 145, 183–84, 206, 219–22, 224–25

intelligence operation, 59, 238n75

intelligentsia, 193

interest rate, 100–102, 116, 121

internal reference 内参, 59

International Consortium of Investigative Journalists (ICIJ), 68–69

involution, 108, 265n90

iPhone, 115

Iran, 42, 140, 151, 154, 160, 168

Islam, *see* Muslim

Italy, 63, 154, 223, 231n4

jail and jail population, *see* prison

Japan, 54, 61, 87, 91, 104, 105, 110, 112, 120, 124, 126, 127, 129, 132, 137, 141, 142–43, 154, 160, 166, 168, 171, 190, 211, 216, 211, 252n67

Jiang Zemin 江泽民, 20, 27–28, 50, 71, 88

jingoism, *see also* nationalism, 47, 157

job report 述职, 17, 234n7

Kashgar 喀什, 212

Khmer Rouge, 20

KMT (Kuomintang or Nationalist Party) 国民党, *also see* ROC, 18–19, 22, 63, 234n10

Korea, 54
North, 48, 100, 160, 236n39;
South, 83, 87, 110, 112, 113,
130, 132, 136, 139, 142, 151,
161, 168, 171, 216, 217, 222,
250n319

Lakeside University 湖畔大学, 77,
249n288
Land Reform 土改, 19, 92, 235n18
land ownership/rights, 27, 37, 56, 62,
89, 100, 106, 125, 128, 253n69
in Vietnam, 253n70
laogai (reform through labor) 劳改,
38, 46, 241n130
laojiao (education through labor) 劳
教, 38–39, 40, 46, 241n130
largest firms, 110, 115, 128, 130–32,
211
latecomer's advantage, 88, 90
latecomer's disadvantage/curse, 90–91
launching satellites 放卫星, 7, 9, 11
legal and judicial system, 22, 27, 29,
37–44, 52, 57, 72, 74, 79, 147,
149, 172, 183, 186
extra- and pre-legal, 44–47, 71, 74,
75–76, 78–79, 147, 241n130
Legalism/Legalist 法家, 18, 22, 26,
33, 46, 50, 51–52, 70, 72, 124,
137, 175, 179, 186, 190, 227,
248n365
legitimacy, political, 7, 16, 26, 88,
101, 104, 110, 152, 166, 173,
196, 193, 228
Lei Feng 雷锋, 143–44, 185, 262n32
Lenin, Vladimir, 22–23, 26, 31,
32–33, 50, 175, 190, 227,
236n40 & n43
Lenovo 联想, 222
Lewis Transition, 88
LGBTQ (lesbian, gay, bisexual,
transgender and queer), 49

Li Keqiang 李克强, 123, 146, 253n61
Li Wenliang 李文亮, 10
life expectancy, 135, 143, 231n4
leading cadres 领导干部, see cadre
and gaogan
Lin Biao 林彪, 272n54
LIO (liberal international order), 85,
229, 285n4
literacy, 135, 231n4
little pinks 小粉红, 54
Liu Shaoqi 刘少奇, 187, 236n40,
272n53
Liu Xiaobo 刘晓波, 45, 193, 284n285
living standard, 21, 53, 85, 91, 92,
93, 96, 110, 112, 114, 135–36,
141–42, 147, 159
lottery, 169, 269n165
LSGs (leading small groups) 领导小
组, 57

Ma Huateng 马化腾, 77
Ma Yun, Jack 马云, 77
Macao/Macau, 54, 90, 138, 168
maintain stability 维稳, 38, 44, 70,
81, 82, 118, 134, 142, 236n41
Manchuria/Northeast 满洲/东北, 6,
215
Mandate of Heaven 天命, 21, 24, 26
Mandate of the People, 24, 26,
236n37
Mao Zedong 毛泽东, 3, 5, 16, 17,
20–29, 31–33, 35–36, 42, 44–49,
51, 71, 77, 85, 103, 104, 109,
133, 141, 144, 152, 184–87,
192–94, 211, 234n7, 235n20 &
n30, 237n54, 238n72, 245n199
& n205, 282n283nuclear
accomplishments of Mao Era,
91–92, 135, 231n4, 235n24;
post-Mao era, 3, 12, 16, 20,
26–27, 37, 42, 45, 50, 85,
87–88, 94–97, 103, 118, 144,

Mao Zedong (continued)
164, 176, 182, 188, 191, 193,
200, 212–13; 220, 235n85,
238n84, 29n94; resistance to,
193, 275n85; tragedy of Mao
era, 9, 17–21, 25–26, 34, 77,
90–94, 135, 145, 164, 170, 175,
176, 182, 188, 195, 200, 201,
210, 213, 220, 231n5, 235n18,
239n94, 240n120, 252n35,
271n25 & n29, 272n53, 275n90,
276n103, 281n228
Mao Zedong Thought, 3, 8, 12,
15–16, 18, 22–27, 30–33, 36,
45, 49–50, 52, 57, 104, 190,
234n11, 236n40
Maotai 茅台, 67, 132, 190
Marx, Karl, 22, 29, 70
Marxism, 23, 26, 28, 31, 32, 49, 50,
190, 191, 201, 227, 236n40 &
n43
mass incidents or riots, 82–83, 105,
171, 250n319
Me Too campaign, 176, 270n2
meat grinder politics, 71
Meiji Restoration, 104
mental health, 23, 42, 45–47, 141,
162–63, 266n113
meritocracy, 51, 52, 69, 186, 207
middle-income trap, 90, 118
military, see PLA
Ming Dynasty 明朝, 70
misinformation, also see censorship,
16, 48, 53–54, 104, 157, 158,
180, 242n143
monetary policy, 12, 86, 89, 98, 110,
118, 120–23
money supply (M2 stock), 115–16,
118, 120
Mongol conquest, 20, 194
moral code/morality, also see ethics,
4, 9, 24, 31, 44, 176–77,
179–82, 187–81

moral relativism, 31, 181, 182, 192
moral vacuum/decay, 49–50, 177–78,
179–84, 186–88, 189–95, 198–
99, 206–208, 212–13, 222–23,
224, 271n15, 281n217
move southern water to the north 南
水北调, 108
multiculturalism, 1, 178
Muslim, 46, 72, 176, 177

naked officials 裸官, 31, 68, 189, 192,
274n81
nanotechnology, 204
national amnesia, 51, 180, 186, 190,
191–92
national character 国民性, 179
national mobilization 举国体制, 108
nationalism, see also jingoism, 18,
33, 49, 56, 191, 227
NATO, 231n2
Nazi Germany, 20, 72, 231n4,
275n94
New Zealand, 167, 168
network newscast of CCTV 新闻联
播, 180
Nobel Prize, 9, 193, 220, 275n89,
284n285
non-state sector, 49, 96–97, 102
nudity-borrowing 裸贷, 102–103,
254n82
numbers game, see games of numbers

obscurantism, 184–85, 180, 192, 220,
222
OECD, 130, 142, 160, 224
Officialdom 官场, see also police
state, 55–69, 72, 74, 110, 182,
189, 195–96, 212
officials-standard 官本位, see also power
fetishism, 47, 52–53, 58, 65, 178–
81, 182, 200, 222–23, 271n19
oil (petroleum), 102, 116, 130, 132,
159

Olympic Games, 78, 108, 219, 233n34, 255n111, 274n83

onanism, *zihai* 自嗨, *yiyin* 意淫, 177–78

organ transplant, harvest of, 43, 67

Orwell, George, *1984*, 48, 170, 180

P2P (peer to peer), 101

Pakistan, 108, 153, 154, 168

Panama Papers, 68–69

PAP (People's Armed Police) 武警, 56, 58

partocracy, *also see* party-state, 16, 22, 34, 37, 55–69, 104, 133, 177, 228, 238

party-state, 1, 3, 4, 11, 15–17, 21–22, 26–28, 30, 33, 35, 37, 38, 40, 47–49, 54–55, 57–58, 60, 63–75, 77, 82–83, 87–88, 91–92, 96, 100–101, 104–105, 108, 115, 123, 127, 133–34, 135–37, 141–43, 145, 147, 152–53, 156–58, 164, 167–68, 172, 175–78, 180–82, 190–91, 193–94, 203, 207, 209, 212, 225, 227–29, 235n24, 237n54, 264n60, 285n2

Pearl Harbor, 104

Pegatron 和碩, 115

Peking University 北京大学, 64, 162, 165, 200, 204, 205

pension, 112, 119, 142, 149, 150, 264n61

People's Bank (central bank) 人民银行, 98, 121, 146

People's Congress 人大, 55, 57–58, 64, 181

People's Political Consultative Conference 政协, 57, 58, 181

People's Daily 人民日报, 27, 59, 203

people's democratic dictatorship, people's democracy, people's dictatorship 人民民主专政, 2,
15–16, 18–19, 30, 37, 49–50, 57, 152, 175, 184, 236n43, 237n64

petition 信访, 46–47, 241n136

petrel syndrome 海燕综合症, 174, 270n193

PhD education, 63–64, 165–66, 197, 201–202, 205

piracy, 131, 223–25

PLA (People's Liberation Army) 解放军, 18, 48, 55, 58–59, 70, 103–104, 150, 181, 216, 245n199 & n200 & n204, 247n240

   corruption in, 181, 189, 216, 272n54, 273n59, 276n103

plagiarism, 185, 196–99, 202, 225, 277n119

Plagiarius Negative Award, 224–25

PM2.5, 216–17, 282n258

police state, *see also* officialdom, 37, 55, 59–64, 69, 74, 78–80, 120, 169

   purge of police, 73; size of police, 63, 70, 245n22; types of police, 38, 45–46, 59–60, 63, 78–80, 95, 169–70, 245n203

political commissar 政委, 59

political tradition and ideation, of China, 1, 4, 20, 124, 138, 185, 228, 224n190

populism, 18, 34, 50, 56, 104, 191, 227

poverty, 3, 7, 22, 86, 110–11, 135–36, 144–50, 152, 159, 253n69, 263n49, 264n63

poverty line, 7, 145–47, 263n42 & n50 & n51

power fetishism, 47, 53, 58, 180–81

PPP (purchasing power parity), 9, 96, 137–38, 253n54, 263n51

PRC Constitution, 17, 31, 50

PRC National Security Law, 30

Prison/jail, 40–42, 46, 60, 74, 239n103, 240n104

   Qincheng 秦城, 239n103

propaganda, 5, 9, 25, 26–33, 48–54, 104, 128, 157, 203, 204, 244n195, 284n298
detoxification of, 54, 176
prostitution, 46, 195–96, 254n82
press and publication, 160, 198, 210–11
purges, political, 17, 20, 35, 37, 44, 71–74, 156, 183, 187, 193–94, 222
Putin, Vladimir, 54, 167

Qin-Han polity 秦汉政体, 1, 4, 15, 18, 20–21, 22–23, 26, 30, 45, 46, 49–51, 72, 88, 94, 103, 137, 141, 179, 184, 190, 221, 227
Qing Dynasty 清朝, 19, 21, 61, 96, 210, 284n283
quantitative assessment, 4–7, 109–32, 261n4
quantum technology, 204, 279n180

R&D, 132, 203, 221
real estate, 68, 87, 124–29, 135, 146, 183
tax of, 105, 128, 142
recuperating and recovery policy 休养生息, 19
rehabilitation, 239n94
religion, 3, 31, 53, 176–77, 190
renewable energy, 259n202
Renmin University 人民大学, 205
return land to farming 复耕, 7
returnees 海归/海龟, 92, 166, 173–74, 252n28, 268n141
reverse-elimination 逆淘汰, 43, 69
Rich State and Strong Military 富国强军, 104
richest Chinese (Hurun) list, 75–76
RMB 人民币, 116, 120–25, 127, 257n146
exchange rate to USD, 127; internationalization of, 122–23

ROC (Republic of China) 中华民国, *also see* Taiwan, 18–19, 22, 24, 36, 66, 96, 137, 210, 220, 234n10, 284n283
rule by law, 44, 52, 233n1
rule of law, 15, 18, 26, 34, 44, 52, 90, 101, 184, 212, 213, 233n1, 243n170
rule of man, 15, 26, 44, 52, 233n1
ruler, ruling class and red aristocracy, 17, 20–21, 24, 26, 30, 31, 33–34, 43, 47, 50, 52, 57–58, 59, 64–69, 70–72, 74, 90, 103, 108, 118, 123, 124, 136, 141, 143, 144, 150, 179, 181, 182, 191–92, 194, 200, 223, 228, 233n1, 237n54, 265n90, 267n125
run-study 润学, 174, 270n293
Russia, 19, 121, 132, 140, 161, 172

Sanjiang Plains 三江平原, 215
SARS, 197, 277n120
SARS-CoV-2, *see* COVID-19
savings rate, 101, 103, 111–12
secret police, *see also* intelligence operations, 38, 40, 45, 56, 59, 71, 245n203 & n204, 274n61
SEE (Shanghai Composite Index) 上证指数, 99
selectorate, 34, 57
sent-down 下放, 93, 182, 196, 252n36
Shanghai Stock Exchange, 99
Shanghai 上海, lockdown of, 82–83, 174
Shostakovich, Dmitri, 231n4
Shenzhen 深圳, 107, 114, 125, 126, 136, 150, 171
Shenzhen Stock Exchange, 99
shuanggui (double designations) 双规, 38–39
Sichuan 四川, 152, 154, 212, 213

Singapore, 54, 87, 111, 171, 223
Social Darwinism, 23
social tranquility, 37, 70, 82–83, 135, 169
 in Korea and the US, 83, 250n319
social welfare, 115, 142, 186
Socialism, with Chinese characteristics, 8, 17–18, 27, 29, 30–32, 85–87, 145, 181, 229, 237n57
socialist core values, 191, 274n75
SOE (state owned enterprise) 国有企业, 49, 68, 88, 97, 101–103, 104–105, 113–14, 123–24, 131–32, 158–59, 186, 189
South Africa, 179, 192, 215
Soviet Union, 9, 19, 20, 21, 45, 48, 55, 56, 59, 67, 72, 108, 190, 194, 211, 222, 231n4, 238n72, 247n242
soy beans, 116, 159
Special Service Bureau 特勤局, 59, 245n206
special supplies (provisions) tegong 特供, 67, 93, 141, 159, 209, 247n242 & n243
Spring of Beijing, 27
Stalin, Joseph, 19, 22–23, 26, 28, 33, 144, 175, 190, 194, 227
State Council 国务院, 57, 207
state-capitalism, partocracy-capitalism, 21, 87, 90, 133, 228
stock market, 98–100, 103, 127
Stoicism, 143, 164, 169
suicide, 8, 72, 75, 92, 141, 158, 163
Summit for Democracy, 30
superpower/giant by the numbers, 3, 17, 89
Supreme People's Court 最高人民法院, 40, 43–44, 57, 240n110
Supreme People's Procuratorate 最高人民检察院, 39, 57

"superiority" of the CCP-PRC party-state, 8, 87, 133, 153, 232n26 & n27, 251n3
surveillance, 38, 59, 70, 78–80, 160, 170, 209
Sweden, 40

Tacitus Trap, 81
Taishan Society 泰山会, 77, 249n288
Taiwan 台湾, also see ROC, 19, 30, 36, 54, 57, 87, 113, 115, 137, 139, 142, 154, 161, 166, 213, 216, 251n4, 270n193
talent-attractions program 引才计划, 201
tangping (nihilistic slackening) 躺平, 173
targeted people 重点人口, 45, 72, 74, 147, 188, 269n170
tax, rate, 106, 123, 142, 145–46, 262n22
Tencent 腾讯, 77, 132, 211, 254n80
TFP (Total Factor Productivity), 109, 112
think tank, 201–202, 278n166 & n167
Third Front 三线, 103, 254n83
thought work 思想工作, also see propaganda, 26, 47–54, 180, 190, 193, 200, 204
Thousand Talents 千人计划, 108, 166, 201
Three Gorges 三峡, 108, 156
three supremacies 三个至上, 50
Tiananmen Movement/Uprising 天安门运动, 17, 27, 120, 192
Tianjin 天津, 151, 156, 171
Tianxia 天下, 21
Tibet 西藏, 152, 209, 212, 215, 284n285
TikTok 抖音, 160, 211
torture, 41, 46, 74, 188, 199, 239n103

Totalitarianism, 15, 18, 26, 49, 69, 227
tourism, 107, 110, 164, 169, 212
treatment 待遇, 67–68, 180
Tsinghua University 清华大学, 63, 165, 200–201, 204, 206
Tu Youyou 屠呦呦, 220–21
Two Mountains Theory 两山理论, 218

Ukraine, 35, 99
unemployment rate, 6, 115, 148, 232n16
United Kingdom, 178, 205, 215, 221
United Nations, 3, 5, 7, 138, 145, 161
United States, 1–2, 5, 10, 30, 33, 40, 41, 45, 63, 64, 76, 78, 80, 83, 92, 96, 99, 107, 117, 127, 132, 134, 145, 153, 155, 164, 165, 166, 199, 203, 208, 223, 229

vacuous employment 吃空饷, 62, 186
velvet prison, 50
Vietnam, 7, 100, 130, 161, 253n70
Vodka politics, 132
Voluntarism, 24, 144
voluntary servitude 自愿为奴, 51
voting with feet, *also see* emigration, 54, 148, 164–25, 169, 205

Wanda 万达, 68, 76
Wang Huning 王沪宁, 237n69
Wang Zhiming 王志明, 244n194
Wangyi 网易, 162
WeChat 微信, 160, 170, 211, 243n180
Wen Jiabao 温家宝, 68, 280n202
Westernization, 3, 27, 137, 276
Westphalian System, 2, 3, 18, 85, 103, 219, 223
whataboutism, 133

white glove 白手套, 76, 183
White Paper Protest 白纸抗议, 83, 250n317
WHO (World Health Organization), 7–8, 11, 143, 163, 216
wolf warriors 战狼, 54
World Bank, 109, 111, 120, 145, 147, 263n46 &n51
world order, 1, 2, 97, 134, 220, 223, 228–29
world peace, 1, 54
World Revolution, 33, 36, 45, 49
World Suboptimality, 137
World War II, 18, 21, 54, 184, 211, 219, 228
WTO (World Trade Organization), 90, 115
Wuhan 武汉, 10–11, 158, 207, 233n42 & n44 & n45, 265n87

Xi Jinping, 习近平, 5, 17, 27–33, 36, 45, 49–50, 57, 68–70, 71, 72–73, 82, 88, 90, 98, 100, 108, 133, 146–47, 152, 177, 180, 192, 193, 195, 197, 199, 204, 205, 218, 219, 236n47, 237n57, 265n90
   anti-Xi, 83, 237n54, 270n193; books by, 28, 236n50; cult of personality & imitation of Mao, 27–29, 90, 234n7
Xi Jinping Thought, 27–33, 44, 49–50, 218, 270n185, 285n4
Xiaomi 小米, 222
Xinhua 新华社, 59
Xinjiang 新疆, 46, 72, 83, 152, 177
Xiong'an 雄安, 218
Xishan Society 西山会, 77, 249n288

Yangtze River 长江, 64, 108, 200, 214, 215
Yellow River 黄河, 215, 282n251
Yugong (Mr. Fool) 愚公, 144

Zhang Yimou 张艺谋, 78, 274n77
Zhao Ziyang 赵紫阳, 87, 187
Zhejiang University 浙江大学, 204
Zhengzhou 郑州, flood of, 8, 156

Zhong Nanshan 钟南山, 11, 196
Zhongnanhai 中南海, 67, 187, 234n11
Zhou Enlai 周恩来, 187, 190, 211,
    272n53